South-Western

Managing Your Personal Finances

3rd edition

JOAN S. RYAN, MBA, PH.D.
Business Administration Department
Clackamas Community College
Oregon City, Oregon

Vice-President/Editor-in-Chief: Dennis M. Kokoruda
Developmental Editor II: Willis S. Vincent
Developmental Editor: Bob Sandman
Production Manager: Carol Sturzenberger
Production Editor: Mark Cheatham
Photo Editor: Fred M. Middendorf

Internal Design: Lamson Design
Unit Opener/Cover Photos: McHale Photography
Cover Design: Ross Design
Composition/Page Makeup: Lachina Publishing Services
Copyeditor: Gary Morris

ISBN: 0-538-62896-0

Library of Congress Catalog Card Number: 95-069635

  6 7 8 9 0   03 02 01 00

Printed in the United States of America

I(T)P
International Thomson Publishing

South-Western Educational Publishing is a division of International Thomson Publishing Inc. The ITP trademark is used under license.

Welcome to the exciting world of personal finance! The approach to the study of personal finance offered in *Managing Your Personal Finances*, 3d edition, focuses on your role as a citizen, student, family member, consumer, and active participant in the business world. The intent of this text is to inform you of your various financial responsibilities and to provide you with opportunities for self-awareness, expression, and satisfaction in a highly technical and competitive society.

In *Managing Your Personal Finances*, 3d edition, you will explore many important areas of interest that will enhance your financial security. You will discover new ways to maximize your earnings potential, develop strategies for managing your resources, explore skills for the wise use of credit, and gain insight into the different ways of investing your money. You will also learn about risk management, laws that protect you, and how to get redress when things go wrong with a purchase. Mostly, you will begin a lifelong journey of personal financial planning.

Goals of the Text

The seven units of this text provide a wide variety of useful and practical information. After completing each unit you will be able to do the following:

- *Unit 1:* Prepare effective career selection tools, such as a resume, letter of application, job application, and thank-you letter.
- *Unit 2:* Describe employee rights and responsibilities in the workplace. Compute gross pay and net pay; complete federal income tax forms; reconcile bank statements; and prepare a month's budget based upon personal information.
- *Unit 3:* Explain savings and investing options, including stocks, bonds, mutual funds, real estate, and retirement planning tools and accounts.
- *Unit 4:* List the advantages and disadvantages of credit, compute the costs of credit, and explain how to avoid and solve problems with credit.

preface

- *Unit 5:* Discuss housing alternatives (particularly renting, buying, or building); explain strategies for buying and maintaining an automobile; and identify issues commonly affecting family relationships (such as a vacation, marriage, divorce, and death).
- *Unit 6:* Define risk management and the need for insurance, including property, health, disability, and life insurance.
- *Unit 7:* Explain the rights and responsibilities of consumers in the marketplace.

Unit and Chapter Format

This text contains 30 chapters encompassing seven units of study. Each unit and chapter has been designed to cover content in a clear and motivating manner.

The Units. All units begin with learning objectives. Learning objectives at the beginning of each unit draw together related chapters of study. A unit overview, entitled Looking Forward, highlights the theme of each unit. At the end of each unit, a culminating project either reinforces or expands the contents. An epilogue (Looking Back) concludes each unit through a review of the main ideas in each chapter.

The Chapters. Each of the chapters contains learning objectives, vocabulary words (Terms to Know), contents divided into several sections, special features, an end-of-chapter summary, and end-of-chapter activities. These aids to learning are included to help you achieve success as you study each chapter.

Learning Objectives. Learning objectives at the beginning of each chapter are fulfilled by studying the chapter narrative, responding to the end-of-chapter activities, and completing the activities in the *Student Activity Guide*. Each major heading within a chapter narrative is correlated with a learning objective.

Vocabulary Words. Key vocabulary terms are listed on the first page as Terms to Know and are also printed in bold and defined within each chapter. Other important terms and concepts are printed in italics.

Special Features. Throughout the book, certain special features will help you see and relate chapter concepts as they apply to the real world of personal finance. Three types of special features are included in this book:

1. Personal Perspectives focus your attention on current topics in personal finance. You are made aware of some of the trends and issues that you will face in the marketplace.
2. Global Connections give you an opportunity to examine the international aspects of a variety of business and consumer topics. They also expose you to other cultures and the practices and policies affecting consumers around the world.

3. Point/Counterpoints highlight contemporary personal finance issues through an examination of pro and con viewpoints.

End-of-Chapter Summary. The chapter summary reviews the content relating to each chapter's learning objectives. Use the summary to review the key points covered within a chapter.

End-of-Chapter Activities. The end-of-chapter activities progress from simple to complex. You can complete these activities in addition to or in conjunction with those provided in the *Student Activity Guide* designed to supplement this text. End-of-chapter learning activities consist of the following:

- Vocabulary Terms—exercises providing you with additional practice in the use and understanding of key terms.
- Facts and Ideas in Review—a set of questions for determining your basic understanding and recall of the chapter material.
- Applications for Decision Making—a set of problems for gauging your ability to apply ideas and concepts introduced in a chapter.
- Life Situation Problem Solving—a set of activities encompassing a number of financial planning situations requiring critical thinking and effective decision making.

Appendices. Appendices A and B contain the federal income tax forms that you will use with Chapter 7. Appendix C contains information on the Internet, the fastest growing means for communicating and sharing information.

Glossary. An alphabetical listing of all key terms used throughout the text are compiled at the end of the book for quick, easy reference.

Message to Students

After studying *Managing Your Personal Finances*, 3d edition, you will have a better grasp of your responsibilities to yourself and society. You will also better understand your own wants, needs, and values, and how these affect personal financial decisions. Understanding the concepts presented in this text will enable you to make wise decisions that will help your financial future and make you a better citizen.

Joan S. Ryan

contents

3 unit: financial security

4 unit: credit management

5 unit: resource management

6 unit: risk management

7 unit:
consumer rights and responsibilities

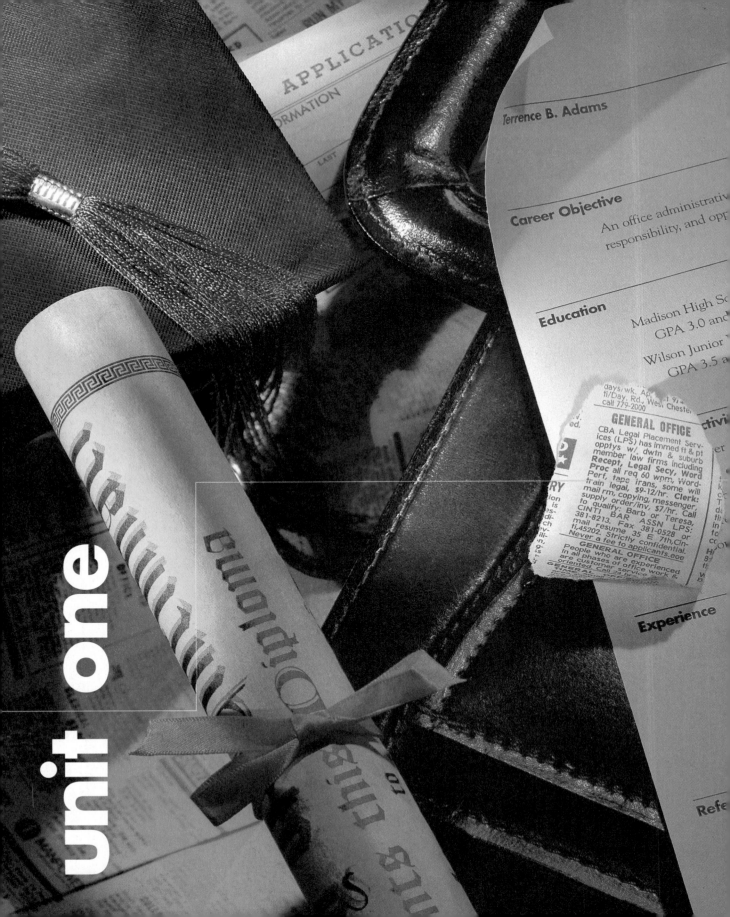

unit one

career decisions

chapters

objectives: *After reading and studying the chapters, and completing the exercises and activities, you will be able to:*

1 Explain the process of job choice and understand how to cope with changes in the job market.

2 List factors affecting career choice, sources of job information, and job search techniques.

3 Prepare job search tools which include an application letter, a resume, an employment application, and a thank-you letter.

4 Explain strategies for adapting to career choices, including how to get along with coworkers, meet employer requirements, and achieve personal goals and needs.

5 Prepare work forms and demonstrate an understanding of employer and employee responsibilities and work laws.

looking forward

Unit 1, Career Decisions, prepares you to analyze choices and develop the tools to secure and maintain temporary, part-time, or full-time employment, now or in the future. This unit is based on the idea that making wise career decisions is crucial to managing your personal finances and all future financial planning.

This unit explores new career options and how to cope with changes that will affect career choices. You will learn why people work, how to begin career planning, and where to find up-to-date information. You will learn how to compete with other applicants in getting a job. Then you will explore how to adapt to and keep the job—important skills that lead to good work relations and work history.

objectives:

After reading and studying this chapter you will be able to:

1-1   Discuss career and job trends and describe sources of job information.

1-2   Complete a job analysis form, listing the positive and negative features of potential career choices.

1-3   Describe the techniques for coping with change.

1-4   Explain changing career patterns in a world economy and the need for job networking.

terms to know:

technology
productivity
job analysis
salary
benefits
promotion
employee expenses
work characteristics
entrepreneur
upgrading
retraining
advanced degrees
college placement center
self-assessment inventory
networks

The first step in building a solid financial future is choosing the right career. This step involves probably the most important decisions you will ever make. Your choice of career will affect your future in many ways: where you will live; how much you will spend, invest, and save; what you do in your spare time and where you go on vacations; and the type of retirement plan you will have. Because choosing the right career is so important, you should consider all possible options and trends, and any factors that may affect that choice both now and in the future. This chapter is an introduction to the world of work—a changing and dynamic arena that will provide many challenges and rewards for you in the years to come.

Choosing Your Career

chapter

1

C areers of the future

Your grandparents or even your parents may have worked for one employer for twenty-five to forty years before comfortably retiring. But your career path will likely look much different. As one philosopher said, "The future isn't what it used to be." New and better products and services, together with global competition, have changed the expectations and needs of employers. Chances are the job you are hired for will be so different within five years that you will have retrained, upgraded, or changed jobs entirely along the way.

Technology creates newer, better, and faster ways of getting things done. **Technology** is a general term for advances resulting from improvements in work methods that increase productivity of people and machines. **Productivity**, the value of a completed product in relation to its cost, must increase for a company to stay competitive. That is, companies today must maximize efficiency in order to be profitable and stay in business.

Major Occupational Groups

In the early 1900s, farmers comprised more than one-third of the total workforce of the United States; now, they make up less than three percent, and that number is decreasing. Today, in most occupations the collection, use, and distribution of *information* is the job. Technology is a key factor in this field, as information is gathered, transmitted, and stored in new and more efficient ways both nationally and internationally.

The second largest career group is in the *professions*, where knowledge is the key job skill. Professional employees also work in the information field, with the creation, processing, storage, and retrieval of information as important parts of the job.

Service jobs are a large—and growing—sector of the market. They also are dominated by technology and information needs which determine what will be produced and how it will be made available to customers. Service employees are using highly sophisticated information storage and retrieval devices, from point-of-sale computers to optical scanners for inventory counting.

Many historians, economists, and futurists foresaw this extraordinary transformation of occupations. It has been variously labeled the "space age," "electronic era," "global village," "technological revolution," "post-industrial society," "information age," and "technetronic age." All of these terms make reference to technology and the rapid increase of knowledge which affect virtually all career choices today.

Job Titles and Descriptions

Some of today's careers may appear to be the same as they were ten or twenty years ago. However, you will find that most are considerably different when you compare present-day job descriptions, job qualifications, and employment opportunities with earlier counterparts.

Careful research into job titles and descriptions of potential careers will help prepare you for making career choices. Several U.S. government publications provide detailed descriptions of many job titles. Three of them are available in most public libraries—the *Dictionary of Occupational Titles* (DOT), the *Occupational Outlook Handbook*, and the *Monthly Labor Review*.

The *Dictionary of Occupational Titles* classifies jobs by nine-digit categories according to functions and duties. Listed within the major categories are numerous jobs available in the United States. Figure 1-1 is an excerpt from the DOT which lists several specific jobs under "Occupations in Writing." To use the *Dictionary of Occupational Titles*, you first consult the index to locate the reference number for "Occupations in Writing." Jobs may be further divided into functions and duties, with a brief description of these.

The *Occupational Outlook Handbook* is a yearly publication of the U.S. Department of Labor. It provides in-depth job descriptions and includes additional information about job opportunities nationwide.

Fig. 1-1

DOT Job Descriptions

131.067-014 COPY WRITER (profess. & kin.)
Writes advertising copy for use by publication or broadcast media to promote sale of goods and services: Consults with sales media, and marketing representatives to obtain information on product or service and discuss style and length of advertising copy. Obtains additional background and current development information through research and interview. Reviews advertising trends, consumer surveys, and other data regarding marketing of specific and related goods and services to formulate presentation approach. Writes preliminary draft of copy and sends to supervisor for approval. Corrects and revises copy as necessary. May write articles, bulletins, sales letters, speeches, and other related informative and promotional material. May enter information into computer to prepare advertising copy.
GOE: 01.01.02 STRENGTH: S GED: R5 M2 L5 SVP: 7 DLU: 89

131.067-018 CRITIC (print. & pub.; radio-tv broad.)
Writes critical reviews of literary, musical, or artistic works and performances for broadcast and publication: Attends art exhibitions, musical or dramatic performances, reads books, or previews motion picture or television presentations. Analyzes factors such as theme, expression, and technique, and makes comparisons to other works and standards. Forms critical opinions based on personal knowledge, judgment, and experience. Organizes material to emphasize prominent features, and writes review. Presents oral review in live or recorded form when working in broadcasting medium. May enter information into computer to prepare reviews. May be designated according to field of specialization as Art Critic (print. & pub.; radio-tv broad.); Book Critic (print. & pub.; radio-tv broad.); Drama Critic (print. & pub.; radio-tv broad.); Movie Critic (print. & pub.; radio-tv broad.); Music Critic (print. & pub.; radio-tv broad.)
GOE: 01.01.03 STRENGTH: S GED: R6 M2 L6 SVP: 8 DLU: 88

131.067-022 EDITORIAL WRITER (print. & pub.)
Writes comments on topics of reader interest to stimulate or mold public opinion, in accordance with viewpoints and policies of publication: Prepares assigned or unassigned articles from knowledge of topic and editorial position of publication, supplemented by additional study and research. Submits and discusses copy with editor for approval. May specialize in one or more fields, such as international affairs, fiscal matters, or national or local politics. May participate in conferences of editorial policy committee to recommend topics and position to be taken by publication on specific public issues.
GOE: 01.01.02 STRENGTH: S GED: R5 M3 L5 SVP: 8 DLU: 77

131.067-026 HUMORIST (profess. & kin.)
Writes humorous material for publication or performance: Selects topic according to personal preference or assignment. Writes and makes changes and revisions to material until it meets personal standards. Submits material for approval and confers with client regarding additional changes or revisions. May conduct research to obtain factual information regarding subject matter. May specialize in writing comedy routines, gags, or special material for entertainers and be designated Gag Writer (profess. & kin.). May write comedy shows for presentation on radio or television and be designated Comedy Writer (profess. & kin.). May work as a member of writing team and be assigned to develop segment of comedy show.
GOE: 01.01.02 STRENGTH: S GED: R6 M2 L6 SVP: 8 DLU: 77

Source: U.S. Employment Service, Dictionary of Occupational Titles (Washington, D.C., U.S. Government Printing Office, Fourth Edition, 1991), p.87.

As you can see in Figure 1-2, the *Handbook* makes reference to the DOT numbers for the jobs it describes. The *Handbook* descriptions include topics such as nature of the work, working conditions, employment, training and qualifications, job outlook, earnings, related occupations, and sources of additional information.

| Fig. 1-2 | **Portions of an *Occupational Outlook Handbook* Job Description** |

Telephone Installers and Repairers

(D.O.T. 822.261-022 and .281-018)

Nature of the Work

Telephone installers and repairers install, service, and repair telephones and other communications equipment on customers' property. When customers move or request new types of service, installers relocate telephones or make changes to existing equipment. In buildings under construction, they install wiring and telephone jacks.

Telephone installers, sometimes called station installers, assemble equipment and install wiring on the customers' premises. They connect telephones to outside service wires and sometimes climb poles or ladders to make these connections. In apartment and office buildings, they make connections to service wires or terminals in basements or in wire closets. After installation, they test equipment to make sure it works properly.

Some experienced installers and repairers have multiple skills. They are considered especially valuable by many small companies. In some areas, installers and repairers handle special cases such as complaints to public service commissions, illegal or unauthorized use of equipment, and electric or acoustic shocks.

Employment

Telephone installers and repairers held about 40,000 jobs in 1992. More than 9 out of 10 worked full time for telephone companies.

Job Outlook

Employment of telephone installers and repairers is expected to decline sharply through the year 2005. Employment will fall as technological improvements make this work less labor intensive. For example, prewired buildings that enable customers to buy telephones and plug them into prewired jacks have effectively eliminated the functions of the installer. The modular assembly of telephones, where components plug in and out, also will reduce the time and skills needed for repair. Also, fewer phones will be worth repairing as prices continue to decline. In addition, the use of portable terminals which hook into a central testing system makes repairers more efficient.

With employment projected to decline, job openings will result exclusively from the need to replace persons who transfer to other occupations or leave the labor force. Traditionally, most openings for telephone installers and repairers have been filled by workers in other telephone company jobs. As technology continues to displace installers and repairers, it will remain difficult for telephone workers without additional training and virtually impossible for "outsiders" without the necessary skills to get these jobs.

Earnings

In 1992, median weekly earnings of full-time electronic equipment repairers were $521. The middle 50 percent earned between $406 and $692. The bottom 10 percent earned less than $312, while the top 10 percent earned more than $729. Earnings vary widely by occupation and the type of equipment repaired, as shown in the following tabulations:

Telephone installers and repairers	$626
Data processing equipment repairers	619
Electronic repairers, communications	
and industrial equipment	484
Office machine repairers	476

Central office installers, central office technicians, PBX installers, and telephone installers and repairers employed by AT&T and the Bell Operating Companies and represented by the Communications Workers of America earned between $752 and $824 a week in 1992.

According to a survey of workplaces in 160 metropolitan areas, beginning maintenance electronics technicians had median earnings of $12.34 an hour in 1992.

Related Occupations

Workers in other occupations who repair and maintain the circuits and mechanical parts of electronic equipment include appliance and powertool repairers, automotive electricians, broadcast technicians, electronic organ technicians, and vending machine repairers. Electronics engineering technicians may also repair electronic equipment as part of their duties.

Source: U.S. Department of Labor, Occupational Outlook Handbook (Washington, D.C., U.S. Government Printing Office, 1992–93), Bulletin 2400, pp. 316–317.

Additional statistics and graphic information are available on a monthly basis in the *Monthly Labor Review*, published by the U.S. Department of Labor. Articles in this publication provide current information about specific *occupation clusters* (groups of similar occupations) across the nation. The *Monthly Labor Review* is found in most libraries.

ob analysis

While considering the type of work for which you will be best suited, you may find it useful to do a job analysis such as the one shown in Figure 1-3. A **job analysis** shows the positive and negative attributes of a given career choice. After careful analysis, you may find that a certain job will not meet most of your career objectives. When this happens, continue with your analyses of other careers that interest you. Because you will probably spend a number of years in your first career choice, selecting the right one is very important.

Positive Features of Employment

You will find that your chosen career will provide you with many positive features. The most important is usually the **salary**, which is the amount of monthly or annual pay for which you are hired. You should also consider whether there are scheduled salary increases after a month, six months, or a year. Some companies offer frequent evaluations, merit raises, and liberal pay schedules. **Benefits** are also important. They include sick pay, vacation time, profit-sharing plans, health insurance provisions, and other company-provided supplements to income, as discussed in Chapter 6.

There will be many positive features to your chosen career, including salary, benefits, and a chance for promotion.

Fig. 1-3   **Job Analysis Form**

JOB ANALYSIS

Job Title: _____

Positive features:	**Negative features:**
Beginning salary: _____	Employee expenses: _____
Benefits: _____	_____
_____	_____
_____	_____
_____	_____
Promotion opportunities:	Work characteristics:
_____	_____
_____	_____
_____	_____
_____	_____
Other considerations:	Other considerations:
_____	_____
_____	_____
_____	_____

Another important feature is the opportunity for **promotion;** in other words, the ability to advance, to accept more responsibilities, and eventually to work your way up to higher positions. Promotions give you recognition for your achievements, higher pay, and more challenging work. For example, a junior accountant will want to work for a company in which advancement to senior accountant and partner is possible.

Other considerations might include travel (the ease and speed of getting to work), company stability in the community, work hours and flexibility, and personnel policies. It's important to examine all of the

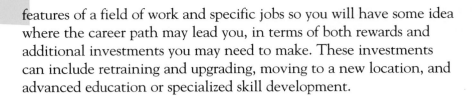

features of a field of work and specific jobs so you will have some idea where the career path may lead you, in terms of both rewards and additional investments you may need to make. These investments can include retraining and upgrading, moving to a new location, and advanced education or specialized skill development.

Negative Features of Employment

Unfortunately, every job or occupation also has its negative features. You should be prepared to see these negatives as challenges that go along with the positive aspects of employment.

Employee expenses include any costs to be paid by the employee that are not reimbursed by the employer, for example, uniforms or other special clothing and their cleaning. Although such expenses may be tax deductible, they can be very costly and can make the job seem less attractive. For example, if you choose to become a real estate agent and work independently (rather than as an employee of an agency), you will pay your own advertising costs, automobile expenses, membership dues to a multiple-listing service, license fees, and many other expenses normally paid by an employer. Carefully balance employee expenses against benefits in a prospective job.

Work characteristics, such as routine or changing tasks, indoor versus outdoor work, working alone or with people, job pressures, time between breaks, supervisory relationships, number of employees with whom you will work, and company rules and policies, should also be of particular interest. Because you will do this work for eight or more hours a day, it is important to match work characteristics to your own needs and preferences.

Other considerations include your transportation arrangements and costs; how you feel about the company, its employees, or your supervisor; your attitude toward the particular job and its responsibilities; and how this job fits into your overall career and life goals.

To gain insight into how employees in actual careers feel about their jobs, the *Vocational Biographies*, published by Vocational Biographies, or *Working*, by Studs Terkel, are examples of books that have information about people and their jobs. Both publications are a series of short descriptions of workers in many different occupations. In addition to discussing their job likes and dislikes, these workers give more details about their jobs than you may find elsewhere. Your library or bookstore will have other material on this subject.

You can continue your in-depth career research by searching the subject headings in your library's card catalog and magazine indexes, such as the *Business Periodicals Index* and the *Readers' Guide to Periodical*

Literature. Most career information sources can be found in the reference section of the library.

Entrepreneurship

Many people would like to own their own business, large or small, and be their own boss. An **entrepreneur** is someone who organizes, manages, and assumes the risks of a business or enterprise. There are many opportunities for people to start their own business, or purchase an existing business or franchise, in order to become independent. While long hours of work and dedication usually accompany such a move, rewards are also great because you can better control your own life and future.

With careful planning, training, advice, financing, and support, many young people today will eventually own and run their own business enterprises. Small business management and entrepreneurship courses, information, and assistance are often available in high schools, community colleges, and through local business organizations such as Junior Achievement. *Incubator projects* (in which cities or counties provide reduced-cost sites with incentives and subsidies to get a small business on its feet) and Small Business Assistance Centers also provide ongoing training, education, and assistance as needed.

An entrepreneur assumes the risks of a business. What type of lifestyle does this store owner seem to have?

oping with change

With increasing numbers of advanced technologies, one thing should be clear to most American workers: Change is certain. Psychologists agree that there are three things you can do about change: accept it, reject it, or ignore it. If you accept change, you can be part of it and help it happen. If you reject change, you will be run over by it; progress and technological advances cannot be stopped. If you ignore change, you will be left behind, wondering what happened. By rejecting or ignoring change, you will be very frustrated, unemployed, or both. By reading, becoming a lifetime learner, taking classes, and completing a self-assessment, you can be aware of changes and be better able to cope.

Read Widely

There are a variety of magazines that follow national and international trends from general technology to specific industries. If you work with computers, one of the many computer magazines will keep you informed of technological advances entering the marketplace almost daily. In addition, we all need to read newspapers and magazines to keep up with what is going on in the United States and in the world. In this way, we will be prepared for the challenge of change that is inevitable.

Be a Lifetime Learner

Both at work and in your personal life, be interested in what is going on. Ask questions; talk to people; follow news and special events; participate in community activities; care about what is going on in your local area, state, and country, and in the world. Joining professional and service organizations will also keep you informed of what's new in specific job areas. Through professional organizations and other groups, you can find out about workshops and seminars that will keep you aware of trends. This will make you a more interesting person to talk to, to work with, and to be around. And it is essential to your successful career development and enhancement.

Take Classes

Sometimes technological advancements are too complex to learn by yourself, so you should actively seek new knowledge by taking classes to gain new skills. **Upgrading** is advancing to a higher level of skill to increase your usefulness to an employer. Many jobs, especially those affected by technological improvements, will require regular upgrading

point counterpoint

M anaging Organizational Change

Change is a fact of life. Most attempts at change are likely to meet some resistance. The first column in the table below suggests why companies are successful in implementing changes; the second, why companies are unsuccessful.

Why Employees Welcome Change

Significant Input—Employees have a great amount of input throughout the change process.

Favorable Manner—Employees have been given plenty of advance notice regarding the change, are participating in it, and are being given consideration and attention throughout the change process.

Well Communicated—There is a continuing free flow of open, candid communication in all directions and across all organizational lines.

Is a Perceived Need—Employees themselves have observed opportunities and suggested changes. They believe the present change effort is in response to their suggestions.

Trust in the Initiators of Change—Employees respect, trust, and support the initiators of the change.

Why Employees Resist Change

No Input—Employees were not involved in initiating the change nor in planning the implementation steps.

Objectionable Manner—The change was entirely unexpected and is being forced upon the employees with no apparent consideration of their feelings and their personal welfare.

Poorly Communicated—There was inadequate and/or distorted communication about the real underlying reasons for the change, how it would actually impact employees, and how it would be implemented.

No Perceived Need—Employees can see no reason why change is required. The present way of operating appears to be going fine. They are perfectly satisfied with the status quo.

Distrust of the Initiators of Change—Employees are highly suspicious, cynical, and distrustful of management and/or the other people who are initiating the change.

critical thinking

1. Why do many attempts to overcome resistance to change fail?

2. Can you think of reasons why employees might resist change?

by employees. **Retraining** is the learning of new and different skills so that an employee can retain the same level of employability. Community college and vocational training is being geared as much to retraining displaced employees as to preparing employees for entry-level positions.

Technical courses are often available through corporations for retraining their own employees. Those who volunteer and are eager to learn will be positioning themselves for advancement. Other training is available through technical schools, vocational centers, job placement services, business colleges, and community colleges. For many careers, applicants will have to have a bachelor's degree before they are hired.

Americans place a high value on education. Young people are staying in college longer before entering the workforce than ever before. **Advanced degrees** are obtained through specialized, intensive post-baccalaureate programs that prepare the recipients for higher level work responsibilities with more challenges and higher pay. Advanced degrees may be a master's, a doctorate in a specialized field, or a professional degree in medicine, law, veterinary medicine, engineering, aerospace technology, and so on. Advanced degrees may require one year for a master's degree and an additional three years for a Ph.D. after a master's degree. It is also possible to earn a Ph.D. without first obtaining a master's degree. This path usually takes longer (up to five years).

A career path can often be better defined through technical training.

Complete a Self-Assessment

As you go through life, your needs and values will change. It is important to look inward to define what is important to you and to use this process in planning your future. You should be thinking often about what you like doing, what you do well, and what skills and knowledge you want to enhance. For those who choose some form of college or technical training, a **college placement center** offers advice and counseling to help you determine a career direction. You may be asked to use an autobiographical approach, writing or tape-recording your life story. Counselors will help you analyze this data and determine where it is you would really like to go with your life. Vocational testing is also available through these college placement centers. You might want to compare your interests with those of successful people in various professions. A values clarification test will help you determine what is important to you both personally and professionally.

Private career counselors are listed in the Yellow Pages, and may be consulted for a fee ranging from $25 to $75 an hour. A less expensive and more productive approach is to do your own research, using the sources listed in this chapter, as well as *The American Almanac of Jobs and Salaries*. The latter book evaluates job opportunities in many career fields and gives a full range of salaries for positions and levels. You can do industry research and look into major job categories (service, professional, and so on, as listed in Chapter 2). Specific company research will help you determine which companies can provide you with the best career opportunities. You might want to check your library to find sources such as *Standard & Poor's Register of Corporations, Directors and Executives, United States and Canada* or *The 100 Best Companies to Work for in America* to read about major American companies and why they are successful. You can learn about their history, structure, and future plans. Finally, you can do field research and talk to people working in careers that interest you. These interviews will show you strengths and weaknesses in some careers that you might not have anticipated. All this information is crucial in determining your needs and matching them to an appropriate career.

A **self-assessment inventory** lists your strong and weak points and gives you an idea of how to prepare yourself for a career. As weak points are improved, they become strengths in your inventory. By keeping aware of your strengths and weaknesses, what is going on in the world, and what you need to do to keep up with technological changes, you will not be left behind in the future.

Figure 1-4 is a self-assessment inventory that lists a typical young person's assets, liabilities, and plans for action. Can you complete a similar inventory based on your personal qualifications?

A comprehensive self-assessment will help you determine areas that need work. You might ask another person to objectively assess your strengths and weaknesses. A different point of view can sometimes help clarify your self-assessment.

Fig. 1-4   **Self-Assessment Inventory**

Strengths	Weaknesses	Plan of Action
Education: High school diploma including business courses	Education: Weak in office skills	Take extra computer classes to learn new word processing and spreadsheet programs.
Experience: Cooperative job in office — part-time summer job as clerk; volunteer work at church	Experience: Need experience using computer programs	Look for work experience which includes computer applications in database management.
Aptitudes and Abilities: Good hand-eye coordination; work well with people	Aptitudes and Abilities: Poor speaker; shy around opposite sex	Practice speaking in small groups; lead a class at church; attend more social functions.
Appearance: Neat and clean; short, well-groomed hair	Appearance: Wardrobe needs more professional work clothes.	Start buying clothes that are appropriate for work.

hanging career opportunities

Career planning is changing as never before. A career choice is not a permanent and final decision, but is subject to rapid, unpredictable change. To understand how the job market will be affected, let's examine some of the major changes sweeping the country and the world.

Long-Term Planning

Businesses must be concerned with what will happen in the long run; otherwise, they will be totally unprepared when new technologies that require massive changes and improvements emerge. Individuals also must look to long-term planning to protect themselves from the effects of a rapidly changing technology—they must be in the midst of the change and help it happen. Career plans must span several decades and must be as broad, diversified, and open to the opportunities and challenges of the future as possible.

A World Economy

The idea that we can isolate ourselves from the rest of the world and live in total peace and security is a myth. We are now part of a worldwide, interdependent economy. As a nation, we must seek ways to survive and grow internationally; as individuals, we must understand and be

aware of the changes occurring worldwide, particularly in *Third World countries*. Third World countries are undeveloped and underdeveloped nations.

The twenty fastest growing economies of the 1980s and into the 1990s were all in Third World nations, including the oil exporting countries, South Korea, Singapore, the Dominican Republic, Taiwan, Mexico, and Brazil. The economic powers of the Third World are taking over the industrial production tasks formerly controlled by more developed countries, and they have the potential workforce to do it.

Should we try to go back and recapture our role as leader of a modern Industrial Revolution? Most experts agree that the answer is "No." Instead, we should adapt and move forward in the area in which we are the leader—information.

Networking

Businesses and individuals are using a new, more relaxed system to get the job done, moving away from formal, individual-oriented structures and toward networks. **Networks** are communication lines established for people to talk to each other and share information. Networking includes making phone calls, sharing lunch, and creating opportunities to give ideas and share resources, and to receive needed information from someone who has it. To find a career, you will need to use a job network for establishing contacts and obtaining information. Through networking, you are able to get inside information without being an "insider."

Adapting to the world of work in the future will require successful networking. You can begin now by creating a master list of people you know through your parents, business acquaintances, and personal friends and associates. By communicating within your network, you will learn how to prepare yourself for a job, where the openings are, and how to pursue them.

 ummary

Technological advances have resulted in a rapidly changing world. All occupations will use information as a major resource, and we can expect our job qualifications and responsibilities to change to accommodate that fact.

Careful job analysis will help you make better career choices as you consider the positive and negative features of your job options. Many of you will become entrepreneurs—owners of your own business.

Coping with change has become an important attribute of survival in the technological age. Many of us seek ways to keep current through upgrading our skills and job retraining. We may need to change the direction of our career paths several times during our lives. Through self-assessment techniques, we can discover and correct areas of weakness and improve our opportunities for advancement.

When we consider how long it took the world economy to pass through the agricultural to the industrial era, and then from the industrial era to the information age, we realize that with rapid technological improvements the future will be very different and will change with unprecedented speed. To cope successfully, we must use long-range planning, become a one-world economy, and develop strong personal and business networking skills.

Vocabulary terms

Directions: Can you find the definition for each of the following terms used in Chapter 1?

advanced degrees
benefits
college placement center
employee expenses
entrepreneur
job analysis
networks
productivity

promotion
retraining
salary
self-assessment inventory
technology
work characteristics
upgrading

1. A procedure used to list the positive and negative attributes of a given career choice.
2. One who organizes, manages, and assumes the risks of a business or enterprise.
3. A source of career counseling available at colleges or technical training institutes.
4. Advances resulting from improvements in work by people and machines.
5. Communication lines established for people to talk to each other and share information.
6. The amount of monthly or annual pay.
7. The daily activities at work, such as indoor or outdoor work, or working alone or with people.
8. Expenses paid by employees and not reimbursed by employers.
9. The chance to advance, accept more responsibility, and work your way up the corporate ladder.
10. Sick pay, vacation time, profit sharing, and other company-provided supplements to income.
11. Specialized, intensive post-baccalaureate programs.
12. Advancing to a higher level of skill.
13. Learning new and different skills in order to remain employable.
14. A listing of strong points, weak points, and plans for action.
15. The value of a completed product in relation to its cost.

acts and ideas in review

1. What do most occupations center on today?
2. What is the second largest career group today?
3. List some of the names given in this chapter and others that you may have heard that describe today's electronic era.
4. List three publications of the U.S. government that will assist you with career choices.
5. Describe the types of information that would be listed on a job analysis.
6. List some employee expenses that you might expect to pay in your first occupation choice.
7. What are the three things you can do about change?
8. List four ways you can keep up with new technologies and stay prepared for tomorrow's career choices.
9. How much education do you need to earn an advanced degree?
10. List some major changes that are sweeping the country and the world.
11. What is meant by a world economy?
12. List some Third World countries that have made great economic gains.

pplications for decision making

1. Can you describe some new technology that has been introduced in the past few months?
2. Can you describe some technological advance made just a year or two ago that is now obsolete?
3. What is the role of information in many of today's careers?
4. How has world interdependence changed our lives as Americans?
5. What are some positive features of employment which you have observed in the work of your parents or others?
6. What are some negative features of employment which you have observed in the work of your parents or others?

7. Describe ways you learn to keep in touch with what is going on in the world technologically.

8. What types of independent research can you do to determine the type of work you want and the company you want to work for?

9. Why is long-term planning necessary for individuals as well as for businesses?

 ife situation problem solving

1. Look up three career choices in the *Dictionary of Occupational Titles*. Summarize your findings in one paragraph about each choice. Look up the same three occupations in the *Occupational Outlook Handbook* and add a second paragraph about each.

2. From a current issue of *Monthly Labor Review*, summarize an article about an industry or employment trend.

3. Complete a job analysis, using the form in Figure 1-3 as a guide, for three different occupations. To get this information, consult one of the sources listed in this chapter, or interview someone working in each occupation field. List your source(s) of information on the job analysis form.

4. Explain to a friend why it is necessary to be aware of what is new and what is happening technologically in the world. Give suggestions as to what she or he can do to keep up with changes.

5. Pick a large company or corporation you think you would like to work for in the future. Do some research to learn more about the company. (Suggestion: *Standard & Poor's The 100 Best Companies to Work for in America*.) Summarize your findings in a one- or two-paragraph article.

6. Develop a networking plan—a list of all possible communication sources you may have—and add to it each time you make a contact. List contacts you plan to set up, people you would like to meet, places you would like to visit.

7. Using the *Occupational Outlook Handbook* and the format shown in Figure 1-3, prepare a career report for one occupation in which you are interested. (Note that the form shown in Figure 1-3 is provided as a worksheet in Activity 1.2 of the *Student Activity Guide*.)

**terms
to know:**

*identity
values
lifestyle
aptitude
interests
personality
goal
experience
locked in
contact
work history*

objectives:

After reading and studying this chapter you will be able to:

2-1   List reasons why people work and factors that affect career choices.

2-2   Identify and describe good career planning techniques.

2-3   List sources of job opportunity information.

2-4   Itemize and explain good job search techniques, and formulate a personal plan of action to get the desired job.

areer planning begins while you are still in school and continues through-out your work life. Without a plan, you may end up someplace you find undesirable; even with good planning, you will need to be careful and revise your strategies frequently. In this chapter, we will explore various aspects of career planning and give you some advice to help you make the best career decisions.

chapter

2

Planning Your Career

hy people work

Most people work most of their lives. After completing high school and additional training or education, you will probably work for twenty-five to forty years! Perhaps you are a teenager with a part-time job; maybe you are from a two-income household; it's even possible that you or a member of your family has more than one job. Many people work even after retirement to supplement fixed incomes and find fulfillment.

People work to meet their needs, wants, and goals. They work to provide food, clothing, shelter, vacations, education, and luxuries. If working does not make it possible to meet personal goals, people are likely to become frustrated or unhappy in the job.

People also work to gain a sense of **identity**—of who they are. Because work is typically the central activity of a person's life, it often becomes a *way* of life, strongly linked to that person's identity. For example, as a student, your main activities center on school. Your identity is that of student. When you are asked what you do, you describe activities, favorite classes in school, sports you play, and events related to your education. When you are finished with school, your identity will probably be based on your career. For example, when adults are introduced, the first question asked is usually "What do you do for a living?" When one person answers, "I'm a financial economist," and another says, "I'm a sports announcer," two entirely different images come to mind.

actors affecting career choice

Because your career will have an impact on nearly every part of your life, the choice of a career is very important. Many factors will affect your decision, among them values and lifestyle, aptitudes and interests, and personal qualities and traits.

Values and Lifestyle

Values are the things in life that are important to you. While you are living at home, your values will probably reflect those of your parents. During high school you begin to form values of your own—keeping some of your parents' values and rejecting others. For example, you may retain your parents' value that it is proper to wear a tie while attending a religious service, while rejecting a value that modern music is worthless.

Lifestyle is the way people choose to live their lives based on the values they have chosen or rejected. Your lifestyle is evident to others from the clothes you wear and the things you buy, rent, use, do, enjoy, and feel. A career is considered an important value in most peoples' lives because it influences lifestyle. With careful planning, a career can be rewarding and satisfying and also provide the money needed to support the lifestyle you desire.

Aptitudes and Interests

An **aptitude** is a natural physical or mental ability that allows you to do certain tasks well. Examples of aptitudes include finger dexterity—the ability to use your fingers to move small objects quickly and accurately; and manual dexterity—the ability to move your hands skillfully. Certain types of work require certain types of aptitudes. Aptitude tests are valuable tools in career planning because they help you realize your strengths and weaknesses. Aptitude tests can be taken through the counseling or career guidance departments of most high schools. You may want to test your physical and mental abilities before you begin making career plans.

Manual dexterity is an aptitude that could determine your career choice.

In addition to your aptitudes, you should think about your **interests**—the things you like to do and the reasons you enjoy doing them. By examining the types of things you enjoy, you can better choose a career that has similar activities and will therefore be satisfying. For example, a person who enjoys being with large groups of people and helping others will likely prefer a job working with others to one working alone. Consider the options listed in Figure 2-1.

Which of these work activities appeal to you?

working alone	outdoor work
following directions	physically inactive work
helping others	repetitive tasks
self-motivated work	thinking work
indoor work	working with others
physically active work	leading and directing
various tasks	creating and designing
manual work	presenting or speaking
working with machines	analyzing and recording

Fig. 2-1

Types of Work Activities

Personal Qualities and Traits

Your **personality** is made up of the many individual qualities and traits that make you unique. Personal qualities include such things as your appearance, intelligence, creativity, sense of humor, and general attitude. Most jobs require an individual with a particular set of personal qualities and traits. For example, a person who represents a company to the public or to potential customers needs a different set of personal qualities and traits than does a machine operator. Examining your personal qualities and traits can help you choose a career that's right for you. How many of the traits listed in Figure 2-2 apply to you?

Check each of these that apply:

1. Has a good attitude toward own work and that of others.
2. Shows courtesy and respect toward others.
3. Is dependable and will do what is promised.
4. Has a desire to succeed and to do a good job.
5. Has enthusiasm for the job and for life.
6. Is clean and has a healthy appearance.
7. Is friendly and helpful.
8. Has a good sense of humor and cares about others.
9. Desires and respects giving a day's work for a day's pay.

Fig. 2-2

Personality Traits

areer planning

Planning for your future career is an important task. Consider the total time spent working: eight hours a day, five days a week, fifty weeks a year totals 2,000 hours each year. If you work the average career span of forty-three years (from age twenty-two to age sixty-five), you will have spent 86,000 hours on the job. In addition, you will have spent time traveling to and from work, getting ready for work, putting in overtime (paid and unpaid) and doing other work-related activities away from the workplace. Because your work will likely take so much of your time, you will need to choose and plan for your career carefully.

Steps in Career Planning

Effective career planning involves careful investigation and analysis—a process that may take years to complete. Career planning involves self-analysis, research, a plan of action, and reevaluation.

1. **Self-Analysis.** Using resources available from schools, employment offices, and testing services, you can explore personal factors that relate to your career choice. You should:
   a. Determine your wants and needs.
   b. Determine your values and desired lifestyle.
   c. Assess your aptitudes and interests and determine how they match job descriptions and activities.
   d. Analyze your personal qualities and traits—those that are satisfactory and those you need to improve.
2. **Research.** Based on a good self-analysis, you can determine which careers interest you most and which suit you best. You should:
   a. Seek information in books, pamphlets, articles, and other resources available from libraries, counseling centers, and employment offices.
   b. Compare some of your interests, abilities, and personal qualities to job descriptions and requirements. Most careers can fit into one of the nine classifications shown in Figure 2-3. Can you choose one or more of these areas whose requirements you can meet? Can you decide which cluster the job of your choice would fit into?
   c. Interview people in the fields of work you find interesting.
   d. Observe occupations, spend time learning about jobs and companies, and seek part-time work to get direct exposure and experience.

Fig. 2-3 **Job Clusters**

Job Classification	Description of Activities	Training Needed	Working Hours	Beginning Salary	Examples
Clerical/Secretarial	Work in office setting. Involves contact with people and machines. Must operate computer, have telephone skills, etc.	High school diploma plus special training in keyboarding, accounting, etc.	40 hours/week during normal business hours.	Urban. $1,000-1,500/mo. w/experience.	Secretary, office assistant, word processor operator
Professional	Involves use of highly specialized knowledge. Often stressful. High-level responsibility implied.	4+ years of college. May require special training and/or apprenticeship.	40 hours/week during normal business hours plus overtime.	Urban. $25,000-50,000/yr.	Physician, lawyer, teacher, accountant
Skilled Labor	Emphasis on use of highly specialized skill. Special clothing required. Involves use of tools, machines, etc.	High school diploma plus special training, apprenticeship, licensing, or bonding.	40 hours/week plus overtime.	Minimum wage to set salary. Urban. $1,500-1,800/mo. w/exp. $1,800-2,100/mo.	Builder, mechanic, construction worker
Sales and Marketing	Emphasis on persuading others to buy products and services. Salesperson represents company, self.	High school diploma plus special training. License usually required.	Varied. Often seasonal.	Commission. Often self-employed.	Real estate agent, insurance agent, retail salesperson
Service	Involves labor that does not produce a material good. May or may not involve personal contact.	None to specialized 2-year degree program.	Varied. Split shift, as needed.	Minimum wage to $1,500/mo. for supervisor trainee.	Custodian, barber, chef, police officer
Management	Emphasis on supervision of operations, decision making, and direction giving.	College degree plus in-service training.	40 hours or more/week.	Urban. $2,000-3,000/mo. w/exp. $3,000-4,000/mo. (middle mgt).	Store manager, bank officer, supervisor
Semiskilled and Unskilled Labor	Involves assembly line and other manual work. Physical fitness and good health needed.	In-service training or vocational diploma.	40 hours/week plus overtime.	Minimum wage. $10-15/hour when advanced.	Assembly worker, farm laborer
Entertainment and Recreation	Emphasis on entertaining people. Special quality or talent needed.	None required. Dancing, singing, and music lessons helpful.	Varied. Often under contract.	$0 to unlimited.	Singer, dancer, athlete, talk show host
Military Service	Emphasis on defense of the country. Discipline and training stressed. Ability to follow orders needed. Must fulfill minimum service requirement.	High school diploma usually required.	Daily during set number of years' commitment.	$12,000 + all expenses, depending on rank.	Armed Forces service people

3. **Plan of Action.** After you have done some job research, you will need to develop a plan of action that will eventually bring you to your career goals.

   a. Use good job search techniques: Get organized, make a plan, follow through, and don't give up.

   b. Develop necessary skills by taking courses and gaining exposure to the area in which you want to pursue a career.

   c. Seek a part-time or volunteer job to gain experience.

   d. Evaluate what you have done. If at any point you think you are following the wrong career path, change your mind before you stay on it too long.

   Choosing and planning for a career in the method just described may seem confusing and complicated. Many people do follow this method, however, either consciously or unconsciously. Those who do not give career choice and planning the proper thought often spend years in a job for which they are not suited before discovering their mistake. Others discover their mistake but are unable to correct it. You can avoid those mistakes. Start your career planning today and continue it throughout your lifetime.

4. **Reevaluation.** Because the world around us changes rapidly, we all need to prepare ourselves to meet the changes and challenges ahead. You may wish to reevaluate your choices and prepare for career changes to take advantage of new opportunities. About every five years you need to think about what you will be doing and where you would like to be in the next five years.

global connection

F uture Career Opportunities

By the year 2000, nearly one-third of all jobs will be directly related to international trade. The number of Americans working abroad will have increased dramatically, but just as importantly, Americans working for non-American companies here at home will also increase substantially. Many students in today's schools will find themselves working for foreign corporations with offices, branches, or operations in the United States. Many of their direct supervisors, fellow workers, and company executives will be internationals.

Expansion in international trade and investments has influenced the job market and employment trends in the United States by creating new job opportunities for those who are prepared to accept them. Sensitivity to cross-cultural differences will enhance relationships between foreign employers and their American employees. Also, understanding the impact of global economic trends on employment is essential to making sound career choices and positioning oneself for promotion opportunities.

The United States is a global partner with many countries. A global economy requires that all workers be internationally literate. The results of several studies prove that Americans' level of intercultural savvy is weak. Many students show little interest in speaking a foreign language. When asked if they read the newspaper for world events, most respond "no." Similarly, many students are not aware of world affairs and differences among cultures. Knowledge of geography—even of the United States—seems to be at an all-time low.

critical thinking

1. How often do you read the newspaper or listen to world news?

2. Choose a foreign country and do a report on its language, its culture, and how it compares to the United States in terms of technology, standard of living, and so on. Explain the differences in education and training of this country's workforce.

3. Are you required to take a foreign language? What is your choice of language? Why?

The Importance of Goals

A **goal** is a desired end toward which efforts are directed. We all need goals in order to have a sense of direction and purpose in life. There are three types of goals: short-term, intermediate, and long-term.

A *short-term goal* is one you expect to reach in a few days or weeks. You must work consistently and with certainty to achieve it because you will have to account for the results in a very short time. A short-term goal could be preparing to pass a math test next week. You know you must plan your studying to be ready for the test or suffer the consequences.

Intermediate goals are those you wish to accomplish in the next few months or years. Some examples are graduation from high school, a vacation trip, or plans for the summer.

Long-term goals are those you wish to achieve in five to ten years or longer. They might include college, career, marriage, and family planning.

It has been said that if you do not work on a goal every day, you do not care about that goal. If goals are to be meaningful, they should be defined and written down, and become a part of your life. Many people find a checklist a handy way to help them reach their goals. Figure 2-4 shows a typical goal checklist that you can look at and work on daily.

Fig. 2-4

Checklist

CHECKLIST

Week of Sept. 1

Accomplished

Short-term goals (today/this week)
1. Buy birthday gift for mom. _____
2. Get haircut (Saturday). _____
3. See counselor about chemistry class. _____

Intermediate goals (next month/year)
1. Get a C or better on chemistry test (test in 2 weeks). _____
2. Prepare for SAT test (test in October). _____
3. Finish term report (due November 9). _____
4. Complete college admission forms (by January 15). _____

Long-term goals (future)
1. Graduate from college.
2. Begin full-time job.
3. Buy a car.

Things to do now
— Extra work in science
— Bring up GPA to 3.5
— Update placement folder
— Get part-time job (save $50 a month)

Making the Right Choices

How do you know what kind of job is best for you? How can you possibly decide now, in high school, what you will want to do for the rest of your life? You may not be able to decide. Yet, unfair as it may seem, what you do now can greatly affect what you will do in the future.

You learn about a career through experience. **Experience** entails the knowledge and skills acquired from direct participation in a certain area. Furthermore, the more experience you gain, the more you learn, and the more qualified you become. The more experience and expertise you gain in an area, the more desirable you become as an employee in that area. Thus, you can set yourself up for a career in a certain area, make yourself worth more to an employer, and increase your earnings by continuing in that area. Your lifestyle will be based on that work and the salary you receive.

Unfortunately, the longer you work at one type of job, the greater the chance of becoming **locked in**—a feeling that you cannot change to another type of work. Often, you cannot afford to take the cut in pay that may accompany starting over. If you take a part-time job as a clerk, for instance, rather than a job that prepares you for your chosen career, you are in the process of locking yourself into the clerk/ secretarial job cluster. Taking a temporary position to earn a living while you are preparing for your chosen career is a common practice. However, to achieve your career goals, you must continue to pursue jobs in your field.

Consider the type of work you want for the future. Will a temporary or part-time position move you closer to that goal?

ources of job opportunity information

There are several sources of job opportunity information: word of mouth and personal contacts; school counseling and placement services; periodicals, books, and other publications; public and private employment agencies; and newspaper, telephone book, and private job listings.

Many job openings are filled before they are advertised. They are filled from within the company, or by people outside the company who have been privately informed of the opening by a friend or other contact within the company. A **contact** is a person you know who can help you get an interview for a job. Relatives, friends, people you have worked for, and others are contacts and are often able to provide you with inside information on job openings. Therefore, the more people you know, the better your chances of hearing about a job opening before it is made public and of getting the job because you had a contact.

If you are seeking a job in an area in which you have no contacts, you'll want to make contacts and get to know people who can tell you about openings. If, for example, you want to work in a bank, you should meet people who work in banks and make yourself known to the personnel manager and other key employees. You can do this through acquaintances and friends in business, professional organizations, and community activities, and through school-sponsored visits, job shadowing, job fairs, or other activities.

School Counseling and Placement Services

Many schools have programs to assist students in preparing for careers, in making career choices, and in securing part- or full-time work. One such program is the cooperative or work experience, or supervised field experience. In this type of program, students receive high school credits for on-the-job experience that directly relates to classroom studies in a chosen career area. Students placed in work situations are given grades on their work and are paid minimum wage for their efforts. Employers receive tax credits for the wages they pay the students during training.

School counselors and teachers are also good sources of job opportunity information. They often know about specific job openings and are asked by employers to recommend students for them. If you are interested in an office job, you should talk to counselors and business teachers as you complete business courses.

Colleges and universities (and some high schools) offer placement centers. Placement centers help students find employment; these services are usually offered free of charge. Job openings are posted at the school, and qualified students are given information so that they can apply. These services also include keeping a placement folder on each student that contains school records, including attendance, academic, and disciplinary records. When employers ask for information about a student, they are given copies of information from the student's placement folder. If your school has a placement center, examine your folder and have teachers and other adults write recommendations to put in it. You should also see that all school records are in the folder. Be sure to check at your school to see what other types of assistance are available.

Periodicals, Books, and Other Publications

Your local public and school libraries are good resource centers for information about jobs. You can find facts about which jobs will be available in the future and which may not be around very long. You can read job descriptions and find other information about opportunities for employment, benefits, and requirements.

One good job sourcebook is the *Occupational Outlook Handbook*, described in detail in Chapter 1. At the library you will also find many government and industry publications that present information about job trends, kinds of jobs, employment possibilities, skills needed, and education requirements.

In addition, many current periodicals contain timely information about selected occupations. You might want to look at magazines such as *Time, Newsweek, U.S. News & World Report, Fortune,* and *BusinessWeek*. The *Readers' Guide to Periodical Literature*, and computerized library databases that permit interlibrary loans and other services, will assist you in locating information by topic, article, title, or author.

Public and Private Employment Agencies

All major cities have public and private employment agencies whose business is to help you find jobs for which you are prepared and help employers locate the best applicants for job openings. Private employment agencies may or may not charge a fee for their services. Such fees vary from agency to agency, so you should compare prices before you sign with one. Some of these agencies charge a fee to the employer, others charge the prospective employee when a job is found, and still others divide the fee between the employer and the hired employee. The state employment office does not charge a fee because it is a government agency.

At the state employment office, you can also obtain information about government jobs training assistance programs, YES (Youth Employment Services), Youth Corps, Civil Service (state and federal), and apprenticeship boards, as well as other government employment programs that exist from time to time. You may qualify for one or more of these types of work programs.

Newspaper, Yellow Pages, and Private Job Listings

The Help Wanted ads in the classified section of your local newspaper consist of job openings in your area. Brief descriptions of the positions are given, often with salary ranges specified. By keeping a close watch on these ads, you can respond quickly when a new job enters the market. Both employers and employment agencies advertise job openings to attract qualified applicants. You may be asked to send a letter of application and a resume to an employer before you will be granted an interview. In Chapter 3 you will learn how to prepare a letter of application and a resume.

Private job postings at businesses or career placement centers are often overlooked as a source of job information.

The Yellow Pages of the telephone book is an alphabetically arranged subject listing of businesses advertising their services. If you are looking for a job in a certain field, determine the subject heading under which that type of work might be classified. You will find under that heading a list of companies that may be offering jobs in your field. You may want to send letters of application and resumes to all those listed, asking to be considered for the next opening.

Many companies, government offices, and schools place job opening announcements on bulletin boards, circulate them within the company, and post them in other special locations. Checking in these places may give you the inside information you need to apply for a position at the right time. Often the first applicants for a job opening have an advantage over those who apply at the last minute.

ob search techniques

Finding and getting the right job takes hard work, careful planning, and often a great deal of time. Nevertheless, it is important that you put in sufficient time and effort to ensure that you get a job you enjoy and can stay with. Dissatisfaction leads to frequent job changing, which may damage your employment chances in the future. Your **work history** is a record of the jobs you have held and how long you stayed with each employer. It will provide important information to future employers. If, for example, your record shows that you changed jobs six times in six months, you will appear immature and unstable to future employers. Thus, your work history, in this example, will hurt your chances of getting a job you might want very much.

Job search techniques that will help you find and get the right job are discussed in the following paragraphs. The key elements in a successful job search involve getting organized, making a plan, following through, and not giving up.

Get Organized

After you have decided what kind of job you want, the first step is to get organized. Assemble all the information you will need about the type of work you want to do. List prospective companies for which you would like to work. Gather your sources of information and research job descriptions, skills and aptitudes needed, and other job requirements. Make lists of personal contacts, places to go, and people to see. Prepare a current resume and letter of application. Ask previous employers, teachers, or others to write letters of recommendation for you and ask them if you may use their names as references for employment purposes. Update your placement folder at school. You may want to prepare a checklist of things to do and check them off as they are completed.

Make a Plan

A plan is important to the success of your job search because it keeps you organized, shows what you have done, and indicates what you need to do in the immediate future. A good plan lists all your goals and shows a time frame for getting them done. As each step or goal is accomplished, it should be checked off. A plan you might want to follow is shown in Figure 2-5.

Follow Through

The most important—and the most difficult—step is following through. After you have contacted a potential employer by letter or by filling out an application for a job opening, or after you have met a personnel manager or had an interview, it is important that you follow through. This means checking back from time to time to say you are still interested in the job. Call back in a day or two to check on the job, and always try to be courteous and upbeat.

Fig. 2-5

Plan to Get a Job

Job Leads:
State employment office
Help Wanted ads (newspaper)
School placement office
Marketing teacher

Contacts:
Uncle Henry (knows manager of local Penney's)

Time Line — Week 1

Day 1:
Type resume and letter of application.
Check Help Wanted ads.
Make list of local stores from Yellow Pages.

Day 2:
Send two application letters.
Get two personal references.
Call Uncle Henry to set a date for lunch.

Note: Any planned activities that are not completed this week should be brought forward to next week's plan

Don't Give Up

Before you get a good job, you will probably not get several other jobs for which you applied. When your first and second efforts appear to be fruitless, remain calm and courteous, and keep checking back for openings. Try all your job leads. Be prepared at all times, so that if you are called for an interview on short notice—even on the same day—you can do so. Continually check the want ads for new openings. Call back when you have established a contact, and check with your contacts frequently. Although a good job search may take several weeks or months, it will pay off. With careful planning and research, you can find the job that will meet your needs, wants, and goals.

ummary

Work provides people with a sense of identity and affects nearly every part of their lives. Career choice is affected by values and lifestyle, aptitudes and interests, and personal qualities and traits. Preparing for a career begins with habits and attitudes formed in high school and earlier.

Career planning is a significant life activity. It involves self-analysis, research, designing a plan of action, and reevaluating choices every five years. Short-term, intermediate, and long-term goals help us attain career objectives. Experience gained makes us more employable, yet can also cause us to be trapped in dead-end jobs because we are locked in by the pay and benefits.

Job opportunity information is available from many sources. The most frequently used source is word of mouth and personal contacts, which tell us about openings before they are advertised. Other sources include school counseling and placement services; periodicals, books, and other publications; public and private employment agencies; and newspaper, telephone book, and private job listings.

Your future employability is built on your work history or record of jobs held. In addition, it is important to be organized, make a plan, follow through, and not to give up when frustrated by the job search.

2

Vocabulary terms

Directions: Can you find the definition for each of the following terms used in Chapter 2?

aptitude   *lifestyle*
contact   *locked in*
experience   *personality*
goal   *work history*
identity   *values*
interests

1. The things in your life that are important to you.
2. A natural physical or mental ability.
3. Individual qualities and traits that make you unique.
4. Person you know in a business who can give you inside information about a job.
5. The record of jobs you have held.
6. A description of who you are.
7. The way you choose to live your life, based on your values.
8. An end toward which efforts are directed.
9. Knowledge, skills, and practice gained for direct participation in a job.
10. Describes the condition of feeling that you cannot change to another type of work because you cannot afford to start over in pay.
11. The things you like to do.

Facts and ideas in review

1. Why do people work?
2. What is your identity at this time in your life? (You may have more than one.)
3. Define *values*. List three of your parents' values and three of your own.
4. What factors affect career choices?
5. What is manual dexterity? Why might it be important to you to know if you have good manual dexterity?

6. What is meant by *personal traits*? List three.
7. What are the four major steps in good career planning? Describe other good career planning techniques.
8. Why do people need to set goals in life?
9. What are (a) short-term, (b) intermediate, and (c) long-term goals?
10. What is meant by the term *locked in*?
11. How can you establish personal contacts within a business where you don't know anyone?
12. What are placement services? What types of placement services are available at your school?
13. List five sources of job opportunity information.
14. Why should you check around with different private employment agencies before signing up with one of them?

Applications for decision making

1. From Figure 2-1, list the activities that appeal to you. Can you think of several occupations that offer these types of activities?
2. Describe your desired lifestyle in ten years. Develop a plan of action to get the desired job that will support your desired lifestyle.
3. Using Figure 2-4 as an example, prepare a checklist that contains short-term, intermediate, and long-term goals. At the end of one week, check to see what you have accomplished.
4. Cut these types of want ads from the classified section of your local newspaper: three ads by private employers; three ads by private employment agencies; one ad for someone to make a cash investment; one ad for someone in a sales position (to work on commission rather than for a salary); and one ad that gives the beginning salary in a dollar amount.
5. Using your telephone book, list ten private employment agencies, their addresses, and their phone numbers. Also list the address and phone number of the state employment office. Call one of the private agencies and ask a counselor the amount of the fee for a job that will pay approximately $1,000 a month, and ask who would pay the fee.
6. Write a paragraph describing your work history. It can be current or what you would like it to be in ten years.
7. List and describe the four steps in an effective job search.

8. Using Figure 2-5 as an example, prepare a plan to get yourself a job using a one-week timetable. List your job leads, your contacts (or potential contacts), and a daily plan to accomplish several things each day.

ife situation problem solving

1. Jory McLean has decided that her long-term goal in life is to become an astronaut. She is now a sophomore in high school and hasn't done any planning. Jory's grades are average; she is active, outgoing, and bright. What can Jory do now, in the next few years, and beyond to prepare herself for a career as an astronaut?

2. Using Figure 2-3 as a guide, classify each of the following job titles into one of the nine job classifications. You may have to do some research to determine types of activities performed, skills and education required, working hours, and beginning pay. Next to each occupation, indicate whether or not you would be interested in the job. Next to job classification, indicate whether or not you would be interested in this type of career.

   a. log scaler
   b. court reporter
   c. sheet-metal worker
   d. technical writer
   e. building custodian
   f. underwriter
   g. mechanical engineer
   h. sonar operator
   i. cosmetologist
   j. physical therapist
   k. computer programmer
   l. radio announcer
   m. singer
   n. infantry officer
   o. administrative assistant
   p. FBI special agent
   q. tailor

3. Jolene Price wants to be an accountant when she completes high school. She is taking accounting courses and is working part-time at an ice cream store. What should Jolene be doing to prevent herself from becoming locked into her job at the ice cream store?

4. Rich Esterbrook would like to work as a merchandising manager for a large department store. He has all the qualifications, education, and skills necessary, but he doesn't know anyone in any large stores, and most openings are filled before he even knows they existed. What can Rich do to find out about job openings in the large department stores?

5. Manny Reese is a sophomore in high school. He plans to use the placement service of his high school to help get a part-time job in his senior year. What should Manny do between now and his senior year to be sure his placement folder is ready when he is ready to find a job?

6. Mike Kriz has worked part-time after school for the past two years. He worked for two weeks as a cook, but rarely got to work on time and was fired. He worked for two months as a busboy but quit because he didn't get enough tips. Mike also worked for three weeks as a janitor but was laid off. Finally, he worked for four months as a plumber's assistant but quit because the work hurt his back. What is Mike's record of job changes called? What does it say to potential employers? Would you hire Mike?

objectives:

After reading and studying this chapter you will be able to:

3-1 Explain the purpose of, describe the parts of, and prepare, a letter of application.

3-2 List the guidelines for, and prepare, a resume.

3-3 Describe the letter of reference and explain why it is useful to job applicants.

3-4 Prepare a job application form, prepare for a job interview, and list methods of making a good first impression.

3-5 Explain the purpose of, describe the content of, and prepare, a thank-you letter.

Job applicants and salespeople are in much the same position. A job applicant competes with other applicants for a job just as a salesperson selling cars, stereos, and other products competes with other salespeople. Instead of selling a product, however, you are selling yourself—your work experience, your education, and your ability to perform a job—to a potential employer.

In Chapters 1 and 2, you learned about careers, choices, and getting started on your career plan. In this chapter, you will examine the job application tools, interview techniques, and follow-up procedures that are critical to the job search. Once you have prepared the letter of application, the resume, and the application form, you will then learn how to use these tools, along with letters of reference, to prepare for an effective interview and to conclude the application process.

chapter

3 Getting the Job

To get a good job you will have to sell yourself. Does this young man appear to be properly prepared for an interview?

The letter of application

To apply for a job opening, or to inform a prospective employer of your interest in a potential or future job opening, job applicants often send a letter of application, together with a resume. The **letter of application** introduces you to the potential employer and gives you a chance to "sell" your qualifications. The letter of application that you write is really a sales letter. It is often your first contact with a new job, and it is important to make a good impression.

Contents of an Application Letter

The letter of application should be specific, interesting, and direct. The first paragraph should identify the purpose of the letter—why you are writing. Be *specific*—tell the reader why you are writing or how you learned about a job opening. Refer to a specific job title or type of position you are seeking.

The middle paragraph or paragraphs should give reasons why you should be considered for the job. Use full sentences which explain your qualifications and interest in the company as well as the job. To make your letter interesting, you might relate experiences you have had, classes you have taken, or skills you possess to satisfy the job requirements. The tone throughout your letter should be enthusiasm in presenting your qualifications. The writing style should be conversational—you should be able to "hear yourself talking" throughout the letter.

The closing paragraph should wrap up the letter in a friendly yet assertive manner. Be *direct*—ask for an interview. For example, give the reader your telephone number and a good time to call. In a friendly manner, make it clear that you would like to hear from the reader soon and that you are available for an interview.

Preparing the Letter of Application

Generally, the letter of application should be on white, standard size (8½-×-11-inch) paper of good quality. The mailing envelope should be of the same color and quality. Personal letterhead stationery, with matching envelope, is also appropriate.

Figure 3-1 shows a typed letter of application which is a response to a newspaper ad. Figure 3-2 on page 46 shows a similar letter of application which was prepared using proportional spacing and a laser printer. Most word processing software programs for microcomputers allow you to choose different fonts, or type styles, when preparing documents. Which letter do you like best?

Along with your letter of application, you may wish to enclose a copy of your transcripts (school records) or a letter of reference and resume. If you enclose a copy of your transcripts or a letter of reference, be sure to refer to it in the letter. Enclosures should also be listed at the end of the letter in a separate notation.

If a handwritten letter of application is required, you should follow the same guidelines for letters. That is, use standard size, plain white paper and leave the same amount of space between parts so that spacing on the final product looks very much like a typed letter.

Parts of the Letter of Application

A letter of application should contain five basic parts. As you can see from Figure 3-3 on page 47, they are the return address, the letter address, the salutation, the body, and the complimentary close.

Return Address

The **return address** shows your address to the person to whom you are writing so that he or she can write back. The standard three-line return address contains your complete address and the date of the letter but does not contain your name.

Fig. 3-1   **Letter of Application (typed); Block Letter Style**

234 Maple Street
Eugene, OR 97401-4321
June 15, 19--

Mr. R.B. Evans, Manager
Magna Music Company
2345 Main Street
Eugene, OR 97401-0013

Dear Mr. Evans

Please consider me an applicant for the office clerk position
advertised in last Sunday's Register-Guard.

My high school course work in business, which includes word
processing, accounting, and computer studies, has prepared me for
an entry-level position. Enclosed is my resume that lists my
education, experience, and skills.

My long-range goal is to work in an office where I can accept
increasing responsibilities and advance toward a position as an
administrative assistant. I gained valuable knowledge and
experience in my cooperative work experience assignment this past
year at Video Image Plus in Springfield, Oregon.

Please call me to set up a time for an interview. I am available
any day after 3 p.m. and can be reached at (503) 555-2000. I look
forward to hearing from you.

Sincerely yours,

Terence B. Adams

Terence B. Adams

Enclosure: resume

234 Maple Street
Eugene, OR 97401-4321
June 15, 19--

Ms. Marcia Evans, Owner
Brock's Music Emporium
P.O. Box 8264
Eugene, OR 97440-8264

Dear Ms. Evans

Please consider me an applicant for the next opening you have for an office clerk in your Eugene store.

I have prepared myself for this type of career and would appreciate the opportunity to work for you. As you can see from my enclosed resume, I have counter experience as well as bookkeeping, clerical, and telephone skills. Most of my course work has been in business and has included training in word processing, computer applications, and accounting.

I am available for full-time work beginning June 30 and plan to enroll part-time at the community college in the fall. I would like to continue my studies in the areas of business and music. I am looking for a permanent position with a company like yours where I can accept responsibility and challenge. My long-range career goal is to be an administrative assistant with a company such as yours.

You can reach me at (503) 555-2000 after 3 p.m. daily. I could come for an interview at your convenience. I would certainly appreciate the opportunity to discuss potential present or future employment with your company.

Sincerely yours

Terence B. Adams

Terence B. Adams

Enclosure: resume

Fig. 3-3 **Parts of a Letter**

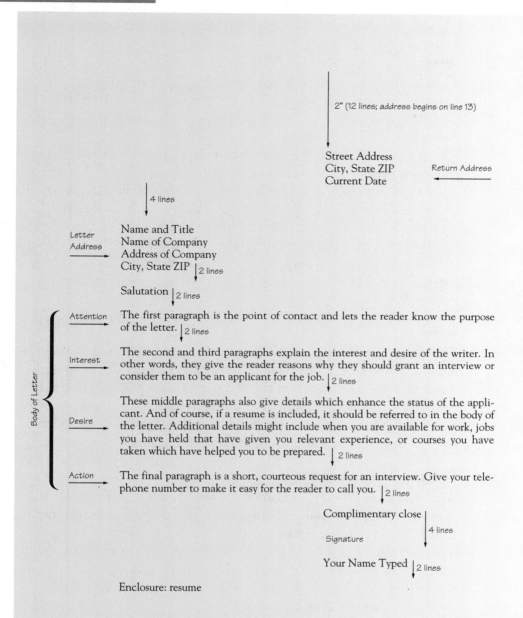

2" (12 lines; address begins on line 13)

Street Address
City, State ZIP   Return Address
Current Date

4 lines

Letter
Address

Name and Title
Name of Company
Address of Company
City, State ZIP | 2 lines

Salutation | 2 lines

Attention The first paragraph is the point of contact and lets the reader know the purpose of the letter. | 2 lines

Interest The second and third paragraphs explain the interest and desire of the writer. In other words, they give the reader reasons why they should grant an interview or consider them to be an applicant for the job. | 2 lines

Body of Letter

Desire These middle paragraphs also give details which enhance the status of the applicant. And of course, if a resume is included, it should be referred to in the body of the letter. Additional details might include when you are available for work, jobs you have held that have given you relevant experience, or courses you have taken which have helped you to be prepared. | 2 lines

Action The final paragraph is a short, courteous request for an interview. Give your telephone number to make it easy for the reader to call you. | 2 lines

Complimentary close |
                                        4 lines
Signature

Your Name Typed | 2 lines

Enclosure: resume

Letter Address

The **letter address** contains the name and address of the person or company to whom you are writing. It is important to determine the name and title of the person to whom you are writing; avoid the use of "Personnel Manager" whenever possible. If you are unable to determine whether that person is male or female, you may wish to use the simplified version of a business letter shown in Figure 3-4.

Salutation

Also known as the greeting, the **salutation** addresses your letter to the particular person you want to read the message. The person's name or other form of address may be followed by a colon, or by nothing at all. Do not use a comma. "Dear Mr. Smith:" and "Dear Sir or Madam:" are examples of salutations. You should avoid addressing application letters "To Whom It May Concern." There is no salutation in the simplified format; instead, there is a subject line. This makes the letter less personal and more businesslike, but also avoids choosing a title for a person, such as Mr., Ms., Mrs., Miss, or Dr.

Body

The **body** of the letter contains four basic parts and should be three or four paragraphs long. These paragraphs should attract the employer's *attention*, state your *interest* in the company and position, arouse the employer's *desire* to interview you, and request that the employer take *action* in the form of an interview. These parts of the body are often referred to as AIDA—attention, interest, desire, and action.

Complimentary Close

After you have stated your business, a **complimentary close** such as "Sincerely yours" or some other appropriate phrase courteously ends your letter. Your name appears several lines below the closing to allow space for your signature. The simplified format does not include the complimentary close, but goes directly to your name, again eliminating the personal touch. Below your typed name are the notations for enclosures that will accompany the letter.

 he resume

The **resume** is often called a personal data sheet, a biographical summary, a professional profile, or a vita. As a concise summary of personal information of interest to a prospective employer, a resume briefly

Fig. 3-4 **Simplified Letter of Application**

2" (12 lines; address begins on line 13)

234 Maple Street
Eugene, OR 97401-4321
June 15, 19--

4 lines

Personnel Manager
Excel Wholesale Company
818 Magnet
Eugene, OR 97401-0011 | 2 lines

(All caps)

POSITION POSTING OF JUNE 11, 19--, NO. 41826, ACCOUNTING CLERK | 2 lines

Please consider me an applicant for the position posting referred to above. | 2 lines

As you can see from my resume, I have completed the course work required to qualify for an entry-level accounting clerk position. In addition, I have worked for six months in a clerk position where I learned about serving customers, keeping cash records, recording purchases, and answering a multiline telephone during busy hours. | 2 lines

It is my long-range goal to be an administrative assistant. I would like to work in a challenging job with increasing responsibilities which utilize my business and accounting skills. I am available for full-time employment now. In the fall, I would like to attend the community college part-time to continue my studies in business and accounting. | 2 lines

I am available for an interview at your convenience. Please call me at (503) 555-2000 if you are available to talk to me about current or future employment with your company. I look forward to hearing from you. | 4 lines

Signature

Terence B. Adams | 2 lines

Enclosure: resume

describes your work experience, education, abilities, interests, and other information such as awards, offices, and activities. The resume is a valuable tool when applying for a job because it tells the employer neatly and concisely who you are, what you can do, and your background and special interests. You can also list references (names and addresses) on the resume. References are people who can tell a prospective employer about your work habits, character, and skills. Always have an up-to-date resume ready for potential employers. Figure 3-5 shows a commonly used resume style.

General Guidelines for a Resume

There are no set rules for preparing a resume. You should choose the style which best presents you to an employer. There are, however, some guidelines which have proven successful, such as:

1. Keep your resume to one page, if possible, by carefully arranging the information you choose to include. If your resume spills onto a second page, but doesn't fill it, place your references on a separate page to keep the resume to one page.
2. Include all information pertinent to the job for which you are applying. An employer wants to know you are interested in a specific job opening. Rather than prepare a "generic" resume to fit all possible openings, use key words from a job posting or ad in the paper so that you appear to be matched to the job opening.
3. Unless a particular employer requests otherwise, prepare the resume on good quality, 8½- × -11-inch paper. Avoid bright colors, odd sizes, and paper with stains or discolorations.
4. Choose a style for your resume that is attractive and easy to read. Place the most important items in the upper one-third of the page.
5. Proofread carefully. There should be no errors or evidence of errors on a resume. Use a good quality laser printer and choose a font or fonts which are attractive and businesslike. The resume shows more than information; it shows an employer how you organize and present yourself.

Parts of the Resume

You may arrange your resume according to personal preference. A simple or basic resume, which is on one page, should include limited personal information, a career objective, education, work experience, additional qualifications and skills or special items of interest, and references. People often choose to list their references on the resume

| Fig. 3-5 | A Resume |

TERENCE B. ADAMS
234 Maple Street
Eugene, OR 97401-4321
(503) 555-2000

CAREER OBJECTIVE

Office or accounting clerk position with challenge, responsibility, and opportunity for advancement to administrative assistant.

EDUCATION

1993-96	Madison High School, Eugene, Oregon (GPA 3.00)
	Major Course of Study: Business and Accounting
1990-93	Wilson Junior High School, Eugene, Oregon

Relevant Course Work:

		Relevant Skills:
Word Processing	Accounting I and II	Typing (70 wpm)
Computer Applications	Marketing I and II	Word processing and
Business Math	Business Law	spreadsheet software

Extracurricular Activities:

Member: National Honor Society, 1994-96
Member: Future Business Leaders of America, 1993-96
Competitor at regional skills event in area of accounting

WORK EXPERIENCE

Accounting Clerk, Video Image Plus, Springfield, Oregon (six months)
Cooperative work experience position through Madison High School.
Duties included answering telephone, preparing statements, serving customers, keeping cash records, recording purchases, and filing.

Office Assistant, Madison High School, Eugene, Oregon (one year)
Work in the front office included helping new students get to classes, answering the telephone, running errands, typing forms, and calling parents.

Paper Boy, Register-Guard, Eugene, Oregon (two years)
Delivered morning newspapers in one route for one year, and on two routes for one year. Duties included keeping good records, collecting from customers, sorting and doing inserts, making special deliveries, and substituting for others.

REFERENCES

Provided gladly on request.

until they have adequate other, more substantial work-related data to substitute for references. When references are not listed on a resume, it is desirable to say "Provided on request," so prospective employers know that such information is readily available. You may wish to have a separate page listing the references in the event the employer asks. Following is a discussion of the basic parts of a resume.

Personal Information

This section usually appears first on the resume and includes your name, address, and telephone number. You may also wish to include a telephone number at which messages can be left. An area code should also be used in most large metropolitan areas. However, information such as age, sex, marital status, number of dependents, or ethnic background does not give information about your skills or qualifications, and therefore should be omitted.

Career Objective

The career objective is a short, assertive statement indicating your career goal (for example, a goal to obtain a particular position title). Make the statement forward-looking, interesting, and specific. This statement both helps the employer identify with your plans and reveals your interest and enthusiasm for the job and for your future. Avoid weak and unimpressive statements such as, "Any type of work in the office." The career objective statement can be omitted in cases where it might be too limiting or too specific. As your resume gets more detailed, this is probably the first part you will drop to add more important information.

Education

List all secondary and postsecondary schools you have attended, starting with the most recent and working backwards. You may wish to include major areas of study, grade point average, extracurricular activities, scholastic honors, specific courses that apply to the job opening, or any other pertinent facts that you think will create a favorable impression on the employer. For example, extracurricular activities tell an employer that you are a well-rounded person and possess many different abilities, interests, and aptitudes. Offices held in school organizations or clubs will show the employer that you have leadership ability.

Work Experience

List all jobs, paid and unpaid, that you have held, including assisting at school functions, working as a teacher's aide, and any part- or full-time summer or vacation jobs (such as camp counselor or errand person).

You may want to write this section of your resume in paragraph or outline form. Include information such as name and address of employer, job title, work duties, and specific achievements while with this employer. Emphasize your work rather than dates of employment or name of employer.

Additional Qualifications

Educational and employment records present an overview of your personal and professional qualifications. However, you may have additional skills and abilities that you wish to bring to a potential employer's attention. For example, you may want to list special equipment you have learned to operate, foreign languages you know, special talents you have (such as playing the piano), or computers and software you have used. You can also list honors you have received or contests you have won. All of these things give an employer a more complete picture of your personality and your achievements.

On your resume, list extracurricular activities and volunteer work to show you possess different abilities, interests, and aptitudes.

References

References are persons who have known you for at least one year and can provide information about your character and achievements. References should be over age eighteen and not related to you. The best types of references include teachers, school counselors, former employers, and adults in business. Be sure to ask permission of the people you wish to list as references before including them on your resume. If you choose not to list references on your resume, you should nevertheless have names, addresses, and telephone numbers ready for employers who ask for them.

Letters of reference

A **letter of reference** is a statement, in letter form, attesting to your character, abilities, and experience, written by someone who can be relied upon to give a sincere report. When you ask someone to write a letter of reference for you, be sure to give the person enough time to prepare it. It is also helpful to give them a copy of your current resume or a short summary of your accomplishments and background. Be sure to ask a business reference to type the letter on letterhead stationery. A sample letter of reference is shown in Figure 3-6.

When you receive the letter of reference, make several photocopies of the original to give to employers along with your resume and letter of application. Keep the original for your files because you may need additional copies for other job applications.

The application form

When you visit a company to interview or to inquire about a job opening, you will probably be asked to complete an **employment application**. When possible, you should ask for an application form, take it home, and type it. If not, then the form should be filled out very carefully, using a good quality black pen. When completing an employment application, you should follow these steps:

1. Print neatly using a black or dark blue pen that does not skip or blot. Keep your responses within the space provided. Handwriting must be easy to read and clear.
2. Fill in all the blanks. When you cannot answer a question, write "N/A" (not available or not applicable), or use a broken line (————) to indicate to the employer that you have not skipped or ignored the question.
3. Be truthful. Give complete answers. Do not abbreviate unless the meaning of the abbreviation is clear.
4. Have with you all information that might be requested on the application form, such as social security number, telephone numbers, driver's license number, or work permit number. Calling later with the rest of the needed information inconveniences the employer and makes you look unprepared.

A completed application for employment is shown in Figure 3-7 on page 56.

Fig. 3-6   **Letter of Reference**

FARWEST TRUCK CENTER
402 First Street, NW
Eugene, OR 97402-2143

June 4, 19--

To Whom It May Concern

RE: Terence B. Adams

I have known Terry Adams as an employee for one and a half years. Terry began working for Farwest as a work-study student in the cooperative education program at his high school. He proved to be such a good employee that, at the end of the school year, we kept Terry as a full-time summer worker. He now works for us part-time after school and on weekends.

Terry is a fine young man. I have found him to be honest and sincere. He is always on time and is genuinely eager to do a good job. Terry gets along well with other employees and customers. He has filled in for vacationing office employees and has been able to assume additional responsibilities very quickly.

Without hesitation I can recommend Terry to you as a fine person and an outstanding employee. He will, I am sure, be an asset to any company for which he works.

If you have any further questions, please do not hesitate to call me.

Sincerely

Harriet Williams

Harriet Williams
Manager

Fig. 3-7   **Application for Employment**

APPLICATION FOR EMPLOYMENT

PLEASE PRINT WITH BLACK INK OR USE TYPEWRITER   *AN EQUAL OPPORTUNITY EMPLOYER*

NAME (LAST, FIRST, MIDDLE INITIAL)	SOCIAL SECURITY NUMBER	DATE
Adams, Terence B.	643-27-1364	6/24/--

ADDRESS (NUMBER, STREET, CITY, STATE, ZIP CODE)	TELEPHONE
234 Maple Street Eugene, OR 97401-4321	(503) 555-2000

IN CASE OF EMERGENCY, NOTIFY:	NAME Thomas and Rita Adams	RELATIONSHIP Parents
	ADDRESS Same as above	

EDUCATION

	SCHOOL NAME	CITY AND STATE	YEARS ATTENDED
HIGH SCHOOL	Madison High School	Eugene, Oregon	1993-1996
JUNIOR HIGH SCHOOL	Wilson Jr. High School	Eugene, Oregon	1990-1993
OTHER			

SKILLS

TYPING	SHORTHAND	ACCOUNTING	FILING
70 wpm	No	Yes (1 yr.)	Yes

OTHER SKILLS (LIST)
Telephone use

MACHINES YOU CAN OPERATE (LIST)
Calculator, IBM PC, IBM Word Processor, Copier, Cash Register

WORK HISTORY (LAST POSITION FIRST)

FROM	TO	EMPLOYER NAME/ADDRESS	POSITION	ENDING PAY	REASON FOR LEAVING
6/98	Present	Farwest Truck Center Eugene, Oregon	Assistant File Clerk	$5.25 /hr	Desire more responsibility
11/97	6/98	Coast Carloading Eugene, Oregon	Office Helper	Minimum Wage	More responsibility
7/96	10/97	Pancake House Restaurant Eugene, Oregon	Host/ Cashier	Minimum Wage	More time for school

REFERENCES

NAME	ADDRESS	OCCUPATION	TELEPHONE NUMBER
Ms. Grace Lawton	Eugene, Oregon	Mgr., Valley Title	(503) 555-6121
Mr. Patrick Bailey	Eugene, Oregon	Business Teacher	(503) 555-0731
Miss Frances Bishop	Eugene, Oregon	Work Experience Coord.	(503) 555-0731

I understand and agree that any false statements on this application may be considered sufficient cause for dismissal.

Terence B. Adams
SIGNATURE OF APPLICANT

personal perspective

H elp Wanted

The following is a typical ad in a newspaper's Help Wanted section. It poses a dilemma for many young people today—how can you have education *and* experience? If no one will hire you, how can you ever get that "experience"?

> WANTED: Sales Trainee. Must have course work in sales and marketing. Degree preferred. Two years sales experience required. Starting salary $21,000 plus benefits.

The situation may seem hopeless. But there are a number of ways you can meet this employer's requirements of both education and experience. But it takes planning and foresight. As you are completing your formal education in the classroom, you can also be preparing for work, in the following ways:

1. **Cooperative Work Experience.** A job after class, part-time, evenings, and weekends—while you are in school—will add valuable experience for your resume. Be sure, however, that the work experience is directly related to the type of job you will be applying for.
2. **Summer Work.** During the summers you may wish to consider working at a related job. To do this, you might try:
   a. *Temporary Work.* A company which places temporary help may have a position for you that would be filling in for a regular employee. While the position is only temporary, it gives you valuable insight and work experience.
   b. *Volunteer Work.* As a volunteer, you may be foregoing pay, but you will gain the needed experience for your resume.
3. **Internship.** An internship is an on-the-job training experience that usually pays only your expenses. In other words, you are learning while you are at the work site. The employer pays you only your cost of getting to work and any extra expenses you incur. You are receiving training and exposure to the job requirements, while the employer is receiving added help without additional payroll costs.

All of the above suggestions will help you find ways to avoid the "education but no experience" dilemma a lot of graduates face. Plan ahead and be ready for that opening!

critical thinking

1. Does the type of career you desire require that you have experience in order to be hired for an entry-level position?

2. What are some ways you plan to have gathered experience at the same time you are completing your formal education?

3. Have you participated in (a) cooperative work experience, (b) summer work (temporary, part- or full-time, or volunteer), or (c) an internship? If so, describe how you benefited.

The job interview

During the job interview, an employer will have your completed job application, together with your resume, letter of application, letter(s) of reference, and any other information you have provided. The **job interview** is a procedure in which you may be questioned about statements you have made on the application for employment or about information contained in the resume and letters. Therefore, you should spend at least as much time and effort in preparing for the interview as you did in getting the interview.

Preparing for the Interview

Preparation is essential to a successful interview. First, you should review your resume so that all your personal information and qualifications will be fresh in your mind. Be prepared to answer open-ended questions such as "Tell me about yourself," "Why do you want to work for us?" or "What would you like to be doing in five years?" These types of questions are designed to see how well you organize your thoughts, how well you speak, and how you think under pressure, as well as whatever information can be obtained without direct questions. Avoid rambling on, talking about your childhood or personal information, and talking negatively about others. Emphasize your skills, achievements, and career plans. Rehearse what you will say if you are asked this type of question.

It is also important to learn something about your potential employer. Find out what the company makes or sells, where its plants and branch operations are, how rapidly it has grown, and what its prospects are for the future. Think of questions you might ask the interviewer about the company and about the position for which you are applying. The prospective employer will be more interested in you as an employee if you show that you are interested in the company. This kind of information can be obtained from such sources as these:

1. The Yellow Pages of the telephone directory, which may have an advertisement that will list products or services;
2. The company itself (simply call and request the information you need);
3. A friend or acquaintance who works for the company and can give you good information (just ask);
4. Annual reports (usually kept on file at public and university libraries), which describe the company and its financial resources; and
5. Current periodicals and newspaper articles, which may discuss the company's economic health or plans for expansion and growth.

Your questions about the company should reflect your research from such sources as annual reports or the business section of local newspapers.

Making a Good First Impression

Since it may affect your whole future, the interview is an important moment in your life, and it is worthwhile to make careful, even painstaking, preparation for it. Several important details should be remembered in preparing to make a favorable impression:

Arrive on Time

Better yet, arrive five to ten minutes early so you have time to check your appearance and compose yourself. Never be late to an interview —the interviewer will consider your tardiness an indication of your expected job performance. Time your travel route before the day of the interview, then allow extra time for traffic and parking.

Dress Appropriately

If you are seeking work in a bank, dress like those already employed at the bank. Whatever you wear, be neat and clean. Do not overuse jewelry, perfume, or aftershave. Be modest and conservative in dress, hairstyle, and appearance. In other words, look like you already have the job and are preparing for the job beyond.

Go Alone

Do not bring along a friend or relative. Only you will perform the job if hired; therefore, the interviewer wishes to talk to you alone.

Dress appropriately for the interview— be conservative in your general appearance.

Be Prepared

Have copies of your resume, reference letters, and school transcripts with you. All should be neat, up-to-date, and accurate. Take a pad of paper and one or two good pens, articles you have found at the library concerning the company, and other information you may need or find useful. Bring your papers in a briefcase or some type of carrying folder to keep them neat and organized.

Appear Poised and Self-Confident

It is normal to be nervous, but don't let your emotions control you. It is important to appear relaxed and comfortable. Maintain good eye contact with the interviewer. Do not chew gum, smoke, or display nervous habits. An occasional smile shows you are relaxed and feel good about yourself. Avoid chattering to fill quiet times; allow the interviewer to lead the discussion.

Be Courteous

Even if you are asked to wait, respond with courtesy and understanding. Convey an attitude of composure and congeniality. Use "please" and "thank you."

Think Before You Answer Each Question

Be polite, accurate, and honest. Use correct grammar; be especially careful of verb tenses. Say "yes" rather than "yeah." Avoid slang and informal speech. Speak slowly and clearly.

Emphasize Your Strong Points

Talk about your favorite school subjects, grades, attendance, skills, work experience, activities, and goals in a positive manner. Negative comments are inappropriate and reflect badly on your personality.

Be Enthusiastic and Interested in the Company and the Job

Show that you are energetic and able to do what is asked with a willing attitude. Let the interviewer know that you are interested in the company, in the job and career, in your future, and in what's going on in the world. Above all, let common sense guide you throughout the interview; look for non-verbal and other cues from the interviewer, listen carefully, and try to understand the needs and wants of the company that is hiring.

Be energetic and positive about your possible association with the company.

When the interview is over, thank the interviewer for his or her time. Say you will check back later, then do so. Leave a copy of your resume, letters of reference, and other information with the interviewer. Exit with a smile and a comment along the lines of "I look forward to working for this company."

The thank-you letter

When your interview is completed and the employer is left to make a decision, a **follow-up** is essential. Positive contact with the employer after the interview will remind the employer of your appearance, personality, and qualifications, and should improve your chance of getting the job. A **thank-you letter** is an excellent follow-up tool to remind the interviewer of your interest in and desire to work for the company.

A brief thank-you letter should be written to the employer to express your appreciation for having been given the interview. This letter will also reaffirm your interest in the job and give you an opportunity to restate some of your qualifications for the position. Figure 3-8 is a sample thank-you letter.

Basic Rules for the Thank-You Letter

The content of the thank-you letter is very important. Follow the same format and guidelines that you used in preparing your letter of application. You may want to enclose an additional letter of reference or other information that may help convince the interviewer to hire

Fig. 3-8   **Thank-You Letter**

234 Maple Street
Eugene, OR 97401-4321
June 25, 19--

Mr. R. B. Evans, Manager
Magna Music Company
2345 Main Street
Eugene, OR 97401-0013

Dear Mr. Evans

Thank you for the time you spent with me during our interview yesterday. I enjoyed meeting you and having the opportunity to see how your company operates.

Your description of the office clerk position sounded very interesting and challenging to me. I believe I have the skills you need, and the desire to do an excellent job for you. You can be assured that I will do my best on the job as well as seek additional and better skills to be of more value to you in the future.

If there is any further information I can supply you, please feel free to call me. I look forward to hearing from you.

Sincerely yours

Terence B. Adams

Terence B. Adams

you. Remember to address the interviewer by name. If more than one person interviewed you during your visit, write a brief letter to each person.

Body of the Letter

The message of your thank-you letter is contained in the body. The first paragraph should remind the interviewer of your interview by making reference to it. A good way to begin is as follows: "Thank you for giving me the opportunity to speak with you on (date and time of interview) concerning . . ."

The second paragraph reminds the interviewer of your interest in and desire to work for the company. At this point, you could also remind the interviewer of your abilities, goals, and qualifications in a subtle, modest manner. You might add the times when you are available and the telephone number where you can be reached.

The final paragraph should express courteously your eagerness to hear from the interviewer when he or she has reached a decision. This paragraph should end on a positive note.

Keep your letter short and to the point, and make sure it is error-free. Your final opportunity to represent yourself to the potential employer through a thank-you letter may make the difference that will get you the job.

 ummary

Getting a job takes time and effort. The process begins with the application letter—whether you are responding to an ad in the paper or writing a letter hoping to match a need. The letter of application is your first impression. It introduces you and what you have to offer; it usually refers to a resume, which is enclosed, for further detail. The resume or data sheet contains all the specific information about you which will impress an employer. It should be arranged to best "sell" you. References may be listed on the resume or on a separate page. In addition, you may wish to obtain letters of reference from those who have worked with you or who have known you and are familiar with your skills, interests, and abilities.

The application form must be filled out with care. Respond fully and truthfully, using "N/A" when information requested is not available or not applicable. Type if at all possible; if not, print clearly and neatly.

Arrive early for the interview and be prepared to answer hard questions. You'll get better at interviewing with each time you practice. Try to be relaxed and enthusiastic; listen carefully and answer slowly. Always follow up the interview with a thank-you letter. It reminds the employer of your interest and qualifications for the job and may be the detail that gives you an edge over your competition.

V **ocabulary terms**

Directions: Can you find the definition for each of the following terms used in Chapter 3?

body
complimentary close
employment application
follow-up
job interview
letter address
letter of application

letter of reference
references
resume
return address
salutation
thank-you letter

1. The part of a letter that shows the writer's street address, city, state, ZIP Code, and date of the letter.
2. The greeting, using a person's name.
3. The part of a letter that shows the name and address of the person or company to whom you are writing.
4. A summary of personal information, education, experience, additional qualifications, and references of a person seeking a job.
5. The main portion of a letter, which has four main parts.
6. People over eighteen, not related to you, who have known you for at least one year and can report on your character and achievements.
7. A written statement from someone who knows you; it should be typed.
8. A form you fill out when you apply for a job.
9. A procedure in which you are asked questions about yourself, your work experience, and your education, to which you respond orally.
10. A letter to an employer asking for a job interview.
11. The phrase that courteously ends a personal business letter.
12. A tool to remind the employer of your interest in the job, written after the job interview.
13. A final contact, usually a thank-you letter, made after a job interview and before the interviewer makes a decision.

Facts and ideas in review

1. What is the purpose of a letter of application? What action is desired? What do the letters AIDA stand for?
2. What size paper should you use for a letter of application or a thank-you letter?
3. List and describe briefly the five basic parts of a letter of application.
4. When would you use the simplified letter format for a letter of application?
5. What is a resume? Describe the parts you will include in your own resume.
6. Why should you list extracurricular activities on your resume?
7. Which kinds of people should be used as references on a resume?
8. List four rules for filling out an application for employment.
9. What is meant by the term follow-up?
10. What is the content of the body of the thank-you letter?
11. Why is it important for you to type your resume, letter of application, and thank-you letter? How could using a computer make them even better?

Applications for decision making

1. Prepare a letter of application to a business or company that you would like to work for. Read the instructions on pages 43–48 carefully. (Figure 3-1 shows the point of contact as a newspaper ad; Figure 3-4 shows a simplified letter of application.)
2. Prepare your resume, using your own design. Include all information that applies to you, emphasizing your strong points.
3. Call, write, or speak directly to each person listed on your resume as a reference (or anyone you would use when asked for references), and ask permission to use their names on your resume or for job interview purposes. Ask one person to write a letter of reference for you to use in seeking a job.
4. Obtain and complete an application for employment from a local business.

5. Write a thank-you letter for a job interview. Assume you were interviewed by the person to whom you sent your letter of application (see Question 1). You should know the interviewer's name now. Address the person by name and title.

 ife situation problem solving

1. Mike Smith wants to work as a forest ranger when he graduates from college. At present, he knows of no openings, but he does know the address of the local Bureau of Land Management, which occasionally hires students during summers to help in the forest. Mike takes science courses and does well. He is available to work all summer, and could even work without pay if his living expenses were covered. Because you are Mike's friend, you have offered to help him write a letter of application. Make up a return address, letter address, salutation (or use Simplified format), body, and complimentary close, using the letters of application as guides.

2. Naomi Rodriguez must provide a resume in order to answer an advertisement in the local newspaper. Write in outline form a summary of the basic rules of writing a resume. On another piece of paper, sketch a resume and label its parts. You do not need to insert fictional information—just describe what kinds of information Naomi should use.

3. Pam Olefson tells you that she has a job interview tomorrow. She has never been on a job interview before, and she is very nervous. Pam asks you to point out to her what she should and should not do during her interview. On a piece of paper, make a list for Pam of at least five things she should be sure to do and five things she should avoid during her job interview.

4. Lee O'Leary has just completed a job interview. The interviewer will see six more applicants over three days before she makes a decision. Lee knows that his competition is tough, but believes he stands a good chance of getting the job because he is available to work right away, his grades are high, and he has taken three marketing courses. Would you advise him to write a follow-up (thank-you) letter? What might he say in such a letter?

objectives:

After reading and studying this chapter you will be able to:

4-1 List and describe effective communication strategies, including listening, informal and formal speaking, communication among employees, and communication among employees and employers.

4-2 Discuss techniques of effective human relations.

4-3 Describe employer expectations and policies such as written and unwritten work rules, attitudes, and absenteeism.

4-4 Explain motivation and levels of need as described by Maslow and discuss the results of job satisfaction.

A successful career brings recognition, respect, and freedom from economic want. Once you make a wise career choice, and plan for and get the job you really want, it is important to be successful and build a foundation for future promotions and career opportunities. Adapting to your job involves understanding and meeting the needs of other employees as well as supervisors and employers. In this chapter, you will learn the techniques that will make you a valuable employee and prepare you for advancement to higher responsibilities.

chapter 4

Adapting to Your Job

ommunicating at work

Today's jobs and those in the future will depend on good communication skills. Of all the job activities you perform in a day, 80 percent involve communication in one form or another. While writing is often considered the most frequent form of communication, 60 percent of job communication involves listening and speaking. Figure 4-1 illustrates the amount of time spent in the four forms of communication (listening, speaking, writing, and reading) during the average work day in America.

Listening

Hearing is not the same as listening. **Hearing** is the process of perceiving sound. It requires little or no thinking and very little effort. **Listening** is the active hearing process that requires mental concentration and

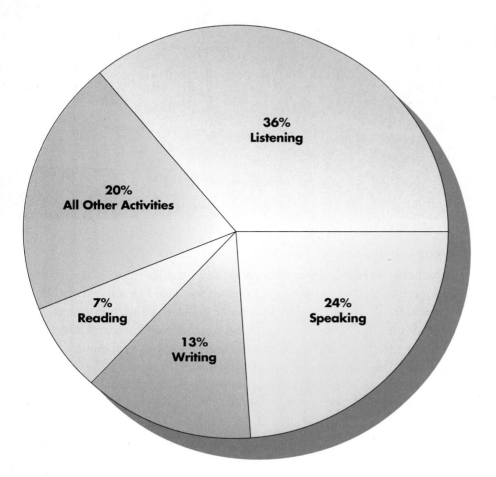

Fig. 4-1

Communication on the Job

36%
Listening

20%
All Other Activities

7%
Reading

13%
Writing

24%
Speaking

effort. Listening carefully is a communication tool that will bring you much reward. There are several rules to follow to become a good listener:

1. Look at the speaker and maintain eye contact to show interest in what the speaker is saying.
2. Ask questions—get actively involved in the conversation.
3. Avoid interrupting or changing the subject.
4. Control your emotions. Listen to what the speaker says, then evaluate it with an open mind.

Different types of listening are needed at different times. The three types of effective listening are sympathetic, critical, and creative.

Listening is a critical element of communication.

Sympathetic Listening

Sympathetic listening, sometimes called empathy listening, is the ability to perceive from another person's point of view and to sense mentally and emotionally what the person is feeling. To listen with empathy, keep your eyes and attention on the speaker; do not interrupt the speaker or interject your opinions; ask questions that lead the speaker to make further explanations and analysis; do not make body gestures or expressions indicating approval, disapproval, or opinion. Your own opinions should not be given unless asked for.

Critical Listening

Critical listening is the ability to differentiate facts from fiction or useless trivia. When analyzing information about a product or service you are considering purchasing, you will need to use critical listening. For example, claims that a product is "the best buy," "top quality," "one of a kind," "really beautiful," or "a sure winner," do not tell you anything about the product. But when you hear descriptors that provide important information describing a product, such as "100 percent cotton," "one-year guarantee," or "wash and wear," you are receiving useful information.

Creative Listening

Creative listening is the ability to hear new ideas that can help you develop a plan of action. Creative listening is often used in problem solving. Brainstorming is a common component of creative listening. In this process, all ideas are written down, regardless of quality. Then, after every possible piece of information is gathered, the best parts are put together to make a workable plan. Creative listening is difficult because it is a group process.

Informal Speaking

At most workplaces, about 24 percent of the average employee's time is spent in oral communication. Most of the speaking you will do will be informal speech. *Informal speech* is used in four major ways: to make contact with others, to exchange information, to influence others, and to solve problems.

1. *To make contact with others*, you greet people, exchange social conversation, chat about the weather, report on people and events, establish personal relationships, and find common ground for discussion. All relationships, formal or informal, begin with this initial contact which often leads to more conversations where common interests are discovered and developed. This type of informal speech is a daily event for most people at work; it's important to be able to initiate conversations and begin relationships this way.

2. *To exchange information*, you explain an idea, clarify a difficult point, and illustrate with examples. This is often accomplished by relating to others through some common experience, which is discovered by asking and answering questions. Information must be passed between and among workers so that the company can produce its goods or services in a timely and efficient manner.

3. *To influence others*, you stimulate feelings, present new viewpoints, and convince through basic appeals of emotion, logic, and evidence. To get people to accept your viewpoint and make it their own as well, you might describe personal experiences, encourage open communication, give advice, and share a conviction (a strong belief). You will need to convince others of the validity of a new idea or suggestion you may have, or when you feel strongly about changing something.

4. *To solve problems*, you identify or define a problem and specify its causes. Then you consider all possible alternatives and propose solutions. Finally, after rational elimination of the least desirable choices, you select the best option. To effectively solve problems, you must have the help and cooperation of others with whom you are communicating. Unfortunately, you can't solve problems if you haven't mastered the first three informal speech methods.

Formal Speaking

There are three basic purposes for formal speaking: to inform, to entertain, or to persuade. Information is presented in different ways, depending on which kind of speech you are making.

1. **To Inform.** In this type of presentation, you are attempting to convey information to your audience. The information should be given in a manner that is easily understood. You can give facts and then reach your conclusions (inductive reasoning), or you can give the conclusions first, followed by the reasons (deductive reasoning).

2. **To Entertain.** This type of speech is humorous from beginning to end. The purpose is to get the members of your audience to relax and enjoy themselves. Entertainment speaking may seem fun and easy, but it is probably the most difficult form of formal speech, because you are dependent on the audience's reaction. For example, if the audience doesn't laugh or respond favorably to you, you may find it difficult to keep going.

3. **To Persuade.** This is a speech designed to convince your audience to take some action or to believe something. To be convincing, you must use solid information based on facts and statistics. You must appear to be honest and to believe in what you are saying. Persuasive speech takes a great deal of practice and motivation. If you are not sincere, your audience will sense it.

To give your formal speeches added dimension and style, you can use audiovisual equipment and aids. Equipment such as overhead projectors, screens, tape recorders, and sound systems, and audiovisual aids such as transparencies, slides, display boards, flip charts, chalkboards, maps and graphs, real objects, models, and handouts, create interest.

Audiovisual aids give added dimension and style to presentations.

The setting, which includes lighting, room layout, seating, speaker's stand, and microphone, can also contribute to the positive acceptance of a speech.

Stage fright (nervousness) is a natural and common reaction. Many experienced speakers are nervous or tense before speaking. There are several things you can do to control stage fright, such as build confidence, be well prepared, and practice speaking.

1. **Build Your Confidence.** Practice in relatively nonthreatening speaking situations. Talk before small groups, including friends and family. Take speech classes and observe other speakers carefully.

2. **Be Well Prepared.** First, outline what you want to say. Then time yourself giving the speech several times. Prepare an additional "comfort zone" of several minutes' worth of material in case time goes faster than you thought it would. Most people talk faster when they are nervous, so make allowances for this. Be sure you have enough material and that the material is appropriate and well developed.

3. **Practice Public Speaking.** Begin with short speeches and build to longer ones. Practice speaking slowly and carefully when expressing your thoughts and opinions. Volunteer to speak before classes, clubs, and groups. Record your voice and evaluate its effectiveness. This will help you keep your voice low and clear, avoiding high pitches, slang, talking too fast, and so on.

Communication Among Employees

While upward and downward exchanges of ideas and information tend to be more formal, **horizontal communication** (communication among employees of equal rank) is usually informal. Within all groups there are invisible hierarchical ranks and communication barriers. These can be minimized through the use of effective communication abilities and interpersonal relations skills. The most common types of horizontal communications are face-to-face conversations (described earlier in the "Informal Speaking" section) and small group meetings.

Small group meetings may be organized (with specific purposes in mind), or they may be spontaneous and informal. Common functions of small group meetings include problem solving, decision making, and information sharing. Usually employees who are in small groups tend to be of equal rank. Ideas and suggestions promoted by a group tend to be implemented more often than when the same information comes from one person. Some companies encourage small group meetings to get good advice, desired feedback, and varied approaches to problem solving. These companies find that involving employees is a good way to increase employees' commitment to the solution of a problem.

Communication Between Employees and Employers

There are two types of communication between employers and employees: downward and upward. **Downward communication** is used to keep employees informed and to give them job-related instructions and feedback about their performances. Downward communication needs to be consistent, fair, and easily understood by employees. Some communications will be public and verbal, some written, and others will occur in private or group meetings. Information and ideas need to be clearly presented so that employees can respond and adjust accordingly.

Upward communication is the transmitting of information from employees to supervisors and employers. Upward communication includes information about job and work-related problems, organizational policies and procedures, and suggestions for improvement of company practices. The effectiveness of this flow of information and ideas depends on relationships between employers and employees, the quality of the employee's presentation of the message, the extent to which the message is positive or negative, the timeliness of the message, and its perceived usefulness to the employer. When upward communication is free-flowing and encouraged, employees tend to be more productive and efficient because they believe they have a significant role, and therefore job security, with the company.

Human relations

Human relations is getting along with others. As technological advances become more complex and sophisticated, our need for genuine and caring human relationships increases. To be truly competent in human relations, you need to have a good understanding of yourself and of others (including their needs, desires, and attitudes), and a genuine concern with the needs and feelings of others.

Techniques for maintaining effective human relations include accepting differences, treating others as individuals, empathizing with others and praising their achievements, describing problems rather than personalities, accepting responsibility, avoiding dogmatic statements, treating others as equals and trusting them, and controlling your emotions.

1. **Accept Differences.** All people are different; we need to accept others as they are, tolerate differences of opinion, and recognize that other ways of doing things may also be effective. It is important to be able to disagree without being disagreeable.

2. **Treat Others as Individuals.** Take time to discover the individuality in others; learn people's names and call them by their names; take an interest in what others are doing. Every person needs and deserves to be respected as a human being.

3. **Empathize with Others. Empathy** is the ability to see others' points of view and understand their feelings. It does not mean you agree with them or with what they are feeling, but rather that you understand what they are saying, feeling, or experiencing.

4. **Praise Others.** Be consistent in praising the achievements of others. False praise doesn't benefit anyone; therefore, seek good things which are true and complimentary, and use them freely. But avoid untrue or exaggerated claims that will appear to be forced and fake.

5. **Describe Problems.** When problems with someone else occur, you will get the person's cooperation by describing the problem rather than the person or personality differences. To do this, you avoid accusations. For example, say "That report was not what was needed by the auditors," rather than "You did not prepare the report properly for the auditors."

6. **Accept Responsibility.** Take responsibility for your actions. Everybody makes mistakes; take responsibility for yours. Your willingness to accept responsibility and say "I goofed" will be respected by coworkers and employers.

7. **Avoid Dogmatic Statements.** A dogmatic statement asserts an opinion as if it were a fact. A user of dogmatic statements soon becomes known as a "know-it-all," or worse, a "loose cannon." To avoid appearing dogmatic, restrict your judgments to possibilities rather than absolutes.

8. **Treat Others as Equals.** Treat each person you associate with as though he or she is making worthwhile contributions. Don't talk down to people by telling them what they should know or should do. Allow others to make their own decisions without criticism.

9. **Trust Others.** People will live up to, or down to, your expectations; therefore, think the best of others and expect the best. When they know you trust them, most people prove to be trustworthy.

10. **Control Your Emotions.** Withhold judgments, comments, or decisions until all information is gathered. Reacting emotionally may affect your decisions, and you may later regret the display of emotions. Be slow to show emotions, holding off as long as you can to be sure you have reached the right conclusion. Showing your initial reaction is often the worst thing you could do!

mployer expectations and policies

Employers have expectations and policies to inform and guide employees in meeting goals and objectives of the business. Many of these expectations are expressed as work rules, work attitudes, and absenteeism policies.

Work Rules

Most businesses have written and unwritten *work rules* that are generally understood by all employees. *Unwritten rules* often are commonly understood without being documented or verbally communicated. A dress code is one example. Before you interview for a job, find out how employees who are already at the job are dressed. An employer expects employees to know from common sense some of the work rules that apply to their jobs. Courtesy and teamwork are expected. Loyalty, a positive attitude, punctuality, good grooming, and appropriate dress are other unwritten and unspoken rules.

Written work rules are usually posted in employee work areas to remind employees of strict policies that must be followed. These rules are generally written for the benefit and protection of all employees.

When everyone adheres to the rules, the work flows smoothly and everyone shares in the responsibilities. Breaking a rule can cause dissatisfaction and hard feelings among employees. Figure 4-2 is an example of work rules that might be posted in an employee lunch room.

COMPANY WORK RULES
Sanders Department Store

1. Work begins promptly at 8 a.m. or 2 p.m. and ends promptly at 5 p.m. or 10 p.m. These are our hours of operation, and the store must be covered.

2. No food, drink, or smoking is allowed in the store.

3. Smoking is permitted in Lounge B during break at 10:15 a.m. and at 2:45 p.m. for the day shift, and at 4 p.m. and at 8:45 p.m. for the evening shift.

4. All employees will be clean and properly groomed at all times. Facial hair is permitted if it is well groomed. Use good judgment in what you wear.

5. When a worker is sick, he or she must call in by 7 a.m. for the day shift, or by 4 p.m. for the evening shift.

6. Vacations are taken according to seniority; no more than three employees may take vacations during the same week. All vacations must be arranged two weeks in advance.

Fig. 4-2

Work Rules

Because the rules shown in Figure 4-2 are basic disciplinary rules, employees who break them are subject to immediate discipline. Employers generally will not tolerate employees who are late for work or who leave work early (except in rare emergencies). When one employee is permitted to break the rules, others will see this and feel justified in doing the same thing, thinking they should be treated in a similar manner. It is important for a new employee to follow all the rules to the letter—and beyond—to show the employer that he can fit in and be a part of the team. A new employee should arrive early, leave on time, and never stay overtime on a break or sneak food into the work area. While these infractions are not acceptable in regular employees, they are tolerated even less in new employees.

Work Attitudes and Absenteeism

Employees' work attitudes are important to employers because they affect morale, output (production), and public relations. Every employee in a company represents that company to the public. When the employee's attitude is good, a favorable impression is made.

Employers appreciate employees who have a positive attitude and do their jobs with enthusiasm.

Good public relations are important to a company's future growth and profitability. Employees in today's best-run organizations follow these simple rules to create a favorable impression:

1. Remember customers' names.
2. Make an unusual effort to help.
3. Demonstrate knowledge, enthusiasm, and interest in customers.
4. Display genuine concern for quality of product and service.
5. Care about people and meeting their needs.
6. Listen sympathetically to customer complaints.
7. Take pride in themselves and their work.

Employers appreciate employees who "go the extra mile"—who do more than what is required, and do it with a positive mental attitude.

Most human resources experts and managers agree that absenteeism is a special kind of problem. How to deal with the problem depends on the reasons for absence. Professor P. J. Taylor (London University) observed that of all absences:

- 60 percent are due to serious or chronic illnesses, injuries, or family emergencies;
- 20 percent are due to acute, short-term illnesses (such as the flu), work-related accidents, or personal problems;
- 10 percent are due to a minor illness such as a cold, and to employees whose decision to report to work or not depends on their attitudes about their jobs; and

- 10 percent are due to a feigned illness so that the employee can enjoy a day off.

The absentees making up the last 20 percent are of greatest concern to businesses. Industrial psychologists call this "voluntary absence syndrome" and warn that these patterns can lead to serious emotional imbalance and disturbance in the absentees' lives. Some authorities on employee absenteeism contend that the person who is chronically absent from work without good reason is mentally ill. They believe that this type of person cannot deal with the reality of work, and that she or he must escape from reality by regularly staying away from work.

Types of Absentees

Absentees usually fall into groups with similar characteristics. Most fit into these six categories:

Chronic

These are the people who seem to have little tolerance for pressure on the job or off. Before they can be counseled, they first need to be aware that their absence is a problem and is causing other problems.

Vacationir g

These are people who work only long enough to pay their bills and put a few dollars in their pocket before they head down the road. Vacationers make a conscious choice to be absent from work as much as work rules will allow, and they rarely will accept or benefit from counseling.

Directionless

This group of employees is generally made up of young people. Until they decide what they want to do with their lives, they are likely to be poor employees and may take advantage of opportunities to be absent from work.

Aggressive

These are people who willfully stay away from work, intending their absences to cause problems. This kind of behavior requires professional counseling to correct.

Moonlighters

People who hold more than one job are often either too tired to come to work or trapped by conflicting work schedules. Very often the moonlighter is forced to make a choice between jobs.

Occasional

These employees' absences are legitimate, and their illnesses are real. But while their absences can cause temporary problems in the workplace, these absentees need a mixture of sympathy, understanding, and good advice.

Causes of Chronic Absenteeism

Of the 20 percent of absentees who are absent due to minor or feigned illness, 60 percent can be helped. Employees who can answer yes to any of these questions are categorized as needing and responding to help.

1. Is getting to work a problem (real or imagined)?
2. Are off-the-job pressures (such as family and marital troubles) so overwhelming that they weaken the employee's resolve to go to work?
3. Is the employee too eager to please or too easily misled?
4. Does the employee feel the work is boring, disagreeable, unattractive, or somehow not measuring up to expectations?
5. Are the employee's working relationships unpleasant?
6. Are there serious problems in the employee's life that need immediate attention (child care, emergencies, serious illness, court appearances, and so on)?
7. Has lateness or absenteeism become a habit the employee finds hard to break?

Employees who can answer yes to any of the following questions are categorized as probably unwilling or unable to respond to help. In other words, overcoming these symptoms involves more action and resolve than the employee is capable of.

1. Does work or pay hold no strong attraction for the employee? Does the employee show general disinterest in life, work, pay, or any other rewards?
2. Do off-the-job pressures and needs have a greater priority than work and a greater payoff in the view of the employee?
3. Is the employee intentionally absent in order to disrupt production or cause problems for the employer or for other employees?

Alcoholism and Drug Abuse

The National Council for Alcoholism reports that the alcoholic is absent two to four times more often than the nonalcoholic and that on-the-job accidents are two to four times more frequent for the alcoholic than for the nonalcoholic. Drug abuse is more difficult to detect by employers, but overall effects and outcomes are similar to those for alcoholics. Work efficiency is impaired, other employees are affected, and general work attitudes are inhibited when employees suffering from drug addiction attempt to perform as usual without professional help. The use or sale of alcohol or drugs on the work site is usually cause for immediate dismissal.

Repetitive Work

The most common reason for absenteeism (other than illness) is the tedium of repetitive work that is considered routine and nonintellectual. Employees who perceive their jobs as nonproductive or unimportant are more likely to have high absenteeism rates.

New Employees

Newly hired employees are often chronic absentees. Employers should request previous employment records of total days and times absent. A letter of reference that specifically details the person's attendance record, as well as other qualifications for the job, may be presented during a job interview. A former employer's letter of reference will probably include specific information about attendance, total days absent while working for that company, dependability, responsibility, and punctuality.

Costs of Absenteeism

High rates of absenteeism cost companies thousands of dollars annually. The U.S. Department of Labor has developed a formula to compute a rate of absenteeism that can be used to calculate total costs to a business.

For example, assume that a small business has an average of twenty-five total employees (including part- and full-time) during a month's payroll period. The average month has twenty-two workdays. If that employer had total absences among all employees of fifteen full days, the absenteeism rate would be about 2.73 percent. Most labor experts agree that an absenteeism rate of 2.0 is low, while a rate of 5.0 is high.

Once the absenteeism rate is known, the cost to the company can be calculated by using the average wages earned. An absenteeism rate of 2.73 percent would cost the company about $17,000 each year in lost time, assuming that the average wage earned was $6.00 an hour.

Effects of Absenteeism

The absentee is not the only one affected by absenteeism, but is usually the most seriously affected. Typically, the results range from penalties, fines (such as payroll deductions), and warnings, to temporary layoffs, poor recommendations, lack of respect (from employers and fellow employees), and eventually to termination of employment.

When action is not taken, businesses are in effect giving their approval (or lack of disapproval) to the absences, thereby encouraging other employees to feel free to be absent often. The working employees resent having to do another employee's work when no corrective action is taken by the employer. The overall effects of absenteeism are well known: demoralization, lack of respect for the employer, increased disciplinary action, tightening of company policy, declining working conditions, and poor employment references.

otivation and needs

All human beings have some needs that are basic to survival and other needs that go beyond mere physical existence. A person's work attitudes and job satisfaction are affected and motivated by the fulfillment of his or her needs. Abraham Maslow, a behavioral psychologist, developed a human behavior model called *Maslow's Hierarchy of Needs*. Maslow's hierarchy divides human needs into five distinct categories, as shown in Figure 4-3.

Hierarchy of Needs

Employment can be the basis for meeting all five levels of need. Levels 1 and 2 are things that are essential to physical survival: pay that is adequate to provide food, clothing, and housing, and sufficient job security to feel safe and comfortable. When basic needs are not provided by the job, the absence of these factors is called a **dissatisfier**. In other words, your work productivity will be reduced because your incentive and desire to work are diminished. (It is important to note that one level of need does not have to be completely satisfied or fulfilled before we can go on to meet needs in the next level or levels.)

Levels 3, 4, and 5 are called **motivators** because accomplishments and recognition in these areas will lead to greater productivity and work satisfaction. **Productivity** is a measure of efficiency that compares the costs of output of a production unit during a specific period of time. A quality standard is often incorporated into the measure of productivity.

Every employee can be motivated because every person needs fulfillment beyond physical requirements. Most businesses consider it the responsibility of management to provide opportunities for employees to meet their needs.

Level 3 is described by Maslow as the need for love and the need to belong to the group: to be accepted, to have friends, and to be valued

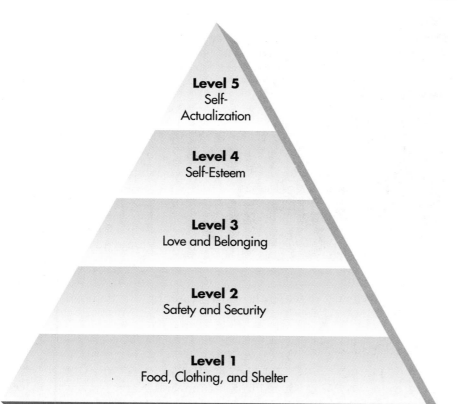

Fig. 4-3

Maslow's Hierarchy of Needs

as a member of the team. In the workplace, love is represented by kindness and caring in work relationships; and belonging, by the feeling that we have a meaningful role in the workplace.

Level 4 is **self-esteem** and self-worth, and it refers to our inner feelings about ourselves and what we do. When work is challenging and rewarding, we feel good about our job and about ourselves, and we want to do more. When employees do not feel good about themselves and their accomplishments, they tend to become negative about others and their accomplishments and often show a decrease in work effort or productivity.

Level 5 is **self-actualization,** the level at which employees are able to meet all their needs of accomplishment and satisfaction; they are able to do the work they choose, as they choose, and receive appropriate rewards for a job well done. To aid employees in achieving this level, many managers try to determine what type of work their employees need for self-fulfillment and self-actualization. Then they introduce this kind of work into their employees' workday gradually until they can handle such work well and use it to realize their full potential.

Job fulfillment is to be found through acceptance and friendship with team members.

Results of Job Satisfaction

The employer is not the only winner when employees are able to meet most of their needs. Employees feel better about themselves; stress levels decline; efforts are rewarded by greater pay, advancement opportunities, and praise; and work is pleasant and enjoyable. Employers benefit from increased productivity, which leads to greater profits, company growth, and income potential.

Increased Productivity

When employees work better, they are more productive. Time is used wisely; more work is produced in less time, and better work is produced in the same or less time. Increased productivity leads to higher profits for the employer, and subsequent rewards for the employees—both tangible (raises, bonuses, or promotions) and intangible (praise, commendation, and self-esteem).

Self-Esteem and Self-Actualization

To put forth your best effort; to win the praise of employer and employees; to strive for new challenges—all are valid bases for career development and satisfaction. As these goals are met and achieved, they bring personal pride and enjoyment that are satisfying beyond the paycheck. Because you will probably work most of your adult life, why not strive to accomplish the most to the best of your ability?

Rewards and Opportunities

Employers often seek to motivate employees using praise and pay as reinforcements for desirable results. Your rewards will vary: oral or written commendations from employers; admiration and respect of other employees; pay raises for exemplary work (often called merit pay); increased opportunities for challenging work (new job assignments with increased responsibilities); opportunities for advancement to higher paying positions with more prestige and status; and respect from others inside and outside your organization for your accomplishments

point counterpoint

M anagement Versus Labor

Business and labor have often been at odds in this country. As our foreign competitors frequently point out, American owners and managers are not on the same "team" as their employees and workers. This causes loss of productivity, job dissatisfaction, and mistrust between owners or managers and their employees.

The Employees' Side

Many employees feel that their employers do not care about them; that they are "only a number" and easily replaceable. They cite low wages and poor or no benefits. They tell of employers who lay off employees at the first sign of economic downturn. They speak of poor evaluation systems, lack of incentives, and worst of all, lack of empathy and communication by employers.

The attitude of many workers in American factories, repair shops, and stores is: "Why should we work ourselves to an early grave for an employer who doesn't appreciate anything we do? When they (the employers) show us that they consider us important, then we'll put in the kind of effort they want. Until then, I'm doing nothing more than I have to until I can find a better job."

The Employer's Side

Employers and managers have to be competitive to stay in business. They report that competition is tough and getting tougher; that wages increase but productivity (output) does not. In order to be profitable, they must cut costs in every way possible. Unfortunately, wages are the largest expense of most businesses, so it's the logical place to make cuts first.

"Many workers are just plain lazy. They want a full day's pay but don't want to give a full day's work," say managers at typical businesses. "I can't pay top wages until this business starts bringing in more cash. Therefore, there won't be better wages or benefits until workers start earning it."

critical thinking

1. Do you agree with the logic of the employee's side? Are there more points that could be made?

2. Do you agree with the logic of the employer's side? Are there more points that could be made?

3. What would you do or advise employees and employers to do to solve this dilemma which is harming American competitiveness?

and quality of work. You could become known as "one of the best in the field" and gain recognition in your community, city, state, or even nation. This makes you valuable not only to your own employer, but it also makes you more employable in the future should you desire to move to another job or another area. Increased opportunities within your field are created by excellence in work accomplishments and should be a part of your long-term career plans.

Summary

Adapting to your job and having successful work experience depends on good listening, speaking (informal and formal), and human relations skills. Employers have written and unwritten rules and work expectations and are concerned with employee attitudes and resulting problems such as absenteeism and tardiness. Workers who understand employer expectations and successful job adaptation strategies will have success in being more productive, satisfied employees. Job satisfaction can be attained through motivation and meeting the needs of employers and other employees. Learning and applying successful communication skills will enhance a person's employability, productivity, and self-image.

ocabulary terms

Directions: Can you find the definitions for each of the following terms used in Chapter 4?

creative listening   *listening*
critical listening   *motivators*
dissatisfier   *productivity*
downward communication   *self-actualization*
empathy   *self-esteem*
hearing   *sympathetic listening*
horizontal communications   *upward communication*
human relations

1. Communication among employees of equal rank.
2. An active process or skill that requires mental concentration and effort.
3. Communication that keeps employees informed, gives instructions, and provides feedback.
4. Diminishes your desire to work.
5. Leads to greater work satisfaction.
6. A type of listening in which you differentiate fact from fiction.
7. Transmitting of information from employees to supervisors and managers.
8. Feelings of self-worth about ourselves and our accomplishments.
9. Getting along with others.
10. A measure of the output of a production unit.
11. The type of listening in which you listen but offer no advice.
12. A type of listening in which all ideas are considered and the most workable parts are saved.
13. A level at which employees meet all their needs of accomplishment and satisfaction.
14. The process of perceiving sound.
15. The ability to see others' points of view or understand their feelings.

end-of-chapter activities

acts and ideas in review

1. List four ways informal speaking is used on the job.
2. In percentages, how much time on the job is spent on these activities:
   a. listening
   b. speaking
   c. writing
   d. reading
   e. other activities (traveling, filing and retrieving, data entry, running errands, cleaning up, organizing, thinking, planning, and so on)
3. What are the differences among the following types of listening?
   a. sympathetic listening
   b. critical listening
   c. creative listening
4. List three purposes of formal speeches.
5. List the three main categories of speaking tools.
6. List three things you can do about stage fright.
7. Distinguish among these types of communication:
   a. horizontal communication
   b. downward communication
   c. upward communication
8. What is meant by good human relations?
9. List five techniques for maintaining effective human relations.
10. What percentage of all absences is due to serious or chronic illness, injuries, or family emergencies?
11. What is voluntary absence syndrome?
12. List six categories of absentees.
13. Give three reasons or causes of chronic absenteeism.
14. What are some effects of absenteeism on the absentee? On other employees?
15. List in order from bottom to top Maslow's five levels of need.
16. What are three major results of job satisfaction?

pplications for decision making

1. What are some things you can do to improve your listening skills?
2. Under what circumstances would you use sympathetic listening? critical listening? creative listening?
3. What type of speech or presentation did you hear recently (informational, entertaining, or persuasive)? Describe it.
4. Have you ever experienced stage fright? What did you do to help make it easier?
5. What are two types of horizontal communication? Describe each.
6. Why are human relations important in any career or workplace?
7. Why is it important for a new employee to observe all unwritten and written work rules?
8. What is meant by a chronic absentee?
9. How do alcoholism and drug abuse affect an employee's performance on the job?

 ife situation problem solving

1. The following formula was devised by the U.S. Department of Labor for computing a rate of absenteeism. Compute the rate of absenteeism based on these facts:

Average number of employees: 45
Number of workdays in period: 22
Worker days lost during period: 26

$$\text{Rate of Absenteeism (\%)} = \frac{\text{Worker Days Lost During Period} \times 100}{\text{Average Number of Workers} \times \text{Number of Work Days in Period}}$$

2. Interview a person working full time and ask how each of the following levels is met through his or her employment: Level 1 (food, clothing, and shelter); Level 2 (safety and security); Level 3 (love and belonging); Level 4 (self-esteem and self-worth); and Level 5 (self-actualization).

3. Salvador works for a small delivery service and believes that he is underpaid. He brags to friends, "When I'm making deliveries, sometimes I stop for a pizza. Sometimes I even visit my girl friend. Why should I knock myself out on what I earn?" What advice would you give Salvador?

4. Make a list of unwritten rules that you observe in your home or in your classroom. Compare your list to a friend's list to see the similarities and differences.

5. Interview employees about the necessity of getting along well at a place of employment. Then ask an employer the same questions:
   a. Do you feel that human relations is an important part of each job where you work?
   b. Does the employer (supervisor) feel that human relations is important?
   c. What types of company policies or unwritten rules are in place to ensure good human relations?

After reading and studying this chapter you will be able to:

5-1 Understand and complete appropriate work forms, such as W-4, social security application, and work permit application forms.

5-2 Understand and recall employee responsibilities at work, including responsibilities to employers and to other employees.

5-3 Describe employer responsibilities to employees.

5-4 List and define provisions of basic employment laws enacted for the protection and security of workers.

terms to know:

Form W-4
allowances
exempt status
social security
  number
minors
Form W-2
marketable
initiative
administrative
  agencies
Social Security Act
unemployment
  insurance
Wage and Hour Act
minimum wage
workers'
  compensation

n Chapter 4 you learned how to successfully adapt to your work; in this chapter you will become familiar with another aspect of the job: employment forms, responsibilities, and laws. This information will assist you in decision making and give you the informed background to work in a safe and productive environment. In this chapter, we will cover three areas: the work forms you will be required to fill out and use for employment and for your personal records; your responsibilities to your employer and your employer's responsibilities to you; and basic employment laws that protect you in the workplace.

Keeping Your Job

chapter 5

 nderstanding and preparing work forms

When you begin your first paying job, you will need to be aware of a number of forms. Most of these forms ask for information that employers are required by law to keep. Some of them are obtained prior to beginning work (social security card and work permit, if you are under sixteen), while others are completed by you when you begin working (W-4) and by the employer after you have worked during the year (W-2). You should be familiar with these forms because you may need to make corrections or changes from time to time, and because you will use the information on some of these forms for reporting income taxes.

Form W-4, Employee's Withholding Allowance Certificate

When you report to work, you will be asked to fill out a **Form W-4, Employee's Withholding Allowance Certificate.** The information you put on this form determines the amount of money your employer will deduct from your paycheck for income taxes. On this form you declare the total number of your **allowances**—persons claimed that reduce the amount of tax withheld from your paycheck. The more allowances you can claim, the less tax you will have withheld. You may automatically claim yourself; other allowances can be for spouse and children.

If you qualify, you may also claim **exempt status** and not have any federal tax withheld from your paycheck; simply write *exempt* on the W-4 form as shown in Figure 5-1. You may claim to be exempt from federal tax withholding if you will not earn enough money to owe any federal tax. The maximum amount of earnings necessary to qualify varies annually. Exemption may be claimed if last year you owed no federal tax and qualified for a full refund and this year you also do not expect to owe any federal tax and should get a full refund.

Social Security Forms

Because all workers in the United States must pay a social security tax from wages earned, all have a **social security number.** Your social security number is your permanent work identification number. While you are working, your employers withhold social security taxes from your pay and contribute matching amounts. The amounts you earn and the amounts contributed for social security throughout your work life are credited by the Social Security Administration to your account under

Fig. 5-1   **Form W-4, Employee's Withholding Allowance Certificate**

Form **W-4**	Employee's Withholding Allowance Certificate	OMB No. 1545-0010

Department of the Treasury
Internal Revenue Service

▶ **For Privacy Act and Paperwork Reduction Act Notice, see reverse.**

1 Type or print your first name and middle initial
Marisa M.   Last name
Clark   **2** Your social security number
682-40-5896

Home address (number and street or rural route)
685 West Circle Avenue

3 ☒ Single ☐ Married ☐ Married, but withhold at higher Single rate.
Note: *If married, but legally separated, or spouse is a nonresident alien, check the Single box.*

City or town, state, and ZIP code
Cincinnati, OH 45227-6287

4 If your last name differs from that on your Social Security card, check here and call 1-800-772-1213 for more information . . ▶ ☐

5 Total number of allowances you are claiming (from line G above or from the worksheets on page 2 if they apply) . | **5**
6 Additional amount, if any, you want withheld from each paycheck . . . . | **6** $
7 I claim exemption from withholding and I certify that I meet **ALL** of the following conditions for exemption:
● Last year I had a right to a refund of **ALL** Federal income tax withheld because I had **NO** tax liability; **AND**
● This year I expect a refund of **ALL** Federal income tax withheld because I expect to have **NO** tax liability; **AND**
● This year if my income exceeds $600 and includes nonwage income, another person cannot claim me as a dependent.
If you meet all of the above conditions, enter "EXEMPT" here . . . . ▶ **7** EXEMPT

Under penalties of perjury, I certify that I am entitled to the number of withholding allowances claimed on this certificate or entitled to claim exempt status.

Employee's signature ▶ *Marisa M. Clark*   **Date** ▶ January 3   , 19 - -

8 Employer's name and address (Employer: Complete 8 and 10 only if sending to the IRS) | **9** Office code (optional): | **10** Employer identification number

your assigned number. When you become eligible, benefits are paid to you monthly based upon how much you have paid into your account.

Figure 5-2 is an application for a social security number. Children at least one year old must have a social security number if they are to be claimed as dependents on a tax return filed by a parent or parents. This application must be filled out completely and sent to the Social Security Administration. They will assign one social security number for your lifetime and will issue you a card bearing a nine-digit number. If the original card is lost or destroyed, you can obtain a duplicate without charge.

From time to time— every few years—you should check to see that your earnings have been properly credited to your

Most workers pay a social security tax; these funds provide income during retirement.

Fig. 5-2 **Application for a Social Security Card**

SOCIAL SECURITY ADMINISTRATION
Application for a Social Security Card

Form Approved
OMB No. 0960-0066

INSTRUCTIONS

- Please read "How To Complete This Form" on page 2.
- Print or type using black or blue ink. DO NOT USE PENCIL.
- After you complete this form, take or mail it along with the required documents to your nearest Social Security office.
- If you are completing this form for someone else, answer the questions as they apply to that person. Then, sign your name in question 16.

1 NAME
To Be Shown On Card

▶ Marisa — FIRST — Melanie — FULL MIDDLE NAME — Clark — LAST

FULL NAME AT BIRTH
IF OTHER THAN ABOVE

FIRST — FULL MIDDLE NAME — LAST

OTHER NAMES USED

2 MAILING ADDRESS
Do Not Abbreviate

▶ 685 West Circle Avenue
STREET ADDRESS, APT. NO., PO BOX, RURAL ROUTE NO.

Cincinnati — CITY — Ohio — STATE — 45227-6287 — ZIP CODE

3 CITIZENSHIP
(Check One)

[X] U.S. Citizen [ ] Legal Alien Allowed To Work [ ] Legal Alien Not Allowed To Work [ ] Foreign Student Allowed Restricted Employment [ ] Conditionally Legalized Alien Allowed To Work [ ] Other (See Instructions On Page 2)

4 SEX

[ ] Male [X] Female

5 RACE/ETHNIC DESCRIPTION
(Check One Only—Voluntary)

[ ] Asian, Asian-American Or Pacific Islander [ ] Hispanic [ ] Black (Not Hispanic) [ ] North American Indian Or Alaskan Native [X] White (Not Hispanic)

6 DATE OF BIRTH 8/21/81
MONTH DAY YEAR

7 PLACE OF BIRTH (Do Not Abbreviate) Cincinnati, Ohio
CITY STATE OR FOREIGN COUNTRY

[ ] Office Use Only
FCI

8 MOTHER'S MAIDEN NAME

Mary — FIRST — Grace — FULL MIDDLE NAME — Jacobs — LAST NAME AT HER BIRTH

9 FATHER'S NAME

Richard — FIRST — Allen — FULL MIDDLE NAME — Clark — LAST

10 Has the person in item 1 ever received a Social Security number before?

[ ] Yes (If "yes", answer questions 11-13.) [X] No (If "no", go on to question 14.) [ ] Don't Know (If "don't know", go on to question 14.)

11 Enter the Social Security number previously assigned to the person listed in item 1.

[ ][ ][ ] – [ ][ ] – [ ][ ][ ][ ]

12 Enter the name shown on the most recent Social Security card issued for the person listed in item 1.

FIRST — MIDDLE — LAST

13 Enter any different date of birth if used on an earlier application for a card.

MONTH DAY YEAR

14 TODAY'S DATE ▶ 1/08/--
MONTH DAY YEAR

15 DAYTIME PHONE NUMBER ▶ (513) 555-8684
AREA CODE

DELIBERATELY FURNISHING (OR CAUSING TO BE FURNISHED) FALSE INFORMATION ON THIS APPLICATION IS A CRIME PUNISHABLE BY FINE OR IMPRISONMENT, OR BOTH.

16 YOUR SIGNATURE

▶ *Marisa M. Clark*

17 YOUR RELATIONSHIP TO THE PERSON IN ITEM 1 IS:

[X] Self [ ] Natural Or Adoptive Parent [ ] Legal Guardian [ ] Other (Specify)

DO NOT WRITE BELOW THIS LINE (FOR SSA USE ONLY)					
NPN		DOC	NTI	CAN	ITV
PBC	EVI	EVA	EVC	PRA	NWR	DNR	UNIT

EVIDENCE SUBMITTED	SIGNATURE AND TITLE OF EMPLOYEE(S) REVIEWING EVIDENCE AND/OR CONDUCTING INTERVIEW
	DATE
	DCL	DATE

Form **SS-5** (9/89) 5/88 edition may be used until supply is exhausted account. The Social Security Administration in Baltimore provides a card for you to complete for this purpose (Figure 5-3). Within 30 days you should receive a report that has your income according to the Social Security Administration's records. There is no charge for this service. Mistakes do happen! If you find any discrepancies, report them immediately.

Work Permit Application

Federal and some state laws require **minors**—persons under the age of legal majority—to obtain a work permit before they are allowed to work. The work permit is signed by the parents or legal guardian of persons under age sixteen. Application for a work permit is obtained from the Department of Labor, a school counseling center, or work experience coordinator. There is usually no charge for obtaining the card, but the applicant will have to provide his or her social security number and proof of age, and have a parent's or legal guardian's signature. Additional information may be required in some states. Figure 5-4 is an example of a work permit application. The form must be filled in completely and clearly. Processing of the work permit application takes three to six weeks, so early application is advisable.

Form W-2, Wage and Tax Statement

When you have worked for a business or company during the year, you will receive **Form W-2, Wage and Tax Statement**, which lists income you earned during the year and all amounts withheld by the employer in your behalf. These amounts include federal, state, and local income taxes, and social security tax. Figure 5-5 on page 98 is a completed W-2 statement. Your W-2 should be compared to payroll slips received with each paycheck to be sure that the right amounts have been reported.

The employer must provide you with a copy of Form W-2 no later than January 31 of the year following the one in which you were employed. This is true even if you only worked part of the year and were not working as of December 31. If you do not receive a W-2 from your present employer (and from all employers you may have worked for during the year), you should contact the employer to get the W-2. Former employers may not have a current address for you. When all else fails, the Internal Revenue Service (IRS) can provide a substitute form.

Fig. 5-3

Request for Social Security Statement of Earnings

SOCIAL SECURITY ADMINISTRATION

Form Approved
OMB No. 0960-0466   [ ] **SP**

Request for Earnings and Benefit Estimate Statement

To receive a free statement of your earnings covered by Social Security and your estimated future benefits, all you need to do is fill out this form. Please print or type your answers. When you have completed the form, fold it and mail it to us.

1. Name shown on your Social Security card:

   Marisa   M.

   First Name   Middle
                     Initial

   Clark

   Last Name Only

2. Your Social Security number as shown on your card:

   6 8 2 – 4 0 – 5 8 9 6

3. Your date of birth 08   21   81
                       Month Day   Year

4. Other Social Security numbers you have used:

   [ ][ ][ ] – [ ][ ] – [ ][ ][ ][ ]
   [ ][ ][ ] – [ ][ ] – [ ][ ][ ][ ]

5. Your sex: [ ] Male [x] Female

6. Other names you have used
   (including a maiden name):

   None
   _____

7. Show your actual earnings for last year and your estimated earnings for this year. Include only wages and/or net self-employment income covered by Social Security.

   A. Last year's actual earnings: *(Dollars Only)*

      $ [ ][ ] 2 , 0 8 4 . 0 0

   B. This year's estimated earnings: *(Dollars Only)*

      $ [ ] 4 , 0 0 0 . 0 0

8. Show the age at which you plan to retire:

   6 5   *(Show only one age)*

9. Below, show the average yearly amount you think you will earn between now and when you plan to retire. We will add your estimate of future earnings to those earnings already on our records to give you the best possible estimate.

   Enter a yearly average, not your total future lifetime earnings. Only show earnings covered by Social Security. Do not add cost-of-living, performance or scheduled pay increases or bonuses. The reason for this is that we estimate retirement benefits in today's dollars, but adjust them to account for average wage growth in the national economy.

   However, if you expect to earn significantly more or less in the future due to promotions, job changes, part-time work, or an absence from the work force, enter the amount in today's dollars that most closely reflects your future average yearly earnings.

   Most people should enter the same amount they are earning now (the amount in 7B).
   Future average yearly earnings: *(Dollars Only)*

   $ [ ] 4 , 0 0 0 . 0 0

10. Address where you want us to send the statement.

    Marisa M. Clark
    Name

    685 West Circle Avenue

    Street Address (Include Apt. No., P.O. Box, or Rural Route)

    Cincinnati   OH 45227 - 6287
    City   State   Zip Code

11. [ ] Please check this box if you want to get your statement in Spanish instead of English.

    I am asking for information about my own Social Security record or the record of a person I am authorized to represent. I understand that if I deliberately request information under false pretenses I may be guilty of a federal crime and could be fined and/or imprisoned. I authorize you to use a contractor to send the statement of earnings and benefit estimates to the person named in item 10.

    +--+
    | **Please sign your name (Do not print)** |
    | |
    | *Marisa M. Clark* |
    | Signature |
    | |
    | 1/9/--   (513) 555-8684 |
    | Date   (Area Code) Daytime Telephone No. |
    +--+

Form SSA-7004-SM (2-93) Destroy Prior Editions

Fig. 5-4   **Work Permit Application**

STATE OF OREGON
BUREAU OF LABOR AND INDUSTRIES

APPLICATION FOR A WORK PERMIT

INSTRUCTIONS: You must be at least 14 years old.

The permit will not be issued unless all blanks are filled in and clearly readable.

Proof of Age must be attached. The following documents are acceptable to prove your age:

> Birth Certificate, Baptismal Certificate, Hospital Certificate, Resident Alien Card, Driver's License or Learner's Permit issued by DMV.

Print your full name (Do not use nickname).

Print your Social Security Number clearly.

You and a parent or guardian must sign this application.

Send complete application, proof of age and self-addressed stamped envelope for postage and handling to: Bureau of Labor and Industries, Work Permit Unit, # 1160, 800 NE Oregon St. # 35, Portland, OR 97232. Telephone No. 731-4074

YOUR PROOF OF AGE WILL BE RETURNED TO YOU.

Duplicate Work Permits: Call the nearest BOLI office.

WORK PERMIT APPLICATION

Work Permit No. _____
(For office use only)

Mitchell	B.	Lewin	
Name (First)	(Middle)	(Birth last name)	(Current)

3/28/81	Male	252-43-4557
Birthdate	Sex	Social Security Number

1350 Harrison Street	555-3485
Mailing Address	Telephone No.

Portland	Multnomah	Oregon	97232
City	County	State	Zip Code

Portland	OR
Birthplace (City)	State

Mitchell B. Lewin
Minor's Signature

Margaret A. Lewin
Parent or Guardian Signature

Fig. 5-5   **Form W-2, Wage and Tax Statement**

1 Control number	22222	OMB No. 1545-0008								

2 Employer's name, address, and ZIP code	6 Statutory employee ☒	Deceased ☐	Pension plan ☐	Legal rep. ☐	942 emp. ☐	Subtotal ☐	Deferred compensation ☐	Void ☐

Hanson Motors
85 Briar Street
Cincinnati, OH 45230-5162

7 Allocated tips	8 Advance EIC payment
9 Federal income tax withheld	10 Wages, tips, other compensation $2,084.00

3 Employer's identification number 93-81256791	4 Employer's state I.D. number OH4422	11 Social security tax withheld $129.21	12 Social security wages $2,084.00
5 Employee's social security number 682-40-5896		13 Social security tips	14 Medicare wages and tips $2,084.00

19 Employee's name, address, and ZIP code	15 Medicare tax withheld $ 30.22	16 Nonqualified plans

Marisa M. Clark
685 West Circle Avenue
Cincinnati, OH 45227-6287

17	18 Other

20	21	22 Dependent care benefits	23 Benefits included in Box 10

24 State income tax $14.04	25 State wages, tips, etc. $2,084.00	26 Name of state Ohio	27 Local income tax $41.60	28 Local wages, tips, etc. $2,084.00	29 Name of locality Cincinnati

Copy 2 To Be Filed With Employee's State, City, or Local Income Tax Return   Department of the Treasury—Internal Revenue Service

Form **W-2 Wage and Tax Statement   19--**

Employee's and employer's copy compared   ☐

Employee responsibilities

As a new employee, you will want to do the best possible job. In order to be successful, you will have a number of responsibilities to meet. These include personal responsibilities to your employer, including doing competent work, being thrifty and punctual, having a pleasant attitude, showing loyalty and respect, dependability, initiative, and interest, and being capable of self-evaluation. You will also be expected to show a sense of teamwork, thoughtfulness, and loyalty to other employees. Finally, you must be helpful and courteous to customers.

Responsibilities to Employers

Your employer hires you and pays you at predetermined intervals. In return for this pay and other benefits you may receive, the employer expects certain things from you, as follows:

Competent Work

You should do your best to produce the highest quality finished product for your employer. The work needs to be **marketable**; that is, of such quality that the employer can sell it or represent the company by use of your product. If, for example, you type a letter that has so many mistakes and erasures that it cannot be mailed, the letter is not a marketable product.

Thrift

When using an employer's materials, you should be as thrifty as possible, conserving supplies and materials with as much care and diligence as if they were your own. Supplies and other materials are expensive.

Punctuality

Workers should consistently arrive at work on time, take allotted breaks, and leave at quitting time. Being punctual means being ready to go to work at the appointed time—not rushing through the door at the last minute. For example, rather than arriving at 8 a.m. (the starting time), you should be at your job at 8 a.m.

Pleasant Attitude

On any job, it is important to be pleasant and easy to get along with. You should be willing to follow orders and take directions. Your employer also has the right to expect you to be courteous to customers, because you represent the company or store to others.

Loyalty and Respect

While working for a company, you should never spread rumors or gossip about your employer or job. As long as you are on the company "team," you are expected to be loyal. Loyalty includes showing respect to the employer and the company on and off the job.

Dependability

When you say you will do something, follow through. The employer should be able to depend on you to do what you are hired to do. A person who is dependable has a good reputation and will be considered for increased responsibilities and promotions.

Initiative

You should not have to be told everything to do. Employees who stand idle when a specific job is completed are of very little value to employers. **Initiative** means that you do things on your own without being told to; you're a self-starter.

Interest

It is important for you to show an interest in your job and your company. You should project an attitude of wanting to learn all you can and of giving all tasks your best possible effort. Being enthusiastic about your job tells an employer your sincere interest in being a cooperative and productive worker.

Self-Evaluation

The ability to take criticism and to assess your own progress is important to you and the employer. Everyone has strong points and weak points, but the weak points cannot be improved unless you are willing to admit they exist and to work on them. Employers are faced with the task of employee evaluation to determine raises and promotions. Employees should be able to recognize their own strong points and limitations and do a realistic self-evaluation of their job performance.

Responsibilities to Other Employees

In addition to your responsibilities to your employer, you also have duties to your fellow workers. These include the following:

Teamwork

You are part of a team when you work with others in a company, and you need to do your share of the work. Employees must work cooperatively in order to produce a quality final product; when friction and personality problems occur, the productivity and efficiency of the whole company decrease.

Thoughtfulness

Be considerate of fellow workers to promote a good work atmosphere for everyone, including customers. Having a pleasant attitude will result in a more enjoyable time for yourself and others. Personal problems and conflicts have no place at work.

Loyalty

In addition to being loyal to your employer, you should also be loyal to fellow employees. This includes not spreading rumors about them. Gossiping leads to a breakdown of teamwork.

Responsibilities to Customers

As an employee, you represent the company. To the customer who walks in the front door, you *are* the company. Thus, your attitude toward a customer often will be the deciding factor in whether he or she returns for future products or services. Therefore, remember that on behalf of your employer you have the responsibility to greet the customer with an attitude of helpfulness and courtesy.

Employees must work cooperatively as a team to be successful.

Helpfulness

When customers come to your employer's place of business, they expect to get reasonable help in finding or deciding what to purchase. It is the employee's responsibility to help customers find what they want or to do what is needed to make a sale. An attitude of helpfulness reflects well on the company and is an important part of any job.

Courtesy

Whether or not you like a customer, that customer actually pays your wages—by keeping your employer in business. Without the customer, the business could not exist. Therefore, your attitude toward the customer should always be respectful and courteous, never hostile or unfriendly. Customer loyalty to a business is often built by friendly, helpful employees.

mployer responsibilities

Employers also have responsibilities to employees. Some responsibilities are required by law; others are simply sensible practices for keeping employees happy and on the job. Failure to meet these responsibilities can result in a high employee turnover rate (with resulting high costs for training new workers), increased premiums for unemployment insurance, and employer fines for unfair labor practices. Some employer duties include adequate supervision, fair personnel policies, safe working conditions, open channels of communication, recognition of employee achievement, and compliance with civil rights and other laws.

Adequate Supervision

Employees need to be properly supervised if the employer expects them to do a good job. Supervision includes providing appropriate instruction in the use of equipment and safety standards, and spending enough time with new employees to adequately train them.

Fair Personnel Policies

Policies on hiring and firing and salary advancement, and procedures for recourse for employee disputes need to be fair and well defined. Employees should know clearly what is considered acceptable and unacceptable performance, what the standards are for advancements and raises, and what constitutes grounds for suspension or discharge.

Safe Working Conditions

All employees must be provided with safe equipment, a safe working environment, and adequate training for working under dangerous conditions. Special protective equipment and clothing and warning signs must be provided to employees working under dangerous conditions. Laws governing working conditions for minors are stricter than those for adults in most industries.

Open Channels of Communication

Employers need to communicate with employees so that all employees have the opportunity to express concerns, ask questions, and make suggestions. Lack of open channels of communication can result in poor morale of workers and low work output. Employees need to know they are an important part of the company and that their opinions are valuable.

personal perspective

Sexual Harassment

A safe working environment also means one that is comfortable and free of unwanted conduct which interferes with work performance. Sexual harassment is any unwelcome advance, request for sexual favors, and other verbal or physical conduct that is offensive.

Workers are protected by the Equal Employment Opportunity Commission (EEOC) from these types of behaviors. Harassment on the basis of sex violates the Civil Rights Act of 1964, and employers have the responsibility to prevent and eliminate sexual harassment in the workplace. EEOC guidelines state that an employer is responsible for the actions of employees as well as nonemployees on work premises.

Unfortunately, sexual harassment is widespread. Studies show that at least 50 percent of working women and 15 percent of working men have experienced sexual harassment on the job. What can be done to reduce and eliminate this problem? Fortunately, steps are being taken and the problem is being examined for future action which will help workers in protecting themselves from sexual harassment and its consequences.

Until a few years ago, the only recourse to sexual harassment was through a lawsuit against the offending person. Today, all complaints are investigated by the EEOC. When sexual harassment is found, the victim may receive a remedy such as back pay, a promotion, or reinstatement if he or she had been fired. When the victim's rights are not protected, the EEOC will sue the employer.

Many companies have policies to prevent and discourage sexual harassment. All employees are entitled to respect, courtesy, and tactful behavior. Abusing the dignity of anyone through ethnic, sexist, or racial slurs or any derogatory or objectionable conduct is cause for disciplinary action. This includes suggestive remarks, physical contact, and intimidation.

It is helpful for all employees to be aware of sexual harassment— what it is and how to avoid it. For example, employees who tell inappropriate jokes or engage in suggestive behavior, such as flirting, may find themselves in embarrassing situations. It is important to dress and act professionally at all times, so that the employee can truly say he or she did nothing to contribute to the situation.

critical thinking

1. What would you do if you received unwanted physical or verbal contact on the job?

2. What are some things you can do to reduce your risk of sexual harassment?

Laws dictate protective clothing and special training for employees working in potentially dangerous jobs.

Recognition of Achievement

Employers need to provide some form of reward for performance by employees. Merit pay raises as well as advancement on a regular schedule provide encouragement for workers to do their best possible work. When achievement is not recognized, employees lose the desire to be as productive as possible. All human beings need to be rewarded and encouraged from time to time; a salary bonus or raise is an excellent method of encouragement.

Compliance with Employment Laws

In the next section we will learn of some of the employment laws enacted to protect workers from unfair labor practices. Employers must obey state and federal laws designed to protect workers from discrimination in employment on the basis of race, color, sex, national origin, religion, age, or disability. The employer is responsible for observing workers' rights. Failure to do so can result in severe penalties for the employer. Complaints of discrimination in employment may be filed with the Equal Employment Opportunity Commission.

 mployment laws

In the last fifty years, many laws have been enacted to provide protections for American workers. Federal immigration law requires that you show a prospective employer an original social security card, together with other evidence of your citizenship and right to be employed, such as a driver's license, birth certificate, passport, or other identification. This law and others are generally enforced by government agencies.

Major employment acts are called administrative laws. Established by Congress and authorized by the executive branch of government, **administrative agencies** are given the power to enforce administrative laws. The Department of Labor is responsible for overseeing several important labor acts and their provisions.

The main provisions of the laws will generally be in one or more of the following areas for all workers:
1. To establish a minimum wage
2. To provide regular working hours
3. To provide unemployment, disability, and retirement insurance benefits
4. To provide equal employment opportunities and eliminate discrimination
5. To establish safe working conditions

Other laws have provisions for specific workers that do not apply to all workers. Minors are given several special provisions:
1. Specific safety precautions and laws governing working conditions that are more extensive than for adults
2. Maximum number of hours to be worked and times during which minors can work during the school year
3. Requirement for those under age sixteen to obtain a work permit

If any employee believes that he or she has not received benefits as required by law, *recourse*, or remedy, is available. If you think you have a legitimate complaint, you should call the state Department of Labor, which will assist you without charge. Employers found in violation of labor laws are subject to fines, payment of damages to employees, and other penalties determined by a court of law.

Social Security Act

Originally called the Federal Insurance Contributions Act of 1935, the **Social Security Act** was the first national social insurance program enacted to provide federal aid for the elderly and for disabled workers. In 1965, the Medicare provision (hospital and medical insurance protection) for elderly retired workers and other qualified persons was added. Five basic types of benefits are paid: (a) disability, (b) survivor, (c) retirement, (d) hospital, and (e) medical. Benefits received depend on the amount of contributions made. Self-employed workers pay their social security contributions when they pay their income tax. For employees in occupations covered by social security, contributions are mandatory. Social security protection is not yet available for some types of employment. Your local social security office will know if your employment is covered. Social security (FICA) tax is deducted from your gross pay and sent to the Internal Revenue Service for proper crediting to your social security account.

The Social Security Act provides federal aid for disabled workers.

Unemployment Compensation

An important part of the Social Security Act provides that every state must have an **unemployment insurance** program that provides benefits to workers who lose their jobs through no fault of their own. After a waiting period, laid-off or terminated workers may collect a portion of their regular pay for a certain length of time. Premiums for unemployment insurance are generally paid by employers. Rates vary according to employers' records of turnover, or how often they hire and fire employees.

The more often employers let workers go, the higher the premium rate they will pay. Each state has its own regulations for waiting period, maximum benefits, deadlines for filing claims, and premium rates. Unless otherwise extended by provision of the state legislature, benefits are paid for a maximum of 26 weeks through the local state employment office. In most states, an unemployed worker must wait for at least one week before receiving benefits. To receive benefits, a worker must have been employed for a minimum period of time (6 months to one year, depending on the state) and for a minimum amount of earnings ($400 or more per month in most states).

Fair Labor Standards Act

Popularly known as the **Wage and Hour Act**, the Fair Labor Standards Act of 1938 stated that persons working in interstate commerce or a related industry could not be paid less than a minimum wage of 25 cents an hour. A **minimum wage** is the legally established lower limit on wages employers may pay. The federal minimum wage reached $4.25 an hour on April 1, 1991. (The hourly rate increases when the Congress and President approve it. Also, many states require higher minimum wages than the federal minimum wage.) Another provision of the act states that hourly wage workers cannot be employed for more than 40 hours a week. Hours worked in addition to the regular hours are considered overtime and must be paid for at one and one-half times the regular rate.

Each state enforces wage and hour laws, which include federal provisions and additional state regulations. These laws, which are regulated by state Departments of Labor, provide that regular paydays be established and maintained by every employer. For example, in the state of Oregon, payment of wages to new employees must begin no later than thirty-five days after the date work has begun. When an employee quits, wages due must be paid within forty-eight hours of the final day worked. When an employee is discharged, all wages are due immediately. Any employee who requests that his or her paycheck be mailed is entitled to have it mailed to an address designated by the employee. An itemized statement of deductions from wages must be furnished to employees with their regular paychecks.

The maximum number of hours that minors may work varies according to state laws. Tips are not considered wages and may not be calculated in the amount of minimum wage due. Any employee who is unduly charged fees or denied any of the legal rights provided by the Fair Labor Standards Act or state laws may file an appeal with the nearest office of the Department of Labor.

The minimum wage law has an exception—those businesses whose annual sales do not exceed $250,000 are exempt from paying the minimum wage. Also exempt are not-for-profit and governmental offices that are providing employment as part of a training program.

Workers' Compensation

Workers' compensation is the name for statutes (laws) that give financial security to workers and their families for injury, illness, loss of income, or death that occurs as a result of the job or working conditions. This law is often labeled "liability without fault" because the employer is responsible for employee injuries and illnesses that are the result of employment, even though the employer may have done nothing to cause the injury or illness. Today all fifty states have workers' compensation statutes. In some states the SAIF (State Accident Insurance Fund) or other designated state agency collects a premium for each working person. The fee is usually based on the number of days worked during a pay period. Employers pay the workers' compensation premium in most states. However, in some states, employees are required to pay all or a part of the premium. The premiums are used to pay benefits to injured employees. Benefits include payments to doctors and hospitals, to the employee for temporary or permanent disability, and to survivors in the event of death.

Employers also may choose to maintain their own workers' compensation insurance program, if they qualify. Upon proof that an employer can meet the expenses of such a liability, a private company will establish the fund on behalf of the employer to insure against the loss. Large companies may provide their own workers' compensation insurance program within the company benefits package.

 ummary

New employees must understand and complete work forms prior to employment; these include Form W-4 and applications for a social security number and a work permit. Knowledge of their responsibilities at work—to employers, other workers, and customers—will help them to be better workers and to keep their jobs. Employers also have responsibilities to their employees, some of which are required by law, and others which make work more pleasant and productive. Many basic employment laws have been enacted to protect workers' rights and to provide for their security.

Vocabulary terms

Directions: Can you find the definitions for each of the following terms used in Chapter 5?

administrative agencies   minimum wage

allowances   minors

exempt status   Social Security Act

Form W-2   social security number

Form W-4   unemployment insurance

initiative   Wage and Hour Act

marketable   workers' compensation

1. Persons claimed on Form W-4 that reduce the amount of tax withheld from your paycheck.
2. Your permanent work identification number.
3. A form completed by your employer and mailed to you no later than January 31.
4. Work of such quality that an employer can use it.
5. Persons under the age of legal majority.
6. Established by Congress to enforce administrative laws.
7. Enacted in 1935, it was our first national insurance program to provide financial help for elderly and disabled workers.
8. A part of the Social Security Act, ensuring that benefits are paid to workers who lose their jobs.
9. A form you fill out when you begin working on which you claim a number of allowances to determine taxes withheld from your paycheck.
10. Persons who will not incur any federal tax liability may claim this status on their Form W-4.
11. The ability to do things without being told.
12. Benefits that protect workers from loss due to on-the-job illness or injuries.
13. The common name for the Fair Labor Standards Act.
14. The minimum amount that employers can pay to workers per hour.

end-of-chapter activities

5

acts and ideas in review

1. What is the purpose of Form W-4?
2. Why do you need to have a social security number before you begin work?
3. Besides retirement income, what other benefits are provided by social security?
4. Why is it important that your employer have your correct social security number?
5. Where can you obtain a work permit application?
6. Besides yourself, who must sign your work permit application if you are under age sixteen?
7. What information is listed on Form W-2?
8. By what date must your employers for the past year provide you with a Form W-2?
9. What should you do if your employer during the past year does not send you a Form W-2?
10. List at least five responsibilities that the employee has to his or her employer.
11. List at least three responsibilities that an employee has to other employees at work.
12. What responsibilities do employees have to the employer's customers?
13. List and describe three responsibilities that employers have to their employees.
14. What is an administrative agency?
15. What are some of the provisions of the Social Security Act?
16. What is unemployment insurance?
17. List the major provisions of the Fair Labor Standards Act.
18. What is meant by the phrase "liability without fault"?

 pplications for decision making

1. Obtain a Form W-4 from the nearest office of the Internal Revenue Service and complete it properly, claiming exempt status if you are entitled to do so.

2. Look up in your telephone directory the address of your nearest Department of Labor office. Go there and pick up a work permit application and fill it out. (Your counseling center or work experience coordinator will probably have work permit forms also.)

3. On a piece of paper list in the order you think most important the responsibilities that employees have to their employers. Then ask a working parent or other working person to list employee responsibilities in order of importance. Compare the two lists. Then, if possible, ask an employer to list in order what she or he considers important responsibilities that employees have to their employers.

4. What responsibilities do you have, as an employee, to customers of your employer? A popular expression used in business today is "total customer satisfaction." What do you think is meant by this expression?

5. What responsibilities do you think employers should have to employees besides the regular payment of wages earned? Ask a person who is working full-time the same question. Compare answers.

6. Look up the Social Security Act in an encyclopedia or historical reference book in your library. Obtain this information: (a) why social security was deemed necessary by the president at the time; (b) who the president at the time was; (c) history of benefits, deductions from paychecks, and purpose of social security.

7. Obtain from your state Department of Labor the provisions of state laws regarding employment of minors. Include (a) maximum hours per week that can be worked, (b) latest hour in the evening that a minor can work, (c) if a work permit is required for workers under sixteen, and (d) any other provisions to protect a minor working part- or full-time.

8. From your state Department of Labor or from an employer, obtain information as to how workers' compensation insurance is handled in your state. Is it handled by a state agency or private insurance programs? What types of benefits are available? How much are the premiums and who pays them? Because all states have workers' compensation laws, determine all you can about the laws in your state.

ife situation problem solving

1. Your friend Bruce has discovered that the amount of wages paid to him during the year appears to be different from the amount listed on the W-2 sent to him by his employer. He asks you what to do. What should you reply?

2. Leah O'Shane worked for three employers last year. Now it's February 1 of the following year, and she has received Form W-2 from only two of those employers. She asks you what she should do about it. What should you tell her?

3. Because last year Gene did not earn enough money on his part-time job to have to pay any federal taxes, his employer has asked him if this year he would like to claim exempt status on his W-4. Explain to Gene how he can claim to be exempt and what this means to him.

4. Marita, 14, has decided that she wants to work part-time this summer doing whatever kind of work she can find to earn money to buy school clothes. Tell her what things she should do to prepare for work. Also tell her what forms she may have to complete when she begins work.

5. Millie Angelino just received her W-2 form from her employer and has noticed that her social security number is wrong on the form. What should she do? What can happen if she does nothing?

6. Jarod Simpson worked for over a year for the same employer, then was laid off because business was slow. He is looking for another job, but he is in need of income to make his rent payment. You told Jarod that he may be eligible for unemployment insurance payments. Explain how he could qualify and whom he should see to find out about unemployment benefits.

7. Chi Wang, who has a visual disability, applied for a position as an assistant credit manager at a local retail store. David Burrow, the store's personnel manager, tests his eyesight by having him read a chart written in small print. Wang fails the test and, on that basis alone, is rejected for the position. Investigate the Americans with Disabilities Act and determine if Wang's employment rights have been violated.

Career Development:
Acquiring Leadership Skill

This special section is designed to help you acquire leadership skill as part of career development. It contains material on how to run a successful meeting, including setting up, implementing meeting strategies, preparing minutes, and handling parliamentary procedure. If you've ever attended a meeting that failed—people were bored, there was no clear direction, nothing was decided—then you know why it is important to run effective meetings.

Planning for a Successful Meeting

If you are merely announcing information, you don't need a meeting —just a memo. The time to have a meeting is when you need input or opinions, when you want the group to make a decision which is binding on them, or when you want everyone to hear an important decision at the same time. There are several rules for having successful meetings.

First, no meeting should last more than one hour. If it does, you should provide for drinks and a break. If a meeting lasts more than two hours, you also should provide food.

Second, give at least one week's notice, or preferably, two. People need time to plan their schedules so they can make it to your meeting.

Third, never call a meeting after 5 p.m. when people are exhausted from a full day's work, unless you also have arranged a time of relaxation and entertainment.

Fourth, send a meeting notice, together with an agenda. Give people time to add items to the agenda. Plan the meeting so that it ends as scheduled. Postpone items to the next meeting if necessary. Stick to the agenda—do not allow other items to be brought up. Put unplanned topics on the next meeting's agenda.

Fifth, follow parliamentary procedure. By using this method of running a meeting, everyone has a fair chance to speak, all decisions come to a closure, and all people are bound by the decision of the majority.

Setting up the Meeting

A meeting notice can be a full sheet of paper, a postcard, or anything in between. It announces the date and time, place, and purpose of a meeting. If the meeting is more than two weeks away, a reminder should be sent (or a phone call) to participants.

MEETING NOTICE

The Strings and Percussion Club will meet on Friday, May 1, 19xx, to adopt its constitution and bylaws.

Place: Westminster Barn
        144 Appleton Road

Time: 7 p.m. to 8:30 p.m.

Please call Mary at (613) 555-3344 if you cannot attend.

If more than one item will be discussed, you should enclose an agenda in addition to the meeting notice (see page 115). The agenda could appear directly below the meeting notice, or it could be on a separate page. The agenda lists the order of business and who, if anyone, is responsible for each item. The president is in charge of running the meeting, and should follow the agenda exactly as it is printed. If there are corrections to the agenda, they should be made immediately after the call to order. Only in emergencies should the agenda be revised; otherwise, the agenda will not be respected in future meetings.

There is a correct order of business, which includes the following 12 steps:

1. Call the meeting to order (record the starting time)
2. Roll call
3. Approval, amendment, or correction of minutes of previous meeting
4. Reading of correspondence
5. Reports of
   a. Officers
   b. Standing committees
   c. Special (ad hoc) committees
6. Unfinished business (from previous meetings)

AGENDA

Strings and Percussion Club
May 1, 19xx
7:00 p.m.

1. Call to order—G. Bates, President
2. Approval of previous minutes—C. Anderson, Secretary
3. Establish new committee to plan concert
   a. Decide on date of concert
   b. Decide location of concert
4. Report from constitution and bylaws committee
   a. Proposed format and content
   b. Vote for adoption or rejection
5. Set date of next meeting
6. Adjournment—8:30 p.m.—G. Bates, President

7. New business
8. Appointment of committees
9. Nomination and election of officers
10. Announcements
11. Setting the date of the next meeting
12. Adjournment (record the ending time)

Minutes are corrected when there is a minor revision, and amended when there is a paragraph or more to change. The changes are recorded in two places—as an insertion in the minutes being corrected, and in paragraph form in the minutes of the meeting during which changes are made.

Changes in the minutes being corrected can be done in longhand, drawing lines through incorrect words and writing correct words above it. Do not erase; it should be clear what was corrected. When the correction is too lengthy to put a line through it and write above it, it is an amendment. To make an amendment, type the corrections or additions on a separate piece of paper and attach it at the end of the minutes. Draw a line through material that has been deleted and make a notation that the corrected (amended) paragraphs are attached. Never retype minutes to correct them. Make changes in such a way that anyone reading them can tell what, when, and how corrections and additions were made.

unit

Preparing minutes is difficult because they must be accurate and must reflect the intent of the meeting. The secretary who takes minutes, often called the recorder, must use the skill of paraphrasing for the essence of the meeting. All motions must contain exact words. Minutes should look like the sample shown below.

MINUTES OF MEETING

Strings and Percussion Club
May 1, 19xx
7 p.m.

The regular meeting of the Strings and Percussion Club was called to order at 7 p.m. by president G. Bates, at Westminster Barn. Present at the meeting were G. Bates, C. Anderson, M. Atkeson, R. Deering, B. Wilson, M. Duncan, L. Andrews, and P. Smith. Absent were R. Harris and P. Adams.

Minutes of the previous meeting of April 3 were approved as mailed.

New Committee for Concert

A committee was selected to organize the next concert. M. Atkeson agreed to chair the committee, with members L. Andrews and P. Smith. The concert will be August 1 at the Fairgrounds in Wheaton.

B. Wilson will provide amplification design as usual. M. Duncan will not be able to play at the concert.

Report from Committee for Constitution

The Constitution and bylaws committee reported on its proposed constitution and bylaws. They are based on a sample provided by the Jazz Ensemble at Ridgewood High School. After considerable discussion, the constitution and bylaws were unanimously approved. It was agreed that the club sponsor will continue to be the Ridgewood Jaycees for at least another year.

Next Meeting

The next meeting will be June 4 at 6 p.m. Location to be announced. The meeting was adjourned at 8:20 p.m.

Respectfully submitted,

C. Anderson

C. Anderson, Secretary

Parliamentary Procedure

Basic rules of order for running a meeting are known as parliamentary procedure. Fundamentals include courtesy to all, one item at a time, majority rule, respect for the rights of the minority, justice for all, and partiality for none.

Principles of parliamentary procedure include the following:

All members are equal. All votes have the same value.

There must be a minimum number of voting members present in order for a decision to be binding—called a *quorum*. For example, a majority of three-fourths of the voting members, as defined by the bylaws, could constitute a quorum. Thus if there were twelve members, nine would need to be present for a decision to be binding. Of the nine, five would have to vote yes (a simple majority).

Only one main proposition, or motion, may be before the assembly at one time. Only one member may have the floor (be allowed to speak) at one time. The issue being discussed, never the person who proposed it, is the item being debated. Personal remarks are always out of order.

A question once settled may not be presented again. A majority vote (of the quorum) decides all issues except members' rights; then a larger vote is required. A two-thirds vote is necessary to deprive a member of his or her rights in any way.

Silence gives consent. Those who do not vote agree by their silence with the decision. A motion is the means by which all business is introduced. The word *motion* means a formal proposal that certain action be taken. Motions are made in the following manner:

1. A member addresses the chair (obtaining the floor);
2. The chair recognizes the member by calling his or her name;
3. The member introduces the motion by saying, "I move that . . ."
4. The motion is seconded by another member who says, "I second the motion."
5. The chair states the motion: "It has been moved and seconded that . . ."
6. The chair opens the discussion by saying, "Is there any discussion?"
7. A member calls the question by stating, "I call the question," which means the group is prepared to vote.
8. The chair puts the question to a vote by stating, "The motion states . . ." "All those in favor say 'Yes' " (or signify by raising their right hand) followed by "All those opposed say 'No.' "
9. The chair announces the vote by saying, "Motion carried," and then repeating the content of the motion; or by saying "Motion defeated," and then repeating the content of the motion.

If there is an amendment to the motion, the amendment must be approved in the same manner as the main motion, followed by approval of the main motion as shown above.

Parliamentary procedure is based on *Robert's Rules of Order*, which contains many more definitions and instructions than those outlined here. The person presiding over a meeting should be familiar with all of the Rules of Order and abide by them.

After the Meeting

When the meeting is concluded, a copy of the minutes should be prepared and mailed (or handed) to each member, whether present or absent. Minutes are often mailed along with the next meeting notice and agenda. A notebook should be kept which contains all of the minutes of meetings of the organization.

Follow-Up Assignment

1. Observe a meeting in your community. Did it follow parliamentary procedure? Was there an agenda? If so, was it followed? Were starting and ending times observed? How did you feel about the meeting—was it organized, respecting all present, and fruitful?
2. Join or set up a new club. Keep minutes and adopt a constitution and bylaws which state its purpose and how it shall conduct its business. You can obtain samples from existing organizations or the public library. Turn in the following project information:
   a. Name of club or group
   b. Meeting notice and agenda
   c. Minutes of a meeting
   d. A one-page analysis of the effectiveness of the meeting—what went right or wrong, and what could be improved

looking back . . .

Unit 1, Career Decisions, examines the process of getting the right job and keeping it. Selecting the right career is the first step; it's important to base your decision on what you find personally rewarding, satisfying, and challenging. Keeping pace with change will be a significant part of any career choice.

There are many sources of career information. Most school and local libraries have magazines, journals, and government publications that outline requirements, qualifications, and opportunities for particular jobs.

The job search is a difficult experience for most people. But it is easier when the applicant is well prepared and equipped to answer questions, write letters, and submit written documentation. The employment application, application letter, resume, and thank-you letter are crucial for that all-important first step—obtaining the job interview. Time-tested interviewing techniques can be used to gain entry-level employment.

Each job is an important part of a person's work history. This means that new employees must learn quickly how to get along with coworkers, meet employer expectations, and satisfy their personal goals and needs through employment.

Finally, work forms are a necessary part of any job. Employer and employee responsibilities should be clearly understood, along with appropriate work laws and regulations.

unit two

money management

objectives: *After reading and studying the chapters, and completing the exercises and activities, you will be able to:*

1 Compute payroll deductions and net pay; identify optional and required employee benefits; list trends in the workplace; and describe the role of labor unions.

2 Explain the purposes, types, and history of taxes in the United States; define basic tax terminology (such as exemptions, dependents, gross income, adjusted gross income, and taxable income); and prepare U.S. individual federal income tax return Forms 1040EZ and 1040A.

3 Prepare personal and case study budgets; describe and prepare a personal net worth statement and a personal property inventory; explain the elements of contracts, negotiable instruments, and warranties; and discuss a personal records filing system.

4 Prepare checks and deposit slips, record transactions in checkbook registers, and reconcile bank statements; explain check endorsements; and list types of checking accounts and banking services available to customers.

looking forward

Unit 2, Money Management, begins with an examination of your paycheck—gross pay, deductions, and net pay. You will explore benefits, which are an important part of your financial security. You will also look at trends in the workplace that impact your career and opportunities for advancement. Then you will learn about preparing your income taxes. You have a responsibility to pay taxes, and you will learn about paying your fair share, no more and no less.

Next you will learn about financial management, beginning with preparing budgets and other financial records. This information will help you meet your financial goals by tracking expenses and planning for purchases and lifestyle changes. You will also learn about contracts, both formal and informal, that you enter into daily.

Finally, you will learn how to use a checking account, including writing checks, keeping a checkbook register, and reconciling your account. All accounts are not created equal, and you will discover how to choose the right bank and services that meet your needs.

objectives:

After reading and studying this chapter you will be able to:

6-1 Compute payroll deductions and net pay from information and tables provided.

6-2 Identify optional and required employee benefits and recognize their value as additions to net pay.

6-3 Explain trends in the workplace such as flexible schedules, job rotation, job sharing, and permanent part-time employment.

6-4 Understand the role of unions and professional organizations in the workplace.

terms to know:

gross pay
overtime
deductions
net pay
incentive pay
employee services
vested
flextime
compressed workweek
job rotation
job sharing
labor union
collective bargaining
fringe benefits
seniority
strike
professional organization
lobbying

There's nothing quite as exciting as receiving your first paycheck—money earned for work performed! Unfortunately, what you agreed to work for, whether an hourly wage or a monthly salary, will not be the amount of your check. Deductions, both required and optional, will be taken. This chapter explains the deductions and what they mean, together with employee benefits and options such as flexible scheduling, telecommuting, and job sharing. You'll also discover the purpose and role of unions and professional organizations in your work life. With this chapter you will begin to focus on money management as you explore the financial aspects of your job—from the paycheck to the parking space.

chapter

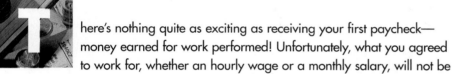

Employee Pay and Benefits

6

Gross pay, deductions, and net pay

When you are hired to work for an employer, you agree to perform certain job tasks in exchange for regular pay. **Gross pay** is the total or agreed-upon rate of pay before any deductions are made. If you work for an hourly wage or work overtime hours, computations must be made to determine the amount of your gross pay. As you can see in Figure 6-1, overtime pay is added to weekly pay for M. J. Smith who is married and has two withholding allowances. As you will notice, there are deductions for credit union payment, health insurance, union dues, and accident insurance. State income tax, if any, would also be deducted from gross pay.

Hourly Wages

Perhaps you will be paid for each hour you work. If so, a record is kept of the hours you work, and the number of hours then is multiplied by your pay rate to determine the amount of gross pay. For example, if your rate of pay is $4.25 an hour and you work forty hours during the week, you will earn gross pay of $170 a week ($4.25 multiplied by forty hours).

Overtime

Overtime is defined as hours worked beyond the regular hours. A standard workday is eight continuous hours with scheduled breaks plus an unpaid lunch period. A standard workweek is forty hours in a five-day period of eight hours each day. According to the Fair Labor Standards Act, overtime is paid at the rate of one and one-half times the regular rate of pay. If the regular rate of pay is $5.00 an hour, the overtime rate is $7.50 an hour ($5.00 times one and one-half). For example, a person may work a regular workweek of forty hours at $4.50 an hour, plus one hour overtime each day. Gross pay for this would be computed as follows:

$$\begin{aligned}
40 \text{ hours} \times \$4.50 \text{ an hour (regular pay)} &= \$180.00 \\
5 \text{ hours} \times \$6.75 \text{ an hour (overtime pay)} &= \underline{33.75} \\
\text{Gross pay} &= \$213.75
\end{aligned}$$

Monthly Salary

Perhaps you will be paid a set amount per month. In most cases you will work regular hours, but you will not receive additional pay for any overtime work. If you work overtime on a regular basis, your employer

Fig. 6-1   **Paycheck with Deductions**

Marshall Manufacturing Co.

14 Ault Street   El Paso, TX 79925-6457

88-0581 / 1120

PAYROLL CHECK

Co. Code	Department	File No.	Clock No. ID	Social Security No.	TO THE ORDER OF	Pay Date	Check No.
R&T	000108	43329	501 A	555 12 3344	M.J. SMITH	02 10 95	BELOW

PAY THIS AMOUNT	NET PAY
Two hundred thirty-four and 83/100 dollars	$234.83

M.J. SMITH
1133 ELM STREET
EL PASO, TX 79930-3264

DISBURSING AGENT FOR ABOVE EMPLOYER

Harry F. Washburn

AUTHORIZED SIGNATURE

EL PASO BANK
EL PASO, TEXAS

⑈112005812⑈ 010450 001995⑈

Marshall Manufacturing Co.

14 Ault Street   El Paso, TX 79925-6457

Co. Code	Department	File No.	Fed. Status	Name	Pay Period Ending	Pay Date
R&T	000108	43329	501 A	SMITH, M.J.	02 10 95	02 10 95

Hours Units	Rate	Earnings	Type	Deduction	Type	Deduction	Type
40 00	6 50	260 00	REG	20 00	CR UN		
5 00	9 75	48 75	OT	11 00	H INS		
				2 50	UN DUES		
				3 80	ACC INS		

This Pay	Gross	Fed. With. Tax	OASD	Medicare	Other Deductions		Net Pay
This Pay	308 75	13 00	19 14	4 48	37 30		
YTD	1,852 50	78 00	114 84	26 88	223 80		234 83

could, if he or she wished, pay an agreed-upon overtime rate computed from your monthly salary. For example, say your salary is $800 a month. The agreed-upon rate might be $6.82 an hour for overtime ($800 a month divided by twenty-two average workdays a month, divided by eight hours a day, times one and one-half). Thus, if you worked a total of twenty hours overtime in one month, your total gross pay would be $800 plus $136.40 (twenty hours times $6.82 an hour).

Overtime pay is allotted for those hours worked beyond the regular workweek.

Annual Salary

Perhaps you will earn an annual, or yearly, salary. Annual pay is usually divided into equal amounts paid each month or pay period. For example, suppose you agree to work for $15,000 a year. Your monthly gross pay will be $1,250 ($15,000 divided by 12). Or, if you are paid every two weeks, your paycheck would be $576.92 every two weeks ($15,000 divided by 26). You should know that you will receive 26 paychecks instead of 24 using this method. In a later chapter, you will learn about budgeting when paychecks are received weekly, biweekly (every two weeks), or monthly.

Deductions

Amounts subtracted from your gross pay are known as **deductions.** Some deductions, such as social security, federal income tax, and state income tax (if your state has an income tax), are required by law. Other deductions are optional and you may elect one or more of them. For example, you can have an automatic deduction for the purchase of savings bonds.

Employers are required to keep detailed records of wages earned and hours worked for inspection by the Department of Labor. With each paycheck, you also must receive a detailed list of all deductions taken from your gross pay. Deductions may not be withheld without your written consent except by court order. This, of course, does not apply to taxes, social security, and other deductions required by federal and state laws which all employees must have withheld from their paychecks.

Net Pay

When all deductions are taken out of your gross pay, the amount left is known as **net pay.** This is the amount of your paycheck, or what you can actually spend. Net pay is often called *take-home pay* because it is what you actually have left over to do with as you wish. In other words:

Regular Wages or Salary + Overtime = Gross Pay
Gross Pay − Deductions = Net Pay

Figure 6-2 is an employee withholding sheet, which lists weekly gross pay, deductions, and net pay. By law, an explanation of the pay computations—including gross pay, deductions, and net pay—must be provided with each paycheck. It is important to save the employee withholding sheet or other form of itemization of withholdings from your gross pay so that you can check the accuracy of the W-2 your employer gives you the following January for filing your income tax return.

To compute gross pay on the employee withholding sheet, the number of regular hours worked is multiplied by the hourly rate. Any overtime hours are multiplied by the overtime rate. Gross pay includes either hourly wages plus overtime, or salary plus overtime.

Required deductions include federal, state, and local taxes, and social security. The tax withholding amounts are determined from tax tables such as those shown in Figures 6-3 through 6-6 on pages 129–132. (These tax tables are samples taken from the employer's withholding tax tables of the Internal Revenue Service and the Department of Revenue for the state of Oregon.) The more allowances a person claims on his or her W-4 statement, the less the amount of tax the employer will withhold or deduct from gross pay. We are using a standard rate—the social security deduction is withheld at the rate of 7.65 percent of the first $61,200 as of January 1, 1995. (Note: This withholding rate and maximum amount will change [increase] because of acts of Congress designed to provide social security benefits and keep the fund solvent.)

In addition to required deductions, those deductions an employee has authorized to have withheld will be subtracted from gross pay. The most common of these deductions are insurance payments, union dues, credit union payments, savings account deposits, retirement contributions, and charitable deductions. These types of deductions cannot be withheld from pay without the written consent of the employee.

Fig. 6-2   **Employee Withholding Sheet**

EMPLOYEE WITHHOLDING SHEET

Employee Name Shari Gregson   Social Security Number 898-40-7426

Pay Period: ☒ weekly   ☐ bimonthly   ☐ monthly

Number of allowances: 1   ☐ married   ☒ single

GROSS PAY

   1. Regular Wages: 40 hours at $ 6.00 /hr.   = $ 240.00

or

   2. Regular Salary: =

   3. Overtime: 4   hours at $ 9.00 /hr.   =   36.00

     GROSS PAY . . . .$ 276.00

REQUIRED DEDUCTIONS

   4. Federal Income Tax (use tax tables) . . . .$ 27.00

   5. State Income Tax (use tax tables) 16.00

   6. Social Security Tax (use 7.65% x gross pay) 21.11

OTHER DEDUCTIONS

   7. Insurance . . . .

   8. Union Dues 3.00

   9. Credit Union 20.00

   10. Savings . . . .

   11. Retirement . . . .

   12. Charity . . . .

   13. Other: _____ . . . . _____

          _____ . . . . _____

     TOTAL DEDUCTIONS (total lines 4 through 14) . . . .$ 87.11

NET PAY (subtract total deductions from gross pay) . . . .$ 188.89

Fig. 6-3

State Tax Withholding Table—Weekly Payroll

Weekly payroll period (Oregon)
Amount of tax to be withheld

WAGE		NUMBER OF WITHHOLDING ALLOWANCES																	
		TWO OR LESS						THREE OR MORE											
		SINGLE			MARRIED			SINGLE OR MARRIED											
AT LEAST	BUT LESS THAN	0	1	2	0	1	2	3	4	5	6	7	8	9	10	11	12	13	14
0—	20	0	0	0	0	0	0	0	0	0	0	0	0	0	0	0	0	0	0
20—	40	1	0	0	0	0	0	0	0	0	0	0	0	0	0	0	0	0	0
40—	60	2	0	0	0	0	0	0	0	0	0	0	0	0	0	0	0	0	0
60—	80	3	2	0	1	0	0	0	0	0	0	0	0	0	0	0	0	0	0
80—	100	4	3	1	2	1	0	0	0	0	0	0	0	0	0	0	0	0	0
100—	120	5	4	3	3	2	0	0	0	0	0	0	0	0	0	0	0	0	0
120—	140	6	5	4	5	3	2	0	0	0	0	0	0	0	0	0	0	0	0
140—	160	8	6	5	6	4	3	1	0	0	0	0	0	0	0	0	0	0	0
160—	180	9	8	7	7	6	4	3	1	0	0	0	0	0	0	0	0	0	0
180—	200	11	10	8	8	7	5	4	3	1	0	0	0	0	0	0	0	0	0
200—	220	12	11	10	9	8	7	5	4	2	0	0	0	0	0	0	0	0	0
220—	240	14	13	11	10	9	8	6	5	4	2	0	0	0	0	0	0	0	0
240—	260	15	14	13	12	10	9	8	6	5	3	2	0	0	0	0	0	0	0
260—	280	17	16	14	13	11	10	9	8	6	5	3	2	0	0	0	0	0	0
280—	300	18	17	16	14	13	12	10	9	8	7	5	3	2	0	0	0	0	0
300—	320	20	19	17	16	14	13	12	11	10	8	7	5	3	2	0	0	0	0
320—	340	21	20	19	17	16	15	14	12	11	10	9	7	5	4	2	0	0	0
340—	360	23	22	21	19	17	16	15	14	13	11	10	9	7	5	4	2	0	0
360—	380	24	23	22	20	19	18	17	15	14	13	12	10	9	7	5	4	2	0
380—	400	26	25	24	22	21	19	18	17	16	14	13	12	11	9	7	5	4	2
400—	420	28	26	25	23	22	21	20	18	17	16	15	14	12	11	9	7	6	4
420—	440	29	28	27	25	24	22	21	20	19	17	16	15	14	13	11	9	7	6
440—	460	31	30	28	26	25	24	23	21	20	19	18	17	15	14	13	11	9	7
460—	480	33	31	30	28	27	25	24	23	22	21	19	18	17	16	14	13	11	9
480—	500	35	33	31	30	28	27	26	25	23	22	21	20	18	17	16	14	13	11
500—	520	37	35	33	32	30	29	27	26	25	24	22	21	20	19	17	16	15	13
520—	540	38	37	35	34	32	30	29	28	26	25	24	23	21	20	19	18	16	15
540—	560	40	39	37	35	34	32	30	29	28	27	25	24	23	22	21	19	18	16
560—	580	42	40	39	37	36	34	32	31	29	28	27	26	25	23	22	21	20	18
580—	600	44	42	40	39	37	36	34	32	31	30	29	27	26	25	24	22	21	20
600—	620	46	44	42	41	39	37	36	34	32	31	30	29	28	26	25	24	23	21
620—	640	47	46	44	43	41	39	37	36	34	33	32	30	29	28	27	25	24	23
640—	660	49	48	46	44	43	41	39	38	36	34	33	32	31	29	28	27	26	25
660—	680	51	49	48	46	45	43	41	39	38	36	35	33	32	31	30	29	27	26
680—	700	53	51	49	48	46	45	43	41	39	38	36	35	34	32	31	30	29	28
700—	720	55	53	51	50	48	46	45	43	41	39	38	36	35	34	33	32	30	29
720—	740	56	55	53	52	50	48	46	45	43	41	40	38	37	36	34	33	32	31
740—	760	58	57	55	53	52	50	48	47	45	43	41	40	38	37	36	35	33	32
760—	780	60	58	57	55	54	52	50	48	47	45	43	41	40	39	37	36	35	34
780—	800	62	60	58	57	55	54	52	50	48	47	45	43	41	40	39	38	36	35
800—	820	64	62	60	59	57	55	54	52	50	48	47	45	43	42	40	39	38	37
820—	840	65	64	62	61	59	57	55	54	52	50	49	47	45	43	42	41	40	38
840—	860	67	66	64	62	61	59	57	56	54	52	50	49	47	45	44	42	41	40

FOR WAGE OF 860 AND OVER—
9.00 PERCENT OF AMOUNT OVER 860 PLUS—

860—OVER		68	66	65	63	62	60	58	56	55	53	51	50	48	46	44	43	42	41

Fig. 6-4

State Tax Withholding Table—Monthly Payroll

Monthly payroll period (Oregon)
Amount of tax to be withheld

WAGE		NUMBER OF WITHHOLDING ALLOWANCES																	
		TWO OR LESS SINGLE			TWO OR LESS MARRIED			THREE OR MORE SINGLE OR MARRIED											
AT LEAST	BUT LESS THAN	0	1	2	0	1	2	3	4	5	6	7	8	9	10	11	12	13	14
0–	40	0	0	0	0	0	0	0	0	0	0	0	0	0	0	0	0	0	0
40–	80	0	0	0	0	0	0	0	0	0	0	0	0	0	0	0	0	0	0
80–	120	1	0	0	0	0	0	0	0	0	0	0	0	0	0	0	0	0	0
120–	160	3	0	0	0	0	0	0	0	0	0	0	0	0	0	0	0	0	0
160–	200	5	0	0	0	0	0	0	0	0	0	0	0	0	0	0	0	0	0
200–	240	8	2	0	0	0	0	0	0	0	0	0	0	0	0	0	0	0	0
240–	280	10	4	0	1	0	0	0	0	0	0	0	0	0	0	0	0	0	0
280–	320	12	7	0	4	0	0	0	0	0	0	0	0	0	0	0	0	0	0
320–	360	15	9	2	6	0	0	0	0	0	0	0	0	0	0	0	0	0	0
360–	400	17	11	5	9	2	0	0	0	0	0	0	0	0	0	0	0	0	0
400–	440	20	14	8	11	5	0	0	0	0	0	0	0	0	0	0	0	0	0
440–	480	22	16	10	13	8	1	0	0	0	0	0	0	0	0	0	0	0	0
480–	520	24	19	13	16	10	3	0	0	0	0	0	0	0	0	0	0	0	0
520–	560	27	21	15	18	12	6	0	0	0	0	0	0	0	0	0	0	0	0
560–	600	29	23	18	21	15	9	1	0	0	0	0	0	0	0	0	0	0	0
600–	640	31	26	20	23	17	11	4	0	0	0	0	0	0	0	0	0	0	0
640–	680	34	29	23	25	19	14	7	0	0	0	0	0	0	0	0	0	0	0
680–	720	37	32	26	28	22	16	10	2	0	0	0	0	0	0	0	0	0	0
720–	760	40	35	30	30	24	18	13	5	0	0	0	0	0	0	0	0	0	0
760–	800	43	38	33	32	27	21	15	8	0	0	0	0	0	0	0	0	0	0
800–	840	46	41	36	35	29	23	17	11	3	0	0	0	0	0	0	0	0	0
840–	880	49	44	39	37	31	26	20	14	6	0	0	0	0	0	0	0	0	0
880–	920	52	47	42	40	34	28	22	16	9	1	0	0	0	0	0	0	0	0
920–	960	55	50	45	42	36	30	25	19	12	4	0	0	0	0	0	0	0	0
960–	1000	58	53	48	44	39	33	27	21	14	7	0	0	0	0	0	0	0	0
1000–	1040	62	56	51	47	41	35	29	24	17	10	2	0	0	0	0	0	0	0
1040–	1080	65	59	54	49	43	37	32	26	20	13	5	0	0	0	0	0	0	0
1080–	1120	68	62	57	51	46	40	34	28	23	16	8	1	0	0	0	0	0	0
1120–	1160	71	65	60	54	48	42	36	31	26	19	12	4	0	0	0	0	0	0
1160–	1200	74	68	63	56	50	45	39	34	29	23	15	8	0	0	0	0	0	0
1200–	1240	77	72	66	59	53	48	43	37	32	26	19	11	4	0	0	0	0	0
1240–	1280	80	75	69	61	56	51	46	40	35	30	23	15	8	0	0	0	0	0
1280–	1320	83	78	72	65	59	54	49	43	38	33	26	19	11	4	0	0	0	0
1320–	1360	86	81	75	68	62	57	52	46	41	36	30	22	15	7	0	0	0	0
1360–	1400	89	84	78	71	65	60	55	49	44	39	33	26	18	11	3	0	0	0
1400–	1440	92	87	82	74	68	63	58	53	47	42	37	29	22	14	7	0	0	0
1440–	1480	95	90	85	77	71	66	61	56	50	45	40	33	26	18	11	3	0	0
1480–	1520	98	93	88	80	75	69	64	59	53	48	43	37	29	22	14	7	0	0
1520–	1560	101	96	91	83	78	72	67	62	56	51	46	40	33	25	18	10	3	0
1560–	1600	104	99	94	86	81	75	70	65	59	54	49	44	36	29	21	14	6	0
1600–	1640	107	102	97	89	84	78	73	68	62	57	52	47	40	32	25	17	10	2
1640–	1680	110	105	100	92	87	81	76	71	66	60	55	50	44	36	29	21	14	6
1680–	1720	113	108	103	95	90	85	79	74	69	63	58	53	47	40	32	25	17	10
1720–	1760	116	111	106	98	93	88	82	77	72	66	61	56	50	43	36	28	21	13
1760–	1800	120	114	109	101	96	91	85	80	75	69	64	59	54	47	39	32	24	17

Fig. 6-5 **Federal Tax Withholding Tables—Weekly Payroll**

SINGLE Persons—WEEKLY Payroll Period
(For Wages Paid in 19--)

If the wages are—		And the number of withholding allowances claimed is—										
At least	But less than	0	1	2	3	4	5	6	7	8	9	10
		The amount of income tax to be withheld is—										
$0	$55	$0	$0	$0	$0	$0	$0	$0	$0	$0	$0	$0
55	60	1	0	0	0	0	0	0	0	0	0	0
60	65	2	0	0	0	0	0	0	0	0	0	0
65	70	3	0	0	0	0	0	0	0	0	0	0
70	75	3	0	0	0	0	0	0	0	0	0	0
75	80	4	0	0	0	0	0	0	0	0	0	0
80	85	5	0	0	0	0	0	0	0	0	0	0
85	90	6	0	0	0	0	0	0	0	0	0	0
90	95	6	0	0	0	0	0	0	0	0	0	0
95	100	7	0	0	0	0	0	0	0	0	0	0
100	105	8	1	0	0	0	0	0	0	0	0	0
105	110	9	2	0	0	0	0	0	0	0	0	0
110	115	9	2	0	0	0	0	0	0	0	0	0
115	120	10	3	0	0	0	0	0	0	0	0	0
120	125	11	4	0	0	0	0	0	0	0	0	0
125	130	12	5	0	0	0	0	0	0	0	0	0
130	135	12	5	0	0	0	0	0	0	0	0	0
135	140	13	6	0	0	0	0	0	0	0	0	0
140	145	14	7	0	0	0	0	0	0	0	0	0
145	150	15	8	1	0	0	0	0	0	0	0	0
150	155	15	8	1	0	0	0	0	0	0	0	0
155	160	16	9	2	0	0	0	0	0	0	0	0
160	165	17	10	3	0	0	0	0	0	0	0	0
165	170	18	11	4	0	0	0	0	0	0	0	0
170	175	18	11	4	0	0	0	0	0	0	0	0
175	180	19	12	5	0	0	0	0	0	0	0	0
180	185	20	13	6	0	0	0	0	0	0	0	0
185	190	21	14	7	0	0	0	0	0	0	0	0
190	195	21	14	7	0	0	0	0	0	0	0	0
195	200	22	15	8	1	0	0	0	0	0	0	0
200	210	23	16	9	2	0	0	0	0	0	0	0
210	220	25	18	11	4	0	0	0	0	0	0	0
220	230	26	19	12	5	0	0	0	0	0	0	0
230	240	28	21	14	7	0	0	0	0	0	0	0
240	250	29	22	15	8	1	0	0	0	0	0	0
250	260	31	24	17	10	3	0	0	0	0	0	0
260	270	32	25	18	11	4	0	0	0	0	0	0
270	280	34	27	20	13	6	0	0	0	0	0	0
280	290	35	28	21	14	7	0	0	0	0	0	0
290	300	37	30	23	16	9	1	0	0	0	0	0
300	310	38	31	24	17	10	3	0	0	0	0	0
310	320	40	33	26	19	12	4	0	0	0	0	0
320	330	41	34	27	20	13	6	0	0	0	0	0
330	340	43	36	29	22	15	7	0	0	0	0	0
340	350	44	37	30	23	16	9	2	0	0	0	0
350	360	46	39	32	25	18	10	3	0	0	0	0
360	370	47	40	33	26	19	12	5	0	0	0	0
370	380	49	42	35	28	21	13	6	0	0	0	0
380	390	50	43	36	29	22	15	8	1	0	0	0
390	400	52	45	38	31	24	16	9	2	0	0	0
400	410	53	46	39	32	25	18	11	4	0	0	0
410	420	55	48	41	34	27	19	12	5	0	0	0
420	430	56	49	42	35	28	21	14	7	0	0	0
430	440	58	51	44	37	30	22	15	8	1	0	0
440	450	59	52	45	38	31	24	17	10	3	0	0
450	460	61	54	47	40	33	25	18	11	4	0	0
460	470	63	55	48	41	34	27	20	13	6	0	0
470	480	65	57	50	43	36	28	21	14	7	0	0
480	490	68	58	51	44	37	30	23	16	9	2	0
490	500	71	60	53	46	39	31	24	17	10	3	0
500	510	74	61	54	47	40	33	26	19	12	5	0
510	520	77	63	56	49	42	34	27	20	13	6	0
520	530	79	66	57	50	43	36	29	22	15	8	1
530	540	82	69	59	52	45	37	30	23	16	9	2
540	550	85	72	60	53	46	39	32	25	18	11	4
550	560	88	75	62	55	48	40	33	26	19	12	5
560	570	91	77	64	56	49	42	35	28	21	14	7
570	580	93	80	67	58	51	43	36	29	22	15	8
580	590	96	83	70	59	52	45	38	31	24	17	10
590	600	99	86	73	61	54	46	39	32	25	18	11

Fig. 6-6

Federal Tax Withholding Tables—Monthly Payroll

MARRIED Persons—MONTHLY Payroll Period
(For Wages Paid in 19--)

If the wages are—		And the number of withholding allowances claimed is—										
At least	But less than	0	1	2	3	4	5	6	7	8	9	10
		The amount of income tax to be withheld is—										
$0	$540	$0	$0	$0	$0	$0	$0	$0	$0	$0	$0	$0
540	560	3	0	0	0	0	0	0	0	0	0	0
560	580	6	0	0	0	0	0	0	0	0	0	0
580	600	9	0	0	0	0	0	0	0	0	0	0
600	640	14	0	0	0	0	0	0	0	0	0	0
640	680	20	0	0	0	0	0	0	0	0	0	0
680	720	26	0	0	0	0	0	0	0	0	0	0
720	760	32	1	0	0	0	0	0	0	0	0	0
760	800	38	7	0	0	0	0	0	0	0	0	0
800	840	44	13	0	0	0	0	0	0	0	0	0
840	880	50	19	0	0	0	0	0	0	0	0	0
880	920	56	25	0	0	0	0	0	0	0	0	0
920	960	62	31	0	0	0	0	0	0	0	0	0
960	1,000	68	37	6	0	0	0	0	0	0	0	0
1,000	1,040	74	43	12	0	0	0	0	0	0	0	0
1,040	1,080	80	49	18	0	0	0	0	0	0	0	0
1,080	1,120	86	55	24	0	0	0	0	0	0	0	0
1,120	1,160	92	61	30	0	0	0	0	0	0	0	0
1,160	1,200	98	67	36	6	0	0	0	0	0	0	0
1,200	1,240	104	73	42	12	0	0	0	0	0	0	0
1,240	1,280	110	79	48	18	0	0	0	0	0	0	0
1,280	1,320	116	85	54	24	0	0	0	0	0	0	0
1,320	1,360	122	91	60	30	0	0	0	0	0	0	0
1,360	1,400	128	97	66	36	5	0	0	0	0	0	0
1,400	1,440	134	103	72	42	11	0	0	0	0	0	0
1,440	1,480	140	109	78	48	17	0	0	0	0	0	0
1,480	1,520	146	115	84	54	23	0	0	0	0	0	0
1,520	1,560	152	121	90	60	29	0	0	0	0	0	0
1,560	1,600	158	127	96	66	35	5	0	0	0	0	0
1,600	1,640	164	133	102	72	41	11	0	0	0	0	0
1,640	1,680	170	139	108	78	47	17	0	0	0	0	0
1,680	1,720	176	145	114	84	53	23	0	0	0	0	0
1,720	1,760	182	151	120	90	59	29	0	0	0	0	0
1,760	1,800	188	157	126	96	65	35	4	0	0	0	0
1,800	1,840	194	163	132	102	71	41	10	0	0	0	0
1,840	1,880	200	169	138	108	77	47	16	0	0	0	0
1,880	1,920	206	175	144	114	83	53	22	0	0	0	0
1,920	1,960	212	181	150	120	89	59	28	0	0	0	0
1,960	2,000	218	187	156	126	95	65	34	3	0	0	0
2,000	2,040	224	193	162	132	101	71	40	9	0	0	0
2,040	2,080	230	199	168	138	107	77	46	15	0	0	0
2,080	2,120	236	205	174	144	113	83	52	21	0	0	0
2,120	2,160	242	211	180	150	119	89	58	27	0	0	0
2,160	2,200	248	217	186	156	125	95	64	33	3	0	0
2,200	2,240	254	223	192	162	131	101	70	39	9	0	0
2,240	2,280	260	229	198	168	137	107	76	45	15	0	0
2,280	2,320	266	235	204	174	143	113	82	51	21	0	0
2,320	2,360	272	241	210	180	149	119	88	57	27	0	0
2,360	2,400	278	247	216	186	155	125	94	63	33	2	0
2,400	2,440	284	253	222	192	161	131	100	69	39	8	0
2,440	2,480	290	259	228	198	167	137	106	75	45	14	0
2,480	2,520	296	265	234	204	173	143	112	81	51	20	0
2,520	2,560	302	271	240	210	179	149	118	87	57	26	0
2,560	2,600	308	277	246	216	185	155	124	93	63	32	1
2,600	2,640	314	283	252	222	191	161	130	99	69	38	7
2,640	2,680	320	289	258	228	197	167	136	105	75	44	13
2,680	2,720	326	295	264	234	203	173	142	111	81	50	19
2,720	2,760	332	301	270	240	209	179	148	117	87	56	25
2,760	2,800	338	307	276	246	215	185	154	123	93	62	31
2,800	2,840	344	313	282	252	221	191	160	129	99	68	37
2,840	2,880	350	319	288	258	227	197	166	135	105	74	43
2,880	2,920	356	325	294	264	233	203	172	141	111	80	49
2,920	2,960	362	331	300	270	239	209	178	147	117	86	55
2,960	3,000	368	337	306	276	245	215	184	153	123	92	61
3,000	3,040	374	343	312	282	251	221	190	159	129	98	67
3,040	3,080	380	349	318	288	257	227	196	165	135	104	73
3,080	3,120	386	355	324	294	263	233	202	171	141	110	79
3,120	3,160	392	361	330	300	269	239	208	177	147	116	85
3,160	3,200	398	367	336	306	275	245	214	183	153	122	91
3,200	3,240	404	373	342	312	281	251	220	189	159	128	97

B enefits and incentives

Types of benefits include insurance, pension plans, paid sick leave and vacations, profit sharing, and the like. Some of these benefits are required by law. Among them are unemployment compensation, workers' compensation, and social security. These federal programs were discussed in Chapter 5. Many employers provide one or more of the following optional (not required by law) benefits.

Profit Sharing

Profit sharing is a plan that allows employees to receive a portion of the company's profits at the end of the corporate year; the more money (profits) the company makes, the more the company has to share with employees. Most companies who provide profit sharing consider it **incentive pay**—a payment or benefit given to encourage employees to do more and better quality work. Employees who have profit-sharing plans are thought to identify more closely with the company and its profit goals, making them more likely to reduce waste and increase productivity.

Paid Vacations and Holidays

Most businesses provide full-time employees with a set amount of paid vacation time, which means that while you are on vacation, you are paid as usual. It is not uncommon to receive a week's paid vacation after a year of full-time employment, two weeks after two years, three weeks after five years' employment, and so on.

A benefit that you are likely to receive for any full-time job is paid time off for holidays. Generally, full-time employees who are receiving a salary are entitled to have off, with pay, those holidays designated as "paid holidays." These include Christmas, Thanksgiving, Fourth of July, Labor Day, and Memorial Day. Other holidays that are considered paid holidays by many companies include New Year's Day, Veterans' Day, and Presidents' Day. An employee required to work on a holiday is usually paid double or more than double the regular hourly rate of pay.

Employee Services

Employee services are the extras that companies offer in order to improve employee morale and working conditions. Many companies offer discounts on merchandise sold or made by the company to their employees. For example, if you work at a clothing store that allows employee discounts, you can purchase your clothing for a reduced price. A typical discount may be 10 percent or more. Other services include social and recreational programs, free parking, tuition reimbursement for college courses, company newsletters, day-care centers, and counseling for employee problems.

Sick Pay

Many businesses also provide an allowance of days each year for illness, with pay as usual. This benefit is usually available for full-time employees only. It is customary to receive three to ten days a year as "sick days" without deductions from pay.

Leaves of Absence

Some employers allow employees to leave their jobs (without pay) for certain reasons, such as having children or completing education, and return to their jobs at a later time. While a leave of absence may be unpaid, it has an important advantage—it gives job security and permits you to take time off for important events in your life.

The Family and Medical Leave Act (known as FMLA) took effect August 5, 1993. Employers with fifty or more employees must give up to twelve weeks unpaid leave per year for the birth or adoption of a child, or care for a spouse, child, or parent with a serious illness, or for the employee's own serious illness. Employers are required to maintain health coverage during the leave, and job reinstatement rights are guaranteed.

Insurance

Most large companies provide group health insurance plans for all employees. A few plans are paid for almost entirely by the employer, as a part of employee compensation. Other plans require paycheck deductions if employees elect to participate in the plan. Insurance plans typically include health, dental, vision, and life insurance.

Health Insurance

A typical health insurance plan might have a $150 (or more for a family) employee-paid amount, or *deductible*. After the deductible has been reached, the plan pays 80 percent of most doctor bills and prescriptions and 100 percent of hospitalization charges and emergency bills. Traditional insurance plans generally will not cover routine physical examinations. As an alternative to a traditional plan, your employer may offer you a health maintenance organization (HMO) plan or another variation of this health care program. Health insurance will be discussed in Chapter 27.

Life Insurance

Many companies offer life insurance. Life insurance pays a cash benefit to a designated person, called a *beneficiary*, when the insured dies. The purpose of life insurance is to partially offset the income lost when a wage earner dies. When you leave current employment, the group policy does not go with you. An employer generally pays an amount each month for coverage to as much as $50,000 on each employee. An employee may pay for additional coverage through monthly payroll deductions. Life insurance is discussed in detail in Chapter 27.

Dental Insurance

Most dental plans provide a maximum benefit of $1,500 to $2,000 per year per family member. In addition, orthodontia (braces) may not be covered. Routine exams and cleanings are usually covered 100 percent, while most other services are covered 80 percent of a predetermined fee range. If, for example, a dentist charges $110 for a composite filling, and the insurance plan pays a high of $80 for this service, the plan will pay 80 percent times $80, or $64, and the patient will pay the remainder. In addition, most nonroutine work, such as crowns, bridges, or root canals, is covered at a lesser rate, such as 50 percent. Dental insurance may have a small deductible, such as $50 per person per year.

Vision Insurance

This type of insurance covers the cost of prescription lenses and eye examinations once every few years. As the employee gets older, more frequent exams are allowed. Generally, frames are not covered, but sometimes coverage is available for contact lenses. Vision and dental insurance are explained further in Chapter 27.

Bonuses and Stock Options

Bonus plans include pay incentives based on quality of work done, years of service, or company sales or profits. A factory manager may offer all workers a $100 year-end bonus as a reward for having no serious on-the-job accidents during the year. Christmas bonuses are often based on years of service. If a division of a company reaches a particular sales goal in a year, all top-level managers would receive a bonus equal to a percentage of their current salaries.

Stock-purchase options give employees (usually executives) the right to buy a set number of shares of the company's stock at a fixed price by a certain time. The employees gain as long as the stock price goes up. Many types of stock option plans exist.

Vision insurance covers the cost of prescription lenses and eye examinations.

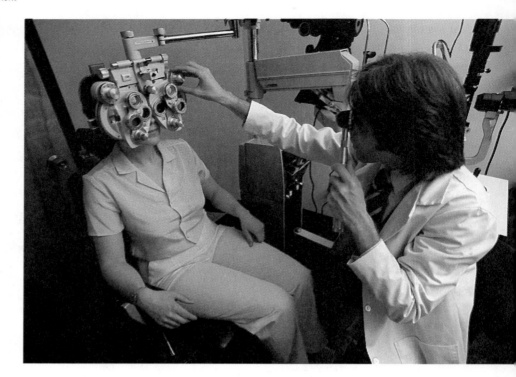

Pension and Savings Plans

Some employers provide retirement plans. When an employee retires, he or she receives a monthly check. In some cases, an employee may withdraw funds early in part or in full, or retire early and begin collecting benefits. Employees are fully **vested**—entitled to the full retirement account—when they terminate employment after a specified period of time—usually five years. We will discuss retirement planning in a later chapter; this benefit will have special value for you as you grow older.

Employer-sponsored savings plans, such as a 401(k) for private employers or a 403(b) for government employers, is also an employee retirement plan. An employee makes contributions that may be partially or wholly matched by the employer. Generally, employees should not withdraw from savings plans until retirement except in cases of hardship or emergency.

Travel Expenses

Companies that require employees to travel in the course of their work often provide a company car or a mileage allowance if they use their own car. Generally, car insurance, gasoline, and repair and maintenance expenses for the company automobile are also provided. While out of town, employees receive a daily allowance, or have their motel, meals, and other travel expenses paid. In some cases, employees are expected to pay the costs of their travel, keep receipts and evidence of purchases, and submit a report in order to be reimbursed.

Evaluation of Employee Benefits

Many of these optional benefits are of great value to employees. Benefits generally are not currently taxable to employees (except bonuses and other benefits paid in cash), yet they provide valuable coverages and advantages. Generally, large companies provide more extensive optional benefits packages.

In recent years, employee benefits have been expanded to meet the needs of different life situations. *Cafeteria-style* employee benefits are programs that allow workers to base their job benefits on personal needs. Flexibility in the selection of benefits has become quite common. For example, a married employee with children might opt for increased life and health insurance, while a single parent may use benefit options for child care services.

rends in the workplace

Many employers are responding to changes in the lifestyles and needs of their employees. Some of the changes that employers make to meet the personal needs of employees and to avoid absenteeism, burnout, and turnover are the implementation and use of flexible schedules and compressed workweeks, job rotation, job sharing, permanent part-time and home work or telecommuting, and on-site child care.

Altered Workweeks

Many firms have experimented with *altered workweeks* to get away from the standard eight-hour-a-day, five-day-a-week work schedule. Flextime is one type of work scheduling system. Another variation is the compressed workweek.

Flexible schedules, or **flextime,** is an arrangement of working hours that provides for all employees to be present at a specified period (core time), with the rest of the workday being completed at employee discretion. Employees negotiate their starting times, usually within a three- to four-hour period. This allows them to begin working as early as 6 a.m. or as late as 9 or 10 a.m. Even though starting times are flexible, most employers require employees to work a required number of hours per day. For example, a person arriving at 6 a.m. would be finished by

3 p.m. (having a one-hour unpaid lunch break), while a person arriving at 10 a.m. would be finished at 7 p.m. The *core time period* is a crucial time during the day when all employees must report to work. This may be between 10 a.m. and 3 p.m., the peak hours for business activity.

Flextime decreases absenteeism and tardiness. Production increases because employees are responsible for working a full day regardless of when they arrive on the job. Employees experience greater job satisfaction because flextime helps them fulfill their personal goals. For example, employees who need to pick up children from school would find it important to be off at 3 p.m. Other employees may like the fact that public transportation is less congested than at peak travel times. Flextime also allows for scheduling of medical or other appointments, and it reduces stress caused by the pressure of meeting strict work schedules.

A **compressed workweek** is the scheduling of the normal forty hour workweek into less than five days. The typical compressed workweek is ten hours a day for four days, followed by three days off. Some types of work are better suited to a compressed schedule than are others. For example, some kinds of taxing physical or mental work are probably not suitable for a compressed workweek.

Job Rotation

Job rotation is a technique for training employees to be efficient in more than one specialized area. Employees "rotate" from one area to another. This technique has a fairly high cost to the employer because training is an expensive procedure. Employees are sometimes allowed to perform tasks in each of the areas, while in other instances they simply observe.

The use of job rotation allows the company to maximize the opportunities for employee growth and development. Job satisfaction improves and productivity increases. Employees benefit from additional training, and the boredom, burnout, and accidents experienced by employees performing the same tasks daily are reduced. A major advantage of job rotation for both employer and employee is that information and ideas are voluntarily and freely exchanged among employees so that no one has absolute control over one area. As employees understand how others' work contributes to the overall production, they can better appreciate personal contributions.

Job Sharing

Job sharing is often considered an employee motivation strategy. In **job sharing,** two people share what was originally a full-time position. Individual salaries and benefits are split according to the amount of each employee's contributions.

Job sharing is especially attractive to people who desire part-time work. Older employees are finding job sharing an attractive alternative to retirement. An increasing number of companies and employees are finding that job sharing helps improve productivity and efficiency. Advantages include reduced absenteeism and tardiness; flexibility for the employee who needs half days for other activities, recreation, or relaxation; less fatigue; and higher productivity levels.

Permanent Part-Time and Telecommuting

Many employees are choosing to work only part-time (sixteen to twenty-five hours a week), and companies can save on salary and benefits by hiring permanent part-time employees. Part-time work usually provides some benefits to the employee, including job security, while also allowing freedom to spend other time away from work. Mothers with small children, older employees, and others find that permanent part-time work is best suited to meeting their financial and psychological needs.

Telecommuting, or working at home, allows employees to work in their own home in such areas as routine data entry, transcription, keyboarding, and software development. Home work is convenient and gives the worker flexibility. In some industries, such as the garment industry, home work is not allowed. In information processing and related fields, however, home work is becoming increasingly popular.

Many employees find themselves well suited to permanent part-time work.

Child Care

A major issue for the 1990s is child care for working parents. Many companies provide on-site child care facilities as well as coverage of child care expenses as a part of employee benefit packages. Federal legislation is likely to change child care significantly in years to come. Legislation will focus on high-quality, affordable programs for children of working parents.

Labor unions and professional organizations

Many jobs involve union membership or participation in a professional organization as a requirement of employment. Unions are groups of people joined together for a common purpose. A **labor union** is a group of people who work in the same or similar occupations, organized for the benefit of all employees in these occupations.

History of Unions

Unions were organized in the United States as early as the late 1800s. The first unions were local groups organized by skilled craftspeople to protect themselves from competition by untrained and unskilled employees. In 1886, the American Federation of Labor (AFL) was organized by Samuel Gompers, who served as its president for 37 years.

Early unions had very little power until 1935, when the National Labor Relations Act (the Wagner Act) gave unions the right to organize and bargain with employers. In 1938, John L. Lewis became the first president of a new union—the Congress of Industrial Organizations (CIO). Unions continued to grow in number, power, and size until 1947, when Congress passed the Labor Management Relations Act, commonly called the Taft-Hartley Act. This act was passed to limit the powers of unions and to curb strikes. In 1955, the AFL and CIO merged under the leadership of George Meany and became the largest and most powerful union in the United States.

Unions grew in numbers, strength, and importance until the middle 1980s. Then, with the pressures of competitiveness and international trade, companies began looking for ways to cut costs. Membership in unions began declining as jobs were lost. In the 1990s, labor unions are struggling to survive in many industries.

global connection

Working Around the World

Conducting business or working in a foreign country requires an awareness of its major cultural characteristics. In general, businesses around the world prefer not to have unions because they slow down business decisions and often increase labor costs, thereby decreasing profits.

South Korea is a country in the Far East. It has traditionally had a low level of unionism, but in the last decade has seen the strength of unions increase substantially. Unionism is a part of democracy, and as this southeast Asian country becomes more like its Western counterparts, it is likely to develop even more unions and the problems and opportunities that accompany them.

For example, not long ago one of Korea's major companies, the Hyundai auto factory, had a strike where 25,000 union members actually went to work as usual but didn't work on automobiles. Instead, they swept floors and maintained the plant and made sure that no damage occurred as a result of strong emotions or the activism of radicals. When the strike was over, they left the plant in good condition and had maintained a good relationship with their employer.

Still, the average worker in Korea works 50 hours a week or more at an average of about one-third of the American minimum wage. While Korea has grown and expanded twentyfold in the last twenty-five years, the average worker hasn't seen a significantly increased standard of living. There is a minimum wage law in Korea, but it is very low and has been slow to increase. The Korean government fears that wage increases will lead to inflation and higher living costs.

critical thinking

1. Have you read about or heard about a labor strike in the United States? How is it different from what you might find in Korea?

2. How are you affected by minimum wage laws in the United States? Do you think we should abandon a minimum wage? Why or why not?

3. Discuss why companies would prefer not to have labor unions today and what this would mean for workers.

Functions of Unions

The importance of labor unions in American life cannot be measured by the number of employees in unions alone. Many nonunion employers are influenced by the standards set by union agreements with other employers; and many employees reap the benefits of unionization even though they do not belong to a union.

Labor unions have four major functions: (a) to recruit new members; (b) to engage in collective bargaining; (c) to support political candidates who are favorable to the union; and (d) to provide support services for members.

Unions exercise power through large numbers of members. Therefore, new employees in occupations that have unions are strongly urged, if membership is not mandatory, to join the union. Political candidates who express opinions favorable to a particular union may receive campaign funds and/or endorsements from union leaders. These endorsements usually mean large numbers of the union members, locally and nationally, will vote for the candidate. Unions provide support for their members by helping to keep them employed, negotiating job transfers, providing credentials for job-seeking employees, and providing the education members need to obtain and keep jobs.

The major function of unions is **collective bargaining,** which is the process of negotiating the terms of employment for union members. Terms of the agreement are written in an employment contract. The contract is usually quite detailed and is divided into these major sections: wages and supplements; employees' rights on the job; union rights in relation to the employer; management rights in relation to the union; and the grievance procedure, which comes into play when a provision of the contract has not been honored. A *grievance* is a formal complaint, by an employee or by the union, that management has violated some aspect of the contract.

The labor contract stipulates wages to be paid for certain jobs and types of work. Paid holidays, vacations, overtime rates, and hours of work are also specified in the contract. Most labor contracts also list fringe benefits. **Fringe benefits** are employee benefits beyond wages or salaries, including health insurance, sick leave, and pensions. Union contracts usually provide for **seniority** rights, which state that the last ones hired should be the first ones laid off. In other words, the longer you work, the more job security you are entitled to. Seniority may be used to determine transfers, promotions, and vacation time according to most union contracts.

When agreement on a contract cannot be reached between the union and the employer, the dispute can be mediated. Congress created the Federal Mediation and Conciliation Service as part of the Taft-

Hartley Act. Through *mediation,* the union and the employer receive the help of a neutral third party (the specialist). The specialist is used to bring about concession and compromise. Specialists (mediators) cannot issue binding decisions. When employers and union officials cannot agree on the terms of a new contract, the labor union may make the decision to **strike,** a process in which union members refuse to work until an agreement is reached.

A strike is an option a labor union may use during a contract dispute.

Types of Unions

Unions are self-governing organizations that can be classified into three types: craft unions, industrial unions, and public employee unions. Major decisions are made by elected leaders. Many unions have developed a high degree of professionalism and are regarded as powerful. Union leaders often work full time in their positions. Unions often employ their own lawyers, doctors, economists, educators, and public relations officials; dues collected from members provide the basis for the services of these professionals.

Craft Unions

Membership in craft unions is limited to those who practice in an established craft or trade, for example, bricklayers, carpenters, or plasterers. Major craft unions include those of the building, printing, and maritime trades, and of railroad employees.

Industrial Unions

Membership in industrial unions is composed of skilled, semiskilled, or unskilled employees in a particular place, industry, or group of industries. Examples include the AFL-CIO, Teamsters, and United Auto Workers. Most of this country's basic industries (steel, automobiles, rubber, glass, machinery, mining) are heavily unionized.

Public Employee Unions

Municipal, county, state, or federal employees such as firefighters, teachers, and police officers may organize public employee unions. These unions are organized much like craft and industrial unions except that they generally do not hire outside officers. In other words, municipal or county workers would also serve as union representatives and officers, sometimes with released time and pay from union dues.

Professional Organizations

A **professional organization** also collects dues from members and provides support services. In some cases, membership in a professional organization may be required. Most notable of professional organizations include the American Bar Association (required) for lawyers and the American Medical Association (optional) for doctors. Each state bar association provides the testing procedures for lawyers' "admission to the bar." Attorneys who are severely disciplined are "disbarred," which means they can no longer practice law.

Professional organizations have six major purposes: (a) to establish and maintain professional standards, including procedures for self-improvement; (b) to support legislation and political action that is beneficial to the profession, called **lobbying**; (c) to encourage individual growth and achievement; (d) to publish a professional journal or magazine; (e) to provide pension, retirement, and insurance benefits for members; and (f) to keep members up-to-date on current information and procedures. Because most doctors and lawyers are self-employed, their professional behavior is not regulated except through membership in these organizations and/or through lawsuits. Exams, accreditations, admission procedures, and other standards are administered through these organizations.

Another professional organization, sometimes called a union (the largest one nationwide), is the NEA (National Education Association). Dues are unified, which means that an educator who joins a local association must also join the state and national associations. Each branch of the NEA charges dues, just as do the national, state, and county bar associations.

Summary

Employee pay and benefits provide financial security for employees and their families. It is the employee's responsibility to understand gross pay (including overtime); deductions (required and optional); and net pay (how to compute it). Employee benefits provide work incentives and are essential to employees. Changes in the workplace such as flextime, compressed workweek, job rotation, job sharing, permanent part-time work, telecommuting, and on-site child care have created opportunities for employees for employment reward, enrichment, and creativity. Finally, unions and professional organizations are often required in the workplace and should be clearly understood from the standpoint of their roles, benefits, advantages, and disadvantages for employers and employees.

Vocabulary terms

Directions: Can you find the definition for each of the following terms used in Chapter 6?

collective bargaining
compressed workweek
deductions
employee services
flextime
fringe benefits
gross pay
incentive pay
job rotation

job sharing
labor union
lobbying
net pay
overtime
professional organization
seniority
strike
vested

1. Similar to a labor union, but membership is required for persons in certain occupations.
2. A process in which employees refuse to work until an agreement with management is reached.
3. An effort to support legislation that would be of benefit to a certain group.
4. The total agreed-upon salary or pay before deductions.
5. Amounts subtracted from gross pay, some required and some optional.
6. Also known as the amount of the paycheck.
7. A condition of having full rights to monies deposited or funds accumulated in a retirement plan.
8. A group of people in the same or similar occupations, organized for the benefit of all.
9. The process whereby unions and employers negotiate terms of employment.
10. The first hired is the last fired or laid off.
11. Encouragement plan to get employees to do more and better work.
12. An arrangement of working hours that varies among employees.
13. A technique for training employees to be efficient in more than one specialized area.
14. Two people share what was originally one full-time position.
15. A work schedule where you work four days, ten hours each, rather than five days, eight hours each.
16. Extras that a company offers in order to improve employee morale and working conditions.

17. Employee benefits beyond wages and salary, including health insurance, sick leave, and benefits.
18. Hours worked beyond the regular forty-hour workweek.

Facts and ideas in review

1. How is gross pay different from net pay?
2. List five optional deductions you may elect to have withheld from your gross pay.
3. How much is the minimum wage?
4. What is required when an employee has worked more than the maximum regular workweek?
5. What is a leave of absence?
6. What is a core time period?
7. What is a major advantage of job rotation to employers?
8. What are the four major functions of labor unions?
9. What are the three types of labor unions?
10. How are labor unions funded? That is, who pays for the services they provide?
11. Describe the collective bargaining process.
12. Explain the principle of seniority.
13. What was the significance of the Wagner Act to American labor?
14. How is mediation used in labor negotiations?
15. Name a professional organization.

Applications for decision making

1. Compute gross pay for these situations:
   a. Regular hours worked: 40
      Overtime hours worked: 5
      Regular rate of pay: $5.85 an hour
   b. Regular salary: $800 a month
      Overtime hours agreed upon: 8 a week (four weeks)
      Overtime rate of pay agreed upon: $7.50 an hour
   c. Total hours worked: 43 (in 5 days)
      Regular rate of pay: $6.10
   d. Annual salary: $18,000
      Compute monthly gross pay:

2. Using the payroll income tax withholding tables on pages 129–132, locate the following answers:

   a. For a single person, one allowance, who made $110 last week:
     State withholding tax:
     Federal withholding tax:

   b. For a single person, no allowances, who made $222 last week:
     State withholding tax:
     Federal withholding tax:

   c. For a married person, two allowances, who made $1,120 last month:
     State withholding tax:
     Federal withholding tax:

   d. For a married person, six allowances, who made $1,479 last month:
     State withholding tax:
     Federal withholding tax:

L ife situation problem solving

1. Joan Valencio, social security number 484-40-9876, works for a weekly paycheck. She is single and claims no allowances. Last week she worked five days for a total of forty-four hours. Her regular rate of pay is $7.60 an hour. In addition to federal income tax, state income tax (use tables shown in Figures 6-3 through 6-6), and social security tax, Joan also has insurance of $16 a week withheld and puts 6 percent of her gross pay into a retirement account. Compute gross pay, deductions, and net paycheck.

2. Martin Etter, social security number 444-33-2121, works for a weekly paycheck. He is single and claims one allowance. Last week he worked five days, for a total of forty-eight hours. His regular rate of pay is $6.80 an hour. In addition to required deductions, he also has $10 a week sent to his credit union account and gives $5 a week to United Fund (charity). Compute gross pay, deductions, and net paycheck.

3. Hector Fuentes, social security number 644-30-2929, works for a monthly salary. He is married and claims four allowances. Last month Hector worked twenty-two days. He does not get paid for overtime. His monthly salary is $1,780. In addition to required deductions, Hector also pays insurance premiums of $23 a month and sets aside for retirement 6 percent of his gross monthly pay. Compute gross pay, deductions, and net paycheck.

4. Margaret Bielke, social security number 331-84-3139, works for a monthly paycheck. She is married and claims two allowances. Her yearly salary is $20,700. Last month she worked twenty-one days, without overtime. In addition to required deductions, Margaret also contributes $14 a week (assume a four-week month) to the Heart Fund and sets aside $50 a month, paid directly to her savings account. Compute Margaret's gross pay, deductions, and net paycheck.

5. Ying Ho, social security number 414-31-3245, works for a monthly salary. He is married and claims no allowances. His monthly salary is $1,500. When Ying works overtime, it is at an agreed-upon hourly rate of $12.75. Last month he worked ten hours that will be paid overtime. He worked twenty-three days. Ying has only the required deductions. Compute Ying's gross pay, deductions, and net paycheck.

objectives:

After reading and studying this chapter you will be able to:

7-1 Understand the purpose of taxes, different types of taxes, and the history of taxes in the United States.

7-2 Describe components of the tax system, including the IRS, the power to tax, and paying your fair share.

7-3 Define and show a working knowledge of exemptions, dependents, and taxable and nontaxable income when preparing tax returns.

7-4 Prepare Forms 1040EZ and 1040A (Individual Federal Income Tax Returns).

As you learned in the previous chapter, income taxes will be withheld from your paycheck (unless you qualify for exempt status, as discussed in Chapter 5). In addition, you will need to file a federal income tax return by April 15 of the following year to show the tax owed or to claim a refund. If you live in a state that has a state income tax, you will also need to file a state tax return. In this chapter, you will discover why and how taxes are collected, as well as income tax terminology, and learn how to prepare income tax returns.

chapter 7

Federal Income Tax

Our tax system

In the democratic, free enterprise society found in the United States, money is collected by the government from citizens and businesses in the form of taxes. This money, which is called **revenue,** is redistributed (spent) according to needs and priorities determined by Congress. The largest source of government revenue is income taxes. Other taxes providing government revenue include social security taxes, unemployment insurance taxes, inheritance and estate taxes, excise taxes, import duties, and personal property taxes, to name a few.

A commonly accepted criterion of tax fairness is that individuals with different amounts of wealth or income should pay different amounts of taxes. This theory is called the *ability-to-pay principle*. **Progressive taxes** are those that increase in proportion to income. Tax rates increase as the level of taxable income increases. Basically, everyone who receives income from employment, or any other source, is subject to paying income taxes. The person with the higher income not only pays more taxes but pays them at a higher rate.

Regressive taxes are those that decrease in proportion to income. With a regressive tax, the person with the higher income pays a lower percentage of income in taxes than a lower income person. Sales taxes are regressive taxes, because those who can least afford to pay the tax (the poor) are assessed the greatest amount in proportion to their income. *Sales taxes* are often called "pay as you go" taxes, because they are levied against your purchases. For example, your state may charge a 5 percent sales tax. If you buy an item worth $10, your tax would be 50 cents, and you would pay $10.50 for the item you are buying. Almost all our consumption taxes turn out to be regressive. Another example of a tax on consumption is an *excise tax*. Excise taxes are imposed on specific goods and services, such as gasoline, cigarettes, alcoholic beverages, air travel, and telephone service.

Proportional taxes or flat taxes are those for which the rate remains constant (stays the same) even though the amount being taxed increases. Property taxes are proportional. For example, all people owning property in the same community pay the same tax rate per every $100 of assessed value. If your parents own a home, they must pay property taxes which are assessed on a yearly basis. This money is paid to the local tax assessor, in either semiannual or monthly payments.

Federal taxes help provide funding for our national parks.

On a local level, taxes provide services such as education, parks and recreation, streets and roads, and police, fire, and health departments. On a national level, they provide salaries for Congress and funds for national defense, highways, parks, welfare, foreign aid, and other services. Most of the services (local, state, and national) are provided for the general welfare of all citizens, although as an individual, you may not benefit directly.

History of taxes

For many years the United States operated without an income tax. Many of the new inhabitants came to America to avoid taxation, and the new society was careful to avoid it. While our country was a colony of England, the British government imposed certain taxes. However, when the Revolutionary War brought independence, there was no direct income tax imposed on citizens. The Constitution, drawn in 1787, included the option to tax, but not to tax individuals directly. Excise taxes and customs duties produced enough revenue to meet the nation's needs at that time.

But while the government did not levy *income* taxes against the citizens, it also did not provide services for them. Such was the case until the mid-1850s.

The Revolutionary War was financed by contributions from sympathetic countries such as France. The War of 1812 brought a temporary income tax, but when the war debts were paid, the tax was dropped.

When the Civil War became an economic burden, an income tax to finance the war became necessary. In 1862, President Lincoln signed into law a bill that provided for progressive income taxes on wages earned; when the war debts were paid off, the tax expired. Congress introduced the first permanent income tax in the form of the 16th Amendment to the Constitution in 1909. The amendment was ratified by three-fourths of the states by 1913. However, only nominal taxes were levied as a result of this Amendment.

World War I (1917) was paid for by income taxes. After WWI, the country prospered until the Great Depression of 1929. At that time the government was providing few services, and many people suffered badly as a result. But President Franklin D. Roosevelt's "New Deal" again brought prosperity through taxation and redistribution of income. In 1935, the Social Security Act was signed into law, creating the Internal Revenue Service (IRS). The IRS was designed to collect taxes and turn them over for the payment of government debt, commitments, and benefits. Money withheld from wages for social security was deposited with the U.S. Department of the Treasury.

During World War II, taxes were increased to finance the war. This increase set a precedent for the changing tax rates we know today. Rates are increased to pay for the growing services and needs of the government.

omponents of the tax system

Our tax system is complex. Both businesses and individuals pay income taxes and must file income tax returns each year. The basic components that allow the tax system to operate efficiently are the IRS, the country's power to tax income, and each taxpayer's willingness to pay his or her fair share.

The IRS

The Internal Revenue Service is an administrative agency of the Department of the Treasury. Its headquarters is in Washington, D.C., with seven regional offices throughout the country. Each regional office is a major data processing center that oversees at least ten district and local offices. The main functions of the IRS are to collect income taxes and to enforce tax laws.

In addition to collecting income taxes and enforcing the law, the IRS performs a number of other services. In local offices, IRS employees assist taxpayers in finding information and forms. The IRS prints brochures and pamphlets to aid taxpayers in preparing their returns. It also furnishes tax information and instruction booklets free to schools and colleges.

The Power to Tax

The power to levy taxes rests with the Congress of the United States. The Constitution provides that "all bills for raising revenue shall originate in the House of Representatives." Proposals to increase or decrease taxes may come from the president, the Department of the Treasury, or from a congressperson representing the interests of a geographic area. The House Ways and Means Committee studies the proposals and makes recommendations to the full House. Revenue bills must pass a vote in both the House and the Senate and then be signed by the president before they become law.

The power to levy taxes rests with the Congress of the United States.

Paying Your Fair Share

Our income tax is a graduated rate—the more income you receive, the more income tax you pay. Tax rates change as Congress seeks ways to bring in more money to balance its budget and reduce the deficit, which results from spending more money than is received from taxpayers. For example, there were three tax brackets (15%, 28%, and 31%) prior to changes initiated by President Clinton. Another bracket was added (36%) for high-income taxpayers (couples earning over $140,000 or individuals earning over $100,000). These additional taxes were earmarked to reduce the national debt.

Our income tax system is based on **voluntary compliance,** which means that all citizens are expected to prepare (or have prepared) and file income tax returns. Taxes owed are due on or before the deadline of April 15 of each year. Responsibility for filing a tax return and paying taxes due rests with the individual. Failure to do so can result in penalty, interest charges on the taxes owed, a fine, and/or imprisonment. Willful failure to pay taxes is called **tax evasion,** which is a felony punishable by a fine or imprisonment or both.

An IRS Audit

Taxpayers called for an IRS **audit** have three choices. First, they can represent themselves all the way to an appeal in Tax Court if necessary. Second, they can give someone the power of attorney to take their place, as long as the designated person is a lawyer, certified public accountant, a member of the immediate family, or an enrolled agent (someone formerly employed by the IRS at the audit level for five years or more). Third, they can bring anyone at all—tax preparer or therapist—for support during the session. Most audit sessions involve nothing more than confirming supporting documentation; therefore, most taxpayers can go alone unless the matter is unusually complicated.

A correspondence audit is much more common than an office audit, where the taxpayer sits down with the auditor to answer questions and produce records. In a correspondence audit, the IRS asks the taxpayer to respond to specific questions or produce evidence of deductions or other entries on the tax return. A field audit is similar, except that an IRS agent or local representative visits the taxpayer to verify information or ask specific questions.

 ## Definitions of terms

Your tax preparation efforts should be geared toward paying your fair share of taxes while taking advantage of tax benefits appropriate to your financial situation. Before you can understand how to prepare tax forms, you need a working knowledge of the tax vocabulary. The terms described in the following paragraphs are found on income tax returns, in IRS instruction booklets, and on forms and schedules you will use.

Filing Status

There are five different ways to file a tax return: (1) as a single person (not married); (2) as a married person filing a joint return (even though only one spouse may have earned income); (3) as a married person filing a separate return; (4) as a "head of household" (a person may qualify as a head of household whether married or single if certain conditions are met in providing a residence for persons dependent on the taxpayer); or (5) as a qualifying widow(er) with a dependent child. You mark your filing status on the front of the tax form. A more complete description of these classifications is found in IRS instruction booklets. After you file your first tax return, each year thereafter you will automatically receive a tax booklet containing the necessary forms in the mail for use in preparing your tax returns.

Exemptions

An **exemption** is an allowance a taxpayer claims for each person dependent on the taxpayer's income. As a taxpayer you are automatically allowed one exemption for yourself unless someone else (such as a parent) claims you on his or her return. If you are filing a joint return, you can take an exemption for your spouse. Once you are divorced, you cannot take an exemption for a former spouse.

An exemption is an allowance a taxpayer claims for each person dependent on the taxpayer's income.

point counterpoint

To Tax or Not to Tax

Taxes collected from individuals and businesses provide our government with the money necessary to provide services. When taxpayers do not pay their fair share of taxes, then the government must borrow money to cover its debts. In addition, because of low revenues from taxes, the government often finds it necessary to raise tax rates and change the rules so they can collect more taxes.

In our country, many people do not pay their fair share of taxes. The tax cheaters represent a cross-section of the economy, from low income individuals to the very rich. An underground economy exists where people buy and sell goods for cash, and the transactions are never reported on tax returns. This occurs at garage sales, flea markets, and other direct sales. Some people simply do not want to pay their fair share of taxes—they believe the government is corrupt or doesn't spend their money wisely. Others feel that taxes are simply too high and they refuse to pay.

Arthur Laffer is an economist who served as a economic advisor to President Reagan. He developed what is called the Laffer Curve, which shows that as tax rates go up, total tax dollars collected by government actually decreases. According to his theory, as tax rates increase, taxpayers avoid and even evade taxes. Some refuse to earn overtime or income that would be subject to tax. Others find tax loopholes, invest overseas, or do whatever else is necessary to avoid taxes.

Any way you look at it, when everyone doesn't pay their fair share, the country as a whole suffers. Then the burden is passed along to others who can't avoid taxation—usually wage earners who have taxes withheld from their paychecks.

critical thinking

1. How do you feel about taxes in this country? What benefits do you receive even though you may not be paying taxes?

2. Do you feel that penalties for tax evaders are too tough? Not tough enough?

3. Why do people consider the IRS their enemy? Find out what happens in an IRS audit of a tax return, and write a report.

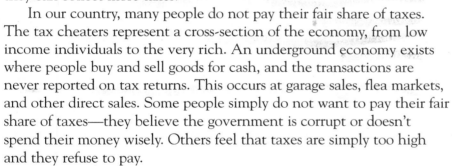

A dependent is a person who lives with you and who receives more than half his or her living expenses from you. This includes a baby born at any time during the year or a person who died during the year. Each exemption claimed on the income tax form excludes a certain amount of gross income ($2,350 per exemption in 1994, with this amount increasing according to the cost of living each year).

Any person who meets all five of the following requirements qualifies as a dependent:

1. The person must be a relative (child, stepchild, adopted child, or foster child; grandchild, great grandchild; son-in-law or daughter-in-law; parent, stepparent, or parent-in-law; grandparent or great grandparent; brother, sister, half brother, half sister, stepbrother, stepsister, brother-in-law, or sister-in-law; and, if related by blood, aunt, uncle, nephew, or niece). Relationships created by marriage are not ended by divorce or death.
2. The person must be a citizen or resident of the United States, or a resident of Canada or Mexico, or an adopted child who is not a U.S. citizen but has lived with you all year in a foreign country.
3. If the person is married, he or she cannot file a joint return with his or her spouse.
4. The person's income must be less than the amount of her or his exemption ($2,450 at this writing). This test does not apply to a child under age 19 or to a student under age 24.
5. You must provide over half of the person's support during the year.

Children of divorced or separated parents are a special case. The parent who has custody of a child for most of the year (custodial parent) generally can claim the child as a dependent. Three exceptions are as follows: (1) if the custodial parent agrees not to claim the exemption; (2) if the divorce decree entered into before 1985 allows the noncustodial parent to claim the exemption and the noncustodial parent contributed at least $600 for the child's support during the year; or (3) if the divorce decree grants the exemption to the noncustodial parent.

Gross Income

Gross income is all the taxable income you receive, including wages, tips, salaries, interest, dividends, unemployment compensation, alimony, workers' compensation benefits, and so forth. Scholarships and grants may be taxable for amounts used for expenses other than tuition and books. For non-degree candidates (people just taking classes but not pursuing a degree), even more may be taxable. In other words, because you are not pursuing a degree, some, most, or all of what you receive for this type of education is taxable. Also, employer-reimbursed tuition is in most cases taxable. Certain types of income are not taxable and are not reported as income; these include child support, gifts, inheritances, life insurance benefits, and veterans' benefits.

Wages, Salaries, and Tips

These items are monies received through employment, as shown on the Form W-2, Wage and Tax Statement supplied by the employer by January 31 each year.

Interest Income

This includes taxable interest from banks, savings and loan associations, credit unions, series HH savings bonds, and so on. You should receive Form 1099-INT from the payers of such interest.

Dividend Income

Dividends are distributions of money, stock, or other property that corporations pay to stockholders. You will receive a Form 1099-DIV.

Unemployment Compensation

By January 31, you should receive Form 1099-G showing total unemployment compensation received. This amount will be entered on a tax return as income.

Social Security Benefits

Eighty-five percent of social security benefits received are taxable if total income (including nontaxable or tax-exempt) exceeds $34,000 for single taxpayers and $44,000 for married taxpayers. Form SSA-1099 lists total social security benefits paid to you during the year. (People receiving railroad retirement benefits in lieu of social security must apply the same rule and will receive Form RRB-1099.)

Child Support

Money paid to a former spouse for support of dependent children is called **child support.** This income is not taxable for the person receiving it, nor is it deductible for the person paying it.

Alimony

Money paid to support a former spouse is called **alimony.** It is taxable for the person receiving it and deductible for the person paying it. (The long Form 1040 is required.)

You are also taxed on other forms of income, including winnings from gambling, bartering income, pensions and annuities, rental income, royalties, estate and trust income, and income on sale of property.

Adjusted Gross Income

Some adjustments, or monies that are spent, are allowed to be subtracted directly from gross income, such as contributions to IRAs (not allowed on Form 1040EZ). If you qualify for an IRA (individual retirement account; see Chapter 11), you may be able to deduct amounts contributed. After these adjustments are subtracted from gross income, the result is **adjusted gross income.** When you look at a tax return, you will see that adjusted gross income is used as a basis for computing other deductions.

Taxable Income

Deductions are expenses the law allows the taxpayer to subtract from adjusted gross income. All taxpayers are allowed to list certain expenses which are called **itemized deductions.** To itemize deductions, you must complete Schedule A and Form 1040. On this form you can list medical and dental expenses (the amount that exceeds 7.5 percent of adjusted gross income); state and local income taxes and property taxes; home mortgage interest; gifts to charity; qualifying casualty and theft losses; moving expenses; and qualifying job and miscellaneous expenses.

Instead of itemizing your deductions, you can choose the **standard deduction.** Most people prefer the standard deduction, as shown in Figure 7-1; you will want to subtract this amount from adjusted gross income unless your itemized deductions are larger. Figure 7-1 shows the standard deduction for most people based on their filing status.

The standard deduction is higher for people age sixty-five or older, and for blind people. Once you have subtracted your standard deduction (or itemized deductions), you need to compute exemptions. An amount is deducted for each exemption to arrive at your **taxable income,** which is used to determine the tax liability from the tax tables. Figure 7-2 shows the formula for determining your taxable income.

Fig. 7-1

The Standard Deduction

STANDARD DEDUCTION FOR MOST PEOPLE

If your filing status is:	Your standard deduction:
Single	$3,800
Married filing jointly or qualifying widow(er)	6,350
Married filing separately	3,175
Head of household	5,600

Fig. 7-2   **Taxable Income Formula**

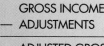

```
        GROSS INCOME
    —   ADJUSTMENTS
        _____

        ADJUSTED GROSS INCOME
    —   STANDARD DEDUCTION OR ITEMIZED DEDUCTIONS
    —   EXEMPTIONS
        _____

        TAXABLE INCOME
```

 reparing to file

Once income and expense records are ready, you can make a rough draft of your tax return. You should also study the tax booklet that accompanies the printed forms. This contains the latest tax information, including new or revised tax laws, you will need to prepare your return. Read the return carefully to be sure you are taking advantage of every possible deduction and are reporting all taxable income. A simple 1040EZ tax return may require only 15 minutes to prepare; the long Form 1040 may require several days after all information has been gathered. In addition to a federal tax return, you may have to file a state income tax return.

Who Must File?

You must file a tax return if your filing status, age, and gross income are as shown in Figure 7-3.

In addition to the requirements given in Figure 7-3, persons claimed as dependents on another person's tax return may also have to file a tax return (see tax booklets). You may also have to file if (a) you owe any special taxes, such as social security tax on tips; (b) you earned $400 or more from self-employment; or (c) you earned $100 or more from a church or church-controlled organization that is exempt from employer social security taxes.

Persons who did not earn enough to owe taxes, but who had taxes withheld from their paychecks, should file a return to reclaim monies withheld. If you do not file, you will not get a refund.

Fig. 7-3 **Who Must File?**

Chart A — For Most People

You must file a return if your **gross income** was at least the amount shown in the last column. **Gross income** means all income you received in the form of money, goods, property, and services that is not exempt from tax, including any gain on the sale of your home (even if you may exclude or postpone part or all of the gain).

Marital status	Filing status	Age	Gross income
Single (including divorced and legally separated)	Single	under 65	$6,250
		65 or older	$7,200
	Head of household	under 65	$8,050
		65 or older	$9,000
Married with a child and living apart from your spouse during the last 6 months of 19--	Head of household	under 65	$8,050
		65 or older	$9,000
Married and living with your spouse at end of 19-- (or on the date your spouse died)	Married, joint return	under 65 (both spouses)	$11,250
		65 or older (one spouse)	$12,000
		65 or older (both spouses)	$12,750
	Married, separate return	any age	$2,450
Married, not living with your spouse at the end of 19-- (or on the date your spouse died)	Married, joint or separate return	any age	$2,450
Widowed before 19-- and not remarried in 19--	Single	under 65	$6,250
		65 or older	$7,200
	Head of household	under 65	$8,050
		65 or older	$9,000
	Qualifying widow(er) with dependent child	under 65	$8,800
		65 or older	$9,550

Source: IRS Instructions for Filing U.S. Tax Returns.

When to File?

You must file no later than April 15 of the year after you earned income. If April 15 falls on a weekend or holiday, your tax return is due on the next regular weekday. If you file late, you are subject to penalties and interest charges.

Short Form or Long Form?

Although there are nearly 400 federal tax forms and schedules, taxpayers have a choice of basic forms when filing their return (see Figure 7-4). You must decide whether to fill out a short form (1040A or 1040EZ) or to itemize your deductions, using the long form (1040). Most recently, 17 percent of taxpayers used Form 1040EZ, 19 percent used Form 1040A, and 64 percent used the regular Form 1040. Which form you choose will depend on the type and amount of your income, the number of your deductions, and the complexity of your tax situation.

Where to Begin?

During the year, save all receipts and proofs of payment for your itemized deduction. You will need these receipts to prove the accuracy of your tax return if you are audited. Save all employee withholding records. By January 31 you should receive your Form W-2, Wage and Tax Statement, from each of your employers. Compare it with your records and check it for accuracy. Any discrepancy between the Form W-2 and your records should be reported immediately to the employer and corrected. Social security tax withholding rates increase periodically, and a current IRS tax preparation booklet will give you the current rates.

It is wise to prepare your tax return early—as soon as you receive your Form W-2 Wage and Tax Statement and any 1099s, which reflect other income received. Gather all other necessary information, including tax preparation booklets and last year's tax return as a model for preparing this year's. If you owe additional taxes, mail your return and the amount due in sufficient time to have the envelope postmarked by April 15. If you have a refund coming, the sooner you file, the sooner you will receive it. If you wait until April, your refund may be delayed for months. You will not receive interest on refunds.

Once you have gathered all your information, prepare both the short and the long form to determine whether you can save money by itemizing deductions. Read all directions carefully and fill out all schedules completely.

Fig. 7-4

Which Form to Use?

Which form should I use?	There are three tax returns for individuals: Form 1040EZ, Form 1040A, and Form 1040. You may use Form 1040 if you want to, but you will probably save time if you are able to use 1040A or 1040EZ.			
	Filing status	**Number of exemptions**	**Taxable income**	**Only income from**
Form 1040EZ	Single (under 65 and not blind)	No more than one personal exemption for yourself	Only taxable income (line 7) of less than $50,000	• Wages, salaries, tips • Taxable scholarships and fellowships • Interest of $400 or less
Form 1040A	• Single • Married filing joint • Married filing separate • Head of household • Qualifying widow(er) with dependent child	All exemptions that you are entitled to claim	Only taxable income (line 19) of less than $50,000	• Wages, salaries, tips • Taxable scholarships and fellowships • Interest • Dividends • Unemployment compensation
Form 1040	• Single • Married filing joint • Married filing separate • Head of household • Qualifying widow(er) with dependent child	All exemptions that you are entitled to claim	Any amount of taxable income (line 37)	• Wages, salaries, tips • Taxable scholarships and fellowships • Interest • Dividends • Taxable social security and railroad retirement benefits • Unemployment compensation • Self-employment • Rents and royalties • Pensions, annuities, and IRAs • Taxable state and local income tax refunds • Capital gains • Gain from the sale of your home • Alimony received • All other sources

Source: IRS Instructions for Preparing U.S. Tax Returns.

If you do not have enough taxes withheld during the year, you are subject to a penalty and have to increase withholdings for the next year. If you receive a large refund, you should reduce your allowance status to have less withheld during the year.

Even if you hire a professional tax preparer, you are responsible for supplying accurate and complete information. Hiring a tax preparer will *not* guarantee you are paying the correct amount. If you discover an error in a tax return after it has been filed, you may file an amended return (Form 1040X) to claim a refund or credit, or to pay additional tax due.

Save copies of the tax returns you file, together with all supporting evidence (receipts) for six years. Tax returns should be kept in a safe-deposit box, together with copies of W-2s and other supporting information.

P reparing income tax returns

The federal income tax return must be completed in ink or typed with no errors or omissions. The booklets provided by the IRS have line-by-line instructions that explain each section and type of income or deduction.

Many people hire professional tax preparers to do their income tax returns. These preparers may do the job manually, although they increasingly are using a tax preparation computer program. This program provides all the necessary forms, and helps prepare simple returns quickly. Computer tax programs are available for all types of computers, and cost from about $20 to $50.

The preparation of tax returns is usually a simple process of following directions and inserting appropriate information. Remember, an unsigned tax return will be returned to the taxpayer before a refund is issued. If a joint return is prepared, both spouses must sign it.

Form 1040EZ

You may use Form 1040EZ if you are single or married and claim no dependents. Taxable income must be less than $50,000. Line-by-line instructions for filling out Form 1040EZ are given on the back of the form. Highlights of the instructions are described in the following paragraphs.

Step 1: Name and Address

Fill in your name, address, and social security number. Check the "Yes" box if you want $3 to go to the Presidential Election Campaign Fund. This is a fund established by Congress so that all taxpayers could share equally in the costs of election campaigns. This method of campaign financing makes it possible for all presidential candidates to compete for votes without taking large donations from special interests, such as large corporations, unions, or wealthy individuals. The $3 comes from taxes already withheld, so income taxes are not increased for the individual. You can contribute to the Presidential Election Campaign Fund by checking the appropriate box on your tax return.

Step 2: Reporting Income

First, enter your total wages, salaries, and tips, as shown on your W-2 form(s). Second, enter interest earned on savings accounts (this amount cannot be more than $400). Add these two figures together—this is your adjusted gross income.

You can make a contribution to the Presidential Campaign Fund by checking the appropriate box on your tax return.

Next, you must indicate if you are claimed as a dependent on another person's tax return. If so, you will lose most or all of the standard deduction. If not, you can enter the total standard deduction and personal exemption allowed on the 1040EZ ($6,250 at this writing). This amount is subtracted from adjusted gross income to obtain your taxable income.

Step 3: Compute Tax

Now enter the total federal tax withheld (as shown on your W-2 forms) and compare it to the tax you owe based on your taxable income. Look up the amount of your taxable income and the amount of tax you owe in the tax tables. (See Appendix A for the EZ tax table.)

Step 4: Refund or Amount Owed

If the amount of federal taxes withheld is larger than the amount of tax you owe, you will receive a refund. If you owe more tax than was withheld, you must pay the difference. Write your check to the Internal Revenue Service and attach it to your return.

Step 5: Sign the Return

Sign your tax return. Make sure your W-2 form(s) and check (if applicable) are attached to the completed return, and mail the return to the regional IRS office designated for your area.

Form 1040A

Form 1040A is printed on four pages. Line-by-line instructions for completing it are available in the booklet "Instructions for Preparing (Year) 1040EZ and 1040A." Instructions as to who may and may not use the form are also in the booklet. This form would be used by individuals who have less than $50,000 in taxable income from wages, salaries, tips, unemployment compensation, interest, or dividends. With Form 1040A, you also can take deductions for individual retirement account (IRA) contributions and a tax credit for child care expenses. The following steps will guide you through the completion of Form 1040A.

Step 1: Name and Address

The first section requires writing in the name, address, social security number, and occupation of persons filing the return. Once you have filed your first tax return, you will receive a tax booklet each January which contains a preprinted mailing label with your name, address, and social security number. This can be affixed to your return, eliminating the need to write out the information. Each person filing can elect to give or not give to the Presidential Election Campaign Fund.

Step 2: Filing Status

In this section, you select your tax filing status. You must fill in spouse's name and social security number if filing separately, names of dependents if head of household, and year spouse died, if filing as widow(er).

Step 3: Exemptions

Form 1040A provides space to declare your exemptions. Claim yourself and your spouse if you are filing jointly, and enter the names of your dependents together with qualifying information.

Step 4: Total Income

Enter wages, salaries, tips, and other income as shown on the Form W-2 you attach to the tax return. You must report any taxable interest income. If you have received over $400 in interest, you must list the name of each payer and the amount on Schedule 1. (See Figure 7-9, page 174.) You must also list tax-exempt interest income, even though it is not taxed. Income from dividends is next. Again, if you have over $400 in dividends, each source must be listed separately on Schedule 1.

You must enter the taxable amount of any money received from IRAs, pensions, and social security benefits. Then you must enter unemployment compensation income. If you received any unemployment compensation during the year, you must attach Form 1099G.

Step 5: Adjusted Gross Income

You can deduct contributions to an Individual Retirement account (IRA). Each employed worker who earns at least $2,000 can contribute up to $2,000 toward an IRA, if they qualify. Rules for eligibility are explained in the guide for preparing taxes (Publication 17). If both taxpayers are eligible, IRA deductions are entered and totaled. The total is then subtracted from gross income, and the difference is your adjusted gross income.

Step 6: Taxable Income

Next you will compute your taxable income. First, the adjusted gross income is entered. Then check if you or your spouse is 65 or older or blind, if you are claimed as a dependent by another taxpayer, or if you are married filing separately. The standard deduction is entered (at this writing, $3,800 for single, $6,350 for married filing jointly or widow(er), $3,175 for married filing separately, or $5,600 for head of household). The standard deduction amount is subtracted from adjusted gross income, and the number of exemptions claimed is multiplied by the amount allowed for each exemption (at this writing, the exemption amount is $2,450). It is also subtracted from adjusted gross income to determine taxable income.

Step 7: Figuring Taxes, Credits, and Payments

This section is used for entering the amount of tax liability, or the amount of taxes due from you based on your taxable income, and credits due you. To find the amount of tax due, consult the tax tables (see Appendices A and B) in the instructions booklet. Then you may claim any credit due for child care expenses. Complete Schedule 2, Part 1, to determine the amount of the credit, and subtract it from the tax liability. (Note that a tax credit directly reduces taxes.) After credits are subtracted, the remaining amount is your total tax liability.

Finally, enter the amount of federal income tax withheld, as shown on your W-2 form, which you will attach to the tax return. You would enter the earned income credit (EIC) as if it were taxes withheld. At this writing, for people who have a child but income of less than $25,296, EIC can be as much as $2,528. Taxes withheld and the earned income credit are added together.

Step 8: Refund or Amount Owed

If the amount withheld plus credits exceeds the tax liability, the difference is your refund. But if you have more tax liability than the amount withheld or computed as a credit, you owe taxes. A check for the amount owed must be attached to your tax return.

Step 9: Signature

In this section, taxpayer and spouse must both sign and date a joint return even though only one may have earned or received income. Anyone who was paid to prepare your tax return for you also must sign and date the return.

Figure 7-5 shows John Calhoun's Form W-2, Wage and Tax Statement. Figure 7-6 on page 170 shows his completed Form 1040EZ

Fig. 7-5   **Sample W-2 Wage and Tax Statement**

1 Control number					
		OMB No. 1545-0008			

2 Employer's name, address, and ZIP code	6 Statutory employee ☐ Deceased ☐ Pension plan ☐ Legal rep. ☐ 942 emp. ☐ Subtotal ☐ Deferred compensation ☐ Void ☐
Blanton School District T-31 23855 SW 85th Portland, OR 97215-4562	7 Allocated tips · 8 Advance EIC payment

	9 Federal income tax withheld $1,501.00	10 Wages, tips, other compensation $14,720.00

3 Employer's identification number 93-899348488	4 Employer's state I.D. number 2384762	11 Social security tax withheld $912.64	12 Social security wages $14,720.00

5 Employee's social security number 465-84-3894		13 Social security tips	14 Medicare wages and tips $14,720.00

19 Employee's name, address, and ZIP code John F. Calhoun 285 SW 28th Street, #8 Portland, OR 97214-4562	15 Medicare tax withheld $213.44	16 Nonqualified plans
	17	18 Other

20	21	22 Dependent care benefits	23 Benefits included in Box 10

24 State income tax $946.00	25 State wages, tips, etc. $14,720.00	26 Name of state Oregon	27 Local income tax	28 Local wages, tips, etc.	29 Name of locality

Copy 1 For State, City, or Local Tax Department   Department of the Treasury—Internal Revenue Service

Form **W-2 Wage and Tax Statement**   **19--**

Employee's and employer's copy compared   ☐

tax return. Mr. Calhoun is single and claims one exemption. His wages are found on the W-2, which he previously checked for accuracy. John earned $134 in interest on his savings account. No one else can claim him as a dependent.

From the tax tables in Appendix A, Mr. Calhoun locates a tax liability of $1,294. When the tax liability of $1,294 is subtracted from taxes withheld of $1,501, the difference is $207. The amount of tax withheld is greater by $207 than John's tax liability, so he should receive a refund for that amount.

Married persons filing jointly with dependents may choose to file Form 1040A or Form 1040. Figures 7-7A and 7-7B on page 171 show the Wage and Tax Statements for Michael J. and Melissa B. Anderson. Figures 7-8A and 7-8B on pages 172–173 show their joint return (1040A).

Sample 1040EZ Tax Return

Department of the Treasury — Internal Revenue Service

Form **1040EZ**

Income Tax Return for Single and Joint Filers with No Dependents (99) 19--

OMB No. 1545-0675

Use the IRS label

Print your first name — John
MI — F.
Last name — Calhoun

If a joint return, print spouse's first name
MI
Last name

Otherwise, please print.

Home address (number and street). If you have a P.O. box, see instructions. — 285 SW 28th St.
Apt. no. — #8

City, town or post office. If you have a foreign address, see instructions. — Portland
State — OR
ZIP Code — 97214-4562

Your Social Security Number
465 84 3984

Spouse's Social Security Number

See instructions in Form 1040EZ booklet.

Presidential Election Campaign

Note: *Checking 'Yes' will not change your tax or reduce your refund.*
Do you want $3 to go to this fund? . . . . ▶
If a joint return, does your spouse want $3 to go to this fund? . . . . ▶

Yes No
x

Income

		Dollars	Cents
1	Total wages, salaries, and tips. This should be shown in box 1 of your W-2 form(s). Attach your W-2 form(s) **1**	14,720.00	

Attach Copy B of Form(s) W-2 here.

Enclose, but do not attach, any payment with your return.

Note: You **must** check Yes or No.

2	Taxable interest income of $400 or less. If the total is over $400, you cannot use Form 1040EZ **2**	134.00
3	Add lines 1 and 2. This is your **adjusted gross income**. If less than $9,000, see instructions to find out if you can claim the earned income credit on line 7 . . . . **3**	14,854.00

4 Can your parents (or someone else) claim you on their return?

Yes. Do worksheet; enter amount from line G here. ☐

No. If single, enter $6,250.00. If married, enter $11,250.00 ☒ For an explanation of these amounts, see instructions..

6,250.00

5	Subtract line 4 from line 3. If line 4 is larger than line 3, enter 0. This is your **taxable income** . . . . ▶ **5**	8,604.00

Payments and tax

6	Enter your federal income tax withheld from box 2 of your W-2 form(s) **6**	1,501.00
7	**Earned income credit.** Enter type and amount of nontaxable earned income below. **7**	- -
8	Add lines 6 and 7 (don't include nontaxable earned income). These are your **total payments** **8**	1,501.00
9	**Tax.** Use the amount on **line 5** to find your tax in the tax table in the instruction booklet. Then, enter the tax from the table on this line **9**	1,294.00

Refund or amount you owe

10	If line 8 is larger than line 9, subtract line 9 from line 8. This is your **refund** **10**	207.00
11	If line 9 is larger than line 8, subtract line 8 from line 9. This is the **amount you owe**. See instructions for details on how to pay and what to write on your payment **11**	

Sign your return

I have read this return. Under penalties of perjury, I declare that to the best of my knowledge and belief, the return is true, correct, and accurately lists all amounts and sources of income I received during the tax year.

Your signature — *John F. Calhoun*
Spouse's signature if joint return

Keep a copy of this form for your records

Date — 3/15/--
Your occupation — Mechanic
Date
Spouse's occupation

For IRS Use Only — Please do not write in boxes below.

Paid Preparer's Use Only

Preparer's signature
Date

Firm's name (or yours if self-employed) and Address
Preparer's SSN
EIN

Check if self-employed ☐

D181 For Privacy Act and Paperwork Reduction Act Notice, see instructions.

Form **1040EZ** (19--)

FDIA0201 12/22/--

Figs. 7-7A, 7-7B　　**Sample W-2 Statements—Melissa and Michael Anderson**

1 Control number											
		OMB No. 1545-0008									

2 Employer's name, address, and ZIP code	6 Statutory employee ☐	Deceased ☐	Pension plan ☐	Legal rep. ☐	942 emp. ☐	Subtotal ☐	Deferred compensation ☐	Void ☐

A & W Welding Supply
85 West Bensington Blvd.
Chicago, IL 60615-2358

7 Allocated tips	8 Advance EIC payment
9 Federal income tax withheld $611.00	10 Wages, tips, other compensation $12,811.40

3 Employer's identification number 92-186848	4 Employer's state I.D. number 33-261	11 Social security tax withheld $794.31	12 Social security wages $12,811.40
5 Employee's social security number 411-86-3214		13 Social security tips	14 Medicare wages and tips $12,811.40

19 Employee's name, address, and ZIP code	15 Medicare tax withheld $185.77	16 Nonqualified plans

Melissa B. Anderson
312 East 34th Street
Chicago, IL 60604-5214

17	18 Other

20	21	22 Dependent care benefits	23 Benefits included in Box 10

24 State income tax	25 State wages, tips, etc.	26 Name of state	27 Local income tax	28 Local wages, tips, etc.	29 Name of locality

Copy B To Be Filed With Employee's FEDERAL Tax Return　　Department of the Treasury—Internal Revenue Service

Form **W-2 Wage and Tax Statement**　19--

1 Control number											
		OMB No. 1545-0008									

2 Employer's name, address, and ZIP code	6 Statutory employee ☐	Deceased ☐	Pension plan ☐	Legal rep. ☐	942 emp. ☐	Subtotal ☐	Deferred compensation ☐	Void ☐

A Art Studios
48 East 11th Avenue
Des Plaines, IL 60601-3132

7 Allocated tips	8 Advance EIC payment
9 Federal income tax withheld $591.00	10 Wages, tips, other compensation $11,028.60

3 Employer's identification number 91-4813141	4 Employer's state I.D. number 226421	11 Social security tax withheld $683.77	12 Social security wages $11,028.60
5 Employee's social security number 323-40-6128		13 Social security tips	14 Medicare wages and tips $11,028.60

19 Employee's name, address, and ZIP code	15 Medicare tax withheld $159.91	16 Nonqualified plans

Michael J. Anderson
312 East 34th Street
Chicago, IL 60604-5214

17	18 Other

20	21	22 Dependent care benefits	23 Benefits included in Box 10

24 State income tax	25 State wages, tips, etc.	26 Name of state	27 Local income tax	28 Local wages, tips, etc.	29 Name of locality

Copy 1 For State, City, or Local Tax Department　　Department of the Treasury—Internal Revenue Service

Form **W-2 Wage and Tax Statement**　19--

Fig. 7-8A   **Form 1040A Joint Income Tax Return**

Form
1040A (99)

Department of the Treasury — Internal Revenue Service

U.S. Individual Income Tax Return   **19--**   IRS Use Only — Do not write or staple in this space.

OMB No. 1545-0675

Label

Your first name: **Melissa**   MI **B.**   Last name **Anderson**   Your Social Security Number **411-86-3214**

If a joint return, spouse's first name: **Michael**   MI **J.**   Last name **Anderson**   Spouse's Social Security Number **323-40-6128**

Home address (number and street). If you have a P.O. box, see instructions. **312 East 34th Street**   Apartment number

City, town or post office. If you have a foreign address, see instructions. **Chicago**   State **IL**   ZIP Code **60604-5214**

Use the IRS label. Otherwise please print or type

For Privacy Act and Paperwork Reduction Act Notice, see instructions.

Note: Checking 'Yes' will not change your tax or reduce your refund.

Presidential Election Campaign Fund   Yes / No

Do you want $3 to go to this fund? . . . .   **X**

If a joint return, does your spouse want $3 to go to this fund? . . . .   **X**

Check the box for your filing status

Check only one box.

1 ☐ Single

2 ☒ Married filing joint return (even if only one had income)

3 ☐ Married filing separate return. Enter spouse's social security number above and full name here . . . . . ▶

4 ☐ Head of household (with qualifying person). If the qualifying person is a child but not your dependent, enter this child's name here . . . . ▶

5 ☐ Qualifying widow(er) with dependent child (yr spouse died ▶ 19   ).

Figure your exemptions

If more than seven dependents, see instructions.

6a ☒ **Yourself.** If your parent (or someone else) can claim you as a dependent on his or her tax return, **do not** check box 6a. But be sure to check the box on line 18b on page 2.

6b ☒ **Spouse** . . . .

No. of boxes checked on 6a and 6b: **2**

c Dependents:

(1) Name (first, initial, and last name)	(2) Check if under age 1	(3) If age 1 or older, dependent's social security number	(4) Dependent's relationship to you	(5) Months lived in home in 1994
Billy B. Anderson	x		Son	6
Diane K. Anderson		612-38-4814	Daughter	12

No. of your children on 6c who:
● lived with you: **2**
● didn't live with you due to divorce or separation:
Dependents on 6c not entered above:

d If your child didn't live with you but is claimed as your dependent under a pre-1985 agreement, check here . . . . ▶ ☐

e Total number of exemptions claimed

Add numbers entered on lines above: **4**

Figure your total income

Attach Copy B of your Forms W-2 and 1099-R here.

If you didn't get a W-2, see instructions.

Enclose, but do not attach, any payment with your return.

7 Wages, salaries, tips, etc. This should be shown in box 1 of your W-2 form(s). Attach Form(s) W-2 . . . .   **7**   **23,840**

8a Taxable interest income. If over $400, attach Schedule 1 . . . .   **8a**   **284**

b Tax-exempt interest. Do not include on line 8a **8b**   **400**

9 Dividends. If over $400, attach Schedule 1 . . . .   **9**   **168**

10a Total IRA distributions . . . **10a**   **0**   **10b** Taxable amount **10b**   **0**

11a Total pensions and annuities . . . . **11a**   **0**   **11b** Taxable amount **11b**   **0**

12 Unemployment compensation **12**   **0**

13a Social security benefits . . . . **13a**   **0**   **13b** Taxable amount **13b**   **0**

14 Add lines 7 through 13b (far right column). This is your **total income** . . . . ▶   **14**   **24,292**

Figure your adjusted gross income

15a Your IRA deduction **15a**   **2,000**

b Spouse's IRA deduction **15b**   **2,000**

c Add lines 15a and 15b. These are your **total adjustments** **15c**   **4,000**

16 Subtract line 15c from line 14. This is your **adjusted gross income**. If less than $25,296 and a child lived with you (less than $9,000 if a child didn't live with you), see 'Earned income credit' in the instructions . . . . ▶   **16**   **20,292**

D181 For Privacy Act and Paperwork Reduction Act Notice, see instructions.   Form **1040A** (19--) Page **1**

FDIA1312   11/16/--

Fig. 7-8B   **Form 1040A Joint Income Tax Return (*continued*)**

Form **1040A** (19--)   Page **2**

Name(s) shown on page 1   Your Social Security Number

Melissa B. and Michael J. Anderson   411-86-3214

	17 Enter the amount from line 16	**17**	20,292

Figure your standard deduction, exemption amount, and taxable income

18a Check if: ☐ **You** were 65 or older ☐ Blind ☐ **Spouse** was 65 or older ☐ Blind **Enter no. of boxes chkd** ► **18a** [ ]

b If your parent (or someone else) can claim you as a dependent, check here ► **18b** ☐

c If you are married filing separately and your spouse files Form 1040 and itemizes deductions, see instructions and check here ► **18c** ☐

19 Enter the **standard deduction** shown below for your filing status. **But if you checked any box on line 18a or b,** go to instructions to find your standard deduction. **If you checked box 18c,** enter -0-.
• Single — $3,800   • Married filing jointly or qualifying widow(er) — $6,350
• Head of household — $5,600   • Married filing separately — $3,175 .... **19** 6,350

20 Subtract line 19 from line 17. If line 19 is more than line 17, enter -0- **20** 13,942

21 Multiply $2,450 by the total number of exemptions claimed on line 6e **21** 9,800

22 Subtract line 21 from line 20. If line 21 is more than line 20, enter -0-. This is your **taxable income** .... ► **22** 4,142

Figure your tax, credits, and payments

If you want the IRS to figure your tax, see the instructions for line 22.

23 Find the tax on the amount on line 22. Check if from:
☒ Tax Table or ☐ Form 8615 .... **23** 619

24a Credit for child and dependent care expenses. Attach Schedule 2 ...... **24a** 0

b Credit for the elderly or the disabled. Attach Schedule 3 .... **24b** 0

c Add lines 24a and 24b. These are your **total credits** **24c** 0

25 Subtract line 24c from line 23. If line 24c is more than line 23, enter 0 .... **25** 619

26 Advance earned income credit payments from Form W-2 .... **26** 0

27 Add lines 25 and 26. This is your **total tax** .... ► **27** 619

28a Total federal income tax withheld. If any tax is from Form(s) 1099, check here ► ☐ **28a** 1202

b 1994 estimated tax payments and amount applied from 1993 return **28b** 0

c **Earned income credit.** If required, att Sch EIC **28c** 0
Nontaxable earned income:
amount ..... ► _____ | and type .... ► _____

d Add lines 28a, 28b, & 28c (don't include nontaxable earned income). These are your **total payments** .... ► **28d** 1,202

Figure your refund or amount you owe

29 If line 28d is more than line 27, subtract line 27 from line 28d. This is the amount you **overpaid** **29** 583

30 Amount of line 29 you want **refunded to you** **30** 583

31 Amount of line 29 you **want applied to your 1995 estimated tax** **31**

32 If line 27 is more than line 28d, subtract line 28d from line 27. This is the **amount you owe.** For details on how to pay, including what to write on your payment, see instructions **32**

33 Estimated tax penalty. Also include on ln 32 ...... **33**

Sign your return

Keep a copy of this return for your records.

Under penalties of perjury, I declare that I have examined this return and accompanying schedules and statements, and to the best of my knowledge and belief, they are true, correct, and accurately list all amounts and sources of income I received during the tax year. Declaration of preparer (other than the taxpayer) is based on all information of which the preparer has any knowledge.

Your signature ► *Michael J. Anderson*   Date 4/15/--   Your occupation Student/cashier

Spouse's signature. If joint return, BOTH must sign. ► *Melissa B Anderson*   Date 4/15/--   Spouse's occupation Student/clerk

Paid preparer's use only

Preparer's signature ►   Date   Check if self-employed ☐   Preparer's SSN

Firm's name (or yours if self-employed) and address ►   EIN   ZIP Code

Form **1040A** (19--)

FDIA1312 12/13/--

Fig. 7-9   **Sample Schedule 1**

Schedule 1 (Form 1040A)	Department of the Treasury—Internal Revenue Service **Interest and Dividend Income for Form 1040A Filers** (99)	**19--**	OMB No. 1545-0085

Name(s) shown on Form 1040A	Your Social Security Number

Part I Interest income

Note: *If you received a Form 1099-INT, Form 1099-OID, or substitute statement from a brokerage firm, enter the firm's name and the total interest shown on that form.*

1   List name of payer. If any interest is from a seller-financed mortgage and the buyer used the property as a personal residence, see instructions and list this interest first. Also, show that buyer's social security number and address.

	Amount
1	

2   Add the amounts on line 1 . . . . **2**

3   Excludable interest on series EE U.S. savings bonds issued after 1989 from Form 8815, line 14. You **must** attach Form 8815 to Form 1040A **3**

4   Subtract line 3 from line 2. Enter the result here and on Form 1040A, line 8a **4**

Part II Dividend income

Note: *If you received a Form 1099-DIV, or substitute statement from a brokerage firm, enter the firm's name and the total dividends shown on that form.*

5   List name of payer

	Amount
5	

6   Add the amounts on line 5. Enter the total here and on Form 1040A, line 9 . . . . **6**

D181 For Paperwork Reduction Act Notice, see Form 1040A instructions.   19-- Schedule 1 (Form 1040A) Page 1

FDIA140   10/20/--

Summary

Income taxes paid by individuals are the government's largest source of revenue. Other taxes are also levied. Income taxes did not always exist, but evolved because of the need to finance wars. Not until 1913 was a progressive tax levied against individual income. Today, the income tax is an important part of the economy. The IRS collects taxes; we voluntarily comply with tax laws; we prepare and file tax returns in a timely manner.

Gross income less adjustments equals adjusted gross income. Adjusted gross income less itemized deductions or the standard deduction and exemptions leaves taxable income. Individuals who have deductions that exceed the standard deduction must file Form 1040 (long form). Preparing tax returns is an important and mandatory activity; willful failure to do so is a federal offense.

7

end-of-chapter activities

Vocabulary terms

Directions: Can you find the definition for each of the following terms used in Chapter 7?

adjusted gross income	progressive taxes
alimony	proportional taxes
audit	regressive taxes
child support	revenue
deductions	standard deduction
exemption	taxable income
gross income	tax evasion
itemized deductions	voluntary compliance

1. Money collected by the government through taxes.
2. A tax based on the more income earned, the more tax paid.
3. A tax wherein the rate remains constant, regardless of the amount of your income.
4. A tax that decreases in proportion to increases in income.
5. A base amount allowed according to filing status in lieu of itemizing deductions.
6. A system whereby citizens are expected to prepare and file appropriate tax returns.
7. Willful failure to pay taxes.
8. A listing of allowable deductions such as medical expenses, mortgage interest and tax payments, and contributions.
9. An allowance for each person dependent on the taxpayer's income.
10. All the taxable income received during the year, including wages, tips, salaries, interest, dividends, alimony, and unemployment compensation.
11. Gross income minus allowed adjustments.
12. Money paid to a former spouse to support dependent children.
13. Money paid to support a former spouse.
14. Expenses allowed by law that are subtracted from adjusted gross income.
15. The net amount of income, after allowable exemptions and deductions, on which income tax is computed.
16. A procedure whereby a tax return is questioned by the IRS.

Facts and ideas in review

1. What is the United States government's largest source of revenue?
2. Describe the three basic types of taxes.
3. List five other taxes providing government revenue besides income taxes.
4. What is the main function of the IRS?
5. List at least five services the government provides for all citizens from taxes collected.
6. When was the first permanent income tax ratified?
7. When was the Internal Revenue Service created?
8. List three services provided by the IRS.
9. Who has the ability to levy taxes on the citizens of the United States?
10. What is meant by a tax system based on voluntary compliance?
11. What can happen to you if you deliberately do not file your tax return and pay taxes due?
12. At what age is a social security number required for a tax return?
13. List five types of income that are taxable.
14. List five types of income that are not taxable.
15. How is child support different from alimony in terms of taxation?
16. Explain the standard deduction and when you should itemize.
17. When must you file your federal income tax return? Why?
18. What should you do if you discover an error after you have filed your tax return?
19. Under what circumstances would you file the long Form 1040 tax return?
20. Why should you file your tax return early when you expect a refund?
21. Explain the purpose of the Presidential Election Campaign Fund. If you check the "Yes" box on your return, does it increase your taxes by $3?

Applications for decision making

1. Explain the need for taxes in this country. How does everyone benefit from taxes?
2. Summarize how taxing income came about in this country. Do you think that the time will ever come when taxation will no longer be needed? Explain.

3. Explain how new federal taxes are imposed.
4. How does your filing status affect the amount of taxes you will pay?
5. How does the number of exemptions claimed affect the amount of taxes you will pay?
6. What are deductible expenses?
7. When should you file Form 1040EZ? 1040A?
8. What is your standard deduction if you are married filing jointly or a qualifying widow(er)?
9. What must you do if you are married and wish to deduct charitable contributions on your tax return?

 ife situation problem solving

1. Acquire a copy of Form 1040EZ. Prepare a tax return for Marla Hunt. Use Appendix A tax tables and the following information:

   Marla M. Hunt (s.s. no. 541-33-9892)
   54 Center Street
   San Francisco, CA 96214-3627

   Marla is a part-time engineer. She wants $3 to go to the Presidential Election Campaign Fund. She is single and claims only herself as an exemption. Marla's salary is $28,200, plus interest of $155. No one else claims her as a dependent, and she had $3,660 in federal taxes withheld.

2. Using Figure 7-8, Form 1040A, and the tax tables in Appendix B, calculate the tax liability of Mack R. Rueoff, an auto mechanic. Mack's gross income is $24,000. He has a $2,000 IRA deduction, claims the standard deduction, and had $2,280 in federal taxes withheld. He is single and is entitled to one exemption. Based on this information and Appendix B tax tables, how much does Mack owe, or how much is his refund?

3. Using Figure 7-8, Form 1040A, and the tax tables (Appendix B), calculate the tax liability of Martin Springer, a part-time teacher. Martin's wages totaled $16,201; interest income, $190; tax-exempt interest, $200. He has an IRA contribution of $500, claims the standard deduction, and had $1,656 in federal taxes withheld from his wages. He is single and is entitled to one exemption. How much does Martin owe in taxes, or how much is his refund?

4. Acquire a copy of Form 1040A and Schedule 1 to prepare a joint tax return for Mell and Janis O'Hara.

Mell K. and Janis B. O'Hara
(s.s. nos. 895-10-9008, 485-01-9089)
2450 West 18th Avenue
Dallas, TX 75201-7242

Mell is a construction worker, and Janis is a preschool teacher. They both want to contribute $3 to the Presidential Election Campaign Fund. Married, filing jointly, Mell and Janis have one dependent child, Mark J. O'Hara, who is under age one and lives with them. They both contributed $2,000 to IRAs. Mell's and Janis's combined incomes totaled $38,400 (Janis's is $18,400). They contributed $700 to qualifying child care expenses and had a total federal tax of $3,672 withheld. Mell and Janis had interest income of $1,400: First National Bank, $300; interest on a private loan to J. Smith, $600; certificate of deposit at State Savings & Loan, $500. Tax-exempt interest income was $400. Dividend income amounted to $1,100: $411 from CDK stock, $621 from Investors' Mutual Fund, Inc., and $68 from I.P.Q. Manufacturing Co. Use Appendix B tax tables.

objectives:

After reading and studying this chapter you will be able to:

8-1 Analyze and understand the budgeting process and prepare personal and case study budgets.

8-2 Understand the purpose of personal record keeping and be able to prepare a personal net worth statement and personal property inventory.

8-3 Explain the elements of legal contracts and negotiable instruments and understand your rights and responsibilities.

8-4 Discuss the need for a filing system for personal records.

In Unit 1 you learned about career planning; in the previous two chapters, you learned about pay and benefits together with income taxes. Your take-home pay is the focus of this chapter—what you have to spend or to save. Careful management of your income will provide you with many benefits: you will meet all of your needs and many of your wants; you will feel financially secure; and you will be able to plan for your future. But most importantly, you will be in control of your financial destiny. You will make decisions rather than simply accept whatever comes your way. This chapter introduces strategies for financial management which are basic to financial success.

chapter 8

Budgets and Financial Records

Budgeting income and expenses

Do you have unlimited resources to buy all the things you want or need? There are people who do, but unless you have inherited wealth, you are probably like most other Americans—in order to achieve financial success, you will have to plan and work for it. Budgeting and maintaining financial records are a significant part of financial planning and provide the road map to financial security. Budgeting is the first step.

Importance of Financial Planning

Your **disposable income** is the money you have to spend or save as you wish after taxes, social security, and other required and optional deductions have been withheld from your gross pay. In order to use this income to your best advantage, you will need to create a financial plan.

All the money you receive is spent, saved, or invested. You may spend it for things you need or want, save it for future needs, or invest it to earn more money. A **financial plan** is an orderly program for spending, saving, and investing the money you earn. You may already understand the need to save part of your income for the future. Financial planning is important because it helps you do the following:

1. Determine and evaluate how wisely you are using your money;
2. Get the most from your income;
3. Prevent careless and wasteful spending;
4. Organize your *financial resources* (sources of income) so that you can maintain a plan of personal financial fitness; and
5. Avoid money worries and problems by understanding the proper methods of saving, spending, and borrowing money.

The first step in attaining financial fitness is to set up a plan. A **budget** is an organized plan whereby you match your expected income to your expected expenses. The purpose of preparing a budget is to plan your spending and saving so that you won't have to borrow money to meet your needs. Careful budgeting will enable you to stretch your money to provide for your present and future needs and also to satisfy your wants.

Figure 8-1 shows a high school student's budget plan for one month. This student expects to receive a total of $380, and plans to use the money for certain needs and wants, and to save part of it as well.

Fig. 8-1

Simple Budget

BUDGET FOR SEPTEMBER

Income

Work (part-time)	$320.00
Allowances for household chores	20.00
Lunch money	40.00
Total income	$380.00

Expenses

Daily lunches	$ 80.00
Supplies	20.00
Snacks	40.00
Entertainment (movies and golfing)	140.00
Total expenses	$280.00

Savings

To Columbia County Credit Union	$100.00
Total expenses plus savings	$380.00

The first step in setting up a budget is to estimate total expected income for a certain time period. Include all money you expect to receive. You may wish to use a weekly, biweekly, or monthly budget, whichever best matches how often you expect to receive money.

The second step is to decide how much of your income you want to save—to set aside for future needs. Most financial experts advise saving at least 10 percent of your disposable income each pay period. By saving at least this amount, you will have money to pay for future needs, both expected and unexpected.

The third step is to estimate your expenses, or money you will need for day-to-day purchases; for example, lunches, fees, personal care items, clothing, and so forth.

A Typical Monthly Budget

Figure 8-2 represents the monthly budget of Mike and Jennifer Harris, a recently married couple. Mike and Jennifer have no children, and both are working. The Harrises estimate their expected income by adding together their two take-home incomes (paychecks), along with anticipated interest on savings and earnings on investments.

BUDGET — Mike and Jennifer Harris

	Monthly	Yearly
Income		
Salary (Mike) after taxes	$ 1,380	$16,560
Salary (Jennifer) after taxes	1,410	16,920
Interest earned on savings (average)	25	300
Earnings from investments (tax deferred)	50	600
Total income	$ 2,865	$34,380
Expenses		
Fixed expenses:		
Rent	$ 800	$ 9,600
Utilities (average)	100	1,200
Car payment	280	3,360
Insurance:		
Car	60	720
Life and Health	50	600
Total fixed expenses	$ 1,290	$15,480
Variable expenses:		
Telephone (average)	$ 45	$ 540
Gasoline (average)	120	1,440
Car repairs and maintenance (average)	60	720
Cable television (average)	28	336
Groceries (average)	400	4,800
Clothing (average)	200	2,400
Personal care (average):		
Dry cleaning, shoe repair, etc.	25	300
Drugs and cosmetics	25	300
Insurance deductible and copay	50	600
Recreation and entertainment (average)	100	1,200
Gifts and donations (average)	200	2,400
Total variable expenses	$ 1,253	$15,036
Total fixed and variable expenses	$ 2,543	$30,516
Cash surplus (total income minus total expenses)	$ 322	$ 3,864
Allocation of Surplus:		
Emergency savings fund	$ 100	$ 1,200
Short-term savings	100	1,200
Long-term investments	122	1,464

Fig. 8-2

Monthly and Yearly Budget for a Married Couple

They would like to save at least 10 percent every month, setting aside money for emergency savings, short-term savings, and long-term investments as shown.

Fixed expenses are those that remain constant, and to remove or change them will take a major revision in lifestyle. Definite obligations are the basis for this portion of a budget. Examples are savings, house payments, utilities, car loans, average gasoline and car maintenance costs, and insurance premium payments. Most financial experts recommend that a family have no more than 50 to 60 percent of take-home pay set aside for fixed expenses. They agree, however, that in the beginning that standard is difficult to achieve. But with time, pay raises, and careful budgeting, a family can attain that goal.

Variable expenses will change according to needs and short-term goals. Sufficient money should be allotted to cover these expenses, because they can change frequently. Variable expenses fluctuate due to the household situation, time of year, health, economic conditions, and a wide variety of other factors. Examples are telephone, cable TV, groceries, dental or medical bills not covered by insurance, entertainment, recreation, charge account purchases, investments, and miscellaneous purchases.

Fixed expenses remain constant and are definite obligations, such as payments on a house. Variable expenses, such as those for entertainment, may vary according to changes in lifestyle.

ersonal records

Good personal record keeping is important. Well-kept records make planning a budget easier, ensure improved long-range financial planning, and form the basis for properly completed income tax returns, credit applications, and other financial forms. There are four types of personal records you will want to keep: records of income and expenses, a statement of net worth, a personal property inventory, and tax records. These basic types of records are important because they enable you to (a) evaluate your family or individual spending, (b) provide information for tax returns, (c) analyze your financial picture and plan for the future, (d) provide a basis for determining future goals, and (e) provide a basis for maintaining an effective, updated budget.

Records of Income and Expenses

W-2 statements sent by employers each January show money earned and deductions made by the employer during the year. The W-2s also state the amount of taxes and social security tax withheld. You may need the W-2s later when you want to collect benefits. Other records of income include statements from banks of interest earned on savings. Expense items include receipts listing charitable contributions, medical bills, or work-related expenses. As we learned in Chapter 7, this information will be needed when preparing budgets and tax returns. These receipts and statements are often referred to as documents and can be used as proof, or evidence, of income and expenses. These documents should be stored in a safe place for future reference.

Statement of Net Worth

A *net worth statement,* such as that shown in Figure 8-3, is a list of items of value, called **assets,** that a person owns; amounts of money that are owed to others, called **liabilities** or debts; and the difference between the two, known as net worth. If your assets are greater than your liabilities, you are said to be solvent, or in a favorable financial position. But if your liabilities are greater than your assets (you owe more than you own), you are said to be insolvent, or in a poor financial position.

Net worth information (lists of assets and liabilities) is most often required when you ask for a loan or apply for credit. The bank or other financial institution will want you to be solvent and a good risk who will likely pay back a loan. It also helps you keep track of how you spent your money and what you have to show for it at the end of the year.

Fig. 8-3

Net Worth Statement

NET WORTH STATEMENT
Nygen Phomn
January 1, 19--

ASSETS		LIABILITIES	
Checking account	$ 500	Loan on car	$1,800
Savings account	800	Loan from mother	100
Car value	3,000	Total liabilities	$1,900
Personal property:			
(inventory attached)	5,000		
Total assets	$9,300	**NET WORTH**	
		Assets minus liabilities	$7,400
		Total	$9,300

Personal Property Inventory

The personal property inventory is a list of all one's personal property. Personal property is usually all items inside the home—clothing, furniture, appliances, and so forth. A personal property inventory is especially useful in the event of fire, theft, or property damage, as proof of possession and value. As a further safeguard, a person may photograph items of value, attach the photographs to the inventory, and keep this information in a safe deposit box or other secure place to use as evidence in the event the property is damaged, lost, or stolen. A personal property inventory also shows you what you have to show for money you have spent. Reviewing it frequently will help you assess your spending patterns. As new items are purchased and others disposed of, the inventory should be revised. Figure 8-4 shows the inventory of personal property of Nygen Phomn.

Tax Records

All taxpayers should keep copies of their tax returns, W-2 statements, and other receipts verifying income and expenses listed on tax returns for three years after the tax return is filed. For good planning purposes, tax returns should be kept much longer, along with W-2s and other important documentation. Information used in preparing tax returns should be kept in a safe place in the event of an audit. The IRS has the legal right to audit your tax returns and supporting records for three years from the date of filing the return (longer if fraud or intentional wrongdoing on your part can be proved).

Fig. 8-4 **Personal Property Inventory**

PERSONAL PROPERTY INVENTORY
Nygen Phomn
January 1, 19--

Item	Year Purchased	Purchase Price	Approximate Current Value
MDV CD player and component system with speakers, stock numbers XG4283, XK4323, and SL3236	1995	$2,800	$2,600
Bedroom furniture (bed, dresser, lamp, clock)	1991	2,000	1,200
Clothing and jewelry	1991	approx. 2,000	700
Trax-T 18-speed bicycle	1994	600	400
TKD microcassette digital tape recorder/player	1993	150	100
		$7,550	$5,000

Legal documents

To manage personal finances, you often need to enter into agreements, fill out forms and applications, and provide personal information and records. It is difficult to function successfully in today's society if you do not master the simple documents explained below.

Contracts and Agreements

A **contract** is a legally enforceable agreement between two or more parties to do or not to do something. We all have many transactions in our daily lives that can be properly classified as contracts or lawful agreements. Contracts are a part of personal business situations even though they may not be consciously acknowledged. If you buy a suit and it needs an alteration, a ticket is filled out by the clerk. Any changes requested and the promised date of completion are written on the ticket. This ticket is a contract under which you, the consumer, promise to pick up the suit and pay for the alteration when it is completed. The store promises to do the work and present it to you on the agreed-upon date for the stated price.

Contracts are a part of most personal business situations even though they may not be consciously acknowledged.

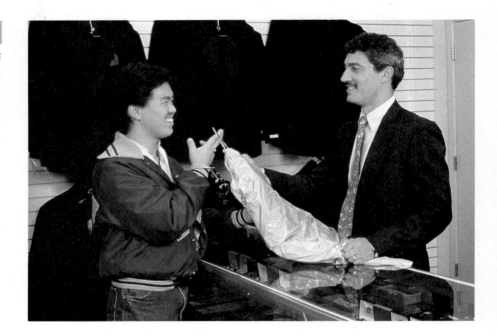

Other examples of situations requiring agreements are (a) retail credit plans, whereby customers either agree to pay for purchases by monthly payments or open a charge account at a store; (b) buying a home and paying for it over a number of years by means of mortgage payments; and (c) renting an apartment, a duplex, or a house. In each of these cases, there is generally an express agreement between two or more persons. *Express agreements* can be oral or written: what makes them express is that the terms have been agreed upon between the parties.

Figure 8-5 shows a charge application from a retail store. In addition to giving certain requested information, you are asked to agree to certain conditions before opening an account. Attached to the application will be an explanation of finance charges and how they are computed. You will sign the application to show that you understand

Fig. 8-5   **Charge Application**

CHARGE APPLICATION

Please print clearly

ACCOUNT IN NAME OF:	First Richard Initial J. Last Washington
	Address 45 Front Street #8
	City Portland State OR ZIP 97201-1072

Phone (503) 555-0181   How long at this address? 4 years
Area Code   Number

Check one: ☐ Own ☐ Lease ☒ Rent ☐ Live with parents ☐ Other*

*Explain _____

Previous address if less than three years _____

_____ How long? _____

Employer O'Toole Paper Co.   How long? 4 years

Employer's Address Portland, OR 97214-4179   Phone 555-0142

Occupation Administrative Asst.   Salary $342   ☒ Weekly   ☐ Monthly

COMPLETE SECTION FOR JOINT ACCOUNT:

Name First N/A   Initial _____   Last _____

Employer _____   How long? _____

Employer's Address _____   Phone _____

Occupation _____   Salary _____   ☐ Weekly   ☐ Monthly

Other income:
Source _____   Amount _____

CREDIT REFERENCES:

Name of Bank First Bank   Bank Address Portland, OR   ☒ Checking ☒ Savings

Name of Creditor Meier & Frank   Account Number 818 424 961   Address Portland

Creditor JC Penney   Number 4891248369   Address Portland

Creditor _____   Number _____   Address _____

NEAREST RELATIVE NOT LIVING WITH YOU:

Name Harry Washington   Address 614 Chevy St., Portland, OR 97216-6172

I understand the terms and conditions of this credit application, including service charges and fees, which will be charged to this account as explained on the reverse side of this application. I have read it completely and agree to all conditions. I testify that all information contained in this application is true and complete.

APPLICANT'S SIGNATURE *Richard J. Washington*   Social Security Number 481-32-8194   Date 4/1/--

the finance charges and agree to pay them if your balance is not paid in full each month. Be sure you have read everything contained in the agreement before you sign it. If something is not clear, be sure to ask for an explanation so that you can understand your rights and responsibilities before you enter into the contract.

In addition to written agreements, there also are many unwritten agreements. When you get a job, ride a bicycle, rent a videotape, or shop in a mall, you have made an *implied agreement*. Whether you realize it or not, you have agreed to certain things by your acceptance of the job, riding on public streets, rental of the videotape, or simply going to a mall. For example, when you ride your bicycle, you agree to abide by appropriate traffic laws, ride in a safe and responsible manner, and observe the rights of other riders, pedestrians, and cars around you. A violation of one of these unwritten agreements can result in a traffic ticket, a fine, injury to yourself, injury to others, or damage to property.

Elements of an Enforceable Contract

To accomplish its purpose, a contract must be binding on all persons who enter into it. Some contracts must be in writing and signed by all persons involved in order to be legally binding. Examples of contracts that must be written are contracts for the purpose of sale of real property (homes and land); contracts that cannot be fully performed in less than a year; contracts involving $500 and over; and contracts in which one person agrees to pay the debts of another.

To be legally binding, enforceable agreements, contracts must have all of the following elements, which are explained in detail.

1. Agreement
2. Consideration
3. Contractual capacity
4. Legality
5. Genuineness of assent
6. Legal form

Agreement. A contract has **mutual assent** when it is offered and accepted. In order to prove mutual assent, two conditions are required by law: a valid offer and acceptance of that exact offer. One person makes the offer, another person accepts it. When one person makes an offer and another person changes any part of it, the second person is making what is known as a *counteroffer*. The counteroffer is a new offer and has to be accepted (or rejected) by the first person.

Consideration. The price involved is called **consideration.** Consideration may be in the form of an object of value, money, a promise, or a performed act. If one person is to receive something but gives nothing in return, the contract may not be enforceable. The idea behind consideration is that each party to the agreement receives something of value. When you buy a pair of shoes, you get the shoes and the store gets your money. The shoes and the money are items of consideration.

Contractual Capacity. Contractual capacity is the competence (legal ability) of the parties. Competent parties are persons who are legally able to give sane and intelligent assent. Those who are unable to protect themselves because of mental deficiency or illness, or who are otherwise incapable of understanding the consequences of their actions, cannot be held to contracts. They are protected from entering into agreements that may prove to be against their best interests. Minors are not considered competent parties and therefore cannot be held to contracts, with exceptions. Generally, any person eighteen or older who is not mentally deficient is considered competent. Married persons under age eighteen are also considered competent to enter into agreements. Furthermore, all persons eighteen or older are considered to be legally competent unless they are declared incompetent by a court of law.

Legality. The purpose of a legally enforceable contract must be of a lawful nature. A court of law will not require a person to perform an agreed-upon act if it is illegal. Without a lawful objective, the agreement has no binding effect on a person.

Genuineness of Assent. It is possible for a contract to be unenforceable even though two parties with full legal capacity have entered into an agreement for a legal purpose and even though it is supported by consideration. This occurs when there is no genuine assent because there is misrepresentation, a mistake, duress, or undue influence. A mistake can be unilateral (by one party) or bilateral (by both parties) and must be of some material (important) fact.

Misrepresentation is also called fraud, and contains four elements: (a) misrepresentation of a material fact with (b) the intention to deceive; (c) the innocent party has justifiably relied on this misrepresented fact and (d) has been injured (damaged) as a result. *Duress* is the use of force or fear (threatening) to make a person enter into a contract. Undue influence arises from special relationships (such as guardian or fiduciary) in which one party's free will is overcome by the other.

Legal Form. State laws provide that contracts must contain the necessary information to be enforceable. The contract may be a printed form, drawn up by attorneys, or it may be in some other readable and understandable form. It must state the date, duration of contract, persons involved, consideration, terms of agreement, and other necessary information to explain the purpose of the contract and the intentions of the persons entering into it. In some cases the contract, or a memorandum of contract, must be recorded. When a contract is recorded it is made a public record, and a photocopy is stored by the county recorder. Before a document can be recorded, it must meet specific requirements that are set out by state law.

Valid, Void, and Voidable Contracts

The enforcement of contracts is necessary for an efficient economic system. Both consumers and businesses benefit from contract enforcement. Without it, dishonest consumers or business owners could refuse to honor their agreements, and our daily business activities would be disrupted. Contracts can generally be classified as valid, void, and voidable.

Valid Contracts. Valid contracts are those that contain all of the essential elements—mutual assent, consideration, competent parties, lawful objective, agreed-upon period of time, and legal format. They are legally enforceable. A valid contract sometimes becomes an unenforceable contract because the time limit for filing suit to enforce it has passed.

Void Contracts. Void contracts are those that are missing one or more of the essential elements. These contracts are null and void, and are not enforceable in a court of law. An example of a void contract is one that will require doing something illegal. In other words, if you enter into an agreement and later learn that you will be doing something against the law, you cannot be forced to fulfill your part of the contract.

Voidable Contracts. A voidable contract can be enforced or avoided by one of the parties. If that party chooses avoidance, or decides to withdraw from the transaction, the contract will not be enforced. An example of a voidable contract is a car payment agreement entered into by a minor. A minor may declare the contract voidable because contracts with minors do not meet the competent party test of a legally binding contract. However, if the minor continues to make payments on the contract after reaching age eighteen, he or she has made that contract valid and is legally responsible for fulfilling the contract.

personal perspective

Minors and the Law

A minor is a person who has not yet reached the age of majority. In most states, the age of majority is eighteen. In other words, when you turn eighteen, you become an adult, with all the rights and responsibilities (except some specially reserved privileges).

As a minor, you have protections afforded to you by the law. One such protection is the right to disaffirm a contract.

That is, a minor who enters into a contract can decide to cancel the agreement. The other contracting party is entitled to receive back that which was agreed to. For example, Joe Williams purchases a car from the XYZ Car Lot for $600, agreeing to pay $100 down and $50 a month for 10 months. After the second month, and while Joe is still 17, he decides he no longer wants the car. He can rescind the contract—return the car and discontinue payments.

There are exceptions to this rule. If the minor has a cosigner, the cosigner is responsible for full payment for the car. Or if the car is considered a "necessary" item for the minor, then the minor can be held to the payments. A *necessary* is an item the minor requires for his or her attained lifestyle and which a parent ordinarily does not provide. The car could be considered a necessary if the minor needs it to get to work and his parents can't buy it for him.

Also, if a minor continues making payments and otherwise abides by the contract until after reaching the age of majority, the contract is said to be ratified. That is, as an adult, the person confirmed the agreement that was reached as a minor.

The laws to protect minors vary from state to state. The right of minors to disaffirm contracts is based on the premise that minority shall be "used as a shield, not as a sword." That is, the minor can use his or her status as a child to be protected from those who would take advantage of him or her. Minors cannot use their status as a minor to take advantage of others.

critical thinking

1. Do you think the laws protecting minors are sufficient? Defend your answer.

2. Do you think minors should have more rights? If so, what would they be?

3. What is the age of majority in your state? What rights are you given when you reach that age? Are there still privileges which are deferred until later?

Consumer Responsibilities in Agreements

As a consumer, you have the following responsibilities regarding the contracts and agreements you enter into:

1. Understand all clauses and terms contained in the agreement. Do not sign it until you have read it; your signature acknowledges that you have read and you understand the contract.
2. Keep a copy of the agreement. Put it in a safe place for future use.
3. Be sure the agreement is dated correctly.
4. Be sure all blank spaces are filled in or marked out and that no changes have been made after you have signed it. Your initials at the bottom of each page will prevent substitution of pages.
5. Be sure all provisions agreed upon are written clearly. Because interpretation may vary, vague phrases are often not enforceable.
6. Be sure all dates, amounts, and other numbers are correct and written clearly.
7. Be sure proper disclosure is made by the seller. The buyer is entitled to proper and complete information about the rate of interest, total finance charges, cash payment price, and so on.
8. Be sure all cancellations and adjustments are made in accordance with the contract.

Although consumers are protected by numerous consumer protection laws, occasionally specific legal services are required. Legal services, in one form or another, are available to every citizen. But your best protection is to guard yourself in advance by understanding the agreements you enter into.

Negotiable Instruments

The word negotiable means legally collectible. A **negotiable instrument** is a document that contains promises to pay monies and is legally collectible. The negotiable instruments most people are likely to use are checks (discussed in Chapter 9) and, to a lesser extent, promissory notes. A negotiable instrument is legally collectible if the following conditions are met:

1. It must be in writing (not oral) and signed by the maker.
2. It must contain an unconditional promise to pay a definite amount of money.
3. It must be payable on demand or on a fixed or determinable future date.

4. It must be payable to the order of a particular person or to the holder of the note.
5. It must be delivered to the payee.

If any one of the above conditions is missing, the document is not a negotiable instrument; it is no longer legally collectible.

A promissory note is a written promise to pay a certain sum of money to another person or to the holder of the note on a specified date. A promissory note is a legal document, and payment can be enforced by law. An example of a promissory note is found in Figure 8-6.

The person who creates and signs the promissory note and agrees to pay it on a certain date is called the *maker*. The person to whom the note is made payable is known as the *payee*. A promissory note is normally used when borrowing a large sum of money from a financial institution.

In some cases creditors (those extending credit) will require cosigners as additional security for repayment of a note. A **cosigner** is a person who is established (has a good credit rating) and promises to pay the note if the maker fails to pay. The cosigner's signature is also on a note. Young people and persons who have not established a credit rating are often asked to provide a cosigner for their first loan.

PROMISSORY NOTE

$ __400.00__   January 15 _____ , 19 _ _

I (we) __Marilyn Huykamp_____ , jointly and severally,
do agree and promise to pay to __Emerald Furniture Co.__
the sum of ____Four hundred and 00/100_____ dollars
with interest at the rate of __9%__ from __January 15, 19--__ , payable in
monthly installments of $__69.67__ beginning __February 1__ , 19 _ _
and on a like day each month until paid in full, the last payment
due __July 1_____ , 19 _ _. Said payment shall include interest.
In the event of default, the maker hereof agrees to pay attorneys' fees and
court costs in collection of this note.

Marilyn Huykamp
Maker

Fig. 8-6

Promissory Note

Warranties

A **warranty,** also called a guarantee, is an assurance of product quality or of responsibility of the seller. The warranty may be in writing or assumed to exist by the nature of the product. However, a warranty is not a safeguard against a poor buying decision.

All products contain implied warranties, and some have written guarantees as well, stating responsibilities that the manufacturer agrees to. A product is supposed to do what it is made to do, whether or not standards are stated in writing. For example, a tennis ball must bounce. If it does not bounce, you can return the defective ball, even if there is no written warranty.

A warranty is an assurance of product quality or of responsibility of the seller.

Specific written warranties often guarantee that a product will perform to your satisfaction for a certain period of time. Many written warranties state that you may return a product for repair or replacement if it ceases to work because of a defect. Warranties will not protect against normal wear and tear of the product.

Figure 8-7 illustrates a limited warranty that might be found when purchasing a home product. Read it carefully to determine what the manufacturer does and does not guarantee.

Fig. 8-7

Limited Warranty

Limited Warranty   12 Y 845

This product is guaranteed for one year from the date of purchase to be free of mechanical and electrical defects in material and workmanship. The manufacturer's obligations hereunder are limited to repair of such defects during the warranty period, provided such product is returned to the address below within the warranty period.

This guarantee does not cover normal wear of parts or damages resulting from negligent use or misuse of the product. In addition, this guarantee is void if the purchaser breaks the seal and disassembles, repairs, or alters the product in any way.

The warranty period begins on the date of purchase. The card below must be received by the manufacturer within 30 days of purchase or receipt of said merchandise. Fill out the card completely and return it to the address shown.

Owner's Name: _____

Address: _____

City, State, Zip: _____

Date of Purchase: _____

Store Where Purchased: _____

Return to: ALCOVE ELECTRICAL, INC.
42 West Cabana
Arlington, VA 23445-2909

Serial No.   12 Y 845

iling systems for personal records

Families often find it to their advantage to keep good records, prepare and file their own tax returns, and plan their own savings and investment strategies. Keeping a good filing system for your personal records will help you organize, store, and retrieve needed information.

Manual Filing System

A typical home filing system would include folders and labels, and a small two-drawer or accordion file. Information accumulated in the files will assist in preparing, revising, or updating a budget, and in writing to companies about problems with products or services. A filing system also helps keep your personal records in a neat and orderly fashion in your home—easy to find, file, and use when needed. Folder labels might read alphabetically as shown in Figure 8-8.

Fig. 8-8

Home Filing System

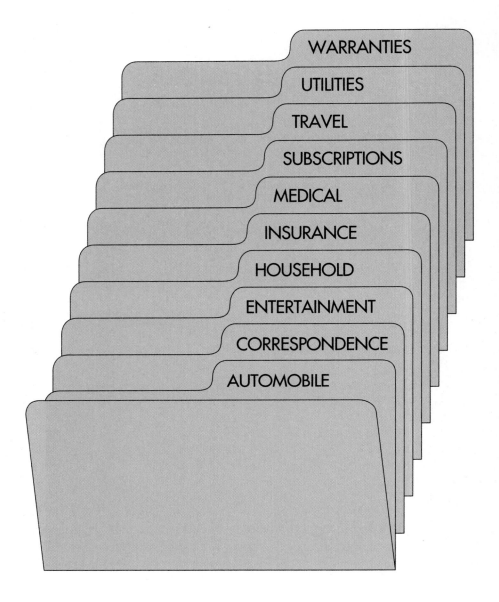

In these files, you would keep records and receipts. For example, in the "automobile" folder, you might want to keep track of mileage, oil changes, tune-ups, repairs, and other car expenses. The "insurance" file would include premium due dates, descriptions of coverages, and so on. Original copies of important documents such as insurance policies and wills should be kept in a safe-deposit box, and receipts and records used for income tax purposes should be taken from the home files to the safe-deposit box when taxes are filed.

Electronic Filing System

Many families are investing in home computer systems for personal financial planning. The advantages of computerized systems include (a) ease of updating information, (b) ease of storage of records, and (c) speed of making new computations, calculations, and comparisons. Many microcomputer software programs are available to consumers at software stores for reasonable prices. A **spreadsheet** program sets information into charts where numbers and words can be visualized and manipulated; formulas can be inserted to automatically change some numbers when others change. A **database management** program allows the storage and use of information so that all or parts of it can be recalled, combined, and manipulated. Such programs allow you to put your budget, household inventory, tax returns, net worth statement, and other tools of investment planning on the computer. In addition, specialized personal finance programs allow storage and use of information for personal record keeping.

 ummary

Financial planning is an orderly program of planning, saving, and investing money earned. It requires budgeting to account for income, saving, and expenses. Good financial planning also includes keeping thorough personal records, including records of income and expenses, net worth statements, personal property inventories, and tax records. It also means having an awareness of contracts (both express and implied), negotiable instruments, and warranties. A filing system (manual or electronic) assists in keeping personal records orderly and systematic so that wise financial decisions can be made.

Vocabulary terms

Directions: Can you find the definition for each of the following terms used in Chapter 8?

assets
budget
consideration
contract
cosigner
database management
disposable income
financial plan

fixed expenses
liabilities
mutual assent
negotiable instrument
spreadsheet
variable expenses
warranty

1. Agreement by two or more persons to the terms of a contract.
2. Expenses that remain constant, at least in the short run.
3. Expenses that vary according to needs and short-term goals.
4. A legally enforceable agreement between two or more parties.
5. A price to be paid, a promise to pay, or a promise to do something or not do something.
6. Things of value that a person owns.
7. A person who promises to pay a note if the maker fails to pay.
8. An assurance of product quality or of responsibility of the seller.
9. An orderly program for spending, saving, and investing your income.
10. An organized plan of matching income and expenses.
11. Amounts of money that you owe to others, also known as debts.
12. A piece of paper containing a written promise to pay.
13. A computer program which sets numbers and words into chart format.
14. A computer program which stores, arranges, and manipulates information as needed.
15. The money you have left over after required deductions, which you can spend or save as you wish.

Facts and ideas in review

1. Why should consumers prepare a budget and be concerned about financial planning?

2. What is the difference between fixed and variable expenses?
3. Which are the four types of personal records all consumers should prepare and keep in a safe place?
4. Why is it important to maintain these four types of personal records?
5. Besides the obvious use for obtaining credit, what is another good reason for preparing a personal property inventory?
6. Why should taxpayers save copies of their tax returns and supporting receipts and evidence?
7. How is an implied contract different from an express contract?
8. In order to be enforceable in a court of law, contracts must contain six elements. Briefly name each.
9. Give three examples of contracts that must be in writing in order to be enforceable in a court of law.
10. What is the difference between a void contract and a voidable contract?
11. What is the most commonly used form of negotiable instrument?
12. List the five conditions of negotiable instruments that make them legally collectible.
13. List five consumer responsibilities when entering into a contract.
14. Explain the concept of a filing system for personal records and list what file labels you would choose.

A pplications for decision making

1. Using Figure 8-1 as a model, prepare a simple budget for yourself, listing expected income, savings, and expenses for a month. How much will you set aside for savings?
2. How will your budget change in the next few years? What are your short-term and intermediate goals?
3. Using Figure 8-3 as a model, prepare a net worth statement, listing as assets those items of value you possess and any debts for which you are responsible. Compute your net worth. How can you use this information?
4. Using Figure 8-4 as a model, prepare a personal property inventory, listing items of personal property in your room at home. Why should you and your family keep a record such as this?
5. After examining Figure 8-5 (charge application), list the kinds of information requested by a retail store. Why do you think a store needs or wants this type of information?

6. Following the example of Figure 8-6, write out in longhand form a promissory note from you to John Doe, payable in one year of monthly payments, in the amount of $50 with interest at 11 percent and monthly payments of $4.63. Are you the maker or the payee?

7. Bring to class an express warranty from a product you or your family recently purchased. What does the warranty specifically promise to do? List any restrictions (exceptions) that the manufacturer has placed in the warranty.

ife situation problem solving

1. Based on the information given, prepare a monthly and yearly budget for Mike and Jan Harbour. Use Figure 8-2 as a model.

Average Income	Net paychecks total $1,800 monthly	
	Interest on savings $50 monthly	
Average Monthly Expenses	Rent payment	$400
	Utilities	120
	Gasoline	100
	Insurance	150
	Groceries	200
	Clothing	100
	Car payment	210
	Car maintenance	50
	Telephone	40
	Entertainment and	
	recreation	200
Cash Surplus	Savings	To be determined
	Investment fund	60
	Miscellaneous	120

2. Based on the information given, prepare a monthly and yearly budget for Elaine Kreitz. Follow the style shown in Figure 8-2.

Average Income	Net monthly pay is $1,400.	

Average Monthly Expenses	Rent	$410
	Insurance	60
	Utilities	50
	Gasoline	60
	Clothing	60
	Entertainment	100
	Savings	120
	Telephone	15
	Car payment	150
	Car repairs	20
	Groceries	150
	Personal care	50
	Miscellaneous	155

3. Revise Elaine's budget when she agrees to share her apartment with a friend. Some expenses can be shared equally. Assume the telephone expense increases to $30; utilities to $60; and insurance to $70. These expenses along with rent are shared equally. What will you have her do with the added funds?

4. Based on the information given, prepare a net worth statement for Sako Masuta. Follow Figure 8-3.
Sako owns a car worth about $3,000, but owes $1,500 on it to the bank. He has $500 in savings and $100 in checking. His personal property totals $3,000, and he also owes $90 to his credit union.

5. Based on the information given, prepare a personal property inventory for Sako Masuta. Follow Figure 8-4.
Sako has these furnishings in his apartment: JWA CD stereo system, Model 252, SN 975923, bought last year for $600, present worth $500; sofa, present worth about $800; Bright alarm clock, SN 630AM and Blare radio, Model 2602, SN 413T, bought four years ago, total worth about $100. Sako also has the following personal items: miscellaneous clothing and jewelry, present worth about $800; Quantex wristwatch, present worth about $100; coin collection, valued last year at $600. Sako has photographs of these items. (List a hypothetical purchase price for all items except the CD system in preparing your property inventory.)

terms to know:

checking account
drafts
demand deposit
canceled checks
overdraft
floating a check
checkbook register
reconciliation
blank endorsement
special endorsement
restrictive
  endorsement
certified check
cashier's check
stop payment order

objectives:

After reading and studying this chapter you will be able to:

9-1 Understand the purpose, uses, and advantages of a personal checking account.

9-2 Prepare checking account documents, including a signature card, checks, deposit slips, checkbook register, and bank reconciliation.

9-3 Explain check endorsements and describe the types of checking accounts available to consumers.

9-4 Define the various banking services available and fees charged to consumers.

n the previous chapter, you learned about the importance of keeping good financial records and budgeting your money. Checking accounts and other banking services are the next topic in financial planning. All checking accounts and banking services are not created equal, however. A bad choice of a bank or a banking product—even one as straightforward as a checking account—could cost you hundreds of dollars a year. For the consumer, shopping for the best buy in banking services is as necessary as shopping for the best buy in, say, a VCR. And it's potentially far more rewarding.

chapter

9 Checking Accounts and Banking Services

Purpose of a checking account

Financial institutions such as banks, credit unions, and savings and loan associations offer a number of different services. The first service you will likely want is a checking account. A **checking account** is a banking service wherein money is deposited into an account and checks, or **drafts,** can be written to withdraw money from the account as needed. This type of account is also known as a **demand deposit,** because you can demand portions of your deposited funds at will. Only you, the depositor or drawer (maker), can write checks on the account. Financial institutions usually charge a fee for checking services, or require that a minimum balance be kept in the account. In shopping for a checking account, you will find a wide variety of services and fees.

A checking account can be a useful and convenient tool. Writing a check is often safer than using cash, especially when making major purchases in person, or when paying bills or ordering merchandise through the mail. **Canceled checks** are those the bank has processed, or cleared. As such, they can be used as proof of purchase or of payment in the event a dispute arises. Checking accounts also have built-in record keeping systems to help you keep track of money received and spent; this makes them a great help in personal budgeting and record keeping. Finally, as a checking account customer, you have access to other banking services, such as instant loans, use of the day and night teller, and free traveler's checks.

In shopping for a checking account, you will find a wide variety of services and fees.

In exchange for the convenience of using a checking account, you must accept certain responsibilities. First, you must write checks carefully and keep an accurate record of checks written and deposits made. Second, you must reconcile your account with your bank statement promptly each month. Third, you must keep canceled checks as proof of purchase or of payment and for income tax records. Canceled checks should be kept in a secure place, such as a safe-deposit box.

In addition, you must maintain sufficient funds in your account to cover all checks written. A check that cannot be covered by the funds in your account is called an **overdraft.** A financial institution receiving an overdraft usually stamps the check with the words "insufficient funds" and returns the check to the payee or the payee's institution. When an overdraft occurs and a check is returned, the check has "bounced." That is why checks that are returned for insufficient funds are often called "rubber checks." In addition, your bank will charge a fee of $15 or more for each NSF ("non-sufficient funds") check processed. When checks are returned, the institution notifies the account holder of its action.

You are **floating a check** when you realize your account contains insufficient funds, but you write a check anyway hoping that you can make a deposit before the check is cashed. Floating a check is more difficult in the computer age when the processing of checks and deposits is faster and more efficient. Purposely overdrawing your account and floating a check are illegal in most states. These acts are felonies that can result in a fine, imprisonment, or both.

Opening your checking account

To open a checking account, a depositor must fill out and sign a signature card, such as the one shown in Figure 9-1. The signature card provides the bank with important information and an official signature to compare with subsequent checks written.

In Figure 9-1, Ardys Johnson completed and signed the left side of the card. The right side is for a joint account holder. (Signature cards look different at various banks, but essentially contain the same information.) Ardys also listed her mother's full name (including maiden name) for use in identification. Anyone forging Ardys's signature is not likely to know her mother's maiden name when questioned by a teller.

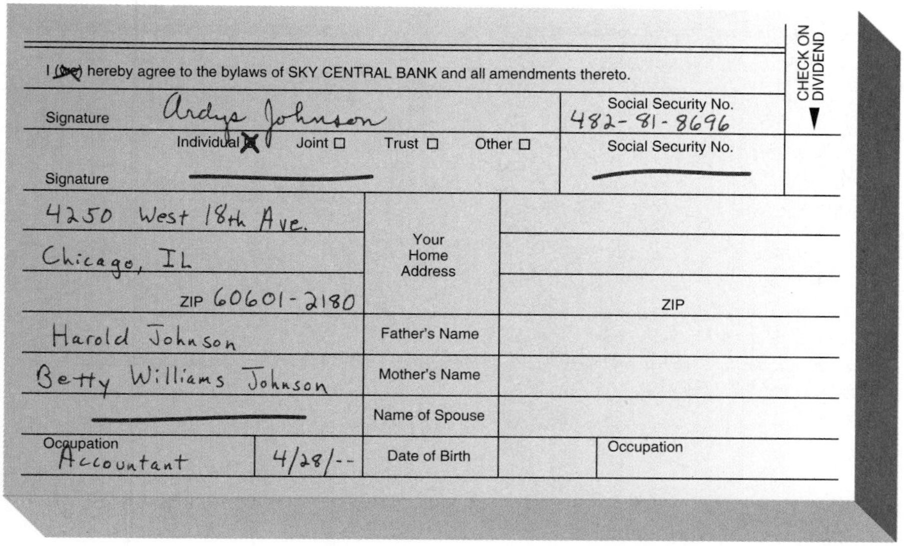

Fig. 9-1

Signature Card

Using your checking account

Checking accounts can help you manage your personal finances, but only if you use them correctly. Careless or improper use of a checking account can result in financial loss. Some tips on using a checking account follow.

Parts of a Check

A check consists of ten parts. Figure 9-2 illustrates these parts.

Check Number. Checks are numbered for easy identification. In Figure 9-2, Check 581 has been prenumbered by the bank (see Part A).

ABA Number. The American Bankers Association (ABA) number appears in fraction form in the upper right corner of each check (see Figure 9-2, Part B). The top half of the fraction identifies the location and district of the bank from which the check is drawn. The bottom half helps in routing the check to the specific area and bank on which it is drawn.

Maker's Preprinted Name and Address. Most checking account owners prefer to have their name, address, and telephone number preprinted on the top left of each check (see Figure 9-2, Part C). Most businesses are reluctant to accept a check unless it is preprinted with this information.

Fig. 9-2

Check

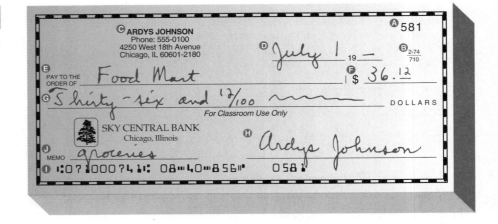

Date. The first item to be filled in is the date on which the check is written (see Figure 9-2, Part D). Do not postdate checks; that is, do not write in a future date. Most banks process checks when they are presented, or charge a fee for holding them. Checks over six months old may not be honored by the bank.

Payee. The payee is the person or company to whom a check is made payable. Food Mart is the payee in Figure 9-2 (Part E).

Numeric Amount. The numeric amount is the amount of dollars and cents being paid, written in figures (see Figure 9-2, Part F). The amount should be neatly and clearly written, and placed as close as possible to the dollar sign, with the dollars and cents distinctly readable. Many people raise the cents above the line of writing, as shown in Figure 9-2, and insert a decimal point between the dollar and cent amounts.

Written Amount. The written amount shows the amount of dollars and cents being paid, written in words. The word "dollars" is preprinted at the end of the line (see Figure 9-2, Part G). The word "and" is handwritten to separate dollar amounts from cents; it replaces the decimal point. When checks are written by computers, the "and" is usually omitted. Always begin writing at the far left of the line, leaving no space between words, and draw a wavy line from the cents to the word "dollars," as shown. In Figure 9-2, the fraction 12/100 means that 12 cents out of 100 is to be paid.

Drawer or Maker. The drawer, or maker, is the person authorized to write checks on the account. Ardys Johnson is the maker of the check in Figure 9-2 (see Part H) because she is the person who opened the checking account and deposits money into it. The bank has a copy of Ardys's signature on file so that they can stop someone attempting to forge Ardys's name on one of her checks.

Account Number. The account number appears in bank coding at the bottom of each check. In Figure 9-2 (see Part I), 08 40 856 is Ardys's checking account number; 581 is the preprinted check number at the top of the check; and 071000741 is the bank's identification code for the electronic sorting and routing of checks.

Memo. A memo line is provided at the bottom left of each check so that the maker can write the purpose of the check (see Figure 9-2, Part J). This line does not have to be filled in; it is provided for the account holder's convenience.

Some banks provide free "stock" checks to customers, but many customers prefer to order checks with special designs or colors rather than use plain stock checks. You will be charged for special design checks at rates from $5 to $15 or more for a standard batch of 200 checks. In addition, you may order special checkbook covers that match or coordinate with check designs (also at extra cost).

Writing Checks

Great care should be exercised in writing a check. Remember to follow these important guidelines in addition to the hints already given:

1. Always use a pen, preferably one with dark ink that does not skip or blot.
2. Write legibly. Keep numbers and letters clear and distinct, without any extra space before, between, or after them.
3. Sign your name exactly as it appears on the check and on the signature card you signed when you opened the account (see Figure 9-1).
4. Avoid mistakes. When you make a mistake, you should void (cancel) the check and write a new one. To cancel a check, write the word VOID in large letters across the face of the check. Save the voided check for your records.
5. Be certain adequate funds have been deposited in your account to cover each check that you write. A check is a negotiable instrument that contains your written promise to pay a certain amount to the payee when it is cashed.

Making Deposits

Just as when you withdraw money from your checking account, you need to complete a form each time you deposit money to the account. Figure 9-3 illustrates this form, which is called a deposit slip.

To prepare a deposit slip, follow these guidelines:

1. Insert the date of the transaction.
2. Write in the amount of currency (paper money) and coin to be deposited.

Fig. 9-3

Deposit Slip

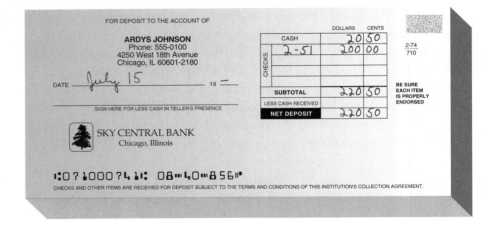

3. If any checks are being deposited, write in the amount of each check, together with the ABA check number (top part of fraction).
4. Total the currency, coin, and check amounts. Write this figure on the subtotal line.
5. If you wish to receive some cash at the time of your deposit, you should fill in the desired amount on the Less Cash Received line. Subtract this amount from the subtotal. Write in the final amount of the deposit on the Net Deposit line. Write your signature on the line above the words "Sign here for less cash in teller's presence."
6. Keep one copy of this deposit slip as proof of the amount of your deposit. Financial institutions have been known to make errors in crediting an account.

Before writing a check you should make sure that adequate funds have been deposited to your account.

When writing deposit slips, you should carefully count the currency and coins you are depositing and recheck all addition and subtraction. Make sure all checks being deposited are properly endorsed (see pages 214–216). Hand the deposit slip to the teller with the currency, coins, and checks you are depositing. Deposits also can be made at automated teller machines (see page 222).

Using a Checkbook Register

A **checkbook register** is a record of deposits to and withdrawals from a checking account. Figure 9-4 shows a page from the checkbook register of Ardys Johnson. Through use of her checkbook register, Ardys can keep track of all checks written, service fees paid, interest earned, and deposits made to the account.

PLEASE BE SURE TO *DEDUCT* ANY PER ITEM CHARGES OR SERVICE CHARGES THAT MAY APPLY TO YOUR ACCOUNT

ITEM NO.	DATE	PAYMENT ISSUED TO OR DESCRIPTION OF DEPOSIT	AMOUNT OF PAYMENT	✓	(−) CHECK FEE (IF ANY)	AMOUNT OF DEPOSIT	BALANCE FORWARD	
							800	*00*
581	7/1	To Food Mart	36 12		.20		Payment or Deposit −36	32
		For groceries					Balance 763	68
/	7/15	To Deposit				220 50	Payment or Deposit +220	50
		For Paycheck					Balance 984	18
/	7/16	To Withdrawal	20 00				Payment or Deposit −20	00
		For Automatic Teller					Balance 964	18
/	7/31	To Service Charge	5 00				Payment or Deposit −5	00
		For Mth. of July					Balance 959	18
		To					Payment or Deposit	
		For					Balance	
		To					Payment or Deposit	
		For					Balance	

Fig. 9-4

Checkbook Register

To fill out a checkbook register, follow these simple guidelines:
1. Write the preprinted check number in the first column. If you are not writing a check, draw a diagonal slash in this column, or use another distinctive notation.
2. Write the month and day of the transaction in the Date column.
3. Enter the name of the payee on the first line of the Description section. On the second line, if one is provided, write the purpose of the check.
4. Enter the amount of the check, service charge, or other withdrawal in the column headed by a minus sign. If the transaction is a deposit, write this amount in the column headed by a plus sign.
5. Transfer the amount withdrawn or deposited to the top line of the Balance column. Subtract this amount from or add it to the previous balance, then write the new balance on the second line of the column.

6. The column headed by a check mark is provided so that you can check off each transaction when it appears on your monthly bank statement. The check mark shows that the transaction has been cleared by the bank and is no longer outstanding.

Always keep your checkbook register handy so that you can write down the necessary information each time a transaction is made. Prompt and correct notations will help you keep track of your personal finances.

 econciling your checking account

Financial institutions that offer checking accounts provide each customer with a regular (usually monthly) *statement of account*. This statement lists checks received and processed by the bank, plus all other withdrawals and deposits made, service charges, and interest earned.

Most financial institutions return your canceled checks with your bank statement. Canceled checks serve as records of purchases and as proofs of payment. *Check safekeeping* (also called truncating) is the practice of some financial institutions of not returning canceled checks. Microcopies are made of the processed checks, and the originals are then destroyed. If necessary, copies of canceled checks may be made from the microform for a small fee ($5 to $10 each).

The process of matching your checkbook register with the bank statement is known as **reconciliation.** The back of the bank statement is usually printed with a form to aid you in reconciling your account. Figure 9-5 represents both sides of a typical bank statement.

On the left in Figure 9-5 is a simple statement of the bank's record of activity in the checking account. Canceled checks and other types of withdrawals are listed and are subtracted from the balance. Deposits are listed and are added to the balance. Bank service charges are subtracted from the balance, and an ending account balance is given.

The balance your checkbook register shows will not always match the ending balance shown on the bank statement. In this case, you can reconcile your account by following these guidelines:

1. Use the reconciliation form printed on the back of your bank statement.
2. Write the ending balance as shown on the front of the statement.
3. List any deposits made that do not appear on the bank statement (they should be listed in your checkbook register).

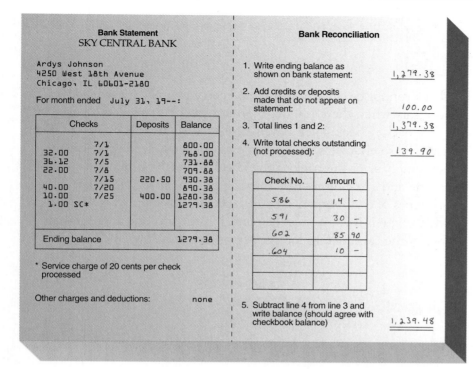

Fig. 9-5

Bank Reconciliation

4. Add the ending bank balance to the deposits made but not yet entered. Write down this subtotal.
5. List all checks you wrote or other withdrawals you made that do not appear on the bank statement.
6. Subtract the total checks outstanding from the subtotal. This should be the same as the balance shown in your checkbook register.

If your attempt at reconciliation is unsuccessful, check your addition and subtraction. Next, go through your checkbook register and check all addition and subtraction for the period covered by the statement. Finally, make certain that you have deducted service charges from and added any interest earned to your register balance. If you still cannot reconcile your account, ask the bank for help in discovering where the error lies. Usually you need to make an appointment for this. Be sure to take your checkbook, canceled checks, and bank statement with you. There normally is no charge for this service.

Reconciliation must be done immediately upon receipt of the bank statement. Any errors or differences should be reported to the bank as soon as possible. Occasionally the bank does make an error, which it will be happy to correct when you report the error immediately.

E ndorsements

A check cannot be cashed until it has been endorsed. A *joint endorsement* is necessary when there is more than one person named as a payee on the face of the check. Each payee must endorse the check before it can be cashed. To endorse a check, the payee named on the face of the check simply signs the back of the check in black or blue ink no more than one and one-half inches from the trailing edge. There are three major types of endorsements: blank, special, and restrictive. Regardless of which type is used, it must be placed in the top one and one-half inches of the trailing edge of a check as shown below.

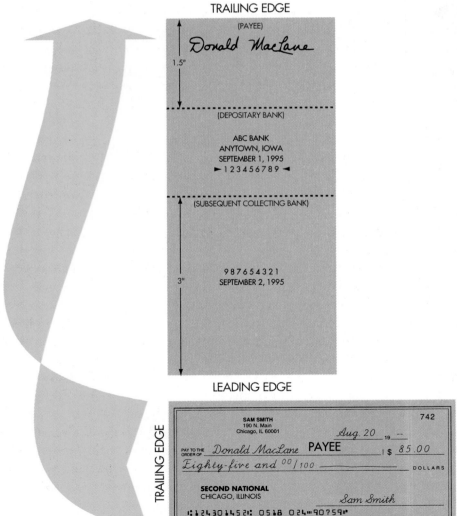

Blank Endorsement

A **blank endorsement** is simply the signature of the payee written exactly as his or her name appears on the front of the check.

(Note: If Donald's name had been written incorrectly on the face of the check, he would correct the mistake by endorsing the check with the misspelled version first, then with the correct version of his name, as shown here.)

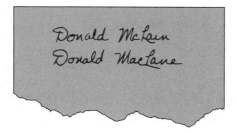

Special Endorsement

A **special endorsement,** or an endorsement in full, is written when the payee signs over a check to a third person. In the following illustration, for example, Donald MacLane uses a check written to him to pay a debt owed to Diane Jones. By using a special endorsement, Donald avoids having to cash the check before repaying Diane. The purpose of the special endorsement, then, is specifically to name the next payee who is entitled to cash the check.

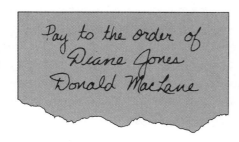

Restrictive Endorsement

A **restrictive endorsement** restricts or limits the use of a check. For example, a check endorsed with the words "For Deposit Only" above the payee's signature can be deposited only to the account specified.

The restrictive endorsement is safer than the blank endorsement for use in mailing deposits, in night deposit systems, or in other circumstances that may result in loss of a check. If a check with a restrictive endorsement is lost, it cannot be cashed by the finder.

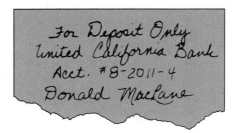

Types of checking accounts

There are many types of checking accounts available at banks, savings and loan associations, and credit unions. You should carefully study your options, because a wise choice can save you money. Some current options include the special account, the standard account, the interest-bearing account, and the share draft account. Most banks still offer free checking (no service fees) if you maintain a certain balance. Free checking is also available to senior citizens, nonprofit groups, and to others during special bank promotions, such as the opening of a new bank or branch.

Accounts can be either joint or individual. A *joint account* is opened by two or more persons. Such an account is also called a *survivorship account* because any person who signs on the account has the right to the entire amount deposited. If one person using the account dies, the other (the survivor) then becomes the sole owner of the funds in the account. All of the checking accounts discussed in this chapter can be joint accounts.

When opening a joint account, you must decide if it will be an "or" account in contrast to an "and" account. If it is specified as an "or" account, any authorized account holder is allowed to write checks on the account. An "and" account with two owners, on the other hand, would require the signatures of both owners on checks.

Special Accounts

Most banks offer a special checking account to customers who write only a small number of checks each month. Service fees are charged at a low flat rate per month with an additional fee for each check written. (For example, $3.00 per month, plus 15 cents for each check cashed). These customers also may be charged service fees only when the number of checks written in a month exceeds the set limit (such as more than 10 checks in a given month). If you write only a few checks each month (like many college students), this plan might be for you.

Standard Accounts

A standard account usually has a set monthly service fee of between $5 and $12, but no per-check fee. Often, if you are able to maintain an average minimum balance, you can avoid service fees entirely. Many banks give a package of services for this type of account, such as free traveler's checks, a teller machine card, or a free safe-deposit box. Some banks offer reduced interest rates on credit card balances to customers who also have checking, savings, and other accounts at their bank.

Interest-Bearing Accounts

Most financial institutions offer what are called interest checking accounts. With these accounts, interest is paid if you maintain a minimum *average daily balance* during the month. If interest is calculated on the basis of a customer's average daily balance, an account holder is required to keep a minimum average amount (often $500 or more) in his or her account each month.

How financial institutions determine the balance you must maintain to waive fees can make a big difference in the cost of an account. With passage of the Truth-in-Savings law in 1993, depositors must receive interest on their full balance every day. Low-balance methods of calculating interest are no longer permitted. Under one such system, interest was earned only on the lowest daily balance for the month. Under another system, an account dipping below the minimum balance would lose interest for the entire month. The *average-daily-balance method* triggers a fee or service charge only if the monthly average of each day's balance drops below a certain dollar amount.

Interest rates rise and fall with economic conditions. When overall interest rates drop, you may receive as low as 1 percent; when overall interest rates rise, you might expect 5 percent or more. Keeping money in a low-interest account can cost you money in interest lost because you could have invested elsewhere, yet it also is useful in avoiding bank service charges.

Share Draft Accounts

Most credit unions offer *share draft accounts*. These are checking accounts with low (or no) average daily balance requirements and no service fees. If you are eligible for credit union membership, this type of account may be the least expensive and most convenient checking method for you. Credit unions and the types of services they offer will be discussed in Chapter 10.

B anking services

A full-service bank is one that offers every possible kind of service, from checking accounts to credit cards, safe-deposit boxes, loans, and automatic tellers. Other services commonly offered are certified checks, cashier's checks, money orders, and debit cards. One guarantee that most banks offer is FDIC (Federal Deposit Insurance Corporation) insurance, which protects the deposits of customers against loss up to $100,000 per account holder.

Certified Checks

A **certified check** is a personal check that the bank guarantees or certifies to be good. The amount of the check is immediately deducted from the checking account, the word *certified* is stamped on the check, and an institution official initials the check. In effect, the bank puts a hold on that amount in the drawer's account so that the money will be there when the certified check is presented for payment. Most financial institutions charge the account holder for this service; typically, the fee ranges from $2.50 to $5 per check.

Cashier's Checks

A **cashier's check** is a check written by a bank on its own funds. You can pay for a cashier's check through a withdrawal from your savings or checking account, or in cash.

Cashier's checks are generally used to pay a person or firm when a cash payment is not desirable. A cashier's check also might be requested instead of a personal check when the payee questions your credit standing, or you do not have a credit history established. A cashier's check also can be used for transactions in which you wish to remain anonymous. The bank is listed as the maker of the check, and your identity need not be revealed. Like certified checks, many banks charge a fee for issuing cashier's checks.

personal perspective

S hopping for the Right Bank

A checking account is a personal choice. Some people choose the bank closest to their home or work. Others choose the biggest bank or the one with the most automatic teller machines. While all of these are good reasons, there are many other considerations in choosing your bank.

Finding that right bank to get started with can take a lot of time. All banks and services are not created equal—they vary a great deal. A good way to start is to make a list of the features that are very important to you. Rank them 1 to 10. For example, #1 may be a low interest rate on a VISA card; #2 may be a low minimum deposit for a free or interest-bearing account; and #3 may be low or no service fees. Then draw a matrix around your ten features, and at the top, list the banks that you are considering. Your matrix might look like this:

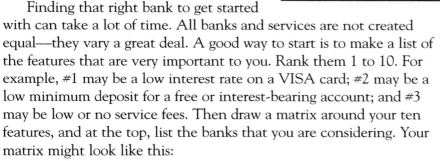

	Bank 1	Bank 2	Bank 3	Bank 4	Bank 5
1. Low rate on VISA card					
2. Low minimum deposit					
3. Low/no service fee					
4.					

For each bank, enter into the matrix the VISA rate, the minimum deposit, and so on, in order to see which bank, overall, gives you the most of what you want. In some cases, banks will be very close on issues important to you and you will make your choice based on factors not at the top of your list. Then you should consider other factors, such as how long the bank has been in existence, whether there are branches where you might likely move, personalities of people who work there, and so on.

critical thinking

1. What is your favorite bank or financial institution? Why?

2. What features do you think are the most important when choosing a financial institution for your checking account?

3. What would cause you to switch from your bank to another one?

Money Orders

Banks sell money orders to those who do not wish to use cash or do not have a checking account. A money order is used like a check, except that it can never bounce. There is a charge for purchasing a money order. It could cost from 50 cents to $5 or more, depending on the size of the money order. You also can purchase money orders through the post office and local merchants.

Debit Cards

Debit cards allow immediate deductions from a checking account to pay for purchases. The debit card is presented at the time of purchase. When the merchant presents the debit card receipt to the bank, the amount of the purchase is immediately deducted from the customer's checking account and paid to the merchant. The debit card transaction is similar to writing a check to pay for purchases. The issuing bank may charge an annual fee for the card or a fee for each transaction. (Note: There is no credit extended to you when you are using a debit card.)

Safe-Deposit Boxes

Safe-deposit boxes are available at most financial institutions for a yearly fee that is based on the size of the box. Annual rental fees may be from between $10 and $30 for a small box to $60 or more for a large box. The customer is given two keys for the box and is allowed to store valuables and documents in the box. Private rooms are available to customers to use when opening boxes to add or remove items. Documents commonly kept in a safe-deposit box are birth certificates, marriage and death certificates, deeds and mortgages, and stocks and bonds. Jewelry, coin collections, and other small valuables also are commonly stored in safe-deposit boxes. Keeping important documents and other items in a safe-deposit box ensures that the items won't be stolen, lost, or destroyed. Keep in mind that some documents can be easily replaced with a duplicate and therefore may not need to be kept in a safe-deposit box.

When you rent a safe-deposit box, you will fill out a signature card similar to that used for opening a checking account. Then each time you enter your safe-deposit box, you will sign a form so that your signature is compared to the one on file. This procedure prevents unlawful entry to your box by an unauthorized person.

Safe-deposit boxes, available at most financial institutions, are most often used to store important documents and small valuables.

Loans and Trusts

Financial institutions also make loans to finance the purchase of cars, homes, vacations, home improvements, and other items. Large banks have departments that assist with loans, and provide advice for estate planning and trusts. (You'll learn more about estates and trusts in Chapter 15.) Banks also act as trustees of estates for minors and others. A *trustee* is a person or an institution that holds or generally manages property for the benefit of someone else under a special agreement.

Discount Brokerage Services

Many larger banks offer discount brokerage services to their depositors. You may buy and sell stocks and bonds through the brokerage service at reduced rates. But you receive no advice or counseling. The purchases and sales are "cleared" through your checking or savings accounts with the bank. Brokerage services will be discussed in Chapter 12.

Many banks also purchase a block of bonds (debt obligations) which they allow their members and depositors to purchase. Generally there is no additional fee to buy or sell these securities (the fee is included in the purchase price). To access this service, however, usually a minimum purchase such as $1,000 is required.

Bank Credit Cards

You can apply to a full-service bank for a bank credit card such as VISA or MasterCard. If you meet the requirements, the card you are issued can be used instead of cash at any business that will accept it.

Banks offering national credit cards usually charge both an annual fee for use of the card and interest on the unpaid account balance. The topics of credit and credit cards will be discussed in detail in Unit 4.

Automated teller machines provide convenient access to bank accounts.

Automated Teller Machines

Certain transactions can be made through an electronic funds transfer (EFT). The main component of the EFT system is the automated teller machine. Using an automated teller machine and an EFT (debit) card, customers may make cash withdrawals from or check deposits to any of their accounts, make payments on loans, pay bills, and receive cash advances using a VISA or Master Card. Using an EFT card is similar to writing a check, except that the amount of payment is instantly deducted from your account. To use 24-hour bank machines, you must have a card that is electronically coded (such as a check guarantee card or bank credit card). You also must know your personal identification number (PIN), which usually is some combination of four or more numbers or letters. For safety, memorize your personal identification number; do not write it down and keep it with your bank card.

Stop Payment Orders

A **stop payment order** is a request that the bank not cash or process a specific check. The usual reason for stopping payment is that the check has been lost or stolen. By issuing a stop payment order, the drawer can safely write a new check, knowing that the original check cannot be cashed if it is presented to the bank. Most banks charge a fee (usually $10 or more) for stopping payment on a check.

Bank fees

Banks charge fees to their customers to cover costs of operation. For example, when you apply for a loan and it is granted, you are charged a loan fee. When the bank acts as a trustee, it charges a fee for this service. Banks also charge noncustomers for services such as check cashing. If you want to cash a check at a bank where you do not have an account, the bank may charge you a fee. Nondepositors pay for other services that may be free to depositors, such as traveler's checks, certified checks, and notary services.

Under the Truth in Savings Act (1993), checking advertised as "free" must carry no hidden charges or conditions. The bank or savings institution cannot charge regular maintenance or per-check fees or require balance minimums to avoid fees. However, it still may charge for a box of checks and for automated teller transactions.

Summary

Checking accounts offer many advantages for people who wish to have proof of purchase, canceled checks, and carry less cash. But checking accounts must be managed carefully, a responsibility which includes reconciling the bank statement each month, keeping an accurate checkbook register, and avoiding unnecessary fees and charges.

To open a checking account, the account holder must fill out and sign a signature card. Personalized checks usually arrive in a few weeks; in the meantime, an account holder can use blank "counter" checks provided by the institution. Checks should be made out in ink, and should be easy to read and understand. Deposit slips should be prepared for all currency or check deposits, and the checkbook register should be easy to read and a new balance computed after each entry.

Check endorsements are important because they determine how a check can be handled for cashing. The three common endorsements for making deposits are blank, restrictive, and special endorsements. Each check you deposit requires an endorsement to authorize the transfer of funds into your account.

Finally, there are many banking services available, and the customers using many of these services are assessed fees. It is important to consider each service carefully and make decisions that benefit you the most.

9

Vocabulary terms

Directions: Can you find the definition for each of the following terms used in Chapter 9?

blank endorsement	draft
canceled checks	floating a check
cashier's check	overdraft
certified check	reconciliation
checkbook register	restrictive endorsement
checking account	special endorsement
demand deposit	stop payment order

1. A banking term to designate that there are insufficient funds to cover a check that has been written.
2. Used to prevent payment on a check after it is lost or stolen.
3. Comparing your checkbook register with the bank statement each month.
4. Checks that have been processed by the bank and returned to you.
5. An endorsement that consists only of the payee's signature.
6. An endorsement, such as the words "For Deposit Only," that limits use of the check.
7. A personal record of checking account transactions.
8. An endorsement signing a check over to a third party.
9. A check guaranteed by the bank to be good.
10. A type of bank account that allows money to be withdrawn at will.
11. A banking service in which money is deposited and checks are written.
12. A form of check for withdrawing money from a demand account.
13. Writing a check on an account without sufficient funds in the hope of making a deposit before the check is cashed.
14. A check written by a bank on its own funds.

Facts and ideas in review

1. What are reasons for having a checking account?
2. What responsibilities do customers (depositors) have when using a checking account?

3. Why is a checking account called a demand deposit?

4. What is a canceled check, and why is it important to a depositor?

5. Why do you need to reconcile your checking account promptly when you receive the monthly bank statement?

6. Why would you be asked your mother's maiden name when opening a bank account?

7. What is a survivorship checking account?

8. List three types of endorsements and give a written example of each.

9. What types of checking accounts are offered by financial institutions? Briefly describe each type of account.

10. How is a bank debit card different from a bank credit card?

11. What is the purpose of a PIN (personal identification number)?

12. List at least four banking services provided by financial institutions.

pplications for decision making

1. List the names, addresses, and telephone numbers of five financial institutions in your community, and list the services provided by each. What type of checking account might you choose? Why? *Note*: Blank checks and deposit slips for problems 2 and 3 can be found in the *Student Activity Guide*.

2. Using Figure 9-2 (check) as an example, and following the rules on pages 207–209, write these checks:
   a. Check No. 12 to Melvin Quigly for $34.44, written today
   b. Check No. 322 to Save-Now Stores for $15.01, written today
   c. Check No. 484 to M. A. Bales for $91.10, written today

3. Using Figure 9-3 (deposit slip) as an example, and following the rules on pages 209–210, prepare these deposit slips:
   a. Today's date; currency $40.00; coins $1.44; Check No. 18-81 for $51.00; no cash retained
   b. Today's date; Check No. 40-22 for $300.00 and Check No. 24-12 for $32.00; $20.00 cash retained

4. Using Figure 9-5 (bank reconciliation) as an example, determine your ending reconciled checkbook balance when all of the following six conditions exist:
   a. Your ending checkbook balance is $311.40 (before the service fee is deducted).

b. You made an error, resulting in $30.00 less showing in your account than should be.

c. The service fee is $6.00.

d. The ending bank balance is $402.00.

e. Outstanding deposits total $100.00.

f. Outstanding checks total $166.60.

5. Determine your ending reconciled checkbook balance when all of the following six conditions exist:

a. Your checkbook ending balance is $800.40 (before the service fee is deducted).

b. The service fee is $3.00.

c. The ending bank balance is $1,100.00.

d. Outstanding deposits total $50.00.

e. Outstanding checks total $352.60.

6. Write out on plain paper the information needed for a signature card, as shown in Figure 9-1.

L ife situation problem solving

1. Find the errors in the following check.

RICHARD McGUIRE	**518**
Phone: 555-0109	
2802 Saratoga Street	
Ogden, UT 79393-4081	

June 1 ___ 19 _--_   97-145 / 1243

PAY TO THE ORDER OF _Best Buys_ | $ _3500_

Thirty five and ⁰⁰/100 _____ DOLLARS

For Classroom Use Only

PEAK BANK AND TRUST
OGDEN, UTAH

MEMO _____   Rick McGuire

⑆124301452⑆ 0518 024⑈90759⑈

2. The deposit slip shown is to deposit the check in Question No. 1. Can you find the errors on the deposit slip?

DEPOSIT SLIP

BEST BUYS FOODS
Ogden, Utah

DATE _June 1_ _____ 19 __

SIGN HERE FOR LESS CASH IN TELLER'S PRESENCE

STATE BANK OF
UTAH
Main Branch   Ogden, Utah

⑈123000 123⑈017 0 30123⑈   FOR CLASSROOM USE ONLY

24/12-7
33

CHECKS	CURRENCY		
	COIN		
	1243	35	00
	TOTAL FROM OTHER SIDE		
	TOTAL	35	00
	LESS CASH RECEIVED		
	NET DEPOSIT	30	00

A hold for uncollected funds may be placed on checks or similar instruments you deposit. Any delay will not exceed the period of time permitted by law.

RM 552 (0584)

3. Complete the bank reconciliation form on the following page by first finishing the checkbook register below, entering the service charge, and then computing balances. (Don't write in your textbook; use another piece of paper.)

PLEASE BE SURE TO *DEDUCT* ANY PER ITEM CHARGES OR SERVICE CHARGES THAT MAY APPLY TO YOUR ACCOUNT

ITEM NO.	DATE	PAYMENT ISSUED TO OR DESCRIPTION OF DEPOSIT	AMOUNT OF PAYMENT	✓	(−) CHECK FEE (IF ANY)	AMOUNT OF DEPOSIT	BALANCE FORWARD	
							100	00
101	3/1	To Grocery Mart	24 75				Payment or Deposit 24	75
		For Groceries					Balance 75	25
102	3/3	To Independent Phone Co.	13 00				Payment or Deposit 13	00
		For Feb. charges					Balance	
/	3/5	To Deposit				30 00	Payment or Deposit 30	00
		For					Balance	
103	3/8	To Local High School	10 00				Payment or Deposit 10	00
		For Band donation					Balance	
104	3/10	To Alan's Bakery	3 80				Payment or Deposit 3	80
		For Bread					Balance	
105	3/15	To Grocery Mart	18 20				Payment or Deposit 18	20
		For Groceries					Balance	
/	3/18	To Deposit				42 00	Payment or Deposit 42	00
		For					Balance	
106	3/20	To Acme Hardware	4 18				Payment or Deposit 4	18
		For Hammer					Balance	

BANK STATEMENT
Hometown Bank

For month ended March 31, 19--

Beginning balance ································· $100.00

Checks cashed		Deposits	Date	Balance
$24.75			3/7	$75.25
13.00		$30.00	3/8	92.25
10.00	$3.80		3/11	78.45
1.20 SC				77.25
Ending balance ············				$77.25

BANK RECONCILIATION

Ending balance as shown on bank statement $ _____

Add deposits not shown on bank statement $ _____

_____   _____

Subtract checks written but not shown
  on bank statement   _____

_____   _____

Adjusted balance (should be same as
  ending balance in checkbook) $ _____

Financial Checkup 1:
Assessing Your Financial Health

This first Financial Checkup is designed to help you begin the financial planning process. In the first section, you will assess your financial health by carefully examining your present financial condition. By taking inventory of where you are now, you can begin to build a plan for the future.

Your Job

We'll begin with your job. The money you earn affects what you are able to purchase and save now as well as your future prospects for financial stability. It's important to rate your job in terms of your opportunities for advancement, the company's chances for survival, and your job satisfaction. If you feel you are in a dead-end job, working for a weak or financially unstable company or in an obsolete industry, start looking for a more promising situation. On the other hand, if you like your work, and the future looks good for the company and the industry, then examine your opportunities for advancement. In addition, consider your own mental attitude, skills, and aptitudes for higher level positions.

Remember that the pay you receive in any job is only part of what you get as an employee. You also should consider fringe benefits, training received, and opportunities for making contacts that could be important in your career plans.

Worksheet 1 (Rate Your Job) is designed to help you assess your current job and any potential job you might consider. Complete Worksheet 1 provided in the *Student Activity Guide* (it also appears at the end of this Financial Checkup). When you examine the scores, you will have a clearer picture of the direction you should pursue. The time to do career research is now, not when you've invested several years of your life in the wrong job, the wrong employer, or the wrong industry.

Your Income and Outgo (Cash Flow)

Having completed the budgeting exercises in Chapter 8, you recognize the importance of keeping track of dollars that regularly flow through your hands. Worksheet 2 is a Cash Flow Statement which will help

financial checkup

you identify where your money comes from and where it goes. In addition, it allows you to make projections for future income and outgo on a yearly basis. It's important to pinpoint your spending habits, analyze them, and take steps to improve your financial picture.

Examine your cash flow closely, looking for places your income may be leaking away. Plugging the small leaks will help you build larger cash reserves and spend money more wisely.

Complete Worksheet 2 which is provided in the *Student Activity Guide* (it also appears at the end of this Financial Checkup).

Your Net Worth

An assessment of where you stand begins with what you own and owe at the moment. Worksheet 3 is a Net Worth Analysis which is used for listing your assets and liabilities and making projections of where you would like to be at some future date, such as a month, a year, or five years.

The purpose of the net worth analysis is threefold: to show you your strong and weak areas; to help you plan for specific short-term changes; and to allow you to project goals into the future based on those decisions.

Complete Worksheet 3 in the *Student Activity Guide* (it also appears at the end of this Financial Checkup).

Your Tax Liability (for Extra Credit)

Based on the income tax returns you prepared in Chapter 7, use Worksheet 4 (Tax Liability) to analyze your tax liability and determine whether or not you can avoid paying taxes through careful planning. Keep copies of your tax returns. Compare tax liability by preparing Forms 1040EZ, 1040A, and the long Form 1040. Use the form that gives the greatest tax advantage (that is, the lowest amount of taxes). Then study tax booklets and other information to see where you can benefit from taking more deductions.

Complete Worksheet 4 (Tax Liability) in the *Student Activity Guide* (it also appears at the end of this Financial Checkup).

Note relating to Worksheet 1: A score of 25 points is possible for each section. A score between 20 and 25 for any section indicates stability and good prospects for the future. A score between 15 and 20 indicates you should examine the characteristics carefully before making long-term commitments. A score between 10 and 15 indicates you should start looking for a new job, a new employer, or a new type of career soon. A score under 10 indicates you are in a hopelessly dead-end job which has no future and should be viewed as only temporary.

WORKSHEET 1
Rate Your Job

Directions: Rate each of the following characteristics on a 1 to 5 point scale. A score of 5 means *always;* a score of 4 means *usually;* a score of 3 means *as often as needed;* a score of 2 means *sometimes;* a score of 1 means *never;* and a score of 0 means *not applicable.* If you do not have a job, complete this worksheet after doing research about your desired future job.

Your Score

1. You enjoy the work you do, and you look forward to going to work each day. _____
2. You are willing to get extra training, education, or extra skills in order to be challenged. _____
3. You seek additional responsibility and can do the job well. _____
4. You like the work environment, and others recognize you as someone who will help and be a team player. _____
5. You receive regular pay raises large enough to keep you ahead of inflation and support your desired lifestyle. _____

Your total _____

Job Score

1. The product or service is in demand and prospects look good for the future. _____
2. The industry is growing as a whole, with opportunities for advancement in other companies similar to yours. _____
3. The product or service is inflation-resistant (rising prices don't greatly affect sales). _____
4. Turnover among employees is generally low. _____
5. Pay scale and fringe benefits compare well with other companies in the same field. _____

Job total _____

Employer's Score

1. Your boss calls on you to handle tough assignments and gives you credit for your accomplishments. _____
2. The boss regularly solicits your suggestions and follows them. _____
3. The company promotes from within. _____
4. The company has a large number of customers rather than just a few big ones. _____
5. The company is well established and still growing. _____

Employer's total _____

Total of all points _____

WORKSHEET 2
Cash Flow Statement

Directions: Keep a record of income and expenses for a month (you might want to do this for a year to build a budget base for the following year). In the first column, list each item you receive or spend in a month. In the second column, project your annual income or expense for each item. In the third column, check any items that need attention. In the fourth column, indicate how much (increase or decrease) each item should change monthly—what you'd like to accomplish. In the fifth column, indicate how much additional money you would save (or spend) annually by making the changes in the fourth column.

Example:	THIS MONTH	YEARLY TOTAL	NEED CHANGE	MONTHLY CHANGE	YEARLY EFFECT
Entertainment expense	$38.00	$456.00	×	−$12.00	+$144.00

	1 THIS MONTH	2 YEARLY TOTAL	3 NEED CHANGE	4 MONTHLY CHANGE	5 YEARLY EFFECT
ITEM					
Income:					
Take-home pay	_____	_____	_____	_____	_____
Bonuses/gifts	_____	_____	_____	_____	_____
Interest income	_____	_____	_____	_____	_____
Other _____	_____	_____	_____	_____	_____
Totals	_____	_____	_____	_____	_____
Outgo:					
	_____	_____	_____	_____	_____
	_____	_____	_____	_____	_____
	_____	_____	_____	_____	_____
	_____	_____	_____	_____	_____
	_____	_____	_____	_____	_____
	_____	_____	_____	_____	_____
	_____	_____	_____	_____	_____
Savings	_____	_____	_____	_____	_____
Totals	_____	_____	_____	_____	_____

Analysis:
List ways you can cut expenses or increase income (such as by substituting activities, buying cheaper products, or working odd jobs in the summer).

unit 2

WORKSHEET 3
Net Worth Analysis

Directions: Fill in the blanks below. In column 1, write in the market value of each item you possess or debt you owe. See Chapter 8 for definitions of terms (assets, liabilities, and net worth). In column 2, write in what each item will be worth in one year. In column 3, indicate the value of each item in five years. You can assume an item will increase it if gains in value over time (through interest or inflation) or if you add to or purchase an item from that category.

ITEM	1 TODAY'S BALANCE	2 ONE-YEAR PROJECTION	3 FIVE-YEAR PROJECTION
Assets:			
_____	$_____	$_____	$_____
_____	_____	_____	_____
_____	_____	_____	_____
_____	_____	_____	_____
_____	_____	_____	_____
_____	_____	_____	_____
_____	_____	_____	_____
_____	_____	_____	_____
_____	_____	_____	_____
_____	_____	_____	_____
_____	_____	_____	_____
_____	_____	_____	_____
Total assets	_____	_____	_____
Liabilities:			
_____	_____	_____	_____
_____	_____	_____	_____
_____	_____	_____	_____
_____	_____	_____	_____
_____	_____	_____	_____
_____	_____	_____	_____
_____	_____	_____	_____
Total liabilities	_____	_____	_____
Net worth	_____	_____	_____

Analysis: List major purchases that you wish to make and how you plan to pay for them.

WORKSHEET 4
Tax Liability

Directions: To complete this worksheet, first list your gross income, taxable income, and tax liability for the last three years you have filed tax returns and paid income taxes. If you have not yet filed a tax return, use the projected gross income that you would receive in the entry-level position of your choice (used for Worksheet 1). Compute taxes owed on that amount (see Chapter 7). Then compute how much you could save in income taxes if you made changes as shown. Finally, list some of the tax deductions available on the Form 1040 in the *Student Activity Guide* that you might use to decrease your tax liability.

YEAR	GROSS INCOME	ADJUSTED GROSS INCOME	INCOME TAXABLE	TAX LIABILITY
1. _____	_____	_____	_____	_____
2. _____	_____	_____	_____	_____
3. _____	_____	_____	_____	_____

How would each of the above years' tax liabilities have changed *if* you could have had the following changes:

YEAR	CHANGE	TAX DECREASE
1	IRA deduction of $2,000	$ _____
2	Child care credit of $500	$ _____
3	One more exemption	$ _____

Analysis:
Examine Schedule A of Form 1040 (itemized deductions) in the *Student Activity Guide.* Identify some deductions you might wish to take advantage of to reduce your tax liability.

Examine Form 1040 in the *Student Activity Guide* and list additional types of income and deductions that are required and/or permitted when this form is used.

looking back . . .

Money management refers to the day-to-day financial activities necessary to handle current personal economic resources while working toward long-term financial security. Unit 2 was an introduction to understanding money management—from the paycheck to income taxes to budgeting to using a checking account. You learned how to compute gross pay and net pay, and the various types of benefits that are available to you in the workplace. Some workplace trends, such as flextime, job rotation, and telecommuting, may seem exciting to you, while others may be unappealing. You may join a labor union and/or professional organizations as you develop your career; whether you join or not, you should be fully aware of the effect of unions and professional organizations on the work world and the benefits you receive because they exist.

To pay only what you owe in income taxes—no more and no less —you learned to prepare the two short form tax returns: the 1040EZ and the 1040A. Then you learned to budget your income and prepare and keep personal records—either manually or electronically. Contracts were explained, including the elements of an enforceable agreement.

You concluded the unit with checking accounts and banking services, where you learned to prepare checks and deposit slips, keep a checkbook register, and reconcile your account. These are important responsibilities. The most difficult part is selecting the right financial institution and account so that you maximize your benefits and minimize your costs.

unit three

financial security 3

chapters

objectives: *After reading and studying the chapters, and completing the exercises and activities, you will be able to:*

1 Explain the goals of savings, how money compounds, financial institutions, and savings options.

2 Discuss the need for and risks of investing, and describe wise investment strategies.

3 Describe the features of common stocks and preferred stock, compute a stock's return, buy and sell stocks, and explain stock investment practices.

4 Identify bond investments, including corporate and government bonds, and explain how to buy and sell bonds using the financial section of a newspaper.

5 Describe the types of mutual funds and how they work, and discuss the advantages and disadvantages of investing in real estate; precious metals, gems, and collectibles; and futures and options.

6 Explain the objectives of retirement planning, and discuss estate planning tools.

looking forward

Unit 3, Financial Security, begins with a basic explanation of saving, including types of financial institutions and accounts from which to choose. You then will explore the fundamentals of investing and investment alternatives. You also will learn about the many risks of investing, and how to invest wisely.

You will explore the two types of stock—common and preferred—as a major source of capital for a corporation. You will look at the many strategies for buying and selling stocks in securities markets. You will learn how to use the financial pages of a newspaper, including the daily stock listings.

Then you will look at the two types of bonds—corporate and government—an investor should consider. You will learn what types of mutual funds are available, and why you might choose one over another. You'll also discover the positive and negative features of investing in nonresidential real estate—houses, duplexes, apartments, and so on. You'll also learn about investments such as precious metals, gems, and collectibles, as well as futures and options.

You'll end this unit learning about retirement and estate planning since do-it-yourself (personal) retirement plans are basic to a successful retirement. Finally, you will study wills, trusts, and the taxation of your estate.

Financial security begins when you can start *saving*—setting aside money for your future. Savings plans enable you to provide for future needs, both foreseen and unforeseen. The existence of some regular savings, even if the amount is small, gives you a measure of financial independence. Successful savings plans depend on a saver's willingness to give some priority to future needs rather than to devote resources only to current desires. In this chapter, you will discover how you can save more effectively, regardless of income.

chapter 10

Saving for the Future

Why you should save

The best reason to save some of your income as you earn it is to provide for future needs, both expected and unexpected. When nothing is set aside for these inevitable needs, frustration, financial trouble, and even bankruptcy can result. Let's begin by examining some reasons why you should start saving regularly.

One of the best reasons for saving a portion of your income is for short-term needs.

Short-Term Goals

Short-term needs often arise that require money, above what is normally allowed by a budget. These needs typically are paid for out of savings. Some short-term goals you might encounter include the following:

1. Emergencies—such as unemployment, sickness, accident, or death in the family.
2. Vacations—short weekend trips and leisure activities.
3. Social events—weddings, family gatherings, or other potentially costly special occasions.
4. Major purchases—a car, major appliances, remodeling, or other expenses that become necessary as time goes by. (Things do wear out and have to be replaced, repaired, or remodeled.)

You can probably think of other short-term goals for which you should save.

Long-Term Goals

Many individuals and families anticipate some major purchases in the future and save to make them possible. These long-term goals include outlays for such things as home ownership, education, retirement, and investments.

Home Ownership

A down payment on a house amounts to thousands of dollars. The larger the down payment you can make, the smaller your monthly payments will be. Many people consider owning their own home a very important part of their future.

Education

Many high school graduates will borrow money, obtain grants and scholarships, and pay for their own postsecondary training. Education for one or both spouses may involve completing a bachelor's or master's degree, an advanced degree (such as law or medical), or mastering some special skill or trade through a vocational or apprenticeship program.

In addition, many couples begin a savings plan when children are born. Then when the time comes for college, money is available for their children's educational needs.

Retirement

Social security payments probably will not provide sufficient support for your old age. Other plans should be made for financial security after retirement.

Investment

To provide a hedge against inflation or to make money for future use, people may invest in a business, real estate, insurance, stocks, collectibles, or a number of other alternatives. Because investments are often risky, they should be made in addition to, not instead of, regular savings. These types of investments will be described in subsequent chapters.

Financial Security

Probably the best reason to save is the peace of mind that comes from knowing that when short-term needs arise there will be adequate money to pay for them. Another reason to save is to ensure enough money for a comfortable retirement. If you set aside money from each paycheck, you will feel secure knowing that there is money available if and when it is needed.

The amount of money you save will vary according to several factors: (a) the amount of your **discretionary income** (what you have left over when the bills are paid); (b) the importance you attach to savings; (c) your anticipated needs and wants; and (d) your will power, or ability to forego present spending in order to provide for your future.

 ow your money grows

The amount of money deposited by a saver is called the **principal.** Money paid by the financial institution to the saver for the use of his or her money is called **interest.** When interest is computed on the original principal plus accumulated interest, it is called **compound interest.** Figure 10-1 illustrates how interest is compounded annually.

Fig. 10-1

Compounding Interest Annually

Year	Beginning Balance	Interest Earned (5%)	Ending Balance
1	$100.00	$5.00	$105.00
2	105.00	5.25	110.25
3	110.25	5.51	115.36

The more often interest is compounded, the greater your earnings. Figure 10-2 illustrates what happens when 5 percent interest is compounded quarterly (every three months) and is added to the principal before more interest is calculated. You will notice that more interest is earned in quarterly compounded than in annually compounded interest.

Fig. 10-2

Compounding Interest Quarterly

Year	Beginning Balance	First Quarter	Second Quarter	Third Quarter	Fourth Quarter	Ending Balance
1	$100.00	$1.25	$1.27	$1.28	$1.30	$105.10
2	105.10	1.31	1.33	1.35	1.36	110.45
3	110.45	1.38	1.40	1.42	1.43	116.08

Daily interest can be computed for each day savings are on deposit. Banks and financial institutions can rapidly compute the compounding of daily interest with computers.

Earnings on savings can be measured by the *rate of return* or *yield*. Yield is the percentage of increase in the value of your savings due to earned interest. Advertisements for savings options at financial institutions often show the annual percentage yield (APY) as depicted in Figure 10-3.

INTEREST OFFERED

Six-month time certificates

Minimum deposit of $500.00

Annual percentage yield (APY): 5.71%

Interest compounded daily.

Fig. 10-3

Interest Rates

W here you can save

The main financial institutions found in most cities include commercial banks, savings banks, savings and loan associations, brokerage firms, and credit unions. Most of these institutions have greatly expanded their services in the last ten or fifteen years to remain competitive.

Commercial Banks

Many people prefer to keep their checking and savings accounts in the same bank for ease in transferring funds and making deposits and withdrawals. Commercial banks offer convenience to customers in the form of services that go along with accounts, including automatic cash transfer accounts, bank cards, use of 24-hour teller machines, overdraft protection, and other services. Ninety-seven percent of banks are insured by the Federal Deposit Insurance Corporation (FDIC). Most large commercial banks have many branches for ease of making deposits and withdrawals. Commercial banks may be either nationally chartered or state chartered. Rates offered on savings accounts will vary among commercial banks, as well as between commercial and savings banks, savings and loan associations, and credit unions.

Savings Banks

Savings banks are usually referred to as mutual savings banks. These financial institutions are few in number—about 500 of them in roughly a dozen states, mostly throughout New England and the Northeast—but substantial in size. Savings banks are state chartered and are insured by the FDIC. Two primary services offered by these institutions are savings accounts and loans on real property, including mortgages and home-improvement loans. Because of deregulation of the banking industry in the 1980s, savings banks also offer checking accounts and other types of consumer loans.

Savings and Loan Associations

Savings and loan associations are organized primarily to handle savings and lend money. Money deposited in savings accounts is lent to people purchasing homes or making home improvements.

Savings and loan associations offer many of the conveniences and services of commercial banks, including interest-bearing checking accounts, special savings plans, loans to businesses, and other investment and planning services. Many savings and loans offer major credit cards and 24-hour teller machines. Rates and services vary among savings and loan associations, so check around before depositing your money.

In the 1980s, many savings and loan associations failed as a result of careless loan practices and poor investments. Many have merged or been taken over by banks. All savings and loan associations today are insured by the FDIC.

Brokerage Firms

Brokerage firms buy and sell different types of securities. **Securities** are investment instruments issued by corporations or by the government. They represent either equity (ownership) or debt (a loan). In other words, when you buy stock, you become an owner of a company. When you buy a bond, you are loaning money to a company or to the government.

Most securities transactions are made through an **account executive,** or stockbroker, who works for the brokerage firm. An account executive is a person who buys and sells securities for his or her clients. Brokerage firms sell certificates of deposits (see page 246) to customers as an alternative to stocks and bonds. When you have an account with a brokerage firm, you may be able to write checks against a money market fund (see pages 246–247). There are often restrictions, such as a minimum deposit requirement, a maximum number of checks that may be written each month, and a minimum amount for which each check must be written.

Credit Unions

Credit unions are not-for-profit organizations established by groups of employees in similar occupations who pool their money. Credit unions generally offer higher interest rates on savings and lower interest rates on loans. They are insured through membership in NCUA (National Credit Union Administration) so that depositors' accounts are insured up to $100,000. A savings account at a credit union is usually called a **share account.** Credit union members save their money in the form of "shares," which are typically $5 each.

Credit unions are not-for-profit organizations established by groups of employees with similar occupations.

From funds accumulated by these shares, loans are made to credit union members. Credit unions also offer IRAs (Individual Retirement Accounts), share draft accounts (checking accounts), consumer loans, certificates of deposit, and other services. Credit unions are growing rapidly in most parts of the country and consequently are offering more diversified services.

avings accounts

Once you have decided to establish a savings program for yourself or your family, you need to know about the different types of accounts available. Money that is set aside for future needs can be deposited in a number of different savings plans. Common options include regular savings accounts, certificates of deposit, and money market funds or accounts.

Regular Savings Accounts

A regular savings account has a major advantage of high liquidity. **Liquidity** refers to assets (resources owned) that can be converted easily to cash without loss of value. A regular account is said to be liquid because you can withdraw your money at any time without penalty. A regular account generally pays the least amount of interest.

Once you have opened the account, you are free to make withdrawals and deposits. Some financial institutions charge service fees when you make more than a maximum number of withdrawals in a certain period of time. Other institutions charge a monthly fee if your balance falls below a set minimum.

Certificates of Deposit

A **certificate of deposit (CD),** or time certificate, represents a sum of money deposited for a set length of time—for example, $500 for six months. A certificate of deposit is less liquid than a regular savings account, and requires that a minimum amount be deposited. The rate of interest is usually higher (although the difference may be small) than on regular accounts. But if you withdraw your money (or part of it) before maturity, you may be penalized; that is, you will receive less interest than stated on the certificate. A certificate of deposit has a set **maturity date**—the day on which your account comes due. Within so many days after the maturity date, your certificate will renew automatically. You may prefer to redeem it for cash or purchase a new certificate for a different time period. Financial institutions offer certificates of deposit that allow the interest to accumulate to maturity. Often you can choose to receive a check periodically for the interest earned or have the interest deposited in a separate regular account.

Money Market Funds and Accounts

A **money market fund** is a combination savings-investment plan in which money deposited is used to purchase certain types of securities. Money market funds are available to customers of brokerage or investment firms. Money may be deposited or withdrawn from a market fund at any time without a charge or fee. Interest is usually compounded daily so your money grows until the day it is withdrawn.

Although not insured by the FDIC, money market funds are generally considered safe because the securities backing these funds are very stable. Managers of these funds frequently purchase short-term (one year or less) securities issued by the U.S. Treasury. Therefore, the chance of losing your money is very low. Money market funds are classified as mutual funds, a topic that will be covered in Chapter 11.

A *money market account* is a type of savings account offered through a banking institution. Money market accounts are similar to money market funds. Interest rates vary and a minimum balance, such as $500 or more, is often required. These accounts also may have restrictions on the number of checks that can be written over a period of time and the minimum amount for which each check may be written. The major difference lies in safety. These types of accounts are covered by federal deposit insurance.

electing a savings plan

There are a number of important factors to consider in selecting a savings account and a savings institution. These factors include (a) liquidity, (b) safety, (c) convenience, (d) interest-earning potential (or yield), and (e) early withdrawal penalties.

Liquidity

Liquidity, or how quickly you turn savings into cash when you want it, may be important to you. The need for liquidity will vary based on an individual's age, health, and family situation. Some types of deposits may be obtained instantly; others will require a waiting period. Some financial institutions impose a penalty for cashing in a CD early. Savings plans such as regular savings and money market accounts provide a high degree of liquidity.

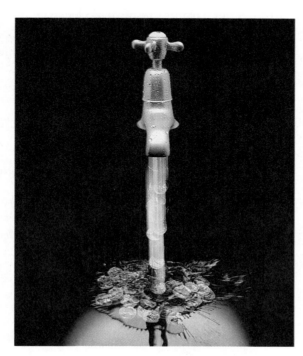

Safety

You want your money to be safe from loss. Most financial institutions are insured by government agencies such as the FDIC.

Accounts protected by this insurance are safe for up to $100,000 per depositor. You should be sure the financial institution of your choice has federal insurance to protect the deposits of customers.

Convenience

People often choose their financial institution because of convenience of location and the services offered. Interest rates on various savings accounts and certificates of deposit may vary only slightly. Fees charged are often very similar.

Many banks have several branches within a limited geographic area, which makes your banking convenient. If a bank has only one branch located several miles from your home, it is more expensive and inconvenient for you to bank there. A very large bank may have branches in other states, giving you banking privileges while out of town.

Many banks offer drive-up windows that open early and stay open later on weekdays and part of the day on Saturday. Day-and-night teller machines may be installed at all branches, offering an added convenience on weekends, holidays, and evenings.

Interest Earning Potential (Yield)

Interest earnings on your deposit should be as high as possible—that is, your savings should be placed in the institution that offers the best rate of return. Usually, the more liquid your deposit, the less interest it will earn. Higher earnings result from leaving money on deposit longer. A regular account usually earns a low rate because savers can maintain a low minimum balance and can withdraw money as needed.

Figure 10-4 is an example of interest rates being paid in a local area. As you can see from the chart, yield depends on the type of account opened.

Fig. 10-4
Current Interest Rates as Reported Weekly

INTEREST RATES FOR CONSUMERS

For the week ended December 10, 19--
(reported at the end of every business week):

REGULAR SAVINGS ACCOUNT:	Commercial banks	3.5%
	Credit unions	3.8%
MONEY MARKET ACCOUNTS:	Commercial banks	3.1%
	Credit unions	3.5%
	Brokerage firms	4.1%

Early Withdrawal Penalties

Each type of account at each institution is controlled by different rules. Before you open an account, be sure to understand the withdrawal restrictions, and any other special conditions that may exist.

Early withdrawal penalties are charged to depositors who withdraw money from their account before maturity. For example, with a certificate of deposit, a time period—such as six months—would be specified. Early withdrawal penalties should be considered when choosing a savings plan. If you need to withdraw all or part of your money before the maturity date, you may be charged a penalty. The penalty is usually the loss of a portion of any interest earned.

Regular savings accounts and money market funds or accounts usually do not carry early withdrawal penalties. Money may be withdrawn in full or in part at any time.

 aving regularly

Everyone should have saving as a goal. In simplest terms, the growth of current savings can be achieved only by spending less than is taken in. It is important not just to save, but to save regularly. By doing so, you can greatly increase your earnings. Figure 10-5 illustrates the effect of compounding when regular deposits are made to savings and interest is earned on interest.

Year	Beginning Balance	Deposits	Interest Earned (5%)	Ending Balance
1	$ 0.00	$100.00	$ 5.00	$105.00
2	105.00	100.00	10.25	.215.25
3	215.25	100.00	15.76	331.01
4	331.01	100.00	21.55	452.56

Fig. 10-5

Compounding Interest and Making Additional Deposits

Obviously, no savings plan is effective unless you have the will power to set aside money. The safe storage of funds for future use is a basic need of every individual. There are ways to make regular saving easier, including savings clubs and payroll deductions.

It is important to save regularly to greatly increase your earnings.

Savings Clubs

Club accounts are savings plans designed for a certain goal or a certain time of the year. Examples are vacation or Christmas club accounts. You make regular deposits into a special account and agree not to touch these funds before a specified date. In this way, you are forcing yourself to save for some event or need, and when the time comes you know you will have the money. Interest paid on savings clubs may be very low; compare them with other savings alternatives.

Automatic Payroll Deductions

Having a certain amount withheld from your paycheck and deposited into a savings account is a method of "paying yourself." Contributions to savings are part of preauthorized payment systems. In this case, money is automatically deducted from your paycheck and deposited in your savings account.

You may authorize an employer to make automatic deductions from your paycheck each month. Many people participate in *payroll savings* plans, in which money is taken out of each paycheck and deposited in a bank or credit union or used to buy government savings bonds.

personal perspective

P reauthorized Payment Plans

When you agree to have preauthorized payments, all the transactions occur electronically without exception. For example, you can authorize *automatic deductions* from a checking or savings account. With automatic deductions, you agree to have money taken directly from an account. House payments can be paid directly from a checking account on the first of each month. Some people have money automatically withheld for insurance payments. Other kinds of automatic deductions are made for the repayment of loans on automobiles, furniture, or appliances, and for the purchase of some types of investments (mutual funds, for example).

But before you authorize automatic deductions, there are several disadvantages you should consider:

1. Your payment is deducted from a checking or savings account automatically—regardless of whether or not your paycheck is deposited on time. If, for some unforeseen reason, your paycheck is not deposited on time, you may have insufficient funds to cover transactions.
2. You do not have control of what should be paid and what should be delayed in the event of a job loss or a financial emergency. In other words, financial decisions are made for you.
3. Closing an account and opening a new account elsewhere can cause problems. You will have to fill out new forms and restart the process of automatic payments.

Many financial experts encourage people to have automatic deductions from checking or savings accounts for convenience. Others don't recommend automatic deductions because you give up control of financial decision-making. You also must remember to enter the automatic deductions in your checkbook register if you wish your checkbook to balance each month. If deductions are made from savings, you also must update your savings register periodically.

critical thinking

1. What kinds of automatic deductions do you see as advantageous?

2. What kinds of deductions might you *not* want to authorize?

S ummary

The purpose of savings is to provide for future needs—short-term, long-term, and unexpected. Future financial security and peace of mind depend on having enough cash reserves for a comfortable living. Earnings on savings can be measured by the yield, or rate of return, which is the percentage of increase in the value of your savings due to earned interest.

Compounding refers to interest that is earned on previously earned interest. Each time that interest is added to your savings, the next interest is computed on the basis of the new amount in the account. Compounding methods vary according to the type of savings plan and the financial institution.

Commercial banks, savings banks, savings and loans, credit unions, and brokerage firms are common places to deposit savings. These institutions offer many savings accounts, including regular savings accounts, certificates of deposit, and money market funds or accounts. To select the right account for you, consider safety, liquidity, convenience, interest earning potential (yield), and early withdrawal penalties.

Saving regularly can help you greatly increase your earnings. Savings clubs and automatic payroll deductions can facilitate regular savings.

Vocabulary terms

Directions: Can you find the definition for each of the following terms used in Chapter 10?

account executive   liquidity
certificate of deposit (CD)   maturity date
compound interest   money market fund
discretionary income   principal
early withdrawal penalty   securities
interest   share account

1. Measure of how easily a deposit can be converted into cash.
2. An ending date on which a certificate is due (must be renewed or redeemed).
3. Money paid for the use of money.
4. The type of account offered to a saver (regular savings plan) at a credit union.
5. A sum of money in a savings account on which interest accrues.
6. Interest computed on the principal plus accumulated interest.
7. The amount of money you have left over when the bills are paid.
8. Another name for a stockbroker who works for a brokerage firm.
9. A combination savings-investment plan in which an investment firm uses your money to purchase a variety of short-term securities.
10. Fee charged to a depositor who withdraws money from a CD before maturity.
11. A sum of money deposited for a set length of time.
12. Investment instruments issued by corporations or by the government.

 Facts and ideas in review

1. List several short-term needs that you may experience in the next few months or years.
2. List any long-term plans you may have that will require money in the next five years or more.
3. What four personal factors determine the amount of money you will save?

4. Why does a regular savings account pay less interest than a certificate of deposit?
5. What things should you consider when choosing a financial institution for your savings?
6. Why might people choose to save their money in a commercial bank when a higher rate of interest might be earned at some other type of financial institution?
7. What is the main purpose of savings and loan associations?
8. How much is an account insured for by the FDIC?
9. List two ways you can force yourself to save.
10. What types of penalties might you face for early withdrawal of all or part of your savings from (a) regular savings, (b) certificates of deposit, or (c) money market funds?
11. What are some advantages of having automatic deductions from checking accounts?

 pplications for decision making

1. Write out your savings plans, listing your short-term and long-term goals and how you plan to achieve them. (How much money will you save to meet them?)
2. What does discretionary income have to do with saving?
3. Select a situation—amount saved and yield—and show the difference between simple and compounded interest. Figure the annual interest earned over a five-year period.
4. Collect advertisements offering various financial services. What factors should a person consider before using these services and the financial institutions that offer them?
5. Visit one or more financial institutions in your community and describe the following:
   a. types of savings accounts
   b. services available to depositors
   c. fees charged for services
   d. requirements, such as minimum deposits, and
   e. other enticements to get your business
6. Explore the reasons for joining a credit union when you have the opportunity.
7. Mike Adams is considering buying a certificate of deposit with the $500 he has in regular savings. Explain to him what factors he should consider when choosing a certificate of deposit.

8. Suppose you need to have the money in a two-year CD before the certificate matures. Ask a local bank what might be the penalty for withdrawing early from a two-year CD. What is the penalty for withdrawing all or part of your money from a regular savings account?

L ife situation problem solving

1. Compute the interest compounded for Harriet Burke, assuming that she deposits $1,000 in a CD with interest compounded every six months at the rate of 8½ percent. The certificate matures in three years. Use this format on a separate sheet of paper:

Year	Beginning Balance	First-Half Interest	Second-Half Interest	Total Interest	Ending Balance
1	$1,000	_____	_____	_____	_____
2	_____	_____	_____	_____	_____
3	_____	_____	_____	_____	_____

2. Marsha Olson wishes to save $100 a month. Her bank computes compound interest monthly. The current rate for a regular savings account is 5½ percent. Compute the ending balance in her account after one year. Use this format on a separate sheet of paper:

Month	Beginning Balance	Deposit	Total	Interest	Ending Balance
1	_____	_____	_____	_____	_____
2	_____	_____	_____	_____	_____
3	_____	_____	_____	_____	_____
4	_____	_____	_____	_____	_____
5	_____	_____	_____	_____	_____
6	_____	_____	_____	_____	_____
7	_____	_____	_____	_____	_____
8	_____	_____	_____	_____	_____
9	_____	_____	_____	_____	_____
10	_____	_____	_____	_____	_____
11	_____	_____	_____	_____	_____
12	_____	_____	_____	_____	_____

3. Compute the interest compounded quarterly on a deposit of $500 for three years at 8 APY. Use the following format on a separate sheet of paper:

| Year | Beginning Balance | Interest | | | | Total Interest | Ending Balance |
		First Quarter	Second Quarter	Third Quarter	Fourth Quarter		
1	$500	_____	_____	_____	_____	_____	_____
2	_____	_____	_____	_____	_____	_____	_____
3	_____	_____	_____	_____	_____	_____	_____

4. Compute your total savings if you keep $1,000 in a regular savings account at 5¼ percent, compounded quarterly, for two years. Use this format on a separate sheet of paper:

REGULAR SAVINGS ACCOUNT

| Year | Beginning Balance | Interest | | | | Total Interest | Ending Balance |
		First Quarter	Second Quarter	Third Quarter	Fourth Quarter		
1	$1,000	_____	_____	_____	_____	_____	_____
2	_____	_____	_____	_____	_____	_____	_____

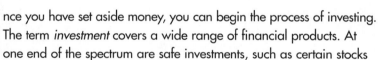

Once you have set aside money, you can begin the process of investing. The term *investment* covers a wide range of financial products. At one end of the spectrum are safe investments, such as certain stocks and bonds. At the other end are risky investments, such as speculative stocks, certain types of real estate commodities, options, and collectibles. In Chapter 10, you learned about the safest, most conservative way to invest. Many investments, such as those presented in Chapters 12 through 15, assume greater risks in order to provide a higher return to the investor. In this chapter, you will learn the basic principles of investing and how to get started as an investor. You also will learn about the basic types of investment alternatives, sources of financial information, and how to make good investment choices.

Managing Your Investments

chapter

11

Investment essentials

Personal investing is the use of your savings to earn a financial return. The overall objective of investing is to earn money with money. As shown in Figure 11-1, personal investing really begins when savings are "permanent" rather than "put-and-take." Initial savings and investments are cautious and conservative. Once a safe cushion of investment is established, more risky (and potentially profitable) investments can be made.

Fig. 11-1   **Essentials of Investing**

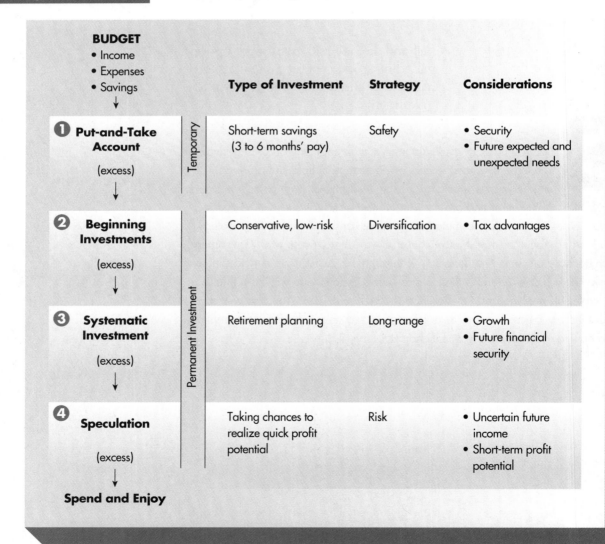

Money that is saved each month first goes into a "put-and-take" account. Savings are *put* first. You *take* money to pay short-term expected and unexpected expenses. For example, you may need money for car repairs, an emergency trip, or new tires. The put-and-take account is temporary. Money is set aside temporarily for short-term needs. Many financial advisers recommend that you have three to six months' net pay set aside for this type of account. Then, should a need arise, you won't dip into permanent, long-term investments to pay for temporary, short-term needs.

Money for short-term needs such as car repairs should come from a put-and-take account.

As you accumulate savings in your put-and-take account, you will eventually have more in a savings account than you need. You want to have enough in the put-and-take account to meet unexpected, short-term needs. When you reach a comfort level, the excess should then be invested to earn more income. *Beginning investments* should be conservative and low risk. These investments can provide certain tax advantages. For example, a two-wage-earner family can benefit from an investment that is tax deductible, tax deferred, or nontaxable. Beginning investments are permanent and therefore should be maintained for the long term. Maximum income is realized when you invest for a number of years.

Once you have accumulated a comfortable amount in beginning investments, any excess can then be used for *systematic investment*— investing for retirement. This type of permanent investment centers on retirement planning.

After you reach the comfort zone in systematic investment, the final level is *speculation*. Taking more chances can yield higher returns. With an emphasis on maximizing your return, excess money is used for speculative investments. A *speculative investment* is made in the hope of earning a relatively large profit in a short time. Profits can be used as desired because they are not needed for present or future financial security.

Reasons for Investing

Investing is an important part of personal financial management. An investment program should begin with the accumulation of an emergency fund. An *emergency fund* is a certain amount of money that can be obtained quickly in case of immediate need. This money should be deposited in a savings account at the highest available interest rate. Other reasons to invest include: (a) to supplement earned income, (b) to make a profit, (c) to minimize tax burdens now and in the future, (d) to provide income for retirement, and (e) to stay ahead of inflation.

Inflation is a rise in the general level of prices. Investors should seek investments for the long term that will grow faster than the rate of inflation. For example, if the annual inflation rate is 6 percent, you will want a higher rate of return. During inflationary times, there is a risk that the return on an investment will not keep pace with the rate of inflation.

At retirement, people need to have more income than social security or retirement benefits will provide. Therefore, retirement planning should include investments that will grow (or increase in value) over time. The chief difference among investments is how fast growth occurs. Often, the greatest opportunity for growth is an investment in common stock. The safest investments, such as certificates of deposit, provide a predictable return but limited growth potential.

Risk

Investing involves some risk. The greater the risk you are willing to take, the greater the potential returns. **Risk** in an investment means a measure of uncertainty about the outcome. On the other hand, safety in an investment means minimal risk of loss. Types of investment risk include short- and long-term, market, company and industry, inflation and interest rate, and political.

One way to mini-
mize many of these risks
is through **diversifica-
tion** or the spreading of
risk among many types
of investments. In other
words, rather than buy-
ing only one kind of
investment, an investor
will choose several types
of investments, such as
stocks, bonds, real estate,
etc. This strategy reduces
risk because not all of
the choices perform
poorly at the same time;
therefore, even if one
choice does not do well,
the others are likely to
make up for any loss.

Short-Term and Long-Term Risks

Short-term investments are generally less risky than long-term investments. You can analyze and predict much more easily what will happen in a week, a month, or a year than in ten or twenty years.

Inflation and Interest Rate Risk

During inflationary times, there is risk that the return on an investment will not keep pace with the rate of inflation. Inflation makes
your fixed-rate investments worth less because they are "locked in" at
lower rates of interest. The value of a fixed-rate investment decreases
when overall interest rates increase and the value increases when overall
interest rates decrease. For example, if you own a security paying a fixed
interest rate (say 5 percent), and interest rates are increasing (to more
than 5 percent), your investment will be worth less.

Political Risk

Government actions that affect business conditions are the basis of
political risk. Increased taxes and certain regulations such as environmental controls can make some investments less attractive.

Market Risk and Company or Industry Risk

Market risk, which affects many types of investments at once, is caused
by business declines, sudden national or world events, or interest rate

fluctuations. Company or industry risk is produced by events that affect only one company or industry. For example, if you invest in the candy industry and the nationwide trend is toward dieting or avoidance of sugar, your investment will be adversely affected. Company or industry risk is associated with investments in corporate securities, such as stocks and bonds.

nvestment strategies

Many individuals never start an investment program because they think they don't have enough money. But even small sums of money grow over a period of time. A wise investment results in financial gain, a poor one, financial loss. Investing wisely over a period of time is a difficult and time-consuming task. The suggestions that follow, however, may make this task easier for you.

Criteria for Choosing an Investment

Some investments increase in value at a rate higher than the rate of inflation; some do not. Some investments provide for increases in value that do not show up as taxable income for many years; others do not. The ideal investment would fulfill all of these criteria:
1. Safety (minimal risk of loss)
2. High liquidity
3. High return (investment income)
4. Growth in value that exceeds the inflation rate

5. Reasonable (low) purchase price (or initial cost)
6. Tax benefits

Obviously, you may not find all of these elements in any one investment. However, all your investments should meet as many of these criteria as possible. The more of these criteria that are met, the more desirable the investment. Most of these criteria will be examined in the context of specific types of investments in Chapters 12–15.

Wise Investment Practices

People commonly make one or more serious mistakes in connection with their investment practices. Some mistakes are minor and can be corrected easily; others cause serious financial damage. If you wish to avoid investment mistakes, follow the wise investment practices described below.

Define Your Financial Goals

In Chapter 8 you were introduced to the importance of setting goals as you developed a budget. If you do not clearly define your financial goals, you will not know which investments to purchase to best meet them. To be useful, investment goals must be specific and measurable.

Go Slowly

Before making investment decisions, gather the information you will need to make a wise decision. Don't act on impulse or because something sounds good on the surface. Provide adequate time to obtain and analyze the needed information and to make a sound choice.

Follow Through

Putting off plans and never taking action will lead to failure in meeting financial goals. If a goal is important, it should be worked on in the present, not put off until some future day that may not come. A common mistake is keeping too much money in the "put-and-take" account and not taking advantage of the higher rates of return of permanent investments.

Keep Good Records

In order to keep a clear view of your future needs and goals, you need to keep good financial records. Your personal net worth statement, plus lists of insurance policies and investments, account balances and the location of bank accounts, contents and location of your safe-deposit box, and so on, are essential information. Unless you know where you have been and where you are, it is difficult to plan where you are going.

Seek Good Investment Advice

Don't be afraid to ask questions. Many people think they can make wise investments without seeking and paying for advice from an expert. In the long run, these investments may prove to be expensive, because poor investments can cost a great deal in lost income. In general, it is wise to seek competent advice from a trained professional before making any investment decision.

Keep Investment Knowledge Current

You should be aware of what is new in the financial market, what is or is not a good investment, when to sell, and when to buy. The economy is a major consideration in making investment decisions, and you need to understand how it works and what various economic indicators mean. Although you should seek advice before making a major investment move, it is your responsibility to know when to ask questions and to make any final decisions about the handling of your investments.

ources of financial information

Because there is more information available about most investments than an investor can possibly digest, he or she must be selective in the type of information used for evaluation purposes. Sources of financial information include (a) newspapers, (b) investor services, (c) financial magazines, (d) full-service brokers, (e) financial advisers, and (f) annual reports of corporations.

Newspapers

Most newspapers contain sections called **financial pages.** Reading these pages daily will help you keep track of financial markets and obtain information needed to make wise investment decisions. In addition, *The Wall Street Journal* is a daily publication that provides detailed coverage of financial information needed for wise investing. *Barron's* is a weekly newspaper that also provides charts of trends, financial news items, and technical analysis of financial data.

The most widely reported and followed financial index is the *Dow Jones Industrial Index*. Often called simply *the Dow*, it is an index of the price movements of thirty major industrial corporate stocks listed on the New York Stock Exchange. Separate Dow indexes are maintained

personal perspective

C hoosing the Right Financial Adviser

Choosing the right financial adviser can be tricky. If you choose the wrong adviser, the financial results could be painful. The most important criterion in selecting a financial adviser is *trust*. You must feel comfortable with your adviser, be willing to give him or her a full and complete picture of your finances and financial goals, and then follow his or her advice.

Many people begin their investing with a trusted family friend who is in the business of giving financial advice at a bank, brokerage firm, or other financial institution. You may know someone who can recommend a competent adviser. If so, your choice will be somewhat easier.

Some people consult with financial advisers at credit unions or through employee assistance plans. Others participate in group seminars offered by employers or professional organizations. In many cases, you can get good general advice about investment strategies that are effective for people with investment goals similar to yours.

The trick to finding and building a relationship of trust with a financial adviser involves taking the time to ask questions and to discuss thoroughly your income, assets, liabilities, and financial goals. Be sure to ask potential financial advisers about their training, background, and experience; philosophy of investing; fees (how they earn money); and investment strategies. You also should know how clients have done in the past with their investment recommendations. Ask for copies of references; take them home and read them carefully. Good advisers will tell you about their past successes. You can also check up on the past performance of stockbrokers through the National Association of Securities Dealers. The association monitors complaints and actions taken against its members. Remember: If you don't feel comfortable with a prospective financial adviser, keep looking until you find one who will help you achieve your investment goals.

critical thinking

1. If you needed financial advice, who would you ask? Why?

2. What are the characteristics you would look for in a successful financial adviser? (What would it take to build your trust?)

3. Can you locate the names and addresses of three or more financial advisers in your area?

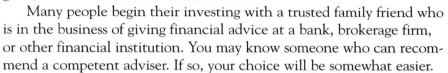

for transportation and public utility stocks. The *New York Stock Exchange (NYSE) Index* includes every stock traded on the New York Stock Exchange. These indices will be explained more fully in Chapter 12.

Investor Services and Newsletters

Companies called **investor services** provide extensive financial data to clients. Main sources of data are *Moody's Investors Service, Standard and Poor's Reports,* and *Value Line.* These publications are found in public libraries and brokerage firms. They contain precise current and historical financial data. Many investors subscribe to weekly or monthly investment newsletters, which give them the latest financial data and information.

Financial Magazines

There are a number of popular weekly and monthly magazines that provide personal financial information. Most of them interpret financial data and give opinions and recommendations. Popular weekly magazines include *Business Week* and *Forbes;* monthly magazines include *Money, Fortune, Kiplinger's Personal Finance,* and *The Economist.*

Full-Service Brokers

Brokers provide clients with analysis and opinions based on their judgments and the opinions of experts in the company they represent. Nevertheless, you cannot expect a broker to pick winners for you every time. Almost all full-line brokerage firms provide monthly market letters giving advice on the purchase and sale of certain securities.

Discount Brokers

Some people are well informed and know what they want to buy and sell. For these investors, there is a service available called discount brokerage. Discount brokers buy and sell securities for clients at a reduced commission. The commission can be half that charged by a full-service broker. A discount broker usually provides little or no investment advice to a client.

Many banks and some savings and loans have discount brokers available to customers desiring to trade securities. In most cases, you will be required to have a checking or savings account at that institution. Money can be transferred from your account to pay for securities purchased, or deposited to your account to reflect securities sold. A bank or savings and loan will also maintain a brokerage account for you, and send you monthly or quarterly account statements showing the current value of your securities.

Financial Advisers

Professional investment planners are called **financial advisers.** They are trained to give intelligent overall investment advice based on your goals, age, net worth, occupation, investment experience, lifestyle, family responsibilities, and other factors. You will be asked to fill out a confidential information packet showing assets, liabilities, net worth, income, and budget as well as your financial goals. The financial adviser usually receives a fee for services rendered, although some advisers receive fees when investment products (such as stocks, bonds, or life policies) are sold. Many people hesitate to use advisers because they are embarrassed about the small amount of money they have to invest. However, financial advisers are available to help most serious investors.

Annual Reports

The **annual report** of a corporation provides the information needed to evaluate that corporation as an investment prospect. The annual report gives the financial history of the company, comparisons of data for several years, and a description of its products and services. In addition, you will find an assessment of the company's future growth plans and prospects, news of any lawsuits against the company, and information about competitors and the company's position in the industry. All major trends are discussed for the company and the industry, including current and future expansions or consolidations that could affect the price or value of the stock.

Most annual reports also include pictures of facilities, officers, and significant events. Charts and graphs are used to display financial trends and comparisons to previous years or similar businesses.

All public corporations are required by the Securities and Exchange Commission (SEC) to publish annual reports. The purpose is full disclosure to stockholders (the owners) and other interested parties (called *stakeholders*). All stockholders of record receive copies of annual reports by mail. If you are interested in investing in a company, or if you would like to know more about a corporation, you can receive a copy of the annual report by writing the company and asking for it. In addition, some large libraries keep copies of annual reports of major corporations on reserve for you to read.

Investment options

For every type of investment opportunity, there are potential investors. And for every potential investor, there are numerous investment choices to make. Once you have established your emergency fund and have some additional money in savings, it's time to consider other investment alternatives. In Chapters 12 through 15, you will explore each type of investment described below more thoroughly.

Stocks and Bonds

Stock represents ownership in a corporation. A *share* of stock is a unit of ownership. The owner of stock is called a *stockholder*. He or she receives a stock certificate, which is evidence of the ownership. When you are a stockholder, you will share in a corporation's profits, which are paid to you as dividends. Investing in stocks is described in detail in Chapter 12.

Bonds are debt obligations of corporations or governments. For example, corporate bonds are issued by public corporations. The corporation pays the owner of the bond a fixed amount of money, called interest, at a fixed interval (usually every six months). The corporation also must repay the *principal,* or amount borrowed, at maturity. The *maturity date* of a bond is the date on which the borrowed money must be repaid. Bonds are explained in detail in Chapter 13.

Government Savings Bonds

When you buy a savings bond, you are in effect lending money to the United States government. A Series EE savings bond is known as a **discount bond.** You buy it for less than its maturity value. The purchase price of a Series EE bond is one half of its maturity value. For example, a $50 bond is purchased for $25; a $100 bond is purchased for $50. At maturity, you receive the full value of the bond. The difference between the purchase price and the maturity value is the amount of interest earned. Generally, EE bonds mature in ten years but can be extended for up to thirty years.

The interest accumulates every six months. Interest is received at the time a bond is cashed in. Interest earned on Series EE bonds is exempt from state and local taxes, and is *not* subject to federal taxation until the bonds are cashed in. These bonds earn a variable rate of interest and have a higher rate of return than regular savings accounts and some CDs.

A Series HH savings bond pays interest semiannually (every six months) and matures in ten years. These bonds can be purchased only in exchange for maturing EE bonds. Series HH bonds may be redeemed at any time after being held for a minimum of six months.

Savings bonds may be purchased from commercial banks or may be acquired through payroll deductions. These purchases are limited to $15,000 ($30,000 maturity value) for individuals and to $30,000 ($60,000 maturity value) for joint owners each year. Savings bond certificates should be stored in a safe-deposit box.

Savings bonds are a good investment because they are considered very safe. Bonds can be quickly and easily converted to cash; their interest is not subject to state or local taxes, only federal; and if they are lost, stolen, or destroyed they can be replaced without cost. Some savings used to finance a college education are free from federal taxation.

Treasury Securities

U.S. Treasury bills (called T-bills) are available in denominations of $10,000, then in increments of $5,000. A Treasury bill is for one year or less; that is, the bill is usually a three-month, six-month, or one-year government obligation. Treasury bills are issued weekly for three- and six-month maturities, and monthly for one-year maturities.

Treasury notes are issued in units of $1,000 or $5,000. Maturities range from two years to ten years. Interest rates for Treasury notes are slightly higher than for Treasury bills.

Treasury bonds are issued in minimum units of $1,000 with maturities that range from ten to thirty years. Interest rates for Treasury bonds are generally higher than interest rates for either T-bills or Treasury notes. Interest paid every six months is taxable for federal income tax purposes, but exempt from state and local income taxes.

Mutual Funds

Suppose you have $500 to invest but do not know which stocks or bonds to buy, when to buy them, or when to sell them. You can buy shares in a large, professionally managed company called a **mutual fund.** A mutual fund pools the money of many investors and buys a large selection of securities that meet the fund's stated investment goals. Two major advantages of a mutual fund to an investor are professional management and diversification, or investment in a wide variety of securities.

Mutual funds are the fastest-growing segment of the United States' financial services industry. Chapter 14 presents a detailed discussion of mutual funds.

Real Estate

Many people like to invest in real estate—houses and land. While this type of investment usually represents a large and often illiquid investment of cash, it has proven to be protection against inflation in some parts of the United States. In some areas, prices of homes have increased faster than the inflation rate. Real estate investments also have tax benefits. Certain costs associated with home ownership are deductible from gross income and therefore lower taxable income. Chapter 14 presents a more in-depth explanation of real estate investing.

Retirement Plans

An **annuity** is a contract or agreement written by an insurance company to provide you with regular income. Generally, you receive income monthly, with payments to continue as long as you live. You usually purchase an annuity contract from a life insurance company. When you buy an annuity, the interest on the principal, as well as the interest compounded on that interest, builds up free of current income tax.

Investments in real estate (houses and land) often offer a measure of protection against inflation.

Taxes are deferred until a person receives payments from an annuity. The payments from an annuity are normally used to supplement retirement income. The annuity is often described as the opposite of life insurance—it pays while you are alive; life insurance pays when you die.

An IRA (*individual retirement account*) is a savings plan whereby an individual sets aside a certain amount of money (up to a specified maximum) each year for retirement. The advantage of an IRA is that the money put into an IRA account each year may be deductible from gross income. You will pay taxes on the IRA when you start withdrawing funds at age 59½ or older.

A Keogh plan is a similar to the IRA but designed more for the self-employed. Available since 1962, Keogh plans allow for larger annual investments than IRAs. Similarly, a Simplified Employee Pension Plan (SEP), introduced in 1979, is aimed at small employers. An employee may contribute to a SEP even if covered by another pension plan; the allowable contribution is higher than for an IRA. Annuities, IRAs, Keogh plans, and SEPs will be discussed in more detail in Chapter 15.

Summary

Investing is a step beyond saving. The process usually involves some risk, but it offers a higher financial return than simply setting money aside in a savings account. An ideal investment would be completely safe, have a high degree of liquidity, and a high rate of return. Investments range from very safe to very risky. The potential return on any investment is directly related to the risk that the investor assumes. Various risks associated with an investment should be carefully considered by an investor.

Wise investment practices include defining goals, moving slowly, following through, keeping good records, getting good advice, and keeping investment knowledge current. Financial information for making good decisions can be found by looking at newspapers, newsletters, and magazines, by consulting full-service brokers and financial advisers, and by reading annual reports of corporations. When reviewing financial information, a potential invester will focus on one or more of the following investment alternatives: stocks, bonds, mutual funds, real estate, and retirement plans. Since investors have more information on investments than most of them can read and comprehend, they must be selective in the type of information they use for making investment decisions.

Vocabulary terms

Directions: Can you find the definition for each of the following terms used in Chapter 11?

annual report
annuity
bonds
discount bond
diversification
financial advisers
financial pages

inflation
investor services
mutual fund
personal investing
risk
stock

1. A bond you purchase for less than its maturity value.
2. A contract whereby you set aside savings to provide future income, such as retirement.
3. The technique of spreading risk among different types of investments.
4. The use of savings to earn a financial return.
5. A rise in the general level of prices.
6. Potential for loss in an investment.
7. A publication that provides information about a company in which you may consider investing.
8. The section of the newspaper that details financial information.
9. Evidence of ownership of a corporation.
10. Companies that provide financial information about companies to investors.
11. Professional investment planners who are trained to give investment advice.
12. An investment that represents the debt of a company or a government.
13. A large, professionally managed company that pools its investors' money and buys a large variety of securities.

Facts and ideas in review

1. Explain the difference between temporary and permanent investments.
2. List at least five reasons for investing money.

3. Briefly describe the types of risks commonly faced by investors.
4. Identify criteria commonly used to select the ideal investment.
5. What are six wise investment practices?
6. What questions might you ask in selecting a financial adviser?
7. Name at least six main sources of financial information.
8. List five magazines providing investment information.
9. What kind of information is typically found in an annual report of a corporation?
10. Explain the difference between stocks and bonds.
11. How does a Series EE savings bond differ from a Series HH bond?
12. Distinguish among T-bills, Treasury notes, and Treasury bonds.
13. List one disadvantage for each of the following:
    a. savings bonds
    b. mutual funds
    c. real estate
    d. IRA

 pplications for decision making

1. Explain the put-and-take concept. Why is it important that money set aside remain a permanent investment? How will you personally design an investment plan? (Will it include a put-and-take account?) Explain.
2. Why is risk such an important consideration when investing? Write a paragraph explaining your comfort level with risk, and how it will affect your investment decisions.
3. Explain why it is *not* possible for one investment to satisfy all the criteria for choosing an investment. Which criteria are most important to you?
4. Read the financial section of your local newspaper. Write a few paragraphs summarizing your findings. In other words, describe the type of information covered and its usefulness to you as an investor.
5. Visit a library and get a copy of a current annual report for a major corporation that does business in your state. Outline the contents of the report and give a brief oral review of your findings to the class.
6. Consult a financial newspaper or magazine and try to find the following information:
    a. the current rate being offered on Series EE savings bonds
    b. the current rate of one-year Treasury bills

c. the current rate of two-year Treasury notes

d. the current rate of thirty-year Treasury bonds

7. Look for current newspaper articles that discuss the real estate market in your area. The real estate section of your Sunday newspaper has extensive current information. Write a paragraph summarizing the prospects for real estate buyers and sellers. Are prices rising or falling in your area? How many homes were sold last month? the previous month?

ife situation problem solving

1. Your friend Amanda, who is nineteen and in college, has just inherited $1,000. The money is not needed for her put-and-take account. What would you tell her to do with it?

2. Rick Felt is considering investing $500. Explain to him what factors he should consider when choosing investment alternatives.

3. Friends of your family, who were recently married, are now finding that they have money left over each month that could be invested. They would like to consult a financial adviser, but don't know one. What tips would you give them about selecting a financial adviser?

4. Lynda Tower would like to invest $10,000 that she inherited from her uncle. She would like to have the money for her daughter's college education starting in eight years. She does not like to take a lot of risk because she cannot afford to lose the $10,000. What course of action would you suggest for Lynda?

5. Johnny McMahon would like to invest in XYZ Corporation. He heard that the company was big and powerful. You've never heard of it. What kinds of information should he have before he invests in this company? Where can he get that information?

6. Choose at least six of the investment alternatives presented in this chapter. Rank the choices from high to low on the factors of safety, risk, and liquidity. Assume that 3 is the highest score and 1 is the lowest score for each factor. Based on the results of your review of possible investments, which three alternatives would *you* select as permanent investments? Why?

objectives:

After reading and studying this chapter you will be able to:

12-1 List the features of common stock and compare it to preferred stock.

12-2 Discuss how to choose the type of stock to buy, what affects the value and price of a stock, and how to compute a stock's return.

12-3 Explain the process of buying and selling stock, including auction exchanges and over-the-counter markets.

12-4 Describe short- and long-term investment strategies when buying and selling stocks.

In the previous chapter you learned why it is important to invest money for the future. Buying and selling stock is an important investment activity for you to consider because potential rewards are high. When you buy stock, you are buying an ownership interest in a company. If the company does well, you may receive a part of the profits. In addition, the value of your stock may increase, which enables you to sell it for a gain. Any stockholder may sell his or her stock to another stockholder. The selling price is determined by how much a buyer is willing to pay. In this chapter, you will learn the ins and outs of buying and selling stock, and whether the stock market best suits your investment strategy.

chapter

Investing in Stocks

12

ypes of stock

Nearly 50 million people in the United States own stocks. There are more than 34,000 publicly held corporations for you to choose from if you decide to become a stockholder (also known as shareholder). A *public corporation* is a company whose stock is traded openly on stock markets.

Stocks are traded in round lots or odd lots. A *round lot* is 100 shares or multiples of 100 shares of a particular stock. An *odd lot* is fewer than 100 shares of a particular stock. Brokerage firms usually charge higher per-share fees for trading in odd lots. Odd lots must be combined into round lots before they actually can be traded.

Common Stock

Common stock is a class of stock in which the owner of the stock shares directly in the success or failure of a business. As a shareholder, you stand to profit when the company profits. You also are entitled to a say in major policy decisions, such as whether to issue additional stock, sell the company to outside buyers, or change the board of directors. The rule is that each share has the same voting power, so the more shares you own, the greater your power.

When the company does well, stockholders receive dividends. **Dividends** are the part of the profits of a corporation that each shareholder receives. A dividend payment must be approved by a corporation's board of directors. Many companies parcel out portions of their annual profits to stockholders in the form of quarterly dividend payments. Dividend payments vary from company to company.

Stockholders can lose all of their investment should the company fail. But one advantage to common stock is that the most a stockholder can lose is his or her investment in the stock. Unlike the owner of a small business where the owner can lose personal assets when the business fails, people who own common stock are not risking other assets.

As a common stockholder, you are legally entitled to vote on major corporate issues. Stockholders may vote in person or by proxy. A **proxy** is a legal form that lists the issues to be decided at a stockholders' meeting and requests that stockholders transfer their voting rights to some individual. When you assign your voting right to someone else, you are giving a proxy. The proxy is valid until you revoke it. As a common stockholder, you can vote for the members of the board of directors. The *board of directors* is a group of people elected by the stockholders to guide a corporation. Annual meetings of stockholders are gatherings of common stockholders who vote on major policies as well as elect the board of directors.

Preferred Stock

In addition to common stock, investors can purchase preferred stock. In **preferred stock,** dividends are fixed, regardless of how the company is doing, making it less risky than common stock. In the event the company fails, the preferred stockholder would be paid first. And like the common stockholder, the preferred stockholder can never lose more than his or her investment in the stock. However, the preferred stockholder does not have voting privileges.

Two types of preferred stock have special features. Please keep in mind that these features will increase the cost of purchasing the stock.

Participating Preferred Stock

The *participating preferred stock* feature works as follows: (1) the required dividend is paid to preferred stockholders; (2) a stated dividend is paid to common stockholders; and (3) the remainder of the earnings available for distribution is shared by both preferred and common stockholders. For example, let's assume the following scenario exists: Company A has 1,000 shares of preferred, and 40,000 shares of common stock outstanding. The preferred stock has a guaranteed annual dividend rate of

5 percent. Dividends are $1 per share for common stock. Total dividends distributed are not to exceed $50,000. When the preferred stock is participating, the dividends for the year would be distributed as follows:

1. Preferred stockholders receive 5 percent on their investment. For the 1,000 shares, valued at $50 per share, the dividend totals $2,500. If you owned 100 shares, your dividend would be $250 ($5,000 × 5 percent).
2. Common stockholders then receive their $1 per share dividend. For 40,000 shares, the dividend totals $40,000. If you owned 100 shares, your dividend would be $400 (100 × $1).
3. The common and preferred stockholders would then receive the balance equally ($50,000 less $42,500 = $7,500). Therefore, preferred stockholders would receive $3,750 ($3,750/1,000 = $3.75 per share) and common stockholders $3,750 ($3,750/40,000 = 9.4 cents per share). If you owned 100 shares of participating preferred stock, your total dividend would be $625.00 ($3.75 × 100 = $375 + 250 = $625). If you owned 100 shares of common stock, your total dividend would be $409.40 ($.094 × 100 = $9.40 + 400 = $409.40).

Cumulative Preferred Stock

If a corporation's board of directors votes not to pay dividends, they can omit dividends paid to both common and preferred stockholders. *Cumulative preferred stock* is a stock issue whose unpaid dividends accumulate and must be paid before any cash dividends are paid to the common stockholders. For example, assume that in 1997 a company has no profits and therefore pays no dividends. In the following year, it has $100,000 available for dividends. Owners of cumulative preferred stock would receive their dividends first, including those that should have been received the previous year, before common stockholders would receive any dividends.

lassification of stock investments

When evaluating common stock investments, investors often classify stocks into different categories. Common categories of stocks include income, growth, penny, blue chip, defensive, and cyclical. Which category is best for you will depend on how much risk you are willing to assume to obtain larger returns on your investments.

Income Versus Growth Stocks

Stocks that have consistent histories of paying high dividends are known as **income stocks.** Investors choose income stocks in order to receive current income in the form of dividends. Preferred stocks pay the most certain and predictable dividend income, and are often the choice of retired people and others investing for income from dividends.

Growth stocks are shares of stock in companies that reinvest their profits into the business so that it can grow and expand. In the long run—ten or twenty years away—these stocks might be worth substantially more than their purchase price today. Growth stocks pay little or no dividends. Investors buy them for the potential increase in value. As such, they are long-term investments. If the value of the stock increases, the stockholder must decide whether to sell it at a high price or continue to hold it. If the stockholder decides to sell, the dollar amount of difference between the purchase and selling price represents a gain.

Penny Versus Blue Chip Stocks

When a stock sells for less than $5 a share, it is classified as a **penny stock.** Although inexpensive, penny stocks are highly speculative. In other words, they can grow substantially in value, or lose all their value if the business does not succeed. Frequently, penny stocks are issued by companies with a "hot" new product or service that may be an enormous success or a total failure.

Blue chip stocks are stocks of large, well-established, and usually profitable businesses. Most people have heard of these companies because their products and services have been around for decades. These companies are in a variety of industries, including automobile production, computer manufacturing, gasoline refining, and banking services.

Defensive Versus Cyclical Stocks

A *defensive stock* is one that remains stable and pays dividends during an economic decline. Generally, companies in this category have a history of stable earnings. A defensive stock is not subject to the ups and downs of business cycles; examples include utilities, drugs, food, and health care. In other words, the demand for these products is consistent regardless of economic conditions; therefore, stocks in these industries protect the investor from sharp losses.

Cyclical stocks do well when the economy is stable or growing, but often poorly during *recessions*, when the economy slows down.

Examples of cyclical stocks are airlines, manufacturing companies, and industries based on travel. For example, if the weather is poor during the month of July when vacations are high, air traffic will be lower and resorts will not do as well. This will result in lower performance for cyclical stocks tied to the travel industry.

A defensive stock, such as a grocery chain, is not sensitive to the ups and downs of business cycles like a cyclical stock (steel manufacturing).

Stock values and the return on an investment

Purchases of shares of stock are evidenced by a stock certificate. The certificate states the number of shares owned, the name of the company issuing the stock, the type of stock (common or preferred), and the par value. The **par value** is an assigned (and often arbitrary) dollar value that is printed on a stock certificate.

When you buy stock you will pay its **market value.** Market value reflects the price investors are willing to pay for a share of stock. How a company currently is doing, its track record, and how well it is expected to perform in the future determine market value. Market value is often very different from par value. Some stocks perform very well, yet their market value seems too low—or a "real bargain." These stocks are called "undervalued." Brokers often think undervalued stocks are worth more than the price for which they are selling. Conversely, stocks can be "overvalued," which means they are selling at a price that is not justified by their earnings potential.

There are several things that affect the price you will pay for a share of stock: the financial situation of a company, current interest rates, the market for a company's products or services, and earnings per share.

1. *The Company.* When a company is performing well (meeting its current obligations and making a profit), the company's stock is attractive. Investors will consider a company's earning power, or its ability to continue to make a strong profit, as well as its debt obligations, or how much the company owes. If the company seems to be in a good financial position, the stock price will continue rising.

2. *Interest Rates.* When interest rates are low, people who would normally put money in savings accounts and certificates of deposit look for more profitable places to invest their money. As interest rates rise, however, people tend to move their money to the safer, less risky, investments. Generally, when interest rates fall below the current rate of inflation, stock prices rise and people buy more stock.

If a company is in a popular industry and products are selling well, the stock's price will rise.

3. *The Market.* The marketplace determines a company's ability to sell its product or service now and in the future. If the company is in a popular industry and products or services are selling well, the stock's price will rise. For example, when people are buying computers, software, and related items, companies in the high-tech industry are considered wise investments. If the demand for a particular product or service declines, the price of the stock will decrease.

4. *Earnings per Share.* **Earnings per share** are a corporation's after-tax earnings divided by the number of common stock shares outstanding. For example, assume that in 1997 XYZ Corporation has after-tax earnings (net profit) of $1,000,000. XYZ Corporation has 100,000 shares of common stock outstanding. Therefore, the earnings per share are $10 ($1,000,000/100,000 = $10). Most stockholders consider the amount of earnings per share important because the computation is a measure of a company's profitability.

How do you make money by buying stock? There are two ways. An investment in common stock can increase in value through dividends and price appreciation, as shown in Figure 12-1. Dividends are usually paid in the form of cash or additional shares of stock. Appreciation occurs when a stockholder purchases a stock and then holds on to it for a period of time.

The *return* is how much money you make from your investment. The return is the difference between what you paid for the stock and what you sold it for, plus any dividends you earned. When computing the return, any commission paid to the stockbroker must be added to the purchase price of the stock. Most brokerage firms have a minimum commission for buying and selling stock. Additional commissions are based on the number of shares and the value of the stock bought or sold.

Computing a Stock's Return

Figuring a stock's one-year return:

$$\frac{\text{Current Price} + \text{Dividends}}{\text{Purchase Price} + \text{Commission}} - 1 \times 100 = \text{Return on Investment}$$

Example: Current stock price: $40/share
Dividends received during the year: $1/share
Purchase price: $38/share
Stockbroker's commission: $125
Number of shares owned: 100

Computations:

$$\frac{(100 \times \$40) + (100 \times 1)}{(100 \times \$38) + 125} - 1 \times 100$$

$$\frac{4,000 + 100}{3,800 + 125} = \frac{4,100}{3,925} = 1.04458 - 1 = .04458 \times 100 = 4.46\%$$

Fig. 12-1

Computing a Stock's Return

he securities market

A securities market is where you buy and sell securities—stocks and bonds. To purchase common or preferred stock, you must work through a broker. Then your broker will buy or sell for you in a securities market-place, which is either a securities exchange or the over-the-counter market.

Bull and Bear Markets

The stock market goes through cycles. For a period of time, stocks go up in value. Then the market corrects itself as people sell (to make a profit) and stock prices decrease. A **bull market** is characterized by rising stock prices and a general feeling of investor optimism. Optimism about how the country is doing also serves to drive up stock prices.

A **bear market** develops when investors are pessimistic about the overall economy and start to sell stocks. Bear markets are characterized by a period of falling stock prices of perhaps 15 percent or more. Bear markets are usually short and savage. The average bull market often lasts three to four times as long as a bear market.

Securities Exchanges

A **securities exchange** is a marketplace where brokers who are representing investors meet to buy and sell securities. The largest organized exchange in the United States is the New York Stock Exchange (NYSE). The smaller American Stock Exchange is also in New York City. Ten other regional exchanges are located throughout the country. To have a stock listed with the NYSE, a company must have at least 1.1 million publicly owned shares with a market value of at least $9 million. For the American Stock Exchange, the minimum is 250,000 shares worth $2.5 million.

The New York Stock Exchange is in a big building at the corner of Wall and Broad Streets in New York City. The trading floor (where stocks are bought and sold) is about two-thirds the size of a football field. Around the edge of the trading floor are booths with computer terminals that are open at both ends, with room inside for a dozen or more floorbrokers. **Floorbrokers** buy and sell stocks on the exchange. Only brokers who are members of the exchange may do business there.

Spaced at regular intervals around the trading floor are trading posts, which are horseshoe-shaped counters, each occupying about 100 square feet on the floor. Behind each counter are *specialists*—the brokers to the floorbrokers. All buying and selling is done around trading posts. About ninety different stocks are assigned to each post. Post display units above each counter show which stocks are sold in each section, the last price of that stock, and whether that price represents an increase or a decrease from the previous price.

Orders received at a brokerage firm are phoned or sent by computer to that firm's booth at the exchange. A message is printed out and is given to the floorbroker to carry out. When the transaction is completed, the clerks for the brokers who bought and sold the stock report back to their respective brokerage firms. The buyer and seller can then be advised that the transaction has been concluded.

The exchange is a form of *auction market* where buyers and sellers are brought together to trade securities. Stock trading happens auction-style because in every transaction, stock is sold to the highest bidder (buyer) and bought from the lowest offerer (seller). Securities listed with the NYSE are traded only during official trading hours—9:30 a.m. to 4 p.m. New York time, Monday through Friday (except holidays).

Over-the-Counter Market

When securities are bought and sold through brokers, but not through a stock exchange, the transaction is over-the-counter (OTC). The **over-the-counter (OTC) market** is a network of brokers who buy and sell the securities of corporations that are not listed on a securities exchange. Brokers in the OTC market do not deal face-to-face. Their marketplace is as large as the number of desks with brokers at work that day. Trades with other brokers are completed by telephone, and a computerized system displays current price quotations on a terminal in a broker's office. Brokers operating in the OTC market use an electronic quotation system called NASDAQ. (The letters were originally an acronym for the National Association of Securities Dealers Automated Quotation System.) To be listed with NASDAQ, companies must have issued at least 100,000 shares of stock worth $1 million.

nvestment strategies

Once stock has been acquired, your investment may be either short or long term. Generally, if you buy and sell stock within a short period of time, you are considered a speculator, or trader. If you hold your investment for a long period of time (a year or more), you are considered an investor.

Short-Term Techniques

When you buy and sell stocks for quick profits, you are "playing the stock market." The goal is to buy a stock that will soon increase in value. Then, when the price rises, the stock is sold. Many investors realize short-term gains through processes called buying on margin and selling short.

Buying on Margin

You can borrow money from your broker to buy stock if you open a margin account and sign a contract called a margin agreement. To establish a margin account, you must deposit a minimum of $2,000 in cash or eligible securities (securities your broker considers valuable collateral) with a broker. Let's assume you have $2,000 in your margin account. You want to buy 100 shares of XYZ Corporation at $20 per share ($2,000). You could use $1,000 from your margin account and borrow $1,000, with interest, from your broker. This strategy is called *leverage*. You use less of your own money and therefore can buy more stocks with less cash. You would still have $1,000 in your margin account to use toward another purchase on margin.

With a margin purchase, you are betting that the stock will increase in value. When it does, you sell the stock, repay the loan, and take your short-term profit. Figure 12-2 shows how margin buying works.

Fig. 12-2

Buying on Margin

Buying on Margin

Example: You buy $2,000 worth of stock with $1,000 of your own money and $1,000 borrowed from your broker at 6% annual interest. The stock increases in value and is sold after 60 days for $2,800. Your broker's commission to buy and sell is $200.

Profit or Gain:

Selling price: $2,800
Less costs: $1,000 (purchase price) + $1,000 (amount borrowed) + $10* (interest) + $200 (commission)

$2,800 − (1,000 + 1,000 + 10 + 200) = $590 profit

$$* \ \$1,000 \times .06 \times \frac{60}{360} = \$10 \text{ interest}$$

Rate of Return:

$$\frac{\text{Gain:}}{\text{Cost Basis:}} \ \frac{590}{2,210} = 26.7\%$$

global connection

T okyo, a Financial Power House

One of the leading stock exchanges in the world is the Tokyo Stock Exchange. The exchange, together with the city's many banks, make Tokyo the financial center of Japan. The Tokyo Stock Exchange handles the stocks of over 1,300 Japanese and foreign companies, more than are handled by the New York Stock Exchange.

Tokyo's banking industry is the major source of loans for businesses throughout Japan. The Bank of Japan is the nation's central bank; its headquarters is in Tokyo. The bank is controlled by the national government of Japan, and the government regulates the nation's entire banking system. In addition, Tokyo has many commercial banks that rank as the world's largest and most influential in terms of both assets and accounts held, and loans made throughout the world. These banks have branches throughout Japan and the world.

Nearly 3,000 companies in Tokyo export products to other countries. These companies account for half the country's export business. The Tokyo Trade Center, a forty-story building, displays Japanese goods for foreign buyers.

Within the city of Tokyo are more than 80,000 factories that manufacture products for sale around the world. Most factories are small, employing fewer than 25 people. There are several large companies as well. Total manufacturing jobs employ more than 1.5 million workers in the city of Tokyo.

Like major cities everywhere, Tokyo also has problems such as overcrowding, traffic, and water pollution. Tokyo's location makes it subject to both floods and earthquakes. Transportation can be very difficult in a city with 2 million registered motor vehicles and more cars than the freeways and streets can handle. Severe traffic jams are common. Air pollution from the traffic makes breathing difficult for traffic police officers, and they often must take oxygen after work. Tokyo is seeking ways to improve mass transit and reduce air, noise, and water pollution.

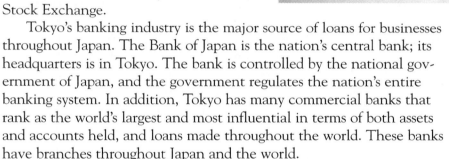

critical thinking

1. Describe the city in which you live in terms of jobs, exports, and problems that need to be solved.

2. What suggestions could you make to Tokyo for solving its traffic and pollution problems?

3. How are Tokyo's problems similar to many of America's large cities?

Unfortunately, if the value of the stock does not increase, you will have to make up the difference. When the market value of a margined stock decreases to approximately one-half of the original purchase price, the investor will receive a margin call from the broker. After the margin call, the investor must pledge additional cash or securities to serve as collateral for the loan. If you don't have the cash, the stock is sold and the proceeds are used to pay the loan.

Selling Short

Selling short is selling stock borrowed from a broker that must be replaced at a later time. To sell short, you borrow a stock certificate for a certain number of shares from the broker. When you sell short, you sell the borrowed stock knowing that you must cover your short position at a later date. When the stock price drops, you cover your position by buying the stock at a lower price than the price it sold for. You then use the stock purchased to replace the stock borrowed from the broker.

A price decrease is especially important to the short seller, who must replace the stock borrowed from the broker with stock purchased at a later date. If the stock increases in value, the short seller will lose money because he or she must replace the borrowed stock with stock purchased at a higher price. Figure 12-3 shows how selling short works. There is usually no broker fee for selling short. The firm receives a commission when the stock is bought and sold.

Fig. 12-3 **Selling Short**	**Selling Short** Example: You borrow 100 shares of stock of XYZ Corporation from your broker. You then sell 100 shares of XYZ at $28 per share and pay a $100 commission (100 shares @ $28 = $2,800 – 100 = $2,700). Two weeks later, the stock price drops to $22. You buy 100 shares at $22 per share and pay a $100 commission (total cost: $2,300). You return a stock certificate for 100 shares of XYZ to your broker. Profit or Gain: $2,700 – 2,300 = $400 profit Rate of Return: $$\frac{400}{2,300} = 17.4\%$$

Long-Term Techniques

As you may already suspect, investing in the stock market for short-term gains can be extremely risky. You cannot beat the market all of the time, but you can make some healthy profits if you study and follow the market carefully. People who buy and then sell stocks with a short time period are called *speculators*, or traders. Most financial consultants advise you to invest for the long term. Records have shown that stock investments have consistently beat rates for savings accounts, CDs, and other conservative options over the long term. People who hold stocks for a long period of time are referred to as *investors*.

Buy and Hold

Most investors consider stock purchases as long-term investments. A stock may go up in value over time. If you sell stock when the price is low, you can lose money. But people who "buy and hold" know that after a number of years the stock will gain value. In addition, many issues of stock pay dividends. Dividends declared by a board of directors provide steady income to stockholders. Stocks that have a history of paying regular dividends are frequently purchased by investors who prefer a steady, predictable source of income.

A stock split also can add to the value of the stock over time. A *stock split* occurs when a company increases shares outstanding, but lowers the selling price in direct proportion. For example, if there were 1,000 shares outstanding with a market value of $60, then a 2:1 (two for one) stock split would result in 2,000 shares outstanding selling for $30. You will notice that the stock is still worth a total of $60,000. A stock split lowers the selling price of a stock and encourages more stock purchasing activity. A lower per-share price makes the shares more affordable. Per-share price sometimes rises as investors buy more stock at the lower price.

Dollar-Cost Averaging

This technique involves the systematic purchase of an equal dollar amount of the same stock at regular intervals. For example, the investor might purchase $100 worth of stock every quarter for one year. When an average is taken (total amount invested divided by total number of shares purchased), the process usually provides a lower average cost per share. See Figure 12-4 on the power of dollar-cost averaging.

Investors who use this technique avoid the situation of buying high and selling low. With dollar-cost averaging, the investor can make a profit if the selling price per share is higher than the average cost per share.

Fig. 12-4

Dollar-Cost Averaging

Dollar-Cost Averaging

Monthly investment amount		Share price ($)		Number of shares
$100	÷	10	=	10
$100	÷	7	=	14.29
$100	÷	5	=	20
$100	÷	10	=	10
$400		$32		54
Total $ invested				Total number of shares

Average share price = $8
$32 ÷ 4

Your average cost per share = $7.41
total $ invested ($400) ÷ total number of shares (54)

Ending value = $540
last share price ($10) x number of shares (54)

Direct Investment and Dividend Reinvestment

With *direct investment*, investors can buy stock directly from a corporation. Often the broker fee is reduced or absorbed by the corporation issuing the stock. With *dividend reinvestment*, dividends can be used to purchase new shares of stock, a method that also avoids a broker fee. For the investor who wants to purchase more stock, these are effective ways to reduce fees associated with buying and selling stock.

tock listings

To make wise investments in the stock market, you will need to track the progress of your chosen investments to see how they are performing. Whether you are reading *The Wall Street Journal* or the financial section of your local newspaper, you should see a listing similar to Figure 12-5 of the stocks that are bought and sold on stock exchanges or over-the-counter. Below the figure, each column is explained so you can understand its meaning.

| Fig. 12-5 | | **Reading the Stock Transactions** |

Reading the Stock Transactions

Excerpt from stock exchange listings:

52 wks High	Low	Stock	Div	Yld %	P/E Ratio	Sales 100s	High	Low	Close	Net Chg.
1	2	3	4	5	6	7	8	9	10	11
58⅞	44	Enger	2.20	4.7	12	109	46⅜	45½	46	−½
45	23	Enger pf	2.25	8.8	10	25	26½	24	25⅜	+⅜
10½	9	Entled	.10	1.0	3	8	10⅛	9½	10	--
24	16	Epsco	1.00	5.0	7	12	21	19	20	+⅞
6⅜	4	ExcLabs	--	--	15	300z	5¾	5⅛	5½	--
57	32	EzemBr	2.50	5.7	11	48	46	43	44	+1

Columns 1 and 2. These columns show the highest and lowest price this stock sold for during the year. For the stock highlighted, the high for the last 52 weeks was 57 and the low was 32. This means the stock sold for $57 a share at one point (high) and $32 a share at another (low).

Column 3. This column lists stocks alphabetically by name. You will notice that stocks are abbreviated. You may see additional abbreviations, such as "pf" which means preferred stock beside the name of the stock. There will be a legend at the bottom of the page that explains what these abbreviations mean. For example, a small "s" means that the stock has recently split. When a stock splits, each share owned is traded for additional shares. A 2:1 split would double your shares. If you owned ten shares worth $50 each, you would now own twenty shares worth $25 each.

Column 4. This column shows the cash dividend per share that is estimated for the year listed in dollars and cents. In the highlighted column, $2.50 means that if you owned 100 shares of this company, you would receive a yearly dividend of $250.

Column 5. Yld % stands for percent yield, or the percentage of the current price the dividends represent. In other words, divide the amount of annual dividends (Column 4) by the closing price (Column 10).

Column 6. The P/E ratio (price/earnings ratio) is the price of a share of stock divided by the corporation's earnings per share over the

To make wise choices in the stock market, you will have to track the progress of your investments.

last twelve months. For example, if XYZ Corporation's stock is selling for $50 per share and XYZ's earnings per share are $10, the P/E ratio is $5 ($50/$10 = $5). The price earnings ratio is a key factor that serious investors use to evaluate stock investments. A low P/E indicates a good investment, and a high P/E indicates a poor one.

Column 7. This column shows sales in hundreds of shares from the previous day—how many shares of stock were bought and sold. Multiply the number by 100 to get the number of shares.

Columns 8, 9, and 10. These columns show the highest, lowest, and closing price for this stock on the previous day. The closing price is the final price at the end of trading for the day.

Column 11. This column, called "net change," compares the closing price today with the closing price of the day before. A minus means the price has gone down. A plus means the price has risen. Stocks that have a price change of more than 5 percent are in boldface.

You will notice there are fractions throughout the columns ($\frac{1}{8}$, $\frac{1}{2}$, $\frac{3}{8}$, $\frac{3}{4}$, $\frac{7}{8}$, and so on). These are fractions of a dollar. Therefore, a stock with a price of 23\frac{7}{8}$ would be selling for $23.875 per share. You would not round to the nearest penny until you multiplied the per-share price times the number of shares bought or sold. For example, 100 of those shares bought at 23\frac{7}{8}$ would cost $2,387.50 (100 × 23$\frac{7}{8}$).

Keeping track of your *stock portfolio* (or stock holdings) can be as simple as checking the closing prices periodically. Some people only check their investments once a year to see if changes should be made to their portfolio. Investors might buy additional shares, sell, or choose a different type of stock after checking their portfolio. The stocks shown in Figure 12-6 have been tracked for ten days straight.

As you can see, some stocks have done better than others in terms of market value as of a certain date. But remember, this chart does not

Fig. 12-6 **Stock Progress Chart**

Stock Progress Chart

Stock Names	Closing Prices for 10 days										Total Change (+ or –)
	1	2	3	4	5	6	7	8	9	10	
1. Enger	28	28¼	29	28	27	28	28½	29	29½	30	+2
2. Glastn	38	40	41	41½	--	40	39	38	38	38	0
3. Karbr pf	61	61¼	61⅛	61	61⅜	61	62	60⅜	61	61⅛	+ ⅛
4. Maxln	50⅛	49	50	50½	51	51	51⅛	52	52	53½	+3⅜
5. Totlmb	10	11	11⅛	11½	11	10⅞	10	9	8	8½	–1½

take into account dividends received or the appreciation in value since a stock was purchased. The stock progress chart is merely a device for monitoring changes in the closing prices of stocks.

Summary

There are two types of stocks: common and preferred. Common stockholders are "owners" of a company, with voting rights. If the company makes a profit, dividends are frequently paid to stockholders. Preferred stockholders have first rights to dividends. Dividend payments to common stockholders must be approved by a corporation's board of directors.

There are several classifications of stocks. Income stocks pay regular dividends, while growth stocks offer the investor hope that the market value of these stocks will "grow," or increase over time. Penny stocks are inexpensive and highly speculative, while blue chip stocks are very safe investments that generally attract conservative investors. Defensive stocks usually maintain a stable market value during declines in the economy, while cyclical stocks follow the business cycle of advances and declines in the economy.

A stock certificate shows the number of shares owned, the issuing company, the par value, and the type of stock being issued. Market value is what you can buy and sell the stock for in the marketplace.

The par value is an assigned (and often arbitrary) dollar value that is printed on a stock certificate. The price paid for stock depends on the financial situation of a company, current interest rates, the market for a product or service, and earnings per share. A stock's return is computed based on dividends as well as appreciation in value.

The securities market is where stocks and bonds are bought and sold. A bull market develops when investors are optimistic, while a bear market reflects pessimism. The New York Stock Exchange and the American Stock Exchange are auction markets where stock brokers buy and sell stocks for their clients. NASDAQ (over-the-counter market) is a dealer market. NASDAQ is a network of brokers who buy and sell the securities of corporations that are not listed on a securities exchange.

Short-term investing techniques include buying stock on margin and selling short. Long-term investing requires that you keep stocks for a number of years. Long-term strategies include "buy and hold," dollar-cost averaging, direct investment, and dividend reinvestment.

Stock listings appear in the *Wall Street Journal* and in the financial section of your local newspaper. Most daily newspapers contain information about stocks listed on the major exchanges and stocks of local interest.

ocabulary terms

Directions: Can you find the definition for each of the following terms used in Chapter 12?

bear market   *income stocks*
blue chip stock   *market value*
bull market   *over-the-counter market*
common stock   *par value*
dividends   *penny stock*
earnings per share   *preferred stock*
floorbroker   *proxy*
growth stocks   *securities exchange*

1. A class of stock whereby the person who owns the stock shares directly in the success or failure of a company.
2. Assigning your vote, as a common stockholder, to another person.
3. Stocks that pay higher than average dividends.
4. A stock that sells for less than $5 a share.
5. The price investors are willing to pay for a stock.
6. A person who buys and sells stocks on the stock exchange.
7. A market that develops when investors are optimistic about the overall economy and purchase stocks.
8. A part of the corporation's profits paid to stockholders.
9. A type of stock in which dividends are fixed and there are no voting privileges.
10. Shares of stock in companies that reinvest their profits into the business so the company can grow and expand.
11. A very safe investment in well-established companies that generally attracts conservative investors.
12. An assigned (often arbitrary) dollar value printed on a stock certificate.
13. A market that develops when investors are pessimistic about the overall economy and sell stocks.
14. A corporation's after-tax earnings divided by the number of shares of common stock outstanding.
15. A marketplace where brokers who are representing investors meet to buy and sell securities.
16. A network of stockbrokers who buy and sell securities of corporations that are not listed on a securities exchange.

end-of-chapter activities

Facts and ideas in review

1. How is common stock different from preferred stock?
2. List the two types of preferred stock and briefly explain each type.
3. Who should purchase income stocks? growth stocks?
4. Which involves the greatest risk—penny stocks or blue chip stocks? Explain the differences between the two types of stocks.
5. Why are defensive stocks not subject to the usual ups and downs of business cycles?
6. Explain the relationship between par value and market value.
7. What causes stock prices to rise and fall? List four factors that affect stock prices.
8. What characterizes a bull market? a bear market?
9. Which is the largest stock exchange in the United States? How does a company get listed on this exchange?
10. What is an auction market (the NYSE)?
11. Why would a stock be listed on the NASDAQ rather than the NYSE or American Stock Exchange?
12. Explain two short-term strategies for investing in stocks.
13. Explain three techniques for long-term investing.
14. In stock listings, what do these symbols stand for: P/E, "S," pf?

Applications for decision making

1. If you own 100 shares of common stock, which you purchased for $28 a share, and a cash dividend of $.88 is declared for the quarter, how much will you receive in dividends?
2. Common stockholders take more risk but have a higher rate of return than preferred stockholders. Explain why.
3. Assume a company has issued the following stock:

   2,000 shares of 5 percent preferred stock at $50 per share
   18,000 shares of common stock at $22 per share

   A cash dividend of $1.30 per share is declared for common stock, after preferred stockholders have received their 5 percent dividend. Compute your total cash dividends for the year if you own:
   a. 100 shares of preferred stock.
   b. 100 shares of common stock.
   c. 50 shares of preferred stock and 50 shares of common stock.

4. If you had an extra $1,000 that you just inherited from a rich uncle, which type of common stock investment would you choose? Explain why.

5. Investing in blue chip stocks is said to be a conservative choice. Can you list several well-known stocks that are considered blue chip? (Hint: Read through the listing of stocks in the financial pages and mark the stocks you recognize. You'll find companies like Coca Cola, General Motors, AT&T, Exxon, and so on. Might these companies be considered blue chip?)

6. Choose a company you would like to learn more about. If it is a large company that is listed on the New York or American Stock Exchanges, you can find information about it in a library or from an annual report. Gather information about the company of your choice and write a report about it—its financial stability, what it produces or sells, and your opinion of its prospects for future success.

7. If you purchased 100 shares of stock in January for $48 a share, received dividends of $1.25 per share on April 1 and July 1, $.95 per share on September 1, and sold the stock in December for $50 a share, what would be the stock's return in one year? Assume a broker commission of 3% on the purchase and sale of the stock.

8. Study the history of bull and bear markets. List the years and months when each type of market occurred during the 1980s and 1990s. Why is it important to understand bull and bear market trends?

9. You have $2,500 in cash in a margin account. You decide to buy stock on margin. You buy 50 shares of stock selling at $100 per share. Assume that the stock rises in value, and thirty days later you sell the stock for $110 a share. Interest on the amount borrowed is 7%. The commission on the purchase and sale is $150. What is the total rate of return?

10. You wish to sell short. You arrange to borrow a stock certificate from your broker for 100 shares of XYZ Corporation on January 2, 1997. You immediately sell 100 shares of XYZ at $60 per share. On April 1, 1997, you instruct your broker to purchase 100 shares of XYZ at $53 per share. You return the stock certificate for 100 shares of XYZ to your broker. Assume the commission was $200. What is the total return on this transaction?

1. Your friend Ashley is considering investing in stocks. She has an extra $5,000 that she wants to invest. She won't need the money for at least five years when she hopes to start medical school. Which of these choices would you recommend—common or preferred? Explain why.

2. Mr. and Mrs. Reynolds are in their late fifties and plan to retire within the next three to five years. They would like to put some of their money into the stock market because interest rates on savings accounts are low. Which of these options would you recommend to them? Give a brief reason for each choice.
   a. income or growth stocks?
   b. penny stocks or blue chip stocks?
   c. defensive or cyclical stocks?

3. Bill Candido has just been given a gift from his grandmother— ten shares of stock in a leading manufacturing company. In the upper right corner, the certificate states PAR VALUE, $10 per share. Bill is confused. His grandmother told him that the closing price for the stock was $50 per share on the day he received the gift. Explain this difference.

4. Jill Rogers bought a stock one year ago. Since then, she has received quarterly dividends of $.50/share. Her fifty shares are now worth $35 each. She paid $29 per share, plus a commission of $180. What is her return? Would you advise her to keep or to sell the stock?

5. Andy and June have been married for less than a year. They are considering buying some stock to have a "nest egg" for their future children. Andy prefers to buy stock in a local company that is small and just getting started. June prefers to buy the stock of a well-known company that is listed on a major exchange. Discuss with them the pros and cons of each course of action.

6. Choose for yourself three types of stocks: one listed on the NYSE, one on the AMEX, and one on the NASDAQ. Pretend that you invested $1,000 in each stock. Compare the closing price for the day on which you purchased each stock to the closing price for each stock approximately three weeks later. Analyze your findings. (What might you have done differently?)

I n the previous chapter, you learned about investing in stocks. In this chapter, you will learn about the different types of bonds, how to buy and sell bonds, and when and why you might choose particular bonds. Stocks and bonds are often mentioned in the same breath, but they represent different kinds of investments. Bonds may seem less glamorous than stocks because, for years, their prices fluctuated less dramatically. And, unlike stock dividends, interest payments on bonds do not increase when a company's profits rise. Today, perceptions of bonds are changing because bond prices tend to fluctuate as much as or more than stock prices. And the bond market, in terms of dollar volume traded, is many times larger than the stock market.

chapter

Investing in Bonds

13

C orporate bonds

While a corporation may use both bonds and stocks to finance business activities, there are two important distinctions between the two. Bonds must be repaid at maturity. Common and preferred stock do not need to be repaid. Interest payments on bonds are mandatory. Dividend payments to stockholders are at the judgment of the board of directors.

Maturity indicates when the bond expires (is "due") and will be repaid. Bond maturities vary widely. Loans can last a year or less or continue for thirty or more years. **Face value** is the amount the bondholder will be repaid when the loan ends. Face value is commonly $1,000. Face value is also referred to as par value.

Corporations may use both stocks and bonds to finance business activities.

Features of Corporate Bonds

Corporate bonds are sold on the open market through brokers just like stocks. Prices asked for bonds appear daily in *The Wall Street Journal* and the financial pages of major newspapers. However, only a tiny fraction of the bonds issued are listed in the newspaper. Bonds are considered "fixed-income investments." A specified amount of interest will be paid on a regular basis. *Interest rate* is the percentage of face value that will be paid in interest to the bondholder on a regular basis. For example, a $1,000 bond might pay 5 percent, or $50 a year. Interest received on money loaned to corporations is fully taxable. Interest earned must be reported as ordinary income on an individual's income tax return. However, the interest paid by a corporation on its bonds is a tax-deductible expense and thus can be used to reduce the taxes a corporation must pay.

You may hear bonds referred to with regard to interest payments as either registered or coupon. A *registered bond* is recorded in the owner's name by the issuing company. Interest checks for registered bonds are mailed semiannually directly to the bondholder of record. A *coupon bond* (also called *bearer bond*) is not registered by the issuing company. To collect interest on a coupon bond, bondholders must clip a coupon and then cash in the coupon at a bank following the procedures outlined by the issuer. Today, most bonds are registered in the holder's name and have no coupons. Bonds with coupons are assumed to belong to whomever possesses ("bears") them. Therefore, if a bond is lost or stolen, interest on it may be collected and it can be redeemed by anyone who has it. For this reason, only "older" bonds are on the market as bearer bonds. Newly issued bonds are always registered.

Many investors have questions about the safety of corporate bonds. Bonds are rated as to their safety. A bond with an AAA rating is the best quality. Highly rated bonds are relatively safe from the risk of default. A *default* occurs when a company is unable to meet its financial obligations. Because corporate bonds are not insured, an investor can lose the investment if a company fails.

A major disadvantage for individual investors is the cost of bonds. Very few corporate bonds are sold in denominations or units of less than $1,000. Bonds are commonly sold in units of $5,000. Bond purchases by an individual investor require a large sum of cash.

A bond may be issued with a call provision. A **callable bond** can be recalled, or paid off, before its maturity date. The date when a bond can be called is identified at the time it is offered for sale. For example, a ten-year bond issued in 1994 with a maturity date of 2004 may be callable in the year 1999. If interest rates have dropped substantially since the bond was issued, the corporation may call the bonds. Corporations usually agree *not* to call bonds for the first five years after issuance. When a call feature is exercised, the corporation generally pays the bondholders a slight premium—an amount above the face value of the bond. A $1,000 bond may be called at 102, or for $1,020.

Types of Corporate Bonds

For corporations, bonds are a primary way of raising capital. The money raised pays for expansion, modernization, and operating expenses. The three types of corporate issues to choose from are debentures, mortgage bonds, and convertible bonds.

Debentures

Debentures are corporate bonds that are backed by the general credit standing of a corporation. In other words, the issuer does not put up any specific assets to assure repayment of the loan. An investor relies on the full faith and credit of the issuer for repayment of the interest and principal. When issued by reliable corporations, debentures are usually relatively safe investments.

Mortgage Bonds

A **mortgage bond,** sometimes called a secured bond, is backed by a specific asset. In the event of a corporation's failure to repay the loan as agreed, the bondholder may claim the property used as security for the debt. The asset or collateral used for security is typically real estate.

Convertible Bonds

A **convertible bond** is one that can be exchanged, at the owner's option, for a specified number of shares of a corporation's common stock. If the bondholder converts to common stock, the corporation no longer must redeem the bond at maturity. Each bond is convertible into a certain number of common shares at a specific price per share. For example, you purchase a $1,000 corporate bond convertible to fifty shares of the company's common stock. You can convert the bond to stock whenever the price of the company's common stock is $20 ($1,000/50 shares = $20) or higher. Assume the company's stock is selling for $22. In this situation, you would have an investment worth $1,100 on conversion ($22 × 50 shares = $1,100).

Earnings on Corporate Bonds

All bonds are issued with a stated face value and interest rate. Figure 13-1 shows interest payments on a $10,000, ten-year, 6 percent corporate bond. Let's assume that the bond is issued January 1, 1995, and interest payments are due June 30 and December 31 of each year. The **maturity date** of the bond is when the principal (face value) must be

Fig. 13-1

Earnings on a Ten-Year Corporate Bond

Year	June 30 Interest	December 31 Interest
1	$300.00	$300.00
2	300.00	300.00
3	300.00	300.00
4	300.00	300.00
5	300.00	300.00
6	300.00	300.00
7	300.00	300.00
8	300.00	300.00
9	300.00	300.00
10	300.00	300.00

January 1, 2005: $10,000 principal is repaid

repaid in full. This ten-year bond would have a maturity date of January 1, 2005, or ten years from the date of issue.

The return on the bond in Figure 13-1 is 6 percent. The yield is also 6 percent; in other words, there is no compounding effect. Simple interest is paid every six months.

However, once a bond has been issued, its market value may be above or below its face value. For example, a $10,000 bond may sell for more than that amount if interest rates are falling. People would be willing to pay more for the bond because it pays an interest rate higher than the current market rate. When bonds sell for more than their face value, they are selling at a **premium.** A $10,000 bond selling for $10,000 is at 100 percent of its face value, or "1." But if the bond sold for "104," there would be a premium of 4 percent. At 104, the purchase price would be $10,400. In this case, the yield would be lower than 6 percent because the purchaser had to pay more than face value to buy the bond.

Bonds also can sell below face value. For example, investors are not willing to pay face value for a bond yielding 6 percent when interest rates are rising. Therefore, the bond may have to be sold at a **discount,** or for an amount lower than face value, to entice buyers. If a bond sold for 96, that would indicate a 4 percent discount. The purchaser of the bond would pay only $9,600 for a $10,000 bond. In this case, the yield to the purchaser would be higher than 6% because less than the face value was paid for the bond.

Figure 13-2 shows how to compute the yield on bonds when they are issued at a premium or at a discount. Yield is not the same thing as the interest rate. In fact, yield may be higher or lower than the bond's stated interest rate, as indicated in Figure 13-2.

Fig. 13-2

Earnings on a Ten-Year Corporate Bond

$$\text{Current yield} = \frac{\text{Interest amount}}{\text{Market value}}$$

	Interest	Yield
If you buy the $1,000 bond at face value	$60	6%
If you buy the bond at 104	$60	5.8%*
If you buy the bond at 96	$60	6.3%*

*Current yield is computed by dividing the annual interest dollar amount of a bond by its current market price ($60/$1,040 and $60/$960).

overnment bonds

In addition to loaning money to corporations, you also can loan money to the government. Government bonds can be issued by the federal as well as state or local government. There are five major types of government bonds: municipal, general obligation, Treasury, savings bonds, and federal agency bonds.

Municipal Bonds

Bonds issued by state and local governments are called **municipal bonds.** The minimum investment in a municipal bond is $5,000, although brokers often ask for a multiple of this amount as a minimum investment. Municipal bonds, often called "munis," can be backed by specific projects, or by the general taxing authority of a revenue-generating governmental unit. For example, a **revenue bond** is repaid from the revenues (income) generated by a special project. Major projects financed by revenue bonds include airports, hospitals, toll roads, and public housing facilities.

Major projects financed by revenue bonds include airports, hospitals, and toll roads.

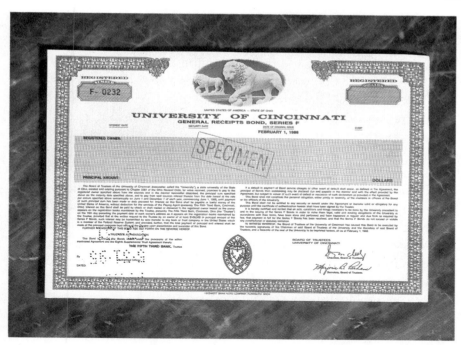

Municipal bonds are often exempt from state and federal taxes.

A **general obligation bond** (or GO) is backed by the full faith and credit of the issuing government unit. In other words, general obligation bonds are secured by the power of state and local governments to levy taxes. As an example, school districts issue bonds to finance construction of new buildings. A city may issue bonds to pay for the cost of a new police or administrative center. States will issue bonds to pay for a new college campus or the development of a new road system.

Municipal bonds generally pay a lower rate of interest than corporate bonds. However, the interest is exempt from federal taxes, so the effective rate is often higher. Municipal bonds exempt from federal taxation also are generally exempt from state and local taxes in the state where they are issued. As Figure 13-3 shows, a person in a 28 percent federal tax bracket is better off with a municipal than a corporate bond, even though the return is lower.

	Corporate Bond	Municipal Bond
Face Value (Principal)	$10,000	$10,000
Rate of Interest	6%	5%
Amount of Annual Interest	$ 600	$ 500
Tax on Interest Earned (28%)	168	0
Net Interest	$ 432	$ 500

Fig. 13-3

Comparing Taxable and Tax-Exempt Bonds

Savings Bonds and Treasuries

As you learned in Chapter 11, U.S. savings bonds can be purchased from commercial banks and through payroll deduction. An individual can buy up to $15,000 worth of these bonds a year. When Series EE bonds are purchased, investors often hold them to maturity. These bonds are issued with maturity values that range from $50 to $10,000. Federal taxation of interest paid on matured Series EE bonds can be postponed if they are converted to Series HH bonds. Series HH bonds pay semiannual interest.

Treasury securities are no longer issued as engraved certificates as are many stocks and corporate bonds. Instead, Treasuries exist as bookkeeping entries in the records of the U.S. Treasury Department itself or in the records of commercial banks. Unlike corporate bonds, Treasury obligations are not rated, since the backing of the U.S. government makes them virtually risk-free. Treasuries are exempt from state and local taxes and are usually *not* callable.

Agency Bonds

In addition to securities issued by the U.S. Treasury, debt securities are issued by federal agencies. Federal agencies that issue debt securities include the Federal Home Loan Mortgage Corporation, Federal National Mortgage Association, Federal Land Bank, Federal Housing Administration, and the Tennessee Valley Authority. When you purchase an **agency bond,** you are loaning money to one of these agencies. Although agency issues are basically risk-free, they offer a slightly higher yield than securities issued by the Treasury. Both can be bought directly through banks or from brokers.

uying and selling bonds

Full-service brokers, who also sell securities, can assist you in purchasing all kinds of bonds. The broker will charge you a commission or a flat fee for this service. Typically, the commission on municipal and corporate bonds is the difference between the bid and ask prices. In other words, the commission is hidden in the price of the bond.

You also can use a *discount broker* to buy bonds. A discount broker charges a smaller fee or commission, usually half or less of what a full-service brokerage charges. You will receive no advice or help in your decisions to buy or sell. Discount brokerage firms are listed in the telephone book. Many banks or other financial institutions provide discount brokerage service.

A Treasury security can be purchased through a Federal Reserve Bank.

If you choose to buy a Treasury security, you can do so through the Federal Reserve System. There are twelve Federal Reserve Banks and twenty-five regional branches spread across the nation. Check with your local financial institutions to find the bank or branch closest to you. They will mail you an application form. You can send your check or money order with the application directly to the Federal Reserve. In recording and storing data about Treasuries, a system called *Treasury Direct* is used. This system stores information on bonds you own. Interest (and principal when the bonds mature) is deposited directly into your bank account. Also, by using Treasury Direct, you can reinvest in Treasury securities automatically when existing securities mature. U.S. government securities also may be purchased through banks or brokers, but you will pay a commission.

In the case of savings bonds, you may wish to purchase them through payroll deductions. Your employer will withhold money as authorized. When your withholdings are sufficient, the bond will be purchased and sent to you. This process takes longer because your employer processes the money through a bank, which in turn purchases the bonds and returns them through your employer. It is often quicker to deal directly with a bank in your area.

Municipal bonds can be purchased through banks or brokers. In most states, you can set up a bank account to buy and sell municipal bonds. Generally, you are purchasing a bond from the inventory your bank has on hand. Banks buy large blocks of municipal bonds and make them available to their customers. There is a fee for this service, although it may be incorporated into the price of the bonds.

Which Bonds to Buy

People invest in bonds for at least three reasons. First, bondholders earn interest for each day a bond is owned. Second, a bond will be redeemed for its face value at maturity. Third, bonds often appreciate in value, and bondholders may be able to sell a bond at a price higher than the purchase price.

Most bond options require a minimum investment of $1,000. Only savings bonds can be purchased with small, regular payments. When you have a large sum of money to set aside, you can consider larger purchases of $5,000 or $10,000.

High-quality bonds are **investment grade.** They are considered safe because the issuers are stable and dependable. For example, U.S. Treasury bonds provide maximum safety of principal since these securities are backed by the Federal government itself.

Corporate and municipal bonds are rated or evaluated by independent rating companies. The two best-known are Standard & Poor's and Moody's. To give a bond its rating, these companies measure the financial stability of the issuing company or municipality. The highest rating is AAA, or triple A. The lowest rating is a D. A D rating indicates a bond is in default; in other words, the issuer is unable to make good on interest and/or principal payments. Any bond with a rating of Baa or higher in Moody's, or BBB or higher in Standard & Poor's, is considered investment grade. Unfortunately, the higher the bond's rating, the lower the rate of interest you will earn. (Note that the lowercase letters in the bond rating indicate more risk than capital letters. The letters stand for company stability, bond security, and general industry risk.)

Junk bonds have a low investment rating—or no rating at all. Any bond with a rating of Ba/BB or lower is called a junk bond. Because of its low or no rating, this type of bond is considered highly speculative. Junk bonds have higher yields and at times appear to have reasonable levels of risk. However, in most cases, interest rates on junk bonds are high because of the risk involved. Most knowledgeable investors should carefully explore the feasibility of buying junk bonds.

personal perspective

T ax Strategies

When choosing investment options, there is an important consideration every investor must keep in mind at all times—taxability. Some investments are fully taxable while others are tax-free. There are numerous options in between. The choice of an investment might hinge on its taxability status.

An investment is *tax-exempt* when there is no tax due, either now or in the future. Tax-exempt investments include municipal bonds sold by state and local governments. However, to be free from both federal and state taxes, you must live in the state where the bond is issued. For example, if you live in California, tax-free bonds in Oregon will be subject to state income taxes in California.

An investment is *tax-deferred* when income will be taxed at a later time. Tax-deferred investments include annuities, which will be discussed in Chapter 15. While earnings are credited to an account now, you do not pay taxes on the earnings until you withdraw them. At that time, your tax rate may be lower, so you will owe less tax.

Taxes also are deferred on assets that appreciate in value. *Capital gains,* the profits from the sale of assets such as stocks, bonds, or real estate, are not taxed until the asset is sold. For example, if shares of stock you own are worth more than what you paid for them, you will owe no taxes on the gain until you sell the shares of stock.

Income and deductions can be *shifted* by postponing them to the following tax year, or accelerating them forward into a current year, when they will do you more good. If your income is higher this year than usual, you can shift some deductions to help offset this increased income. For example, extensive dental work can be scheduled with taxes in mind. Small dental expenses several years in a row may not produce any taxable deduction at all, but if all dental deductions are bunched into one year, a tax deduction may be realized. This practice sometimes requires the advice of tax planning specialists.

Taxes can be *avoided* by selling securities on which you lost money to offset gains on the sale of other securities. In other words, you can deduct losses to reduce capital gains on securities. This strategy is in contrast to *tax evasion,* which is the use of illegal actions to reduce your taxes.

critical thinking

1. Why is it important to consider tax consequences when choosing investment alternatives?

2. What type of investor would likely choose a tax-exempt investment? What type of investor would choose tax-deferred?

3. Why should you seek professional advice when shifting income and avoiding taxes?

Buying Bond Funds

Bonds are available for people who have smaller amounts to invest, but do not want to buy U.S. savings bonds. A bond fund provides diversity and professional management of your money. Bond funds are a kind of mutual fund, which will be discussed in Chapter 14. Generally, a bond fund is a collection of bonds purchased by many small investors and managed by a professional investment company.

Zero-Coupon Bonds

A **zero-coupon bond** is one that makes no interest payments. These bonds, whether issued by the U.S. government, corporations, or municipalities, are sold at a deep discount—as much as 50 to 75 percent below the face value of the bond. With a zero-coupon bond, the buyer receives a return based on the bond's dollar appreciation (increase in value) as its maturity date approaches. A bondholder makes money based on how deep the discount was when the bond was purchased.

With a zero-coupon bond, you must pay taxes on any interest earned each year (even though you don't actually receive it) until the bond is paid at maturity. Interest on zero-coupon municipal bonds, however, is not subject to taxation. Prices on zero-coupon bonds are volatile. The value of your bond can fluctuate widely. Should you need to sell the bond before maturity, you may face a loss.

 ond listings

Only one factor has a real effect on bond prices—interest rates. When interest rates rise, the value of bonds decreases. The bonds are paying less in comparison to other fixed-rate investments. Conversely, when interest rates are dropping, fixed-rate bonds will be attractive because they are "locked in" at higher rates.

When considering buying or selling bonds, you should be familiar with the bond price listings in the financial section of your newspaper. Not all local newspapers contain bond quotations, but *The Wall Street Journal* publishes complete and thorough information on bond transactions.

Purchases and sales of corporate bonds are reported in tables similar to the one shown in Figure 13-4. In bond quotations, prices are given as a percentage of face value, which is usually $1,000.

	Cur.			Net
Bonds	**Yld.**	**Vol.**	**Close**	**Chg.**
1	**2**	**3**	**4**	**5**
PenPac 6s07	6.25	31	96	+½
PlnCr 7 02	6.8	25	103	. . .
Pennzl 7s99	6.94	7	100⅞	−⅛
Prent 6 05	6.1	8	99	. . .
PhilP 5 06	5.2	22	96¾	+¼

Fig. 13-4

Reading the Corporate Bond Transactions

Column 1. The first column lists the name of the bond, followed by its interest rate, and year of maturity. The first bond, PenPac, pays a fixed rate of 6 percent. It matures in the year 2007.

Column 2. The *current yield* of a bond is its return. Divide the annual interest by the current market value of the bond to determine the yield. For example, for the PenPac bond, the current yield of 6.25 percent is found by dividing 6 percent annual interest by 96, the closing price.

Column 3. The volume column lists the number of shares traded that day, in hundreds. In other words, PenPac bonds bought and sold were 3,100 that day.

Column 4. This column lists the closing price, or current selling price of the bonds at the end of the trading day. The closing price is not the same as the face value of the bond. For example, PenPac is currently selling for 96.

Column 5. The net change column compares the last price paid for the bond today with that paid on the previous day. The last price paid on this day for PenPac was +0.5% x $1,000, or $5 higher than the last price paid on the previous trading day. In other words, the PenPac bond "closed up ½" on this day.

 ummary

Investing in bonds is a safe and dependable choice for many Americans. While they are not insured, corporate bonds provide a long-term investment for people who wish to loan money to corporations at competitive rates of interest.

Callable bonds can be redeemed by the corporation at some point before maturity (usually when interest rates are dropping). Debentures are corporate bonds backed by the general credit of the corporation, and mortgage bonds are backed by a specific asset. Convertible bonds can be exchanged for a specific number of shares of common stock.

At maturity date, the principal (face value) of the bond is repaid in full. Semiannual interest payments are earned during the term of the bond. When bonds sell above their face value, they are sold at a premium. When they sell below face value, they are sold at a discount.

Government bonds have a unique and attractive feature—some of them are tax-exempt. Municipal bonds, called "munis," are not taxable for state or federal income taxes. Treasury bonds are federally taxable and pay competitive rates of interest. Interest on U.S. savings bonds is also federally taxable.

Bonds are bought and sold through brokers or through financial institutions. Bonds are rated according to their quality and risk by Moody's and Standard and Poor's. The rating systems of these two organizations are similar but not identical. Junk bonds have the lowest rating and are very speculative.

Some bond prices are quoted daily in the financial section of newspapers, along with stocks and other investments. In bond quotations, prices are given as a percentage of the face value, which is usually $1,000. Thus, to find the actual closing price paid, you must multiply the face value ($1,000) by the newspaper quote.

V ocabulary terms

Directions: Can you find the definition for each of the following terms used in Chapter 13?

agency bond	*junk bond*
callable bond	*maturity*
convertible bond	*maturity date*
debentures	*mortgage bond*
discount	*municipal bonds*
face value	*premium*
general obligation bond	*revenue bond*
investment grade	*zero-coupon bond*

1. A bond with a very low rating, or no rating at all.
2. A type of bond that can be exchanged for stock.
3. A type of bond that allows the issuer to redeem it before its maturity date.
4. Debt security issued by federal agencies.
5. A bond sold at a price far below its face value, with no semiannual interest payments, and redeemable for its face value at maturity.
6. Corporate bonds backed by the general credit standing of the corporation.
7. A bond that sells for less than face value.
8. A corporate bond backed by specific assets, such as buildings.
9. The date when a bond is repaid in full.
10. A bond that sells for more than its face value.
11. A bond which is backed by the full faith and credit of an issuing municipality.
12. A high-quality bond considered to be a safe investment.
13. The time when a bond expires or is due to be repaid.
14. Bonds issued by state and local governments.
15. The amount a bondholder will receive when a bond is repaid.
16. A government bond backed by the general taxing authority of the governmental unit.

13 end-of-chapter activities

Facts and ideas in review

1. How is bond investing different conceptually from stock investing?
2. Can small investors choose bonds as an investment? Why or why not?
3. How are debentures different from mortgage (or secured) bonds?
4. How does a bondholder make money buying bonds?
5. Why would a corporation issue callable bonds?
6. How do state or local governments pay off the principal and interest of municipal bonds issued?
7. Why do municipal bonds pay lower rates of interest than corporate bonds?
8. What is "Treasury Direct"?
9. Why should you be concerned about a bond's rating before you buy it?
10. Why would anyone buy junk bonds?
11. How do you make money on zero-coupon bonds?
12. How do interest rates affect the price (value) of bonds?

Applications for decision making

1. Why do investors buy more bonds than stocks?
2. As a bondholder, would your investment in a corporation bond be more secure than a stockholder's investment? Why or why not?
3. Why might you choose a secured bond rather than an unsecured bond?
4. You bought a $10,000, 6 percent corporate bond at face value that matures in 5 years. What would be your total earnings during that five-year period?
5. Explain why you might choose a municipal bond paying 5 percent over a corporate bond paying 7 percent.
6. When buying Treasury bonds, which would you choose: full-service broker, discount broker, Treasury Direct? Why?
7. You have the choice of buying a municipal bond with a rating of Aaa paying 4 percent or a corporate bond with a rating of Ba paying 8 percent. Which bond would be your choice, and why?

8. You can buy a $1,000 face value zero-coupon bond for $600. The bond matures in ten years. Describe the circumstances under which you would consider buying the bond.

9. A new bond issue you are considering has a face value of $1,000, an interest rate of 5 percent, and a maturity date of eight years. The bond is currently selling at 104. What is the current yield? What amount of interest would be earned in that time period?

10. Three $1,000 bonds have the following closing prices: 95⅜, 103¼, and 99. What are the prices of the bonds in dollar amounts?

 ife situation problem solving

1. Your friend Mary has just inherited $10,000. She considers the stock market too risky. She wants to preserve the safety of the principal invested. Explain to her why buying a bond would be a safer investment.

2. Having convinced Mary to buy a bond, she now asks you if she should consider a corporate bond. Explain to her how debt financing works, and the difference between the types of corporate bonds. What type of corporate bond would you recommend? Why?

3. Mike Ortega has just purchased a $10,000, 7.5% corporate bond that will pay interest semiannually for the next eight years. Prepare a chart showing how much in interest he will receive for the next eight years (total interest payments are 16).

4. Katie McDonnel has chosen to buy a 5.5%, $1,000 corporate bond. The bond currently sells for 104. Compute her current yield on the bond, and explain to her why it is not the same as the stated interest rate.

5. Arnold Osaga is considering purchasing a $10,000 corporate bond yielding 9 percent. He also found that he could buy a municipal bond for 7 percent. His federal income tax rate is 28 percent. Determine his net interest. Show your work.

6. Bob has a regular job and is considering using payroll deductions to pay for savings bonds. If he could set aside $10 per month, how long would it take to buy a $500 EE bond? Explain to him how savings bonds work.

7. Using information from *The Wall Street Journal* or a local newspaper, answer the following questions on the corporate bond issues you select:

Newspaper _____ Date _____

	Current Yield	Volume	Close Price
_____	_____	____	_____
_____	_____	____	_____
_____	_____	____	_____

8. Mel is considering buying some junk bonds. He has some money set aside to use for speculation. He is willing to take the risk. Investigate how these bonds work. Then explain to him what junk bonds are.

9. Andrea has narrowed her choice of bond purchases to two issues: MelMac, a 7 percent corporate issue selling for 102, or BrgPort, a 5 percent municipal issue selling for 96. Compute the current yield of each bond and advise her about which bond to choose.

10. Brian has $10,000 to invest. Brian is considering buying high-quality corporate bonds because interest rates on bonds are somewhat higher than on CDs. He has rejected stocks because of the risk involved. Brian feels that interest rates are going to continue to rise but, in the meantime, he needs a relatively safe place for his money. Explain to Brian how bond prices are affected by interest rates. Is he making the right decision? Why?

11. Choose a corporate bond listed on the New York Bond Exchange and use *Moody's Industrial Manuals* (available at many public libraries) to answer the following questions about this bond issue.
    a. What is Moody's rating for the issue?
    b. What is the purpose of the issue?
    c. Does the issue have a call provision?
    d. What collateral, if any, has been pledged as security for the issue?
    e. Based on the information studied, would the bond be a good investment for you? Why?

In this chapter, we will continue exploring investment alternatives that are available to beginning and experienced investors. Risk will still be the key consideration in decision making. At one end of the spectrum are very safe investments that attract conservative investors. Mutual funds and real estate are often in this category. At the other end are the very risky investments that offer potentially large dollar returns. If they are unsuccessful, however, the investor could lose most or all of the initial investment. Commodities, gem stones, and collectibles are considered risky investments.

Investing in Mutual Funds, Real Estate, and Other Alternatives

chapter 14

utual fund investments

As you will recall from Chapter 11, a mutual fund is an investment alternative for individuals who pool their own and other investors' money to buy stocks, bonds, and other securities sold by an investment company. An *investment company* is a firm that, for a management fee, invests the pooled funds in different types of securities.

Investors buy shares of a mutual fund. The funds thus raised are invested by a mutual fund manager. Professional fund managers devote substantial time to picking just the "right" securities for a fund.

Some mutual funds invest in only one kind of security, such as tax-free bonds, while others are more diversified. Most mutual fund companies offer several different funds, known as a **family of funds.** You are allowed to move back and forth among the funds. You can purchase one type of fund, such as a stock fund, and switch to another, such as a bond fund, at a later time.

Professional managers buy and sell according to their interpretation of market conditions, economic conditions, trends, and other factors. Funds have experienced managers who develop elaborate systems and procedures to help make the right selections. The investor shares in any profits made by mutual funds. Profits are received as dividends which are either reinvested in the fund or distributed to investors as cash payments.

For most funds, you will have to make an initial deposit of $500 to $3,000 or more. Once your account is open, you can make additional purchases as often as you like. Many people make regular payments of $50 to $100 a month. To receive your money, you may be able to simply call the fund and place an order to sell your shares. The sale takes place at the end of the day (in some funds, sooner), and money is available to you the next morning.

Why Investors Purchase Mutual Funds

Mutual funds are convenient for the investor. You don't have to worry about following stock and bond markets, or looking for hot new investments. Professionals are doing the work for you.

When you invest in mutual funds, you are diversifying because mutual funds purchase numerous and diverse stock and bond issues. You can make transfers by telephone, and your investment is liquid. You can get your money quickly if you need it.

When you make regular monthly payments to a mutual fund investment, you are *dollar-cost averaging*. As you learned in Chapter 12, you invest the same amount periodically regardless of what's happening in the financial market. Sometimes you will be paying more for each share in the fund, at other times less. By dollar-cost averaging, you will smooth out the fluctuations in the purchase price of fund shares.

Types of Mutual Funds

Individual funds within a family have different investment goals and strategies. You should choose goals and strategies that match your interests. There are many different types of funds to choose from, including growth, income, balanced, bond, global, and index funds.

Growth Funds

A **growth fund** invests in the common stock of established companies and industries. An aggressive growth fund invests in common stock of new or out-of-favor companies and industries. Growth funds are somewhat risky; aggressive growth funds are very high risk. The goal is strong price increases which take the form of capital gains.

Income Funds

An **income fund** specializes in income-producing securities which consistently pay good dividends. Income funds are considered to be of moderate risk. The goal is current dividend income.

A fund could be called a growth-income fund. In this case, the fund seeks to buy common and preferred stocks that pay good dividends. These stocks also are expected to increase in market value. The goal of the fund is to take advantage of a price rise and current income. The risk level of this type of fund is moderate.

Balanced Funds

A **balanced fund** invests in a mixture of stocks (preferred and common) and bonds (corporate and municipal). The purpose is to reduce risk while maintaining both current income and growth. Balanced funds are generally considered low-risk investments. The goal of a balanced fund is current income and long-term growth with safety.

Bond Funds

A **bond fund** invests in government, corporate, or tax-exempt bonds with different maturity dates. Bond funds are considered *high-yield funds* when the fund invests primarily in lower-rated junk bonds. A bond fund that invests solely in tax-exempt bonds has as its goal tax-free income for investors. Tax-exempt funds appeal to investors in high-income tax brackets. Bond funds are considered low to moderate risk, except for the high-yield funds, which are considered high risk.

Global Funds

A **global fund** purchases international stocks and bonds as well as U.S. securities. These funds appreciate when stock markets abroad are strong and world conditions favor certain overseas markets. International stock values are influenced by fluctuations in exchange currency rates. These funds are considered moderate- to high-risk investments.

Index Funds

An index fund holds stocks or bonds that react the same as the stock or bond markets as a whole do. Many of these funds are tied to a specific market average such as Standard & Poor's index of 500 large company stocks. The goal of these funds is to mirror the movements of certain market indices, going up as the indices rise or down as they fall. These funds are considered moderately risky.

Money Market Funds

These funds invest in short-term corporate obligations and government securities. The average time to maturity for money market fund investments ranges from three weeks to six months. These short maturities provide current income and maximum safety. The goal of any money market fund is the preservation of principal and very high liquidity.

Evaluation of Mutual Funds

The responsibility for choosing the right mutual fund rests with the individual investor. After all, you are the only one who knows how a particular mutual fund can help you achieve your financial objectives. Although investing money in a mutual fund provides professional management, individual investors should continually monitor the fund. Some funds consistently outperform the average. When considering the purchase of a fund, always examine the prospectus, determine costs and fees, and assess the fund's ranking.

The Prospectus

By law, investment companies must provide detailed information about their funds. A mutual fund company must provide a prospectus for each fund offered. The **prospectus** contains information about how the fund operates, a summary of its investments (called a *portfolio*), and its goals

An investment company must provide a *prospectus,* or detailed information about their funds.

and objectives. Annual or quarterly reports of the fund will summarize its performance, or how well the fund has performed during the past year or quarter. Before choosing a mutual fund, an investor should read the prospectus carefully and compare a fund to others being considered.

Costs and Fees

If you buy a mutual fund through a broker, it will likely be a load fund. In a **front-end load,** you pay a commission on your initial purchase and sometimes on reinvested dividends. In a **back-end load,** you pay a commission when you sell your shares before a certain period of time has elapsed. Either way, loads can range from 2 to 8 percent of the value of the shares purchased. Load funds are usually purchased through a broker.

In some cases, you can buy mutual funds directly from mutual fund companies. These are called **no-load funds.** No-load funds do not charge commissions when you buy because they have no salespeople. The usual means of contact is telephone or mail.

Other fees you should consider include annual management/administrative fees, which average about 1 percent of a fund's total assets. This charge is for the advice of professional fund managers and the cost of maintaining your account. The investment may also levy a *12b-1 fee* to defray the costs of marketing and distributing a mutual fund.

Fund Rankings

There are many publications that regularly review and rank mutual funds. Their one-year, five-year, and ten-year performances are compared to other companies with similar goals and objectives. Occasionally, entire sections of business magazines are devoted to listing, describing, and ranking mutual funds.

Earnings on Investments

Except for tax-free mutual funds, earnings on mutual funds are taxable. Earnings are in the form of income dividends, capital gains distributions, or both. Dividends are taxable, and gains are taxable when you redeem or sell your fund shares. When you exchange or trade one fund for another, any gain on the exchange is also taxable.

 ## Real estate investments

Have you ever wondered what it would be like to own real estate? There are many ways to own real estate through direct and indirect investments. In this section, you will learn primarily about commercial real estate investments. The term *commercial property* refers to land and buildings that produce lease or rental income. Such property includes office buildings, stores, hotels, and duplexes and multiunit apartments. Many investors have been able to acquire sizable commercial property holdings by first investing in a duplex and then "trading up" to larger units as the value of the original property increased. (Home ownership will be explained in Chapter 21.)

Direct Real Estate Investments

Real estate is a good hedge against inflation, usually increasing in value over the years, often at rates equal to or higher than inflation. However, real estate is one of the least liquid investments you can make. An investment can take months or even years to sell.

Let's look at some common forms of direct real estate investments. In *direct investments*, the investor holds legal title to the property. Direct real estate investments include land, single-family dwellings, duplexes, apartments, and nonresidential real estate.

personal perspective

H ow to Read the Mutual Funds Section of a Newspaper

When reading the mutual fund listings in the financial section of a newspaper, you will want to be familiar with the columns, abbreviations, and designations that appear. Although investing money in a mutual fund requires professional management, individual investors should continually evaluate their fund investments. Some of the basic means for doing this are described below.

Mutual Fund Quotations

1	2 Inv. Obj.	3 NAV	4 Offer Price	5 NAV Chg.
Ables Fund:				
AciBt1A	GRO	9.63	10.11	...
BiClo	BND	1.51	NL	–.01
CoxDli	SML	8.61	NL	+.01
DrixLt	G&I	26.54	NL	–.07
BB&B Fund:				
Globl B	WOR	6.25	6.25	–.03
MtgLtd	MTG	2.80	2.80	+.02

Column 1—The sponsoring mutual fund company's name is listed first. Its funds appear below in alphabetical order.

Column 2—The investment objective of the fund family is identified. Investors have a choice of growth, bond, small company growth, growth and income, global, and mortgage funds.

Column 3—NAV stands for net asset value. It refers to the dollar value of one share of the fund based on closing quotes.

Column 4—The offer price reflects the net asset value plus sales commission, if any. An "NL" indicates a no-load fund.

Column 5—NAV change indicates the gain or loss based on previous NAV quotation.

critical thinking

1. Which of the mutual funds at left seems to be the best investment as compared to the other choices given? Why?

2. Would you consider investing in mutual funds?

Raw Land

Vacant land, or unimproved property, is considered a speculative investment. You hold the property expecting it to go up substantially in value. Thus, you can sell it for a profit one day. Many people purchase a vacant lot with plans for building a house on it later, either when they can afford it or at retirement. In either case, you will likely have to pay cash for vacant land. Because it is considered speculative, banks are often unwilling to make loans on vacant land.

Detached Houses

You can purchase a single family house and rent it to others. Because the property is not owner-occupied, you may find banks reluctant to make a loan. As a condition for a loan, you may have to make a larger down payment or pay a higher interest rate. When a renter takes possession of your house, you still have responsibilities. For example, as the owner, you must maintain the premises in a livable condition. In other words, you must provide running water, electrical circuits, sewer or septic hook-ups, and normal repairs and maintenance. If the roof leaks or a pipe breaks, it is your responsibility to fix it.

Duplexes, Apartments, and Condominiums

A **duplex** is a building with two separate living quarters. For example, one side of the duplex may have two bedrooms while the other side has three bedrooms. The owner of a duplex has the same responsibilities to renters as the owner of a single-family home.

Other combinations of rented property are possible, such as triplexes (three units), quads (four units), or buildings with five to a hundred or more apartments. When investing in large tracts of real estate, most people join investment groups. By pooling your cash with other investors, you can afford to buy larger and more expensive pieces of property. For example, if you and three others formed a partnership to buy an eight-unit apartment building, each of you would have to pay only one-fourth of the total costs of buying and maintaining the property.

Condominiums, or condos, as they are popularly called, are individually owned units in apartment-style complexes. The owner of a condo owns the individual apartment as well as a proportional share of common areas, such as the lobby, yard, and hallways. Condos are generally cheaper than detached houses because they utilize less land per unit and share roofs, walls, plumbing, and so on. Condos are particularly appealing to single and young people, childless couples, and the elderly.

Recreation and Retirement Property

Many people buy second homes for vacations or for their retirement years. Often these properties are rented to others during the times when the owners are not there, generating income for the owners. Of course, when these properties are rented to others, they will not be in brand new condition when the owner retires to live there full time.

Recreation property includes beach and mountain cabins, and even vacant land near vacation sites such as rivers, lakes, or an ocean. The owner can use and enjoy the property on weekends and during vacations, and at other times rent the property.

Indirect Real Estate Investments

In *indirect investments,* investors appoint a trustee to hold legal title on behalf of all the investors in a group. (A *trustee* is an individual or institution that manages assets for someone else.) Mortgages, limited partnerships, real estate investment trusts, and mortgage pools (in the form of participation certificates) are examples of indirect investments.

Mortgages

The borrowing of money for a house purchase is called a **mortgage.** Mortgage money can be obtained from different places, and different types of mortgages are available. Mortgages and other debt contracts are commonly purchased by wealthier members of a community.

Many people purchase second homes for recreation or retirement.

Often, mortgages are purchased by individuals willing to take on more risk than financial institutions that normally finance mortgages would be willing to assume. Investments of this kind may provide relatively high rates of return because of the special risk involved.

Limited Partnerships

A **limited partnership** is comprised of a group of investors who pool their money to buy high-priced real estate. A limited partnership is often referred to as a *real estate syndicate*. This is a temporary association of individuals organized for the purpose of raising a large amount of capital. The organizer of the syndicate is called the *general partner* or *syndicator*. The people who contribute the capital are the *limited partners*.

Limited partnerships work as follows. The partnership is formed by the general partner who assumes unlimited liability for all the obligations of the partnership. The general partner then sells participation units to limited partners whose liability is restricted to the amount of their initial investment—perhaps $5,000 or $10,000. Limited liability is especially important in real estate partnerships because the mortgage acquired to purchase real estate often exceeds the net worth of the partners.

A limited partnership often owns several properties for diversification. The commercial properties acquired are usually professionally managed.

Real Estate Investment Trusts (REITs)

A **real estate investment trust (REIT)** is similar to a mutual fund. Your money is pooled with other people's money, and the REIT invests your money in real estate. Like a mutual fund, the REIT makes all buy and sell decisions. You can buy and sell REIT shares at will. REITs trade on stock exchanges or over-the-counter. Like stocks, REIT shares fluctuate with market conditions, and dividends are paid when real estate does well. There are many types of REITs—investing in everything from rental properties for monthly income to mortgages for long-term income. REITs are found in the financial section of the newspaper along with stock, bond, and mutual fund price quotations.

Participation Certificates

A **participation certificate** is an investment in a pool of mortgages that have been purchased by one of several government agencies. Participation certificates are sold by federal agencies such as the Government National Mortgages Association (Ginnie Mae), the Federal Home Loan Mortgage Corporation (Freddie Mac), and the Federal National Mortgage Association (Fannie Mae). Maes and Macs are issued by agencies closely tied to the federal government and are about as secure as Treasury securities.

At one time, you needed a minimum of $25,000 to invest in these certificates. However, many mutual funds invest entirely in them, making it possible to buy shares for as little as $1,000.

Property Ownership

When buying real estate, most people make a down payment and get a loan secured by a mortgage to pay the balance. This type of purchase is called **leverage,** which means you borrow money to make the purchase. Only a small amount of the purchase price is your own money. For example, if you buy a duplex for $100,000 and make a down payment of $20,000 (a 20 percent down payment is usually required for rental property), you are borrowing $80,000 from the bank. As the property gains in value, the mortgage remains fixed. When the property eventually is sold, the owner keeps the difference between the sales price and the mortgage, which is called *equity,* or ownership interest.

As the tenant makes rent payments, the owner will make the underlying mortgage payment to the bank. The difference between the amount of rent and the underlying mortgage payment should be used to pay property taxes and the cost of upkeep on the property. When money is left over after these expenses are paid, it is called *positive cash flow.* If, however, the owner cannot collect enough rent to pay the underlying mortgage, property taxes, repairs and maintenance, the difference is called a *negative cash flow.* The owner must pay expenses out-of-pocket to cover the shortfall in income.

In managing a property, the owner may be a resident landlord. Another option is to hire a resident landlord or property manager. A resident landlord lives at the rental site, takes care of all repairs and maintenance, collects the rent, and assures suitable living conditions.

A property manager collects rent, hires and pays people to make repairs and maintain the property, charges a fee for his or her services, and remits the difference to the owner of the property.

The owner of the real estate can deduct **depreciation** over the years. An *annual depreciation charge* is taken to reflect the decline in the value of property due to normal wear and tear. Depreciation is an expense that will reduce the owner's taxable income. In addition, property taxes and other expenses of maintaining property are also deductible. Thus, the owner of real estate can take advantage of tax savings by offsetting rental income with expenses of ownership.

When property is sold, the gain is taxable. But real estate can be difficult to sell. During slow economic times, when people are not able to buy property, an owner may have to lower the price of property substantially in order to sell.

Additional considerations include risks of renting. Renters can damage or destroy property to a degree far exceeding what a security deposit can pay for. When property vacancy rates increase and rental income declines, the property owner must pay for any shortfall out-of-pocket, thus cutting into profits.

Real estate is also subject to zoning laws and other local use restrictions. Cities have laws that regulate what type of structure (single-family residence, apartment complex, office building, for example) that can be built in each area of the city. Before buying property, you should carefully check the applicable zoning laws.

In Chapter 21, the advantages and disadvantages of owning real estate will be explained further.

Metals, gems, and collectibles

Investments in this category are considered speculative. They can return large profits or losses when sold. In some cases, the enjoyment of having and using the investment will far exceed any resale value. Although not inexpensive, precious metals, gems, and collectibles are easy to purchase. However, they can be very difficult to sell in a hurry and do not provide any current income in the form of interest or dividends.

Precious Metals

Gold, silver, and platinum are examples of **precious metals.** They are desirable natural substances whose value usually increases. Precious metals can be the best hedge against inflation. *Inflation* causes prices of precious metals to go up when the quantity and quality of a metal remains the same. However, prices of precious metals are world-based, and can be volatile.

Because gold is rare and valuable, it is a universally acceptable basis for money around the world. The price of gold fluctuates with world economic conditions. Figure 14-1 shows how gold and silver prices have fluctuated since 1967.

Date	Gold (Troy oz.)	Silver (Troy oz.)
6/1/67	$ 35.00	$ 1.80
6/1/80	850.00	32.00
6/1/83	437.50	11.80
6/1/89	368.30	5.27
6/1/93	364.20	3.25
9/1/94	390.20	3.55

Fig. 14-1

Gold and Silver Prices

Gold and silver may be purchased as coins, medallions, jewelry, and bullion. Storing and securing precious metals may be a problem because of bulk and weight. Gold and silver also can be purchased in the form of a certificate stating how much gold or bullion is being held in storage. You also can hold gold indirectly by investing in gold-mining stocks or in mutual funds specializing in these stocks.

Other metals in which you can invest include aluminum, tin, copper, lead, nickel, and zinc. Prices for metals can be found in the financial section of newspapers. Prices vary greatly with changes in world economic conditions.

Gemstones

Gems are natural precious stones, such as diamonds, rubies, sapphires, and emeralds, that are commonly purchased by the gem investor. Diamond prices are high and subject to drastic change. Prices have fluctuated enormously in the last twenty years. For example, a flawless, Grade D, one-carat diamond purchased for $1,900 in 1970 would have sold for $50,000 in 1980, dropped to $17,500 in 1983, and then risen to $23,000 in 1994. Rubies, sapphires, and emeralds often increase in value during inflationary periods.

Precious metals and gems have their greatest value as jewelry. Stones that are one carat or more are rare and are much more valuable than smaller stones. Keep in mind, however, that the markup in jewelry made

from precious metals and gems is typically 50 to 500 percent—or more! When you, as an investor, purchase jewelry at retail prices, you are paying large markups. You will not be able to resell the jewelry for close to what you paid. Prices must increase substantially in the world market before you come near to recovering what you paid for the gem.

Semiprecious stones, such as garnets, spinels, and opals are often a good investment. A one-carat semiprecious stone might cost between $1,000 and $2,000. Cultured pearls, however, are a poor choice for the average investor. While the demand for pearl jewelry has increased in the last fifteen years, so has the supply of the most popular sizes. Consequently, only perfectly round black or rose pearls of a certain diameter are rare enough to be considered good investments—and these pearls are much too expensive for the average investor to consider. Semiprecious stones, like gems, have incredibly high markups when purchased at retail; therefore, any gains will be in the very long term.

The biggest disadvantage of investing in gems (as well as precious metals) is that the market to resell them is very small and unpredictable. If you are eager to sell, you will face a loss. When purchasing gems and metals for an investment, remember that while it is easy to buy them, it is very difficult to resell them. No ready market exists. You must try to find an interested buyer.

Collectibles

Collections of valuable or rare items, from antiques to comic books, are called *collectibles*. They are valuable because they are old, no longer made, unusual, irreplaceable, or of historic importance.

Coins are the most commonly collected items. Silver coins (rather than today's alloy coins) often are worth more than 20 times their face value. For example, a 50-cent piece dated before 1964 contains almost pure silver and is worth about $10, depending on its year and condition.

People like to collect favorite items, from porcelain figures to hubcaps, and hope someday their collection will be valuable. Collecting can be a satisfying hobby. One advantage of collectibles is that you can start small and buy in small quantities. Unfortunately, collectibles can be hard to sell and are considered

Collectibles are often irreplaceable or of historic importance.

illiquid—not easily convertible to cash. You may find it difficult to locate a buyer who is willing to pay you the value of your collection, even when the value is well known. The trick is to collect wisely. Purchase only the highest quality of what you like. Buy what you can enjoy through the years with the assumption the item will appreciate in value.

Futures and options

A **futures contract** is an agreement to buy or sell a commodity at a guaranteed price on some specific future date. Commodities include farm products such as wheat, corn, and soybeans; cattle; and metals such as gold and silver. Commodity prices are volatile because the pressures of supply and demand are disrupted by all kinds of mostly unpredictable situations from political upheaval to the weather.

Commodities are traded in both cash and futures markets. In a *cash market*, the commodity physically changes hands. Most of us are familiar with one aspect of commodities trading—the local farmer's market. Cash is exchanged for a farm product such as tomatoes or strawberries. Unlike the cash market, a commodity is not physically needed for trading in the futures market. For example, a farmer could sell a futures contract to deliver 5,000 bushels of wheat (one contract of wheat) one year from today. The *futures market* was created for those who want to know in advance what they will be paid. The farmer routinely sells in the cash market. He or she enters the futures market only for protection against volatile prices. The futures contract is like an insurance policy against changes in prices. In this case, the farmer knows in advance what he or she will be paid for wheat.

A futures contract is an agreement to buy or sell a commodity (such as wheat, corn, or soybeans) at a guaranteed price on some specific future date.

An **option** gives the investor the right, for a fee, to buy or sell 100 shares of a stock at a predetermined price within a specified period of time. A *call option* is the right to buy 100 shares of stock at a set price by a certain expiration date. You can exercise the right at any time before the option expires. A *put option* is the right to sell stock at a fixed price until the expiration date. An investor who thinks a stock's market value or price will increase during a short period of time may decide to purchase a call option. On the other hand, an investor who feels a stock's price will decrease during a short period of time may purchase a put option to safeguard the investment. Needless to say, options are risky business and not for the inexperienced investor. Options also apply to the purchase and sale of futures contracts.

ummary

Mutual funds are convenient and easy to purchase; they offer moderate rates of return and less risk than stocks and many bonds. With mutual funds, professional managers invest your money for you. When the mutual fund does well, you share in the profits through increased dividends.

There are many types of mutual funds, including growth funds (for long-term investments), income funds (for monthly income), balanced funds (both growth and income), bond funds (which invest only in bonds), global funds (which purchase international stocks and bonds), index funds (which buy stocks based on averages), and money market funds (which invest in short-term debt obligations of organizations).

A prospectus describes the fund and its goals and objectives. Funds are ranked according to their performance over one year, five years, and longer. Funds may be purchased either as load or no-load funds. Investors in funds pay management and administrative fees. Gains on sales of securities in a fund are taxable. Funds also distribute earnings in the form of income dividends which are taxable except for tax-exempt funds.

Real estate is a long-term, illiquid investment for people who want to own real property. You can invest directly in vacant land, single-family houses, duplexes and apartment buildings, or recreation property. You also can invest indirectly in property through mortgages, limited partnerships, real estate investment trusts, and participation certificates. Owning real estate may provide you with a positive cash flow; that is, money received as rental income can exceed your underlying costs—mortgage payments, insurance, repairs, and maintenance. When you must contribute your own cash to cover expenses, you have a negative cash flow. Real estate permits many deductible expenses for tax purposes. Depreciation on commercial property is a deductible business expense.

Metals, gems, and collectibles are collected by many people who enjoy them for their value as jewelry and decorations in their homes. While these items are often difficult to sell, they also offer personal pleasure to the collector.

The commodities market, whether in futures contracts or call or put options, is the most risky and speculative of all investment alternatives. More people lose than gain in this market, but large profits can be made when the timing is right.

14

Vocabulary terms

Directions: Can you find the definition for each of the following terms used in Chapter 14?

back-end load
balanced fund
bond fund
condominiums
depreciation
duplex
family of funds
front-end load
futures contract
global fund
growth fund

income fund
leverage
limited partnership
mortgage
no-load fund
option
participation certificate
precious metals
prospectus
real estate investment trust

1. Silver, gold, and platinum.
2. Information published about a mutual fund.
3. The wear and tear on real estate over the years.
4. A group of different types of mutual funds.
5. A type of mutual fund that specializes in the stock of established companies.
6. A type of mutual fund that invests in a mixture of stocks and bonds.
7. A type of mutual fund where you pay a commission at the time you buy the shares.
8. The type of mutual fund where no commission is charged.
9. A building with two separate living quarters.
10. Buying property but paying only a small part of the purchase price in cash.
11. A mutual fund specializing in stocks and bonds that pay consistently good dividends.
12. A type of mutual fund that invests in Treasury, corporate, or municipal bonds.
13. An agreement you make today for commodities to be bought or sold in the future.
14. A mutual fund that purchases stocks and bonds from around the world.

15. The right to buy or sell stock, for a fee, at a later date for a pre-determined price.

16. A type of mutual fund where you pay a commission when you sell your shares of stock.

17. Individually owned units, as well as a proportional share of common areas, in an apartment complex.

18. A real estate group formed to purchase high-priced real estate for its participants.

19. The borrowing of money for financing the purchase of real estate.

20. An investment in a pool of mortgages that have been purchased by one of several government agencies.

21. A firm that pools investor funds and invests them in real estate or uses them to make mortgage loans.

 ## Facts and ideas in review

1. Give some advantages to buying mutual funds rather than individual stocks or bonds.

2. List six types of mutual funds, and briefly describe each.

3. Explain the difference between a front- or back-end load fund and a no-load fund.

4. How are mutual funds ranked?

5. What kinds of responsibilities does a landlord or property manager have to tenants?

6. Why is vacant land considered speculation?

7. Why do people join investment groups rather than purchase real estate individually?

8. Explain the concept of a positive cash flow.

9. List some disadvantages of owning rental real estate.

10. Why are precious metals considered speculative?

11. List five or six precious metals.

12. Why are gems and semiprecious stones not a good investment?

13. What are some advantages and disadvantages of collections as investments?

14. Describe the difference between a cash market and a futures market.

15. Explain the difference between put and call options.

Applications for decision making

1. Discuss why a person would choose a mutual fund over individual stock and bond purchases. List advantages and disadvantages.
2. Describe the type of investor (in terms of goals and risk aptitude) who would be interested in each of the following types of mutual funds:
   a. growth funds
   b. income funds
   c. municipal bond funds
   d. global funds
3. Why would a person choose a front- or back-end load fund over a no-load mutual fund?
4. Why should a new investor read the prospectus of a mutual fund carefully before purchasing the fund?
5. Describe what it would be like to be a landlord (your responsibilities and duties) if you owned
   a. a single-family house that you rented to a family
   b. a duplex that you rented to two families
   c. an eight-unit apartment building where you were the on-site manager.
6. Why would you wish to buy a piece of vacant land? Describe what your plans might be for the property in ten or twenty years, including where you would buy such a lot and its potential uses.
7. Describe the investor who might choose a second home, such as a cabin in the woods. Why should the investor purchase the property now rather than in the future when it will be used full time for retirement?
8. Explain what is meant by leverage in buying real estate. Why is it desirable to have a positive cash flow after real estate has been purchased?
9. What is meant by the phrase, "Real estate is an illiquid investment"?
10. Precious metals are a good hedge against inflation, but they can also be very unpredictable. Why would anyone want to invest in these items?
11. List some disadvantages of owning gold or silver as investments.
12. What types of gems and semiprecious stones do you prefer? What are the advantages and disadvantages of buying them for investments?

13. Collections are fun to have and can gain in value over the years. Name some collectible items you have seen, collected, or read about that have increased substantially in value over the years. What would you like to collect?
14. Commodities are said to be very risky investments. Are you interested in commodities as investments? Why or why not?

Life situation problem solving

1. Your friend Amy has decided that it is just too much trouble to invest in individual stocks and bonds as a beginning investor, so she thinks mutual funds are the answer for her. Explain to her how much money she will need for an initial investment, and the features of mutual funds that might make them desirable investments.
2. Mark and Mindy have been married for three years, and have managed to save some money to invest. They have decided on mutual funds, but don't want to take too much risk. Still, they would like to have some additional income, and yet sell the shares for a good profit in five to ten years. Explain to them their choices of mutual funds for an investment. Which fund(s) would you choose for this young couple?
3. Obtain a prospectus for a mutual fund company. You can write to an address provided in an ad that you may find in the financial pages of your newspaper or *The Wall Street Journal,* or get one from a brokerage firm or a financial counselor. Read the prospectus and report on your findings: objectives (goals) of the fund, tax status (are investments taxable or tax-free?), and performance of the fund for the last year or so.
4. Your friend Matthew has saved almost $10,000 for a down payment and has decided to buy a small, single-family house that he will fix up and rent. He figures he can get at least $800 a month in rental income. He also has the money to cover the cost of $2,000 to fix up the house. Explain to Matthew the concept of leverage, and about the need for a positive cash flow once the house is fixed and rented.
5. Marc has decided to invest in real estate. He can't decide whether to buy a vacant lot for $25,000 or a one-fourth interest in a four-unit apartment building selling for $400,000. Explain to him the pros and cons of both of these alternatives.

6. Mr. and Mrs. Rodriguez will be retiring in less than ten years. They are considering purchasing a house at the beach that they can use on weekends now and have as their home upon retirement. Explain to them the concept of buying recreation property and its potential as an investment.

7. Your grandmother has a wonderful collection of crystal, gold coins, diamond jewelry, and silver dating back to the early 19th century. When purchased, it cost very little, but today it could be worth a great deal of money. Explain to your grandmother, using a current issue of the newspaper, what today's prices are for silver, gold, gems, and other valuables.

8. Your friend Elizabeth wants to buy a ruby ring at a local jewelry store. She believes it will make an excellent investment for the future, and that she can always sell the ring and get most of her money back. Explain to her the pros and cons of this type of investment.

9. George is a very nervous person. He is worried that his money is not earning enough interest to keep up with inflation. He was reading about commodities and thinks it would be a great way to make some quick money. Explain to him the risk factor involved in trading commodities.

objectives:

After reading and studying this chapter you will be able to:

15-1 Describe the objectives of retirement planning, financial maturity, and preparing for rest, leisure, travel, and use of avocational skills.

15-2 Understand the features of personal retirement plans, including Keoghs and IRAs.

15-3 Explain basic benefits available through employer and public pension plans.

15-4 List the features of wills, powers of attorney, trusts, and joint ownership.

15-5 Discuss inheritance, estate taxes, and gift taxes.

terms to know:

financial maturity
reverse mortgage
Individual Retirement Account (IRA)
Keogh
defined-benefit plan
vested
defined-contribution plan
estate
estate planning
will
heirs
codicil
power of attorney
trust
estate tax
inheritance tax
gift tax

There comes a time when everyone decides to retire from the workforce and focus on doing the things they've waited and planned to do. For some people, these plans include travel and recreation; for others, pursuing a hobby they never had time for. Retirement planning will help you achieve your goals when you are no longer able or willing to work. It is vital to engage in basic retirement planning activities throughout your working years and to update your retirement plans periodically.

This chapter also discusses a subject most people would rather avoid: death —your own or that of your spouse. Most people give little attention to preparing for death. This chapter will help you plan for your family's financial security in the event of your death or the death of your spouse. The strategies presented in this chapter will help you minimize taxes paid on your estate.

Retirement and Estate Planning

chapter 15

lanning for retirement

When you get ready to retire, you will want to have enough financial resources to live comfortably. Many people want to do more than sit around. They want to do the things they didn't have time for when they were working and raising families. To enjoy retirement, you must have a solid retirement plan. Social security and a company pension may be insufficient to cover the cost of living. Inflation may erode the purchasing power of your retirement savings.

Many financial advisors tell clients that they will need approximately 80 percent of their before-retirement salary to live comfortably when they retire. This percentage may seem high. You may wonder how you can have that kind of income when you are no longer working. A comfortable retirement can be realized only by saving now and curtailing current spending.

For now, you are at the beginning your work life. And like it or not, the time to start planning for your retirement is now—with your first paycheck! There will be times when you won't have cash to set aside. You'll be paying for a college education, children, cars, houses, furniture, and so on. But the time will come when you will reach financial maturity. **Financial maturity** is that point in your life when

A comfortable retirement can only be realized through good investments and savings.

you are able to concentrate on your retirement plans. Your children will be grown and on their own. You will own your home and your car will be paid for.

Review your assets to make sure they are suitable for retirement. Make necessary adjustments to fit your circumstances. In reviewing your assets, consider the following factors: housing, investments, insurance, and inflation.

Keep the House or Move?

Once the kids are gone, many couples choose to sell their big home and find something smaller and less expensive. Current tax law provides a "once in a lifetime" exclusion. After age 55, you can sell your house and the first $125,000 of profit is tax-exempt. This is an important opportunity that might be taken at the right time. Other people choose to keep their house because it is paid off; monthly mortgage payments are no longer made. Before moving, consider the negative aspects. Moving is expensive, and if you are not satisfied in your new location, returning to your previous home may be impossible.

Plans are being offered to assist individuals with low incomes who have a high equity in their home. A **reverse mortgage** provides the elderly homeowner with tax-free income in the form of a loan that is paid back (with interest) when the home is sold or the homeowner dies. The reverse mortgage may have a set term at the end of which the loan would be due. A reverse mortgage would provide monthly income for a specified period of time until all equity in the home was used up; at that point, the loan would come due. For example, if you own a home worth $50,000 and your underlying mortgage is $5,000, your equity is $45,000. With a reverse mortgage, the monthly payments to you would add up, together with mortgage interest, until there was no equity remaining. Once the loan is due, you may have to sell the home in order to pay off the loan.

What Type of Investments?

People who are retired view investments from a different perspective than when they were younger. Monthly income is often the main goal for investments. The investor, for example, may want to take dividends rather than reinvest them. Rather than saving for the future, the investor at this stage is trying to preserve his or her financial position; that is, safeguard principal while earning a reasonable interest rate or yield. Fixed-income investments become a more practical choice. A diversified portfolio (group of investments) guards against loss of principal while giving a moderate rate of return. And many retired persons prefer to avoid making investment decisions at this time. They hope that their previous decisions will provide ample income, protection from inflation, and liquidity.

What Type of Insurance?

With financial maturity, insurance needs also change. In Unit 6, we will cover risk management thoroughly. While the need for life insurance has diminished, the retired person must channel those dollars into other insurance needs. You may have set up your life insurance to provide support and education for your children. Now you may want to convert some of this asset into cash or income.

For the retired person, the crucial need for insurance falls in the area of health—being sure that an illness or injury will not wipe out a lifetime of saving and investing. When you qualify for Medicare, you may need supplemental insurance to cover expenses not covered by Medicare. But there may be an interim period—between your retirement from work and when Medicare begins (typically age 65). For some people, this can be five or more years. National health care may lessen the worry about being without insurance coverage during those years. Until such time, however, the retired person or couple must provide for possible contingencies.

How Do You Tackle Inflation?

The possible loss of buying power due to inflation is what makes planning for retirement so important. As you may recall, inflation is the increase in the cost of living. For the retired person on a fixed income, price increases diminish spending power. If inflation is increasing at 8 percent while your retirement income is increasing at only 3 or 4 percent, you'll have to cut out something from your budget. Therefore, budgeting must continue through retirement. Supplemental or part-time work is, often the choice of seniors who enjoy or are able to work, or who need more income to offset inflation.

P **ersonal retirement plans**

These sources of retirement income consist of money you set aside for yourself. You can select from among several personal retirement plans. The two most popular are individual retirement accounts (IRAs) and Keogh accounts. Either of these can be set up at a bank or other financial institution, brokerage firm, mutual fund company, or insurance company. Also popular are annuities, which are typically issued by insurance companies.

Individual Retirement Accounts (IRAs)

An **individual retirement account (IRA)** is a tax-sheltered retirement plan. To be eligible for a tax-deductible IRA, you must have income from employment. (Income from investments does not qualify.) If you received less than $2,000 from employment, the maximum you can put into the IRA is what you earned. However, if earned income exceeds $2,000, the maximum you can put into an IRA as an individual is $2,000 a year. For working couples, the maximum is $4,000. For couples with only one spouse working, the maximum is $2,250.

IRA contributions are tax-deductible (subtracted from gross income). Earnings on IRA accounts are also tax-deferred, which means earnings are not currently taxable. The biggest benefit of an IRA lies in its tax-deferred earnings growth; and the longer the money accumulates tax deferred, the bigger the benefit.

If you are single, with adjusted gross of income between $25,000 and $35,000, your eligibility for a tax-deductible IRA is phased out (reduced). For couples, this figure is between $40,000 and $50,000. Figure 15-1 shows how IRA deductions are phased out. Beyond $35,000 on a single tax return and $50,000 on a joint return, the IRA deduction is completely eliminated. However, you can still make nondeductible IRA contributions. All of the income your IRA earns will accumulate tax-deferred until you withdraw money from it. The IRA reduction or

Fig. 15-1

IRA Deductions

If a pension plan at work covers you or your spouse, the IRA deduction may be reduced or eliminated for both of you as follows:

Adjusted Gross Income		
Single Person	**Couple**	**IRA Deduction**
$25,000	$40,000	100%
26,000	41,000	90%
27,000	42,000	80%
28,000	43,000	70%
29,000	44,000	60%
30,000	45,000	50%
31,000	46,000	40%
32,000	47,000	30%
33,000	48,000	20%
34,000	49,000	10%
35,000	50,000	0

For example, if a single person had $30,000 in adjusted gross income, he or she could have a $1,000 IRA deduction ($2,000 x 50%).

elimination applies only to workers covered by employer pension plans. The full $2,000-per-employee contribution is allowed, regardless of income, for persons not covered by company pension plans.

You cannot withdraw your money from an IRA before age 59½ without a penalty. For early withdrawals, a 10 percent penalty is imposed on the amount withdrawn. In addition, the money you withdrew is subject to federal and state income taxes. You must report such income on your tax return and pay taxes on the amount withdrawn.

Keogh Plans

A **Keogh** is a retirement account available to self-employed individuals and their employees. Keogh contributions are restricted to $30,000 or 25 percent of earned income in any one year, whichever is less. Earned income is your net income after business expenses, including contributions to the plan for employees. Employees must be covered in the plan in a nondiscriminatory manner. Thus, if you contribute 15 percent of your earnings to the plan as an employer, you must contribute 15 percent of any employee's salary as well.

The amounts an employer contributes are fully tax deductible. Earnings on Keogh plans are also tax-deferred. Withdrawals cannot be made before age 59½ without penalty, and withdrawals must begin by age 70½.

Because Keogh plans can be complicated, professional advice should be sought by anyone considering them. Keogh plans must be administered by a trustee. A bank, insurance company, brokerage firm, mutual fund, or other institution dealing with money management can act as a trustee.

Simplified Employee Pension (SEP) Plans

SEP plans were authorized by Congress to encourage smaller employers to establish employee pension plans with IRAs as a funding method. Each employee sets up an IRA account at a financial institution. Then the employer makes an annual tax-deductible contribution up to 15 percent of the employee's salary or $30,000, whichever is less. Employees also can make contributions up to a $2,000 limit. Employee contributions to these plans are also tax-deductible (subtracted from gross income).

For example, assume you earn $15,000 a year. Your employer contributes $1,500 to your plan or 10 percent of your salary. You may then contribute $500 to your plan. On the other hand, assume your employer is contributing $2,250 to your plan. In this case, you could make no personal tax-deductible contribution. The total going into the plan exceeds $2,000. As long as your annual salary remains at $15,000, the most your employer can contribute to the SEP is $2,250 (15% × $15,000).

Annuities

As you learned in Chapter 10, an *annuity* is a savings or investment plan that provides monthly income at a later stage in life. You can buy an annuity as your individual retirement account or as supplemental retirement income. An annuity can be bought with a single payment or with periodic payments. In recent years, *deferred annuities* have become popular because of the tax-free buildup of interest or dividends during the time the annuity contract remains in effect. Such annuities are often used by younger people to save money toward retirement. Annuities will be discussed further with life insurance in Chapter 27.

Employer pensions and government benefits

Employer Retirement Plans

Another source of income for you may be the pension plan offered by your company. With employer plans, your employer contributes to your retirement benefits—and sometimes you contribute too. Contributions and earnings on employer plans accumulate tax-free until you receive them. Let's look at two types of private pension plans.

Defined-Benefit Plans

Many larger companies provide defined-benefit plans for their employees. A **defined-benefit plan** specifies the benefits promised to the employee at normal retirement age based on wages earned and number of years of service. The employer makes the entire contribution to the plan. When the employee retires, he or she is entitled to monthly retirement benefits. After a certain number of years of employment, the employee becomes **vested.** If he or she were to leave the company before retirement, the account balance could be withdrawn in cash or transferred to an IRA. Many of these plans provide that you would receive part, but not all, of the money in such cases.

Each employer pension plan has different rules, provisions, and options. For example, you may be able to choose a fixed monthly payment for your lifetime. If you die, your spouse may continue to receive your pension at a lower amount. Another option might be payments for your lifetime only. You should read the plan document to understand your rights.

If a company goes bankrupt or experiences serious financial difficulties, your plan may be protected by federal legislation. The Employee Retirement Income Security Act of 1974 (ERISA) sets minimum standards for pension plans in private industry and protects millions of workers from inadequately funded pension plans.

Defined-Contribution Plans

A **defined-contribution plan** specifies the minimum contribution that an employer and an employee have to make annually. Each plan has an individual account for every employee; thus, these plans are sometimes called individual account plans. The plan describes the amount the employer will contribute, but does not promise any particular benefit. When a plan participant retires or otherwise becomes eligible for benefits, the benefit is the total amount of money accumulated in the employee's account, including investment earnings on amounts put into the accounts. Two examples of these accounts are the 401(k) and 403(b) plans.

401(k) Plans

Employees of companies that operate for a profit may participate in 401(k) plans. Under a *401(k) plan*, an employer makes nontaxable contributions for your benefit and reduces your salary (or gross pay) by the same amount. The amount withheld is deposited in an account managed by an investment company. Your contributions are not taxable until you withdraw the funds, usually at retirement. Earnings on contributions are also tax-deferred. The employee often has a choice of investment options earning either a fixed or variable rate of return.

Frequently, employers match salary contributions by some percentage. For example, for every $1 of salary contributed to the plan, the employer may add 50 cents (a 50% match). Companies usually set limits on how much they will match of an employee's salary contributed to a 401(k). Withdrawal restrictions and penalties apply when money is withdrawn early, except in the event of death, disability, or financial hardship.

403(b) Plans

Employees of government or not-for-profit businesses may participate in 403(b) plans. A *403(b) plan* is an account for employees of schools, tax-exempt organizations, and government units. While the rules may vary slightly, the 403(b) plan operates similarly to 401(k). These plans have been called tax-sheltered annuities (TSAs) because originally the law permitted only deferred annuities to be purchased by employees who were qualified under this section of the tax code. In 1974 the law was amended to permit investments in mutual funds.

Earnings are tax-deferred, and early withdrawal penalties apply. Should an employee leave this type of employer, the 403(b) funds can be put into an IRA.

Public Pension Plans

You may be entitled to government benefit checks—in the form of social security, military retirement, or veterans benefits. The Railroad Retirement System is the only retirement plan administered by the federal government that covers a single private industry. Many state, county, and city governments operate retirement plans for their employees.

The Railroad Retirement System is the only retirement plan administered by the federal government that covers a single private industry.

Social Security Benefits

When you retire, you will be eligible for social security benefits if you paid social security taxes during your lifetime. The amount of your benefit is based on your earnings and contributions to social security. Remember, these withholdings from your paychecks were matched by your employer(s).

If you were married for 10 years or more, you may be entitled to receive social security benefits based on your spouse's income. This benefit is available even if you are divorced.

Maximum social security retirement benefits are available at age 65. You can retire early, at age 62, and receive reduced benefits. As you are working, you should check your potential social security retirement benefits. Some Federal government employees and railroad employees are not covered by social security retirement benefits although recent federal employees are now paying into social security.

Remember, too, most or all of social security retirement benefits are taxable if your total income from all sources exceeds amounts set from time to time. In addition, thirteen states currently include social security benefits in income subject to their state income tax.

Military Benefits

Retired military personnel receive pensions after twenty years active duty in the U.S. Armed Forces. Pensions are payable in full regardless of other sources of income and are subject to income taxes. In addition, military retirees may have special privileges that accrue from this status, such as the ability to purchase goods through military posts. These benefits can be very attractive, especially for someone who retires in his or her early forties and continues working for another fifteen or twenty years.

Veterans Benefits

The Veterans Administration provides regular pensions for many survivors of men and women who died while in the Armed Forces, and disability pensions for eligible veterans. In addition, veterans may be entitled to benefits ranging from low-interest mortgage loans to financing of a college education to low-rate car, life, or home insurance. Veterans should check to see what benefits are available—both now and at retirement.

state planning tools

While a person is living, all that he or she owns, less debts owed, is called an **estate.** When that person dies, these possessions pass to other people, either as directed by the person who died (called the *decedent*), or by the laws of the state in which the person died. At the time of a person's death, an estate is formed that may be taxed by the federal and/or state governments. **Estate planning** is the process of preparing for the administration and transfer of property during one's lifetime and at one's death. Some tools of estate planning include wills, powers of attorney, trusts, and joint ownership of assets.

Wills

A **will** is a legal document that tells how you want your estate to be distributed after your death. A will also names a person (executor) to act as personal representative of the estate, states preferences for guardians of minor children, and lists powers given to representatives, guardians, or trustees. Any person who is eighteen or older and

A will is a legal document that explains how you want your estate to be distributed after your death.

of sound mind can make a legally valid will. Also, anyone who is legally emancipated—living independently from parents—can make a valid will.

A *simple will* is a short (one- or two-page) document that lists spouse and children and provides how each shall inherit an estate. Simple wills for a husband and wife take a short time to prepare and usually cost less than $150. A will must be witnessed by two persons not mentioned in the will. Witnesses must be 18 or older, not related, and able to attest to the mental competency of the person making a will at the time it is written. An example of a simple will is shown in Figure 15-2.

A *trust will* is a long and complex document that creates a trust for the benefit of a person who cannot take possession of assets. A trust will is usually prepared by a lawyer. A trust is many pages long and lists specific provisions for holding property, assets, and money for minor children or others. A *trustee* is named to manage the money, and all duties and powers are described. The trustee may be a bank, a financial institution, or a person. The *testator* (person who makes the will) lists all persons who may have a claim to his or her estate, specifies all bequests of property to other persons, and lists any specific needs and how they will be fulfilled.

In order for money and property to be left to a minor child, the child must have a legal guardian who makes accountings of the child's property and money. Parents of small children typically create trust wills to provide for their children's education and living expenses. Then the balance of the estate is given to the children at some later age, such as twenty-five or thirty, when all of them have reached adulthood.

A *holographic will* is one written in a person's own handwriting. A handwritten will is legally valid in nineteen states and should be witnessed just as one typed and prepared by a lawyer. Because a handwritten will is often easier to contest (question), a typed will is recommended. Those persons who act as witnesses to a will must not be mentioned in the will itself.

When a person dies without a will, he or she is said to be *intestate*. In that event, the person's property is distributed according to the laws of the state where the decedent died. A typical intestate distribution might be as follows:

If the person is:	*Then distribution is:*
Married	All to spouse
Never married	All to parents
Married, one child	Half to spouse; half to child
Married, two children	Half to spouse; one-fourth to each child

Fig. 15-2   **Simple Will**

LAST WILL AND TESTAMENT OF ANTHONY JOHN HINTON

I, Anthony John Hinton, of the city of Dayton and state of Ohio, do make, publish, and declare this to be my Last Will and Testament in manner following:

FIRST: I direct that all my just debts, funeral expenses, and the cost of administering my estate be paid by my personal representative hereinafter named.

SECOND: I give, devise, and bequeath to my beloved daughter, Carol Hinton Campbell, now residing in Englewood, New Jersey, that certain piece of real estate, with all improvements thereon, situated in the same city and at the corner of Hudson Avenue and Tenafly Road.

THIRD: All the remainder and residue of my property, real, personal, and mixed, I give to my beloved wife, Kimberly Sue Hinton, personal representative of this, my Last Will and Testament, and I direct that she not be required to give bond or security for the performance of her duties as such.

LASTLY: I hereby revoke any and all former wills by me made.

IN WITNESS WHEREOF, I have hereunto set my hand this tenth day of October, in the year nineteen hundred --.

Anthony John Hinton
_____
Anthony John Hinton

We, the undersigned, certify that the foregoing instrument was, on the date thereof, signed and declared by Anthony John Hinton as his Last Will and Testament, in the presence of us who, in his presence and in the presence of each other, have, at his request, hereunto signed our names as witnesses of the execution thereof, this tenth day of October, 19--; and we hereby certify that we believe the said Anthony John Hinton to be of sound mind and memory.

_____ residing at 251 Wonderly Avenue
                                    Dayton, Ohio 45419-2521

_____ residing at 3024 James Hill Road
                                    Kettering, Ohio 45429-2454

_____ residing at 423 Goldengate Drive
                                    Centerville, Ohio 45459-2459

By having a valid will, you can control who gets how much, rather than allowing the state to make those decisions. Property reverts to the state when a person dies without heirs. **Heirs** are people entitled to inherit property or assets (such as parent, child, brother, uncle, and so on).

A person can make a will and later make small changes with a document called a **codicil.** The codicil lists one or two changes, and then reaffirms the rest of the original will document. A will cannot be legally amended by crossing out or adding words, or by removing or adding pages, or by making erasures. A codicil is drawn by an attorney and is executed and witnessed the same as a will.

Power of Attorney

At some time in your life, you may become ill or incapacitated. A **power of attorney** is a legal document authorizing someone to act on your behalf when you need someone to handle your personal affairs or attend to your needs. The power of attorney may be limited or general in time or in scope. A limited power of attorney may be good for thirty days or a year, or it may pertain to a particular transaction. A general power of attorney gives another person the right to act completely for you. When you give a power of attorney to another person, you give that person the power to do anything you could have done.

With this document, a person could take steps on your behalf in the event something happened to incapacitate you. For example, if you became physically impaired, the power of attorney would allow your business to go on without you. Of course, you must fully trust the person who receives this legal right because he or she can transact business as you might do. Figure 15-3 on page 354 shows the legal form for a power of attorney.

Trusts

A **trust** is a legal document giving a person or institution (the trustee) custody of someone else's property or money (*trustor*), for the ultimate distribution to another person (called the *beneficiary*). A trust can exist during the lifetime of the trustor. This type of trust is called *inter vivos*, or a living trust. You simply transfer some property to a trustee, giving him or her instructions regarding its management and disposition while you are alive and after your death. The other type of trust is called a *testamentary trust;* it comes into being upon the death of a trustor. Such a trust can be valuable if your beneficiaries are inexperienced in financial matters or if you wish to avoid potentially high taxes on your estate.

personal perspective

C hallenging a Will

Sometimes it doesn't pay to get the cheapest deal possible. When you think you need a will, there are several ways you can do it and save money. For example, you can get a copy of your cousin Millie's will and write your will using hers as an example. Or you can go to a local stationery store and buy a fill-in-the-blanks will that is supposed to be good in all states. Or you can simply sit down and write out your wishes in your own handwriting—a holographic will—which is legal in many states.

But while the above choices may be legal, the question remains: Can these wills stand up in court if they are contested?

A person can contest the validity of the will of another person if he or she feels excluded or forgotten, believes the testator was mentally incompetent, or *under undue influence*. When a person makes decisions under pressure from another person, they are said to be "influenced." The will may contain provisions that were not truly the "will" of the decedent. The court may agree with a person contesting the validity of a will in any of the above circumstances. In addition, if you wait to draw your will until you are seriously ill, it could be contested based on your mental condition at the time.

If you want to *disinherit* a person who would ordinarily be entitled to an inheritance, you'll need a well-drawn will that will stand up to a court challenge. The most common challenge is from a possible heir who was omitted because of an outdated will. A child not mentioned in a will nor specifically disinherited will automatically share in the distribution of the decedent's estate. Adopted children inherit the same as do natural children.

How do you know for sure you have a will that can withstand a court challenge? The best way is to have an attorney prepare your will according to the laws of your state. You must mention all individuals who would normally inherit from you, and specifically disinherit any of them. To overcome a claim of insanity, undue stress, or physical illness impairing your ability to make decisions, many attorneys videotape the signing of your will. On the tape, you clearly state your intentions and your understanding of their consequences.

critical thinking

1. Have you considered to whom you would like to leave your property should something happen to you?

2. Under what conditions would you attempt to challenge the will of another person?

3. Why would you choose to have a will drawn by an attorney rather than a less expensive, do-it-yourself will?

Fig. 15-3 **Power of Attorney**

FORM No. 654 — GENERAL POWER OF ATTORNEY — DURABLE — (Short Form). COPYRIGHT 19-- STEVENS-NESS LAW PUBLISHING CO., PORTLAND, OR 97204

NL

KNOW ALL MEN BY THESE PRESENTS, That I, _____ ,

have made, constituted and appointed, and by these presents do hereby make, constitute and appoint
_____

my true and lawful attorney for me and in my name, place and stead, and for my use and benefit to demand, sue for, recover, collect and receive all such sums of money, debts, rents, dues, accounts, legacies, bequests, interests, dividends, annuities and demands whatsoever, as are now or shall hereafter become due, owing, payable or belonging to me, to have, use and take all lawful ways and means in my name or otherwise for the recovery thereof, and to compromise, settle and adjust and to execute and deliver acquittances or other sufficient dis-ch arges for any of the same; to bargain, contract for, purchase, receive and take lands, tenements, hereditaments, and accept the seizin and possession thereof and all deeds and other assurances in the law therefor and to lease, let, demise, bargain, sell, remise, release, convey, mortgage and hypothecate lands, tenements and hereditaments, including my right of homestead in any of the same for such price, upon such terms and conditions and with such covenants as my attorney shall think fit; to sell, transfer and deliver all or any shares of stock owned by me in any corporation for any price and receive payment therefor and to vote any such stock as my proxy; to bargain for, buy, sell, mortgage, hypothecate and in any and every way and manner deal in and with goods, wares and merchandise, choses in action, and other property in possession or in action, and to make, do and transact all and every kind of business of whatsoever nature or kind; for me and in my name and as my act and deed, to sign, seal, execute, acknowledge and deliver all deeds, covenants, indentures, agreements, trust agreements, mortgages, pledges, hypothecations, bills of lading, bills, bonds, notes, evidences of debt, receipts, releases and satisfactions of mortgages, judgments and other debts payable to me and other instruments in writing of whatever kind and nature which my attorney in his/her absolute discretion shall deem to be for my best interests, to have access to any safety deposit box which has been rented in my name, or in the name of myself and any other person or persons; to sell, discount, endorse, deliver and/or deposit all checks, drafts, notes and negotiable instruments payable to my order, to withdraw any moneys deposited in my name with any bank, by check or otherwise, and generally to do any business with any bank or banker on my behalf; to complete, sign, and deliver any tax return or form and pay taxes thereon or collect refunds therefrom; also

GIVING AND GRANTING unto my attorney full power and authority to do and perform all and every act and thing whatsoever requisite and necessary to be done in and about the premises, as fully to all intents and purposes as I might or could do if personally present, with full power of substitution and revocation, hereby ratifying and confirming all that my attorney or my attorney's substitute or substitutes shall lawfully do or cause to be done by virtue of these presents.
     This power shall take effect: (delete inapplicable phrase)
          (a) on the date next written below;
          (b) on the date I may be adjudged incompetent by a court of proper jurisdiction.
     If neither phrase (a) nor (b) is deleted, this power shall take effect on the date next written below.
     My attorney and all persons unto whom these presents shall come may assume that this power of attorney has not been revoked until given actual notice either of such revocation or of my death.
     In construing this instrument, and where the context so requires, the singular includes the plural.

     IN WITNESS WHEREOF, I have hereunto set my hand on _____ , 19____ .

_____

     STATE OF OREGON, County of _____) ss.
          This instrument was acknowledged before me on _____ , 19____ ,
     by _____

_____
                                                                       Notary Public for Oregon
                                                       My commission expires _____

POWER OF ATTORNEY		*STATE OF OREGON,* } ss.
_____		County of _____ }
_____		I certify that the within instrument
_____		was received for record on the ____ day
To		of _____ , 19____ ,
_____		at ____ o'clock ____.M., and recorded in
_____	SPACE RESERVED FOR RECORDER'S USE	book/reel/volume No. _____ on page
_____		_____ and/or as fee/file/instru-
After recording return to (Name, Address, Zip):		ment/microfilm/reception No. _____ ,
_____		Record of _____
_____		of said County.
_____		Witness my hand and seal of
_____		County affixed.

_____
                                                       NAME   TITLE
                                         By _____ , Deputy

The purposes of a trust are twofold. First, trusts provide for trustors or their heirs who might not effectively manage property, money, or other assets for themselves. A trustee is held accountable for how money is spent and how the trust is administered. The trustee must file papers yearly with the court reporting on how the trust is progressing. Also, the trustee typically receives a fee for these services. Second, a trust can minimize inheritance or estate taxes as well as probate proceedings. Property held in trust is not subject to probate; therefore, the property can pass to beneficiaries quickly without a prolonged court proceeding. *Probate* is a court proceeding in which a will is validated and processed. An attorney is required to complete the process of probate. The estate pays the costs of probate before heirs receive any property.

Joint Ownership

There are several ways to hold title to property. By putting property in *joint ownership*, two or more persons own an undivided interest in property. Joint ownership of property between spouses is very common. Joint ownership also may exist between parents and children, other relatives, or any two or more persons. If you and your spouse own property as *joint tenants with right of survivorship* (JTWROS), the ownership is split fifty-fifty for estate tax purposes. If one spouse dies, the surviving spouse automatically becomes the sole owner of the property. No legal action is necessary to transfer title. This form of ownership is commonly used for land, automobiles, residences, bank accounts, and securities. Joint tenancy is a convenient and automatic way to pass property. It is perhaps the most widely used property ownership arrangement.

By putting property in joint ownership, two or more persons own an undivided interest in property.

Two or more people can own property without survivorship. As joint tenants without right of survivorship, when one person dies, his or her interest in the property passes to his or her heirs, not the remaining owners.

When a person holds ownership singly, with no joint owner or named beneficiary, that asset becomes part of an estate upon death and will be distributed according to the terms of the will. Joint ownership is an effective way to avoid probate and inheritance taxes in some states.

Taxation of estates

Federal and state governments levy various types of taxes that must be considered in planning your estate. Three major ones are estate, inheritance, and gift taxes. Let's look at how these taxes are levied, and strategies for avoiding them.

Federal Estate Taxes

The federal government levies an **estate tax** on the value of an estate. An estate must be worth more than $600,000 to be subject to this tax. The tax is paid from the assets of the estate, before anything can be distributed to heirs. An estate may have to sell property or investments in order to pay this tax.

Under present law, with intelligent estate planning and properly drawn wills, you may leave all of your property free of federal estate taxes to your surviving spouse. In addition to property transferred to a spouse, all property passed on to qualified charitable organizations remains free of estate tax.

State Inheritance Taxes

Some states also levy an **inheritance tax** on an heir who receives all or part of the estate of a decedent. The basic difference is clear—the estate tax is deducted from the value of the estate, but the heirs pay inheritance taxes on property received. The tax payable depends on the value of the property in an estate, and on the relationship of the heir to the deceased. In states where inheritance taxes are imposed, laws vary widely as to the rate of taxation and the treatment of property to be taxed.

Federal Gift Taxes

The federal government levies a tax on the privilege of making gifts to others. Gifts are a popular way of disposing of property to avoid estate and inheritance taxes. Making gifts prior to death may be inadvisable if you are giving away property you need in order to live comfortably. One way to retain possession is to create a *life estate*. You may pass title to real property but retain your right to live on the premises as long as you are alive. This means that your children cannot evict you even after the property is in their names. If gifts are made to avoid taxes, they should be made in good faith and the resulting change in ownership should be observed carefully.

There are exclusions on the taxation of gifts. You can give $10,000 per person per year without having to pay a gift tax. For gifts that exceed this amount, the gift tax rate is the same as the estate tax rate. A **gift tax** is levied on the person giving—not receiving—a gift exceeding $10,000 a year. Gifts from a husband or a wife to a third party are considered as having been made in equal amounts by each spouse. Therefore, a husband and wife may give as much as $20,000 per year to anyone without incurring tax liability.

A final issue is when you give away cash or property. Any gift given within three years of death is usually considered a "gift in contemplation of death." In this event, the estate still must pay taxes on the value of the gift, and the one receiving the cash or property would have to pay inheritance taxes.

Federal/State Income Taxes

Income taxes must be paid on the income of the decedent for the partial year when he or she was living. This tax return is filed and taxes are paid before an estate is distributed to heirs. The estate may owe state as well as federal income taxes. Estate income tax returns are prepared by attorneys representing the estate and the taxes are paid from the estate before any money is given to heirs.

 S ummary

Once you reach a point in your life called financial maturity, you will be able to concentrate on retirement planning. Retirement planning is important because you will probably spend many years in retirement.

Public and private retirement plans may be insufficient to cover the cost of living. Therefore, other sources of retirement income need to be planned. Other retirement options include personal retirement plans such as IRAs, Keoghs, SEPs, and annuities. These retirement plans are tax-deferred and in some cases tax deductible. These alternatives should be an important part of your retirement planning. You are able to control when and how much to contribute. Employer-sponsored pension retirement plans and public pension benefits are also an important aspect of planning effectively for retirement.

There are many estate planning tools, including wills, powers of attorney, trusts, and joint ownership. Wills, joint ownership, and trusts are three major methods for transferring property at death. To minimize taxes on estates, you should consult an attorney who specializes in estate planning. Estate taxes, inheritance taxes, and gift taxes may be due in addition to income taxes on an estate.

V **ocabulary terms**

Directions: Can you find the definition for each of the following terms used in Chapter 15?

codicil
defined-benefit plan
defined-contribution plan
estate
estate planning
estate tax
financial maturity
gift tax
heirs

Individual Retirement
  Account (IRA)
inheritance tax
Keogh
power of attorney
reverse mortgage
trust
vested
will

1. All a person owns, less debts owed, while he or she is living.
2. Specifies the benefits promised to the employee at the normal retirement age.
3. A plan whereby you receive monthly payments from the bank based on the equity in your home.
4. A common plan for retirement, where you set aside as much as $2,000 per year, and the income is tax-exempt until you retire.
5. A condition whereby you have full rights to withdraw funds deposited on your behalf.
6. A document that gives directions as to how a decedent wishes his or her property to pass to others.
7. People who are entitled to inherit property from another person.
8. A legal document (agreement) that empowers a trustee to hold property for the ultimate benefit of a beneficiary.
9. A tax levied against the property of a decedent by the federal government.
10. A tax levied by a state government on an heir who receives assets from an estate.
11. A point in your life when you can concentrate on your own financial plans.
12. A retirement account available to self-employed individuals.
13. A plan that describes the amount an employer will contribute, but does not promise any particular benefit.
14. The process of planning for your last wishes, including minimizing taxes, attorney's fees, and other expenses.
15. An amendment to a will.

16. A legal document giving another person the power to do something in your absence.

17. A tax levied on an individual who gives more than $10,000 to a person within a year's time.

Facts and ideas in review

1. When does a person or couple finally reach "financial maturity"?

2. Why is housing a major consideration during retirement years?

3. What is meant by "using your home equity"?

4. How are investments made during retirement different from those made while you are working?

5. Why is insurance so important to people on fixed-income retirements?

6. What are four types of personal retirement plans?

7. Who can establish a Keogh retirement plan?

8. Explain the "tax-deductible" features of IRAs, SEPs, and Keogh plans.

9. How is a 401(k) plan different from a 401(b) plan?

10. Why should retirees not rely entirely on social security benefits?

11. What type of military benefits are available to retirees from branches of the armed forces?

12. Why is estate planning important?

13. Why should a person have a will?

14. What is the difference between a simple will, a trust will, and a holographic will?

15. Why would you need a power of attorney?

16. What is the difference between an *inter vivos* trust and a testamentary trust?

17. What governmental unit levies inheritance taxes? Who pays them?

18. Why would a person give property to another person during his or her lifetime rather than wait to pass property by a will?

pplications for decision making

1. At what age would you like to retire? After how many years of work? Briefly describe your plans for retirement—for example, travel, leisure, and recreation.

2. Interview your colleagues and friends to get their views on retirement planning. Why are many young people who worry about the future often reluctant to plan for retirement?

3. Explain how you might invest your money to be sure your income keeps up with inflation. Assume that you will receive social security and pension benefits from an employer.

4. Explain the advantages of using either a Keogh, IRA, SEP, 401(k) or 403(b) as part of retirement planning. Can you also list some disadvantages?

5. Explain why you should not rely solely on social security benefits for your retirement income.

6. Prepare a simple will for yourself, following Figure 15-2. What would happen to your property if you did not have a will?

7. Mary and Tom Kremer, husband and wife, both work. They have adjusted gross income of $45,000, and they are filing a joint tax return. What is the maximum IRA contribution they can make? How much of that contribution is tax deductible?

8. If you had minor children, you might create a trust to provide for them in the event something happened to you. Explain why a trust fund is important for managing the financial needs of minors.

9. When you own property jointly with another person, what might be the advantages? Why would people own property as joint tenants with the right of survivorship?

10. In 1995, you give a $20,000 gift to a friend. Would you pay a gift tax on $20,000 if you were single?

ife situation problem solving

1. Mr. and Mrs. Anderson are now reaching financial maturity. Their kids are grown and through college. Their home is nearly paid off. In five more years, they both plan to retire. Explain to them how their investment strategies today must be different from when they still had children to support.

2. Mrs. Wilson is a widow. She has an employer-paid pension of $300 a month, together with social security benefits of $600 a month. She owns her home free and clear but has high medical bills. Explain to her how she can use her house equity to generate monthly income for her retirement years.

3. Georgina is self-employed. Every year, she has extra money she could save, but instead she spends it on trips and jewelry. She also pays high taxes because she earns considerable money from her business. Explain to her why she should strongly consider a Keogh plan for her retirement years.

4. Micah works and earns under $25,000 a year. He has never had an IRA because he thinks social security will be enough for retirement income. Explain to him how an IRA works, and why he should consider one.

5. Bill has worked for over forty-five years. He served in the military for twenty of those years. He is qualified to retire next year when he reaches age sixty-five. Explain to him what type of benefits he might expect to receive.

6. Your grandmother and grandfather have built a considerable estate. They are worried about how to avoid large estate and inheritance taxes. Their only heirs are your father and your uncle. Explain to them what type of will they could use. Do they need to create a trust, particularly for their grandchildren?

7. Sherry and Alan own a new car jointly, with right of survivorship. Can Sherry leave her share of the car to another person when she draws up her will? Why or why not?

8. Your rich uncle has come to you for advice. How can he avoid estate taxes and inheritance taxes? He would be willing to give some of it away now and consider other options to avoid taxes, such as a trust. Should your rich uncle establish a gift-giving program for his heirs? What type of trust arrangements might this uncle consider?

Financial Checkup 2:
Assessing Your Financial Security

You began your financial planning process with a checkup that helped you carefully examine your financial position. Financial Checkup 2 involves building and protecting your financial security through savings, investments, and retirement and estate planning.

Your Savings Plan

Saving is often defined as postponed spending. The money you set aside today will allow you to make purchases later. A good financial plan begins first with setting aside a portion of your current income to provide for future needs.

In Chapter 10, you learned how to calculate interest on savings deposits. When money is set aside, it gains interest until some point in the future when it is withdrawn and spent. Future value is the final compounded value of a deposit or series of deposits. Using future value tables (which are built into modern financial calculators), you can determine how much money you need to set aside today in order to reach a future goal.

Figure FC2-1 shows the future value (compound sum) of an amount deposited at several interest rates and allowed to compound for a number of compounding periods. Rather than compute interest for each period and add it to the previous balance, you can use this table. For example, if you deposit $5,000 at 8 percent and leave it for 5 years, compounded semiannually, you would use the table as follows: 8 percent a year is 4 percent per compounding period (8 divided by 2); five years, compounded semiannually, is ten compounding periods (5 times 2). Look up the factor on the chart for 4 percent, ten periods (1.48024). Multiply $5,000 times 1.48024 and the total of the account will be $7,401.20 after five years, at 8 percent interest, compounded semiannually.

When you make regular payments (rather than deposit a lump sum at irregular intervals) to your account, you can use another chart to shortcut the calculations. Figure FC2-2 on page 365 is the future value (compound sum) of an annuity. (You will recall that an annuity

Fig. FC2-1   **Future Value (Compound Sum) of $1**

Period	3%	4%	5%	6%	7%	8%	9%	10%	11%
					Percent				
1	1.03000	1.04000	1.05000	1.06000	1.07000	1.08000	1.09000	1.10000	1.11000
2	1.06090	1.08160	1.10250	1.12360	1.14990	1.16640	1.11810	1.21000	1.23210
3	1.09273	1.12486	1.15723	1.19102	1.22504	1.25971	1.29503	1.33100	1.36763
4	1.12551	1.16986	1.21551	1.26248	1.31080	1.36049	1.41158	1.46410	1.51807
5	1.15927	1.21665	1.27628	1.33823	1.40255	1.46933	1.53862	1.61051	1.68506
6	1.19405	1.26532	1.34010	1.41852	1.50073	1.58687	1.66710	1.77156	1.87042
7	1.22987	1.31593	1.40710	1.50363	1.60578	1.71382	1.82804	1.94872	2.07616
8	1.26677	1.36857	1.47746	1.59385	1.71819	1.85093	1.99256	2.14359	2.30454
9	1.30477	1.42331	1.55133	1.68948	1.83846	1.99901	2.17189	2.35795	2.55804
10	1.34392	1.48024	1.62890	1.79085	1.96715	2.15893	2.36736	2.59374	2.83942
11	1.38423	1.53945	1.71034	1.89830	2.10485	2.33164	2.58043	2.85312	3.15176
12	1.42576	1.60103	1.79586	2.01220	2.25219	2.51817	2.81266	3.13843	3.49845
13	1.46853	1.66507	1.88565	2.13203	2.40985	2.71962	3.06581	3.45227	3.88328
14	1.51259	1.73168	1.97993	2.26090	2.57853	2.93719	3.34173	3.79750	4.31044
15	1.55797	1.80094	2.07893	2.39656	2.75903	3.17217	3.64248	4.17725	4.78459
16	1.60471	1.87298	2.18288	2.54035	2.95216	3.42594	3.97031	4.59497	5.31089
17	1.65285	1.94790	2.29202	2.69377	3.15882	3.70002	4.32763	5.05447	5.89509
18	1.70243	2.02582	2.40662	2.54035	3.37993	3.99602	4.71712	5.55992	6.54355
19	1.75351	2.10685	2.52695	3.02560	3.61653	4.31570	5.14166	6.11591	7.26334
20	1.80611	2.19112	2.65330	3.20714	3.86968	4.66096	5.60441	6.72750	8.06231
25	2.09378	2.66584	3.38636	4.29187	5.42743	6.84848	8.62308	10.83471	13.58546
30	2.42726	3.24340	4.32194	5.74349	7.61226	10.06266	13.26768	17.44940	22.89230
35	2.81386	3.94609	5.51602	7.68608	10.67658	14.78534	20.41397	28.10244	38.57485
40	3.26204	4.80102	7.03999	10.28572	14.97446	21.72452	31.40942	45.25926	65.00087
45	3.78160	5.84118	8.98501	13.76461	21.00245	31.92045	48.32729	72.89048	109.53024
50	4.38391	7.10668	11.46740	18.42015	29.45703	46.90161	74.35752	117.39085	184.56483

is a sum of money set aside regularly for the future.) Instead of calculating interest, adding a deposit, calculating interest, and so on, the table shown in Figure FC2-2 simplifies the procedure. For example, say you deposit $1,000 per year for twelve years, earning 6 percent interest a year. Using the chart, look up the factor for 6 percent, twelve periods (16.86994). Multiply $1,000 times 16.86994 ($16,869.94) to obtain the value of the deposits at the end of twelve years.

Using the two tables shown in Figures FC2-1 and FC2-2, complete Worksheet 1 (Future Values) in the *Student Activity Guide* (and illustrated at the end of this Financial Checkup).

For your own personal savings plan, you should set aside a predetermined amount each month. Complete Worksheet 2 (Your Savings Plan) in the *Student Activity Guide* (and illustrated at the end of this Financial Checkup).

Calculate the future values of money you could set aside.

| Fig. FC2-2 | **Future Value (Compound Sum) of an Annuity (Base Value $1)** |

Period	Percent								
	3%	**4%**	**5%**	**6%**	**7%**	**8%**	**9%**	**10%**	**11%**
1	1.00000	1.00000	1.00000	1.00000	1.00000	1.00000	1.00000	1.00000	1.00000
2	2.03000	2.04000	2.05000	2.06000	2.07000	2.08000	2.09000	2.10000	2.11000
3	3.09090	3.12160	3.15250	3.18360	3.21490	3.24640	3.27810	3.31000	3.34210
4	4.18363	4.24646	4.31013	4.37462	4.43994	4.50611	4.57313	4.64100	4.70973
5	5.30914	5.41632	5.52563	5.63709	5.75074	5.86660	5.98471	6.10510	6.22780
6	6.46841	6.63298	6.80191	6.97532	7.15329	7.33593	7.52334	7.71561	7.91286
7	7.66246	7.89829	8.14201	8.39384	8.65402	8.92280	9.20044	9.48717	9.78327
8	8.89234	9.21427	9.54911	9.89747	10.25980	10.63663	11.02847	11.43589	11.85943
9	10.15911	10.58280	11.02656	11.49132	11.97799	12.48756	13.02104	13.57948	14.16397
10	11.46388	12.00611	12.57789	13.18080	13.81645	14.48656	15.19293	15.93743	16.72201
11	12.80780	13.48635	14.20679	14.97164	15.79360	16.64549	17.56029	18.53117	19.56143
12	14.19203	15.02581	15.91713	16.86994	17.88845	18.97713	20.14072	21.38428	22.71319
13	15.61779	16.62684	17.71298	18.88214	20.14064	21.49530	22.95339	24.52271	26.21164
14	17.08632	18.29191	19.59863	21.10507	22.55049	24.21492	26.01919	27.97498	30.09492
15	18.59891	20.02359	21.57856	23.27597	25.12902	27.15211	29.36092	31.77248	34.40536
16	20.15688	21.82453	23.65749	25.67253	27.88805	30.32428	33.00340	35.94973	39.18995
17	21.76159	23.69751	25.84037	28.21288	30.84022	33.75023	36.97371	40.54470	44.50084
18	23.41444	25.64541	28.13239	30.90565	33.99903	37.45024	41.30134	45.59917	50.39594
19	25.11687	27.67123	30.53900	33.75999	37.37897	41.44626	46.01846	51.15909	56.93949
20	26.87037	29.77808	33.06595	36.78559	40.99549	45.76196	51.16012	57.27500	64.20283
25	36.45926	41.64591	47.72710	54.86451	63.24904	73.10594	84.70090	98.34706	114.41331
30	47.57542	56.08494	66.43885	79.05819	94.46077	113.28321	136.30754	164.49402	199.02088
35	60.46208	73.65223	90.32031	111.43478	138.23688	172.31680	215.71076	271.02437	341.58956
40	75.40126	95.02552	120.79977	154.76297	199.63511	259.05652	337.88245	442.59257	581.82607
45	92.71986	121.02939	159.70016	212.74351	285.74931	386.50562	525.85874	718.90484	986.63856
50	112.79687	152.66708	209.34800	290.33591	406.52893	573.77016	815.08356	1163.90853	1668.88115

Investments and Risk

After you have provided for saving, you can then begin investing. The purpose of investing is to earn a higher return than you can earn on savings. In order to do this, you must take more risk. When choosing investments, it is important first to decide how much risk you are comfortable taking. For example, investing in the stock market may be profitable but it may not be appropriate for the person who gets very nervous and upset when the stock market goes down.

Worksheet 3 shown on page 372 is a Risk Aptitude Test that lets you assess your tolerance for risk. If you find you are risk-averse, you should choose lower-risk investments to avoid the stress that accompanies high-risk investments. If, however, you are a risk-taker, then you can take maximum risks and enjoy the uncertainty. Most people fall somewhere between the two extremes; they must try to balance their investments to provide for maximum return for the risk involved.

unit

Complete Worksheet 3 (Risk Aptitude Test) in the *Student Activity Guide*. Write a paragraph summarizing your findings about your own aptitude for risk.

Investment Strategy

An **investment strategy** is a plan which examines potential returns and rates investments according to desirability.

To measure investment potential, there are two standards that apply—the rate of inflation and the overall performance of the stock market. Inflation may be averaging 4 to 6 percent, and if your investment matches or exceeds that rate, you've done well. To estimate the return you're getting, follow the formula in Figure FC2-3.

Fig. FC2-3

Average Rate of Return Formula

Current market value of investment	$_____ A
minus price you paid for it	_____ B
Gain (+) or Loss (−)	$_____ C
plus dividends, interest, and other cash received	_____ D
Total Gain (+) or Loss (−)	$_____ E
Average yearly gain: *divide* by number of years you've owned it (divide E by number of years)	$_____ F
Average rate of return: *divide* average yearly gain (F) by original price (B)	_____% G

For example, let's say you purchased ten shares of stock at $35 each four years ago. It is now worth $38.50 a share. You have received dividends of $.50/share for four years. Computation of the average rate of return is shown in Figure FC2-4.

If inflation was less than 3.9 percent on the average during those four years, your investment was worthwhile. However, if the inflation rate was higher than your average return of 3.9 percent, you should sell that investment and buy something else.

Calculate the average gain per year and average rate of return on investments shown, and rank the investments in order of desirability on Worksheet 4 (Investment Analysis) in the *Student Activity Guide* (and illustrated at the end of this Financial Checkup).

unit

Current value $38.50 × 10	$385.00 A
Original price 35.00 × 10	350.00 B
Gain (A − B)	$ 35.00 C
Dividends (.5 × 10 × 4)	20.00 D
Total gain	$ 55.00 E
Average yearly gain $55 ÷ 4	$ 13.75 F
Average rate of return $13.75 ÷ 350	3.9% G

Fig. FC2-4

Calculation of Average Rate of Return

Your Investment Plan

A good investment plan is to begin slowly, choosing low-risk, predictable, and stable options. Then, as your comfort level increases and you have more money to risk, expand into moderate and high-risk ventures with greater potential profits (and losses). Complete Worksheet 5 (Investment Plan) in the *Student Activity Guide* (and illustrated at the end of this Financial Checkup). You may wish to refer to Chapters 12–14 to examine your options as you plan for future investments.

Your Retirement Plan

The time to begin planning for retirement is now—at the beginning of your work career. Otherwise, unforeseen events may prevent implementation of plans needed to provide a secure retirement. Because people are living longer and healthier lives, it is important for all of us to consider those post-working years. With adequate financial resources, retirement can offer activities and opportunities that are both satisfying and enjoyable.

The most difficult part of retirement planning is estimating your post-retirement income and needs. Generally, living expenses decrease following retirement. Bureau of Labor statistics show that retired couples are able to maintain a similar standard of living with about half the spendable income needed by the average family of four. Some financial advisers recommend that retiring individuals have 80 percent of their take-home pay to maintain their pre-retirement lifestyle. The types of expenses will also change. Health care and food become major budget items while house payments generally disappear because mortgages are paid off. Other expenses, such as utilities and property taxes, do not change significantly.

unit

Between today and the day you retire, inflation will likely increase at a regular rate. However, your investments and savings should also increase at the same proportional rate. Therefore, when planning for retirement needs, prepare a budget based on today's dollars, knowing that in the future the costs will be higher but that the revenues (savings and investments) will also be higher to offset inflation.

To prepare for retirement, you can cut your costs and increase your income. Worksheet 6 (Retirement Plan) will help you determine how much of each you need to do.

Complete Worksheet 6 (Retirement Plan) in the *Student Activity Guide* (and illustrated at the end of this Financial Checkup).

Social security payments probably will not be adequate to meet retirement expenses. Completing the retirement plan in Worksheet 6 should convince most people of the need to provide additional sources of income. Some of these will have a tax advantage; others will not. For example, IRA contributions that were deducted from gross income are now taxable when withdrawn. Therefore, when you withdraw money from an IRA account, you will pay income taxes on the full amount of principal and earnings. When computing the future monthly income to be derived from such sources, be sure to subtract the taxes (28 percent, for example).

Estate Planning

We learned about estate planning in Chapter 14. But there are several other matters to consider which were not covered in the text. For example, when a person dies there are many decisions to make and expenses to pay. The costs involved when a person dies can range from a few hundred dollars to several thousand dollars. These expenses include final medical and hospital charges, the funeral and a casket, and burial.

By preparing instructions and making provisions for these costs in advance, you spare survivors the emotional decision-making process. Survivors who are grieving the loss of a loved one often are unprepared to make the many decisions involved in planning a funeral and burial. At such an emotional time, a family may incur excessive expenses neither they nor the estate can afford.

Cremation is a process of reducing a body to ashes in a high-temperature oven. The ashes are placed in an urn that is presented to the family or placed in a vault. Cremation is less expensive than burial, but there are special requirements. When a body is not cremated within a certain time span, usually two days, it must be embalmed or otherwise prepared for burial. These costs must be paid even though cremation is later chosen.

Funeral services, which usually last a half-hour, may be performed in a church or in a funeral home. The cost can be $1,500 or more, which includes embalming, preparations, music, printed remembrances, and newspaper notices. All decisions about these matters must be made in a relatively short period of time.

Many funeral homes have prearranged plans available at guaranteed costs. Money for the funeral is placed into an account that is insured by the FDIC or NCUA and earns interest. Although the money is for the funeral, it can be withdrawn in an emergency. Written instructions will save the family from overspending at the time of death, minimize emotional and financial distress, and assure the family that the type and cost of the funeral is as desired by the loved one.

A typical letter of final instruction is shown as Figure FC2-5. It outlines a person's wishes and helps others to implement them.

Prepare Worksheet 7 ("Letter of Instruction"), which is in the *Student Activity Guide*, to outline your wishes.

Fig. FC2-5

Letter of Instruction

Date: _____

To my family,

This is a list of my last wishes and arrangements I have made which I hope will make decisions easier for you.

1. I wish to be cremated. I have prearranged services at the Bennet Funeral Home. These arrangements include the details of announcements, selection of urn, etc. I have prepaid these services, and the receipt is attached to this document.

2. I do not wish to be an organ donor. Please do not sign forms to indicate otherwise.

3. My Last Will and Testament is in my safe-deposit box at First Independent Bank, Main Branch, this city. A copy is also in my attorney's office (Anderson & Anderson, this city).

4. I have the following accounts and policies which should be included in my estate:

   Checking Account . . . . First Independent Bank
   Savings Account . . . . First Independent Bank
   Life Insurance Policy ($100,000) . . . New York Life
   Mortgage Insurance. . . . . Veterans Services

5. My safe-deposit box contains deeds to property I own, past tax returns, and lists of credit and charge accounts I hold.

_____
J. B. Adams

unit 3

WORKSHEET 1
Future Values

Directions: For numbers 1–4, use Figure FC2-1 to compute the value of each deposit at the rate given. For numbers 5–8, use Figure FC2-2 to compute the value of each annuity at the given rate.

Future Value (Compound Sum) of $1

Deposit	Time	Annual Rate	Value
1. $5,000 Compounded quarterly	4 years	12%	$_____
2. $1,000 Compounded semiannually	10 years	6%	$_____
3. $7,500 Compounded annually	8 years	8%	$_____
4. $3,850 Compounded semiannually	2 years	8%	$_____

Future Value (Compound Sum) of an Annuity

Deposit	Time	Annual Rate	Value
5. $500/year	5 years	6%	$_____
6. $100/year	10 years	9%	$_____
7. $75/month ($900/yr)	2 years	8%	$_____
8. $250/year	10 years	5%	$_____

unit 3

WORKSHEET 2
Your Savings Plan

Directions: In the spaces, project what you could save presently (either lump sum or monthly payment), and calculate the future value in 5, 10, and 20 years at the interest rate shown. Then project what you would like to be able to save (lump sum or monthly payment) in 5, 10, and 20 years.

Savings Amount	**Interest Rates**	**Future Value**
$_____ What you could set aside today	6% per year, compounded annually, in 5 years	$_____
	6% per year, compounded annually, in 10 years	$_____
	6% per year, compounded annually, in 20 years	$_____
$_____ What you want to be able to save 5 years from now	8% per year, compounded annually, in 10 years	$_____
	6% per year, compounded semi- annually, in 20 years	$_____
$_____ What you want to be able to save 10 years from now	5% per year, compounded annually, in 20 years	$_____
	6% per year, compounded semi- annually, in 5 years	$_____

Make a plan for the amount of money you will set aside now and in the future.

Directions: In the spaces below, write when you will set aside money, how much you will set aside and how often, your goal amount, and the future purpose of the amount saved.

Date	**Amount Set Aside/How Often/Goal**	**Future Purpose of Saved Amount**
_____	$ _____/_____/_____	_____
_____	_____/_____/_____	_____
_____	_____/_____/_____	_____

unit 3

WORKSHEET 3
Risk Aptitude Test

Directions: Answer the following questions, recording your answers in the spaces provided. Then compute your risk aptitude score as shown.

_____ 1. You have an extra $100 left over from your year-end bonus. Would you rather (a) put it all in savings, (b) spend some and save a little, (c) bet it on a lottery.

_____ 2. You are ready to buy a new car. Will it be a (a) small economy car, (b) conventional, standard car with a variety of options, (c) sports car emphasizing speed, style, or performance.

_____ 3. You have won a weekend trip of your choice. Will you (a) take cash instead, (b) go on a cruise or sightseeing trip, (c) fly to a mountain lodge for skiing.

_____ 4. You are considering a job offer. Which of these is most important to you? (a) job security (permanent employment), (b) higher salary with moderate security, (c) higher pay and less job security.

_____ 5. You are betting on a horse race. Which wager will you make? (a) bet on the favorite, even though winnings will be small, (b) select a horse with a good chance of winning and moderate payback if it does, (c) pick a long shot with high payback.

_____ 6. You have a mortgage on your home. Will you (a) make regular payments, paying off the loan on schedule, (b) repay the loan quicker than required so you can save interest, (c) refinance the loan and use the extra cash for other investments.

_____ 7. You are considering changing jobs. Which sounds best? (a) joining a well-established firm and doing similar work, (b) associating with a new company in a newly created position, (c) going into business for yourself.

_____ 8. You have a schedule conflict. The following three events are all scheduled for the same day and time. Which will you choose? (a) attending a seminar, (b) working on a committee, (c) giving a speech to a group of students.

_____ 9. Your dinner is "on the house." Which will you choose? (a) cold turkey sandwich and salad, (b) enchilada with hot peppers, (c) rare sirloin with fries.

_____10. You have a delayed flight and your plane will be four hours late. Will you (a) read a book and wait, (b) take in a short sightseeing trip, (c) book another flight.

Scoring: Give yourself 1 point for each question you marked (a); 3 points for each (b); and 5 points for each (c). Scores 40 and above indicate willingness to take risk (you are a risk taker); scores between 25 and 40 indicate a willingness to take moderate risk; and scores below 25 show high risk aversion. A score of 30 is average.

Your score: _____

Based on your score, what are some investments that have the amount of risk you are willing to take? (See Chapter 11.)

unit 3

WORKSHEET 4
Investment Analysis

Directions: Calculate the average gain per year and average rate of return on investments shown, and rank the investments in order of desirability.

Asset Purchased	Original Price	Years Held	Current Value	Dividends or Interest Received	Avg Gain/ Year	Avg Rate Return	Rank
H&H Stock 25 shares	$14.00/sh	10	$16.00	$.30/share/ year	_____	_____	_____
Time CD	$5,000	5	$5,000	$1,055	_____	_____	_____
Mutual Funds 33 shares	$18.50/sh	7	$17.50	$.35/share/ year	_____	_____	_____
Gold 50 troy oz.	$410/oz.	3	$422	0	_____	_____	_____
ATZ Stock 50 shares	$29.50/sh	5	$35.50	$.50/share/ year	_____	_____	_____

WORKSHEET 5
Investment Plan

Directions: Complete the following worksheet by listing your investment and how much you expect to invest, how long you will keep the investment, and your potential return.

	Investment Choice	Initial Cost	Time Kept	Expected Profit
Example:	Time CD	$1,000	1 year	$80

Beginning Investments

1. _____
2. _____
3. _____

Systematic Investments

1. _____
2. _____
3. _____

Speculative Investments

1. _____
2. _____
3. _____

unit 3

WORKSHEET 6
Retirement Plan

Directions: Fill in the amounts you project for each category in the spaces provided. In order to obtain realistic amounts, you may need to talk to a retired person or other person about projected benefits and costs.

1. Projected Income (monthly)

a. Anticipated benefits:
Social security $ _____
Pensions   _____
Annuities   _____
Part-time work   _____
Other   _____

b. Assets used for income:
Savings accounts $ _____
IRAs   _____
Investments   _____
Other   _____

Total projected
    monthly income $ _____

| Projected − | Projected = | Surplus |
| Income | Costs | (Shortage) |

_____ − _____ = $ _____

2. Projected Costs (monthly)

a. Fixed costs:
Property taxes $ _____
Insurance premiums   _____
Other   _____

b. Variable costs:
Food   _____
Utilities
    Gas or oil   _____
    Electricity   _____
    Telephone   _____
Household maintenance   _____
Transportation   _____
Clothing and cleaning   _____
Personal care   _____
Health care and medical   _____
Recreation/entertainment   _____
Miscellaneous   _____
Other   _____

Total projected expenses $ _____

looking back . . .

Unit 3, Financial Security, explored options for saving and investing money. Wise investing will provide for future goals, including retirement. The time to begin saving, investing, and planning for retirement is now—with your first paycheck!

There are many savings options to consider. Initial investing should begin with liquid savings. Once a reasonable sum has accumulated, the rest should be used for permanent (long-term) investments.

Investing in stocks is considered risky. A stockholder is actually an owner of a corporation and shares in its successes or failures. Successful corporations provide big gains to their stockholders; unsuccessful corporations, big losses. Stockholders must carefully evaluate a corporation before investing in it to determine the potential of its stock.

Traditionally, corporate and government bonds have offered a steady source of income and eventual repayment of the principal amount at maturity. There are many different types of bonds that are considered safe and provide a dependable source of income.

Mutual funds are for smaller investors. The major reasons investors purchase mutual funds are professional management and diversification, or investment in a wide variety of securities. Mutual funds invest in stocks and bonds.

Retirement planning includes many different choices. The wise investor prefers do-it-yourself options, such as an IRA, to government or employer-based pension plans. As a person reaches financial maturity, he or she should also prepare a will and begin estate planning to be sure that federal and estate taxes are minimized.

unit four

credit management

chapters

objectives: *After reading and studying the chapters, and completing the exercises and activities in this unit, you will be able to:*

1   Describe the history of credit and define basic credit vocabulary; list advantages and disadvantages of credit, kinds of credit, and sources of credit.

2   Explain credit records, creditworthiness, credit ratings, and credit laws.

3   Discuss the responsibilities of using consumer credit; compute the costs of credit; discuss methods of reducing credit costs.

4   Explain how to solve credit problems; list major causes of bankruptcy; identify the advantages and disadvantages of bankruptcy; discuss bankruptcy laws and their purpose.

looking forward

Unit 4, Credit Management, begins with a chapter on credit in America that reviews the history of credit, advantages and disadvantages of using credit, kinds of credit available, and sources of credit in America. Chapter 16 serves as a general introduction to what credit is and why it is important to you as a consumer in the American economy.

In Chapter 17, you will learn about credit bureaus, credit files, credit ratings, and credit reports, and your rights and responsibilities as a credit user. You will also discover many credit laws that have been enacted to protect consumers.

In Chapter 18, you will learn about the responsibilities of consumer credit and its cost. You will learn how to compute simple interest as well as the true annual percentage rate, along with how finance charges are assessed on revolving charge accounts. You will also explore ways to minimize the cost of credit.

Finally, in Chapter 19, you will discover what happens when people become overextended and run into problems with credit. You'll begin with learning ways to solve credit problems. You will discover that, if you cannot meet your obligations, you should contact your creditors immediately as a first step. Bankruptcy should be the last step taken by debtors to resolve credit problems.

objectives:

After reading and studying this chapter you will be able to:

16-1 Describe the history of credit in America and define credit vocabulary.

16-2 List advantages and disadvantages of using credit in today's changing economy.

16-3 List and describe the kinds of credit available to the American consumer.

16-4 Describe and compare sources of credit in the American economy.

terms to know:

credit
line of credit
deferred billing
open-ended credit
installment loan
closed-end credit
installment purchase
  agreements
service credit
layaway
retail stores
finance companies
consumer finance
  company
sales finance company
loan sharks
usury laws
pawnshop

f people waited until they had cash to pay for all their purchases, most of us would have a significantly lower standard of living. In other words, we wouldn't be able to purchase a lot of things we have come to expect and enjoy in our everyday living. Credit has become synonymous with the good life—a means by which the vast majority of wage earners can acquire merchandise that they otherwise could not afford. But credit is not a right—it is a privilege based on responsibility and must be taken very seriously. In this chapter, you will learn about the history of credit—how it got started, how it has changed, and what to expect today and in the future. You'll also learn how credit can be your best friend or your worst enemy. You'll study the kinds of credit available to you, and explore the sources of credit to consider when making choices in today's changing marketplace.

Credit in America

chapter 16

The history of credit

When you borrow money or use a charge account to pay for purchases, you are taking advantage of the most commonly used method of purchase in the United States: credit. Over 80 percent of all purchases made in the United States are made through the use of credit. **Credit** is the privilege of buying something now, with the agreement to pay for it later, or borrowing money with the promise to pay it back later. For the privilege of charging purchases or accepting a loan, you often will pay a finance charge.

The need for credit arose in the United States when the country grew from a bartering and trading society to a currency exchange economy. Most historians place this transition at the time of the Industrial Revolution. During that period, items were first manufactured for sale. People no longer produced everything exclusively for their own use.

Americans began to be dependent on one another. Instead of each family being wholly self-supporting, growing its own food and providing its own clothing and shelter, family members began working for others to earn wages. With their earnings, they bought the things they used to make themselves—beginning with food, clothing, and other essentials. Soon the need developed for sources of credit to help families meet their financial needs. Consumer credit had begun.

The need for credit arose when our country grew from a bartering and trading society to a currency exchange economy as at the small-town general store.

One of the earliest forms of credit was the account at the local mercantile or general store. The wage earner or farmer would pick up supplies and put the amount due "on account." Accounts would accumulate for a month, for a season, or even for a year. When a paycheck was received or a crop harvested, the account would be paid in full, and the charging process would begin again. Interest was rarely charged. Credit was more a convenience provided by the store owner for the customer. The account was paid off as soon as possible. But only those customers who were well known to and trusted by the business owner were offered credit.

Banks lent farmers lump sums of money as large as $500 to put in crops at the start of the planting season. The loans were repaid after the harvest. This type of credit was very expensive, however. In the 1800s bank interest rates were very high (25–50 percent), and loans generally were made only in emergency situations. Most people, including bankers, knew very little about credit and how it worked. Consequently, bankers and others making loans charged high interest rates and were very reluctant to lend large sums of money. Credit wasn't easily accepted by most people, for it signified debt and dependence on others.

The Early 1900s

Since 1900, interest rates have dropped. The decrease is attributed to a new awareness and understanding of the advantages—especially the financial rewards—of lending money. At the turn of the century, the United States was changing from an agricultural economy, where the main occupation was farming, to an industrial economy of laborers and manufacturing. Lending institutions began to ask for security on loans (the pledging of property and income); consequently, they became more willing to make loans.

As the use of credit expanded, individual purchasing power also increased. Because more people were willing and able to buy more goods and services, the American economy grew at a healthy pace. Conveniences as well as necessities were purchased with the help of credit, and the average American's standard of living rose. Businesses and consumers benefited from credit. New jobs were created in the extension, processing, and maintaining of credit and its records; the economy grew until World War I, which created significant debt. The war debt was paid off, however, and the United States entered the 1920s in a secure position with credit stronger than ever.

The Next Sixty Years

Between 1920 and 1980, buying on credit became the American way of life. No longer was credit saved for emergencies. Many different forms of credit developed to meet changing consumer needs and wants.

In 1929, many Americans lost their savings when the stock market crashed. Banks went bankrupt, and loans went into default because jobs were lost. It took almost a decade to restore confidence in credit and investments. But recovery was followed by war again, and World War II proved costly. The federal government went heavily into debt and was no longer able to balance its budget. However, consumer credit continued to grow and flourish. Interest rates were low throughout the '40s, '50s, and '60s, and inflation rates were stable and under 10 percent.

The 1970s brought unusually rapid economic growth, overuse of credit, worldwide dependence on oil, and high inflation rates. The decade closed with double-digit inflation. Interest rates were so high that many people could not afford to buy a new home or car even with the use of credit.

The 1970s brought the first powerful consumer credit protection legislation. No longer was "buyer beware" the rule in credit transactions. Laws were enacted to protect consumers from fraudulent practices. Both government and private agencies were formed to assist consumers with their rights and responsibilities.

The late 1970s brought a new occupation—credit counseling. Credit counselors advise others on how to use credit wisely, pay bills, and get out of trouble with credit; when to seek legal advice; and how to avoid damaging their credit ratings.

The 1980s

From 1981 through 1985, the United States experienced a recession that cost many jobs and saw a rapid decline in the use of credit. The recovery that followed was slow and painful. Credit was often seen as an enemy as record numbers of bankruptcies occurred and hundreds of financial institutions failed. Some areas of the country suffered more than others; areas dependent on one industry, such as automobiles or timber, lost the most jobs and confidence in credit.

The 1980s saw a new wave of credit assistance in the form of certified financial planning. Planners assist consumers who have overextended themselves to the point of insolvency (the inability to pay one's debts) by setting up payment plans with creditors and getting the customer back on his or her feet again.

Certified financial planning became a popular career, offering services such as banking and investment advice, assistance in budgeting and planning, and selecting insurance and investment alternatives.

Financial planners earn fees based on options chosen by the investor, often in the form of commissions or a percentage of the purchase price of an investment.

Credit Today

Credit is a major marketing tool across industries in corporate America today. For example, consumers can choose from a multitude of credit cards. Each one has its special features. Car manufacturers give credit toward a new car purchase. Airlines give bonus air miles when travel is charged on their travel cards. Telephone companies give discounts on long-distance calls or service.

In industries such as automobile sales, credit is a major marketing tool.

The 1990s brought lower interest rates which stimulated continued growth in the credit industry. Many nonbanks have begun to issue general credit cards (VISA and MasterCard) to American consumers —from General Motors to United Airlines, Eddie Bauer, Nordstrom, and even gasoline companies. These companies give credit users special bonuses for charging purchases on their accounts. For example, General Motors gives points which can be applied to a new car purchase. Based on purchases, United Airlines gives air miles toward free air travel. Some companies give cash rebates, prizes, and other incentives for using credit cards for purchases.

Nevertheless, credit remains fairly tight in some areas, such as real estate financing and other large loans. Banks and other lenders are very cautious when granting loans and do extensive credit and financial checks to be sure that their risk is reduced. The average consumer may find credit in the '90s a dilemma—while some forms of credit are easy to get and offers abound, other forms of credit are elusive and difficult to qualify for.

The vocabulary of credit

To understand credit fully, you must know certain terms that are commonly used to describe credit, its availability, and its cost. Look for these terms when you start thinking about using credit, and learn their meaning before you sign any credit agreement.

1. **Balance Due.** The amount that remains due on a loan, including both principal (amount borrowed) and interest.
2. **Billing (Closing) Date.** The last date of the month that any purchase you made with your credit card or any payment made on your account is recorded in the account.
3. **Borrower.** The person who borrows money or uses credit (when you charge something, you are, in effect, borrowing).
4. **Capital.** The property you possess that is worth more than your debts (one of the requirements for credit).
5. **Collateral.** Personal property (bonds, stocks, automobiles, livestock, proceeds from an insurance policy, and so on) pledged to a lender to secure a loan.
6. **Creditor.** Person or company to whom one owes money or goods.
7. **Due Date.** The date on or before which payment is due (typically twenty-five to thirty days after the billing date with open-ended credit).
8. **Finance (or Handling) Charge.** The amount a borrower must pay for the use of credit, including interest and service charges.
9. **Installment Purchase (or Sales) Contract.** A written agreement to make regular payments on a specific purchase.
10. **Prorate.** To divide proportionately over a period of time (interest or handling charge, for example).
11. **Secured Loan.** A loan wherein the borrower pledges property or other assets to assure the creditor of repayment.
12. **Service (or Carrying) Charge.** Amount charged to borrowers or customers by merchants or banks for servicing an account or loan.

The advantages and disadvantages of consumer credit

Some people use credit extensively while others pay cash for all purchases. Many people get into trouble each year by not using credit carefully. Whether or not you use credit, you need to be aware of its many advantages and disadvantages.

Advantages of Credit

The wise consumer can gain many advantages from the use of credit. Used correctly, credit can greatly expand a family's purchasing potential and raise its standard of living in many ways.

Credit can, for example, provide emergency funds. A sudden need for cash can be solved by a **line of credit,** which is a preestablished amount that can be borrowed on demand. To establish a line of credit, you fill out the application at your bank and an amount is approved based on your income and financial position, which show the bank you can repay a loan. With a line of credit, money is always available should you need it.

Budgeting and increased buying power can be achieved through the use of credit. Major purchases may be paid for over a period of time, and establishing a good credit record by the early and wise use of credit makes future use of credit for major purchases easier.

Credit is convenient. Credit customers often get better service when they make a purchase because they can withhold payment until a problem is resolved. Regular charge customers receive advance notices of sales and special offers not available to the public, such as deferred billing. **Deferred billing** is a service available to charge customers whereby purchases are not billed to the customer until later. For example, merchandise purchased in October might not be billed to the customer until November, with no payment due until December.

The proof of purchase provided by a charge slip is usually more descriptive than a cash register receipt and helps in making adjustments when merchandise is returned. Finally, shopping is safer with the use of credit. Carrying a credit card makes for faster shopping and is safer than carrying large sums of cash.

Disadvantages of Credit

There are also disadvantages associated with the use of credit. For instance, credit purchases may cost more than cash purchases. Gasoline is an example of a good that sometimes costs a few cents more per gallon when credit is used. In addition, an item purchased on credit and paid for monthly costs more because of finance charges. A finance charge of 18 percent a year is 1½ percent a month. On a $100 purchase, the interest would be $1.50 a month. The larger the purchase and the longer the period of time taken to pay the balance due, the greater the finance charges.

Using credit reduces the amount of comparison shopping. Many consumers shop only in stores where they have credit. Comparing prices and quality at several different stores can save money.

Future income is tied up when credit is used. Buying something that will require payments for several years reduces funds available for items that may be needed in the months to come. This situation can put a strain on the budget.

Credit can provide advantages such as convenience or emergency funds; however, disadvantages may include finance charges and tying up future income.

Buying on credit can lead to overspending. People get into trouble with credit when they buy more than they can pay back comfortably. At the end of the month, when the bills come in, they may be surprised at how much they have really spent.

inds of credit

There are many different credit opportunities to explore. An awareness of the kinds and sources of credit available will help you make wise choices in your credit purchases. Most credit purchases or uses can be divided into these major categories: open-ended credit agreements, closed-end agreements, service credit, and layaway plans.

Open-Ended Credit

Charge card accounts are open-ended forms of credit. With **open-ended credit,** the lender places a limit on how much a qualifying customer can borrow during a given period. The borrower usually has a choice of repaying the entire balance within thirty days or repaying it over a number of months or years. Open-ended credit can be used again and again, generally until you reach a certain prearranged borrowing limit.

Issuers of credit cards keep a record of transactions made in your account during the month and bill you at the end of the month for all purchases. Usually you do not pay a finance charge if you pay the total bill each month. Figure 16-1 is a credit card application.

Open Thirty-Day Accounts

In an open thirty-day credit agreement, a consumer promises to pay the full balance owed each month. Travel-and-entertainment cards, such as American Express and Diner's Club, are examples of these credit cards. On all charges, the balance must be paid in full when the bill is received. There is no credit extended beyond the thirty-day billing cycle. In some cases, the billing cycle may be less than thirty days. A twenty-five-day billing period is common. These cards are widely accepted nationwide and overseas, usually have high or no credit limits, and provide instant purchasing power.

Revolving Credit Accounts

In a revolving credit agreement, a consumer has the option of paying in full each month or of making a minimum payment based on the amount of the balance due. Department stores, gas and oil companies, and banks typically issue credit cards based on revolving credit. Most merchants accept credit cards such as VISA, MasterCard, or Discover in order to increase their business by attracting customers who do not have accounts with their stores. Figure 16-2 shows a credit card statement for a revolving credit account.

Fig. 16-1 **Credit Card Application**

The figure shows a Credit Card Application form titled "CREDIT APPLICATION" with five numbered sections.

Section 1:
APPLICANT LAST NAME | FIRST NAME | MIDDLE INITIAL | HOME PHONE | DATE

STREET ADDRESS | CITY | STATE | ZIP + 4 | YEARS

MAILING ADDRESS | CITY | STATE | ZIP + 4 | YEARS

PREVIOUS ADDRESS | CITY | STATE | ZIP + 4 | YEARS

BIRTHDATE | AGE | SOCIAL SECURITY NUMBER | NUMBER OF DEPENDENTS | AUTO YEAR & MAKE | AUTO COLOR | AUTO LICENSE NUMBER | DRIVER'S LICENSE NO.

Section 2:
EMPLOYER AND SUPERVISOR | TELEPHONE | MONTHLY GROSS WAGE

ADDRESS | CITY | STATE | ZIP + 4 | YEARS

PREVIOUS EMPLOYER AND SUPERVISOR (IF WITHIN LAST 3 YEARS) | TELEPHONE | MONTHLY GROSS WAGE

ADDRESS | CITY | STATE | ZIP + 4 | YEARS

Section 3:
INCOME/EMPLOYMENT — ALIMONY, CHILD SUPPORT OR SEPARATE MAINTENANCE NEED NOT BE REVEALED IF YOU DO NOT WISH TO HAVE IT CONSIDERED AS A BASIS FOR REPAYING THIS OBLIGATION.

OTHER INCOME COMMISSIONS $ | CHILD SUPPORT $ | ALIMONY $ | SOCIAL SECURITY $ | RETIREMENT $ | OTHER $ | TOTAL PAYMENTS $ | MTG/RENT $ | BANK $ | CREDIT CARDS $ | FINANCE COMPANY $ | CREDIT UNION $ | OTHER $ | TOTAL $

LANDLORD/MORTGAGE HOLDER NAME? ☐ OWN ☐ BUYING ☐ RENT ☐ OTHER | ANY COLLECTIONS OR JUDGMENTS? | DECLARED BANKRUPTCY?

NEAREST RELATIVE | TELEPHONE | PERSONAL REFERENCE | TELEPHONE

CO-APPLICANT — IF THIS IS TO BE A JOINT ACCOUNT OR IF ANOTHER PERSON, OR PERSONS WILL USE, COMPLETE SECTIONS 4 & 5. ALL AUTHORIZED PURCHASERS MUST AGREE TO THE TERMS AND SIGN THE AGREEMENT. DO NOT COMPLETE SECTIONS 4 & 5 IF THIS IS AN APPLICATION FOR AN INDIVIDUAL ACCOUNT.

Section 4:
CO-APPLICANT (IF ANY) LAST NAME | FIRST NAME | MIDDLE INITIAL | HOME PHONE | DATE

STREET ADDRESS | CITY | STATE | ZIP + 4 | YEARS

MAILING ADDRESS | CITY | STATE | ZIP + 4 | YEARS

PREVIOUS ADDRESS | CITY | STATE | ZIP + 4 | YEARS

BIRTHDATE | AGE | SOCIAL SECURITY NUMBER | NUMBER OF DEPENDENTS | AUTO YEAR & MAKE | AUTO COLOR | AUTO LICENSE NUMBER | DRIVER'S LICENSE NO.

Section 5:
EMPLOYER AND SUPERVISOR | TELEPHONE | MONTHLY GROSS WAGE

ADDRESS | CITY | STATE | ZIP + 4 | YEARS

PREVIOUS EMPLOYER AND SUPERVISOR (IF WITHIN LAST 3 YEARS) | TELEPHONE | MONTHLY GROSS WAGE

ADDRESS | CITY | STATE | ZIP + 4 | YEARS

I certify that information given in this application is true and accurate. I give McAdams Department Store permission to check my credit rating.

Date _____ Signature _____ Signature _____

Applicant   Co-Applicant

Fig. 16-2   **Monthly Credit Card Statement**

McAdams

Account Number	Payment Due Date	New Balance	Minimum Payment Due	Indicate Amount Paid
779 19 9171	05/24/--	$244.61	$20.00	

0 7 7 3 4 2 7 0 4 2 0 0 0 0 2 4 4 6 1 0 0 0 0 2 0 0 0 4   70

ADDRESS CHANGE

IIlılılıdılIlıdıdıdılIIlıııııIlıdıllılıllılıdılIIlıııIIlıll

ADDRESS

ELIZABETH SANCHEZ
3410 MAIN STREET
VANCOUVER WA 98684-0129

CITY/STATE/ZIP

(AREA CODE) PHONE   5008440

Please return this portion
with your payment. Detach here ▼

Account Number	779 19 9171	To avoid additional **FINANCE CHARGES** being applied to your current purchases on next month's statement, pay the new balance on this statement in full by the due date.	Page
			1 of 1

Date	Store	Reference	Description	Charges	Payments Or Credits
3/28	021	108475936	SPECIAL CARE TREATMENT COSMETICS	60.00	
4/07	021	108476335	COSMETICS CLEANSERS, TONERS, MOISTURIZERS	80.00	
4/12	311	071070078	PAYMENT-THANK YOU		189.16
4/24	097		FINANCE CHARGE	4.61	

ANNIVERSARY TO DATE PURCHASES $1,853.39
ANNIVERSARY TO DATE DIVIDEND $5.96
YOU WILL EARN A 1% DIVIDEND ON MCADAMS PURCHASES
MADE PRIOR TO YOUR NEXT BILLING.
DIVIDEND WILL BE CREDITED ON YOUR JUNE 19-- STATEMENT.

Previous Balance	+ New Charges	− Payments Or Credits	Average Daily Balance (For Finance Charge Only)	+ FINANCE CHARGE (50¢ Minimum)	+ Late Payment Fee	= New Balance
289.16	140.00	189.16	307.19	4.61		244.61

Billing Date This Month	Payment Due Date	**PERIODIC RATE**	**ANNUAL PERCENTAGE RATE**	Credit Line	Amount Past Due	Minimum Payment Due
04/24/--	05/24/--	1.50	18.00	2,000		20.00

McAdams

Payments or credits received after payment due date will appear on next month's statement. For customer service inquiries, please call 1-800-555-6200. **AMOUNTS DUE HEREUNDER MAY BE ASSIGNED. NOTICE: SEE REVERSE SIDE FOR IMPORTANT INFORMATION.**

Credit Card Terms

Credit card offers may seem attractive, but remember a credit card is a form of borrowing that usually involves a finance charge and sometimes other charges as well. Before selecting a credit card, learn which credit terms and conditions apply. Each affects the overall cost of the credit you will be using. Be sure to consider and compare the following terms.

- **Annual Percentage Rate.** The annual percentage rate, or APR, is disclosed to you when you open the account and is noted on each monthly bill you receive. It is a measure of the cost of credit, expressed as a yearly rate.
- **Free Period.** A free period—also called a grace period—allows you to avoid the finance charge by paying your current balance in full before the due date shown on your billing statement. Knowing whether a credit card plan gives you a free period is especially important if you plan to pay your account in full each month. If there is no free period, the card issuer will impose a finance charge from the date you use your credit card or from the date each credit card transaction is posted to your account.
- **Annual Fees.** Most credit card issuers charge annual membership or other participation fees. These fees range from $15 to $35 for many cards.
- **Transaction Fees and Other Charges.** A credit card also may involve other types of costs. For example, some card issuers charge a fee when you fail to make a payment on time or when you go over your credit limit. Some charge a flat monthly fee whether or not you use your card.
- **Method of Calculating the Finance Charge.** If your plan has no free period, or if you expect to pay for purchases over time, it is important to know how the card issuer will calculate your finance charge. This charge will vary depending upon the method the card issuer used to figure your balance. The method used can make a difference, sometimes a big difference, in how much finance charge you will pay. Examples of how finance charges based on identical APRs can differ are explained in Chapter 18.

Tips for Using Credit Cards

Fraud costs credit card companies millions of dollars a year. Counterfeiting of cards, wrongful use of lost or stolen cards, and falsifying computer records have been major problems. To protect your card, you should take these steps:

- Sign newly issued cards immediately.
- Carry only the cards you need.
- Notify creditors immediately when a card is lost or stolen.

- Destroy (cut) expired cards.
- Don't give credit card numbers and expiration dates by phone to people or businesses you don't know.

Closed-End (Installment) Credit

To pay for very expensive items, such as cars, furniture, or kitchen appliances, consumers often use installment credit. Most credit cards have spending limits; and for those that don't, the balance due must be paid back by the due date listed on the billing statement. Whenever a loan is repaid in fixed payments that include principal and interest, it is called an **installment loan** (rather than open credit).

Federal credit laws do not use the word *installment*. Instead, this kind of transaction is referred to as closed-end credit. **Closed-end credit** is for a specified amount. The contract issued tells, among other things, the amount of the purchase, the total finance charge, and the amount of each payment. Usually a down payment is required, and the seller retains a security interest in the item sold. This interest entitles the seller to take back, or repossess, the goods sold if payments are not made according to the schedule in the contract.

Installment Purchase Agreements

Installment purchase agreements with retailers are contracts defining the repayment of the purchase price plus finance charges in equal regular payments (installments). For example, if an item with a purchase price of $800 is bought on a two-year payment plan with a 15 percent APR, the total installment price is $1040 ($800 plus $240 finance charge). Regular monthly payments of $43.34 ($1040 divided by 24) include both principal and finance charges. More purchases cannot be added to an installment purchase agreement, although another agreement can be drawn up, requiring separate, additional payments.

Installment purchase agreements generally are used for large purchases such as automobiles, appliances, and furniture. A signed contract is evidence of the agreement. The items purchased serve as *collateral* and will be repossessed if the agreed-upon payments are not made. In the case of an automobile or mobile home, the lender retains the title until the full purchase price is paid. As a consumer, it is your responsibility to read and understand any contract or note before signing it.

Installment Cash Loans

Agreements for installment cash loans with financial institutions are often similar to installment contracts with sellers. To get an installment cash loan, you must sign a promissory note. A *promissory note* is a written agreement stating the amount of a loan, the annual percentage rate, the terms, and the due date. The item purchased is used as collateral for the loan.

Installment cash loans involve a down payment on the merchandise purchased. Few financial institutions will give you a cash loan for the entire cost of a purchase. The major difference between an installment purchase agreement and an installment cash loan is the lender. Installment purchase agreements are contracts with the seller; cash loans are agreements with a financial institution that lends you the money to purchase an item.

Many businesses, such as repair shops, provide service credit.

Service Credit

Almost everyone uses some type of **service credit** by having a service performed and paying for it later. Your telephone and utility services are provided for a month in advance; then you are billed. Many businesses—including doctors, lawyers, dentists, hospitals, dry cleaners, repair shops, and others—extend service credit. Terms are set by individual businesses. Some of these creditors do not impose finance charges on unpaid account balances, but they do expect regular payments to be made until the bill is paid in full. Others, such as utility and telephone companies, expect payment in full within a time limit; however, they usually offer a budget plan as well, which allows you to average bills to get lower monthly payments.

Layaway Plans

Many retail businesses offer **layaway** plans whereby merchandise is held in your name. You make regular payments and claim the merchandise when it has been paid for in full. Most merchants require 25 percent or more as a down payment, with regular payments to be made once or twice a month. A service fee, ranging from $1 to 5 percent of the purchase price, is usually charged. A coat purchased for $100 on layaway, for instance, might require a deposit of $26 (25 percent plus a $1 fee). Then, three monthly payments of $25 each would pay off the balance, and you would receive the coat.

If you change your mind about a layaway purchase, a portion of the payments already made may be forfeited. The merchant has provided a service—credit and storage of the merchandise—and is entitled to payment for that service.

Because layaway account terms vary among merchants, it is wise to compare service fees, down payment requirements, and penalties. The advantage of layaway credit is that payment can be made over a period of time. Layaway credit is available to most customers whether or not they have any other form of credit with a particular merchant. A disadvantage to layaways is that you don't get the merchandise until a later date. During the waiting period, you may find something you like better, or you may change your mind.

Sources of credit

Credit is a service consumers buy. As with other things consumers buy, it pays to shop around to get the best deal. There are many sources of consumer credit. Some of the major sources are retail stores, commercial banks, credit unions, finance companies, pawnshops, and private lenders.

Retail Stores

Retail stores include department stores, drugstores, clothing stores, hardware stores, and all types of service businesses. Retailers purchase from wholesalers, who purchase from manufacturers and producers. Consumers buy directly from the retailers.

Retail stores take advantage of credit because customers like to shop where they have credit established. Many retail stores offer their own accounts, and also accept bank credit cards and other well-known charge cards. Credit customers receive discounts, advance notice of sales, and other privileges not offered to cash customers.

Commercial Banks and Credit Unions

Commercial banks and credit unions make loans to individuals and companies based on collateral, capital, and credit records. Interest rates vary with location or financial institution and according to what is being purchased. Good reasons for a loan, such as the need to purchase a car or a home or the desire to take a vacation, are required. Regular bank customers who have established credit are able to get loans more easily than noncustomers.

Banks and credit unions also extend credit through credit cards available to account holders. In many cases, the rate of interest charged on these cards will be considerably higher than on loans that are arranged for specific purchases. Credit card interest rates tend to fluctuate with national interest rates and therefore are often as high as the law will allow.

When a person already has a bank (or nonbank) credit card, he or she has an automatic line of credit up to the credit limit of the card. A *credit card advance* is money borrowed against the credit card limit. A card holder can access this money at a teller machine, at a customer service desk in the bank, or by writing an *access check* against the credit card account. Access checks look just like regular checks; they are supplied by the credit card company and when written, are treated like a purchase.

Credit unions make loans available to their members only. Interest rates are generally lower than those charged by banks because credit unions are nonprofit and are organized for the benefit of members. Credit unions are more willing to make loans because the members who are borrowing also have a stake in the success of the credit union.

Finance Companies

Often called *small loan companies*, **finance companies** usually charge high rates of interest for the use of their money. The reason for the high rates is that finance companies are willing to take risks that banks and credit unions will not take. In many cases, people who are turned down by banks and credit unions can get loans at small loan companies. Finance companies are second only to banks in the volume of credit extended.

There are two types of finance companies. A **consumer finance company** is a general-purpose company that extends mostly consumer loans to customers buying consumer durables. (Consumer durables are items expected to last several years, such as an automobile, refrigerator, or stereo. Nondurable goods, such as food products, are consumed in a few days or months. Durable goods may be financed because the purchase price is several hundred to several thousand dollars.) Well-known companies include Household Finance, AVCO, and Beneficial Finance.

The second type of company is the manufacturer-related **sales finance company** that makes loans through authorized representatives.

point counterpoint

L oyalty versus Shopping Around

Mary and John had something in common —both had recently purchased a new bicycle. When they discovered that they had both purchased the same bicycle, the conversation went like this:

"Hi, John," said Mary. "I see you bought a new Trek. Did you get yours down at Johnsons' Cycle?"

"No," said John. "I got mine down in Culvert. Saved $50 because I shopped around until I found this bike at the lowest possible price."

"But Culvert is almost a hundred miles from here," commented Mary.

"Yes," said John, "but when I buy something, I always get the best deal I can find. Johnsons' doesn't put things on sale, and their lowest price just can't beat the discounters. I know I won't get the service, but it's worth it to me to save the money."

"You've got a point, John," said Mary. "But my family has done business with Johnsons' for years. They know us and I feel that I will get my value in the after-the-sale service on my bike."

"Did you pay cash?" asked John.

"No," said Mary, "I'm making 10 monthly installments to Johnsons'. I just didn't have $350 cash to spare, so they let me put down $50 and pay the rest over the next 10 months."

"Are they charging you interest?" asked John.

"Yes, at the same rate I could have got at the credit union. Because I'm a member of the credit union, I can get personal loans at 9 percent," said Mary.

"Not bad," said John. "I borrowed the money using my VISA card. I shop around for banking services too, and I switch banks when I find a better deal on checking accounts, savings rates, or whatever."

"Well, anyway, we both got really good bikes. This teal green and black was my favorite, so Mr. Johnson ordered it for me," said Mary.

"Really? I took this color because it was the only kind they carried," said John. "When you get a great price, you don't always get the color you want."

critical thinking

1. What advantages do you see to establishing a good relationship with a merchant and a bank or credit union? Are there disadvantages?

2. What advantages are there to always shopping around for everything from bicycles to credit? Are there disadvantages?

3. Who do you think got the better deal in terms of total customer satisfaction for the money spent— John or Mary?

For example, General Motors Acceptance Corporation (GMAC) finances General Motors automobile dealers and their customers. Both types of finance companies borrow money from banks and lend it to consumers at higher rates.

Small loan companies take more risk than banks. Therefore, they must be more careful to protect their loans. When payment is not received when due, an officer calls the customer for an explanation. Constant contact is kept to make sure payments are made as agreed. Phone calls, letters, and even personal visits can be expected if the customer deviates even slightly from the agreed-upon payment schedule. High interest rates are another form of protection for the small loan company.

Finance companies lend relatively small amounts of money repayable in monthly installments. These companies are regulated by states under the Uniform Small-Loan Law, which permits fairly high interest rates to cover the costs of making many small loans. Typically, the law permits loans of up to $5,000 and allows interest rates of up to 42 percent a year. The growth of finance companies is the result of efforts to eliminate **loan sharks**—unlicensed lenders who charge very high and usually illegal interest rates. Nevertheless, it is difficult to eliminate such practices, which take advantage of the poorest members of society who can least afford to pay.

Usury laws set maximum interest rates that may be charged. In states where usury laws exist, finance companies charge the maximum. Where no usury laws exist, finance companies charge as much as the customer is willing to pay. When an emergency or other extreme need arises, consumers often feel forced to pay these higher rates of interest to get the money they need.

Pawnshops

A **pawnshop** is a legal business where loans are made against the value of specific personal possessions. Merchandise that is readily salable, such as guns, cameras, jewelry, radios, TVs, and coins, is usually acceptable. The customer brings in an item of value to be examined and appraised. A loan made against the property is considerably less than the appraised value of the item. Some pawnshops give only 10 to 25 percent of the value of the article; most give no more than 50 or 60 percent. For example, if you have a ring appraised at $500, you could probably borrow between $50 and $250. You will be given a receipt for the ring and a certain length of time—from two weeks to six months —to redeem the ring by paying back the loan plus interest. If you do not pay back the loan and claim the ring, it will be sold. Merchandise

taken in a pawnshop is considered collateral for the loan because it is something of value that may be sold if you fail to pay off the loan.

Private Lenders

The most common source of cash loans is the private lender. Private lenders include an individual's parents, other relatives, friends, and so on. Interest may or may not be charged on loans made by private lenders.

Other Sources of Consumer Credit

Life insurance policies can be used as an alternate source of consumer credit. As some life insurance policies build cash value, the policyholder can borrow at low rates of interest against his or her policy. The loan does not have to be repaid, but interest will be charged, and the amount of the loan will reduce the face value of the life insurance policy. (See the section on life insurance in Chapter 27.)

If you have a certificate of deposit with a bank, credit union, or savings and loan association, you can borrow money against the certificate. The certificate is used as collateral, and the interest rate charged is usually only 2 to 5 percent above the interest rate you are receiving on the certificate. If you cash in the certificate before maturity, you incur a penalty; but if you borrow money using the certificate as collateral, you get a moderate rate of interest on the loan, and the certificate retains its full value.

Credit is an important privilege that consumers have the opportunity to use wisely. Credit began in this country when we entered the industrial era and it has grown in importance since then. Credit today is a crucial part of the purchasing power of consumers, and it is important to understand credit terminology.

Credit has several advantages: it provides emergency funds; it increases our standard of living; it is convenient and safe. Credit also can have disadvantages: it can lead to overspending; it reduces comparison shopping; it ties up future income.

There are many kinds of credit available, such as open-ended credit, installment plans, service credit, and layaway plans. Credit card applications are easy and quick; monthly credit card statements list charges, credits, and payments. Credit card terms should be understood by credit customers. Otherwise, the overall cost of credit may be much more than planned. To use credit cards wisely, be sure to carry only the cards you need and notify creditors immediately when cards are lost or stolen. Be responsible with credit accounts.

There are many sources of consumer credit. Merchants, banks, credit unions, finance companies, pawnshops, and private lenders offer credit to consumers. We all can benefit through credit; when used wisely, credit makes life pleasant and comfortable.

Vocabulary terms

Directions: Can you find the definition for each of the following terms used in Chapter 16?

credit
closed-end credit
consumer finance company
deferred billing
finance companies
installment loan
installment purchase agreements
layaway

line of credit
loan sharks
open-ended credit
pawnshop
retail stores
sales finance company
service credit
usury laws

1. A plan whereby merchandise is set aside in a customer's name until it is paid for.
2. Paying at a future date for the present use of money, goods, or services.
3. Having a service performed and paying for it at a later date.
4. Businesses offering goods and services to consumers, including department stores, drugstores, clothing stores, and so on.
5. Laws setting maximum interest rates that may be charged.
6. A legal business where loans are made based on the value of merchandise pledged as collateral.
7. A preestablished amount that can be borrowed on demand.
8. A service to credit customers whereby purchases are not billed for several months.
9. Unlicensed lenders who charge elevated and illegal rates of interest.
10. Small loan companies that charge high but legal rates of interest.
11. Credit whereby you can add purchases up to a set credit limit.
12. Closed-end credit using a contract that defines payment of purchase price plus finance charge.
13. A general-purpose finance company that extends mostly consumer loans.
14. A manufacturer-related company that makes loans through authorized representatives.
15. Installment credit that involves a contract specifying amount of purchase, finance charge, down payment, and amount of monthly payments.
16. Contracts with retailers which define repayment of the purchase price plus interest in regular monthly payments.

acts and ideas in review

1. When credit first began in this country, did loans have high interest rates?
2. Why, when credit began, were bankers and merchants reluctant to lend money and give credit?
3. How has credit affected the American economy?
4. What kinds of jobs are created by credit?
5. List four advantages of using credit.
6. List four disadvantages of using credit.
7. What are four major kinds of credit?
8. How is open-ended credit different from installment (closed-end) credit?
9. Explain the concept of layaway credit. Why is it a good way to begin establishing credit?
10. Give three or four examples of service credit.
11. How are consumer finance companies different from sales finance companies?
12. List the five major sources of credit for consumers.
13. Why do retail stores accept VISA, MasterCard, or Discover Card in addition to their own credit cards?
14. Why do credit unions offer lower interest rates on loans than do commercial banks?
15. Why do finance companies charge high rates of interest on their loans?
16. Explain how a pawnshop works.

pplications for decision making

1. Give an example of a situation in which you would use collateral when making a purchase on credit.
2. How does your family make use of credit? Do you see credit use in your family as a good or bad thing? Explain your answer.
3. Do you think a consumer is being unfair when he or she accepts a "free ride" based on a "grace period" for credit cards? Give reasons for your answer.

4. One major advantage of credit is that it helps consumers deal with emergencies effectively. How does this advantage have special meaning where service credit is concerned?

5. Visit three stores and obtain charge account applications. If possible, also obtain copies of their credit agreements. Compare the forms.
   a. What information is required on all three applications?
   b. In what ways do the credit agreements differ?

6. If you were going into business for yourself, you would have to decide whether or not to accept credit cards from customers. Explain the points in favor of both positions.

7. Would it be possible to live without ever using coins, paper money, or checks? Explain how you might live on credit alone.

8. Does your state have usury laws? You can find out by consulting a current almanac or other references at your library. Identify some of the finance rates that states allow, including your state and neighboring states.

 ife situation problem solving

1. Friends of your grandparents have never used credit. Having lived through the Great Depression, when they lost their life savings, they have never trusted others enough to pay for anything except with cash. What types of problems can result from not using credit? What would be your advice to them, knowing that they have a good income from investments and have no need to buy on credit?

2. Interview three or four adults about credit. Ask them the following questions. Prepare a short report.
   a. How do you feel about the use of credit in America?
   b. Do you use credit cards, such as store credit cards or bank credit cards?
   c. Do you think the rates of interest charged by stores and banks on unpaid balances are reasonable?
   d. What rate of interest is charged by some creditors?
   e. How would you advise a young person just starting out about credit?

3. Do you feel that the advantages of using credit outweigh the disadvantages? Write a paper in paragraph form, either defending the use of credit or explaining why it should be avoided.

4. A friend of yours wishes to buy a new car. She has picked one out at a local dealer, but has only enough money to make a down payment. She asks your advice about where she can finance the balance of her loan for $6,000. What will you tell her?

5. Your cousin Bill needs $100 immediately. He has a portable stereo worth at least $800 and wants to take it to a pawnshop. Explain to him how much he can borrow against the stereo, and what will happen with pawnshop credit.

Building a credit history takes time and patience. You may have to start in a small way and build up slowly. The sooner you begin, the quicker you will realize the benefits of having credit. If you believe that you are creditworthy, keep trying to establish your credit. Don't be discouraged. Shop around. Persistence has a way of paying off.

In this chapter, you will learn about credit records and why they are so important. You will discover what factors are considered when determining a person's creditworthiness. Finally, you'll examine credit laws that protect your rights as a user of credit.

chapter

Credit Procedures and Laws

17

redit records

Before granting you credit, a *creditor* (a person or company that gives you credit) will ask about past credit performance: Were your bills paid on time? Were your debts paid as agreed? How much total credit did you receive? What is the amount of credit you have outstanding at this time? Your **credit history,** which is the complete record of your credit performance, will provide answers to these questions and thus help the creditor gauge your ability to pay back new debts.

Your Credit File

Every person who uses credit has a credit file. The **credit file** is a summary of a person's credit history. Each time credit is used and reported, information on the transaction will appear in the credit file. Your social security number is generally the key piece of information in locating your file and differentiating you from others.

Maintaining credit files is big business. A company that operates for profit in accumulating, storing, and distributing credit information is a **credit bureau.** Credit bureaus, numbering about 1,200 across the nation, assemble and disseminate detailed credit information concerning an estimated 150 million consumers. Normally, whenever a new account is opened, a credit clerk keys into a computer the relevant information from a customer's application, along with details about the initial credit transaction. Once a month, the accumulated contents are transmitted electronically to one or more of the three big national credit bureaus as shown in Figure 17-1. Local and regional credit bureaus hook into the Big Three's computer networks, making everybody's files widely accessible.

Fig. 17-1

Major U.S. Credit Bureaus

Equifax	TRW Credit Data	TransUnion
P.O. Box 740241	P.O. Box 2350	Customer Relations
Department P	Chatsworth, CA 91313	P.O. Box 390
Atlanta, GA 30374	(800) 682-7654	Philadelphia, PA 19064
(800) 685-1111		(800) 851-2674

Credit bureaus issue credit reports about consumers. A **credit report** is a written report issued by a credit bureau to its subscribers. The report contains relevant information about a person's credit history.

You can get a consolidated credit report which would show information gathered by all three major credit bureaus. The cost is approximately $30. Creditco, 2141 Palomar Airport Road, Suite 200, Carlsbad, CA 92009 provides this service for consumers concerned about information being collected. You should check your local telephone book for the names and addresses of credit bureaus in your area that also can provide a credit report about you. Ordinarily, a credit bureau will charge $5 to $15 to give you your credit file information. (If you are denied credit, you can get a free credit report if you ask within 30 days of being denied.)

How Information Is Gathered

Credit bureaus gather information from businesses, called **subscribers.** A subscriber pays a monthly fee to the credit bureau. Each subscriber supplies information about its accounts with customers—names, addresses, credit balances, how payments are being handled, and so forth. Credit bureaus also gather information from many other sources. Articles about consumers found in local newspapers are clipped and added to files. Public records are searched for information to add to a file. When someone applies to a business for credit, a credit report showing all accumulated data on the applicant is provided to the subscriber. Information in the credit report is then used as the basis for granting or denying credit. Usually credit grantors (banks and retail businesses) and employers, landlords, and insurance companies have an interest in credit reports.

Types of Information Stored

Any public information becomes a part of your credit record. For example, if you fail to pay your property taxes, file for bankruptcy, file for a divorce, or apply for a marriage license, this information will appear in your credit record. Birth announcements published in newspapers, job promotions, lawsuits, and other visible activities are recorded. When you fill out a credit application, information requested such as occupation, length of employment, spouse's name and occupation, residence, length of occupancy, number of children and other dependents, and other related data, is sent to the credit bureau by the subscriber.

reditworthiness

Before potential creditors will grant credit to you, they must determine whether you are a good risk—that is, creditworthy. If you meet certain standards that creditors believe are important, you usually will qualify for the credit you desire.

A person who is considered a good credit risk usually meets five basic qualifications, called the five Cs of credit: character, capacity, capital, conditions, and collateral.

1. *Character: Will you repay the debt?* A person with good **character** is one who willingly and responsibly lives up to agreements. One distinctive sign of good character is a responsible attitude toward paying bills and meeting obligations on time. *Stability* is an important personal trait that shows character. For example, a person who has moved six times during the past year might not be considered a good credit risk.

2. *Capacity: Can you repay the debt?* The ability to repay a loan or make payments on merchandise with present income is known as **capacity.** Creditors want to make certain that you will have enough money left over each month after other fixed expenses have been met to pay your debts.

3. *Capital: Is the creditor fully protected if you fail to repay?* Property and other assets that total more than debts are known as **capital.** In other words, when you add up all that you own (assets) and subtract all that you owe (liabilities), the difference (net worth or capital) should be sufficient to ensure payment of debt.

4. *Conditions: What general economic conditions can affect your repayment of debt?* Creditors like to know about **conditions** which affect your ability to repay, such as job security: How secure is your job? How secure is the firm you work for?

5. *Collateral: If your capacity to pay suddenly changes, what can you sell to give creditors their money?* Property or possessions that can be used as security for payment of a debt are known as **collateral.** If a debt is not paid as agreed, the collateral is repossessed and sold to pay the debt.

It is lawful and proper for creditors, in determining your creditworthiness, to ask you for the following personal information: name; age (provided it is not used as the basis for denying credit); source and amount of income; number of dependents, their ages, and other obligations to them; obligations to pay alimony, child support, or other such payments; permanent residence and immigration status; a list of assets;

personal perspective

T eenage Credit

Some businesses are finding it very financially rewarding to offer credit to teenagers. The logic is simple! Teenagers have a lot of money to spend, whether it is earned or supplied by parents. Because teenagers make many buying decisions, from clothing to automobiles, they are a market worth targeting.

Retail businesses that sell merchandise to teenagers are the first to admit that their teenage customers are important to them. By extending credit to teens, they are winning loyalty and at the same time helping teens get established with credit.

A typical teenage credit account might begin at age 16. The applicant (teenager) should have some steady source of income, whether it is from part-time, full-time, or summer jobs, or from parents. In most cases, the teenager needs permission from her or his parents. Permission is expressed in the form of a *cosignature* on the account. What this means to the parent is simple: If the teenager fails to make payments, the parent is responsible not only for the payments, but for the entire balance owed.

Why would parents consider such a deal? Teenagers would be turned down if they asked for credit in their own name. A parent's signature on the credit application allows the credit grantor to rely on the parent's credit rating at first.

Typically, teen credit accounts also have a low credit limit, or maximum amount that can be charged. For example, a $300 credit limit would allow a teenager to charge purchases, pay them off responsibly, and build a good credit record. By keeping the credit limit low, merchants and parents are assured that those beginning in credit won't get carried away and make excessive purchases.

critical thinking

1. Are there stores in your area that extend credit to teenagers? If so, under what conditions?

2. Would you like to get established in credit early? How would you pay for purchases you make?

3. Pick several stores where you would like to have a credit account. Why were these stores chosen?

place and length of employment; history of employment; outstanding debts and accounts; telephone number (or whether you have a telephone); whether you rent or own your home; length of residence at present address; residence history; and savings and checking accounts in your name. A creditor may ask you about marital status only if you are making a joint application or credit is to be secured by property in which your spouse has a legal interest. In either case, a creditor may ask only whether you are married, unmarried, or separated.

Getting started with credit

Everyone has to get started in credit sometime. The sooner you can begin establishing a good credit rating, the better for you and your financial future. It is a slow process, and depending on your age, can take several years to get well established.

Begin with a Savings Account

Open an account with a credit union if you are eligible; if not, open a savings account at a bank. You will want to start at a financial institution that will not charge you a monthly fee when your savings account balance is small. Many banks allow minors to establish accounts with small balances and waive normal fees charged to other depositors. Also, choose a financial institution that has full services available as you prove yourself: checking accounts, loans, and credit cards.

Each month or pay period, make a deposit to your savings account. Keep your account growing through regular saving.

Open a Checking Account

As soon as you have enough money in your savings account to allow you a little "cushion," open a checking account. This will provide you with a convenient method of paying your bills when you have credit accounts and will serve as a record keeping system for your budget. Choose a checking plan that is the least expensive and most convenient for you.

Maintain Your Checking Account Diligently

Do not write checks when there are insufficient funds to cover them. Bouncing checks causes a negative effect on your creditworthiness. Balance your checkbook as soon as you receive the statement of account.

Use Parents to Get Started

You may need your parents' assistance in opening your first account. They may need to act as cosigners, or you may have to rely on their credit rating at first. Many department stores and other creditors will allow you to open a small account ($100 minimum, for example) with your parents' signature, or based on your parents' permission.

Make small purchases on your new accounts and pay the bills promptly using your checking account. Be sure your monthly payments are made on or before the due date—never be late.

Get a Small Loan

Take out a small loan from the credit union or other financial institution where you have your savings and checking accounts. Even though you may not really need the cash, borrowing will establish your credit. Pay back the loan as agreed; make early payments if possible. A six-month loan is sufficient. Again, you may need to rely on your parents or other cosigner for that first loan.

Apply for a Bank Credit Card

With credit established for a couple of years, a part-time job, and a few credit references, you might now be eligible for a VISA or MasterCard account. Check the application carefully and ask about the income limit. If you do not make enough money to qualify for the card, do not apply until you do. In some cases you will have to be working full time and for the same employer for three years. Once you have a bank credit card, you will find it very easy to obtain all the additional credit you want.

 redit applications

Your credit application will reveal to a potential creditor whether you have the character, capacity, capital, conditions, and collateral to gain access to credit. Information on your application concerning your income, previous credit accounts, employment record, and various personal factors will affect a creditor's decision.

Your credit application will reveal your qualifications to receive credit to a potential creditor.

On an application for credit, you will be asked how much your gross or net pay is each pay period. Part-time employees who earn only a few hundred dollars a month generally will not qualify for credit without a cosigner. Unless you can show that your expenses are so low that you have enough money left over to pay extra bills adequately, part-time jobs are not enough. Many credit card companies, such as American

Express and VISA, require an annual income of $15,000 to $25,000 or more before they will grant credit to an applicant. Income other than regular pay, such as interest income, child support or alimony, spouse's income, or dividend income, may be listed. It is wise not to apply for credit until you are earning enough income or have enough personal wealth to afford the payments.

Your payment record is a list of your previous credit accounts. Based on your payment record, the credit bureau will assign you a credit rating (credit ratings will be discussed later in this chapter). If you have paid your bills on time, your credit rating will be favorable. Consequently, potential creditors will be more likely to grant you additional credit based on your bill paying record.

Many creditors require that an applicant has worked steadily at one job for at least six months or longer before they will extend credit. If your work history shows that you switch jobs several times a year, you will not be considered a good risk. Creditors will assume that at some future time you may be unemployed and unable to make your credit payments. You are considered stable in your employment if you have worked for a number of years for one company, or in one particular job. The longer you work consistently, the better your stability rating.

Personal factors that are often considered by creditors include occupation, geographic area, type of residence (renting or owning), age or age group, bank affiliations (types of accounts), and purpose for the credit (a good reason).

credit ratings

Many different systems are used nationwide in rating consumers' credit-worthiness. In a **point system,** you are given points for employment, amount of income, length of residence, type of residence, and so on. If your points total a certain score, you are given credit. But if you don't have enough points, then your personal factors don't total enough to warrant the risk of extending credit to you. Your score, of course, is based on data provided by credit bureaus. If the data is wrong, so is the score.

A rating system, which is accepted by many creditors, rates consumers according to how well they pay back money borrowed or charged. Credit bureaus merely supply credit files (names of customers, account balances, and payment records) to their subscribers and allow the subscribers to make their own rating decisions. Consumers may earn ratings such as excellent, good, fair, or poor.

To earn an *excellent credit rating*, sometimes called an *A Rating*, a customer must pay bills before the due date. If a payment is due on the fifth of the month, it must be received *before* the fifth. An excellent rating also means that the customer is well established (has used credit successfully for many years), has not missed any payments, and has made larger payments than the minimum amount required (paying off debts early).

To earn a *good credit rating*, which is designated a *B Rating*, a customer must pay bills on the due date or within a ten-day grace period. That is, if the payment is due on the first of the month, it must be received no later than the tenth of the month. (When a bill is paid within ten days of its due date, this is considered an automatic grace period.) A good customer pays around the due date, but never outside the grace period, and does not miss any payments.

A *fair credit rating* is earned by a customer who usually pays all bills within the grace period, but occasionally takes longer. Late charges are sometimes necessary, but normally no reminder is needed. This person is often described as slow in paying, but fairly dependable.

A person with a *poor credit rating* is usually denied credit because payments are not regular. Months are often missed in making payments, and frequent reminders must be sent. In many cases, this person has failed entirely to pay back a debt, has filed for personal bankruptcy, or has otherwise shown that he or she is not a good credit risk.

redit reports

All information included on the credit report is written in abbreviated form. A listing of key words and abbreviations is necessary for understanding information included on the report. Files are updated continuously and information stays in the file for seven years. In bankruptcy cases, information stays in the file for ten years.

Credit reports legally may be requested for investigations of credit applications, employment applications, and insurance matters. Anyone making unauthorized use of a credit report is liable for a $5,000 fine and/or one year in jail.

A separate credit file is kept for each creditor, although spouses are listed on each credit report. Each report is divided into the following sections: identification, summary of information, public records and other information, inquiries, and trade. Figure 17-2 is a sample credit report.

Fig. 17-2 **Credit Report**

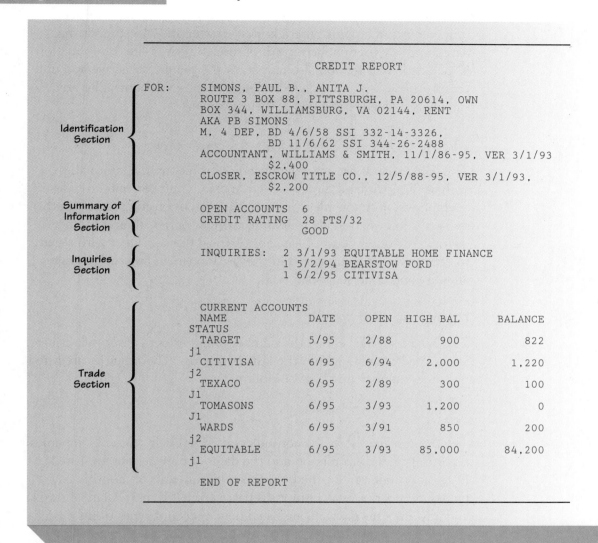

```
                        CREDIT REPORT

            FOR:   SIMONS, PAUL B., ANITA J.
                   ROUTE 3 BOX 88, PITTSBURGH, PA 20614, OWN
                   BOX 344, WILLIAMSBURG, VA 02144, RENT
                   AKA PB SIMONS
                   M, 4 DEP, BD 4/6/58 SSI 332-14-3326,
                          BD 11/6/62 SSI 344-26-2488
                   ACCOUNTANT, WILLIAMS & SMITH, 11/1/86-95, VER 3/1/93
                          $2,400
                   CLOSER, ESCROW TITLE CO., 12/5/88-95, VER 3/1/93,
                          $2,200

                   OPEN ACCOUNTS   6
                   CREDIT RATING   28 PTS/32
                                   GOOD

                   INQUIRIES:   2 3/1/93 EQUITABLE HOME FINANCE
                                1 5/2/94 BEARSTOW FORD
                                1 6/2/95 CITIVISA

                   CURRENT ACCOUNTS
                   NAME          DATE    OPEN   HIGH BAL        BALANCE
                   STATUS
                     TARGET      5/95    2/88        900            822
                   j1
                     CITIVISA    6/95    6/94      2,000          1,220
                   j2
                     TEXACO      6/95    2/89        300            100
                   J1
                     TOMASONS    6/95    3/93      1,200              0
                   J1
                     WARDS       6/95    3/91        850            200
                   j2
                     EQUITABLE   6/95    3/93     85,000         84,200
                   j1

                   END OF REPORT
```

Identification Section

Summary of Information Section

Inquiries Section

Trade Section

Identification

The *identification section* is the first part of the report, and it identifies the subject. Included is such information as full name of consumer, spouse's name, how long the file has been active, last file activity date, present address, previous addresses, any nicknames, marital status, number of dependents, date of birth, social security number, and social security number of spouse.

Following the personal data is employment information, which includes dates and types of employment; salary; spouse's employment, dates, and salary; and other household income sources.

Summary of Information

The *summary of information section* may show total (composite) credit rating points, if a point system is used; newest and oldest reporting dates; and whether public records or foreign (out-of-area) information is included. This section also may show the number of active accounts the consumer has and the credit ranges of those accounts, plus any statements added to the file by the consumer.

Public Records and Other Information

The *public records and other information section* contains information such as filing for bankruptcy—court and case number, liabilities, assets, exemptions, and how filed (individual, joint, or business). Also in this section is information about loan repayment or default and balance owing. Any other court proceedings against the consumer with regard to debt payment are reported in this section (including such things as alimony and child support).

Inquiries

The *inquiries section* shows the number of inquiries made by subscribers to the credit bureau within the last six months. The inquiries are listed by name, number, and date of inquiry.

Trade

The *trade section* shows the consumer's present credit status. Companies reporting credit information and the dates of their reports are listed. Dates accounts were opened, credit limits, amounts of monthly payments, number of years or months paying or left to pay, balances owed, and any amounts past due are listed here. Account types (joint or individual) and account numbers, number of months the accounts were late, and previous high balances are also shown. Any out-of-area (foreign) information would be reported in this section, along with the reporting bureau, in-file date, and date given to the local bureau.

Credit laws

A number of credit laws have been enacted for consumer protection purposes and to provide assistance to consumers using credit. Each of these laws was intended to remove some of the problems and confusion

from consumer credit which, as it became more widely used in our economy, also grew more complex. Together, these laws set a standard for how individuals are to be treated in their daily credit dealings. Several of these laws are summarized in the following paragraphs.

Consumer Credit Protection Act

The Consumer Credit Protection Act of 1968, known as the Truth-in-Lending Law, requires that consumers be fully informed about the cost of a credit purchase before an agreement is signed. Regulation Z of this act provides that the creditor (lender) must disclose all of these facts, in writing, to a debtor (borrower):

1. Cash price
2. Down payment and/or trade-in price
3. Amount financed
4. Insurance costs, filing costs, and other miscellaneous added costs of any kind
5. Finance charge
6. Annual percentage rate
7. Deferred payment price (deferred means "at a later time" or by the end of the credit agreement)

8. Amount(s) and date(s) of payment
9. Description of security interest (item being purchased)
10. Method of computing unearned finance charge (in case of early payoff)
11. Any other information that may be applicable or necessary

In addition, Regulation Z requires a grace period of three business days in which the purchaser can change his or her mind about a credit agreement. The Truth-in-Lending Act also limits your liability to $50 after your credit card is reported lost or stolen. There is no liability at all if the card is reported lost prior to its fraudulent use.

Fair Credit Reporting Act

If you are denied credit based on a credit report, inaccurate information in your file may be the cause. Under the Fair Credit Reporting Act, you have a right to know what is in your file and who has seen your file. A listing of requests made for your file for credit purposes in the last six months, and for employment purposes in the last two years, must be available to you. You may see your credit file at no charge within thirty days of a credit denial. A small fee may be charged in the event you want to see your file at any other time for any reason. You have the right to have inaccurate information investigated, corrected, and deleted from your file and have a new report furnished to creditors. Or, if the information is essentially correct, you can write your own statement giving your side of the story. Your statement must be added to the file.

Fair Credit Billing Act

Under the Fair Credit Billing Act, creditors must resolve billing errors within a specified period of time. A *statement* is an itemized bill showing charges, credits, and payments posted to your account during a billing period. Suppose your monthly statement shows purchases you did not make, or items you returned. Perhaps you are billed for merchandise you ordered but have not received. Creditors are required to have a written policy for correction of such errors.

If you believe there is an error on your bill, you should act immediately. Do not write on the bill that has been sent to you. On a separate piece of paper, write a letter explaining what you believe the problem to be. Write clearly and give a complete explanation of why you believe there is an error. Be specific about the amount in dispute, when you noticed the error, and any details relevant to the disputed amount. Figure 17-3 illustrates what you might say.

Date
Name and Address of Company
Account Number

I have just received my December bill. I noticed
today that there is a charge dated November 24
for Wyatt's Department Store in Calooga,
Wisconsin, in the amount of $42. I have never
shopped at Wyatt's, and I have never been to
Calooga, Wisconsin. I have not lost my credit
card, nor have I authorized anyone else to use
it. Therefore, I would appreciate your looking
into this matter at your earliest convenience.

Fig. 17-3

**Letter Notifying
Creditor of Error**

Your complaint must be in writing and mailed within sixty days
after you receive the statement. The error or amount disputed must be
dealt with by the company in a reasonable manner and within a reasonable period of time. The creditor must acknowledge your complaint
within thirty days. Within ninety days after receipt of your letter, the
creditor must either correct the error or show why the bill is correct.
Customers are still liable for amounts not disputed while the error
dispute is being settled.

Figure 17-4 is an example of one company's written policy for
handling billing errors.

Equal Credit Opportunity Act

As a result of the Equal Credit Opportunity Act, new accounts must
reflect the fact that both husband and wife are responsible for payment. In this way, both spouses establish their own credit histories.
Existing accounts should be changed to assure that the wife, as well
as the husband, is being given credit for the payment record.

The Equal Credit Opportunity Act is a federal law. Many states
also have similar laws; these laws vary widely from state to state and
are changing rapidly. Many state laws are stricter than federal laws.

Fair Debt Collection Practices Act

The Fair Debt Collection Practices Act was designed to eliminate
abusive collection practices by debt collectors. A **debt collector** is a

Fig. 17-4

Error-Correction Policy

IN CASE OF ERRORS OR INQUIRIES ABOUT YOUR BILL:

The Fair Credit Billing Act requires prompt resolution of errors. To preserve your rights, follow these steps:

1. Do not write on the bill. On a separate piece of paper, write a description as shown below. A telephone call will not preserve your rights.

   a. Your name and account number.
   b. Description of the error and your explanation of why you believe there is an error. Send copies of any receipts or supporting evidence you may have; do not send originals.
   c. The dollar amount of the suspected error.
   d. Other information that might be helpful in resolving the disputed amount.

2. Mail your letter as soon as possible. It must reach us within 60 days after you receive your bill.

3. We will acknowledge your letter within 30 days. Within 90 days of receiving your letter, we will correct the error or explain why we believe the bill is correct.

4. You will receive no collection letters or collection action regarding the amount in dispute; nor will it be reported to any credit bureau or collection agency.

5. You are still responsible for all other items on the bill and for the balance less the disputed amount.

6. You will not be charged a finance charge against the disputed amount, unless it is determined that there is not an error in the bill. In this event, you will be given the normal 25 days to pay your bill from the date the bill is determined to be correct.

person or company hired by a creditor to collect the overdue balance on an account. The fee charged by the debt collector is often half of the amount collected. The use of threats, obscenities, and false and misleading statements to intimidate the consumer into paying is prohibited when there is a legitimate reason for nonpayment, such as an error. Time and frequency of collection practices, such as telephone calls and contacts at place of employment, are restricted. Debt collectors are required to verify the accuracy of a bill and give the consumer the opportunity to clarify and dispute it.

redit discrimination

There are many legitimate reasons for denying an applicant credit. Some reasons, however, are considered discriminatory. **Discrimination** is defined as treating one applicant less favorably than others. The Equal Credit Opportunity Act of 1975 was designed to prevent discrimination in judgments of creditworthiness. The act provides that:

1. Credit may not be denied solely because you are a woman, single, married, divorced, separated, or widowed.
2. Credit may not be denied specifically because of religion, national origin, race, color, or age (except as age may affect your ability to perform, or your ability to enter into contracts; for example, minors cannot be held liable for their contracts because they are not considered competent parties).
3. Credit may not be denied because you receive public assistance (welfare), unemployment, social security, or retirement benefits.
4. Credit applications may be oral or written. However, a creditor is prohibited from asking certain questions either orally or in writing such as: Do you plan to have children? What is your ethnic origin? What church do you attend?
5. A creditor may not discourage you, in writing or orally, from applying for credit for any reason prohibited by the act (such as being divorced).

In addition to these prohibitions, the act states that creditors must notify you of any action taken on your credit application within thirty days of submittal. If you are denied credit, the denial must be in writing and must list a specific reason for the denial. After a denial of credit, the creditor must keep for twenty-five months all information used to

The Equal Credit Opportunity Act was designed to prevent discrimination in judgments of creditworthiness.

determine the denial and any written complaint from you regarding the denial. You have the right to appeal, and the creditor must give you the name and address of the federal agency that enforces compliance with the law.

ummary

Credit records are important for all consumers who wish to buy now and pay for things later. Some people get started very early with credit. It takes considerable time to build a good credit history and establish a good credit record. Credit reports are issued by credit bureaus based on information provided by subscribers and from public information.

Creditors, or those granting credit, consider many things in determining a person's creditworthiness. The five Cs of credit are character, capacity, capital, conditions, and collateral.

Credit records give important information about a person's creditworthiness, or ability to repay existing debt and take on new debt. Information in your file includes your income, payment records, employment record, and other personal factors. If you are denied credit, you have rights, including the right to see your credit file, without charge, to see why credit was denied.

Credit scoring systems rate a person's creditworthiness. There are many different systems, including a point system based on rating points. Other ratings may be more qualitative, such as "excellent," "good," "fair," or "poor."

Many credit laws have been enacted to protect consumers and assist them in obtaining and using credit. These laws include the Consumer Credit Protection Act, the Fair Credit Reporting Act, the Fair Credit Billing Act, the Equal Credit Opportunity Act, and the Fair Debt Collection Practices Act. There are some reasons why denial of credit may be legitimate; however, discrimination on the bases of gender, marital status, religion, national origin, and a host of other factors is considered unlawful. A person who is denied credit has the right to know why credit was denied and the right to appeal the decision.

Vocabulary terms

Directions: Can you find the definition for each of the following terms used in Chapter 17?

capacity   *credit history*
capital   *credit report*
character   *debt collector*
collateral   *discrimination*
conditions   *point system*
credit bureau   *subscribers*
credit file

1. Businesses that pay fees to a credit bureau in exchange for credit information collected and compiled into reports.

2. A person or company hired by a creditor to collect the balance due on an account that has not been paid by a customer.

3. A summary of a person's credit history that is kept at a credit bureau and from which a credit report is made.

4. A business that accumulates, stores, and distributes credit information to subscribers.

5. A type of rating used by credit bureaus in determining a person's general creditworthiness.

6. A responsible attitude toward paying bills and meeting obligations on time.

7. Factors that affect your repayment of debt, such as job security.

8. A written statement about a person's creditworthiness, issued by a credit bureau, that summarizes credit history, present indebtedness, public records, and other information available.

9. Ability to repay a loan or make payments out of present income.

10. A complete record of a person's credit performance.

11. The act of treating one credit applicant less favorably than others.

12. Property and assets that total more than debts owed.

13. Property or possessions that can be used as security for payment of a debt.

acts and ideas in review

1. What does a credit bureau do to earn money? Who pays for its services?
2. What is the advantage for businesses of becoming members (subscribers) of credit bureaus?
3. What types of public records become a part of your credit record?
4. Why is it important to pay your bills when they are due rather than a few days late?
5. Why do creditors care about how long you have worked at your present job and about how many jobs you have had?
6. List personal factors that are often considered by creditors.
7. What are the five Cs of credit?
8. What types of discrimination are unlawful in granting or denying credit?
9. What types of personal information can lawfully be asked of credit applicants?
10. What is the name of the federal law enacted in 1975 to protect consumers from unlawful discrimination in credit?
11. Do you have a right to see your own credit file? Explain.
12. What is the purpose of the Truth-in-Lending Act?
13. What should you do if you are denied credit based on your credit file? What can you do if information in your credit file is basically correct but damaging to you as is?
14. What is the purpose of the Fair Credit Reporting Act?
15. What should you do if there is an error on your statement from a creditor?

 pplications for decision making

1. Go to a local credit bureau and see what type of system is being used for locating, storing, and using credit information. Write a one-page report describing the process. Be sure to include the credit rating system used and explain how customers are rated and by whom (the creditor or the credit bureau). Before visiting the credit bureau, prepare a list of questions to ask and call first to make an appointment.

2. You have filled out an application for credit at a local department store. The store has notified you that they cannot give you credit because you have a poor credit rating. What are your rights, and what are some things you should do? You really have no bad payment records, and you have paid previous debts as agreed. Suppose there is an error; what responsibilities to you does the credit bureau have?

3. As a teenager, you would like to get started in establishing a good credit history. Based on your personal situation and the stores and banks in your area, prepare a plan that you might follow in getting started using credit.

4. Describe what you must do if you believe a statement you receive from a creditor contains an error. Describe the process for error correction, including your responsibilities and time limits and the responsibilities and time limits of your creditor.

5. What kinds of credit do you think you will be using in five years? How will you establish a good credit rating to be eligible for increasing credit limits and privileges?

ife situation problem solving

1. Obtain a credit application from a local merchant or national credit card company. On a separate piece of paper, list each question on the form in a column on the left. To the right of the column of questions, make another column. Indicate beside each question whether it is a(n) (a) personal question, (b) payment record question, (c) employment stability question, or (d) income question.

2. You have just received your monthly VISA bill. There is a charge on your bill of $42, but you have a receipt showing the amount should have been $24. The purchase was made at a local clothing store (you supply the name and address) one month ago. Write a letter to the bank that issued the VISA (choose a local bank) and explain the error.

3. Obtain a written error policy supplied by a local or national credit card company or other creditor. Compare it to Figure 17-4 and state how it is different (if at all) or similar.

4. Your friend Alice has just been turned down for credit. She works part-time and would like to buy clothing and jewelry on credit from a local department store. The department store stated lack of credit history as the reason for credit denial. Is there anything Alice can do?

5. A friend of yours was denied credit and asked for a copy of his or her credit report from one of the national credit bureaus. On examination of the report, your friend discovered several errors. For example, the report showed a previous employer and account which your friend never had. It also showed a previous address in another state that is not correct. What can your friend do about this incorrect information?

6. Your neighbor recently purchased a refrigerator but was unable to continue making payments because he lost his job. In the last week he has had abusive telephone calls at home. A collector has come to your house looking for him and has made false and degrading comments about the neighbor's character. Your neighbor has volunteered to return the refrigerator, but the bill collector refuses and threatens him with public humiliation and all sorts of recriminations. What is your advice to your neighbor? What law protects him?

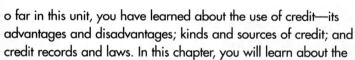

So far in this unit, you have learned about the use of credit—its advantages and disadvantages; kinds and sources of credit; and credit records and laws. In this chapter, you will learn about the costs of credit. If you are thinking of borrowing money or opening a credit account, your first step should be to figure out how much it will cost you and whether you can afford it. Then you should shop for the best terms. Credit costs vary. By remembering the interest rate and finance charges, you can compare credit prices from different sources. Under the Consumer Credit Protection Act (Truth-in-Lending Law), the creditor must inform you, in writing and before you sign any agreement, of the finance charge and the APR. All creditors, including banks, stores, car dealers, credit card companies, and finance companies, are required to disclose these two pieces of information so that you can compare credit costs.

Cost of Credit

chapter 18

esponsibilities of consumer credit

Once you have established credit, you have the responsibility to manage it carefully. Failure to take this responsibility seriously can result in having your credit limited, or in some cases, withdrawn. Because using credit is important to your financial future, you should be aware of your responsibilities to yourself and to creditors.

Once you have established credit, you have the responsibility to manage it carefully.

Your Responsibilities to Yourself

As a credit user, your most important responsibility is to yourself. You are responsible for using credit wisely. This responsibility includes checking out businesses and companies before making credit purchases. Better Business Bureaus and Chambers of Commerce have information about businesses and complaints that have been filed against them.

Another important aspect of the credit user's responsibility is to do comparison shopping. A wise buyer does not make a purchase the first time an item is inspected, nor does the buyer limit his or her shopping to one store because that store offers credit. Before making a major purchase, the wise buyer comparison shops and thinks about the purchase for at least twenty-four hours.

To use credit wisely, the consumer should be familiar with billing cycles, annual percentage rates, and any special charges related to each credit account. As a credit user, you should understand state and local laws regarding the use of credit. Finally, as a credit user, you should have the right attitude about borrowing and using credit. Enter into each transaction in good faith and with full expectation of meeting your obligations and upholding your good credit reputation.

Your Responsibilities to Creditors

When you open an account, you are entering into a relationship with a store, bank, or other creditor. You are pledging your honesty and sincerity in the use of credit.

All credit users have the responsibility to limit spending to amounts that can be repaid according to the terms of their credit agreements. By signing a credit application, you agree to make all payments promptly, on or before the due date.

In addition, the credit user has a responsibility to read and understand the terms of all agreements, including finance charges, what to do in case of error, how to return items, and any other provisions of the agreement.

It is the consumer's responsibility to contact the creditor or merchant immediately when there is a problem with a bill or merchandise is discovered to be defective. In an emergency situation, when a payment cannot be made, the consumer must contact the creditor to make arrangements for payment at a later date.

Creditors' Responsibilities to You

Creditors also have responsibilities when extending credit to individuals and businesses. Some of these responsibilities include the following:

1. Assisting the consumer in making wise purchases by honestly representing goods and services, with all their advantages and disadvantages.
2. Informing customers about all rules and regulations (such as minimum payments and due dates) and fees.
3. Cooperating with established credit reporting agencies, making credit records available to the consumer, and promptly discussing and clearing mistakes in records when they occur.
4. Establishing and carrying out sound lending and credit extension policies that do not overburden or deceive customers. (Setting reasonable guidelines and standards for credit use to prevent additional credit from being extended to customers who cannot afford it.)
5. Establishing and maintaining fair and reasonable methods of contacting customers who fail to meet their obligations, assisting whenever possible with payment schedules and other means for solving credit problems.

How to Prevent Credit Card Fraud

The most common type of fraud is the illegal use of a lost or stolen card. While the credit card holder's liability is limited to $50, the merchant is not protected from such losses. Consequently, merchandise prices are often raised to cover such losses.

It is your responsibility to protect your credit cards from loss. Some tips for using credit cards were explained in Chapter 16, pages 390–391. Always keep a list of credit and charge cards and their numbers in a safe place—not in your wallet. Notify issuers immediately when a loss occurs, both on the phone (immediately) and with a follow-up letter. Keep a copy of all sales receipts so you can verify the accuracy of the monthly statement. Put your cards in your wallet immediately after completing a credit purchase. Be sure any carbons of your credit card transaction are destroyed.

hy credit costs vary

How much you will pay for the use of credit is determined by several factors. One of the most important factors is the method used to compute finance charges explained on pages 429–436. Other important factors include the following:

1. Source of credit
2. Total amount financed
3. Length of time credit extended
4. Ability to repay debt
5. Type of credit selected
6. Collateral or security offered
7. Interest rates
8. Economic conditions
9. Costs of providing credit by businesses

As you learned in Chapter 16, the source of credit is important; some creditors are able to offer better credit plans than others. The more money you borrow and the longer you take to pay it back, the more you will pay in finance charges. The greater your ability to repay and, consequently, the higher your credit rating, the better your chances of being granted credit. The type of credit plan selected will also determine the total amount of the finance charge.

When you buy an item that serves as collateral (security) for the loan, it is called a *secured loan*. Real estate is often considered the most solid collateral; personal property pledged as collateral, such as an automobile, is often considered less secure.

The current rate of interest charged for the use of credit is often affected by the **prime rate,** which is the rate of interest lenders offer to their best commercial (business) customers. Individuals pay more than prime rate customers because the risk is greater to the lender. Inflation has an effect on the cost of credit, too. Borrowers pay more for the use of credit during inflationary economic periods.

In recent years, business costs for granting credit have risen. These business costs are related to delinquent accounts (overdue, but still collectible), bad debts (probably uncollectible), and bankruptcy. These debts add unpredictable and, in some ways, uncontrollable costs to offering credit. Other costs of issuing credit include postage, printing (monthly statements), electronic authorization of credit charges, salaries, computer support, and facilities for a credit center or department. As you can see, credit can be a major cost of operating a business.

 omputing the cost of credit

Determining the cost of credit is easy using the formula for simple interest. The formula for calculating the total cost of installment credit is somewhat more complicated. The cost of a revolving charge account can be calculated using the previous balance method, the adjusted balance method, or the average daily balance method.

Simple Interest Formula

Simple interest is computed on the amount borrowed only and without compounding. The simple interest method of calculating interest assumes one payment at the end of the loan period. The cost is based on three elements: the amount borrowed (or principal), the rate of interest, and the amount of time for which the principal is borrowed. The formula for computing simple interest is as follows:

Interest (I) = Principal (P) × Rate (R) × Time (T)

Principal

The amount borrowed, or original amount of debt, is called the **principal.** When you ask for a loan, the principal is the amount loaned to you before interest is added. For example, if you borrow $5,000 to buy a car, that $5,000 is the principal, or amount of the loan.

Rate

The interest rate is expressed as a percentage. The higher the rate, the less desirable the loan for the consumer.

Time

The length of time the borrower will take to repay a loan is expressed as a fraction of a year—twelve months, fifty-two weeks, or 360 days (in most business transactions, the standard practice is to use 360 as the number of days in a year for computing simple interest). For example, if a loan is taken for six months, the time is expressed as ½. If money is borrowed for three months, the time is expressed as ¼. When a loan is for a certain number of days, such as 90, the time is expressed as $^{90}/_{360}$, or ¼.

point counterpoint

T ackling the Trade-Offs

When you choose credit cards, there are trade-offs between the features you prefer (interest rate, size of payments, grace periods, acceptability, annual fee) and the cost of credit. Below are some major trade-offs you should consider.

The annual percentage rate (APR) is the percentage cost (or relative cost) of credit on a yearly basis. Some people look for the lowest rate so they can minimize the interest they will pay each year on purchases. APRs on credit cards vary widely. For people who make monthly payments, the APR is most important; but for people who pay the balance due in full each month, the APR is relatively insignificant.

Other people say the most important feature determining their choice of a card is the minimum monthly payment. Because some people use ongoing credit accounts to make major purchases, they need small monthly payments that are manageable. For example, some cards require that you repay 2 percent or less of the current balance each month. This feature is very appealing to people who use credit cards to make major purchases.

Still others insist that the most important feature is the grace period. By timing their purchases, they can buy something one month, get the bill for it the next month, with payment not due until the third month. This stretches the time period for repayment. In the meantime, they can earn income to pay the bill and avoid finance charges.

Other credit users claim that the best credit card is the one accepted in the most places. They want a card that can get them instant credit worldwide. They want the assurance that they can get credit at any time, any place.

Some credit users pay off the balance in full every month and consider the most important feature the annual fee. Because they do not pay finance charges, they want to avoid an annual fee that adds to the cost of using credit.

In any case, the best credit card is the one that suits your needs or situation.

critical thinking

1. Which credit card feature appeals to you the most?

2. Which credit card feature is the least appealing to you?

3. When you use bank credit cards to pay for purchases, do you plan to pay the balance in full each month? Why or why not?

Figure 18-1 contains a simple interest problem showing the dollar cost of borrowing. In this problem, a person has borrowed $500 and will pay interest at the rate of 12 percent a year. The loan will be paid back in four months.

Fig. 18-1

Simple Interest

$I = P \times R \times T$

$I = ?$
$P = \$500$
$R = 12\%$
$T = 4$ months

To multiply by a percent, first change it to a decimal: drop the percent sign, then move the decimal point two places to the left.

$I = 500 \times .12 \times \frac{4}{12}$ (Four months is $\frac{4}{12}$ or $\frac{1}{3}$ of a year.)
$= 500 \times .12 \times \frac{1}{3}$
$= 60 \times .3333$
$= \$20$

The simple interest formula also can be used to find principal, rate, or time when any one of these factors is unknown. For example, in Figure 18-2, the rate of interest is 18 percent, and the loan was repaid in 18 months. What was the principal?

Fig. 18-2

Simple Interest (Principal)

$I = P \times R \times T$

$I = \$26$
$P = ?$
$R = 18\%$
$T = 18$ months

$26 = P \times .18 \times \frac{18}{12}$
$= P \times .18 \times \frac{3}{2} \ (1.50)$
$= P \times .27$

$P = 26 \div .27$
$= \$96.30$

Or change the formula to read:

$$P = \frac{I}{R \times T}$$

$$= \frac{\$26}{.18 \times 1.50}$$

$$= \frac{\$26}{.27}$$

$$= \$96.30$$

To find the missing rate, the formula may be used again. See Figure 18-3 for an illustration. Note that the rate stated, 9 percent, is also the **annual percentage rate (APR).** The APR is the percentage cost of credit on a yearly basis.

Fig. 18-3

Simple Interest (Rate)

$$I = P \times R \times T$$

I	= $18
P	= $300
R	= ?
T	= 240 days

$$18 = 300 \times R \times {}^{240}/_{360}$$
$$= 300 \times \tfrac{2}{3} \times R$$
$$= 200 \times R$$

$$R = 18 \div 200$$
$$= .09 \text{ or } 9\%$$

Or change the formula to read:

$$R = \frac{I}{P \times T}$$

$$= \frac{18}{300 \times \tfrac{2}{3}}$$

$$= \frac{18}{200}$$

$$= .09 \text{ or } 9\%$$

As shown in Figures 18-2 and 18-3, you can either plug the numbers into the existing formula or rearrange the formula. Either way, you can find the unknown amount by simple mathematics.

Annual Percentage Rate Formula

The installment plan is used for the purchase of major items such as boats, cars, TV sets, and furniture. The installment plan is often referred to as the "time payment plan." If two or more payments are to be made (as is the case with installment credit), then the APR formula in Figure 18-4 must be used.

A retail installment contract requires a *down payment,* or amount

The installment plan is a method of payment most often used to purchase major items, such as boats, cars, or furniture.

given as security to ensure that other payments will be made. When you buy a car, the car you traded in is often considered the down payment because the older car is worth money. Many merchants require that a down payment be at least 10 percent of the purchase price.

In Figure 18-4, the finance charge is computed on an installment purchase in which a down payment was made. The total number of payments is multiplied by the amount of each payment to determine how much, in addition to the down payment, will be paid for the merchandise. Each payment includes principal and interest. When the cash price is subtracted from the installment price, the difference is the amount of the finance charge.

By law, installment contracts must reveal the finance charge and the annual percentage rate. There are two ways to calculate APR—

Fig. 18-4

Computing the Finance Charge and APR

To get a quick picture of finance charges being paid, use this quick formula:

TOTAL PRICE PAID
(number of installments times amount of each payment, plus down payment)
− CASH PRICE
(what you would have paid if you had paid cash at the time of purchase)
FINANCE CHARGE

Example: The Kramers are buying a new sofa. The cash price is $800. Instead, they can put down $100 and pay the balance in 12 monthly payments of just $66 each. What is their total finance charge?

1. Down payment	$100	
+ Payments (12 x 66)	792	
= Total price paid	$892	
2. Cash price	800	
3. Finance charge	$ 92	

The following formula approximates the true annual percentage rate (APR):

$$R = \frac{2 \times n \times I}{P(N+1)}$$

R = annual percentage rate
n = number of payment periods in one year
I = total dollar cost of credit (finance charge)
P = principal, or net amount borrowed
N = total number of payments to pay off amount borrowed

Using the formula for the Kramers, the APR for the installment purchase would be:

$$R = \frac{2 \times 12 \times 92}{700\ (12+1)} = \frac{2,208}{9,100} = 24.26\%$$

an APR formula and the APR tables. The APR tables are more precise; the formula only approximates the APR. See Figure 18-4 for the formula and a sample problem.

Credit Card Billing Statements

The cost of using an open credit account varies with the method a creditor uses to compute the finance charge. Creditors must tell you the method of calculating the finance charge. Finance charges are usually calculated by computer and are based on the monthly billing cycle. Purchases made up to the closing date are included in the monthly bill. Finance charges are computed on the unpaid balance after the billing date. Creditors must tell you when finance charges begin on your account, so you will know how much time you have to pay your bills before a finance charge is added. Most creditors offering revolving credit give you a 25- to 30-day grace period to pay your balance in full before imposing a finance charge. Creditors may calculate finance charges on open credit accounts using the adjusted balance method, the previous balance method, or the average daily balance method. The way a creditor determines the finance charge can make a big difference in the size of a consumer's credit card bills.

Adjusted Balance Method

When the adjusted balance method is used, the finance charge is applied only to the amount owed after you've paid your bill each month. For example, suppose your previous month's balance was $400. When the bill comes, you pay $300. If the creditor uses the adjusted balance method, you will pay a finance charge only on the unpaid balance ($400 − $300 = $100). As you can see in Figure 18-5, the adjusted balance method has the lowest finance charge.

To find the finance charge, the balance due of $100 is multiplied by 1.5 percent or .015 (18 percent APR divided by 12) to derive a finance charge of $1.50. The finance charge is then added to the balance to determine the new account balance for the next billing cycle.

Previous Balance Method

When the previous balance method is used, the finance charge is imposed on the entire amount owed from the previous month. This method allows no deductions for payments made. If the creditor uses the previous balance method, a finance charge will be imposed throughout the whole month for the entire $400 (the previous balance shown in Figure 18-5). This is the most expensive way to figure a finance charge for the credit user.

Fig. 18-5   **Three Billing Systems**

The adjusted balance method, the previous balance method, and the average daily balance method produce different results. This example is based on a billing period of 30 days:

	Adjusted Balance Method	Previous Balance Method	Average Daily Balance
Monthly Interest Rate	1.5%	1.5%	1.5%
Previous Balance	$400	$400	$400
Payments	$300	$300	$300 (on the 15th day)
Interest Charge	$1.50	$6.00	$3.75
	($100 × 1.5%)	($400 × 1.5%)	(average balance of $250 × 1.5%)*

*To figure average daily balance:

$$\frac{(\$400 \times 15 \text{ days}) + (\$100 \times 15 \text{ days})}{30 \text{ days}} = \$250$$

Average Daily Balance Method

Most creditors use the average daily balance method for computing finance charges. Using this method, the creditor works out what your balance is on each day of the billing cycle. This average daily balance is computed by adding together all daily balances and dividing by the number of days in the cycle (usually twenty-five or thirty). Payments made during the billing cycle are used in figuring the average daily balance. Because payments made during the period reduce the average daily balance, the finance charge using this method is often less than when the previous balance method is used. To determine the average daily balance, creditors add your balances for each day in the billing cycle and then divide by the number of days in the cycle. The example in Figure 18-5 assumes a billing cycle of thirty days.

Avoiding unnecessary credit costs

Credit can be very advantageous to the consumer when it is used wisely. Before deciding whether to borrow money, ask yourself these three critical questions: Do I need credit? Can I afford credit? Can I qualify for credit? If you can answer "yes" to these questions, then you should follow certain guidelines to minimize the cost of credit. Most credit costs can be minimized by adhering to the following guidelines:

1. *Accept only the amount of credit that you need.* Although having credit available when you need it may seem comforting, unused credit can count against you. **Unused credit** is the amount of credit above what you already owe that could be used to charge purchases. For example, if the maximum credit limit on your credit card is $1,000 and you owe $200, your unused credit is $800. Other creditors may be reluctant to loan money to you because you could at any time charge the other $800, thereby reducing your ability to pay back another debt. Potential creditors, then, may view you as a bad risk because of your unused credit. Unused credit accounts are also temptations for you to use more credit than you need.

2. *Keep credit spending steady when your income increases.* Instead of spending that extra income, put it into savings or invest it. Avoid the trap of increasing spending with each increase in your income. It is wiser to reduce existing debt or invest the additional income for future use.

3. *Keep credit cards to a minimum.* Most credit counselors recommend carrying only two or three credit cards. The more credit cards you have, the more temptation you have to make purchases. A bank credit card is good at most places where you do business, which eliminates the need for having several individual charge accounts.

4. *Pay cash for purchases under $25.* If you make yourself pay cash for small purchases, you won't be surprised with a big bill at the end of the month. Paying cash will help you realize the importance of a purchase; consequently, you will buy less and only when you really need an item.

5. *Understand the cost of credit.* You should compute for yourself the finance charges, monthly payments, length of time you will be committed to payments, and so on, for all credit purchases. Most likely, this information will be provided to you in writing. Study the costs carefully and consider how this commitment of future income to paying off debt might affect your budget in the months to come.

6. *Shop for loans.* The type and source of your loan will make a big difference in cost. The cost of credit from three different sources should be compared. Decisions to make major purchases should be planned carefully—never made on the spur of the moment. Don't sit and figure costs in a lender's office. Go home, figure all costs, and consider the purchase carefully without the lender being present.

Make yourself pay cash for purchases under $25 to avoid receiving a large bill at the end of the month.

7. *Use credit to beat inflation.* With the help of credit, you can often purchase needed items on sale that you would not buy if cash were your only payment option. In this way, you can avoid higher prices and save money.

8. *Let the money you save by using credit work for you.* When you purchase on credit (rather than using cash), you can put your cash into savings or investment options that will earn interest or dividends. Many people find it very difficult to save any money. But by putting aside some money ordinarily used for purchases, you provide a source of future income.

9. *Time your credit card purchases carefully.* By purchasing immediately after the closing date of your billing cycle, you can delay your payment for approximately two months rather than one month. Your repayment time is usually 25 to 30 days. You can extend your time to repay to 60 days, interest free, if your timing is right. Know the closing dates and billing cycles for all your open credit accounts and use them to your advantage.

10. *Use service credit to the best advantage.* Don't pay bills that will be covered by insurance. If your medical or dental insurance will pay for 80 percent or more of a claim, do not pay your share until the insurance company has been billed and has paid its portion. In this way you will have full use of your money and will not overpay a bill and have to wait for a refund. Hospitals, doctors, and others often take weeks or months to refund overpayments. Service credit, which is available to most consumers, should be used wisely.

11. *Take full advantage of rebate programs.* Many credit cards, from cards issued by retailers to car manufacturers to airlines, provide rebates. A **rebate** is the return of part of a payment based on the amount you charged during a period of time. The rebate may be computed monthly, quarterly, or annually. For example, XYZ card pays a percentage of all purchases back to customers. If you charged $1,500 during the year, you could receive a check for $15 or more. Some credit cards allow you to accumulate points that can be used for free hotel accommodations, airline tickets, or car rentals. Still others pay cash or prizes for use of the card. You should not use cards to get rebates when it means paying higher finance charges than you might ordinarily pay.

Many credit companies issue credit card rebates that can be used for car rentals, airline tickets, or hotel accommodations.

 ummary

The use of credit involves many responsibilities. You owe it to yourself to do comparison shopping, to wait before making major purchases, to understand costs and charges, and to have the right attitude toward credit. You also have the responsibility to limit spending, to read and understand agreements, to contact creditors immediately when a problem arises, and to observe credit policies. Creditors also have responsibilities to you, including clear and honest dealings, giving complete information about costs, and using sound credit policies. Credit users also have the responsibility to avoid credit card fraud by taking several precautions when using credit.

Because credit can be expensive, you should compare the finance charge and the annual percentage rate as you shop for credit. Under the Truth-in-Lending law, creditors are required to state the cost of borrowing so that you can compare credit costs and shop for credit. Credit costs vary according to many factors, such as the source of credit, amount financed, length of time credit is extended, and type of credit selected.

To compute the cost of credit, you can use a table or a formula. Installment credit involves the use of the annual percentage rate formula. The finance charge on open-ended credit can be calculated in one of three ways: adjusted balance, previous balance, average daily balance.

To avoid unnecessary credit costs, there are many wise practices you can follow, such as not taking advantage of unused credit, keeping credit cards to a minimum, paying cash for small purchases, and shopping at least three places for loans.

V ocabulary terms

Directions: Can you find the definition for each of the following terms
used in Chapter 18?

annual percentage rate   rebate
   (APR)   simple interest
prime rate   unused credit
principal

1. The total amount borrowed.
2. The amount of credit available up to your maximum credit limit.
3. Interest computed on the principal only and without compounding; the dollar cost of borrowing money.
4. The rate of interest lenders offer to their best commercial (business) customers.
5. The amount returned to a credit user as a bonus for charging purchases on certain credit cards.
6. The percentage cost of credit on a yearly basis.

F acts and ideas in review

1. What are the responsibilities of creditors to consumers?
2. What is your liability and responsibility if your credit card is lost or stolen?
3. What kinds of things can you do to protect yourself from losing your credit cards and having large purchases made with your credit cards?
4. List several factors that affect the cost or rate of interest a customer will have to pay to get a loan.
5. What is the formula for computing simple interest?
6. What is the formula for computing the APR on installment credit?
7. Explain the three methods for determining the finance charge on revolving credit?
8. List eleven things you can do to avoid unnecessary credit costs.
9. How can unused credit work against you when you are applying for a new loan?
10. What is meant by "timing your purchases to your advantage"?

Applications for decision making

1. Using the formula for simple interest (I = PRT), solve the following problems, rounding to the nearest penny.

   a. I = ?
      P = $500
      R = 18 percent
      T = 6 months

   b. I = ?
      P = $1,000
      R = 13.5 percent
      T = 8 months

   c. I = ?
      P = $108
      R = 15 percent
      T = 3 months

   d. I = ?
      P = $89.50
      R = 8 percent
      T = 9 months

2. The following simple interest problems have different elements missing. Either change the formula to find the missing element, or insert the given elements into the formula and solve as shown in this chapter.

   Round to the nearest penny. Use the formula I = PRT.

   a. I = $8
      P = ?
      R = 12 percent
      T = 60 days (60/360)

   b. I = $54
      P = ?
      R = 18 percent
      T = 18 months (18/12)

   c. I = $510
      P = $2,100
      R = ?
      T = 2 years (24/12)

   d. I = $36
      P = $108
      R = ?
      T = 18 months (18/12)

3. Using the procedure illustrated in Figure 18-4, determine the APR for the following problems:

   a. The purchase price of an item requires a down payment of $60, with the balance to be paid in twelve equal payments of $60 each. The cash price is $700.

   b. The purchase price of an item that has a down payment of $100 and 24 equal payments of $90. The cash price is $2,000.

   c. The cash price of an item is $200. The down payment is $20, and ten equal payments of $22 each are to be made.

   d. The cash price of an item is $895. With $95 down, the balance is payable in fifteen payments of $60 each.

4. The previous balance method of computing interest is determined by first calculating the finance charge, then subtracting the monthly payment to determine the new balance. Complete the following chart, using a calculator and rounding to the nearest penny. The APR is 12 percent. What is the total finance charge paid?

Beg. Balance	Finance Charge	Adj. Balance	Payment	New Balance
$100	_____	_____	$20.00	_____
_____	_____	_____	20.00	_____
_____	_____	_____	20.00	_____

Total Finance Charge _____

5. With the adjusted balance method of computing interest, the monthly payment is subtracted before the finance charge is calculated. The amount of the finance charge is then added to obtain the new balance. Complete the following chart, using a calculator and rounding to the nearest penny. The APR is 18 percent. What is the total finance charge paid?

Beg. Balance	Payment	Adj. Balance	Finance Charge	New Balance
$500	$50.00	_____	_____	_____
_____	50.00	_____	_____	_____
_____	50.00	_____	_____	_____

Total Finance Charge _____

L ife situation problem solving

1. Your friend Marty is unable to determine whether he is getting a good deal on a loan of $100 for 6 months when he pays back $114. What is the simple interest rate he is paying? (Use I = PRT)

2. You are considering buying a used piano. The cash price of the piano is $600. The company selling the piano is willing to sell it to you for $50 down and 12 equal payments of $50. What is the installment price? What is the finance charge?

3. If you were to purchase a major appliance and pay for it this year, borrowing $800 at 18 percent for 8 months, how much would you pay to finance this purchase?

4. You buy a new car that sells for $14,000 by trading in your car and using the trade-in allowance of $2,000 as a down payment. You pay the balance at $295 a month for 48 months. What is the APR?

5. Your friend Jack is proud of his ability to have and use credit. He buys his lunch every day on credit, and at the end of the month pays only the minimum balance due. When one credit card is at its limit, he switches to another credit card. He figures he can just go on charging forever because he can just make minimum payments. Do you see any problems with this behavior? Explain to Jack how he is incurring finance charges.

6. Your cousin is considering whether to buy a new sound system. She can use installment credit at the store (18% APR), or she could put the purchase on her credit card. Her credit card has a variable rate, which is 9.9% right now, but is likely to increase in the next few months. What is your advice?

A family or an individual that is actively involved in budgeting can easily determine if more debt can be assumed. Unfortunately, from time to time some families and individuals find themselves overextended—trying to cope with more debt than they can possibly handle. While responsible management of credit usually results in a good, solid credit history without blemishes, there are nevertheless times when a person will have trouble meeting debt obligations. Bankruptcy is an extreme legal action available to individuals (as well as corporations) unable to make payments on debts.

In this chapter, you will learn about procedures for managing excessive debt, including bankruptcy as a final option. You will also learn about bankruptcy laws, property exemptions, the causes of debt, the advantages and disadvantages of bankruptcy, and a form that is commonly filed in declaring bankruptcy.

chapter 19

Problems with Credit

olving credit problems

One of the major disadvantages of credit is that it can lead to over-spending. When credit is not budgeted wisely, credit problems can arise. Many people get into trouble with credit every year, and they represent all levels of income and social standing.

Some of the most common abuses of credit are overspending and impulse buying.

Credit problems do not happen suddenly. They usually arise after months and years of poor planning, impulse buying, and careless budgeting. If an excessive debt problem is detected early enough, the cure is simple and easy. However, it is best to plan to use your credit wisely and manage debt carefully from the beginning, so that you don't find yourself with a serious financial problem.

The 20/10 Rule

Credit counselors often suggest use of the **20/10 Rule** to people beginning to use credit: Never borrow more each year than 20 percent of your yearly take-home pay, and never agree to monthly payments that are more than 10 percent of your monthly take-home. The 20/10 Rule applies to credit purchases other than for housing; that is, it applies to closed and open-ended credit.

As an example, suppose that you and your spouse have yearly take-home pay of $21,000 (monthly take-home pay of $1,750). Your borrowing should not exceed a total of $4,200 (20 percent of yearly take-home pay), and your monthly credit payments should not be more than $175. By following the 20/10 Rule, you avoid tying up future income with large credit payments. You can make reasonable house payments; pay insurance, utilities, and other necessary fixed expenses; and still have money left over for entertainment, clothing, and miscellaneous purchases.

Not-for-Profit Credit Counseling

When you get into serious problems with credit, you can seek advice and counseling from one of many private or government-sponsored counseling services. Sometimes fees are charged, usually according to your ability to pay. A counselor will help you set up a good budget and show you how to make your income do the most for you. The credit plan is voluntary; you are under no legal obligation to use or to continue to use the plan.

You cannot get loans from a credit counseling service, but you can get good advice for finding a workable plan for your situation. You can learn about credit counselors by looking under consumer credit counseling services in the Yellow Pages. A local, nonprofit organization affiliated with the National Foundation for Consumer Credit is the Consumer Credit Counseling Service (CCCS). Anyone overwhelmed by credit obligations can phone, write, or visit a CCCS office. There are over 200 CCCS offices nationally. The CCCS requires that an application for credit counseling be completed. Then an appointment is arranged for a personal interview with an applicant. CCCS counseling is usually free.

Some churches, private foundations, universities, military bases, credit unions, and state and federal housing authorities provide similar services. These nonprofit groups that assist in credit counseling are also found in the Yellow Pages of your telephone book.

Commercial Debt-Adjustment Firms

There are numerous companies operating for profit that charge a fee to help you get out of credit trouble. Services provided and fees charged vary widely, and any fee charged will increase the debt you owe. Often you will be asked to turn over your checkbook, paychecks, and bills to the debt-adjustment company. A credit advisor will contact your creditors to work out repayment plans and will make payments for you. Generally, the services provided include a five-step plan, as shown in Figure 19-1.

Fig. 19-1

**Debt-Adjustment
Service Plan**

1. Contact creditors and arrange for payments that can be made from your earnings.

2. Take your paycheck and checkbook and make debt payments for you. You are given an allowance until all bills have been paid off. This arrangement can take two years or more if you are in deep trouble.

3. Counsel you so that you understand how you got so far into debt and how to avoid doing so again in the future.

4. Work with you to create a reasonable budget that you can live with. Credit cards are taken away and given back slowly as the advisor becomes certain that you understand how to use them wisely.

5. Supervise your budget and help you make any needed changes or adjustments.

When you are desperate and cannot seem to control your purchases, you should seek professional credit counseling. You may not like the strictness or discipline involved, but the valuable training can help you avoid getting too deeply into debt again. Debt-adjustment companies, like credit counseling services, are listed in your Yellow Pages and in business directories.

Legal Recourse

But what if a debtor is suffering from an extreme case of financial woes? Is there any relief? When credit problems arise that cannot be solved by your own actions or through assistance, the final step for relief is bankruptcy. When you are *bankrupt*, you are unable to meet your bills. **Bankruptcy** is a legal process whereby you are declared legally *insolvent*—having insufficient income and assets to pay your debts (liabilities).

The U.S. Constitution, Article I, Section 8, states: "The Congress shall have the power . . . to establish . . . uniform laws on the subject of bankruptcies throughout the United States." The inclusion of this clause reflects the belief of our nation's early leaders that debtors should be given a second chance. A **debtor** is a person who owes money to others.

Under old English law, people hopelessly in debt were put in debtors' prisons with no chance of recovering. The drafters of the Constitution opposed this treatment of debtors and gave Congress the authority to pass laws to help people seriously in debt. Since 1880, Congress has passed various bankruptcy laws, the most recent of which is the Bankruptcy Reform Act of 1978. This law was amended in 1984; currently, proposed amendments are likely.

Bankruptcy laws and their purpose

Bankruptcy law in the United States has two goals. The first is to protect a debtor by giving her or him a fresh start, free from creditors' claims. The second is to give fair treatment to creditors competing for a debtor's assets. Many creditors complain that the bankruptcy code requires them to tighten credit because it is too easy for people to give up their debts rather than accept responsibility for them. On the other hand, bankruptcy still casts a black shadow over an individual's credit record. Further revisions of the bankruptcy laws are likely to keep current with trends and problems in the credit industry.

Bankruptcy laws treat two general classes of debt: secured and unsecured. With secured loans that we learned about in Chapter 18, the debtor has pledged specific assets as collateral for payment. If the debt is not paid, the creditor can repossess the asset that has been

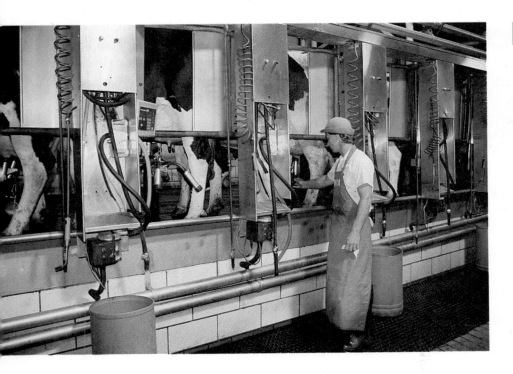

For unsecured debt, no specific assets are pledged and all the debtor's resources may be considered in the bankruptcy action.

pledged. For **unsecured debt,** no specific asset is pledged, but all of the debtor's resources are considered in a bankruptcy action.

Involuntary versus Voluntary Bankruptcy

There are two basic types of bankruptcy: voluntary and involuntary. **Involuntary bankruptcy** occurs when creditors file a petition with the court, asking the court to declare you bankrupt. Under the Federal Bankruptcy Code, an involuntary bankruptcy cannot be started against a farmer or a charitable organization. The court makes a determination as to whether or not you should be so declared. If the court agrees with your creditors, it takes over your property and other assets and pays off your debts proportionally. Involuntary bankruptcy does not occur very often because most creditors prefer to be repaid in full over a period of time rather than settle only for a portion of your remaining assets.

Voluntary bankruptcy, the most common kind, occurs when you file a petition with a federal court asking to be declared bankrupt. Notice of your pending bankruptcy is given in local newspapers and by letters to your creditors. Once notice is given, creditors may file claims. The court collects your assets, sells your property as needed, and distributes the proceeds equitably among your creditors.

A **proportional share** is a percentage based on total debt. For example, let us say that your total debt is $15,000 and your total assets are $5,000. You owe one creditor $1,500. The proportional share owed this creditor is 10 percent of your assets, or $500. The remainder of that debt is *discharged* (no longer owed) after the bankruptcy is complete. **Discharged debts** are those set aside by the court; creditors can no longer seek payment for these debts. Be aware, however, that some debts, such as taxes, child support, and alimony, continue after bankruptcy (cannot be discharged).

Chapter 11 Bankruptcy

For businesses, **Chapter 11 bankruptcy** provides that existing management retains control of a business unless a trustee is appointed by the court. The trustee is a person who will oversee the assets of the business and file court reports. The trustee has substantial powers to administer the operations of a business. The main purpose of Chapter 11 bankruptcy is to reorganize the debt structure of a business. A court can impose a reorganization plan over objections of creditors if it is deemed to be fair and in the best interests of those involved.

For individuals, there are two basic ways to file bankruptcy: Chapter 7 and Chapter 13.

Chapter 7 Bankruptcy

Liquidation is the most familiar type of bankruptcy proceeding. With liquidation, a person's property and assets are sold or otherwise disposed of, in order to get cash to pay off the debts. Commonly called a straight bankruptcy proceeding, **Chapter 7 bankruptcy** wipes out most, but not all, debts. Some debts must still be paid, including child support, alimony, income taxes and penalties, student loans, and court-ordered damages due to malicious (intentional) acts. Once declared bankrupt, an individual cannot file for straight bankruptcy again for six years.

To get debts discharged, debtors must give up all their property except for certain exempted items. **Exempted property** is an asset or a possession that the debtor is allowed to keep because it is considered necessary for survival. Federal laws allow a number of items to be exempted, as shown in Figure 19-2.

1. $7,500 equity in a home

2. $1,200 interest in a motor vehicle

3. Items worth up to $200 each under the categories of household goods and furnishings, appliances, clothing and personal items, animals, crops, and musical instruments

4. $500 in jewelry

5. $750 in tools or books required for work

6. Proceeds from life insurance policies, unemployment insurance income, pension income, and veterans benefits

Fig. 19-2

Federally Exempted Items (as of January 1, 1995)

Thirty-two states require a debtor to use a state exempted item schedule rather than a federal schedule. The remaining eighteen states allow a choice of either federal or state exempted item schedules. Some state exempted item schedules are more generous than the federal list.

New legislation is periodically introduced to tighten up the code revisions of 1978. Many creditors are afraid of the liberal bankruptcy code and desire legislation that gives more rights to creditors while making bankruptcy less desirable for debtors. The only precaution creditors can take is careful screening of applicants and higher requirements of income, employment, and credit stability.

Chapter 13 Bankruptcy

An alternative proceeding that avoids much of the stigma of straight bankruptcy is **Chapter 13 bankruptcy,** which allows creditors to get some of their money back. Debtors keep all their property and work out a compulsory, court-enforced plan to repay a portion of the debts over a period of time, usually three years. Under Chapter 13, often referred to as the wage earner's plan, some debts are totally discharged, but family obligations still remain for child support and alimony.

Chapter 13 bankruptcy may seem more equitable and better for the debtor in terms of reestablishing credit. However, the blemish on the debtor's credit record caused by any form of bankruptcy is hard to overcome for a number of years.

Legal Advice

A person considering bankruptcy should seek good legal advice. In most states it is possible to file for bankruptcy without an attorney. But the law is complicated, and a good bankruptcy attorney can tell you which of your assets will be protected and which exempted items you can claim. The attorney can also assist you in deciding which bankruptcy plan will work best to help you solve your credit problems. Attorneys' fees for handling bankruptcies can range from $150 to $1,500, depending on the case, but good legal advice can save you that much and more.

Reaffirmation of Debts

Creditors may ask debtors to agree to pay their debts after bankruptcy is completed. This agreement is called **reaffirmation.** Reaffirmation requires a court hearing, and the debtor is given thirty days to change his or her mind about making a promise to repay. A creditor is prohibited from harassing the debtor to reaffirm after the court proceedings are over.

While there is little incentive for debtors to reaffirm debts, an honest and sincere person might want to choose one debt over another and try to pay back some of what he or she is not legally obligated to pay.

personal perspective

Credit Strategy

Bankruptcy can be used for personal advantage, as the following story will indicate. It shows how a person can stretch the use of credit for personal indulgence.

John Smith (not his real name) was well established in credit when he lost his job. When he checked his existing credit cards, he held over ten charge cards from retailers and four bank credit cards.

He maintained his lifestyle during the period of being unemployed (which lasted over two years) just like nothing had happened. He charged merchandise on his accounts to the maximum available, and was careful to make all minimum monthly payments in a timely manner. As the months rolled by, he stretched every credit card to its absolute maximum credit limit, taking cash advances against the bank cards and buying all sorts of luxuries from watches to trips.

He sold his house, bought a smaller house with less than $7,500 equity, and hid away the profits from the sale in foreign bank accounts. He sold his fancy car and purchased a smaller one with a value of less than $1,500. He made sure all property in his name fell within the "exempt" category of bankruptcy law in his state. Meanwhile, he continued to use credit and make expensive purchases.

Finally, his credit ran out and he could charge no more. He had amassed over $50,000 in debt. With no job, and no assets remaining that could be used for collateral, he declared bankruptcy.

critical thinking

1. Do you see any ethical problems in this story? If so, what?

2. Were the bankruptcy laws designed to protect someone like John?

3. What lessons can be learned from this story?

ajor causes of bankruptcy

Bankruptcy is a last-resort solution to credit problems. The most common reasons for claiming bankruptcy are business failure, emotional spending, failure to budget and develop a good financial plan, and catastrophic injury or illness. Unfortunately, the Bankruptcy Recovery Act of 1978, which made declaring personal bankruptcy easier, is also considered a factor in the number of people declaring personal bankruptcies.

Business Failure

Every year thousands of small businesses fail. People invest their life savings and more to start a business. Unfortunately, for a number of reasons from ruinous economic conditions to poor financial planning, many small businesses do not make it beyond the first year. Other small business owners borrow more money and go further into debt in order to keep afloat until times get better. Owning and operating a small business can be very risky. Success depends on a great deal of luck—in addition to good financial plans, knowledge of the product or service, favorable business location, and good economic conditions.

Emotional Spending

Emotional rather than rational reasons for buying lead many consumers to eventual bankruptcy. Purchases in excess of what can be afforded, often made for instant gratification; money spent to impress others

Owning a business can be risky—every year thousands of small businesses fail.

(to "keep up with the Joneses") rather than for needed purchases—all result in overuse of credit. Overuse occurs when purchases exceed what can be handled comfortably with present income. Usually overuse of credit is temporary and often not a serious problem. A job loss, a business failure, or some other disaster, however, can put sudden and severe pressure on an already weak financial structure. Then, before the deficiency can be corrected, debt rises beyond the debtor's capability to pay it off. In most cases there is very little to show for the thousands of dollars spent unwisely—nothing that can be sold to pay off debt. Extensive travel, long vacations, or extravagant parties and entertainment are expensive pleasures that have no resale value.

Failure to Budget and Plan

Most people who go bankrupt often have no goals or plans. They neither have nor follow a budget. Many do not know how to set up or keep a budget and are not willing to ask for help or advice in solving their credit problems.

Bankruptcy is not a condition limited to poor people. All classes of people find themselves in trouble with credit. Poor planning can occur at any income level in any financial circumstance. At whatever financial level a person may be, spending and borrowing must be kept in proportion to income. Most causes of bankruptcy can be avoided by careful planning and decision making based on good financial judgment, advice, and goals.

Catastrophic Injury or Illness

Medical care costs a great deal. Some insurance policies have dollar limits for major illnesses. While not all catastrophic injuries or illnesses result in bankruptcy, they often damage a person's or family's financial health for many years to come. For example, a person hospitalized for six months to a year with a critical illness could easily owe $100,000

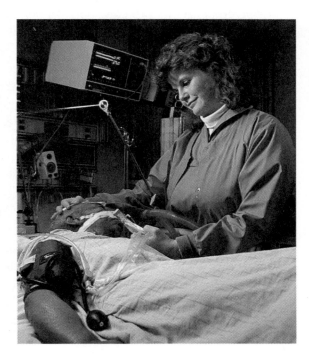

Catastrophic injuries or illnesses can damage an individual's financial health for many years.

a month for medical care, drugs, room charges, and other fees. If there is no insurance, that person's savings can be wiped out in the first month. Many people with this type of debt try to pay it back—at the rate of $1,000 a month, or whatever they can afford. It may be years, even decades, before this type of debt can possibly be repaid, if ever.

Advantages of bankruptcy

For those individuals whose situation seems hopeless, bankruptcy offers a solution to credit problems. While this solution is not without a price, bankruptcy does offer a number of advantages. A brief list of the advantages follows.

1. **Debts Are Erased.** Straight bankruptcy (Chapter 7) offers a fresh start. Overwhelming bills can be reduced or eliminated, and the debtor can start over. With good financial planning and counseling, future credit problems can be avoided. However, obtaining future credit may be more difficult for someone filing a Chapter 7 bankruptcy and making no effort to repay her or his debts than for someone filing Chapter 13 bankruptcy and making an effort to repay some of her or his debts.

2. **Exempted Assets Are Retained.** While the majority of assets must be given up in order to erase debts under straight bankruptcy, certain amounts and types of properties are not taken. With these exempted items, a new start is possible. When a husband and wife file joint bankruptcy, the cushion for a new start becomes even softer because the dollar amounts for exempted items are doubled.

3. **Certain Incomes Are Unaffected.** Bankruptcy will not affect certain types of income a debtor may have, such as social security; veterans benefits; unemployment compensation; alimony; child support; disability payments; and payments from pension, profit-sharing, and annuity plans. These sources of income need not be considered even in a Chapter 13 bankruptcy, in which a compulsory payment plan is established.

4. **The Cost Is Small.** Attorneys' fees and court costs in bankruptcy are relatively small in comparison to the amount of financial relief provided. When total debts reach such a level that income cannot stretch to pay them off, the relief is considerable in comparison to

the cost involved. On the first visit to an attorney's office, a debtor will be given total cost estimates and information about the options available in bankruptcy proceedings.

Disadvantages of bankruptcy

While bankruptcy offers several advantages to the debtor, there is a price to be paid. Bankruptcy should be considered a last resort, and then only after a thorough investigation of the consequences of bankruptcy. Some of the disadvantages of bankruptcy are discussed in the following paragraphs.

1. **Credit Is Damaged.** Despite the more liberal bankruptcy regulations, a bankruptcy judgment still casts a heavy cloud over an individual's credit record. The judgment cannot be wiped off credit records for ten years. Bankruptcy is a notice to creditors and others

that, at one time, the debtor was not able to meet his or her responsibilities.

Depending on the circumstances that caused the bankruptcy, mistrust of a debtor in personal and business affairs may result and continue well beyond the ten years.

2. **Property Is Lost.** A person who declares bankruptcy does not necessarily get to keep exempt assets. Consider this example. Assume that you own a house worth $60,000 that has a mortgage of $25,000 against it. Your equity is $35,000. While the bankruptcy code allows you to keep the first $7,500 of equity in your home, you may be required to sell the home. You will be allowed $7,500 and the other $27,500 must be used to pay off creditors. Or, if you own a car valued at $3,000 and you owe $1,800 on the car, your equity is $1,200. Since this amount equals the allowance for a car, you will not have to sell the car. However, if you have a car valued at $8,000 with a loan of $5,000, your equity is $3,000. You are allowed only equity of $1,200, the legal limit. In this case, you will probably have to sell the car and use all proceeds over $1,200 to help pay off your creditors.

3. **Some Obligations Remain.** Regardless of the type of bankruptcy selected, all debt is not erased. Certain obligations, such as child support, must be paid in full. Other debts also remain: income taxes and penalties, student loans, court-ordered damages in connection with intentional acts of mischief, and other debts at the discretion of the bankruptcy court.

4. **Some Debts Can Be Reaffirmed.** If a lender can prove that there was any type of false representation on the debtor's part in connection with a debt, the debt will not be discharged. In other cases, creditors may ask debtors to reaffirm a debt—to promise to pay it back even though it was discharged. By reaffirming old debts, the debtor does not get the fresh, clean start that is probably needed.

5. **Cosigners Must Pay.** A cosigner can be held responsible for guarantee of a debt after the borrower has been declared bankrupt. A cosigner does not have to pay if the debtor has chosen a Chapter 13 bankruptcy, however. Creditors receive an equitable share of the debtor's assets as payment.

Forms for filing bankruptcy are complicated and lengthy. The first form filed in a bankruptcy proceeding is the bankruptcy petition. An example of a bankruptcy petition prepared and submitted by an attorney is shown in Figure 19-3. Numerous other forms requiring specific information and declarations are required to complete the bankruptcy procedure.

Fig. 19-3   **Bankruptcy Petition**

IN THE FEDERAL BANKRUPTCY COURT FOR THE <u>Eastern</u> DISTRICT OF <u>Kentucky</u>

IN THE CASE OF _____) DEBTOR'S PETITION FOR BANKRUPTCY

<u>Matthew Franklin</u>_____)

_____ , Debtor,)   Chapter 7

_____)   Case No.   <u>89-202</u>

Petitioner, herein called debtor, appears before the Court and alleges as follows:

1. Petitioner's address is <u>513 Main Street, Biggs, KY 43721-0132</u> , and the above court has jurisdiction over this matter.

2. Petitioner has resided in this federal district for the last 180 days, or six months, prior to the filing of this petition.

3. Petitioner is entitled to the benefits of the bankruptcy laws of the United States, and files this petition as a voluntary debtor, seeking relief under Chapter 7 of the United States Bankruptcy Code.

WHEREFORE, petitioner prays for relief according to the provisions of said bankruptcy Chapter 7, and files herewith all supplemental information necessary for the court to make said determination of voluntary bankruptcy.

Patricia Van Schark
_____
Attorney for Petitioner
5101 Third Street
_____
Address of Attorney
Cincinnati, OH 45201-6735
_____

ATTESTATION:

I, <u>Matthew Franklin</u>_____ , petitioner (debtor) named in the foregoing petition, do hereby certify that I have read the foregoing petition and its documents attached thereto, and they are true and correct.

Matthew Franklin
_____
Petitioner

STATE OF <u>Kentucky</u>_____)
) ss.
County of <u>Pike</u>_____)

On <u>May 3</u>____ , 19<u>--</u> , the petitioner, <u>Matthew Franklin</u> , did appear before me and acknowledge that s/he did sign the foregoing petition of his/her own free will.

Geoffrey Combs
_____
Notary Public for <u>Kentucky</u> (state)
My Commission Expires: <u>March 14, 19--</u>

Summary

Credit problems can happen to anyone. Many people find themselves in trouble with credit every year. But there are many ways to get out of trouble and then stay out!

The 20/10 Rule is a guideline for how much debt is comfortable. There are not-for-profit credit counseling centers that provide assistance for a small fee. Commercial debt-adjustment firms also provide assistance. Bankruptcy is a final recourse for insurmountable credit problems.

Involuntary bankruptcy occurs when creditors petition to have a person declared insolvent. Voluntary bankruptcy occurs more often. It may be in the form of Chapter 11, Chapter 7, or Chapter 13. Bankruptcy laws provide for exempted property, or those possessions that will not be taken from a person and sold to pay debts. People considering bankruptcy should get good legal advice to save time and money.

Major causes of personal bankruptcy (of individuals) include small business failure, emotional spending, failure to plan and budget, and catastrophic illness or injury. There are many advantages and disadvantages of bankruptcy; therefore, it should be a well-considered decision. The bankruptcy petition form is simple and easy to follow.

ocabulary terms

Directions: Can you find the definition for each of the following terms used in Chapter 19?

bankruptcy   *involuntary bankruptcy*
Chapter 7 bankruptcy   *proportional share*
Chapter 11 bankruptcy   *reaffirmation*
Chapter 13 bankruptcy   *20/10 Rule*
debtor   *unsecured debt*
discharged debt   *voluntary bankruptcy*
exempted property

1. Legally insolvent—a situation in which a person (or business) is not able to pay debts on time.
2. A plan designed to prevent credit problems that allows 20 percent of yearly take-home pay or 10 percent of monthly take-home pay to be used for paying off open and closed-end credit.
3. A percentage of the debtor's total assets received by a creditor, based on how much is owed that creditor, in proportion to the debtor's total debts.
4. A type of bankruptcy in which creditors file a petition with the court asking the court to declare the debtor bankrupt.
5. A type of bankruptcy in which the debtor files a bankruptcy petition with the court asking to be declared bankrupt.
6. A value or possession in which the debtor is allowed to retain a certain equity because that item is considered necessary to the debtor's fresh start.
7. A type of bankruptcy proceeding with the primary purpose of discharging debts to give a person a chance for a fresh start.
8. A type of bankruptcy that is often called the wage earner's plan.
9. Agreement to pay back a debt to a creditor after the debtor has been declared bankrupt and the debt has been discharged.
10. A debt for which no specific asset is pledged, but all of the debtor's assets are considered.
11. A type of bankruptcy for businesses that attempts to reorganize the debt structure of the business.
12. A person who owes money to others.
13. The legal avoidance of debt which, prior to bankruptcy, was due and owing.

end-of-chapter activities

19

F acts and ideas in review

1. List the four commonly used plans for solving credit problems.
2. Where can you find out about the not-for-profit credit counseling services in your area?
3. What is the purpose of bankruptcy?
4. What are the two types of bankruptcy (one is initiated by creditors, the other by debtors)?
5. Which types of family obligations are not discharged by bankruptcy?
6. List six exempted items under Chapter 7 bankruptcy. Are the amounts for these items doubled for married persons?
7. Once declared bankrupt, how much time must pass before you can again file straight bankruptcy? How long does a bankruptcy judgment remain on your credit records?
8. How does Chapter 13 bankruptcy differ from Chapter 7?
9. Why is it a good idea to seek advice from an attorney before filing for bankruptcy?
10. How long does a debtor have to change his or her mind about reaffirmation of a debt?
11. List the four most common reasons for claiming bankruptcy.
12. List four advantages and five disadvantages of filing bankruptcy.
13. Which types of income are not subject to the claims of creditors?
14. On the bankruptcy petition (Figure 19-3), identify the following:
    a. Who is the petitioner (debtor)?
    b. Is this a petition for straight bankruptcy or the wage earner's plan?
    c. What is the address of the petitioner?
    d. Who signed the petition?
    e. Who signed the attestation (verification that the petition is true)?
    f. Is this petition filed as voluntary or involuntary bankruptcy?

A pplications for decision making

1. Read the classified section of your newspaper every day for one week, checking for bankruptcy notices. Cut all you can find from the legal notices section and answer these questions:
    a. How many total bankruptcies were filed in a seven-day period?

b. How many of the bankruptcies were joint bankruptcies (husband and wife)?

c. What is the lowest amount of debt claimed?

d. What is the highest amount of debt claimed?

e. How many of those filers represented themselves? How many used an attorney?

f. What was the lowest amount of property claimed as exempt?

g. What was the highest amount of property claimed as exempt?

2. Search through the Yellow Pages of a telephone book and through business directories and make a list of the following:

a. Not-for-profit credit counseling services

b. Commercial debt-adjustment firms

c. Attorneys specializing in bankruptcy

d. Classes or other credit counseling services provided in the community, either for a fee or free.

3. Look up the original federal Bankruptcy Act of 1898 in a reference book and write a report covering the following:

a. Provisions of the law (in outline form)

b. Exempted items allowed and types of income excluded

c. Procedures or steps involved in filing bankruptcy

4. Look up the Bankruptcy Reform Act of 1978 and answer these questions:

a. How has the law changed to help consumers?

b. What are the new provisions not found in the old bankruptcy laws regarding exempted items and excluded income?

5. Does the state in which you live require you to use a state exempted item schedule rather than the federal schedule?

6. Is it possible in your area to file bankruptcy without the aid of an attorney? What is the procedure for filing a bankruptcy, with or without an attorney? (You can find out by calling your local legal aid society or by asking at a courthouse.)

ife situation problem solving

1. Your friend Alice has trouble paying her bills. She has taken a second job in order to make all her payments, but the long hours and hard work are causing her health problems. What suggestions do you have in helping her manage her credit problems?

2. Mark and Janice have decided to get help with their credit problems rather than declare bankruptcy. They want to extend the

time for repaying loans but they don't want to hand over their checkbook and credit cards to a debt-adjustment service. What other options do they have?

3. Bill owns a small store. The store has been losing money for some time. Bill is the sole owner of the store and his personal assets are the store's assets as well. Explain to Bill the differences among Chapter 7, 11, and 13 bankruptcy.

4. Jack and Marcene Churchwell are considering bankruptcy. They have the following assets. How much (total) will they be allowed in exempted items?
   a. $18,000 equity in home
   b. $5,000 interest in motor vehicle
   c. $500 in household goods and furnishings, $2,000 in appliances, $1,000 in personal items and clothing, and $2,000 in musical instruments
   d. $5,000 in jewelry

5. M. J. Majesky has filed for bankruptcy and has the following debts. After the bankruptcy, which debts will remain?
   a. $500 owed to a chiropractor
   b. $300 owed in child support
   c. $870 owed in student loans
   d. $1,200 owed in back taxes
   e. $530 owed to a department store
   f. $650 owed to an automobile repair shop
   g. $950 owed to a jewelry store

6. Jeffrey Luther has the following assets. What amounts would be considered exempted items?
   a. $3,500 equity in a home
   b. $3,000 interest in a motor vehicle
   c. $150 in household furnishings
   d. $300 in appliances
   e. $150 in personal items
   f. $300 in a pet parrot
   g. $1,500 in musical instruments
   h. $300 in jewelry
   i. $600 in tools
   j. $15,000 life insurance proceeds
   k. $300 a month in unemployment insurance benefits

Financial Checkup 3:
Managing Spending and Credit Use

The first two financial checkups concentrated on examining your financial position, followed by building and protecting savings, investments, and retirement/estate planning. In this third financial checkup, you will learn more about credit, debt load, and how to protect yourself from fraudulent use of your credit cards.

Your Use of Credit

Credit will enable you to enjoy a standard of living that otherwise would not be possible. Nearly everyone uses credit. A wise consumer analyzes the use of credit on an annual basis, comparing sources, interest rates, minimum payments, and other features (such as rebates) of accounts. Figure FC3-1 (Credit Analysis) is used to analyze your creditworthiness.

Complete Worksheet 1 (Credit Analysis) in the *Student Activity Guide* to give you an idea of how you are handling credit in your life.

When examining your use of credit, you may find it advantageous to keep control sheets that enable you to track your progress in paying off debts. A sample control sheet is shown in Figure FC3-2; you can make similar sheets for each credit card or account to track each monthly payment. At the end of the year, you can total the finance charges. Just keeping the control sheets will assist you because it will make you aware of the cost of credit card purchases. The amount of the finance charge is shown on the monthly statement from the creditor, along with the previous balance, payments and returns (credits), new charges (debits), and the new monthly balance.

Your Debt Load

A **debt load** is the amount of outstanding debt at a particular point in time. Whether your debt load is acceptable to you will depend on

Credit Analysis

Directions: List each type of credit you have and its features. Then complete the analysis to determine what action can and should be taken.

	Monthly Payment	No. of Payments Left	Outstanding Balance	APR	Special Features	Ranking
Installment credit:						
Personal loans:						
Automobile	_____ × _____ =		_____	____	_____	_____
Home improvement	_____ × _____ =		_____	____	_____	_____
Other: _____	_____ × _____ =		_____	____	_____	_____
_____	_____ × _____ =		_____	____	_____	_____
Charge accounts:						
1. _____	_____		_____	____	_____	_____
2. _____	_____		_____	____	_____	_____
3. _____	_____		_____	____	_____	_____

Total debt outstanding . . . .$_____

Average APR . . . . _____

How long will it take to pay off the outstanding debt? (Total outstanding debt divided by total monthly payments) _____

Which debts do you feel comfortable with? _____

Which debts do you feel uncomfortable with? _____

Which debts will you pay off first (those with lowest ranking)? _____

_____

What are some anticipated future debt needs? _____

_____

Which credit sources will you use for future debt (those with highest ranking)?

_____

your ability to meet the regular payments, your ability to pay off the debt quickly if a need or reason arises, and your level of comfort with the amount of debt you owe.

Figure FC3-3 (Your Debt Load) is used to determine whether you have a comfortable debt load. One rule says that installment debt

**Control Sheet:
VISA Account**

(1) Date	(2) Previous Balance	(3) Payments (Credits)	(4) New Charges (Debits)	(5) Finance Charge	(6) New Balance (2−3+4)
1/1	$280.63	$35.00	$20.00	$7.22	$265.63
2/3	265.63	35.00	0	7.01	230.63
3/2	230.63	35.00	15.00	6.88	217.51
3/4	217.51	35.00	0	6.55	189.06

should not exceed 20 percent of yearly take-home pay. Another holds that you should be able to pay off all installment debts in one year at your current monthly payments. Still another says that you should be able to pay off your debts within thirty days if absolutely necessary (with all the cash you can raise).

Complete Worksheet 2 (Your Debt Load) in the *Student Activity Guide* to analyze your personal debt load. Compute your self-score.

If you sense trouble with debt, the solution is to pay off old debts before taking on new ones. Assessment of your debt load will help you find ways to correct the potential problems with debt. Debts are future earnings already spent; unfortunately, many people never assess how much future income is committed to debt and whether the types and sources of credit they use are most advantageous to them.

Protection from Credit Fraud

The cost of credit card fraud is in excess of $3 billion a year and growing. Maybe you will never be a victim, but everyone pays for credit card fraud through higher interest charges, membership fees, and other costs that are passed along to customers.

To protect yourself, there are many things you should do. For example, you should:

- discard receipts and carbons so that numbers cannot be read;
- not allow store clerks to write your credit card numbers and expiration dates on checks;
- pay cash in cases where you suspect your credit information may not be secure;
- never give credit information over the telephone to someone you do not know;
- never sign blank credit slips; draw a line through blank spaces when you sign;

Fig. FC3-3   **Your Debt Load**

Your Debt Load

Directions: Answer the following statements with a "Yes" or "No." Then read the information following the statements to make an assessment of your debt load.

1. You pay only the minimum amount due each month on charge and credit accounts.   YES   NO

2. You make so many credit purchases that your debt load (total debts outstanding) never shrinks.   YES   NO

3. You are usually not able to make it until the end of the month and must borrow from savings.   YES   NO

4. You have borrowed from parents or others and do not have plans to repay the debt.   YES   NO

5. You are behind on one or more of your payments.   YES   NO

6. You worry about money often and are discouraged.   YES   NO

7. Money is a source of arguments and disagreements in your family.   YES   NO

8. You often juggle payments, paying one creditor while giving excuses to another.   YES   NO

9. You really don't know how much money you owe.   YES   NO

10. Your savings are slowly disappearing, and you are unable to save regularly.   YES   NO

11. You've taken out loans to pay off debts, or have debt consolidation loans.   YES   NO

12. You are at or near the limit of your credit lines on credit and charge accounts.   YES   NO

13. You worry more about the amount of the payment than the amount of interest (interest rate) you are paying on loans.   YES   NO

ASSESSMENT: Total number of "Yes" answers_____

If you answered yes to 8 or more statements, you need immediate action to correct your debt load. If you answered yes to 4-7 statements, you should seek to remedy the defects in your debt load soon. If you answered yes to 1-3 statements, you are in pretty good shape and can solve your debt problems. If you answered no to all the statements, congratulations—keep up the good work!

unit 4

- verify your monthly statements to be sure you have been properly charged;
- notify creditors in advance of an address change;
- never lend your credit cards to anyone;
- never put your account number on the outside of an envelope or on a postcard.

You can probably think of many more ways to protect yourself from credit fraud. One bad experience will convince you that it's worth your time and trouble to take precautions. After reading the description of two credit practices that mislead many consumers every year, ask yourself how you can avoid becoming a victim.

Credit Repair Fraud

Phony credit repair companies guarantee you that they can fix your credit history, get you out of debt, or get credit cards for you. They often use 900 numbers so you can contact them. These services cost you a large fee even though they are often provided at no charge by credit bureaus and not-for-profit credit counseling services. In some cases, you can get the information yourself without going through any agency.

In reality, the credit repair company cannot fix your credit history. Once you have a poor credit history, bankruptcy, or other information in your record, it cannot be removed or changed. Instead, these companies find other sources of credit you can apply for. They sell you a list of companies that will issue credit cards to people with poor or no credit ratings. You could do this research yourself. For example, you can buy the *Low Interest, No Annual Fee List* of reputable card issuers with competitive interest rates and no annual fees. Contact BankCard Holders of America, 560 Herndon Parkway, Suite 120, Herndon, VA 22070.

Advance-Fee Loans

These advertisements guarantee you a loan after you have paid a fee in advance, claiming bad credit or no credit is not a problem. You may hear on television or radio a claim that "no applicant is ever turned down." But what really happens is this: The applicant fills out an application and pays the advance fee. The fee is often substantial —from $25 to $200. Then credit is arranged and all payments are closely monitored. The borrower is not allowed to get even one day behind on payments or aggressive debt-collection practices begin.

unit 4

A legitimate lender usually does not charge a fee for applying for open-ended credit, nor will the lender guarantee that you will qualify for credit. Whenever it seems too easy, there is likely a good reason to be suspicious.

Ethical Decisions

Ethics are principles of morality or rules of conduct. Ethical behavior conforms to these rules; unethical behavior violates them.

You may have many opportunities to take advantage of other people. When these opportunities come your way, stop and think how you might feel if you were victimized. Figure FC3-4 lists some circumstances involving credit. Think about how you might react to each circumstance.

Complete Worksheet 3 (Situational Analysis) in the *Student Activity Guide* to develop skill analyzing ethical situations involving credit.

Fig. FC3-4

Situational Analysis

Situational Analysis

For each situation described below, explain how you would respond and why. Are ethical issues involved in each decision?

1. You walk by a day-and-night teller machine in a mall. You see a bank credit card that was left there by a previous user. You look around and there is no one nearby to claim the card. If you leave it there, someone else may find it. What will you do?

2. You make a payment on your credit account at a customer service center. The worker, who is new and in training, accidentally credits your account for more than you paid. For example, you gave her $25 and she credited your account for $50. What will you do?

3. A person you know returns merchandise to the store and gets a credit on his or her charge account, knowing that the merchandise was purchased elsewhere. What will you do?

4. Your friend frequently buys clothing on credit, wears it to a special event, and returns it to the store before the account is due, claiming the garment is damaged or dirty. She then receives a credit or a refund for the merchandise. What will you do?

looking back . . .

Unit 4, Credit Management, explored many aspects of credit in America today. Consumer credit—the use of credit for personal needs but not a home mortgage—dates back to colonial times. Using credit to purchase goods and services may allow consumers to have a more satisfying lifestyle, but credit also requires a responsible attitude. When considering the use of credit, remember that credit costs money and often leads to overspending.

Each person builds a credit rating through responsible use of credit. Credit bureaus collect information about consumers and prepare credit reports that assist creditors in making decisions about granting credit. There are many credit laws that have been passed to protect consumers and users of credit. The concepts of "fair" and "equal" credit have been written into laws that ban discrimination in credit transactions, require that consumers be told the reason when credit is denied, give borrowers access to their credit records, and set up a method to settle billing disputes.

Credit is not free. Even if you don't use credit, the cost of credit is reflected in the prices you pay for goods and services. Some costs of credit are hidden; others are disguised as handling fees, service fees, and the like.

People in trouble with credit should seek credit counseling and perhaps the advice of an attorney if bankruptcy is contemplated. Bankruptcy is a final resort for people who are hopelessly under the burden of debt. Bankruptcy has advantages as well as disadvantages which should be weighed carefully. Bankruptcy will leave a black cloud over your credit record for many years.

PORTABLE
CD PLAYER
$119.99

7729530187927

SALE

RIGHT

unit five

resource management

objectives: *After reading and studying the chapters and completing the exercises and activities, you will be able to:*

1 Explain the process of personal decision making, which is based on wants, needs, values, and factors such as marketing strategies that affect spending habits.

2 Describe housing alternatives and living arrangements as well as landlord/tenant responsibilities, advantages and disadvantages of home ownership, and moving costs.

3 Define real estate terminology and discuss the step-by-step process of buying a home, real estate investment options, and benefits of investing in real estate.

4 Explain the steps in buying a car, the costs of operating a car, ways of extending the life of a car, and laws designed to protect car buyers.

5 Discuss family decisions that begin with marriage and progress to making financial decisions, planning a vacation, dealing with emergencies, getting a divorce, and preparing for death.

looking forward

Unit 5, Resource Management, begins with a chapter on personal decision making where you will learn how to make good decisions based on your needs and wants. You'll examine your personal values, discover how they are influenced by societal values, and learn how marketing techniques encourage certain spending decisions.

When you leave home for the first time, you will have many housing options from which to choose. There are many advantages to renting, but there's also a lot to know about rental applications, leases, landlord/tenant responsibilities, and your rights as a tenant. You'll also learn about moving costs—hook-ups, installation charges, deposits, and other expenses. You'll find that owning real estate as an investment may also be a good choice when you have the opportunity.

Driving your first car will be (or is now) an exciting new part of your life. The buying process takes considerable thought and preparation. You'll consider all the costs—from depreciation to accessories—and you'll learn ways to maintain your car's resale value.

The chapter on family decisions covers a wide range of family-related problems, situations, and opportunities. You will begin with marriage. From there you will examine family financial responsibility, the costs associated with divorce, and the financial aspects related to the death of a family member.

Making personal decisions is an important part of effectively managing your personal finances. Wise decisions keep you on track and give you a sense of achieving your goals. Throughout your life, you will make buying decisions that reflect a wide range of factors: personal, social, and economic. These factors are the basis for the spending, saving, and investing that lead to the achievement of personal financial goals. The emphasis in this chapter will be on personal, social, and economic factors that influence buying decisions. You will learn about the personal decision-making process; about needs, wants, and values that influence decisions; about personal and societal factors that affect decisions; and about marketing strategies that influence the buying habits of all consumers.

Personal Decision Making

chapter

20

Buying decisions are determined by personal, social, and economic factors.

The personal decision-making process

Buying decisions play an important role in your efforts to manage your personal finances. Good decisions can save you money; bad ones can be expensive. For this reason, your decision to purchase a product or service should always be based on careful consideration of available information and alternatives, or other choices you could make. Each daily buying decision requires a trade-off between current spending and saving for the future.

The five-step personal decision-making process presented in this chapter is a logical plan to use in solving problems caused by wants, needs, and goals. By following this process, you can make wise and economical buying decisions.

Step 1—Define the Problem

The first step in the personal decision-making process is simple: define the need or want to be satisfied and state it in a short, concise sentence. Then when your want or need has been pinpointed, you can proceed to the goal of satisfying it in a manner that fits your financial resources.

For example, let's say you need a computer to do schoolwork. Your problem is that you want and need a computer; your goal is to find an economical way to satisfy this need. By solving the "problem," you will achieve your goal of obtaining a computer and will satisfy that need in a way that will give you the most value for the money spent. This first step in the personal decision-making process is an important one because it is at the problem level that you make decisions concerning the purchase of products and services.

If you can't define a problem or describe a need, then perhaps you should think more carefully about spending your money. Would it be an impulsive purchase? Will you be satisfied with your choice in a week or in a month? How badly do you really want this item?

Step 2—Obtain Accurate Information

Once you have determined the problem, you must then gather information relating to your problem or need. List all alternative solutions to the problem and the cost of each. In the computer problem example, there are three basic solutions:
1. Use a computer at school (on campus).
2. Buy a new computer and printer.
3. Buy a used computer and printer.

In order to make a wise decision regarding your problem of obtaining a computer, you will need to know what products and services are available and how much it will cost you to use or purchase them. For instance, you will need to know where computer labs are located on the school campus. The cost of use will include a lab fee, as well as mileage to and from campus, and the time involved. For the possible purchase of a new or used computer, you will need to list desired features and then visit various computer stores, department stores, and discount stores for comparative shopping. At each location, you should make a note of the brands available, features, costs, and warranties. The classified ads are a good source for used computers and printers.

Whenever possible, keep a written record of the information you collect on choices of products and services. By doing so, you can make comparisons of alternatives and costs more easily. Figure 20-1 shows information collected for comparison in the computer problem.

Step 3—Compare Alternatives

When comparing total costs, you must consider time and convenience factors as dollar amounts. In some cases, convenience may be more important than cost, as long as the cost is reasonable. Using the computer example, you may decide that the convenience of having your

Fig. 20-1

**Information on
Comparison Shopping**

COST COMPARISON

		Per Month	Per Year
Option 1. Use Computer Lab			
Time:	Average 5 hours each weekend at school lab	20 hrs.	240 hrs.
Gas:	6-mile round trip, once/weekend, 52/year	$ 3.00	$ 36.00
Lab Fee:	$1.00 per hour (includes paper)	20.00	240.00
		$23.00	$276.00
Option 2. Buy New Computer and Printer			
With student discount		$1,500 one-time cost	
Monthly payments, financed on 3-year loan at 8 percent interest		$51.66	$620.00
Cost of disks, paper, toner, service contract, etc., are additional. Machine should last five years.			
Option 3. Buy Used Computer and Printer			
From private individual		$600 one-time cost	
Monthly payments (12-month loan at 8 percent)		$54.00	$648.00
Costs of supplies, repairs, and upkeep are additional. Machine should last three years.			

own computer is worth the extra dollar cost. You may also decide that even though the cost will be greater, you prefer to avoid the expense of possible repairs on used equipment. Purchasing used computers and printers may be riskier because previous owners may not have maintained them properly.

On the other hand, if you continue to use the computer in your classes and expand your knowledge, you will want to have a computer for both school and personal use. These are just a few of the factors you should consider in this step of the personal decision-making process.

Step 4—Select an Alternative

If you follow the steps outlined in the preceding paragraphs, the decision you make will be based on a careful analysis of the problem, thorough information gathering, and analysis of that information. In this example, the decision is to determine whether to use a campus computer lab or to buy a computer and printer. The cost is the price you will pay for what you decide to do. The wise decision in this or any situation is the one that is within your budget and that gives you the most value for your dollar investment.

Step 5—Take Action

After you have selected the best alternative, you must take action to accomplish the goal of satisfying your need. Because you have made a thorough analysis of information necessary to solve your problem, you can be sure that you have made a wise decision.

Reflect on decisions you have made in the past. Are there some decisions you made that you now regret? If so, did you use a decision-making process or did you buy the first model you saw? While using a decision-making process won't make every decision perfect, it will help you make better decisions in many of the important aspects of your life.

conomic needs and wants

Basic survival needs include (a) food and water, (b) shelter, and (c) clothing. As you can see, **basic needs** are those ingredients necessary for maintaining physical life. Some people would add safety and security to this list. Until these basic needs are met, there is little necessity for any of the other things life has to offer.

Life-enhancing wants and needs include, but are not limited to, the following:
1. Food, clothing, and shelter beyond what is necessary for biological survival.
2. Medical care to improve the quality and length of life.
3. Education to achieve personal goals, both social and economic.
4. Travel, vacations, and recreation to improve personal enjoyment of life.
5. Gadgetry or extra items to make life more fun and give it extra excitement, challenge, or meaning.

You may have decided that many of the life-improving needs and wants are necessary for your happiness. But you must admit they are not absolutely necessary to your physical survival—you may simply have become used to them and therefore expect to have them.

Basic needs such as food are those things necessary to maintain life.

Individual Needs and Wants

What each of us decides we need and want depends on a number of factors. These factors are different among individuals and among societies. All factors may change at different points in our lives. Individual factors include personal style, income, education, security level, and leisure time.

1. **Personal Style.** Each person has his or her own set of values and personal preferences. Personal taste may be formal or informal, flashy or subdued, dominating or easygoing. One person may prefer dark colors; another may choose pastels. One person may enjoy a weekend alone in the mountains hiking, while another would choose a visit to Disneyland. Based on those personal tastes, styles, and preferences, we make choices; we fulfill our wants and needs according to personal values.

2. **Income.** What a person is able to earn and spend will influence the type of consumer choices she or he can make. The more **disposable income**—money left over after expenses are paid that you can spend as you wish—the higher the quality and quantity of your selections. The ability to afford goods and services to fulfill wants and needs considered important will affect a person's satisfaction or dissatisfaction with employment, personal life, goals, and other personal factors such as self-worth or self-esteem.

You can evaluate the career you are considering from the standpoint of the income it provides. For example, you might be considering a career as a systems analyst. By researching the average earnings of a person in this type of work, you might find that in your area the annual level of pay you could expect is $33,000. You need to evaluate how well the salary will be able to meet your needs and wants as well as fulfill your goals of status, social standing, and prestige.

3. **Education.** Formal education is knowledge gained through attending institutions of learning. The end result is a diploma or degree, which is evidence that the recipient has accomplished a certain educational goal and has met the standards for graduation. The level of education achieved will affect future income and will influence a person's needs and wants and choice of methods to fulfill them.

4. **Security Level.** A person acts and reacts in accordance with the degree of safety, security, and peace he or she enjoys. These factors include personal safety as well as personal freedoms and fears for life, liberty, and property. Being secure from physical harm—whether from civil conflicts or robbery and property damage—influences our perceptions and therefore our needs and wants.

   Job security is another important factor. If you feel secure and satisfied in your employment, your choices will be different from those you make when you feel threatened or dissatisfied.

5. **Leisure Time.** Individual needs and wants are often satisfied in our choices of pleasure and recreational activities during our free time. Those who are retired or not employed have more leisure time to allocate. Wise choices in this area can make life rewarding and satisfying. Wasting and making poor use of leisure time results in frustration, loneliness, and depression.

Collective Values

Collective values are those things important to society as a whole; all citizens share in their costs and in their benefits. The society in which you live influences your values, goals, and choices because it demands responsibility from citizens. Society also provides for citizens' legal protection, employment, progress, quality environment, and public and government services.

1. **Legal Protection.** One of the primary needs of the individual that is met by society is preservation of legal and personal rights, and protection from others who would deny someone those rights. Law enforcement is the result of society's value of protection for citizens and property.

2. **Employment.** Most people who are able will work because it is expected and demanded in order to survive in this society. Most of us are aware of this subtle, yet very real, pressure to perform in the work arena. Therefore, we strive to do the best we can—to get a job that pays us well for the effort we put forth. In this way, we can be personally satisfied with our productivity and at the same time satisfy society's demand for citizens who contribute.

3. **Progress.** The relative state of progress of the country in which you live—its technological advances and perceptions about the importance of those advances—will affect your personal goals. In the United States, our society is technologically advanced and places a high value on positive innovations. **Innovations** are new ideas, methods, or devices that bring about changes in the way we live.

4. **Quality of Environment.** Natural resources are of great value and concern to society as a whole because they are very limited, and some cannot be replaced. Because of our priority of preserving a quality environment for ourselves and future generations, we concentrate on activities such as land-use planning, preserving natural beauty and wildlife, and establishing air pollution standards. We also place a great importance on the environmental effects of a given product or service. Environmental quality is important to society as a whole, and individuals respond to this concern by acting and purchasing accordingly.

Collective values are those things important to society as a whole, such as the environment.

point counterpoint

P rivacy versus the Right to Know

Most Americans consider privacy one of their basic rights. The Constitution and its amendments set forth individual rights to protect the right of free speech, the right to bear arms, the right of religion, and so on. But the advent of the computer age has brought to light new concerns about privacy.

When does the gathering and use of information about individuals constitute an invasion of privacy? Today, more than 70 percent of American consumers feel they have lost control over how information about them is circulated and used. This includes data gathered from a multitude of sources, including mail orders, telephone records, credit card purchases, banking transactions, and numerous other computer and electronic transactions that occur daily.

In April of 1990, Lotus Development Corporation, now part of IBM, announced plans to release a new and exciting product called the Lotus Marketplace: Households. This computer program could be bought at computer stores for a modest price of $79.99. It promised personal computer users, primarily small businesses, that they could have current and accurate data about potential customers that included names, addresses, demographic information, and prior purchasing behavior. (Demographic information includes age, lifestyle, children, income, and so on.) This would revolutionize the mailing list concept, putting at the fingertips of businesses a massive amount of data that could be used to target customers from a base of 120 million consumers.

An article followed in *The Wall Street Journal* explaining the product —how information is gathered and used. Public concern mounted and privacy violation outcries were expressed in thousands of phone calls and letters opposing the product. In January of 1991, Lotus canceled the project. They cited consumer concerns and "the substantial, unexpected additional costs required to fully address consumer privacy issues."

Many, if not most, major companies do in fact keep databases of information about their customers. Through these systems they are able to understand individual consumers better and to develop and successfully market new products. According to marketing experts, successful companies profile their customers and target new customers with similar traits.

critical thinking

1. Do you object to information being gathered about your personal buying habits? If so, why?

2. Do you feel that consumers should have control over how personal information about them is collected and used?

3. Do you think that new privacy protection laws are needed to regulate the use of information in the computer age?

5. **Public and Government Services.** Our country is organized to be "of the people, by the people, and for the people." We have a highly advanced and intricate system of government made up of the people, performing services for the people, with money contributed (through taxes) by the people. Our system of taxation takes money from those who have it and redistributes it to those who need it. High value is placed on providing services for all citizens—from police protection to public parks.

actors that influence spending decisions

Consumer purchasing decisions are influenced by personal factors and by outside factors that work together and separately as incentives or deterrents to spending. Planning for major purchases requires analysis and thought to be sure that motives and rationale are appropriate.

Personal Factors

There are many personal factors that influence consumer spending decisions. **Personal factors** are those influences in a person's or family's life that determine spending patterns, preferences, and choices. Some persons and families may be influenced greatly by one or more of the following factors: personal resources; position in life; customs, background, and religion; and values and goals.

1. **Personal Resources.** Your **personal resources** include your time, money, energy, skills and abilities, and available credit. The greater the quantity and the higher the quality of any one of these factors, the greater your purchasing power. For example, the amount of time you have available to compare prices and options before purchasing a product (time quantity), or the level of skill you possess in order to make money quickly at a job (quality), will affect your ability to make wise choices and to earn more money. Generally speaking, the more resources you have available to you, the greater your earning potential and purchasing power.

2. **Position in Life.** Your position in life includes such factors as age, marital status, gender, employment status, and lifestyle. Spending patterns of single people are different from those of married couples and families. A higher income influences spending patterns and therefore lifestyle.

3. **Customs, Background, and Religion.** A **custom** is a long-established practice that may be considered an unwritten law. Families

may be faithful to traditions that have been followed for generations. A dedication to traditions is particularly true of religious groups or of cultures in which strict rules and policies are followed. Persons in these religious or cultural groups may observe special holidays and occasions that are not observed nationally. Buying patterns of these groups are greatly influenced by the values and priorities in their lives. In many cases, custom overshadows all other buying preferences.

Customs, traditions, and religious beliefs often affect buying patterns.

4. **Values and Goals.** Values, which are at the base of all our purchasing decisions, are slow to change. Goals change often. You accomplish one goal and then move on to others. Your total value system may change as your goals in life are met or not met. Individual and family values and goals are expressed through choices of entertainment, literature, sports, luxuries, and so on. These choices are reflected in decisions to purchase goods and services, use of time and energy, and attitudes toward possessions and their accumulation.

Outside Factors

To understand how the world in which you live plays a role in your decision-making process, you must consider the following: the economy, technological advances, the environment, and social pressures.

1. **The Economy.** The **economy** is the system or structure of economic life in a country. This term describes the financial well-being of the nation as measured by economists. The general condition of the economy affects every one of us, and we react to it accordingly. For example, when interest rates on automobile loans are high, fewer people are able to buy new cars. Consequently, older cars are kept longer.

2. **Technological Advances.** You may be fascinated or even obsessed with new electronic games. Or you may be interested in the world's

first mass-market electric-powered automobile. Perhaps you want to add a new solar heating device to your home to make it more energy-efficient. In America, a high value is placed on new technological advances. Many people want to have the newest, most convenient, modern, and interesting gadgets. As new goods and services are created to raise our level of comfort and standard of living, we willingly purchase them.

3. **The Environment.** Concern for the environment can affect consumer buying decisions. Citizens are concerned with home projects, community activities, and statewide programs to beautify and preserve, recycle, and protect existing resources and environment. Thus, this interest in the environment affects consumers' actions and also their product preferences. Products purchased must be ecologically safe and biodegradable (or otherwise recyclable) to meet present and future environmental standards.

4. **Social Pressures.** Social pressures often induce consumers to buy goods and services beyond their real wants and needs. People can be influenced to make purchases by their friends, relatives, and coworkers. The media (radio, television, newspapers) also act as sources of social pressure for consumers. Through advertising, the media convince consumers to buy goods and services designed to keep them young, good-looking, healthy, and sexy. Understanding how outside factors such as the economy, technological advances, the environment, and social pressures influence our spending patterns can help us make wise consumer decisions.

Major Purchase Factors

Because major purchases generally tie up future income or take a big bite out of accumulated savings, carefully consider your needs and wants before committing to a large purchase. Ask yourself these questions, think about it for at least twenty-four hours, and then make a final decision based on a rational—not emotional—perspective.

1. Why do I need or want this product?
2. How long will this product last?
3. What substitutes are available and at what cost?
4. By postponing this purchase, is it likely that I will choose not to buy it at a later date?
5. What types of additional costs are involved, such as supplies, maintenance, insurance, and financial risks?
6. For what other purposes might I use the money spent or committed for this purchase?
7. What is the total cost of this product (cash price, deferred price, interest, shipping charges, and so on)?

Once you have made a decision that you will purchase the good or service, you need to determine whether to pay cash or use credit. Even though you may have the cash available, you should not automatically pay cash for all purchases. If you do, your cash reserves will dwindle, or you may have to do without many conveniences you could have now with wise use of credit. Figure 20-2 is a comparison of various options available, with positive and negative consequences.

Fig. 20-2

Cash or Credit Purchase?

Item	Cash	Credit
Refrigerator		
Price	$800 + $15 delivery charge	$50/month ($900 total) + $15 delivery charge
Total cost	$815	$915
Substitute Used refrigerator		
Price	$400 + $15 delivery charge	$30/month for 15 months + $15 delivery charge
Total cost	$415	$465
Considerations	Ties up cash; cannot make other purchases. No monthly payments. Reduces savings balance. No interest charges.	Allows for budgeting; ties up future income. Can make other purchases. Establishes credit. Interest charged.

Comparison shopping will allow you to determine whether you are getting the best quality for the price you are paying. Name brands often sell at considerably different prices depending on the seller (or markups); by shopping various retail outlets you may be able to save money. In addition, many stores offer sale prices at various times of the year or at regular intervals. Before making a major purchase, ask if and when the merchandise will be placed on sale.

You should also take advantage of store policies that allow you to be refunded part of your purchase price if the item you bought goes on sale within the next two weeks or month. This policy, together with a liberal return policy, should greatly affect your choice of merchants. For example, a store that allows you to return a gift or other purchase within a reasonable period of time from its purchase (a month or more) is much better than a store that will not accept returns, will not give refunds, or requires the receipt for an exchange.

The fact that you are paying a high price does not necessarily mean you are getting the best quality merchandise. It pays to be aware of what is good quality and what you need and expect from the merchandise. Magazines such as *Consumer Reports* make quality comparisons of products. Yearly buying guides that show quality comparisons for many major purchases, from electric mixers to air humidifiers, are also available. You can do a similar analysis while doing your own comparison shopping. Figure 20-3 is an illustration of how to compare cost with quality and utility (usefulness) of product selections. Considering the cost difference for quality and usefulness, the buyer would probably buy either Product A or B because quality and utility make them more reasonable for the price paid.

Fig. 20-3

Cost Analysis

Item	Cost	Quality	Utility
Product A hair dryer	$25.00	High; five-year warranty; metal	3 Speeds 3 Attachments
Product B hair dryer	$18.75	Good; two-year warranty; plastic	3 Speeds 2 Attachments
Product C hair dryer	$15.00	Good; no warranty; plastic	1 Speed 1 Attachment

Marketing strategies that influence spending decisions

Numerous marketing strategies lure us into stores to buy goods and services. Many of these strategies are subtle, and we are often unaware of their impact on our buying patterns. Some frequently used marketing strategies explained in this chapter are advertising, pricing, sales, and promotional techniques.

Advertising

The primary goal of all advertising is to create within the consumer the desire to purchase a product or service. Some advertising is false and misleading; other advertising is informational and valuable.

A variety of media are available for advertising—billboards, television, radio, newspapers, magazines, leaflets, balloons, and T-shirts— all carefully coordinated to reach specific consumer groups. Advertising agencies create colorful and attractive campaigns. They hire well-known athletes and role models, compose jingles and catchy tunes, develop slogans and trademarks, design colorful logos, and choose mascots to identify their products. There are three basic types of advertising: product, company, and industry.

1. **Product Advertising.** Advertising intended to convince consumers to buy a specific good or service is called **product advertising.** The name of the advertised product is repeated several times during radio and television commercials. Famous athletes, actors, authors, or other personalities are often hired to wear or use the product. Testimonials from people who have used the product, giveaways, promotional gimmicks, and other clever and catchy methods are used to persuade consumers to purchase products and services. Advertisements are carefully planned to appeal to specific types of consumers. A **target audience** is a specific consumer group to which the advertisements for a product are directed. Day of the week, time of day, and type of program are taken into consideration

Advertising, as shown by this billboard, can be very attention-getting and creative.

by television advertisers. Products advertised during football games differ from products advertised during daytime television because the target audiences are different.

2. **Company Advertising.** Advertising intended to promote the image of a store, company, or retail chain is known as **company advertising.** Usually price is not a consideration, and specific products are not mentioned. Emphasis is placed on the quality of the products or services the company sells, warranties and/or guarantees offered, or social and environmental concerns of the company. In a store advertisement, you may hear or read about the company's friendly employees, its wide selection of products or services, or its claim that you can find everything you want in one place. These advertisements are designed to promote a favorable attitude toward the company so that you develop a loyalty to the store and will not shop anywhere else. Company advertisements may be accompanied by catchy slogans and tunes, upbeat cartoons, or pleasant scenes to which products of this company make a contribution.

3. **Industry Advertising.** Advertising intended to promote a general product group without regard to where these products are purchased is called **industry advertising.** For example, the dairy industry emphasizes the nutritional value of milk and other natural dairy products. Consequently, the whole dairy industry benefits when people drink more milk and eat more dairy products. Often, industry advertisements stress concern about energy conservation, environmental protection, and the search for new alternative forms of fuels. General health and safety advertisements are often presented in industry advertising campaigns, such as the Smokey the Bear fire safety commercials and the anti-smoking ads.

Pricing

The price of merchandise depends on several factors. Supply and demand determine what will be produced and the general price range. The cost of raw materials and labor, competitive pressures, and the seller's need to make a reasonable profit are some of the factors that determine the price of a product. But there is more to pricing than adding up the production costs and including a profit. Retailers understand the psychological aspects of selling goods and services and use pricing devices to persuade consumers to buy. For example, if buyers believe they are getting a bargain, or are paying a lower price, they are more inclined to buy a product or service. **Odd-number pricing** is the practice of putting odd numbers on price tags—99 cents instead of $1.00, for example. Because the price is under a dollar, it appears to be lower. By paying $5.98 instead of $6.00 the customer is happy because he found a sound buy; the retailer is happy because she has made a profitable sale.

Discounts or low unit prices are often available for buying in large sizes or quantities. However, you cannot assume that because you are buying the large economy size you are actually paying less per ounce than if you bought a small size. Compare unit prices on all sizes.

Sales

Stores advertise end-of-month sales, anniversary sales, clearance sales, inventory sales, holiday sales, preseason sales, and so on. Merchandise may be marked down substantially, slightly, or not at all. In order to be sure that you are actually saving money by buying sale items, you must practice comparative shopping and know the usual prices. When an advertisement states that everything in the store is marked down, check carefully for items that only appear to be marked down in price.

A **loss leader** is an item of merchandise marked down to an unusually low price, sometimes below the store's actual cost. The store may actually lose money on every sale of this item because the cost of producing the item is higher than the retail price. However, the loss leader is used to get customers into the store to buy other products as well. Sales on other items are expected to make up for the loss sustained on the loss leader. There is nothing illegal or unethical about a loss leader as long as the product advertised is available to the customer on demand. A customer who buys only loss leaders and "super" sale items is called a **cherry picker.** Retailers rely on customers to buy other products to make up for the loss caused by sales of the loss leader. Consequently, cherry pickers are not highly favored by retailers.

Promotional Techniques

In order to get customers into stores, retailers may use one or more promotional techniques: displays, contests and games, trading stamps, coupons, packaging, sampling, and direct mail micromarketing.

1. **Displays.** Retail stores often use window displays, special racks of new items, or sampling promotions to entice customers. Products are arranged attractively, and the promotion may carry a theme centered on the nearest holiday—Halloween, Thanksgiving, Christmas, Valentine's Day, Mother's Day, Father's Day, or the Fourth of July. Color schemes, decorations, music, and special effects often set off the products being offered in a way that will appeal to consumers' ego needs.

2. **Contests and Games.** Grocery stores, department stores, fast-food restaurants, and other retail stores that depend on repeat customers often use contests and games to bring customers into the store. Individual product packages, such as cereal boxes, may contain game cards. The possibility of winning something or getting something for nothing appeals to many people. Large and small prizes are offered with the intention of getting customers to come back and buy more so that they can get more game cards, have more chances to win, and receive some of the minor prizes. Careful reading of the rules on the reverse side of the game card or other token reveals the customer's chances of winning. Usually, the chances of winning a major prize are small.

3. **Coupons.** Manufacturer coupons offer cents off on specifically described products from a specific manufacturer and may be redeemed wherever the product is sold. Store coupons offer discounts on specific products, usually for a short period of time, and only at a specific store. Manufacturer and store coupons may be inside or outside of the package, in newspapers or magazines, or on a store shelf. Coupons may not be redeemed for cash, but may be used to give cents off on the product promoted on the coupon. The effect of the coupon is to lower the price of the product in an attempt to convince customers to choose that product or the store offering the bargain over its competitors. Stores that accept manufacturer coupons return the coupons to the manufacturer for a refund in the amount given to the customer.

Manufacturer and store coupons are among the most common promotional techniques used by retailers.

4. **Trading Stamps.** Some stores use **trading stamps** or punch cards that can be redeemed for merchandise at a future date. Trading stamps are used to build customer loyalty and repeat business for future purchases. With punch cards, the customer buys the first ten and then gets the eleventh item free. This technique is also used to build customer loyalty.

5. **Packaging.** Packages are designed to appeal to the eye with the necessary information correctly and attractively arranged. Distinc-

tively designed packages are used to attract the customer's attention away from competitive products. Company logos, brightly colored designs, pictures of people promoting or using the product, and other attention-getters may appear on product boxes. Special features are emphasized, such as "sugar free," "no saccharin," "fortified with eight vitamins and minerals," "new and improved," "safe for children," and many others. Manufacturers know that the package or container must be attractive because it plays such an important role in inducing purchases. Size and shape of packages are significant— containers that appear to hold more of the product or are reusable as storage devices also attract consumers. Often, a game or prize inside the box is also shown on the outside, or coupons are contained inside or on the package. A cents-off price means that the price on the package is reduced by a certain amount, usually shown in large print.

6. **Sampling.** Many companies use direct advertising of their products through sampling. Small sample-size free packages of a product may be sent directly to households; or, company representatives may give out samples, free drinks, or tastes of products in selected stores, in shopping centers, or on street corners. Usually when a new product is first introduced into the marketplace, sampling allows potential customers to try the new product. Some companies advertise in magazines and newspapers, with offers for free samples by mail. All you have to do is fill out the coupon with your name and address and mail it in. In addition to a sample of the product, you may receive a coupon to be used on future purchases of the new product.

7. **Direct Mail Micromarketing.** Many companies buy information about consumers in order to target their potential buying habits. Information about a person's lifestyle, marital status, family, age, and buying habits is known as psychographics. This information is gathered from previous purchases using credit cards or checks, public information, and other sources that are provided by government, the post office, banks, credit bureaus, and other sources. The purpose of gathering the information is to target specific customers with specific products and services that will meet their needs.

While mass marketing may involve television ads, coupons, and other techniques that are spread out to reach millions, micromarketing is designed to target specific people with products that they are likely to want. **Micromarketing** is a marketing strategy designed to target the specific needs of specific customers, including the development of specialty or customized products.

In order to achieve success in micromarketing, the business must have access to specific personal information about potential customers

—their buying habits, income, age, sex, number of children, and so on. For example, when a couple has their first child, they are likely to receive advertisements, samples, and coupons based on their need for baby products and services. The birth record of the child is public information and is gathered to make such micromarketing possible. While many consumers call this "junk mail," it is designed to reach potential customers just like any other marketing strategy.

 ## ummary

The personal decision-making process is a five-step procedure that includes defining the problem, obtaining accurate information, comparing alternatives, selecting an alternative, and taking action. Our economic needs and wants consist of basic needs and life-enhancing wants and needs; individual needs are affected by personal style, income, education, security level, and leisure time available. Collective (societal) values include legal protection, employment, progress, quality of environment, and public and government services. Personal factors and outside factors affect individual spending decisions—from personal resources to social pressures. In addition, we are affected by marketing strategies of advertising, pricing, sales, and promotional techniques.

ocabulary terms

Directions: Can you find the definition for each of the following terms used in Chapter 20?

basic needs   *loss leader*
cherry picker   *micromarketing*
collective values   *odd-number pricing*
company advertising   *personal factors*
custom   *personal resources*
disposable income   *product advertising*
economy   *target audience*
industry advertising   *trading stamps*
innovations

1. Ingredients necessary for maintaining physical life.
2. Things that are important to society as a whole; all citizens share in their benefit and in their cost.
3. An item of merchandise marked down to a very low price, often below actual cost.
4. The practice of putting uneven price numbers on merchandise to make the price appear low.
5. Factors present in one's life that influence spending patterns.
6. New ideas, methods, or devices that bring about changes.
7. A long-established practice that is the same as an unwritten law.
8. A system or structure of life in a country that describes its financial well-being.
9. Advertising that attempts to convince you to buy a certain good or service.
10. Technique used to promote and maintain customer loyalty.
11. A specific consumer group.
12. A type of promotion that attempts to sell a general product group without regard to where it is purchased.
13. One who goes to a store and buys only the loss leaders (items priced below the store's cost).
14. The amount of money a person or family has left over after expenses are paid.
15. A marketing strategy designed to identify specific needs of potential customers in order to sell a product or service.
16. Time, money, energy, skills, and other factors that enhance your purchasing power.

17. A marketing tactic that gives the customer some type of "credit" to redeem at a later date.

acts and ideas in review

1. List the five steps in the personal decision-making process. Briefly describe each.
2. What are some personal factors that influence a person's or a family's spending patterns?
3. What are some outside factors that determine a person's or family's spending patterns?
4. Of the life-improving needs and wants, how many are met in your life?
5. List six different advertising media. Which one(s) do you see most frequently?
6. What is a "target audience"?
7. What is "odd-number pricing"? Is it used frequently in the advertising that you see most often?
8. Why don't retailers like to see cherry pickers?
9. On what theme do promotional displays often center?
10. What types of businesses often offer contests and games to attract customers?
11. What is a "store coupon"?
12. What is a "manufacturer coupon"?

pplications for decision making

1. Using the steps in the consumer decision-making process, make a decision that will satisfy your need for a piano.
2. How do your spending patterns differ from those of your parents? What things do you buy that your parents also purchase? Can you trace any of these purchases to strong family custom, background, or religion?
3. How are you or the members of your family affected when interest rates are very high? Do you benefit, or are you hurt? How? Can you think of anyone who is affected in an opposite way from you? Why is this so?

4. What community-centered and national environmental concerns do you have? What can you do as a single concerned citizen to help preserve the quality of the environment?

5. Spend an evening viewing television or listening to the radio. List the jingles, tunes, key words, phrases, and slogans used in each commercial. How many commercials can you automatically sing along with? What famous athletes, movie stars, and other well-known persons participate in advertisements for particular products or services?

 ife situation problem solving

1. Watch a television program for one hour any time during the day. Determine the program's target audience (teenagers, children, homemakers, sports fans, families, adults only). Pay close attention to all commercials shown during the hour. Write your answers to the following questions on a separate piece of paper.
   a. List all the commercials. Categorize them as either product, company, or industry advertising. (Public-service advertisements and political campaigns are industry advertisements.)
   b. Rate each commercial as good, fair, or poor, depending upon how well it is directed to the television program's target audience.
   c. Rate each commercial according to tastefulness (either good taste or poor taste). Do you find it offensive, degrading, insulting? Explain why you liked or disliked the commercial.

2. Bring to class an advertisement insert from a newspaper. It should be from a department store, local discount store, or grocery store. Write your answers to these questions on a separate piece of paper:
   a. How many individual advertisements show odd-number pricing?
   b. How many mention how much money will be saved or what the regular price is?
   c. Are there any coupons or references to coupons?
   d. Are trading stamps, games, or special incentives mentioned?
   e. Is it attractively arranged?
   f. Is it in color or black and white?
   g. Rate it as to quality, attractiveness, and readability.
   h. Do you see any loss leaders or "super" buys?
   Attach the advertisement insert to your paper. On the insert, write comments next to items to identify them as examples of loss leaders, odd-number pricing, and so on.

3. Describe a store display built around the theme of the most recent major holiday. Describe colors used, products displayed, product arrangement, location in the store, and other aspects. Were there any actual price reductions?

4. List any stores in your area that use one or more of the following promotional techniques. Beside each store name, describe the specific techniques used.

    a. Contests and games   d. Sampling

    b. Trading stamps   e. Other

    c. Coupons

objectives:

After reading and studying this chapter you will be able to:

21-1 Describe the various housing alternatives and potential living arrangements.

21-2 List the advantages and disadvantages of renting a residence, complete a rental application, and understand a lease and an inventory.

21-3 Discuss landlord/tenant responsibilities, including inventory and condition report and appropriate notices.

21-4 Discuss considerations of home ownership (positive and negative).

21-5 List moving costs and installation charges that arise from physical change of residence.

f you walk down any residential street, you are likely to see a variety of housing types. What makes people select a certain type of housing?

A very important personal decision in your future relates to your choice of housing. Initially, you will probably choose to rent or lease. Once you are ready to accept the responsibilities of home ownership, you may decide to buy your place of residence. Your needs, lifestyle, and financial resources will determine whether you decide to rent or buy. In this chapter, you will explore possible housing alternatives and features of each, including agreements, responsibilities, landlord/tenant laws, and the costs of moving into a new residence.

21 Housing

chapter

ousing alternatives

Most people spend half or more of their time at their place of residence —before and after work or school, on weekends and holidays. A person's home should be pleasant, comfortable, and enjoyable. Your first home away from your parents will be very exciting and fun, but it will also take some careful thought and planning for the best choice to meet your needs. Because those needs will change through the years, you are likely to move several times before you buy a home. Nevertheless, each housing decision you make will provide you with a measure of comfort, convenience, affordability, and utility. We'll begin our discussion of housing with several alternatives you will consider initially in your life as a tenant, including on-campus housing, apartments, duplexes, condominiums, and houses. A **tenant** is one who rents or leases property.

On-Campus Housing

Many college students prefer to live on campus while attending a college or university. **Dormitories** are buildings containing many small rooms with beds, dressers, closets, and study areas. Typically, you would have a roommate, or for an extra charge, you might be able to have your own private room. Most dormitories have centrally located lounges for watching television and facilities for doing laundry. Dormitories provide a convenient location, plus eating facilities, with the meals included in the cost. Although individual rooms are small, with limited space for living and studying, the cost per school term may be less than for other available private housing.

Other on-campus housing might be provided through sororities or fraternities. To live in one of their buildings, you would become a member in a process called "pledging." Typically, sororities and fraternities seek new members with goals, plans, abilities, and ideals that are similar to those of the organization. For example, some require a certain grade point average; others look for an interest in community service. To be invited into a sorority or fraternity, you must meet special requirements. College catalogs and brochures explain which sororities and fraternities are available. You must contact them for information about joining.

Housing cooperatives are also available on many larger campuses. When you live in a cooperative, you get a room similar to one in a dormitory. But the difference is in your responsibilities. In addition to

keeping your room clean and usable, you also share in cooking, cleaning, and maintaining of the building. In exchange, your monthly rent is less because you help provide services for yourself.

Major advantages of on-campus housing include closeness to classes and campus activities, access to campus resources such as a library and health center, and a feeling of being a part of campus life. On the other hand, students pay a flat fee for housing and meals, often a term or semester in advance, and do not have the opportunity to budget their resources.

Apartments

An apartment is often the preferred choice for the first residence away from home, particularly for young people attending vocational or community colleges or starting their first full-time job. The amount of rent paid for an apartment is based on the size of the apartment and facilities provided, as well as the amenities provided from saunas to weight rooms. The larger the apartment and the more facilities provided, the higher the rent.

Efficiency apartments provide the least amount of living space, but are also the least expensive. In an efficiency, or studio apartment, there is only one large room serving as the kitchen, living room, and bedroom. Larger apartments with separate living and dining areas are available in a variety of floor plans, including two-story models, called townhouses.

Apartments are usually located in multiunit buildings in which the number of units may be as few as two or as many as several hundred. Facilities provided may include a laundry room, storage area, swimming pool, tennis courts, and clubhouse. In addition, all or part of the utilities (heat, light, and garbage service) may be included in the rent payment.

Apartments provide the greatest amount of independence and flexibility but also require responsibility and good judgment. Most apartment buildings have rules that make close living more enjoyable for all: no pets, no music or noise after 11 p.m., and restricted hours for use of some facilities, such as a pool.

Duplexes

A *duplex* is a two-family house. Usually both halves of the house are exactly the same, but there are separate entrances for each. Generally located in quiet residential areas, duplexes offer more space than apartments. Duplexes also offer more privacy, with only one close neighbor, and may include a garage or carport, private laundry facilities, and other privileges and responsibilities similar to a house. For example, a tenant at an apartment is not expected to perform maintenance activities; a duplex tenant is expected to mow the grass and maintain the landscaping outside and surrounding the unit.

A condominium is an individually owned unit in a multiunit structure.

Condominiums

A *condominium* is an individually owned unit in a multiunit structure. The condominium owner, upon purchase of a unit, becomes a member of the home-owners' association, which is responsible for the property management. A monthly fee is paid by each owner to cover the cost of maintaining the common areas and the outside portion of the units.

The individual owners are responsible for maintaining the interior of the units. Common areas may include a variety of athletic and recreational facilities. Condominium ownership is similar to home ownership but with shared responsibility for common areas enjoyed by all owners.

Houses

A house is a single-family detached home. The purchase price of houses varies with size, facilities, and location. Having a place to call one's own is a primary motive of many home buyers. Stability of residence and a personalized living location are important to many people. Home ownership also has financial benefits. One benefit is the deductibility of mortgage interest and real estate tax payments for federal income tax purposes. A potential benefit is an increase in the value of the property that results from rising property values. These concepts are explained later in this chapter.

Rental houses are private and offer many attractive features. Unfortunately, they are often considerably more expensive to rent than apartments. You are paying for neighborhood living, garage space, privacy, and the other comforts of home ownership. But you are also likely to find many of the same restrictions as with all other rentals, such as no pets allowed. Because rented houses are investment properties that may be sold, you may find the property shown to prospective new owners while you are living there. You may be asked to move if a new owner is purchasing it for private use rather than as a rental.

 ## iving arrangements

Major decisions about your living arrangements must be made before you sign a rental agreement. With whom to live, where to live, what to take, when to move—all are considerations that must be given careful thought.

With Whom to Live

Choosing a roommate is sometimes a difficult task. Is there someone, or ones, among your friends and acquaintances with whom you would enjoy living? Be sure you are compatible with your potential roommate(s) before you move in together. Discuss possible areas of disagreement that may cause trouble if not settled in advance. Some questions that should be answered before making a commitment to share living quarters include these:

1. Do you smoke or drink? How do you feel about others who do?
2. Do you like a clean living area at all times, or are you easygoing and casual about your environment?
3. Do you have steady employment or another source of income to ensure that you can be depended on to pay your share of the common expenses?
4. What are some of your goals? Do you want to continue your education, work full-time, travel?
5. What are your leisure activities? What activities will you share with (or impose on) your roommate(s)?
6. What type of transportation do you and your roommate(s) have? What is the approximate cost? Will you share expenses? If so, how will you divide them?

You might want to consider having more than one roommate. The more personalities involved, however, the more difficult it becomes to have problem-free relationships. Matching similar personality types will increase the chances for a successful living arrangement.

The more you know about each potential roommate, the better you will be able to get along and work out problems. It is a good idea to get to know each person before moving in together. Spend time with each other at school, after school, in the evenings, and on weekends participating in group activities. In this way, you can see what interests you have in common, how each of you interacts with the other(s) and in groups, and what personality traits are strongest. It is not necessary that roommates be completely alike in order to get along. However, they do need to be aware of, and be able to accept, each other's qualities and traits.

Where to Live

The decision of where to live will depend largely on finances. For students attending college and choosing on-campus housing, many of the decisions discussed in this chapter will be predetermined. Off-campus housing involves more planning and careful consideration. Those who will not attend college or who choose an off-campus residence must begin their housing plan with a solid financial analysis: What is a realistic amount to pay for rent payments? You must determine how much you can comfortably pay. Then you can begin shopping for the best housing plan to meet your needs. Some costs to consider when deciding where to live include the following:

1. Deposits and fees to rent or purchase a residence. A **deposit** is a pledge, or down payment.

2. Deposits for and average monthly costs of utilities. A **utility** is a service such as light, power, or water provided by a public utility company.
3. Length of time you plan to live in the residence.
4. Distance from place of work or school.
5. Distance from laundry, shopping facilities, and other frequently used services.
6. Costs of maintenance you are expected to perform.

Most financial experts advise allotting between 15 and 30 percent of your total budget for housing. At first, you may need a roommate to share costs. Later, you may be able financially to carry the burden of living alone.

What to Take

Other than on-campus housing, which is usually furnished, most rental residences can be rented furnished or unfurnished. *Furnished* means that the basics are provided—bed and dresser; sofa, chairs, and lamps; dining table and chairs; and essential appliances. An *unfurnished* rental residence may or may not include basic kitchen appliances such as stove and refrigerator. Usually the fewer the items furnished, the lower the rent. If you have enough items or can acquire the essentials for an unfurnished residence, the savings in rent payments can be considerable.

Home or apartment furnishings can be purchased or rented. Purchase and rental payments should be carefully compared before any decision is made. Renting furnishings can be very expensive. Many companies rent furniture with an option to buy. Each rent payment applies toward the purchase. Your option may be for a specified period of time, at the end of which you will have paid for the furniture entirely. An alternative is that at the end of the one-year rental period, you have the option to buy the furniture at a price reduced by the portion of each rental payment made during that year. Be sure to compute total costs and compare them to any other financing method available for purchasing furniture.

Basic household and personal items necessary for setting up housekeeping include the following:
1. Towels, sheets, tablecloths, and cleaning cloths
2. Cleaning supplies (including mops, brooms, buckets, vacuum cleaner, detergent, and cleansers)
3. Personal items (including shampoo, cosmetics, soap, lotions, medicines, and other personal hygiene items)

4. Clothing, shoes, and other apparel
5. Dishes, silverware, pots, and pans
6. Lamps, clothes hangers, clocks, radio, television, plants, and other decorations.

Carpeting is usually provided, but you may need to supply such items as throw rugs, draperies, a shower curtain, and mirrors. Some of these may be contributed by the roommate(s); some may be purchased jointly. A list of things to be purchased jointly should be made before moving. Each roommate should have available his or her share of the expenses prior to making the purchases. If some things are purchased jointly and one of you decides to move, you must then divide the purchases. At the time of purchase, each person should agree to take some items and give up other items. To avoid arguments later, keep a written record of these agreements.

When to Move

The timing of your move can be an important factor in its initial success or failure. At least six months before you actually plan to move, you should begin making preparations. Others who have experienced a similar move can be of great help to you with advice and contributions of household items.

You should make careful preparations at least six months in advance of a move to a different residence.

At the time you are ready to move from your present home, you should make these preparations:

1. Set aside money in savings to cover cleaning deposits, first and last months' rent, fees, and initial expenses and purchases. In most cases $500 or more may be necessary. If you have a pet, an additional deposit or fee may be charged. Most *deposits* are refundable if you meet your obligations. *Fees* are not refundable.

2. Have a steady and reliable source of income with which you can pay the obligations you agree to pay, such as rental agreements, utility bills, and shared expenses.

3. Accumulate what you need to have in order to live independently, such as clothing, towels, sheets and other bed items, small appliances, and dishes. You may have been accumulating these things through the years. If so, you will have to purchase few items when you move.

4. Discuss with your roommate(s) all options, requirements, expenses, and other concerns. Decide whether you are prepared financially and emotionally to meet the challenges. Be aware of each other's strengths and weaknesses, and decide if you are willing to make changes to meet each other's needs.

5. Plan the move with your career goals in mind. If it is your goal to finish college, then your plan should work in harmony with that goal and help you achieve it. For example, if you are planning to go to college in September and live on campus, it would probably not be wise to go out on your own for the three summer months. The expenses would be too high, and you would be better off saving your money to help meet college expenses. Your goals and those of your roommate(s) should be discussed in detail.

6. Make arrangements for transporting furnishings.

A good way to organize your preparations is to make a needs inventory, such as the one shown in Figure 21-1. You and your roommate(s) will decide what will be needed and check off each item when it is acquired or accomplished.

Group Financial Decisions

All roommates will have a responsibility to meet the obligations they agree upon. Rent is an example of a joint obligation; each person must pay his or her share so that the total rent is paid on time. Utilities probably will be shared equally, as will garbage service, cable TV, monthly telephone charges, and group activity expenses. Long-distance telephone calls should be paid for individually. But expenses such as gasoline or groceries might be divided according to percentage of use. Laundry services usually are an individual expense.

Fig. 21-1

Needs Inventory

What Is Needed	Date Needed	Cost	Date Completed
1. Dishes/towels	Oct. 1	$100	_____
2. First and last months' rent	Oct. 1	$700	_____
3. Cleaning deposit	Oct. 1	$100	_____
4. Car (one to share)	Sept. 1	$100/mth.	_____
5. Radio/television	Oct. 1	$300	_____
6. Job for self and/or roommate	Aug. 1	$--	_____
7. Household budget	Sept. 1	$--	_____
8. Discussion with roommate(s)	June 1	$--	_____
9. Discussion with parents	June 1	$--	_____

Group budgeting allows for the careful allocation of expenses, so that each person pays his or her share. The budget should be prepared and put into writing following a good discussion. Figure 21-2 is an example of a group budget.

Fig. 21-2

Group Budget

Expense	Monthly Cost	Cost Per Roommate		
		Robin	Helen	Arlene
Rent	$450	$150	$150	$150
Utilities (avg.)	75	25	25	25
Gasoline	60	30	20	10
Groceries	150	50	50	50
Household supplies	45	15	15	15
	$780	$270	$260	$250

A method of paying these expenses is for each person to have a separate account for individual expenses, and for the group to have a joint account from which shared expenses are paid. Each person is required to deposit a certain amount into the joint account by the first of each month. Then checks are written from the joint account to pay for rent, utilities, and other expenses incurred throughout the month. Individual expenses are paid individually.

Any plan for taking care of expenses should be agreed upon by all roommates so that everyone is satisfied. Each will know how group and individual expenses will be paid.

 enting your residence

A **landlord** is the owner of the property that is rented or leased to another person. The variety of rental housing provided by landlords emphasizes the advantages of renting. The lack of many conveniences and facilities provided by landlords, however, adds to the disadvantages of renting your residence.

Advantages of Renting

Rental living is the most popular choice among singles and young married couples. As shown in the following list, renting provides a number of advantages, such as mobility, convenience, social life, and lower living expenses.

1. **Mobility.** Many single persons prefer to rent because of the ease and speed with which they can move when a good job opportunity comes along. One of the advantages of renting is that the living arrangement need not be permanent. If you plan to work or go to school for only a few months, renting a residence for that short period is wise.

2. **Convenience.** Many landlords provide a number of conveniences for their tenants. For example, some rental properties have laundry facilities in each unit; others have them located in a central area for all tenants. Extra storage space also may be provided. Recreational facilities are available on many rental properties. Finally, many apartment or condominium complexes are conveniently located near major shopping areas, downtown areas, or important industrial and professional business centers.

3. **Social Life.** Apartments located in multiunit buildings of any size offer the opportunity to meet others and socialize on an informal basis. You are not isolated, without neighbors and other people nearby, when living in a rental complex. In addition, recreational facilities at many large complexes provide numerous opportunities to socialize regularly.

4. **Lower Living Expenses.** Apartments usually are less expensive to rent than houses. But the most important factor in lowering individual living expenses is sharing expenses with roommates.

One of the conveniences often provided by a landlord is laundry facilities.

Disadvantages of Renting

Anyone who has lived in apartments or other rental properties can list numerous disadvantages of these living arrangements. Some frequently mentioned disadvantages of renting are as follows:

1. **Noise.** Those who live in apartments, duplexes, or condominiums share common walls with neighbors above, below, or beside them. Consequently, music, conversations, and other activities of neighbors can be overheard. Late hours or unusual habits of neighbors can be very irritating.

2. **Lack of Privacy.** Because conversations and other activities can be overheard through common walls, tenants often feel that their neighbors know too much about their private lives. Problems associated with shared facilities—laundry and recreation, for example —also become annoying to some tenants after a time.

3. **Small Quarters.** The typical apartment is smaller than some other housing alternatives. Five hundred to 1,000 square feet of living space is average for an apartment. A house may have 1,200 or more square feet of living space.

4. **Lack of Storage Area.** The small size of many apartments means that less cabinet and closet space is available. Also, few rental prop-

erties offer more than a small amount of additional storage space for rarely used items.

5. **Lack of Parking Space.** Many rental properties do not provide garages or off-street parking, especially in city centers. Tenants' automobiles are subjected to the hazards of the weather and those associated with parking on busy streets. In complexes that provide parking lots, visitor parking is often very limited.

Rental Applications

Whenever you rent a residence, you may be expected to fill out an application. The purpose of the application is to allow the landlord to check out your employment (income), previous rental experience, credit rating, and so on. This type of checking is done to assure the landlord that you are a good risk—that you pay your bills and will be a good tenant. A landlord may refuse to rent you property because of your past rental history, employment record, or credit rating. Rental may not be denied, however, solely on the basis of race, religion, national origin, sex, or marital status. Some states have passed laws to prohibit denial of rental to tenants with small children. Figure 21-3 is an example of a rental application.

RENTAL APPLICATION

Name _____ Date _____

Address _____ Phone _____

Name(s) of other person(s) to be living here _____

_____

Previous Address _____

_____ How Long? _____

Employer _____ Phone _____

Address _____ How Long? _____

Bank _____ Savings _____ Checking _____

Credit References

Name _____ Address _____

Name _____ Address _____

Fig. 21-3

Rental Application

Leases and Month-to-Month Agreements

Basically there are two types of agreements used when renting: leases and month-to-month tenancy agreements. A **lease** is a written agreement to rent certain property at a certain price for a specified time period. You may sign a lease for six months, one year, two years, or any period agreed upon. Rent will not be raised until the lease expires, except as agreed upon in the lease. But if you decide to move before the lease expires, you are still responsible for the remaining rent payments. At least thirty days prior to the end of your lease, the landlord should inform you of the rent increase. If you do not wish to stay longer than the time of your lease, you must notify the landlord in writing at least thirty days prior to departure. Figure 21-4 is an example of a lease agreement.

A **month-to-month rental agreement** is an agreement, oral or written, to rent certain property at a set price on a month-to-month basis; that is, with thirty days' notice, a tenant may move out and not be held responsible for additional rent payments. The ease of moving in and out is an advantage. But, because the time length of the agreement is not specified, the rent may be raised at any time. You also can be asked to leave at any time.

A lease and a month-to-month rental agreement will include provisions for deposits and their return, termination of rental, rent payments, tenant and landlord responsibilities, and various other matters. If you do not understand any part of the agreement, ask the landlord about it. If the answer is not satisfactory, get a legal interpretation or refuse to sign the agreement. Both a lease and a month-to-month rental agreement are legally binding documents when you have placed your signature on them. Therefore, it is very important that you fully understand the agreement before signing it.

Rental Inventory

If you reside in a rental property, you are expected to leave it as you found it. Normal wear and tear is expected and accepted. However, anything broken or misplaced is not acceptable. Therefore, to assure that you are not accused of such acts as breaking, damaging, or taking furnishings, take an inventory of the premises at the time you move in. The inventory should list and describe the conditions of the property. Note such things as broken windows, missing window screens, holes in walls, torn carpeting, plumbing problems, and appliance damage or problems. This inventory should be taken with the landlord, and a copy made for each of you. When you move out, you and your landlord should once again take an inventory. Figure 21-5 shows an inventory and condition report that can be used in a variety of rental situations.

Fig. 21-4   **Lease**

RESIDENTIAL LEASE AGREEMENT
AND SECURITY DEPOSIT RECEIPT

THIS INDENTURE, made this ___29th___ day of _____October_____ , 19 ‑‑ , between

___Brendan Martin_____ , hereinafter designated the Lessor

or Landlord, and _____Teresa Thomas_____ , hereinafter designated the Lessee,

WITNESSETH: That the said Lessor/Landlord does by these presents lease and demise the residence

situated at ___614 Dundas Street_____ in _____Cincinnati_____ City,

___Hamilton_____ County, _____Ohio_____ State,

of which the real estate is described as follows:

614 Dundas Street, Cincinnati, Ohio.

upon the following terms and conditions:

  1. **Term:** The premises are leased for a term of ___one (1)___ years, commencing the ___1st___ day of ___November___ , 19‑‑ , and terminating the ___31st___ day of ___October___ , 19 ‑‑ .

  2. **Rent:** The Lessee shall pay rent in the amount of $ _____$400.00_____ per month for the above premises on the ___1st___ day of each month in advance to Landlord.

  3. **Utilities:** Lessee shall pay for service and utilities supplied to the premises, except ___None_____ which will be furnished by Landlord.

  4. **Sublet:** The Lessee agrees not to sublet said premises nor assign this agreement nor any part thereof without the prior written consent of Landlord.

  5. **Inspection of Premises:** Lessee agrees that he has made inspection of the premises and accepts the condition of the premises in its present state, and that there are no repairs, changes, or modifications to said premises to be made by the Landlord other than as listed herein.

  6. **Lessee Agrees:**
     (1) To keep said premises in a clean and sanitary condition;
     (2) To properly dispose of rubbish, garbage, and waste in a clean and sanitary manner at reasonable and regular intervals and to assume all costs of extermination and fumigation for infestation caused by Lessee;
     (3) To properly use and operate all electrical, gas, heating, plumbing facilities, fixtures and appliances;
     (4) to not intentionally or negligently destroy, deface, damage, impair, or remove any part of the premises, their appurtenances, facilities, equipment, furniture, furnishings, and appliances, nor to permit any member of his family, invitee, licensee or other person acting under his control to do so;
     (5) Not to permit a nuisance or common waste.

  7. **Maintenance of Premises:** Lessee agrees to mow and water the grass and lawn, and keep the grass, lawn, flowers, and shrubbery thereon in good order and condition, and to keep the sidewalk surrounding said premises free and clear of all obstructions; to replace in a neat and workmanlike manner all glass and doors broken during occupancy thereof; to use due precaution against freezing of water or waste pipes and stoppage of same in and about said premises and that in case water or waste pipes are frozen or become clogged by reason of neglect of Lessee, the Lessee shall repair the same at his own expense as well as all damage caused thereby.

  8. **Alterations:** Lessee agrees not to make alterations or do or cause to be done any painting or wallpapering to said premises without the prior written consent of Landlord.

  9. **Use of Premises:** Lessee shall not use said premises for any purpose other than that of a residence and shall not use said premises or any part thereof for any illegal purpose. Lessee agrees to conform to municipal, county and state codes, statutes, ordinances, and regulations concerning the use and occupation of said premises.

  10. **Pets and Animals:** Lessee shall not maintain any pets or animals upon the premises without the prior written consent of Landlord.

  11. **Access:** Landlord shall have the right to place and maintain "for rent" signs in a conspicuous place on said premises for thirty days prior to the vacation of said premises. Landlord reserves the right of access to the premises for the purpose of:
     (a) Inspection;
     (b) Repairs, alterations or improvements;
     (c) To supply services; or
     (d) To exhibit or display the premises to prospective or actual purchasers, mortgagees, tenants, workmen, or contractors. Access shall be at reasonable times except in case of emergency or abandonment.

  12. **Surrender of Premises:** In the event of default in payment of any installation of rent or at the expiration of said term of this lease, Lessee will quit and surrender the said premises to Landlord.

  13. **Security Deposit:** The Lessee has deposited the sum of $ ___400.00_____ , receipt of which is hereby acknowledged, which sum shall be deposited by Landlord in a trust account with ___Citizens_____ bank; savings and loan association, or licensed escrow, ___Cincinnati_____ branch, whose address is ___201 Main Street, Cincinnati, Ohio_____
All or a portion of such deposit may be retained by Landlord and a refund of any portion of such deposit is conditioned as follows:
     (1) Lessee shall fully perform obligations hereunder and those pursuant to Chapter 207, Laws of 1973, 1st Ex Session or as may be subsequently amended.
     (2) Lessee shall occupy said premises for ___one (1)___ months or longer from date hereof.
     (3) Lessee shall clean and restore said residence and return the same to Landlord in its initial condition, except for reasonable wear and tear, upon the termination of this tenancy and vacation of apartment.
     (4) Lessee shall have remedied or repaired any damage to apartment premises;
     (5) Lessee shall surrender to Landlord the keys to premises;
Any refund from security deposit, as by itemized statement shown to be due to Lessee, shall be returned to Lessee within fourteen (14) days after termination of this tenancy and vacation of the premises.

  IN WITNESS WHEREOF, the Lessee has hereunto set his hand and seal the day and year first above written.

/s/ *Brendan Martin*   /s/ *Teresa Thomas*
_____   _____
           LANDLORD   LESSEE
      610 Dundas Street
_____
      Cincinnati, Ohio
_____
            ADDRESS

(Acknowledgment)

Fig. 21-5   **Rental Inventory**

INVENTORY AND CONDITION REPORT

Use this report to record the contents and condition of your unit when you move in and before moving out. If you mark anything as being either dirty or damaged, describe it fully on an additional sheet. Use the blank before each item to indicate how many there are. Ask the landlord to sign your copy.

		Dirty Yes* No	Damaged Yes* No				Dirty Yes* No	Damaged Yes* No
Living Room								
___ Couch	1	☐ ☐	☐ ☐	___ Oven racks	43	☐ ☐	☐ ☐	
___ Chair	2	☐ ☐	☐ ☐	___ Broiler pan	44	☐ ☐	☐ ☐	
___ End table	3	☐ ☐	☐ ☐	___ Working refrigerator	45	☐ ☐	☐ ☐	
___ Easy chair	4	☐ ☐	☐ ☐	___ Ice trays	46	☐ ☐	☐ ☐	
___ Floor lamp	5	☐ ☐	☐ ☐	___ Working sink	47	☐ ☐	☐ ☐	
___ Table lamp	6	☐ ☐	☐ ☐	___ Working garbage disposal	48	☐ ☐	☐ ☐	
___ Coffee table	7	☐ ☐	☐ ☐	___ Counter tops	49	☐ ☐	☐ ☐	
___ Light fixture	8	☐ ☐	☐ ☐	___ Range hood w/working fan	50	☐ ☐	☐ ☐	
___ Rug or carpet	9	☐ ☐	☐ ☐	___ Working dishwasher	51	☐ ☐	☐ ☐	
___ Floor	10	☐ ☐	☐ ☐	___ Hot and cold running water	52	☐ ☐	☐ ☐	
___ Walls	11	☐ ☐	☐ ☐	___ Drawers	53	☐ ☐	☐ ☐	
___ Ceiling	12	☐ ☐	☐ ☐	___ Dinette table	54	☐ ☐	☐ ☐	
Bedroom				___ Dinette chairs	55	☐ ☐	☐ ☐	
___ Bed frame(s)	13	☐ ☐	☐ ☐	___ Light fixture	56	☐ ☐	☐ ☐	
___ Headboard(s)	14	☐ ☐	☐ ☐	___ Floor	57	☐ ☐	☐ ☐	
___ Mattress	15	☐ ☐	☐ ☐	___ Walls	58	☐ ☐	☐ ☐	
___ Mattress cover	16	☐ ☐	☐ ☐	___ Ceiling	59	☐ ☐	☐ ☐	
___ Bed springs	17	☐ ☐	☐ ☐	**Bathroom**				
___ Dresser	18	☐ ☐	☐ ☐	___ Towel racks	60	☐ ☐	☐ ☐	
___ Nightstand	19	☐ ☐	☐ ☐	___ Tissue holder	61	☐ ☐	☐ ☐	
___ Drapes or curtains	20	☐ ☐	☐ ☐	___ Mirror	62	☐ ☐	☐ ☐	
___ Mirror	21	☐ ☐	☐ ☐	___ Medicine cabinet	63	☐ ☐	☐ ☐	
___ Light fixture	22	☐ ☐	☐ ☐	___ Counter top	64	☐ ☐	☐ ☐	
___ Rug or carpet	23	☐ ☐	☐ ☐	___ Working sink	65	☐ ☐	☐ ☐	
___ Floor	24	☐ ☐	☐ ☐	___ Working tub	66	☐ ☐	☐ ☐	
___ Walls	25	☐ ☐	☐ ☐	___ Working shower	67	☐ ☐	☐ ☐	
___ Ceiling	26	☐ ☐	☐ ☐	___ Working toilet	68	☐ ☐	☐ ☐	
Bedroom				___ Toilet seat	69	☐ ☐	☐ ☐	
___ Bed frame(s)	27	☐ ☐	☐ ☐	___ Shower curtain	70	☐ ☐	☐ ☐	
___ Headboard(s)	28	☐ ☐	☐ ☐	___ Cabinet	71	☐ ☐	☐ ☐	
___ Mattress	29	☐ ☐	☐ ☐	___ Light fixture	72	☐ ☐	☐ ☐	
___ Mattress cover	30	☐ ☐	☐ ☐	___ Hot and cold running water	73	☐ ☐	☐ ☐	
___ Bed springs	31	☐ ☐	☐ ☐	___ Floor	74	☐ ☐	☐ ☐	
___ Dresser	32	☐ ☐	☐ ☐	___ Walls	75	☐ ☐	☐ ☐	
___ Nightstand	33	☐ ☐	☐ ☐	___ Ceiling	76	☐ ☐	☐ ☐	
___ Drapes or curtains	34	☐ ☐	☐ ☐	**Miscellaneous**				
___ Mirror	35	☐ ☐	☐ ☐	___ Door key	77	☐ ☐	☐ ☐	
___ Light fixture	36	☐ ☐	☐ ☐	___ Windows	78	☐ ☐	☐ ☐	
___ Rug or carpet	37	☐ ☐	☐ ☐	___ Window screens	79	☐ ☐	☐ ☐	
___ Floor	38	☐ ☐	☐ ☐	___ Mailbox	80	☐ ☐	☐ ☐	
___ Walls	39	☐ ☐	☐ ☐	___ Mailbox key	81	☐ ☐	☐ ☐	
___ Ceiling	40	☐ ☐	☐ ☐	___ Thermostat	82	☐ ☐	☐ ☐	
Kitchen				___ Other	83	☐ ☐	☐ ☐	
___ Working stove	41	☐ ☐	☐ ☐	___	84	☐ ☐	☐ ☐	
___ Working oven	42	☐ ☐	☐ ☐					

Do all the windows work? ....
Does the heat work properly? ....

_____ Tenant

_____ Witness

_____ Date

_____ Landlord

_____ Date

*Describe fully on an additional sheet.

personal perspective

C areers and Opportunities in Real Estate

There are many career opportunities for people who are interested in real estate as a career.

A *real estate salesperson* is licensed to sell real estate in a state. He or she must meet education requirements and pass written examinations. As a real estate salesperson, you are an independent contractor. Therefore, you are responsible for your own expenses, including advertising, transportation, dues, health insurance, and so on. You place your real estate license with a licensed real estate broker. The broker oversees your transactions—whether you represent the buyer or the seller—and collects a percentage of the commission.

A *real estate appraiser* is licensed to appraise, or estimate, real estate value, in a state. To be an appraiser, specific classes must be taken and exams passed to prove knowledge. Appraisers are also self-employed but often group together to form a business. Appraisers are paid flat fees, but those fees compensate the appraiser for time and materials.

Real estate property management is representing owners in the renting and maintenance of rental or income property. An on-site property manager lives in an apartment or other unit that is being rented to many tenants. He or she selects renters, arranges and makes repairs, and tends to the day-to-day operations of the property. Free or reduced rent is usually part of the compensation paid to these managers. Other property managers simply keep an inventory of rental properties, select tenants, collect rents, arrange repairs and maintenance, and prepare accountings to owners. For their services, they are paid a percentage or flat fee.

Many people find real estate investing a great way to make money. Real estate can be purchased, repaired and revitalized, and sold for a profit. As a real estate owner, you are entitled to deductions for depreciation, property taxes, and maintenance and repairs. Income from rentals can be a healthy source of income.

critical thinking

1. Do you think real estate would make an interesting career? Do you know anybody who is in a real estate career? If so, describe that person's career.

2. What is the difference between an independent contractor and an employee?

3. Which area of real estate interests you the most?

andlord/tenant responsibilities

Although most states have passed landlord/tenant laws, there are no national laws. However, landlord/tenant laws for residential rental units generally include similarly worded landlord and tenant obligations.

Landlord Obligations

Housing laws in most states require that landlords provide a dwelling that is habitable (livable) at all times. A dwelling is considered habitable if the following conditions are met:

1. The exterior (including roof, walls, doors, and windows) is weather-proof and waterproof.
2. Floors, walls, ceilings, stairs, and railings are in good repair.
3. Elevators, halls, and stairwells meet fire and safety regulations. (Smoke detectors are required in each unit in most states. Tenants are responsible for testing the alarms, replacing batteries, and reporting any defects.)
4. Adequate locks are provided for all outside doors, working latches are provided for all windows, and exits meet fire and safety regulations.
5. Plumbing facilities comply with local and state laws and are in good working condition.
6. Water supply provided is adequate.
7. Lighting, wiring, heating, air conditioning, and appliances are in good condition and comply with local and state building and safety codes.
8. Buildings and grounds are clean and sanitary; garbage receptacles are adequate. (Tenants may be responsible for garbage removal charges.)

Tenant Obligations

Tenant obligations usually are stated specifically in the lease or month-to-month agreement. If they are not stated, the following obligations and responsibilities are implied:

1. To read, understand, and abide by the terms of any lease or month-to-month agreement.
2. To pay the rent on or before the due date. Failure to make a rent payment as stated in the rental agreement may result in late fees, termination of the agreement, or eviction. Through **eviction,** a landlord may legally demand that a tenant move from the premises.

3. To give thirty to sixty days' notice of intent to move. This notice will prevent the forfeiture of deposits and allow the landlord time to rent the unit before you move (see Figure 21-6).

4. To keep the premises in good, clean condition and to prevent unnecessary wear and tear or damage to the unit.

5. To use a dwelling unit only for the purposes for which it is intended. For example, you should treat appliances and other furnishings in a reasonable manner. If the landlord pays for any or all utilities, you should use them in a reasonable manner. If a washer and dryer are provided in individual living units, commercial usage is prohibited.

6. To allow the landlord access to the living unit to make repairs or improvements.

7. To obey the rules of the apartment complex or other community living area covering such things as quiet hours, use of recreational facilities, use of laundry facilities, and parking regulations.

Date ___8/15/-- _____

Dear __Ms. Paula Liang_____ :
      Landlord's Name

I will vacate the premises located at __16 Rosewood Ave._____
Apt. ____10____ , on ____9/15/--_____ . This letter constitutes 30 days' notice as required in my lease.

Attached is a copy of the Inventory and Condition Report that I completed when I moved in. You will note the items for which I am not responsible. I believe the premises will be left in the condition in which they were found, with these exceptions: _____

_____A cracked window pane in kitchen_____
for which I know I am responsible. Other than those listed, I know of no other damages to the premises, and I believe I am entitled to a refund of $__400___ of my original deposit of $__500___ , made when I moved in.

My new address will be __215 John St._____

_____

Please mail my deposit check to the address within 30 days of vacancy.

        Yours truly,

        John H Keller
        Tenant(s) Name(s)

Fig. 21-6

Notice to Landlord

uying your residence

Many people reach a point in their lives when they must decide whether to buy a house or continue to rent. Because the purchase of a home is probably the most important and most expensive decision people make, the advantages and disadvantages should be weighed carefully. Although many single people own their own homes, marriage and family usually create the greatest need for home ownership. To provide more space and room for expansion, hobbies, and recreation for children are often the reasons given for buying a home. Most financial experts advise that the purchase price of a house should be no more than two-and-a-half times your gross income.

Advantages of Home Ownership

Some of the more important advantages that home ownership provides are the savings in taxes, an increase in equity with each payment, and increased privacy and personal freedom. Home ownership likewise provides a sense of security, permanence, and belonging to a neighborhood or city. The personal values that cause a desire for home ownership are hard to describe, but nevertheless they are important factors in the decision to buy a home.

Tax Savings
Interest paid on a real estate loan, along with property taxes levied against the property, are deductible for income tax purposes. (These topics are discussed further in Chapter 22.) The effect of these deductions is to lower the cost of home ownership. Renters cannot deduct any part of their rent payments from their income taxes.

Equity Increases
Equity is the difference between the appraised value of your home and what you owe on it. For example, if you purchase a home valued at $75,000 and have a loan of $50,000, your equity is $25,000. With each loan repayment, you decrease the amount of debt but increase the amount of equity. When you sell the home for more than you paid for it, you will make money because you will have the amount of your equity and a profit returned to you.

Privacy and Personal Freedom
Home ownership offers privacy and personal freedom not available to renters. In your own home you make all the decisions and have free

use of all facilities. Owning a home also provides a feeling of security and independence. Knowing that the home is yours to do with as you wish and when you wish can be very satisfying. With home ownership comes the freedom to have pets, a backyard to work and play in, and possibly space to plant a garden.

Disadvantages of Home Ownership

Most of the disadvantages of home ownership relate to cost. In addition to a monthly mortgage payment, other costs generally not found in renting are necessary for homeowners. Some of the costs involved are the down payment, mortgage, closing, property taxes, insurance, utilities, and maintenance and repairs.

Down Payment

Most conventional (not government backed) loans require a 10 to 30 percent down payment. For example, if you are purchasing a home for $50,000, you will need $5,000 (10 percent) to $15,000 (30 percent) for the down payment. For many singles and young married couples, saving enough money for the down payment takes a number of years.

Mortgage

The balance of the purchase price, after the down payment, is usually borrowed from a bank or other financial institution. A **mortgage** is a long-term loan on a specific piece of property, such as a home or other real estate. Payments on a mortgage are made over an extended period, for example, fifteen or thirty years. The larger your down payment, the lower your monthly mortgage payments. Property taxes and the cost of property insurance are often included with the mortgage payments.

Closing

The **closing costs,** also referred to as *settlement costs,* are the fees and charges paid when a real estate transaction is completed. Closing costs may add another $1,000 to $3,000 to the purchase of your home (as discussed further in Chapter 22). The purchaser usually pays for a title search to have the abstract on the property updated. The **abstract** is a summary of all previous transactions involving the property you wish to buy. Additional costs that the purchaser may pay are for a personal credit report, loan fees, assumption fees (to assume someone else's mortgage), closing fees, recording fees, tax and interest prorations, and fire insurance.

Property Taxes

The real estate property tax is a major source of funding for local governments. Homeowners pay property taxes based on the assessed value of land and buildings. The **market value** is the highest price a property

will bring in a competitive and open market. A local taxing authority determines the *assessed value* for your property, usually a percentage of the market value. A new home worth $300,000 might have an assessed value of $150,000 (or 50 percent of its actual value). If the property tax rate is $24 per thousand of assessed value, you will pay 150 times $24, or $3,600 a year, in property taxes. The total amount of property taxes paid annually is deductible on your income tax return.

Insurance

A homeowner must have insurance covering the structure as well as the contents of a home. A more detailed explanation of homeowners insurance is presented in Chapter 26.

Utilities

Because most homes are larger than apartments or other rental units, the utility bills are also usually larger. The homeowner pays for all utilities and garbage services, whereas a renter may pay for some but not all of these items. In addition, when any repairs are needed to water or sewer lines, the homeowner is fully responsible for the costs involved.

One of the responsibilities of the homeowner is maintenance and repair of the structure.

Maintenance and Repairs

Maintenance and repairs, inside and outside the home, are the responsibility of the owner. These include such responsibilities as painting, mowing, trimming, landscaping, fertilizing, pulling weeds, and spraying for insects. Roofs are generally good for fifteen to twenty-five years. If you purchase an existing (not new) home, you may have to replace the roof after only a few years. The amount of insulation necessary to keep the house warm in winter and cool in summer may need to be increased.

aking the move

Several costs are involved in the actual, physical change of your residence. Two that you will need to be prepared for are moving costs and installation charges.

Moving Costs

Moving costs may involve time and money in careful packing, storing, transporting, loading and unloading, and unpacking. The distance you move is an important factor. The greater the distance, the greater the expenditure of time, energy, and money. A move across town is much less expensive and time-consuming than a cross-country move. If you have your own automobile, the problem is eased somewhat. Still, careful planning and packing are essential to be sure you move the items that you really need and will use.

In order to move, you may need to rent a truck or trailer; borrow a van or pickup; have friends or family help; or send some items by mail, freight, bus, or other available carrier. You may also decide to store some items because you have no immediate need for them and because they would take up valuable space.

If you rent a truck or trailer, you may find a local rental agency that will rent one that you can leave in the city to which you are moving. One-way truck and trailer rental fees are based on a flat rate, plus mileage and gasoline. The rates vary and should be compared to get the best price. A typical rate is $100 a day, plus twenty cents a mile and gasoline. Some one-way rental agencies will not accept cash in payment of a rental. They require a credit card number or may charge you a deposit of $300 or more, which will be refunded when you return the truck to the designated location.

Of course, if you hire a moving company to move your possessions to your new residence, the charges will be considerably more because you will pay for labor as well. By renting a truck or trailer and using your own labor for loading, driving, and unloading, you save money. But you also accept the responsibility involved in using the equipment of others.

Installation Charges

As a new occupant of a house or rental unit, you will pay some installation charges. Although fees vary with the type and location of the residence, there are usually charges for installation of a telephone and cable TV, and for turning on the electricity and other utilities.

To obtain these services, most of which are essential, you may be required to show your ability to meet your financial obligations. Many utility companies charge a deposit that is refundable after a year or two, when you have proved your ability to pay your bills.

Other companies, such as the telephone company, charge a one-time fee that is not refundable. You may be charged $75 to $100, depending on your city, to have a telephone installed. The installation charge is added to your first bill. Then monthly service rates vary according to the type and number of phones you choose, kinds of services selected, and other factors. Many people buy their telephones to avoid paying monthly telephone rental fees. You will pay more to have an **unlisted number.** If your telephone number is unlisted, it is not listed in the telephone directory and cannot be obtained through directory assistance. An unlisted number assures privacy and prevents many unwanted calls.

 ummary

When you first move into your own residence, you have many choices to consider. For students attending colleges and universities, on-campus housing alternatives should be considered carefully because they are convenient and conducive to learning. Apartments offer many advantages but are not as private or spacious as duplexes, condominiums, or rental houses. Each of these options has many positive and negative features.

Your choice of roommates and where you plan to live will greatly affect your selection of housing alternatives. In sharing accommodations, you will need to provide basic household and personal items as well as joint furnishings for the apartment. As important as roommate choices and location is a decision about when to move. You must prepare financially before making a move.

There are many advantages to renting, including mobility, convenience, social life, and lower living expenses. But disadvantages are also numerous and include noise, lack of privacy, and lack of space. Rental applications and agreements can be difficult to understand. You can protect yourself with a rental inventory listing the condition of the property when you take possession.

There are many landlord and tenant responsibilities. You will find that you are expected to take care of the property as if it were your own and return it in the condition you received it. Otherwise, you will be assessed fees and lose your deposit.

Buying property also has many advantages, including tax savings, an increase in equity, privacy, and personal freedom. But ownership also requires a cash down payment, mortgage payments, property taxes, insurance, and expenses for maintenance and repairs.

Moving can be an arduous task. There are many moving costs to consider, such as renting a truck or trailer and installation and start-up charges.

21

Vocabulary terms

Directions: Can you find the definition for each of the following terms used in Chapter 21?

abstract	*lease*
closing costs	*market value*
deposit	*month-to-month rental*
dormitories	*agreement*
efficiency apartment	*mortgage*
equity	*tenant*
eviction	*unlisted number*
landlord	*utility*

1. A landlord's legal method of removing someone from a rental unit.

2. A service, such as light, power, water, or gas, that is provided by public companies or corporations.

3. The difference between the value of your home and what you owe on it.

4. A pledge or a down payment.

5. One who rents or leases property from a landlord.

6. A summary of all previous transactions involving a certain property.

7. The highest price a property will bring in a competitive and open market.

8. On-campus buildings that contain small rooms for student living.

9. A telephone number that is not listed in the telephone directory and cannot be obtained through directory assistance.

10. The owner of the property rented or leased to another person.

11. A written agreement to rent property at a certain price for a specified time period.

12. A studio apartment that is one large room that serves many purposes.

13. A written agreement to rent certain property at a set price on a month-to-month basis.

14. A long-term loan on a specific piece of property.

15. Costs incurred before a buyer can take possession and a seller can pass title to the buyer of a piece of real estate.

Facts and ideas in review

1. How soon before a move should you begin making plans?
2. List four advantages of renting a residence.
3. List four disadvantages of renting a residence.
4. What is the difference between a furnished and an unfurnished residence?
5. How does a condominium differ from an apartment?
6. What is the purpose of a rental application?
7. How does a lease differ from a month-to-month tenancy agreement?
8. Why should you complete and have a landlord sign an inventory when you move into a rental unit?
9. List five tenant obligations when renting.
10. List six conditions a landlord must meet in order to make rental property habitable.
11. What are some advantages of owning your home?
12. What would be the typical down payment on a $100,000 home?
13. What is the market value of a home?

Applications for decision making

1. Ask two persons each of the questions below. Based on the answers, determine if the three of you would be a compatible living group.
   a. Do you smoke or drink? How do you feel about persons who do?
   b. Are you a clean, fussy housekeeper or easygoing, casual, and relaxed about your surroundings? How often do you clean?
   c. Do you work steadily, part-time or full-time? How would you pay your share of the rent and other shared expenses?
   d. What are some of your goals regarding college, your job, or recreation?
   e. What do you like to do in your spare time? What are your group activities? your individual activities?
   f. What type of transportation do you have or plan to have? What are the costs involved? Which costs will be shared?

2. What have you accumulated that you would want to take with you to a new residence? (Examples: radio, television, towels, furniture, cleaning items, dishes.)
3. What basics would you have to buy to live independently?
4. Make a list of things you should do before moving out on your own.
5. In order to move your possessions from your present home to a new residence, what types of transportation are available to you? What is the best and least expensive for you?

ife situation problem solving

1. Prepare a report comparing the rental prices and availability of apartments, duplexes, condominiums, and houses in your area. To compare prices, living conditions must be comparable; you must compare two-bedroom unfurnished apartments to two-bedroom unfurnished duplexes, and so forth. Also, note how many are available in each category at the present, the high and low prices, and the average rental prices.
2. Study the listings of homes for sale in the classified ads of your newspaper. Answer these questions:
   a. What is the lowest sale price you can find?
   b. Describe the house with the lowest sale price.
   c. What is the highest sale price you can find?
   d. Describe the house with the highest sale price.
   e. How many houses are for sale in one day's newspaper ads? What is the name and date of the newspaper?
   f. How many homes are listed for sale by the owner?
   g. Describe the house that you would choose to own; include size, price, features, and location.
3. Using the community resources in your area, find out the hookup or installation deposits and fees for the following services:
   a. Telephone
   b. Electricity
   c. Cable TV
   d. Water or garbage services
   Are any of these fees partially or fully refundable? If so, under what conditions?

4. Find out the monthly rates for the following telephone services in your area:
   a. Standard phone
   b. Touch-Tone service
   c. Conference call
   d. Speakerphone
   e. Private line
   f. Call Forwarding
   g. Call Waiting
   h. Unlisted telephone number
   i. Additional phone jack installed

terms to know:

real property
personal property
fixture
lot and block
metes and bounds
eminent domain
police power
fee simple
encumbrances
easement
lien
multiple listing
  service
offer
earnest money
deed
proration
time sharing
appreciation
depreciation

objectives:

After reading and studying this chapter you will be able to:

22-1 Define real estate terminology, including legal descriptions of property, rights and interests in property, and ownership of property.

22-2 Describe the step-by-step process of buying a home.

22-3 List and explain real estate investment options, including single-family houses, duplexes, multiplexes, apartment buildings, and land.

22-4 Explain the benefits and risks of real estate investments.

The biggest and best investment you will ever make is the purchase of your own home. Owning real estate is a financial goal of many people. Having a place to call your own is a primary motive of many home buyers. While personal preferences and tastes are the foundation of many home buying decisions, financial factors may modify your final choice.

In the previous chapter, you learned some of the advantages and disadvantages of owning your own home. In this chapter, you will continue to study home ownership as you learn about the process of buying your own home. You will then explore real estate investments—the purchasing and holding of rental properties as short-term and long-term investments, including houses, duplexes, multiplexes, apartment buildings, land, REITs, and other choices. You will also discover the many rewards and risks involved in home ownership and real estate investments.

chapter

22 Real Estate Principles

eal estate ownership

Real property is land and anything permanently attached to it, such as buildings, fences, and sidewalks. Real property within a county and state is a matter of public record. By visiting your county courthouse, you can select a piece of property and find out where it is located, who owns it, its legal description, and other public information. **Personal property** refers to items that are not permanently attached to real property but are removed when the property is sold, such as cars, lawn mowers, and furniture. When an item of personal property is permanently affixed to real property, it is called a **fixture.** A fixture becomes a part of real property when removing it would cause substantial damage to the building or land. For example, if you attach a bookshelf to the wall of a room using fourteen molly bolts, the removal of the bookshelf would do considerable harm to the wall. Therefore, the bookshelf is considered a permanent feature, or fixture, of the home.

Legal Descriptions

Land is measured by federal and state governments using base lines and prime meridians. From the intersection of these points, surveys are made into townships, square miles, or sections. Local areas are also divided into townships, sections, and acres, then into subdivisions and lots for resale to individual buyers. There are five common ways to describe real property: informal reference, lot and block, metes and bounds, government survey, and assessor parcel number.

Informal Reference

A street address is one way to describe land with a building on it. For example, a property could be described informally as, "the house at 235 Sycamore Street, Dallas Texas," or "the ranch known as the Lazy M Ranch located 15 miles south of Alturas, California."

Lot and Block

Using the **lot and block** method of describing real estate, a house located at 1400 Elm Street would be identified as follows:

> Lot 3, Block 6, of the Sunshine Addition to the City of Portland, Multnomah County, Oregon.

This description identifies the property by its lot number and block number within a subdivision. Both the lot number and the block number of individual pieces of real property are shown on a map of subdivisions on file in the county recorder's office called the *recorded plat*.

Metes and Bounds

Another type of legal description is **metes and bounds,** which is a detailed method of identifying a parcel of property by specifying its shape and its boundaries. Such a description would read like this:

> Commencing at the permanent reference mark which designates the Sunshine Addition to the City of Portland, thence north 80 degrees 0 minutes 0 seconds east, 152.0 feet to the point of beginning; thence south 80 degrees 0 minutes 0 seconds east, 180 feet; thence south 15 degrees 0 minutes 0 seconds west, 160 feet; thence south 85 degrees 0 minutes 0 seconds west, 151 feet; thence north 4 degrees 11 minutes 18 seconds east, 199.5 feet back to the point of beginning.

A map based on the foregoing metes (distance) and bounds (direction) would look like Figure 22-1. Metes and bounds are based on benchmarks, which are used as permanent reference marks, and degrees in a circle, which move in a clockwise direction from the point of beginning.

Government Survey

The rectangular survey system was authorized by Congress in May 1785 as a fast and simple method of surveying property. Rather than using existing monuments, it was based on imaginary lines that circle

The rectangular survey system was authorized by Congress in May of 1785.

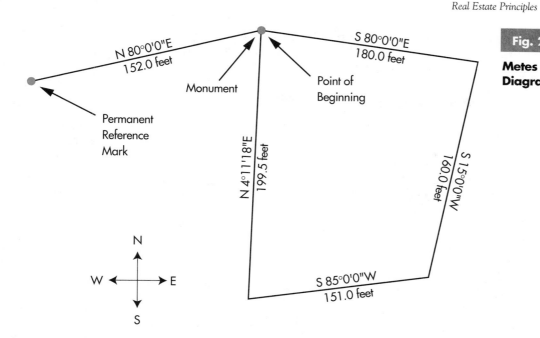

Fig. 22-1

Metes and Bounds Diagram

the earth. These lines are east-west (latitude) and north-south (longitude). Certain longitude lines were selected as prime meridians; for each of these meridians, an intercepting latitude line was selected as the baseline. Every twenty-four miles north and south of a baseline, correction lines were established (because the earth is a sphere rather than a flat surface). Ranges are marked every six miles east and west of prime meridians; townships intersect range lines every six miles north and south. With this type of legal description, a piece of property would be described as follows:

> The northwest quarter of the southwest quarter of Section 32, Township 2 North, Range 3 East of the Sixth Prime Meridian.

Assessor's Parcel Numbers

In most counties, the tax assessor assigns a parcel number to each parcel of land in the county. A parcel could be assigned a number like 15-8-44, which would mean Book 15, page 8, Parcel 44.

Rights of Government

Owners of real estate are free to do whatever they please with the property they possess, subject to several government-imposed restraints. As an owner of real property, you have the right to build or tear down your building within the government's building codes. Some of these rights are limited by law and by building codes, or by zoning laws of cities and/or counties. *Zoning laws* restrict how property in an area can be used. These laws are imposed to control lands and subdivisions to assure the highest and best use of the lands.

Property Taxes

Government has the right to impose taxes on real property. Property taxes are called *ad valorem* (imposed at a rate percent of value) taxes because they are based on value. Real estate taxes are an important source of money for cities, counties, and states. In many states, schools, fire and police, parks, and libraries also depend on property taxes to operate.

Eminent Domain

The right of the government to take away privately held real property regardless of the owner's wishes is called **eminent domain**. Land is usually taken for the public good for such things as schools, freeways, streets, parks, urban renewal, garbage disposal site, or public parking. The legal proceeding is called *condemnation*; the property owner must be paid the fair market value of the property taken.

Police Power

The right of the government to enact laws and enforce them for the public health, safety, morals and general welfare is called **police power.** Examples of police power include zoning laws, building codes, health and fire regulations, and rent control. Police power does not take away property (like eminent domain), but it does restrict how an owner may use the property.

Rights of Owners

Real estate ownership is a right in the United States. Each citizen has the power to own real property. If you own property, you have the right to determine its use and its management; therefore, you are called the *owner*. Ownership is a bundle of rights. If you own all the rights to property, you own it in **fee simple.** After the rights of government are held in reserve (property taxes, eminent domain, and police power), the remaining fee simple interest can be held by a person and his or her heirs forever.

Limitations of property rights are called **encumbrances** and are grouped into public rights such as the right to tax, the right to acquire property (eminent domain), and police power for the general welfare. Private rights are incidental to ownership. Easements and liens are examples of private rights.

Easements

An **easement** is the right or privilege one party has to use the land of another person for some special purpose. For example, an easement for telephone or electricity enables the telephone or power company to erect poles or bury cables on and across the property. Easements also may be given for people to walk or drive across the land.

Liens

Because of the permanence (immovability) of real estate, it is good security for a loan, debt, or judgment. A **lien** is a hold or claim that one person has on the property of another person to secure payment of a debt. In addition to property tax liens (by government), there are several other types of liens placed against real property, such as mortgage liens, judgment liens, and mechanic's liens.

1. A *mortgage lien* is a pledge of property by its owner to secure repayment of a debt. In contrast to a property tax lien imposed by law, a mortgage lien is created by the property owner. If the mortgage is not repaid, the creditor can foreclose and sell the pledged property.

2. A *judgment lien* arises from a lawsuit for which money damages are awarded by the judge or jury. The law permits a hold against property of the debtor until the judgment is paid. The judgment remains attached to the property until the debt is paid, and the creditor can force the sale of the property to pay the debt.

3. A *mechanic's lien* gives anyone who has furnished labor or materials for the improvement of property the right to place a lien against that property; a sale of the property can be forced to recover the money owed. To be entitled to a mechanic's lien, the work or materials must have been provided under a contract with the property owner. The legal theory behind mechanic's lien rights is that labor and materials enhance the value of the property, and the property should be security for payment. The mechanic's lien must be filed within a set period of time (60 to 120 days after work completion) and expires in a year or two (depending on state law). Unfortunately, if the property owner pays the contractor, but the contractor fails to pay a subcontractor for labor or materials, the mechanic's lien can force double payment by the owner.

When a person owns a property "free and clear," it does not mean that the property has no other interests against it. Public rights always remain; easements and other private rights may also apply. Free and clear means that no mortgages or other types of liens are placed against the property. When a debt is secured by a *mortgage*, the borrower signs a document that gives the lender a lien on the property.

he process of buying a home

In buying real estate either for a residence or for investment, you should consider the location, accessibility, climate, nearness to employment, type and quality of construction, cost and effort of maintenance, and numerous other factors. If you are uncertain or inexperienced as to how to go about gathering and assessing such facts, you can always obtain information and advice from a real estate agent. Banks, savings and loan companies, builders, and appraisers are also good sources of real estate information.

After you carefully consider all the factors involved in a real estate purchase, you can begin the process of purchasing real property. This process can take many weeks or even months. Generally, the procedure can be summarized as in the following paragraphs.

A real estate salesperson can be helpful to you in your search for the right home.

Finding and Selecting Property

In order to find the property you want to buy, you will need to see many houses. You can look by yourself or work with a real estate salesperson, who is trained to know the market, help you find the right home, and assist you with the purchase, financing, and closing. There is no charge to you, the purchaser, for these services. Either way, you will visit many homes listed with the real estate agency, advertised for sale in the newspaper, or that you just drive past and want to see. In the newspaper classified ads, homes are listed by area of town or geographic location. Some are for sale by the owner; others are listed with real estate agencies.

Real estate agencies that belong to a **multiple listing service** offer a valuable service to homeowners: wide exposure to people in the business of selling homes. Most metropolitan, urban, and suburban areas have many real estate sales offices located within their boundaries. When these real estate agencies form the multiple listing service organization, all listings from each office are combined into one book. All salespeople within that geographic area have access to all real estate listings and can sell any of the properties listed to a buyer. Thus, when you list your house for sale with one real estate salesperson, you really have all the salespeople in the area working for you. The person who lists your house receives half of the sales commission; the person who sells your house receives the other half. The cost to you is the same, yet your exposure to the sales market is much greater.

A multiple listing service gives persons seeking to buy a home in a specific area greater exposure to available homes. They can see many listings in all parts of the city. The cost to the buyer is the same; real estate commissions are included in the sale price of a home. Most multiple listing books come out twice a month. Homes are listed according to location and value. The less expensive homes are listed first in each section.

After you have viewed many homes in the area you prefer, you may decide you want to buy one of them. Before you can take possession of the property, however, you must complete the formal buying process, which may take several weeks or months.

Making an Offer

To let the seller (owner) know you want to buy his or her home, you sign an agreement called an **offer.** This formal document explains the terms of the purchase—the down payment; the mortgage you will assume or acquire on your own; and the dates when you will pay what is due, close the deal, and take possession. This agreement is also known as an "earnest money offer." **Earnest money** is a portion of the purchase price that the buyer deposits as evidence of good faith to show that the purchase offer is serious. This money is held in a trust account until the transaction is closed.

If you fail to meet the terms of the agreement, you will have damaged the seller. The house may have been held off the market for awhile and therefore could not be sold to anyone else. You may forfeit your earnest money to the seller if you do not buy the home according to the terms of the agreement. One way to avoid losing your money is to make your offer contingent on obtaining financing and the property passing an inspection.

When the seller accepts your offer exactly as it is stated, you have what is called an *acceptance*. You may withdraw your offer at any time until the seller accepts it. If any conditions of the offer are changed, the seller makes what is known as a *counteroffer*. You have the choice of accepting or rejecting the counteroffer. For example, the seller may want a different date of possession or a larger cash down payment.

Obtaining Financing

After you have come to an agreement with the seller, you will probably borrow to buy the property. To finance your property purchase, you will need to obtain funds for a down payment, meet certain requirements of your lending institution, and assess different types of mortgages.

Down Payment Sources

The most common source of down payment money is from parents or relatives. Most lending institutions will not allow mortgage applicants to also borrow their down payment. In other words, there cannot be another lien against the property other than the mortgage at the time the sale is closed. Because the down payment can be $5,000 to $10,000 or more, many first-time home buyers have difficulty saving the money and must "borrow" it from parents.

Qualifying for a Mortgage

To qualify for a mortgage loan, borrowers must complete extensive loan applications. Credit history will be checked, along with banking and other references. The borrower must prove to the lender that he, she, or they are capable of meeting the monthly payment. Lenders will look for evidence that the borrower is able to meet current bills, type and amount of debt already incurred, amount and source of income, and the borrower's creditworthiness. Generally, lenders will expect that the monthly mortgage payment will not exceed 30 percent of the borrower's take-home pay. The purpose of loan qualifying is to assure the lender that the borrower can and will meet the debt obligation.

Types of Mortgages

There are two basic types of mortgages: *fixed-rate mortgages* and *adjustable-rate mortgages* (ARMs). With a fixed-rate mortgage, the interest rate is set and does not change during the term of the mortgage, which is usually fifteen to thirty years. With an adjustable-rate mortgage, the interest rate is usually lower than the fixed rate to begin with, but the interest rate changes as economic conditions vary. For example, a fixed rate of 8 percent would remain unchanged for thirty years. An adjustable rate of 5 percent may escalate to 10 or 12 percent as interest rates go up in the economy. Most adjustable-rate mortgages specify maximum rate increases (such as 2 or 3 percent a year) and ceilings (such as a top of 12 percent) to which the interest rate can rise.

Taking Title to Property

After both parties have reached an agreement, and financing has been obtained, title to the property must be transferred. A title simply means the right to ownership of property. The **deed** is the document that transfers title of real property from one party to another. The form of ownership of property should be reviewed and proper advice sought before deciding upon taking title to property under a deed. The following are different ways of taking title to property: joint tenancy, tenants in common, partnership, and corporate.

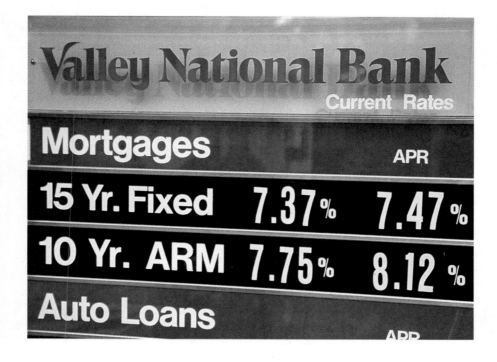

The two basic types of mortgages are fixed rate and adjustable rate.

Typical property buying transactions involve a number of procedures that can limit the buyer's chances of getting a defective title. A buyer should order a *title search*, which lists all the facts about the property being purchased: name(s) of owner(s), liens against the property, easements and assessments (such as sidewalk or street lighting), property taxes, and so forth. A *title insurance company* will issue a preliminary title report (and eventually the title insurance policy). This report gives the buyer detailed information about the property: mortgages and other liens, the owners, legal descriptions, map, and any restrictions on the property. Title insurance provides the buyer with insurance for any claims arising from a defective title. Most lenders require that the borrower buy title insurance.

As part of the closing process, loan papers are ordered from lending institutions, and all necessary papers are prepared. If any problems arise, the buyer and seller are notified. For example, some deeds may carry restrictions that limit the kind of building that can be erected and the use of the property. Inspections, such as termite examinations, are carried out. A credit report is issued. Proper prorations are computed, and the closing documents are prepared. A **proration** is a divided cost or expense. For example, if property taxes are paid for a year at a time, and the buyer takes possession half way through the year, the buyer's "proration" is one-half of the prepaid taxes. In other words, the buyer must reimburse the seller for half of the taxes that were prepaid.

When all these procedures are completed, the seller and buyer are notified of a closing date. The *closing* involves a meeting of the buyer, seller, and lender of funds, or representatives of each party, to complete the transaction. In some parts of the country, the closing is known as settlement, or close of escrow. First the buyer, then the seller, signs the necessary documents. A hodgepodge of local customs dictates how a closing is handled. Your local real estate agent, lender, or attorney can brief you on the procedures in your area. At closing, the buyer takes possession of the property. On closing day, the buyer will pay a variety of fees and charges. The *closing costs*, also referred to as settlement costs, are paid when a real estate transaction is completed. Figure 22-2 is a list of typical closing costs for a real estate transaction.

 eal estate investments

Real estate is a very popular investment for many Americans as you learned in Chapter 14. After making substantial investments in real estate, a person may quit his or her job to work full time managing

Fig. 22-2

Typical Closing Costs

TYPICAL REAL ESTATE CLOSING COSTS

Type of Cost	Typical Amount	Who Pays
Credit report (on buyer)	$50	Buyer
Property appraisal fee	$150-$500	Buyer
Pest and damage inspection	$50	Buyer
Mortgage loan origination fee	varies	Buyer
Mortgage loan assumption fee	varies	Buyer
Document preparation (deeds, closing costs, etc.)	$50-$100	Buyer and Seller
Notary fees and filing fees	$10-$50	Buyer and Seller
Title search; title insurance	$100-$750	Seller
Survey	$150-$500	Seller
Attorney's fees	$500-$1,000	Buyer and Seller
Escrow fees	$50-$500	Buyer and Seller
Escrow payments	varies	Buyer and Seller
Transfer taxes and fees	varies	Seller

investment properties. Most people begin with an initial purchase of a single-family house or small apartment building. Then they may purchase an inexpensive run-down property (but in a good neighborhood), make a low down payment, and refurbish the property. After it is refurbished, this property may be sold (to obtain more cash for subsequent purchases), or it can be rented to bring in monthly income to pay off the underlying mortgage.

The excess of rental income over underlying mortgage payment plus repair and maintenance expenses is *positive cash flow*. If the owner of real estate does not receive enough money from rent to pay the underlying mortgage and other expenses, the result is *negative cash flow*.

Figure 22-3 is a cash flow statement prepared for the owner of a triplex. Examine this statement carefully.

You may notice no entry for cleaning deposits or for last month's rent. These payments by tenants are probably being held in trust on their behalf. Since deposits and last month's rent are not earned income to the landlord, the amounts are not listed as revenue. These deposits will show as income when used by the landlord to pay for cleaning or to cover the last month's rent. A cleaning deposit is used to offset the expense involved in cleaning rental property after a tenant vacates the premises. Property owners cannot keep monies deposited with them unless there is damage or cleaning expenses incurred.

Another factor to consider that affects cash flow is *vacancy*. When a rental unit is not being rented, no income is received to offset the

Fig. 22-3

Cash Flow Statement

CASH FLOW STATEMENT
For Property at 875 Sycamore Street
For the Year Ended December 31, 19--

Rental Income Received:

Unit 1	($800/month x 12 months)	$ 9,600
Unit 2	($700/month x 11 months)	7,700
Unit 3	($500/month x 5 months and	2,500
	$550/month x 6 months)	3,300

Total Income $23,100

Expenses:

Unit 1	New bathroom heater	$350	
	New paint	175	
	Repair screen door	75	
	Repair stove	50	$ 650
Unit 2	Repair leaking roof	$400	
	Repair bathtub	250	
	Replace locks	75	725
Unit 3	Repair counter	$300	
	Clean carpet	100	
	New paint	175	
	Replace wiring	300	875

Mortgage payment, First Bank ($1,100 x 12)	13,320
Property taxes	2,850
*Property management fee (10%)	2,310

Total Expenses $20,730

Net Cash Flow (income minus expenses) $ 2,370

*Note: The management fee is 10% of rental income.

mortgage payment and other expenses. Vacancies occur from time to time as tenants come and go. If a long time is taken to get a unit rerented, the owner may experience a negative cash flow as a result.

Single-Family Houses

A small house is often the best way to get started as an investor. In determining which property to buy, the most important factor to consider is the future resale value. Location is the key to good resale value. More popular and well-maintained neighborhoods always hold value.

Houses on quiet streets, next to more expensive properties, and consistent with other houses in the neighborhood will best hold their value. Most experts advise you to buy the smallest or least expensive house in the neighborhood. In this way, the higher-valued homes around you will bring up the value of your property.

Duplexes and Multiplexes

A *duplex,* or building with two living units, is usually located in a residential neighborhood, often at a corner location. A *triplex* or *quad* is also likely to be tucked within a neighborhood setting. These types of units are rented to families and others who are attracted to a residential neighborhood, or a less traveled street. Duplexes and multiplexes generally do not rent for as much money as single-family houses, but offer many of the same advantages.

Apartment Buildings

To invest in an apartment building, you may need to form a partnership or joint venture with several other investors in order to have enough cash to make the down payment. For example, you may pool your resources with three others, each contributing $100,000. You might assume an underlying or existing mortgage, or you might apply for a new loan. You would have to contribute your share toward the expenses not covered by rental income.

Investors in apartment buildings often form a partnership or joint venture to pool their resources.

Land

Most people who buy a tract of land assume that the value will increase in the future. Because land is considered speculative, most banks will not grant a mortgage; therefore, you must purchase land for cash. Nevertheless, land located in the right location can sell for many times its original value if property values are rising. For example, a vacant lot purchased 20 years ago for $15,000 could be worth several hundred thousand dollars today if it were in a commercial (business) area.

REITs

For those who do not want to invest directly in real estate, that is, who do not want to purchase and own specific property, there is an option called REIT (Real Estate Investment Trust). REITs were explained on pages 326–327 of Chapter 14.

A Real Estate Investment Trust trades like a stock and works like a mutual fund. Your investment is pooled with other people's money, and the trust invests the money in real estate. For many people, REITs are attractive because the trust makes the investment decisions, shares are easily traded, and the current yields are fairly high. Share prices of REITs fluctuate in response to economic conditions, the size of the dividend paid by the trust, and the changes in real estate values. Long-term gains depend on the underlying values of the real properties held by the trust and the quality of the trust's management. You will find REITs listed in the funds section of *The Wall Street Journal*.

Other Choices

Other real estate investment choices include condominiums, cooperatives, PUDs, and time shares. These choices are often considered quite risky. Owners may have trouble reselling these kinds of property without careful planning and considerable luck.

Condominiums

A condominium owner has partial responsibility for land and building maintenance and management as well as some other ownership costs. In addition to the mortgage, the owner must pay a monthly or yearly fee to cover these costs. Often, existing apartment complexes are converted to condominiums. (Condominiums were also discussed in Chapters 14 and 21.)

Cooperatives

A cooperative is similar to a condominium. You would sign a *proprietary lease*, which is an owner's agreement to meet the conditions of the owners' association. A proprietary lease entitles you to own an apartment in a building with numerous other similar units, subject to rules established for the benefit of all owners. But rather than have your own mortgage for a unit within the building, as is the case with a condominium, there is one big mortgage on the entire building. A group of people called *cooperators* go in together and contribute equal shares to make the large mortgage payment. For example, a cooperative building may contain ten apartments. The underlying mortgage of $500,000 may involve a monthly payment of $5,000. Each cooperative owner would have to pay 1/10, or $500 per month for the mortgage payment. In addition, each owner would pay a share of the utilities bill, the property taxes, the insurance, and so on. Like condominiums, cooperatives are organized under a management agreement. A monthly fee is charged for maintaining the building and grounds.

PUDs

A PUD is a planned unit development. PUDs have features common to both condominium and cooperative ownership. You buy a house and the lot as separate property. You also must pay a monthly fee to a community association that owns the common areas. Common areas are open green spaces and may include parks, pools, clubhouse facilities, jogging trails, boat docks, and so on. These areas are not maintained by the city; the owners all contribute to the maintenance.

Time-shares

Time-sharing is a method of selling living units within a vacation facility to many owners. Each owner has a fractional ownership interest in a unit. Units are typically sold for one week a year. However, a buyer can usually purchase an additional week (or weeks) if he or she so desires.

The idea began in Europe in the 1960s when groups of individuals would jointly purchase units at ski resort lodges and summer vacation villas. Each owner would take a week or two of vacation each year. In 1969, the first time-share opened in the United States. Since then, hotels, motels, condominiums, townhouses, lodges, villas, recreational vehicle parks, campgrounds, and even cruise ships have been time-shared.

For a purchase price ($5,000 to $15,000), you get the right to vacation at a location (from Hawaii to Mexico to the Caribbean) for one or more weeks a year. When you own a time-share, the dates you can stay at the vacation location are guaranteed each year. You must pay a monthly or yearly fee to help cover the maintenance costs of the property. When the owners are not vacationing, their units are often rented to the public.

Generally, time-shares are good for only a set number of years: 10, 20, 25, or 40. At the end of that time, your interest expires. During the term of the time-share you can sell your interest, but finding buyers can be difficult. You may not get back your original investment or make a profit. Nevertheless, this type of vacation alternative is attractive to some people, such as ski enthusiasts who like to spend two weeks every year at a certain ski lodge.

 he financial benefits of real estate

A potential benefit is increases in the value of property. **Appreciation** is the increase in property value while a person owns the property. For example, if you buy a piece of real estate for $50,000 and a year later it can be sold for $60,000, the appreciation is $10,000. Appreciation is not taxable until property is sold, and the cash is actually received.

As an owner of real estate, you can deduct from your adjusted gross income on your tax return the property taxes you pay to the local government. You can also deduct the interest you pay on a mortgage loan. Real estate is a *tax shelter* because the owner is able to take advantage of these income tax deductions.

For the owner of rental property, in addition to normal operating expenses, interest on a mortgage, and property tax payments, you are permitted to deduct a *depreciation allowance* based upon the expected life of the property. **Depreciation** is the using up of property value. Most rental properties are depreciated over twenty-five to thirty years. For example, if an apartment building is purchased for $200,000, with an estimated value of $20,000 on the land (land is not depreciable) and an estimated life of twenty years, the annual depreciation expense (tax write-off) would be $9,000 ($200,000 − 20,000 ÷ 20).

If you use *leverage* (that is, you borrow money to pay for your investment) you can make a healthy return investing only a limited amount of your own money. It enables you to acquire more expensive property than you could buy on your own. This is an advantage when property values are rising. Unfortunately, when you use leverage (other people's money), you can still lose money (your initial investment) if real estate prices go down.

Assume that you buy a $100,000 property with no loan and then sell it for $120,000. The $20,000 gain represents a 20 percent return on your $100,000 investment. Then assume that you invest only $10,000 of your own money and borrow the other $90,000 (90 percent financing). Now you have made $20,000 on your $10,000 investment, or a 200 percent return.

personal perspective

Who Needs a Real Estate Professional to Sell Property?

In order to sell real estate for others, you must have a real estate license in the state in which you do business. Anyone assisting buyers or sellers and receiving any type of fee, such as a commission or a referral fee, must have a license. Real estate law protects prospective buyers and sellers from receiving advice and help from people who do not have the appropriate education and experience to provide assistance.

If you are buying and selling real estate for yourself, you do not need to have a real estate license. Many real estate investors hold a real estate license, even though it is not necessary. However, if you are employing a licensed real estate professional, make sure he or she declares in all purchase offers, listing agreements, newspaper advertisements, and other documents that he or she is a licensed real estate professional.

When selling real estate, contact several agents for a listing presentation in your home or property. What you want to learn from each agent is pertinent information about the agent and the company, the terms of the listing, a price estimate for your property, and the marketing steps the agent will take.

Past performance is a pretty good indicator of future success. Find out how many homes your prospective agent and firm have listed and sold recently and how many times she or he was responsible for finding the buyer.

Reject any agent whose company is not a member of the local Multiple Listing Service. The MLS provides a master list of all the properties for sale in a community through its member real estate companies. MLS is perhaps the only benefit a real estate agent can provide that you couldn't get on your own.

critical thinking

1. Provide a list of questions you might ask an agent before signing a contract to have the agent sell your home.

2. Talk to several real estate professionals (realtors, brokers, loan officers, appraisers), and ask them to explain their responsibilities to buyers and sellers in a real estate transaction.

he risks of owning real estate

There are considerable risks along with potential rewards with real estate ownership. For example, a rental property purchased right before an economy goes into a recession is likely to have a negative cash flow. When people cannot afford to pay a high rent, landlords are forced to lower rents or offer special incentives ("first month's rent free," for example) to attract tenants. On the other hand, when rental housing is scarce and the location is desirable, owners of real estate can raise rents and still keep the property fully occupied.

Real estate wears out. The roof will need replacing every fifteen or so years; pipes break and must be replaced; painting, inside and out, must be done every few years. If renovation does not occur, the property loses real value over the years. Remodeling may be needed to stay competitive and to attract high-quality tenants.

One risk of owning real estate is that it is fairly illiquid.

Unfortunately, real estate is prone to uncontrollable factors as well. If the surrounding neighborhood is changing adversely, the property will lose value. Population shifts into or out of any area can affect rental income. A community depending on servicemen to fill the supply of rental units would be severely hurt by a military base closing, for example.

Real estate offers many opportunities to investors, but real estate is also fairly *illiquid*. Property cannot always be sold quickly; in fact, it may take several months or even longer to sell a rental property. Many people consider real estate a long-term investment—one that builds up equity over the years until the underlying mortgage is paid in full.

Summary

Real estate investing is challenging and fun, but also requires considerable thought and preparation. It isn't as easy as it seems. You can own real property (land and anything permanently attached) and personal property. Real property is described by informal reference, by lot and block, by metes and bounds, by government survey, or by an assessor's map number. The rights of government in real property include property taxes, eminent domain, and police power. Ownership rights are what's left after the above interests.

To buy a home, you first begin the long and careful selection process. Cautiously consider the location and desirability of the property. An offer expresses your interest in purchasing property and includes a deposit of several thousand dollars (earnest money). If you arbitrarily change your mind, you can lose this deposit. Closing is the process of preparing papers and gathering evidence so that the property can be transferred from the current owner to the new owner.

Financing a new home involves a significant down payment ($5,000 or more) that is often borrowed from parents or saved by the borrowers. To qualify for a mortgage, borrowers must have a good credit history, a good source of income, and enough money left over to make a house payment after other debts are paid. Fixed-rate mortgages have a specified set interest rate for the length of the loan. Adjustable-rate mortgages (ARMs) have an interest rate that varies according to economic conditions. While the initial interest rate is usually lower with an ARM, it is likely to increase over the length of the loan.

Real estate is a good way to diversify an investment portfolio. Examples of these investments include single-family homes, duplexes and multiplexes, apartment buildings, land, REITs, and other choices. A real estate investment should be considered a long-term investment.

Benefits of investing include appreciation in value, tax savings, positive cash flow, and leverage. Disadvantages include weak economic conditions, repairs and maintenance, renovations to keep the value of property increasing, and illiquidity.

ocabulary terms

Directions: Can you find the definition for each of the following terms used in Chapter 22?

appreciation
deed
depreciation
earnest money
easement
eminent domain
encumbrance
fee simple
fixture
lien

lot and block
metes and bounds
multiple listing service
offer
personal property
police power
proration
real property
time sharing

1. The increase in property value while a person owns the property.
2. A property owner's interest in real property after legal limitations, zoning laws, easements, and the like that could interfere with your use of the property.
3. A claim, right, lien, or other liability limiting title to real property.
4. The right of the government to take away privately held real property.
5. An organization that combines real estate listings for a number of real estate offices to facilitate buying and selling.
6. The using up, or wearing away, of real property value.
7. Items that are not permanently attached to real property, such as cars and furniture.
8. An item of personal property that is permanently affixed to real property.
9. A formal, written proposal to buy a home or other piece of real property.
10. A legal description of a parcel of property by its shape and its boundaries.
11. The right of the government to enact laws and enforce them for the public health, safety, morals, and general welfare.
12. Land and anything that is permanently attached.
13. A description of property by its lot number and block number within a subdivision.
14. The right or privilege one person has to use the land of another person for some special purpose.

15. A hold or claim that one person has on the property of another person to secure payment of a debt.
16. A portion of the purchase price that the buyer deposits as evidence of good faith to show that a purchase offer is serious.
17. A document that transfers title of real property from one party to another.
18. Dividing costs or expenses, a process done at closing.
19. A method of selling living units within a vacation facility.

Facts and ideas in review

1. List the five common ways of describing real property.
2. List the three encumbrances described and briefly explain each.
3. Explain these three types of liens: mortgage liens, judgment liens, and mechanic's liens.
4. Summarize the four steps in the process of buying a home.
5. What is a multiple listing service? Can you name this service in your local area? (Hint: Look in the Sunday newspaper in the classified section or an advertisement of realtors belonging to this service.)
6. What is an earnest money offer?
7. What is the purpose of a title search and title insurance?
8. How do most people get started investing in real estate?
9. Distinguish between positive cash flow and negative cash flow.
10. Briefly describe the different investment options for the purchase of real estate.
11. What are the financial benefits that are derived from owning real estate?
12. What are some of the risks associated with owning real estate?

Applications for decision making

1. Make a visit to your county courthouse. In the assessor's office or records division, look up the property where you live. To start, all you need is your street address. Locate and write down your lot and block, metes and bounds, government survey, and assessor's

parcel number, if available. Look at the map that shows where you live, and draw a rough map of the lot on which your home is located.

2. Write a one-page summary of government-imposed restraints to real property ownership, including property taxes, eminent domain, and police power. Analyze why these laws are enacted and what they mean to property owners. Talk to a person who owns real property and ask his or her opinion of these and other restraints on their property rights.

3. Discuss with a property owner or real estate salesperson the process of purchasing real estate, including steps taken, length of time, and costs involved. Ask them what they would have done differently and things to watch out for when buying real estate. Write a paper summarizing what you have learned.

4. Visit a title insurance company in your area and ask them what they do, how they gather information, and how they are able to insure titles.

5. "Ownership of real estate is one of the best investments you can make." Explain why you would consider (or not consider) real estate as an option for your investment portfolio. Include advantages and disadvantages.

6. Of all the real estate investment options, which one is the most appealing to you? Write a paragraph explaining your choice and your reasons for eliminating the other possibilities.

7. Obtain the home mortgage rates from your local commercial bank, a savings and loan association, and a credit union. Compare these rates and such terms as the down payment, loan costs (points), loan length, and maximum amount available to determine which of the three offers the best financing rates.

8. You might ask, "Why should I go to the expense of hiring someone to sell my property for me?" Because of the complexities of real estate ownership today, it is often wise and less expensive in the long run to engage the services of a professional who knows what she or he is doing. Find out through research or an interview with one or more real estate salespersons at least five services that a professional can provide in selling your home.

L ife situation problem solving

1. Your friend Margaret wants to know more about a house she is thinking about buying. All she knows is the address of the property.

How can she find out more about the property, including its legal description, owner of record, and liens against the property?

2. An owner of real property advertises in the paper that he owns a home free and clear. What does this mean?

3. Eric has decided to buy some real estate. He can't decide whether to buy vacant land or a small house and fix it up. Explain to him the steps involved in buying property, and contrast these two investment options.

4. You have just inherited $25,000 and you are considering some type of real estate investment. You could put down the $25,000 on a house, fix it up, and resell it or rent the property for a period of time. As an alternative, you could invest in a partnership and own a one-fourth interest in an apartment building. The options are endless. Which investment option will you choose? Explain.

5. Your friend Hans has just spent a free weekend at a time-share facility. He is excited about buying a time-share unit for one week. He can "trade" his week for another week in a time-share unit in almost any part of North America and Europe. His initial cost is only $7,500. What other costs may he incur as an owner? Discuss the pros and cons of this type of investment.

6. Ask students to clip an advertisement from the newspaper on a duplex, multiplex, or small apartment building for sale that includes the total price of the unit. From the same newspaper, they can determine the average rental prices for similar types of units. Based on Figure 22-3 (Cash Flow Statement), have students prepare a hypothetical cash flow statement for the ad. To be certain their numbers are realistic, they should ask a parent or other property owner, or someone in the real estate industry, to check their work.

objectives:

After reading and studying this chapter you will be able to:

23-1 Describe the process of buying a new or used car, including selection, financing, and wise buying practices.

23-2 Explain automobile leasing costs, processes, advantages, and disadvantages.

23-3 List the costs of owning and operating a car, from depreciation, gas, and taxes to the cost of accessories.

23-4 Describe methods for extending the life of your car and maintaining its resale value.

23-5 Discuss consumer protection available for new car buyers.

F ew of us live, work, and shop within a small geographic area. Most of us need transportation to go to work or school or for other reasons. Transportation, and more specifically the automobile, has become a necessity for most of the people in our society.

Your selection and use of an automobile is a fundamental part of your personal financial plan. Whether you buy a new or a used car, there are proven strategies that will make the experience better and minimize your costs. In this chapter, you will investigate the steps in buying a car and in financing the purchase. You will determine the costs associated with owning and operating an automobile. You'll discover ways to extend the life of your car and maintain its resale value. Finally, you'll learn about the legal and social concerns associated with car ownership.

chapter

23

The Automobile

uying a car

The first step in buying a car is deciding what type of car you want, need, and can afford. Almost everyone would like to drive a small, red sports car—a convertible with two seats, a floor shift, and a high-powered engine. Unfortunately, for most people this type of car is probably the worst choice they can make. The purchase price of the car is only one factor. You must also consider the cost of insurance, licensing and registration, gas, maintenance, and repairs.

Buying an automobile involves a number of choices and alternatives. The process should begin with some basic decisions related to vehicle size, style, and model, and to finances.

Steps and Strategies

The steps in buying a new or used car include identifying your top three choices of vehicles, researching and comparing, getting credit preapproval, visiting dealerships, test-driving your choices, and making an offer.

Narrow the Choices

Select potential vehicles that make the best match with your needs. You may need an automobile that is large enough to carry three or more passengers, along with packages or containers. You may also need one with good fuel economy because you'll be driving over 100 miles a week. Your price range will also help narrow your choices.

Before purchasing a car, you must consider not only style but the purchase price and the cost of insurance.

A primary decision is whether to buy a new automobile or a used one. This decision is based primarily on financial factors. Can you afford the costs involved in buying a new automobile? A used car is less expensive to buy than a new car.

Research and Compare

Before you head for the dealerships, stop by the local library. Look up the cars you are considering in magazines such as *Consumer Reports, Edmund's New Car Prices*, and *Car and Driver*. Look for articles about specific models, performance, repair records, safety features, and suggested prices. Look for overall reliability ratings. You may drop some models from your list while adding others. Now add to the list the options that are important to you, such as power steering, antilock brakes, air bags, air-conditioning, power seats, and so on. When comparing costs, be sure to compare models with the same options.

Get Credit Preapproval

Find out how much money you will be qualified to borrow *before* visiting automobile dealers. This process is called **preapproval.** You may or may not use the preapproval; however, it is an effective tool to use when considering how much to spend on an automobile. Knowing ahead of time how much money you have to spend will be a major influence on your choice of vehicle.

Visit Dealers

When you first visit new car dealerships, you should be gathering information only. Collect brochures, ask questions, write down information. Be sure vehicles you are considering come equipped with options that are important to you. An important source of information is on every new car. The **sticker price,** displayed in printed form on the vehicle, is the suggested retail price of a new car with its optional equipment.

Once you are certain you have the right new vehicles on your list, make a second visit to dealerships. Ask for the salesperson you talked to the first time. Don't negotiate yet, just focus on exact information—the sticker price (including transportation charges), taxes, and licensing fees.

If you are in the market for a used car, new car dealers usually have a good supply of used vehicles. These are late-model vehicles that have been received as trade-ins for new car purchases. Other sources of used cars include used-car dealers, individuals selling their own cars, and auto rental companies.

Your first visit to a car dealership should be to gather information.

Used-car dealers usually offer vehicles that are older than those offered by new car dealers. They are unlikely to have a service department, and if they give you a warranty, its coverage is very limited. Individuals selling their own cars can be a good bargain if the vehicle was well-maintained. However, few consumer regulations cover the purchase of a car from a private party. You may also consider cars from rental firms. The automobiles of auto rental companies are usually serviced regularly, but most of them have had many different drivers or may have undergone extreme use.

Test and Inspect Each Car

Test-drive the vehicles of interest to you. Compare ride, handling, features, and cost at several dealers. Go slowly—never be in a hurry when you are shopping for an automobile. Some salespersons will try to pressure you into buying right away. Resist that temptation. You will enhance your bargaining position with patience and knowledge of the car you are planning to purchase. When buying a used car, have a trained and trusted mechanic of your choice check it to estimate the costs of current or potential repairs.

Experts recommend never purchasing before the third visit; and before buying, take the time to check a dealer's reputation. A call to the Better Business Bureau will give you valuable information about the number of and types of complaints consumers have made.

In many larger cities and urban areas, automobiles must pass a **vehicle emission test,** which means the car must meet minimum clean air standards. The fee for the emission test is usually only $10 to $25; however, repairs needed to meet the test requirements may cost an additional $150 or more. Before deciding to purchase an automobile, you should check to see if it has passed vehicle emission tests and if not, whether there is a guarantee provided for this requirement.

Make an Offer

Decide what price you feel is fair before you make any offer for a car. Make up your mind that you will not be pressured into paying more. Either go alone or with a person who is more experienced than you. Stick to facts and don't reveal emotions to salespersons. For example, don't make statements like, "This car is really beautiful; it's just what I want." This type of information can weaken your bargaining position. Make your initial offer, which should be lower than your top price. Be prepared to bargain. But don't pay more than you feel comfortable with. According to the AAA (Automobile Association of America), you can use this rule of thumb: For a compact or subcompact car, the dealer has paid about 90 percent of the sticker price; for mid- and full-size cars, 84 to 87 percent; and for luxury cars, 84 percent.

Before the sale is complete, you must sign a sales agreement. The **sales agreement** is the legal document that contains the specific details of an automobile purchase. As with any contract, make sure that you understand the sales agreement before signing it.

Price Bargaining Schemes

In the bargaining process, sometimes a salesperson will say he or she needs approval from a supervisor or the owner. The salesperson leaves you for several minutes, and then returns to say your low offer just isn't acceptable. You'll be turned over to a "closer," a person who may take advantage of your eagerness to buy. The best thing to do is be polite but remain firm about your offer. Walk away from a deal if you feel you are being pressured.

Two deceptive bargaining techniques are lowballing and high-balling. **Lowballing** occurs when a new car buyer is quoted a very low price or *lowball*. Lowball is a salesperson's term for making the customer a ridiculously low offer for a trade-in. After the customer vigorously protests the low offer, the salesperson pretends to be talked into a better trade-in allowance and thus a sale. **Highballing** occurs when a new car buyer is offered a very high price for a trade-in. However, at the last moment, usually just before the sales agreement is to be signed, the salesperson remembers that all contracts must be cleared through a higher level authority. The salesperson disappears for a few minutes and then reappears with the following news: "Too much is being allowed for a trade-in." At that point, the salesperson indicates the trade-in would be "good" on a more expensive car or the same car with more options.

To prevent confusion in determining the true price of a new car, do not mention a trade-in vehicle until the cost of the new car has been determined. Then ask how much the dealer is willing to pay for the old car.

After the price has been agreed upon, the dealer may try to increase the purchase price by the use of **packs**—high-priced, high-profit dealer services that add little or no value. For example, dealer preparation is nothing more than cleaning the car and checking the air in the tires and the oil in the engine. These services should be provided without extra charge. Other common packs include protective wax or polish, rustproofing, and extended warranties. Rarely are these special services worth the cost. Just say no!

Financing Your Car

The best way to buy a car is with cash. You'll get the best deals that way. Unfortunately, most people don't have enough money to buy a car for cash. Therefore, you must finance the purchase of an automobile. Many lenders will preapprove you for a certain loan amount. Preapproval separates financing from the process of negotiating the price of the car.

Credit Unions

In many cases, your local credit union will have the best loan for your new or used car. Often, they will finance more of your purchase (requiring less of your own cash), have lower interest rates, and require smaller monthly payments. Get an estimate—of interest rates available, length of loan, and so on—and compare the loan to the others available to you.

For example, some credit unions offer free or low-cost car-buying support. This ranges from advice on what price you should pay to the actual purchase of the car. While a car-buying service is usually not free, you may find that experts can get an automobile for you at a lower cost than you can buy it yourself.

Car Dealers

Most new car dealers offer financing. On particular models and at particular times of the year, they may offer you better terms than those available from many other sources. These special deals are sponsored by the manufacturers or their financing agencies to stimulate sales or to promote a particular model. GMAC (General Motors Acceptance Corporation) is an example of a finance company that makes loans on cars through dealerships. Ford, Chrysler, and most other manufacturers offer similar programs. Your payments will be to the finance company —not the dealer. You will have to qualify for the credit just as if you were applying for credit at a financial institution.

Banks and Other Institutions

Commercial banks, savings banks, and even insurance companies often make car loans. These loans are repaid in equal monthly payments of 36, 48, or 60 months on cars, trucks, vans, and other passenger vehicles. The automobile serves as collateral; the bank or other institution has an interest in the car until the loan is repaid.

easing a car

Rather than purchasing a new car, you might consider leasing. **Leasing** is a contractual agreement under which monthly payments are made for the use of an automobile over a set period of time. No ownership interest in the vehicle is given. For example, you may lease a car for two years. At the end of two years, you can turn in the car and get a new one, or you can buy the car for its *residual value*. Residual value is the expected value of the vehicle at the completion of the lease. Individuals

When you lease a car, you obtain no ownership interest in the vehicle.

who lease automobiles are protected by the Consumer Leasing Act, administered by the Federal Trade Commission. This act requires disclosure of various terms and conditions of the leasing agreement.

With interest on automobile loans no longer deductible on federal tax returns, auto leasing is more popular than ever. Leasing has forever changed the car business. Individuals can afford to lease a more expensive automobile than they could buy on credit. In 1993, one-fourth of all cars and trucks were leased rather than sold. The reason is simple: many people cannot afford the big price tag on new cars. Leasing provides an alternative—no large down payment or trade-in to worry about. Just drive away for a set monthly payment!

ost of operating a car

Most people spend more of their income on an automobile and related expenses than on any other item except housing and food. After the initial outlay for the vehicle (down payment, taxes, title, and other fees), there are expenditures for interest on an auto loan and insurance. But there are also other costs that add considerably to the cost of vehicle ownership. These ownership costs include gas and oil, depreciation, licensing fees, and maintenance and repairs.

Gas and Oil

The cost of gasoline depends on the size of your automobile and the number of miles you drive. Cars with big engines get less gas mileage than smaller vehicles. Nevertheless, cars of the '90s get substantially better gas mileage than their counterparts in the '60s and '70s. Gasoline and oil are variable operating expenses. Your cost depends on how many miles you drive each day; therefore, your gas bill could vary from $50 to $100 a month or more.

Depreciation

Depreciation is the loss in value of the vehicle during its lifetime. This occurs as a result of normal wear and tear, style and model changes, and the passage of time. As the car ages, the number of miles driven increases, the physical condition begins to deteriorate, and mechanical difficulties arise. All these factors cause loss in value. However, not all automobiles depreciate. Very old vehicles in excellent condition may *appreciate*, or increase in value.

Depreciation is the single greatest cost of owning newer vehicles. The cost of gasoline comes second. In most cases, the age of a car is the most important factor in determining its resale or trade-in value. Other factors include mileage, brand popularity, body style, size, and color.

While depreciation is a fixed cost of automobile ownership, the actual amount of the decreased value hinges on two factors: the amount that the automobile is used and how well it is maintained. Low-mileage, well-maintained cars retain a larger portion of their original value than do other automobiles. Also, certain well-made, often expensive models, depreciate at a slower rate than other models.

Registration and Titling

A fee to register a car title is charged in all states. A **car title** lists the legal owner (usually the bank or other lending institution) and the registered owner (you). Title registration fees and sales taxes occur only at the time a car is purchased. A license fee occurs as an annual fixed cost. This licensing fee may include an excise tax based on the value of the car, the weight of the car, and/or the size of the engine, depending on the state in which you live. For example, in the states of Washington and California, an excise tax is based on the value of the car. A new car's annual licensing or registration fee includes a flat fee plus an excise tax of $50 to $1,000. As an example, in 1995, the total licensing cost in Washington for a 1995 Ford Taurus was $655 ($23.65 for registration and the remainder for excise tax).

Maintenance and Repairs

The owner's manual will tell you what services are needed and how often. Typically, you can expect to change oil every few thousand miles, have a major engine tune-up every 20,000 to 30,000 miles, and perform other maintenance at scheduled intervals. Systems of your car that should be monitored and maintained include emissions control, air-conditioning, brakes, transmission, and so on.

You also should plan on unscheduled repairs. Such things as flat tires, broken belts, and leaky hoses happen from time to time—and the repairs can be costly. Planning for these expenses is easier if the number of miles you drive during a given period of time is more or less uniform.

As your car gets older, maintenance and repair costs usually increase. You should expect to replace such relatively low-priced parts as fan belts, hoses, the battery, and the muffler. Buying new tires for your car can be very expensive. Based on the size, traction, and type of tire, you can pay from $50 to $200 a tire for new quality tires.

Accessories

Many people choose to add certain features to make their vehicles more functional and attractive, or to perform more efficiently. These items include extra tires (snow), floor mats, seat covers, litter containers, wheel covers, striping and paint features, and sound systems. In some cases, these costs will add to the value of the vehicle; in other cases, they will subtract from it.

xtending the life of your car

Because vehicles are expensive, you will get your best value (cost versus benefit) when you take care of your investment. There are many strategies you can use to keep your car going, to preserve its exterior and interior, and to avoid the costly replacement of parts. Strategies include regular oil changes, routine maintenance, use of a garage, washing and waxing, preserving interiors, and good driving habits.

Change the Oil on Schedule

Most newer cars can run 7,000 or more miles between oil changes. But service technicians report that changing oil more frequently can add years of life to a car. The slogan "oil is the life of your engine" means that the oil lubricates the moving parts of the engine and keeps it clean. Oil must be changed to eliminate accumulated dirt and sludge. Your individual driving habits will dictate how often oil should be changed. For example, short trips and regular city driving require more frequent oil changes.

Experts advise changing oil every 3,000 miles, or every three months, whichever comes first, for suburban and urban driving. Likewise, the oil filter should be replaced when oil is changed to clean oil circulating through the engine. Lubrication, oil change, and oil filter replacement (called "lube, oil, and filter") should cost from $18 to $30, depending on the size of the vehicle engine. Figure 23-1 points out differences in engine oil and helps you decide which one is right for your vehicle.

Follow Routine Maintenance

Don't wait for trouble before checking fluid levels and inspecting belts, hoses, and tire pressure. Most car owners find that by replacing parts periodically, they are able to avoid major problems. These ongoing

Fig. 23-1

All Oil Is Not the Same

ENGINE OIL GRADES AND VISCOSITY

All engine oils are not the same. There are various service grades, depending on additives that are mixed in.

Service Grade

Service SF is the highest grade of engine oil for gasoline-powered vehicles. If you drive a late model car, the owner's manual will specify service grade, or may simply say "heavy duty." Service SF will work in these cars.

Viscosity

Oil thickness requirements vary with temperature ranges in your area. Viscosity is indicated by the letters "SAE." The higher the number, the thicker the oil. For example, SAE 40 means the oil is thicker than SAE 30. If your area has great variations in temperature, you will likely want a multigrade oil for changes in temperature.

Multigrade oil is marked with two numbers, such as 10W-40. In this example, the 10 applies to cold weather and the 40 applies to hot weather. If, for example, the rating is 5W-30, then the car needs more viscosity to get started, and then evens out once it is warm. Usually a 10W-30 or 10W-40 can be used year-round.

routine checks and fixes should cost $100 to $250 a year, but will save you major repairs in the long run. The owner's manual will tell you mileage or time intervals for certain servicing. Since automobile maintenance and repairs can be expensive, be sure to seek out competent service for your money.

Keep Your Car in a Garage

A car kept in the garage at night, and when its owner is at home, is safe from theft and vandalism. It is also protected from the weather, which can damage or destroy its finish and even affect its mechanical condition. Low temperatures, for example, affect almost every component. The engine is harder to start, and the battery is weaker. Thus the starter has to work harder, and the charging system is stressed. Low temperatures can also cause oil in the engine, transmission fluid, and differential fluid to thicken, which can cause more wear on the vehicle. Even an unheated garage is better for your car and its engine than no garage at all.

personal perspective

H ow to Sell a Used Car

If you sell your old car yourself, here are some steps that will help you make a quicker sale.

1. Make sure that you have the title, registration, and other documents that are required when a car is sold. Meet the buyer at the motor vehicles division and transfer title when you receive the cash or cashier's check. Never let a new owner drive away with a car that is still in your name.

2. Prepare the car for sale. Wash and polish the outside, vacuum and clean the inside, and shampoo the upholstery. Check fluid levels and tire pressure, and make certain all lights are functioning.

3. Set a reasonable price. Check a recent National Automobile Dealers Association (NADA) "Blue Book" for high and low book values. Check the classified ads in your newspaper to be sure this price is in the appropriate range.

4. Tell the facts. Present the truth to prospective buyers—what's good about the car as well as its weaknesses, parts that are no longer working, and so on. Disclose the last time you had a tune-up, and allow prospective buyers to check maintenance records.

5. Always ask for cash or a cashier's check. Remove the license plates if they cannot be transferred. Do not allow a new owner to drive a car for which you are still legally registered or responsible.

6. Notify your insurance company immediately that you have sold the car. During the time you are attempting to sell your car, be sure to maintain the minimum coverage (usually liability) required in your state.

Advertise your vehicle in local newspapers. Usually weekend classified ads capture the attention of more readers. When showing your vehicle, go along on the test drive and observe any inspections performed by a mechanic.

critical thinking

1. When you get ready to sell your car, you might want to avoid selling it to a friend, neighbor, or relative. Why?

2. Why should you insist on cash or a cashier's check before you allow a new owner to drive away?

3. Why is it important for you to be sure the vehicle title and/or registration is transferred from you to the new owner?

Clean and Wax Your Car

It's important to keep your car clean. When water sits on the surface of metal, it can cause rust. Cars that are washed more often will have a shining exterior for years. If you live in an area that is warm most of the year, then you'll need to use protective wax to guard your paint from the damaging rays of the sun. If you live in an area that is cold most of the year, you'll need to preserve your car's exterior with frequent cleaning and waxing. In addition, keep your car garaged during the cold hours of the evening and night.

Make sure to keep your car clean to help preserve its value.

Most cars should be waxed twice a year: before the cold and rainy winter and before the hot and dry summer. Once your car has begun to **oxidize** (permanently lose its color and shine), it is very difficult to restore the original gloss. In most cases, a car with oxidized paint must be repainted to restore its shine. A **polishing compound** can be used to get rid of surface scratches, scuffs, and stains. Polishing compounds, often called cleaners and prewaxes, can be tricky to use. They often contain **abrasives,** which are coarse and contain strong chemicals. Used gently, an abrasive can remove the top layer of paint. An abrasive will expose the shiny paint underneath. But used too vigorously or too often, an abrasive will strip the paint right down to the primer.

Just as important as washing and waxing is fixing and repairing dents and paint chips. You can get a container of vehicle paint that matches your car's color. When you get a paint chip, usually from a rock or other hard substance that hits your car when you drive, you should touch up the ding. First make sure the surface is clean and dry; then apply the touch-up paint in very small amounts. Touch-up paint dries very quickly, and you can use more than one layer. You should know that dents, dings, and other breaks in the paint can lead to rust and corrosion.

Preserve the Interior

The inside of your car is also very important for good resale value. The type of **upholstery,** or covering on seats, isn't as important as how it is maintained. Generally, cloth upholstery is more durable than vinyl. While cloth upholstery is more difficult to clean from spills and dirt, vinyl can crack and tear when it gets too hot or cold, or is punctured by sharp objects. The best type of upholstery is leather, which is more expensive, but holds up the best of all. Leather, however, must be cared for with regular cleaning and lubricating to keep it soft and clean.

Regardless of the type of interior, a wise car owner takes precautions. Floor mats will protect the carpeting and are a good investment. Using an old blanket or cloth fabric will protect the interior of the trunk. Avoid eating messy foods in the car. And frequent cleaning—vacuuming and dusting—will keep the car's interior from deteriorating as rapidly. Cars with vinyl upholstery should not be left in the sun for long periods of time. Dropcloths should be used over the dashboard and in the rear window area to protect fabric from color fading and damage.

Cars owned by smokers will have permanent odors and possibly stains. To alleviate the odor of smoke, the windows should be opened frequently, and a deodorant air freshener should be used. Finally, always keep a trash bag in your car to hold wrappers and other waste material.

Follow Wise Driving Habits

To keep your car running efficiently for years, there are many wise habits to observe. For example, when your car is new, there is a "break-in period." At this time, avoid high-speed driving and hard acceleration. The oil and filter are usually changed earlier than regular maintenance schedules suggest. Additional suggestions follow.

When the car is new:
1. Don't drive for long stretches at a constant speed. Vary speed as driving conditions permit.
2. During the first thousand miles, drive progressively faster, accelerating gradually.

3. Avoid fast starts, sudden stops, sharp turns, and rapid gear changes to help your brakes get broken in.
4. Drive at moderate speeds and around town, avoiding long trips so your tires can get adjusted. You may need additional wheel balancing and front-end alignment.

For all cars:
1. Don't race a cold engine—give it time to warm up. On the other hand, the idling or warming up should be for only 10 or 15 seconds. Start the engine and drive off gently as soon as the engine is running smoothly.
2. Keep coolants in your car's radiator during hot weather and antifreezes during very cold weather.
3. When driving a car with a manual transmission, shift deliberately, pausing as you move through the neutral position.
4. Don't shift into a forward gear when your car is rolling backward, or vice versa.
5. When stopped in traffic, hold the car in place with the brakes rather than engaging the clutch.
6. Don't turn the steering wheel when the car is motionless. This strains the front-end components. Turn the wheel only when the car is moving.
7. Keep the windshield and back window free of ice, using a scraper rather than your windshield blades. Running wipers over a dry surface can scratch the glass.
8. Glance at gauges and warning lights as you drive. When your car signals you to stop or to get something checked, do it right away. For example, if the oil pressure gauge or warning light shows, it could mean a loss of oil pressure and may indicate your engine is about to self-destruct. When your engine shows it's too hot, turn off the air-conditioner and drive slower. If overheating is severe, pull over and stop the engine quickly. Open the hood, but do not unscrew the radiator. Get to know features of your car and how to handle them properly.

Finally, always wear your seat belt. It can save your life!

 ## onsumer protection for car buyers

A *warranty* is a written guarantee of the soundness of a product. A warranty clearly states what the manufacturer will do if the product does not perform as it should. A new car warranty provides a buyer with some assurance of quality. Car warranties vary in the time and mileage of the protection they offer and in the parts they cover. The main aspects of a warranty are the coverage of basic parts against manufacturer's defects; the power train coverage for the engine, transmission, and drive train; and the corrosion warranty that usually applies to holes due to rust, not to surface rust.

Sometimes, however, being aware of warranty provisions is not enough. Some cars have so many problems (or such hard-to-assess problems) that warranty coverage is of little comfort to their owners. In the past, when major functional problems occurred with a new car and warranty service didn't resolve the difficulty, most consumers had no recourse. As a result of consumer frustration, many states have enacted lemon laws.

Lemon Laws

Even the most careful purchases can turn out to be lemons. Because some vehicles just seem to lead from one repair to another, many states have **lemon laws.** Connecticut started the trend in 1982, and thirty-two other states have followed suit. According to most state laws, you have a lemon if, in the first year of ownership or 12,000 miles, (a) you've taken the car into the dealer for four unsuccessful attempts to repair the same substantial defect, or (b) your car has been out of service for a total of at least 30 days. Lemon laws allow you to get a new car or your money back. Unfortunately, this protection is not automatic. You need to have good documentation and be prepared for a long process. A proceeding called arbitration and a possible lawsuit may be necessary to enforce your state's law. Figure 23-2 indicates what to do if you have a lemon.

Fig. 23-2

**What to Do If You
Have a Lemon**

Here are some things you can do to protect yourself in the event you end up with a lemon:

1. When you take the car in for repair, give the dealer a written list of problems. Make sure these problems are in the dealer's repair records. Keep copies of each list and the repair receipts you are given.

2. Any time you are returning to have the same item repaired, point it out to the dealer. Make the dealer aware that the problem is continuing and not new. Again, keep copies of each list and their attempted repairs.

3. If your car qualifies as a lemon, tell the car dealer. Bring copies of your records. If the dealer is not responsive, contact the manufacturer's zone office. Talk to the consumer relations office, or go all the way to their national headquarters if necessary. Follow up the conversation with a letter and copies of your records. Be sure you keep your own copy of the letter and the original documentation.

4. If the defect is serious and the car is dangerous to drive, file for arbitration immediately. Make sure you fill out all necessary forms. State the problem clearly and, once again, provide copies of your documentation.

5. Demand a quick hearing date. Remind the arbitrators that under Section 703 of the Magnuson-Moss Warranty Act you are entitled to an arbitration decision within forty days of filing.

6. You are under no obligation to accept a prolonged hearing. You can demand that the arbitration panel meet and make a decision.

7. If you are not satisfied with the arbitrator's decision or the process, you might want to contact a lawyer who specializes in lemon-law cases. The Center for Auto Safety in Washington, D.C., may be able to help you.

The FTC Used-Car Rule

For people who buy previously owned vehicles, there's the concern that the vehicle may have some hidden or potentially expensive repairs ahead. The Federal Trade Commission has a rule, called the "Used Car Rule," that is designed to help used-car buyers. All used-car dealers must inform consumers about who will be responsible for payment of repairs after the sale. This rule doesn't guarantee that there won't be problems, but it does assure the buyer about who will pay the repairs if something breaks.

The rule requires that a sticker, called the "Buyer's Guide," be placed on all used cars. Figure 23-3 illustrates this sticker which tells consumers where they stand. If the "As is" box is checked, the buyer will pay all repair costs. If any items are under warranty, they must be declared. Cars bought from a private party do not carry a warranty and

BUYERS GUIDE

IMPORTANT: Spoken promises are difficult to enforce. Ask the dealer to put all promises in writing. Keep this form.

Chrysler	New Yorker	1993	A0A085C147961
VEHICLE MAKE	MODEL	YEAR	VIN NUMBER

T6204B
DEALER STOCK NUMBER (Optional)

WARRANTIES FOR THIS VEHICLE:

☒ # AS IS – NO WARRANTY

YOU WILL PAY ALL COSTS FOR ANY REPAIRS. The dealer assumes no responsibility for any repairs regardless of any oral statements about the vehicle.

☐ # WARRANTY

☐ FULL ☐ **LIMITED WARRANTY. The dealer will pay ___% of the labor and ___% of the parts for the covered systems that fail during the warranty period. Ask the dealer for a copy of the warranty document for a full explanation of warranty coverage, exclusions, and the dealer's repair obligations. Under state law, "implied warranties" may give you even more rights.**

SYSTEMS COVERED: **DURATION:**

_____   _____
_____   _____
_____   _____
_____   _____

☒ **SERVICE CONTRACT.** A service contract is available at an extra charge on this vehicle. Ask for details as to coverage, deductible, price, and exclusions. If you buy a service contract within 90 days of the time of sale, state law "implied warranties" may give you additional rights.

PRE PURCHASE INSPECTION: ASK THE DEALER IF YOU MAY HAVE THIS VEHICLE INSPECTED BY YOUR MECHANIC EITHER ON OR OFF THE LOT.

SEE THE BACK OF THIS FORM for important additional information, including a list of some major defects that may occur in used motor vehicles.

Fig. 23-3

Buyer's Guide

are often not a good choice. While you may save money by buying directly from the previous owner, you cannot expect the previous owner to make repairs or stand by the condition of the vehicle.

 ummary

The automobile provides us with basic transportation, but for many people it is much more than that. It gives us our freedom and, for some people, it is an expression of personality. But automobiles are expensive to own and operate.

The process of buying a vehicle can take weeks or even months. First, the buyer narrows his or her choices and does research on those models of interest. Preapproval is an important step in establishing financing for the purchase. When visiting dealerships, ignore high-pressure sales tactics and go slowly. The first visit is for information gathering; the second is for asking questions and getting firm prices; the third involves test-driving. When preparing to deal, have a price range in mind and do not allow emotion to rule your decision making. Watch out for low- and highballing tactics. Avoid packs when buying a new car.

Financing your car should take considerable research as well. In many cases, credit unions or banks will offer complete services and low costs; but in some cases, the dealer will offer better rates through a financing company or the manufacturer. For some people, leasing is a good option. You don't have a large down payment. At the end of the lease period, your vehicle is returned to the leasing company.

The cost of car ownership is increasing. Gas and oil, depreciation, licensing, maintenance, and repairs are some of the ownership costs.

To extend the life of your car, you will need to change oil and filters regularly, follow routine maintenance schedules, keep your car dry and out of the sun and bad weather, clean and wax the car, preserve the interior, and observe wise driving habits.

There are several protections available to car buyers. Warranties usually accompany new cars and are good for several years or a specified number of miles. Lemon laws protect consumers from vehicles that can't be repaired. The used-car rule informs consumers about the expenses of potential repairs. The best protection for car buyers is to go slowly—check out a vehicle carefully before you buy it.

Vocabulary terms

Directions: Can you find the definition for each of the following terms used in Chapter 23?

abrasive   *packs*
car title   *polishing compound*
depreciation   *preapproval*
highballing   *sales agreement*
leasing   *sticker price*
lemon laws   *upholstery*
lowballing   *vehicle emission test*
oxidize

1. Laws enacted to protect car buyers who purchase cars that are in constant need of repairs.
2. A deceptive technique where a new car buyer is offered a very high price for a trade-in.
3. A deceptive technique where a new car buyer is quoted a very low price for a trade-in.
4. A document that lists the legal owner and the registered owner of a vehicle.
5. The process of qualifying for a loan before you begin looking for a car.
6. High-priced, high-profit dealer services that add little of value to your car purchase.
7. A legal document specifying the details of an automobile purchase.
8. The suggested retail price shown on the window of a new car.
9. A vehicle test required in many urban areas to verify that a vehicle meets clean air standards.
10. A cleaning substance used to remove surface scratches, scuffs, and stains.
11. Ingredients that are coarse and contain strong chemicals that can remove paint.
12. Interior seat coverings.
13. A contractual agreement under which monthly payments are made for the use of an automobile over a set time period.
14. Permanent loss of color and shine in the paint on a car.
15. Loss in value of a vehicle during its lifetime.

acts and ideas in review

1. What is the first step in the car-buying process?
2. What are some sources of information about cars—their safety, repair record, reliability, and so on?
3. What is meant by getting "preapproval"?
4. What is the purpose of visiting several car dealerships?
5. What steps should you follow in preparing to deal on a car?
6. Explain the difference between lowballing and highballing.
7. Identify three sources of loans for the purchase of automobiles.
8. What are the costs of operating a car?
9. What are some factors that cause a car to depreciate?
10. What are some steps you can take to extend the life of your automobile?
11. Why is it important to change the oil regularly?
12. Give an example of routine maintenance.
13. What is the purpose of cleaning and waxing your car?
14. List three things you can do to protect your upholstery.
15. Explain five wise driving strategies.

 pplications for decision making

1. Make a list of car dealerships in your local area. Divide up the dealerships and, as a group of students, visit each one. Collect brochures on various car models and bring them to class. Each group can report their findings—kinds and types of brochures, how they were treated, and so on.
2. Look up current issues of consumer protection magazines, including *Consumer Reports*, that give you information about products and services. Also look for magazines such as *Car and Driver* that give specific information about car choices, accessories, and related products. Choose a topic, such as which is the best car stereo, or which motor oil works best for a particular kind of car, and so on, and write a one-page report on your findings.
3. Talk to a loan officer about the process of preapproval for a car loan. Ask to see application forms and discuss qualifications. Based on the information gathered, prepare a summary of income require-

ments for an auto loan. For example, would it take an income of $2,000 a month to be able to afford a Ford Taurus with monthly payments of $300?

4. Do research about vehicle leasing in your area. Begin by looking in the Yellow Pages to find several companies that offer lease programs. Call or visit them to get information on how leasing works, the costs, and the benefits. If possible, talk to a person who leases a vehicle, or who has leased one, to get a picture of the advantages and disadvantages of leasing.

5. Prepare a budget that lists potential costs a car owner may face. Ask a parent or other person who has owned a car to help you complete the list. For example, in computing the year's depreciation, check want ads to see what that year and model car is selling for. Deduct this from the purchase price of the car and divide by the years of age. Keep in mind that a vehicle depreciates more in the first few years than it does later. Determine a total cost and summarize in a paragraph your findings about the costs of operating a vehicle.

6. Call your state motor vehicles division or visit a local office and get information about registration and title fees in your state. You may have to wait in line to get the information, or you may be able to locate brochures or pamphlets that explain these costs. While you are there, pick up a copy of the driver's manual and other information about your state's vehicle laws.

7. In groups, prepare a list of options that you feel are very important to have in a car. Then research the price of each of these options. For example, if you choose air conditioning as vital, then what would it cost to add this feature to the base price of a car? You will find prices for these items in consumer magazines in your library, or visit dealerships and study the sticker prices on cars of your choice.

8. Borrow an owner's manual and read through it. In the section marked regular maintenance schedule or something similar, find out how often the oil needs to be changed, how often a major tune-up is required, and what things must be checked, repaired, or replaced at regular intervals. Based on this information, prepare a cost summary for a year of regular maintenance.

9. Do research on different types of waxes and cleaning compounds that you might use on a vehicle. Compare their features—what they will do and what are the costs, together with possible hazards. Estimate the cost of keeping a car clean, waxed, and touched up for a year.

10. For a week's time, observe drivers as you are riding to and from school or at other times of the day. Keep a list of things drivers do to avoid injuries and accidents. Also keep a list of things drivers do that could potentially cause harm to themselves and others. Make a summary of what you have learned.

11. Consult your local library consumerism section and ask about lemon laws in your state. You should be able to find out what consumer protections are available to you in the purchase of new and used cars. Write a one-page report on your findings.

 ife situation problem solving

1. Your friend Marsha is considering buying a small, older car. She works part-time, after school and on holidays. In the summer, she makes good wages, but is saving for a college education. She visits a local dealer who suggests that buying an older car is not a good idea. The dealer points out that the car may break down, will likely cost a lot to maintain, and wouldn't be dependable. Do you agree? What advice would you give Marsha?

2. Your friend Roger has decided to buy a car. Because he is working at a regular job, he thinks he can afford a new car. He isn't sure how much money he can afford to pay for monthly car payments, and he doesn't know how much of a down payment he might need to make. How would you advise him to get started in the car-buying process?

3. Jack Adams has already purchased two cars. He is ready to buy a third car but frankly, he tells you, the experience is so negative that he's putting it off for as long as possible. When you talk to him, you discover that the problem lies in the buying process itself. When Jack gets into a dealership he feels pressured; he then buys something that he later regrets. What advice can you give him to have a more positive experience?

4. Jenny Bell has just purchased a new car. Now she faces the decision: Should she add to the cost of her purchase with undercoating and rust prevention, a polish shine application, and a three-year extended warranty? Altogether, these items will add almost $1,000 to the price of the car. She's concerned because the dealer told her that these will add to the life of the car and she plans to keep it for a long time. What is your advice?

5. You are looking at a vehicle for possible purchase. A sticker on the window called the "Buyer's Guide" says this vehicle is sold strictly "As Is." What does this mean?

6. You are buying a new car and are considering whether to trade in your old vehicle. The dealer tells you that you are paying $1,500 less on the new car because of your trade-in. But you find that in reality you would get a $1,500 reduction in price for having no trade-in and for paying cash. Discuss the pro's and con's of trading in your car versus selling it yourself.

7. Your friend Brett is excited about buying his first car. He is paying cash for the car. This purchase will deplete his savings, but he has a part-time job that pays $100 a week. Explain to him the costs of operating a car.

8. Bill Clark has just purchased a new car. He plans to drive the car at least 100,000 miles and then he hopes to get as much money as he can for it. What advice can you give him about extending the life of the car and improving its resale value?

9. Your friend Jane has a car that has been fixed four times for the same problem—a faulty starter. Advise her about lemon laws.

**terms
to know:**

*wedding party
formal wedding
semiformal wedding
informal wedding
financial plan
family financial
    planning
itinerary
reservation
travel agency
overbooked
dissolution of
    marriage
property settlement
    agreement
alimony
cremation*

objectives:

After reading and studying this chapter you will be able to:

24-1 Describe the steps, costs, and planning involved in getting married and making family living decisions.

24-2 Discuss the planning and costs involved in maintaining a household and being prepared for emergency situations.

24-3 Outline the steps needed in planning a successful vacation.

24-4 Define the steps and costs in a divorce.

24-5 Discuss why a person needs a will, identify types of survivors' benefits, and explain "last expenses."

When two people decide to get married and establish a household, a new and exciting adventure begins. But there are many hazards along the way. In this chapter, you will follow a couple's wedding plans through family living decisions, vacation planning, coping with emergencies, divorce, and death. While all of these events won't happen at once, and in most cases will be spaced over a lifetime, you will preview many situations that can occur in a lifetime to discover some basic information essential to all consumers.

chapter

24 Family Decisions

arriage: a new beginning

You will most likely make an important decision about marriage at some time during your life. For some people, the decision will be made within a few years of graduation from high school. For others, the decision will be made much later.

Most couples take the last step before marriage by appearing before the city or county clerk and applying for a marriage license. In the vast majority of states, couples over eighteen years of age do not need their parents' consent. With parental consent, most states allow minors as young as sixteen to marry.

The decision to marry should be preceded by several important decisions, such as: Will you and your spouse both work? What are your desires about rearing children? What are some joint family goals you want to plan? Family decisions such as these should be discussed and made jointly; for those that are extremely important to either person, decisions should be made before marriage. For example, if one person feels strongly about having children while the other person absolutely does not want children, then marriage plans should be cancelled or postponed until this issue is resolved.

Let's look at the process of getting married, including the engagement, premarital counseling, ceremony plans and costs, and the honeymoon.

Engagement

When two people decide to be married, they become engaged. If an engagement ring is chosen, it is worn on the third finger of the left hand of the prospective bride. The choice of style, size, and kind of stone and setting will determine the price of the engagement ring, which may range from a few hundred to a few thousand dollars or more. Some couples prefer matching wedding bands, in which case an engagement ring often is not worn.

An engagement period of six months to a year is customary in most parts of this country. Once the engagement is announced, careful planning of the many steps to ensure a smooth and memorable wedding begins.

Premarital Counseling

In order to have a wedding in some religions, counseling sessions are required. The couple meets with a member of the clergy or other counselor, together and separately, to discuss issues that will be vital to the success of the marriage and later family life. There may be a predetermined number of sessions, or the number of sessions may vary according to how well prepared for marriage the counselor or cleric thinks the couple is. Topics most often discussed include money and budgeting, the meaning of the marriage commitment, in-laws and other potential problems, and religious aspects of marriage that are unique to each faith. The counseling sessions should be planned early, well before final preparations are being made for the wedding.

Ceremony Plans and Costs

Planning for the wedding ceremony should begin at least six months in advance. Figure 24-1 is a bride's budget worksheet, which shows the many preparations to consider. This worksheet should be completed in rough draft form as the wedding planning progresses. The cost of each item will vary according to style, quantity, and preferences. As costs begin to add up, the bride and groom may decide to eliminate, expand, or reduce some of the expenses involved.

Guest lists are prepared by the bride and groom and by each set of parents; these lists are then combined. Guests may include relatives and friends of the couple. The number of guests being invited and the size of the wedding party will determine the number of invitations needed, size of the church, cost of the reception, and so forth. The **wedding party** consists of the persons who are active participants in the wedding ceremony: the bride and groom, best man, maid or matron of honor, bridesmaids, ushers, flower girl, and so on.

Fig. 24-1   **Bride's Budget Worksheet**

Engagement Party

Invitations . . . . $_____
Food . . . . _____
Beverages . . . . _____
Music . . . . _____
Rental fees . . . . _____
Decorations . . . . _____
Professional services . . . . _____
Gratuities . . . . _____

Total . . . . $_____

Stationery

Invitations . . . . $_____
Announcements . . . . _____
At-home cards . . . . _____
Personal stationery . . . . . _____
Stamps . . . . _____

Total . . . . $_____

Clothing

Wedding dress . . . . $_____
Headpiece/veil . . . . _____
Shoes . . . . _____
Accessories . . . . _____
Personal trousseau . . . . . _____

Total . . . . $_____

*Denotes expenses usually
shared by both families

Bridesmaids' Luncheon

Invitations and
   place cards . . . . $_____
Food . . . . _____
Beverages . . . . _____
Rental fees . . . . _____
Decorations . . . . _____
Professional services . . . . _____
*Gratuities . . . . _____

Total . . . . $_____

Photographs

Engagement portrait . . . . $_____
Wedding portrait . . . . . . _____
Formal photos . . . . _____
Reprints . . . . _____

Total . . . . $_____

Wedding Ceremony

Sanctuary rental . . . . $_____
Music . . . . _____
Decorations . . . . _____
Flowers for attendants . . . _____
Aisle runner . . . . _____
Transportation
   to/from ceremony . . . . _____
*Gratuities . . . . _____
Miscellaneous . . . . _____

Total . . . . $_____

Reception

Hall rental . . . . $_____
Decorations . . . . _____
Music . . . . _____
Food . . . . _____
Beverages . . . . _____
Wedding cake . . . . _____
Favors . . . . _____
Professional services . . . . _____
*Gratuities . . . . _____

Total . . . . $_____

Other

Bridal consultant fees . . . $_____
Accommodations for
   out-of-town
   attendants . . . . _____
*Security guard . . . . _____
Sound recording of
   ceremony . . . . _____
*Insurance for
   wedding gifts . . . . _____
Bride's blood test
   (if required) . . . . _____
Groom's ring . . . . _____
Gift for groom . . . . _____
Gift for attendants . . . . . _____
Special effects . . . . _____
Other fees . . . . _____
_____
_____
_____

Total . . . . $_____

GRAND TOTAL . . . . $_____

In the past, almost all wedding expenses were paid by the bride's family. This custom is changing. Now, the groom's family usually pays some of the expenses—such as rehearsal dinner or reception—or splits the expenses with the bride's family. Generally, however, the following expenses belong solely to the groom:

1. Bride's ring(s)
2. Marriage license
3. Wedding gift for the bride
4. Gifts for the best man, groomsmen, and ring bearer
5. The bride's bouquet and going-away corsage, corsages for mothers and grandmothers, and boutonnieres for the men in the wedding party
6. Cleric's or judge's fee
7. Bachelor dinner (unless given and paid for by the best man)
8. Lodging (if necessary) for out-of-town groomsmen
9. Groom's special clothing, including clothing for rehearsal dinner, wedding, and honeymoon
10. Delivery of wedding presents to new home
11. Honeymoon costs (which may be shared equally between bride and groom if the bride is working)

The planning of the wedding is usually done jointly by the bride and groom, with much consideration given to cost. The size of the wedding, the time of day, the location, and the formality of the bride's dress are what determine the style of the wedding. A **formal wedding** may be held in the daytime or in the evening, and all guests and participants wear formal attire (which, for evening, includes long gowns and tuxedos). A **semiformal wedding** usually is held during the afternoon or early evening, with less formal wear required of guests. While the wedding party may still dress as formally or informally as they choose, guests generally wear suits and dresses normally chosen for special occasions. An **informal wedding** may be held outside, in a church, or almost anywhere. No special clothing is required for the wedding party or for the guests.

Other types of weddings are preferred by some couples. A civil ceremony is performed by a public official, such as a judge or justice of the peace. This is a quick, inexpensive ceremony and requires the presence of two witnesses in most states.

The Honeymoon

Immediately following the wedding reception, the newly married couple usually takes a honeymoon trip. Most couples plan a trip out of town. Resort areas and places that provide different types of entertainment are popular. A honeymoon may last from several days to several weeks and cost as much as several thousand dollars. A couple generally plans the honeymoon together, carefully considering preferences and costs involved.

Honeymoons may be inexpensive automobile trips, elaborate cruises, or flights to exotic islands. The length and type of honeymoon will depend on time available, cost, and desires of the couple. More elaborate plans usually involve using travel agencies and other sources of travel information. Travel options are discussed thoroughly in the vacations section of this chapter.

amily financial decisions

When two people are married, they form a new family unit. Decisions are made by the family unit based on each person's needs and wants. Ideally, decisions regarding goals, the budget, and division of responsibilities must be open to discussion at all times.

Decisions regarding whether or not to have children may affect your career goals and professional life.

Family Goals

A family unit must examine needs and priorities and set goals for the future. Short-term goals involve decisions about where to live for now; whether both partners will work; what major purchases to make this year and next; and what leisure activities a couple will participate in, jointly and separately. Intermediate goals include what will happen in the next five or ten years: whether children are wanted, where the couple will live in the foreseeable future, and whether a job or career change should be completed. Long-term goals include decisions about children's education (savings and investments), special events, and retirement.

In order to guide your financial decision making, your financial goals should be stated with the following considerations in mind:

1. Financial goals should be realistic and based on your income and life situation. An annual vacation in the Caribbean would not be realistic on a modest income.
2. Financial goals should be listed in specific measurable terms. The goal of "accumulating $10,000 in a mutual fund within five years" is a clearer goal than "saving money for future expenses."
3. Financial goals should indicate a time frame. In the previous example, five years was the goal. A time frame helps you measure your progress toward your financial goals.
4. Your financial goals should specify the type of action to be taken and should serve as the basis for various financial activities.

As you do family financial planning, assess your current family financial situation. A **financial plan** is a formalized report that summarizes your current financial situation, analyzes your financial needs, and suggests a direction for your financial activities. You can create this document yourself or use the assistance of a professional financial planner.

The Family Budget

Every family has a unique financial situation and must plan accordingly to meet specific needs and goals. **Family financial planning** is the process of managing your money to achieve economic satisfaction. A planning tool that lets a family take control of their financial situation is the family budget.

A family budget allows for spending, saving, borrowing and investing to meet future goals. Joint decisions are often complicated and difficult to reach because more people are involved in the decision making. Nevertheless, family budgeting is an essential part of a successful marriage. Continually communicate with the other members of your household about financial goals and the financial activities needed to attain them.

Dividing Responsibilities

In addition to household chores and duties, a family also needs to divide financial responsibilities. Individual as well as joint checking accounts may be desirable. If there is only one checking account, it makes balancing the account much easier when only one person writes checks on that account. However, who will carry the checkbook and be responsible for paying the bills? Many couples choose to have individual checking accounts, where each spouse is responsible for part of the income and part of the bills. For example, one spouse may choose to pay utilities, groceries and household expenses, and the car payment. The other spouse may choose to pay the rent or house payment, entertainment, insurance, and miscellaneous expenses. Then each spouse is responsible for balancing his or her checking account each month and meeting his or her part of the budget.

Perhaps one spouse is in charge of collecting, storing, and retrieving tax information for the preparation of tax returns. The other spouse might be responsible for making vacation arrangements, reservations, and itineraries. By dividing and sharing the responsibilities of the household, goals can be achieved in an orderly manner with each spouse contributing equally.

acation planning

Vacations are an important part of our lives. Planned vacations maximize the time available for fun and enjoyment. Vacation decisions include determining the kind of vacation, making plans and reservations, at-home preparations, and covering last-minute details.

A successful vacation is dependent upon careful planning.

Kind of Vacation

The first decision is to determine the kind of vacation you want: relaxation, excitement, travel, adventure, special events, visiting relatives, or a combination of these. The vacation plans for any type of vacation also depend on how much time you have, including travel time, and how much money you will have to spend.

Based on the kind of vacation desired and the time and money available, you can list your alternatives, as shown in Figure 24-2. Then you can discuss and weigh the alternatives and make a final decision. Creativity in decision making is vital to effective choices. Considering all of the possible alternatives will help you make more effective and satisfying decisions.

Fig. 24-2

Vacation Analysis

VACATION ANALYSIS

$299 or less	$300 – $1,000 to spend	More than $1,000
Camping	Car trip	Car or plane trip
Visiting relatives	Sports (skiing, other	Tours/group travel
Sports events	adventure)	Varied entertainment
	Amusement parks	options
Three days or less	Three to five days	Five days or more

The more money available, the longer and more expensive the vacation can be. Your choices may be different from those listed in Figure 24-2. Each family needs to decide what type of vacation is desired, budget income to allow money to meet that need, and plan the vacation accordingly. While a camping trip may be very attractive to one family, it may be totally unappealing to another. Having a successful vacation depends on properly defining the type of vacation desired, having the money to spend on it, and planning it carefully.

Plans and Reservations

To make maximum use of available vacation time, it is a good idea to write out what will happen, when, at what cost, and what needs to be done. An **itinerary** is a detailed schedule of events, times, and places. You can make your own for the entire trip, listing each day's activities. An example of a vacation trip itinerary is found in Figure 24-3. Before going on vacation, leave a copy of your itinerary with a neighbor or friend in case of emergency.

Fig. 24-3

Itinerary

ITINERARY

Date	Time	Activity
Monday	8:00 a.m.	Arrive at airport (Flight 739 leaves at 9:05 a.m.).
	10:00 a.m.	Arrive at Los Angeles airport. Take hotel shuttle service; arrive at hotel by 10:45 a.m.
	12:00 noon	Lunch at hotel restaurant.
	1:30 p.m.	Disneyland for remainder of day. Dinner at Disneyland.
Tuesday	8:00 a.m.	Breakfast at Howard Johnson's.
	9:00 a.m.	Knott's Berry Farm (20 minute ride by tour bus). Spend day there; eat lunch there.
	7:00 p.m.	Leave Knott's Berry Farm; go to dinner at Bob's Big Boy.
	8:00 p.m.	Return to hotel.
Wednesday	8:00 a.m.	Breakfast at Pancake House.
	9:00 a.m.	Universal Studios. Tour begins at 10:00 a.m., lasts until noon.
	12:00 noon	Lunch at nearby restaurant. Catch tour bus at 1:30 p.m. to return to hotel.

All the different places you plan to go and things you plan to do should be listed on the itinerary. You may want to list the time it takes to do certain activities, distances to get to and from activities, methods of transportation, and special notes, such as "bring camera." When designing your itinerary, be sure to leave enough time to do the planned activities in comfort and relaxation. Check on seasonal adjustments that may change operating days, amounts of fees, and opening or closing times.

Reservations should be made whenever possible. A **reservation** is an advance commitment whereby you are assured of receiving a service. A room reservation guarantees that when you arrive at the hotel or motel a room will be waiting for you. Hotels and motels may be booked up, or full, well in advance of your vacation date; therefore, reservations should be made early—a month or more before your vacation is not too soon. Reservations should also be made for airlines, buses, trains, boats, or car rentals. Airline boarding passes and seat assignments may be obtained a few days before your trip.

At-Home Preparations

Before leaving on your vacation, you should take care of many things at home. Ask a neighbor to pick up your newspaper, or have the paper stopped if the vacation is longer than a few days. Mail delivery should be stopped, also; have your mail held at the post office. This can be done at the post office by filling out a form that tells the post office the date to begin holding your mail and the date to resume delivery. When this is done, mail and papers will not accumulate in your mailbox, giving evidence to others that you are away from home.

Arrange for the feeding of pets, caring of plants, mowing of the lawn, and other normal duties around your home. Use an automatic timer for lights so that they come on in the evening and go off a few hours later. Also play soft radio music. All doors and windows should be locked securely, and the curtains and drapes should be closed. It is also a good idea to ask a neighbor to keep an eye on things while you are away. Finally, it is common to alert the local police so an officer can check the security of your home while you are on vacation.

Last-Minute Details

Careful packing of clothing and supplies is necessary. Make a list of things you will need, including cameras, special clothing, shoes, and personal items. Take only what you need in the smallest possible containers. Be sure to pack enough clothing to last the entire vacation without laundering (unless it is a very long vacation). Any rented equipment should be obtained as early as is convenient without incurring additional cost. All bottles and other containers should be closed tightly to avoid leakage. Do not forget any prescriptions or other medications frequently needed.

You may wish to take major credit cards. However, leave at home in a safe place all those cards you do not need. Take enough cash to pay those expenses that require cash only; others can be charged on a bank card or paid for by traveler's checks. Traveler's checks may be purchased at any bank or other financial institution in denominations of $10, $20, $50, and up. The smaller denominations are usually easier to cash. If traveler's checks are lost or stolen, they will be replaced if you produce the list of check numbers. Always keep the list separate from the checks.

Reservations may need to be confirmed because flights are often canceled or changed. You should check at least twenty-four hours in advance to be sure your flight is confirmed. You may choose to use a **travel agency,** which is an authorized agent for all airlines to issue tickets and make reservations and confirmations in your behalf.

personal perspective

A voiding Household Accidents

Thousands of injuries occur each year in the home, many of them serious. Household injuries can be avoided, however, through the use of certain commonsense preventative measures.

The kitchen, with cupboards, shelves, drawers and storage areas, food, and appliances, is an especially attractive area for small children. Cleansers, detergents, and other products that are *toxic* (poisonous) can cause serious injury or death. Cooking ingredients should be placed in high cupboards, out of the reach of small children. Poisonous products should always be stored in their original containers: a soda bottle should not be used to store cleaning fluid. Any product containing a questionable substance should be stored away from food.

The bathroom is a potentially deadly play area for small children. The toilet lid should always be kept down when a toddler or infant is in the house. Children should never be left unattended while bathing, swimming, or otherwise in or near water. Appliances such as hair dryers should be unplugged and kept away from sinks and tubs. Personal care items should be kept out of the reach of children.

Because of lack of space, many families store infrequently used items in attics, garages, high cupboards, and basements. Retrieval of stored items can be dangerous. Ladders should be placed firmly with a second person holding the legs for support. Falling is a common household accident that can be avoided with care and thought.

Weapons, including guns and knives, should be locked away with ammunition locked in a separate place. Tools and power devices stored in garages and work areas should be kept out of the reach of children. Chemicals, fertilizers, oil, gasoline, and other such products should be stored securely, following rules of storage safety for combustible and flammable products. Fire hazards are created by cleaning rags, papers, and cluttered possessions. Unused refrigerators or other storage containers should have the doors removed so that children cannot become trapped in them.

critical thinking

1. Have you been involved in some type of household accident? Describe what you did and how you felt.

2. What other types of emergency situations have you heard or read about? How were they handled?

There may be no fee for the services of a travel agent. When you pay a fee to a travel agent, you may get more specialized service than loyalty to an airline or hotel. Travel agents do not work for any specific airline; however, some airlines pay higher commissions or fees to travel agents. Travel agents can find flight connections that will result in less waiting time between flights, lower air fares, and better departure times. Sometimes, however, you may need to change planes more often to get a lower rate or better flight time.

Plan to arrive at the airport at least an hour before your flight's departure time. This gives you time to check in, get a seat assignment, and go through the appropriate steps for boarding. Often, flights are **overbooked,** which means that the airline has sold tickets for more seats than are available. Airlines overbook flights because many people make more than one reservation or do not show up for a scheduled flight. Should you be a victim of overbooking (bumping), the airline must ask people who are not in a hurry to give up their seats voluntarily in exchange for a future free ticket and a later flight. Passengers bumped against their will are, with few exceptions, entitled to compensation usually in the form of cash, a coupon, or a free flight. By arriving ready to check in, you can avoid an overbooking problem.

If you travel frequently, you may be eligible for discount flights or special bonuses through airlines' frequent flyer plans. These plans are usually based on air miles traveled; you are given credit for miles each time you take a regular flight aboard an airline. In most cases, there is no charge to participate in the plan.

Be sure that all appliances are turned off before you leave home. As a precaution, do not use any appliances the morning of your departure. In the excitement of preparing to leave, you could easily forget to turn off or unplug them. A last check before leaving will reassure you that nothing has been left on.

ivorce: expensive and difficult

In all but a few states, a divorce is now called a **dissolution of marriage,** which means that irreconcilable differences have led to the breakdown of the marriage. Furthermore, one partner does not have to prove fault by the other partner to be granted a divorce. If one partner wants the marriage to be dissolved, it can be done. The only time fault is considered is when the issue of child custody arises.

Cost of Divorce

Expenses involved in divorce are high. Attorneys' fees (one attorney for each party), court costs and filing fees, child support and alimony, division of property, and settlement costs may be included. The more issues there are to settle, the higher the attorneys' fees will be.

When child custody is an issue and a court hearing is necessary, the fees are even higher. Often parties can agree outside of court and enter into a **property settlement agreement.** This is a document specifying the division of property and assets agreed to by both parties and entered into court for the judge's approval. The more that can be settled outside of court, the less divorce proceedings cost.

In most cases, the parent who is granted custody of the children will receive child support from the other parent. *Child support* consists of monthly payments made by the noncustodial parent to help provide food, clothing, and shelter for children of the marriage. The amount of child support is based on the income and ability of the parties, on the assumption that both parties are responsible for supporting the children to the best of their abilities. **Alimony** consists of a lump sum or monthly payments, usually for a set number of years, until the former spouse can support herself or himself. Alimony is awarded in some cases when one spouse has been dependent on the other for a number of years and has little means of self-support. Most alimony awards are for a limited number of years, or may be based upon a former spouse completing education or training for employment. Child support and alimony are at the discretion of the judge and become binding on the parties under the divorce decree. Amounts of child support and alimony can only be modified by another court order.

Steps in Divorce

Dissolving a marriage is often a lengthy and unpleasant matter. Usually the papers are not actually filed until the couple has been separated for some time and it appears to be in everyone's best interest to pursue a legal dissolution of marriage. One party goes to an attorney, and the attorney prepares the documents, which are filed with the court. The other party is served with copies of the papers, called Petition for Dissolution of Marriage, and given a short time to appear (file papers) if there is a disagreement with the proposals set forth in the petition. The petition sets forth how the first party proposes to divide property and award custody, amounts desired for child support, visitation rights, and so on. If the second party fails to appear (defaults), then the first party is awarded whatever is asked in the petition. In most cases, the second party does appear and a court date is set to decide the issues that cannot be settled between the parties.

Often it takes many months, even a year or more, for the case to be heard in court. Consequently, a hearing will be held to establish temporary custody, child support, visitation rights of the noncustodial parent, and other matters. Many of the temporary provisions tend to become permanent. That is, often both parties agree in writing to property settlement and other matters prior to the court date. When the judge approves the agreement, it is entered as part of the *decree*, which is a final statement of the dissolution decisions. A decree is final and binding on both parties until modified by the court.

If the parties cannot agree on a settlement, the case then goes to court. There is no jury in divorce cases. Both parties testify and present their cases. Witnesses may be called in the issue of child custody to determine which parent would be the better custodial parent. The judge's decision is based entirely on the best interests of the child or children of the marriage. All other matters—property, alimony, amount of child support, visitation rights—are also decided in court. The court hearing may last several days; once the decree is entered, a waiting period of sixty to ninety days before either party may remarry is usually imposed.

 eath: a final plan

Aging and death are parts of living and need planning and attention. Preparations are not only for those who are about to die; they should be considered by all responsible adults.

Writing a Will

Many people do not understand the need for a will. A will expresses a person's wishes for disposal of property after his or her death. (Wills, as you will recall, were explained thoroughly on pages 349–352 of Chapter 15.) A will only passes title to property that does not otherwise pass.

For example, if you own a home jointly with another person, on your death the home will go to that other person. Although jointly owned property passes directly to the joint owner and may be appropriate for some assets, such as a home, only with a will can you distribute your property exactly as you wish. One of the most vital records you should have is a will. Every adult should have a written will.

Survivors' Benefits

Surviving spouse and children are usually provided with some kind of death benefits. Survivors need to check thoroughly to see what benefits have accrued through the years.

Life insurance benefits are not taxable to the recipients. Benefits from a life insurance policy can be obtained by mailing a copy of the death certificate, the original life insurance policy, and a claim form to the life insurance company. (Life insurance is described in detail in Chapter 27.)

The Veterans Administration pays a stipend to survivors of veterans. The benefit may include a grave marker, funeral services, and cash of $400 or more, depending on type and length of service and branch of armed forces. Children of veterans may also be entitled to scholarships and educational grant benefits.

Many employer pension plans pay lump-sum or monthly benefits to widows and families. Employer-paid benefits may not be automatic, and the widow(er) may have to apply to receive these benefits.

Last Expenses

The costs involved when a person dies can range from a few hundred dollars to several thousand dollars. These expenses include final medical and hospital charges, funeral expenses and casket, and burial. By preparing instructions and making provisions for these costs in advance, you spare survivors the emotional decision-making process at a time of vulnerability. Survivors who are grieving the loss of a loved one are often unprepared to make the many decisions involved in planning a funeral and burial. At such an emotional time, a family may incur elaborate final expenses that they or the estate cannot afford.

Funerals

The cost of a funeral can range from $1,500 to $5,000 or more, depending on type of casket and burial. Typical funeral charges include moving the body (to funeral home, church or synagogue, and cemetery); embalming and preparation for public viewing; casket; use of facilities;

funeral director's and staff fees; hearse; family limousine; pallbearers' car; flower car; escort to cemetery; obituary (newspaper death notice); clergy fees; printed memorial folders, memorial book, and thank-you cards; death certificate; and all necessary permits. The cost of a burial plot and marker are additional expenses.

Many funeral homes have prearranged plans available at guaranteed costs. Money for the funeral is placed in trust and earns interest. You should be able to get a full refund if you cancel the plan. Look over carefully any "preneed" or prepayment plan that may be offered. It may lock you into using the services of a particular funeral home at uncertain future prices. If you move away or the home goes out of business, you may have trouble getting your money back.

Cremation

Cremation is a process of reducing a body to ashes in a high-temperature oven. The ashes are placed in an urn. The urn is presented to the family for safekeeping or burial. Cremation is a less expensive alternative to embalming and "cosmetizing" the body for public viewing. When a body is not cremated within a certain time span, usually two days, it must be embalmed or otherwise prepared for burial. Cremation, like immediate burial without a funeral, permits the survivors to hold a memorial service at any time or place, without having the body present. This procedure is not only less expensive, but may be more comfortable for families and other mourners.

 ummary

Marriage is a commitment between two people to begin a new life together. Traditionally, the law sees husband and wife as parties to a marriage contract for life and for the benefit of each other. The most important duty of both spouses is to provide for the support, nurture, welfare, and education of their children. Other practical and legally recognized purposes of marriage (besides procreation and the rearing of children) include the fulfillment of sexual, economic, and companionship needs.

Once married, couples must make some serious decisions about the family unit's finances. The financial planning process allows a family to take control of its financial situation. Every family has a unique financial position, and any financial activity must therefore be unique—that is, carefully planned to meet specific needs and goals. One of the most effective tools in the planning process is the budget.

Vacations are fun for everyone. But a vacation can be even more exciting if all arrangements have been carefully planned. You won't have to worry about finding a place to stay or having the right accommodations. A travel agent can assist you in the planning of your trip.

A marriage usually ends through death of either spouse or a divorce. The divorce rate in the United States has remained at about 50 percent for a number of years: one-half of all marriages will end in divorce. Divorce is the process of dissolving a marriage; when children are involved, the process can be long and difficult. Costs of divorce can also be high. Matters such as the division of property, child custody, visitation rights, and so on, must be settled.

Preparing for death should begin long before death occurs. Planning for death prevents important decisions from being made by survivors who may be unaware of the final wishes of a loved one. Also, at the time of death, loved ones are often incapable of effective decision making because of grief. When a person dies, the law looks for instructions to resolve some basic legal issues that arise. The necessary instructions are found in a valid will left by the deceased person.

24

 ocabulary terms

Directions: Can you find the definition for each of the following terms used in Chapter 24?

alimony
cremation
dissolution of marriage
family financial planning
financial plan
formal wedding
informal wedding

itinerary
overbooked
property settlement agreement
reservation
semiformal wedding
travel agency
wedding party

1. An advance commitment whereby a traveler is assured of a plane seat or a motel room.
2. Persons who participate in the wedding ceremony: bride and groom, best man, maid of honor, bridesmaids, ushers, flower girl, ring bearer, candle lighters, and so on.
3. A type of wedding in which everyone, including guests, wears formal attire.
4. A type of wedding in which only the wedding party is dressed formally.
5. A detailed list of events, times, and places planned for a trip or vacation.
6. The result when an airline sells more tickets for a flight than it has seats available.
7. Another term for a divorce, meaning irreconcilable differences have led to the breakdown of the marriage.
8. A written agreement by husband and wife to dispose of and divide the assets of a marriage.
9. A lump sum or monthly payments to support a former spouse.
10. The process of reducing a body to ashes in a high-temperature oven.
11. The process of managing your money as a group to achieve economic satisfaction.
12. A formalized report that summarizes financial needs and sets a direction for financial activities.
13. An authorized agent for airlines that issues tickets and makes reservations for travelers.
14. A wedding requiring no special clothing or location; it is often held outside.

Facts and ideas in review

1. What is the purpose of premarital counseling?
2. How long before the wedding should a couple begin making preparations?
3. List some responsibilities (expenses) that are traditionally accepted by the bride and her family.
4. List some responsibilities (expenses) that are traditionally accepted by the groom and his family.
5. What are the differences among a formal wedding, a semiformal wedding, and an informal wedding?
6. What are some advantages and disadvantages experienced by couples who work for several years before having children?
7. What types of vacation options are available?
8. What types of things are listed on a vacation itinerary?
9. List some preparations that you need to make before leaving on vacation. Include those preparations designed to keep people from realizing that you are gone.
10. What is the purpose of using traveler's checks instead of carrying cash?
11. How much does a travel agency charge a customer for making reservations and issuing airline tickets?
12. What are some of the costs involved in getting a divorce?
13. What are the steps of getting a divorce?
14. What types of survivors' benefits are available when a person dies?
15. What are some costs of death and burial?

Applications for decision making

1. Describe a wedding that you have attended in the last year or two (include wedding party, dress, flowers, reception, and so on).
2. Describe the wedding you would choose for yourself, including setting, type of ceremony, wedding party, total cost, number of guests, honeymoon plans, and so on.
3. How does a family's budget differ from an individual's budget?
4. Design a three-day itinerary for a trip to a resort area within about a thousand miles of where you live. Include all necessary information.

end-of-chapter

24

5. What property or money do you own that is not jointly held with someone else? To whom would you like to see your property go at your death? Make a list of what you have and to whom you would like to make bequests.

ife situation problem solving

1. Write a report describing different engagement ring options:
   a. Diamond solitaire with matching bands. Compare costs of different size diamonds.
   b. Gold and silver bands. Compare quality, width, and costs.
   c. Costs of stones other than diamonds: rubies, emeralds, and sapphires. Compare different sizes of each.
   d. Financing plans available to young couples.

2. Tom Nielsen and Teresa Kimball will be married in a month. Both are working and plan to work at least five years before having children. They have asked for your opinion on how household duties should be divided because both of them work eight hours a day, five days a week. Devise a plan for dividing duties and responsibilities; include checkbook balancing and financial planning.

3. You and a friend have decided to take a trip. Based on the following three hypothetical cases, describe the kinds of trips you would take and list all of the costs that would be involved in each.
   a. You each have $75 to contribute and could get away for a three-day weekend. You have one automobile that does not need maintenance or repairs.
   b. You each have $500 to spend and could get away for three to five days.
   c. You each have $1,500 to spend and could be away for ten days.

4. What types of divorce/dissolution laws are in effect in your state? Are they no-fault or fault laws? What are the waiting periods? Describe the procedures for dissolution.

5. In your area, what would be the approximate total cost of a funeral? Visit a funeral home or get information through research about the costs and services provided, including cremation, mausoleum, and other choices.

Financial Checkup 4:
Managing Your Resources

This feature focuses on Unit 5, in which personal decision making (Chapter 20) was followed by a discussion of housing alternatives and real estate principles (Chapters 21 and 22) and then automobile ownership and family decisions (Chapters 23 and 24). Additional topics for further study are presented here so students can learn more about related areas.

Personal Decision Making

There are many ways the unwary consumer can be "taken to the cleaner's." Home improvement, car purchase, and other major expenses are common ways to take advantage of unsuspecting people whose objective is to take good care of their property, to extend its life, and to build its value. Let's look at some situations you may face in the future.

Don't Call Me, I'll Call You

When people knock on your door to sell you goods or services, be sure to go slowly, ask questions, and check them out before you buy. A typical home improvement fraud would work like this: A person knocks on your door and compliments you on your well-maintained yard. They notice that your trees are wilting or that your roof could use cleaning. They assure you that they are qualified to perform the work and could do the job more quickly and much cheaper than a large company. Because they are a small-scale operation, however, they need payment up front to buy materials and cover expenses. In reality, the work may never be performed. Or it may be of such poor quality that you would be no better off than before it was done. Or even worse, damage could be done to your property that could cause you further expense.

Figure FC4-1 is a list of things you should and should not do when confronted with this type of pitch.

Check Before You Sign

When you are solicited at home:

1. Don't sign today. Any agreement that is worthwhile can wait until you have time to think about it.

2. Don't give cash. When you give a check, you may have the option of stopping payment. But you must act quickly. It is better to avoid giving cash or check until you have had time to reconsider. Many states have laws (called "green river laws") that allow you three business days after a purchase over $25 with a check or credit card to change your mind and revoke the transaction.

3. Check it out. Ask the Better Business Bureau or your state attorney general's office for consumer complaints about the individual or company. Are they authorized to do business in your state? Are there consumer complaints on file against them?

4. Compare prices. Compare the prices for labor and materials with other sources. This may take several days but is worth it.

5. Don't hurry. If you didn't originate the sale, don't allow others to "create demand" for a product. Don't allow others to talk you into something you don't want.

6. When in doubt, don't. Make this your motto. As the saying goes, "If something seems too good to be true, it probably is." Get all the information you need, then evaluate it carefully. If you still have doubts, wait.

Promises, Promises

An "unconditional, lifetime, money-back" guarantee is only as good as the ability of the guarantor (the one making the promise) to perform. It is often easy to find exceptions; when a company goes out of business, the guarantee goes with them. Another common guarantee says, "Good as long as you own this car." The guarantor is counting on the fact that you won't keep the car more than a few years; when things start to go wrong, you will no longer be the owner.

All That Glitters

This investment scheme capitalizes on your desire to get rich quick, coupled with an attraction to beautiful and rare objects (from gold to diamonds). There are thousands of counterfeit Krugerrands (gold coins) circulated across the nation; investors have no idea they are fake until they try to sell them. By then the seller has vanished. Gold-painted lead also appears to be the real thing—gold bullion. Investors who pay up front, before true value is verified, get stuck with worthless lead. Junk gems are passed off as valuable rubies, sapphires, emeralds, and

unit

diamonds. These "phenomenal bargains" are no bargain—they are advertised as rough stones that need polishing, but they are junk. When these items are purchased by mail, you may find yourself with little recourse.

Complete Worksheet 1, Before You Buy: Ripoffs and Warning Signals, in the *Student Activity Guide* to analyze situations involving good consumer decision making. (This worksheet is also illustrated at the end of this Financial Checkup.)

Mortgage Loans

First-time home buyers need to know the anticipated monthly payment when they purchase a house. The monthly payment will depend on the type of mortgage: fixed rate or variable rate.

Computing the Payment Amount

Clearly, the largest cost of home ownership (whether the home is new or previously owned) is the house payment. The total payment is based on (a) amount of loan, (b) interest rate charged, and (c) length of time to repay the loan. On a **fixed-rate mortgage**, the interest rate remains constant over the life of the loan. Under a fixed-rate mortgage, a $50,000 loan at 8 percent amortized over fifteen or thirty years would result in the following payment:

	30-year loan	**15-year loan**
Monthly payment:		
Principal and interest	$366.85	$477.68
Property taxes (based on assessed value of $70,000 and tax rate of $15 per thousand)	87.50	87.50
Fire insurance premium	10.00	10.00
Total monthly payment	$464.35	$575.18

It is important to note, however, that while monthly payments are higher, the fifteen-year loan will save the borrower interest charges over the life of the loan. For example, under the thirty-year plan, the borrower will repay $132,066 ($366.85 × 360 payments); under the fifteen-year plan, the borrower will repay $85,982 ($477.68 × 180 payments). [Twelve payments per year × thirty years is 360; twelve payments per year × fifteen years is 180.] This is a savings of $46,084!

The **adjustable rate mortgage (ARM)** is one where the interest rate starts low but changes as the loan progresses. For example, for the first three or five years, the rate may be several percentage points below the fixed rate. But then the lender can raise the rate as much as two or three percentage points a year, with a cap or maximum rate that can be charged. Typically, when fixed mortgage rates are 8 percent, an ARM might start at 5 percent for three years but increase to as much as 12 percent, if interest rates continue to rise. This type of loan is ideal for the person or family that will be moving frequently and can sell the house and move when it is time for a mortgage rate increase.

Loan Fees

When financial institutions (lenders) loan money to home buyers, they charge **loan fees** that pay the costs of setting up the loan. Loan fees may range from $100 to $2,500 or more, depending on the loan. In most cases, if the loan does not go through for some reason, the borrower forfeits the loan fees.

Points may be charged by certain lenders as their origination or loan fee. One point is one percent of the loan amount. For a $50,000 loan, if the point rate is 3, then the borrower will have to pay a 3 percent fee, or $1,500 ($50,000 × 3% = $1,500).

If a home is purchased on a land sale contract, attorneys' fees for preparation of the contract and for advice on the sale will run from $500 to $2,500 or more, depending on the time required to prepare documents and assess the situation. Any person using an attorney should ask for an estimate of fees, including the hourly rate, for preparation of documents, filing fees, and advice. Generally, each party (the buyer and the seller) pays their own attorney's fees.

Mortgage Payment Amount

The chart below provides a simple way to estimate what your mortgage payment amount would be. The higher the rate of interest you are paying on the mortgage, the higher your monthly payment will be. To estimate your monthly mortgage payment (for principal and interest only), complete the following steps:

1. Determine the mortgage rate amount and the length of the loan.
2. Using the chart below, pick the appropriate mortgage loan factor. For example, for a 7 percent, thirty-year mortgage, the factor is $6.64.
3. Multiply this factor times the number of thousands in the mortgage principal. For example, in $50,000, there are 50 thousands. Multiply $6.64 times 50. Your monthly payment would be $332.

Monthly Mortgage Payment Factors (per $1,000 of loan amount)	Loan Rate	30 Yrs	25 Yrs	20 Yrs	15 Yrs
	6.0%	5.94	6.40	7.16	8.40
	6.5%	6.29	6.73	7.46	8.69
	7.0%	6.64	7.06	7.76	8.98
	7.5%	6.99	7.39	8.06	9.27
	8.0%	7.34	7.72	8.36	9.56
	8.5%	7.69	8.05	8.68	9.85
	9.0%	8.05	8.39	9.00	10.14
	9.5%	8.41	8.74	9.32	10.44
	10.0%	8.78	9.09	9.65	10.75

Complete Worksheet 2, Computing Mortgage Payments, in the *Student Activity Guide* to determine estimated mortgage payments for different potential mortgage rates and amounts. (This worksheet is also illustrated at the end of this Financial Checkup.)

Housing Option: Building a Home

When a person or family decides to build a new home rather than buy an existing one, they hire a builder and the process begins. First, house plans are chosen. The buyer must decide on the size and style of the house. Often the builder has real estate lots for sale, and the buyer must select a lot from the builder's inventory. In other cases, the buyer may own a vacant lot or purchase a lot and contract with the builder for only the house itself.

The first cost of building a house is the **architect's fee** for drawing up the house plans. Based upon the buyer's desires and what the buyer can afford, a house plan is prepared. The architect's fee ranges from $1,000 to $2,500 or more, depending on house size and value. The more complicated the floor plans, the higher the fee. Floor plans can take several weeks, or in some cases, the builder already has floor plans from which the buyer can choose. While choosing a preexisting plan is more limiting in choices, the buyer is not faced with paying an architect's fee.

Once the buyer and the builder (often called a building contractor) agree upon the house specifications and the price, a building contract is drawn. It specifies what is to be done, what materials are to be used, and a timetable for completion. Generally, the buyer must make a large down payment so that the builder can purchase materials. The buyer generally can get loan approval only after the house is completed; therefore, the contractor may provide a **construction loan** that finances construction and is paid off when the house is completed. While the buyer does not pay for a construction loan, the interest costs on such a loan are a part of the builder's costs of operation and are included in the price of the house.

unit

A buyer should know that any changes in the original plans will result in increased costs to the buyer. For example, as the house is being built, the buyer may want an improvement, such as a bay window or a slightly larger room. A separate agreement is then required to account for the added costs of this construction.

To build a new home will require several months' time. Most buyers find that it takes from six months to a year from the time they first begin to negotiate with a builder. Along the way there are decisions to make, such as color of carpeting, type of tile or countertop, and choices of paint or wallpaper. Within a prescribed price range, the buyer selects desired choices. If a choice exceeds the agreed-upon allotment, the buyer pays the added charge.

Inspections are also necessary at regular intervals—for electricity, plumbing, and so on. While the builder is responsible for these charges (as a part of the total price), delays can result when inspectors are busy.

Closing costs are similar to those for buying a previously owned home, except that the builder replaces the seller. At closing, all subcontractors (those working for the contractor) and all expenses of construction would be paid. The buyer would also have prorations and other closing costs as well.

The experience of buying a new home can be very rewarding because the buyer sees the house in its various stages of construction and is able to make small changes along the way. But it can also be frustrating because of time delays due to weather, inspections, or shortage of materials.

Complete Worksheet 3, Building Your Dream Home, in the *Student Activity Guide* to get an idea of the type of house you would like to build. (This worksheet is also illustrated at the end of this Financial Checkup.)

Auto Repair Ripoffs

Overcharging and needless repairs cost motorists billions of dollars each year according to the U.S. Department of Transportation. This agency has concluded that at least 50 cents of every dollar spent for auto repairs is unnecessary due to inflated prices or needless work!

Some states require repair shops to give customers written estimates. The final bill cannot be increased by more than 10 percent without authorization from the customer. Many states require that the repair shop return defective or worn-out parts to customers rather than discard them. This practice allows the owner to view the damaged, worn-out, or defective part that has been replaced.

Motorists should be wary of allowing others to check engines, tires, belts, fluid levels, or other areas of their vehicles. For example, a motorist asks that oil be checked while receiving gas. The attendant finds worn-out hoses, a need for new tires, or engine problems that need fixing immediately.

Dishonest mechanics find work that doesn't need to be done, add inflated time (labor) charges and parts to a bill, and remove parts in good condition and replace them with used or rebuilt parts.

Figure FC4-2 is a list of tips from New York City's Department of Consumer Affairs to help you know what to do when you experience car trouble.

Complete Worksheet 4, Ripoffs and Warning Signals, in the *Student Activity Guide* about suspicious situations related to car repairs. (This worksheet also appears at the end of this Financial Checkup.)

Fig. FC4-2

When You Run into Car Trouble

Tips from New York City's Department of Consumer Affairs

- Look for a reliable mechanic before you are faced with an emergency. Ask friends for references.

- If you suspect your car needs repairs, have it checked before it becomes a big repair.

- For large repairs, get two estimates and compare the charges. Let the shops know you are comparison shopping.

- List all symptoms so you won't forget anything when you are talking to a mechanic. Give a copy of the list to the mechanic and keep a copy for yourself. Make sure all of the symptoms are taken care of before you accept the work for full payment.

- Don't authorize work unless you understand what is being done. Add-on work that does not apply to the reason for your repair should be suspect.

- Don't tell a mechanic to "get this car in good running order." This is a blanket opportunity for them to do anything whether or not it is essential.

- Don't sign a repair order unless you understand what is being done to your car. Question each line item.

- Keep itemized bills. Good records will help you in the event work is not satisfactory. Mechanics should stand behind their work. Be able to tell the mechanic, "I had this fuel pump replaced by you two months ago. It should be working." Have the documentation with you to prove it.

- If you suspect you are being overcharged, ask to see the supplier's parts price list.

- Find out which local and state government agencies have jurisdiction over auto-repair complaints. Use the agency if necessary to get satisfaction.

unit

WORKSHEET 1

Before You Buy: Ripoffs and Warning Signals

BEFORE YOU BUY. . .

Directions: Analyze the following situations and determine what might be wrong.

Situation 1. You receive a tantalizing offer in the mail. There's a new development being constructed at your favorite mountain skiing area. You have failed on several occasions to get reservations in the area, so you are excited at the prospect of having a place of your own. The invitation spells out what the new development will look like—buildings, ski lifts, and other amenities. At the bottom it invites you to an informational meeting. You must attend the meeting to be considered for this opportunity. You are asked to bring your checkbook or credit card. Free food will be provided and prizes will be given.

Situation 2. You receive a telephone call that offers you free products for answering a few simple questions. All you have to do is give them your name, social security number, address, and other personal information, and they will send you free samples of merchandise that you use or would like to try based on your lifestyle.

Situation 3. You see an ad in the classified pages where a desperate investor is seeking to unload his collection of rare baseball cards and comic books at lower-than-market prices. He needs the money right away and will sell to the highest bidder. You call to get the address, and when you show up, there are several others there who are interested in the merchandise and are bidding on it.

WORKSHEET 2

Computing Mortgage Payments

Directions: Compute the following estimated mortgage amounts, using the chart supplied on page 601.

What is your estimated mortgage payment for:

30-year mortgage		25-year mortgage		15-year mortgage	
1. $50,000	8%	2. $70,000	6%	3. $80,000	7.5%
4. $100,000	6%	5. $100,000	7%	6. $100,000	8%
7. $150,000	7.5%	8. $150,000	9%	9. $150,000	10%

WORKSHEET 3
Building Your Dream Home

Directions: Answer the following questions and complete the research suggested to specify your dream home. Be sure to list your sources of information.

1. What style of house do you prefer? (two-story, ranch, Victorian, Tudor, and so on)

2. Attach a picture of a house that closely resembles the home of your dreams.

3. Prepare a floor plan that details the rooms and configuration, along with windows, doors, and so on.

4. What is the total square footage of your home?

    How many bedrooms?

    Bathrooms?

    Describe the kitchen and eating area(s).

    Describe the general layout of the house, starting at the front door and ending at the back door or on the second floor.

5. Describe the lot and landscaping, including lot size and shape.

6. Describe the block—what part of town, city or country, the neighborhood or region.

7. Based on today's costs of building real estate, what would it cost to build this house? (Hint: You need to consult the newspaper ads that describe similar new properties or interview a builder or other reliable source.)

8. Prepare a report of your findings, including a cover page, drawings or exhibits, narrative of information, and list of sources of information.

WORKSHEET 4

Ripoffs and Warning Signals (Your Car)

Directions: Read each of the following statements that could be a potential ripoff. Write the warning signal (a point that makes you uncomfortable) and what you would do about it.

1. Your car is making pinging noises every time you accelerate to pass another car or go up a hill. You stop by a service station and while your car is being filled with gas, you casually ask what could be wrong. The attendant replies that he would be happy to take a look at it when he gets off work, and that he could probably fix it in his spare time. Repairs could cost as little as $50 or as much as $250.

2. You are on vacation and driving the family car. You had it tuned up before you left, and your tires are fairly new. Along the way, you stop for gas. While checking the oil, the attendant notices that one of your hoses is loose. He fixes it (no charge) but then sees that you have an oil leak. He offers to make the repair within an hour for $100 plus parts.

3. You take your car in for its regular tune-up and maintenance. You take a list of things that need to be done. An hour later, you receive a telephone call and are asked to authorize extra repairs that total $500. These repairs are not related to the tune-up or regular maintenance. But when the car is up on the rack, the mechanic sees that the work needs to be done.

looking back . . .

In Unit 5, we first learned about personal decision making and how it is influenced by individual, group, and societal factors. Decisions such as purchasing of goods and services are frequently induced by wants, needs, and values. But they also are influenced by marketing strategies that are often subtle, indirect, and targeted to create and satisfy needs.

Living on your own also can be very expensive and wasteful without careful examination of your alternatives. There are many advantages to renting. But all renters have responsibilities as well as rights; knowledge of these rights and responsibilities will save you time, effort, and money.

The American dream of buying your own home does not guarantee a glamorous existence. This investment has financial risks, limited mobility, and higher living costs. After you select a home you desire, your efforts must turn to determining an initial offer price and negotiating a final buying price. To finance your home purchase, you will need to obtain funds for a down payment, meet the requirements of your lending institution, and assess different types of mortgages. The last step in purchasing real estate involves closing the transaction.

Owning your first car will also be an exciting occasion. Gathering information, selecting options for your car, and settling on a price are the primary phases of buying a car.

Last, you explored group decisions that you will encounter, beginning with marriage and progressing through death. While some of these events won't occur in your life for many years, most assuredly you will be affected by all of them.

unit six

risk management

objectives: *After reading and studying the chapters and completing the exercises and activities, you will be able to:*

1 Explain risk management and evaluate the methods of managing risk.

2 Discuss the need for property and liability insurance and the types of coverages available.

3 Describe the need for health insurance, disability insurance, and life insurance, and the types of coverages available.

looking forward

Unit 6, Risk Management, begins with a discussion of risk—what it is and how individuals manage it, usually through insurance. In Chapter 25, you will examine different types of risks and their potential for serious financial consequences, and you will examine a strategy to manage those risks. You will learn many new vocabulary words that apply to all types of insurance. Finally, you will begin to develop a personal insurance program.

In Chapter 26, you will learn the specifics of property insurance— how to protect your residence and personal possessions, your automobile, passengers, and others, and how to protect yourself from liability as a result of your negligence, mistake, or errors in judgment. There are many types of insurance coverages and options; some are expensive and others are a good value for the money spent. The most important thing you will learn is how to assess potential risks and manage them in the most cost-effective manner.

In Chapter 27, you will learn about rising health costs and the need for health insurance. You will explore the types of coverage and types of health plans from which to choose. You will also discover disability insurance—the most neglected and misunderstood form of insurance. Finally, you will learn about life insurance: who needs it, how it works, and the types available.

After reading and studying this chapter you will be able to:

25-1 Explain the concept of insurance: what it is and how it works.

25-2 Define basic insurance terminology and types of risk.

25-3 List the steps and discuss the process of risk management.

24-4 Plan a personal insurance program.

insurance
risk
insurance company
policy
premium
policyholder
indemnification
probability
personal risks
property risks
liability risks
pure risk
insurable risk
speculative risk
risk management
insurable interest
risk avoidance
risk reduction
risk assumption
agency

As soon as you acquire assets, earn a good income, and establish a solid financial base, you must design a plan to protect you and your family against financial hardship due to hazard, accident, or death. Insurance gives you peace of mind because you know that money will be available to meet the needs of your survivors, to pay medical expenses, to protect your home and belongings, and to cover personal or property damage caused by your car. In this chapter you will explore the concept of insurance and how you can make it work to your benefit. You will learn about risks and methods of managing them, along with the vocabulary of insurance. Then you will design a preliminary insurance program. Your plan will be revised and further developed in the chapters that follow.

chapter

Personal Risks
and Insurance

25

How insurance works

Insurance is a method of spreading the risk to protect assets and income. **Risk** refers to the possibility of a loss that faces a person or property covered by insurance. There are many types of insurance, including life, health, homeowners, and automobile. They all provide one important thing: relief from fear of financial loss due to events beyond your control.

Let's take a simple example. Suppose your textbook for this class costs $30. If you lose it, you will have to pay that amount to replace it. An average of ten out of every 100 textbooks are lost each school year. Based on this statistic, the losses in a class of thirty students should come to three books, or $90 (3 × $30). The class could establish an insurance company to help lower the cost of these expected losses to students. Every student would contribute $3 to the company.

An **insurance company,** or insurer, is a business that, for a fee, issues policies to protect individuals and companies against some kind of loss. When a person buys insurance, he or she joins a risk-sharing group (the insurance company) by purchasing a written contract (a **policy**). Under the policy, the insurance company agrees to assume an identified risk for a fee (the **premium**) paid by a person (**policyholder**). The insurance company collects insurance premiums from policyholders under the assumption that only a few policyholders will have financial losses and that the premiums collected will more than cover those needs. In years where a major disaster occurs, such as a hurricane, flood, or earthquake, an insurance company may pay out more in benefits than it receives in premiums.

A major disaster, such as a hurricane, can cause an insurance company to pay out more in benefits than it receives in premiums.

As you probably guessed, insurance is not meant to enrich, only to compensate for actual loss incurred. This principle is called indemnification. **Indemnification** means putting the policyholder back in the same financial condition he or she was in before the loss occurred. **Probability** is the mathematics of chance and the root of indemnification. Every event can be described in terms of probability or likelihood that something will happen.

Insurance companies assess insurance premiums based on statistical probability. In other words, they estimate the likelihood of a potential loss. They gather and analyze large amounts of data. For example, in a sample of 100,000 drivers under the age of 18, an insurance company can predict how many will have accidents in a given year. Based on the law of large numbers, they can actually determine a pattern and predict the risk they are taking. The higher the probability of a loss occurring, the higher the premium for insuring against it.

Insurance terminology

To understand all types of insurance, let's begin with some basic vocabulary. Here are some typical words that relate to insurance:

1. *Actuarial table*—a table of premium rates based on ages and life expectancies.
2. *Actuary*—one who calculates insurance and annuity premiums, reserves, and dividends; a specialist on insurance statistics.
3. *Agent*—a trained professional salesperson who acts for the insurance company in negotiating, servicing, or writing an insurance policy.
4. *Beneficiary*—a person named on an insurance policy to receive the benefits (proceeds) of the policy.
5. *Benefits*—sums of money to be paid for specific types of losses under the terms of an insurance policy.
6. *Cash value*—the amount of money payable to a policyholder upon discontinuation of a life insurance policy.
7. *Claim*—a demand for payment for a loss under the terms of an insurance policy.
8. *Coverage*—protection provided by the terms of an insurance policy.
9. *Deductible*—a specified amount subtracted from covered losses; the insurance company pays only the amount in excess of the deductible.
10. *Exclusions*—circumstances or losses that are not covered under the terms of an insurance policy.
11. *Face amount*—the death benefit of a life insurance policy.

12. *Grace period*—the period following the due date of an unpaid premium during which the policy is still in effect (usually thirty days).

13. *Hazard*—a condition that increases the likelihood of some loss. For example, defective house wiring or a smoke detector with a dead battery increase the likelihood of fire.

14. *Insurance*—a cooperative system of sharing the risk of financial loss.

15. *Insured*—the person, partnership, or company protected against loss (not always the owner of the policy).

16. *Loss*—an unexpected reduction or disappearance of an economic value; the basis of a valid claim for repayment under the terms of an insurance policy.

17. *Peril*—an event whose occurrence can cause a loss; people buy policies for protection against such perils as a fire, storm, explosion, accident, or robbery.

18. *Policyholder*—the person who buys an insurance policy.

19. *Premium*—the sum of money the policyholder agrees to pay to an insurance company periodically (monthly, quarterly, annually, or semiannually) for an insurance policy.

20. *Proof of loss*—the written verification of the amount of a loss that must be provided by the insured to the insurance company before a claim can be settled.

21. *Risk*—the chance of a loss.

22. *Standard policy*—the contract form that has been adopted by many insurance companies, approved by state insurance divisions, or prescribed by law (modifications are made to suit the needs of the individual).

23. *Unearned premium*—the portion of a paid premium that has not been earned by the insurance company and is returned to the policyholder when a policy is canceled.

isks

Each of us faces risks every day. From the moment you get out of bed, you take chances. You could slip and fall; you could have an accident in the kitchen or bathroom. You could be hit by a car or fall off your bicycle or rollerblades. You could have your stereo stolen or injure another person or property while driving your car. Insurance gives you financial protection from the losses associated with these types of risks.

Insurance provides financial protection from the losses associated with risk.

There are three major risks: personal, property, and liability. Each of these risks must be considered as you make plans to protect your financial interests.

Figure 25-1 illustrates risks that occur at various stages of life.

Personal Risks

Personal risks are those possible losses involving your income and standard of living. To insure protection, you purchase life, health, disability, and unemployment insurance. You insure against personal risks when others are depending on your income to provide food, clothing, shelter, and the comforts of life. As you will learn in Chapter 27, this type of insurance can be very expensive. You will be faced with many choices in coverage, costs, and potential benefits.

Property Risks

The possibilities of loss or harm to personal or real property are called **property risks.** For example, your home, car, or other possessions could be damaged or destroyed by fire, theft, wind, rain, accident, and other hazards. To protect from such losses, you purchase property insurance. As you will learn in Chapter 26, insurance for your home and your car requires many decisions that will affect premiums and coverages.

Fig. 25-1

Individual and Family Events

Risks	Causes (Perils)	Strategies to Reduce Monetary Impact
1. Losing job (income)	Poor economy Company's financial condition	Unemployment insurance Learn new skills; make yourself more valuable
2. Illness or injury	On-the-job accident Chronic health condition or handicap	Disability insurance Retraining programs
3. Death of wage earner	Dangerous activities including sports or job; illness	Life insurance Get training/lessons Take safety precautions
4. Liability for others' injuries	Careless driving Hazard at home/place of work	Liability insurance Signs, warnings, supervised uses
5. Loss of property to theft	Vehicle stolen Robbery	Locks/security devices Park in well-lit and secure places Property insurance

Liability Risks

Both your income and your assets can be protected from **liability risks** arising out of your errors or negligence. For example, you can accidentally cause injury or damage to others or their property by your conduct while driving a car. Or a person could suffer a fall while visiting your home. Liability insurance will protect you when others sue you for injuring them or damaging their property.

 ## isk management

Personal, property, and liability risks are all types of pure risk. With a **pure risk,** there is always a chance of loss if certain events (perils) occur. Therefore, pure risks are accidental, unpredictable, and unavoidable. The financial loss can be determined and is therefore an **insurable risk.** In contrast, a **speculative risk** is one in which there may be either gain or loss. When you buy stock, you could either make or lose money. But because these risks are not accidental, unpredictable, or unavoidable, they are also uninsurable.

An organized strategy for protecting assets and people to help reduce financial loss is called **risk management.** An important aspect of risk management is the assessment of potential losses, their likelihood of occurring, and possible financial damage that could result. As shown in Figure 25-2, risk management is much more than buying insurance for every possible type of peril that could occur. To buy insurance, you must have an insurable interest to protect. An **insurable interest** is any interest in life or property such that, if the life or property were lost, you would suffer financially.

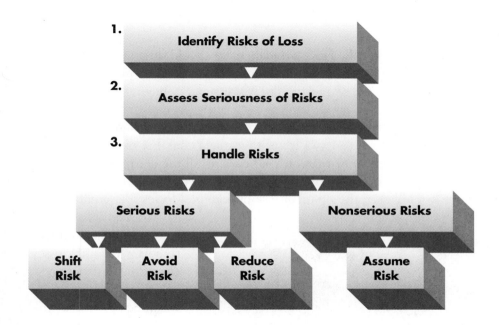

Fig. 25-2

Risk Management Process

While you cannot eliminate risk, you can improve your chances of protecting assets and income against loss. Risk management helps you lower risks and manage them to your greatest financial benefit. The three-step process involves identifying, assessing, and handling risks.

Step 1: Identify Risks

Ask yourself what types of risks you take when you drive a car, own a house, or plan a party. As you will see in subsequent chapters, there are many potential losses that could occur; even though they may not happen as a result of your error or fault, you still can be responsible for damages to others and to property.

Step 2: Assess Risks

Human activities and the ownership of property reflect a certain amount of risk. Some risks are high priority because they could have serious financial consequences. For example, when driving your car, you could destroy the property of others, injure others, or even kill someone. Because potential losses are very great, driving is a high priority risk. Other types of risk may be less significant, less likely to result in loss, and are therefore of a lower priority.

Step 3: Handle Risks

There are four risk management techniques: avoid, reduce, assume, or shift. A good risk management program means you use a combination of the above strategies to balance risks, costs of insurance, and potential losses.

To *avoid* risk, called **risk avoidance,** you avoid situations that involve risk. For example, instead of having a party at your house, you decide to reserve a section of a restaurant. Or instead of buying a house, you decide to rent.

To *reduce* risk, called **risk reduction,** you take measures to lessen the frequency or severity of losses that may occur. For example, you may put studded snow tires on your car, install fire alarms or sprinklers in your home, or insist that seat belts be used in your car. All these steps would lessen the financial risk of potential losses that could occur.

Risk reduction, such as using seat belts, will lessen the frequency and severity of losses.

To *shift* or *transfer* risk, you buy insurance to cover financial losses caused by destructive or damaging events. Insurance provides protection against many risks of financial uncertainty and unexpected losses. Most Americans acquire protection against many different types of risk—fire, theft, injury, illness, and old age.

To *assume* risk, called **risk assumption,** means you will self-insure, or pay for losses personally. *Self-insurance* is the process of establishing a monetary fund that can be used to cover the cost of a loss. This strategy can reduce the cost of insurance. In some cases it may be too expensive to purchase insurance, and the probability of a loss is too low to justify paying an insurance premium. In other words, the likelihood that a given event will occur does not justify the expense of insuring against the potential loss.

As you probably guessed, you can use more than one of these strategies in your risk management plan. For example, you may have just purchased a car. Because driving a car is a serious risk, you will acquire auto insurance. (It's also required in most states.) To avoid risks, you will not drive at especially dangerous times, such as after midnight or in icy weather. To reduce risks, you will have purchased a car with safety features, such as air bags and antilock brakes. To assume some risk, you would have a $250 or $500 deductible for damage to your car. (A higher deductible lowers your insurance premium because you will pay a larger portion of the damages yourself.)

Planning a personal insurance program

Each person and family will face risks and the potential losses they bring. Some people choose to do nothing—but this is in fact a choice. When you allow events to control your life, they also drain your finances in unpredictable and expensive ways. To avoid this type of disaster, you can begin to plan a personal insurance program. Figure 25-3 is an out-line of the type of insurance program a young person just getting started might wish to develop. A very different plan will be needed as you make future choices in lifestyle (such as marriage, having children, and so on). You can use the model, presented as Figure 25-3, for developing an insurance program for any stage in life.

In order to develop a personal insurance program, you should begin with an assessment of the types of risks you are facing and will likely encounter in the next few years. In general, financial advisers say that a basic insurance program should help reduce or alleviate the following.

1. Potential loss of income due to the premature death, illness, accident, or unemployment of a wage earner.
2. Potential loss of income and extra expense resulting from the illness, disability, or death of a spouse or other family member.
3. Potential loss of real or personal property due to fire, theft, or other hazards.
4. Potential loss of income, savings, and property resulting from personal liability (injuring a person or damaging the property of others).

Fig. 25-3 **Insurance Action Plan: Young, Single Adult**

Risk	Reduction	Avoidance	Assumption	Insurance Purchases
1. Auto accidents: car damages	Take drivers education course; practice defensive driving.	Avoid rush hour traffic; avoid driving late at night.	$250 or $500 deductible on collision insurance	Collision insurance
injuries (to self and others)	Wear seat belts; require passengers to buckle up.	Avoid drinking and driving; use public transportation.	Self-insure	Medical insurance; self-health insurance
2. Traffic citations: speeding	Use cruise control and radar detectors.	Obey speed laws; allow extra time before leaving home.	Driving without using care	N/A
3. Injuries: sports	Take lessons, practice, and use appropriate techniques and equipment.	Don't participate; avoid overly dangerous activities.	Pay for costs as incurred.	Health insurance (at work or at school)
4. Preventive care: medical and dental	Use low-cost clinics, get rest and exercise, and practice good nutrition.	Practice naturopathy to minimize problems.	Deductibles; co-pays; pay for all preventive care.	Health insurance

personal perspective

C hoosing an Insurance Agent

The agent you choose can be as important as the insurance company and coverages you select. The insurance agent is an important person because he or she explains to you the best options and helps you plan for your insurance needs.

The agent should

1. Be available to you locally. You should be able to reach the agent by telephone and have a personal visit every few years to keep your insurance needs current.
2. Give you full-service counseling for all your insurance needs, including advice about when you do *not* need insurance.
3. Not exert pressure on you or try to sell you coverages or policies that are not appropriate. He or she should also inform you of when to reduce coverage (when property values decrease) and when to drop coverage.
4. Be professional, knowledgeable, and up-to-date about insurance. In addition, he or she should be able to explain to you, in language you can understand, exactly what is covered and what is not, and how policies work.
5. Be willing and able to answer your questions and keep you informed as to company changes and laws that affect you and your insurance policies.

Choosing the right agent is important. You can buy directly from an insurance company, or you can buy through an insurance agency. An insurance **agency** represents many different insurance companies and can match you with the company and policy that meets your needs. An insurance agent may work directly with a company or be independent (and work for an agency). It is not unusual for a relationship with an insurance agent to extend over twenty or thirty years.

CHARLES S. CAVADINI INSURANCE

Personal	*Financial*	*Business*
AUTO	IRA'S	WORKMENS COMP.
HOMEOWNERS	TERM LIFE	CONTRACTORS LIAB.
RENTERS	ANNUITIES	BUSINESS OWNER
PERSONAL UMBRELLA	UNIVERSAL LIFE	UMBRELLA
FUR-JEWELRY	MUTUAL FUNDS	TRUCKS
SILVERWARE,ETC.	MORTGAGE LIFE	EMPLOYEE
BOAT-CYCLE	DISABILITY	BENEFIT

critical thinking

1. Do you know an insurance agent through your parents or other persons? If so, does the agent work independently or for an insurance agency?

2. Would you consider buying insurance from an out-of-state company if the premiums were considerably less but the company would not have any local agents?

3. Describe the kind of person you would like to have as your insurance agent.

For each risk that you will face, you can determine ways you can reduce, avoid, or assume the risk yourself. However, when a risk is significant and can have drastic consequences, then purchasing insurance is a good idea. In this unit, you will learn more about specific types of insurance. As you consider an insurance action plan, you should also think about the following practices that will help you save on insurance costs: higher deductibles, group insurance, payment schedules, discount opportunities, and comparison shopping.

Increase Deductibles

As you learned earlier in this chapter, a deductible is a specified out-of-pocket amount that you will pay before insurance begins to pay for a loss. Generally, the higher the deductible, the lower the insurance premium. For example, premiums for a policy with a $100 deductible will be considerably higher than for a policy with a $500 deductible.

Purchase Group Insurance

Group plans usually result in premiums that are considerably less expensive than purchasing an individual plan. In the area of health insurance, a group plan is much more affordable than an individual plan. Group plans are available through your job, credit union, a social or professional organization, or other similar group.

Consider Payment Schedules

Believe it or not, how you pay premiums can save you considerable money over a short period of time. Monthly payments usually contain an extra charge, while semiannual payments do not. Typically, premiums are paid annually or semiannually. When you have an automatic deduction from your checking account, there may be a reduction in premium costs. Always compare payment options and weigh the differences in costs.

Look for Discount Opportunities

Many insurance companies offer discounts to policyholders for special conditions. For example, nonsmokers can get lower premiums on fire insurance. Taking drivers education and getting good grades can reduce automobile insurance costs for teenagers. Having more than one vehicle or more than one insurance policy with a company can allow multiple policy discounts. By purchasing all of your insurance through one agency or insurer, you can save money on premiums. You should also check your credit union and other professional or social groups to see if discounts are available.

Engage in Comparison Shopping

Like many other things you buy, it pays to shop around. Consumers should be aware of the variety of available insurance products. Variety makes it possible to find flexible insurance plans tailored to your special needs.

Get quotes from several different companies, and be sure to give each one the same information so you can compare exact coverages and costs. When getting cost estimates for many types of insurance, it is your responsibility to know what your property is worth. In addition, maintaining a good driving record is important when getting price quotes for automobile insurance. It's also important to know exactly what coverages you need—and don't need—before talking to insurance companies.

Shop around for the best insurance company or agency. When rating insurance companies, remember that the most reputable companies provide good coverage at reasonable prices. The financial strength of the insurance company may be a major factor in keeping down insurance costs for consumers.

Ask people you know about local insurance agencies and companies—your family, friends, coworkers, and other acquaintances will recommend good companies and agents.

Summary

Insurance is a method of spreading risk. Risk management is an important part of personal financial planning. All people face risks—or potential losses that are likely to occur. There are three major types of risks: personal, property, and liability. There are many different types of insurance to cover these risks—property insurance, life insurance, automobile insurance, just to name a few.

Personal risks involve your income and your standard of living. Property risks involve your car, home, and other personal possessions that could be lost, stolen, damaged, or destroyed. Liability risks are those that you incur when you are negligent and cause injury to someone else or damage to their property.

Risk management is more than just buying insurance. You must analyze your risks and then design a plan to manage them all effectively. A three-step process begins with identifying, assessing, and then man-

aging risks. Methods of managing risks involve risk avoidance, risk reduction, and risk assumption. All of these strategies should be used together to minimize losses and maximize insurance benefits.

The most common method of dealing with risk is to shift or transfer it to an insurance company. A specific type of insurance should be identified for particular risks where possible. In addition, you must consider deductibles, group insurance, payment schedules, discount opportunities, and company reputation when designing your best personal insurance plan.

V ocabulary terms

Directions: Can you find the definition for each of the following terms used in Chapter 25?

agency
indemnification
insurable interest
insurable risk
insurance
insurance company
liability risks
personal risks
policy
policyholder

premium
probability
property risks
pure risk
risk
risk assumption
risk avoidance
risk management
risk reduction
speculative risk

1. A method of spreading risk to protect assets and income.
2. Potential losses that involve income and a person's standard of living.
3. With this type of risk, there is always the chance of loss if certain events occur.
4. An organized strategy for protecting and conserving assets and people.
5. Taking measures to lessen the frequency or severity of losses that may occur.
6. A company that represents many different insurance companies.
7. The mathematics of chance; the likelihood that something will happen.
8. The possibility of a loss.
9. The possibilities of loss or harm to personal property or real estate.
10. Risks that arise because you make mistakes or errors in judgment.
11. A risk that may result in either a loss or a gain.
12. Choosing actions that would make a risky situation less likely.
13. Establishing a monetary fund to cover the cost of a loss.
14. Putting the policyholder back in the same financial condition as before a loss occurred.
15. Any interest in life or property such that a policyholder would suffer loss.
16. A financial loss that can be determined.
17. A business that issues insurance policies to individuals and companies.
18. A written insurance contract.

25 end-of-chapter activities

19. The amount paid regularly by a policyholder to an insurance company.
20. The person who owns or holds an insurance policy.

 acts and ideas in review

1. Why do people buy insurance?
2. Explain the concepts of probability and indemnification.
3. Define the words *risk, peril,* and *hazard.*
4. List the three major types of risks.
5. Explain the three-step risk management process.
6. Explain the concepts of *risk avoidance, risk reduction, risk assumption,* and *risk transfer.*
7. What are five practices you should consider when designing a personal insurance plan?
8. What qualities should you consider in selecting an insurance agent?

pplications for decision making

1. Prepare a list of insurance companies in your area. Include the types of insurance sold by each company. For each insurance agency, list the insurance companies represented. (Hint: the Yellow Pages of your telephone directory should have these all listed under "Insurance.")
2. Based on Figure 25-1, add any current or anticipated risks you or your family faces or will face in the near future. You might include risks for recreation and travel opportunities, injuries on the job, and so on.
3. Based on your personal situation, analyze your current personal, property, and liability risks. Then assume that you are now ten years older. Based on being where you would like to be and doing what your current goals dictate, analyze your personal, property, and liability risks for this stage in your life.
4. Using Figure 25-2 as a guide, do an assessment of what you consider your most significant risks. Ask your parents to help you identify and assess these risks, along with devising your plan to handle risks.

5. Using Figure 25-3 as a guide, prepare an insurance action plan for yourself. You may need assistance from parents to determine your current insurance coverage. As an alternative, interview a person at a different life stage and ask for advice on an appropriate personal insurance plan.

life situation problem solving

1. Friends of the family, Jan and Dean, are planning to get married next summer. They don't own a car and plan to rent an apartment. They intend to have children in the next few years. What advice can you give them about risk and risk management? When should they consider purchasing insurance?

2. Your cousin Arthur has decided to take up snow skiing. He has asked you how he can avoid paying for high medical bills if he gets injured. Currently, he is under his parents' group policy, but his parents have informed him that he will be responsible for all costs of learning to ski, including any costs not paid by insurance. How can he maximize his opportunities while minimizing his risks and costs?

3. A neighbor of yours has asked for your advice regarding insurance. She owns her own car, works full time, and is buying a house. While she is single, she must pay student loans and other financial debts. She would like to know what risks she is facing and what she might do about it. Can you help her identify, assess, and manage risks based on her situation?

4. A friend, Barry West, made this statement: "I don't take any chances. Everything I own is insured, including my life and ability to provide money for my family. In fact, I pay so much in insurance premiums that there isn't much money left for doing fun things. Am I doing something wrong?" Discuss how handling risk does not always mean buying insurance.

5. Carole Adams is single and under age 25. She just started her first full-time job with group health insurance. She has a car. She has had no accidents or traffic tickets. She has an apartment that contains furnishings and personal belongings. Prepare a list of the risks she may face. What types of insurance coverage may she need?

6. Interview a qualified insurance agent. Find out what a competent insurance agent can and will do to help you purchase various types of protection.

objectives:

After reading and studying this chapter you will be able to:

26-1 Describe the need for fire, theft, and other forms of property insurance and types of policies.

26-2 Discuss the types of automobile insurance coverages available and what each coverage is designed to protect.

26-3 Explain the concept of liability insurance as it relates to an umbrella policy.

n the previous chapter, you learned what insurance is and how it works. In this chapter, you will learn about two specific types of insurance that you will likely purchase during your lifetime. Your home and your personal belongings are a major portion of your assets. Loss of some or all of these possessions could cause financial disaster. Homeowners insurance protects you from loss in the event your home or belongings are damaged or destroyed. Automobile insurance protects you from loss in the event your car is damaged or destroyed in an accident, stolen, or causes injury to another person or damage to another car. As a licensed driver, you have a responsibility to yourself, your passengers, and others using the highways. The automobile is one of the greatest sources of liability risks in our society.

chapter

26

Property and Liability Insurance

omeowners insurance

Property owners face three basic types of risks. The first is *physical damage* that may be caused by hazards such as fire, water, wind, and smoke. These hazards cause destruction of your property or temporary loss of its use. The second type of risk faced by property owners is the threat of *robbery*, *burglary*, *arson*, or *vandalism*. The third type of risk is from *liability*—the legal responsibility for the financial cost of another person's losses or injuries. Doing something careless, such as improperly supervising a swimming pool or not removing items from a staircase, may be classified as negligence in a lawsuit.

A renters or homeowners policy will provide fire insurance.

A **renters policy** protects your personal possessions that are kept on the premises of someone else's property. A renters policy will protect from loss due to fire, smoke, and other types of damage such as water or moisture, freezing, or heat. For example, if you rent an apartment and there is a fire in the building, your personal property (couch, chairs, bed, clothing, and so on) may suffer damage. A renters policy will cover the costs of repairing or replacing damaged or destroyed property.

A **homeowners policy** is more than fire insurance—it also contains coverage for theft or damage to contents as well as accidents that may occur in the house or on the property. Also covered are attached structures, such as garages and tool sheds, as well as shrubs, trees, plants, and fences. If a fire prevents the owner from using the property while it is being repaired or replaced, the homeowners policy also covers temporary housing for a limited time (usually six months or less).

Homeowners policies may be very basic or very broad in the coverages provided. Figure 26-1 is an example of the types of insurance policies that are available, together with the coverages provided by each. Package policies provide coverages for a lower premium than if these coverages were purchased separately. Until the mid-1950s, a person had to buy separate insurance coverage for fire, theft, or other risks.

Fig. 26-1

Homeowners Policies

HO-1	Basic Coverage	Fire, lightning, windstorm, hail, explosion, riot, civil commotion, aircraft, nonowned vehicles, smoke, vandalism, malicious mischief, theft, and glass breakage. Limits apply, such as $500 or 5 percent of policy value, whichever is less.
HO-2	Broad Form	Broader list of perils; broader definitions; still has restrictions and limits, such as fire from fireplaces being excluded; limit of $1,000 or 10 percent of policy value, whichever is less.
HO-3	Special Form	All-risk coverage on dwelling itself; a loss not specifically excluded (such as flood) is covered.
HO-4	Renters	Insuring personal property on a broad-form basis with advantages of homeowners policy (such as special coverage in event of flood or water damage).
HO-5	Comprehensive	Most comprehensive policy available; dwelling and contents are covered on all-risk basis.
HO-6	Condominium Owners	HO-4 coverage for condominium owners (wording is adjusted to fit legal status of condominium owner).
HO-7	Older Homes	Meets special needs of owners of older buildings that have been remodeled and would have high replacement costs (actual cash value basis rather than replacement cost basis).

How Much Coverage Do You Need?

Generally, insurance for contents of a house is half the value of the building or more. For example, a building insured for $100,000 is likely to have contents covered for $50,000 to $75,000. This includes all types of personal possessions, from furniture and furnishings to clothing, appliances, utensils, artwork, and other personal property. To be sure you are reimbursed for all damaged or destroyed property, you should complete a household inventory, as shown in Figure 26-2. You will recall preparing a personal property inventory in Chapter 8; for the homeowner, a more comprehensive household inventory is needed.

Your household inventory should include documentation that shows proof of ownership and value. Some people keep receipts and take pictures or a home video; this documentation should be kept in a safe place (such as a safe-deposit box). Most insurance agents provide household inventory forms to their customers. You should also realize that some things are not covered by property insurance. Figure 26-3 on page 633 lists items that generally are excluded (not covered).

Overinsuring property (buying more insurance than is necessary to cover the value) is unwise. An insurance company will pay only the actual replacement value of the home. For example, if a home valued at $75,000 with contents of $45,000 is totally destroyed, the insurance company will pay no more than $120,000. The principle of indemnity, a legal doctrine, limits recovery under an insurance policy to the lesser of the actual cash value of a loss or the amount that will restore the insured to his or her position prior to the loss.

Claim adjustors, also known as *insurance adjustors*, determine the value of what was destroyed or damaged by a fire or other event causing a loss. In addition, insurance companies employ *insurance investigators* who look for evidence of destroyed or damaged property. They also look into cases where people try to claim damages that did not occur. Fraudulent insurance claims can result in criminal charges, fines, or both.

For a small added premium, a property owner can extend coverage with an **endorsement.** An endorsement specifically lists the property and its value and has an added premium. For example, flood or earthquake insurance can be obtained as an endorsement, or additional coverage, to your homeowners policy. Coverage added onto the existing policy is often called *extended coverage*. Instead of adding coverages to existing policies, some homeowners may save money by purchasing a more comprehensive form of homeowners policy.

Most homeowners policies contain a provision requiring that the building be insured for at least 80 percent of the replacement value. Only 80 percent is required because even if your property is completely destroyed, the land and the building foundation will probably still be

Fig. 26-2   **Household Inventory**

HOUSEHOLD INVENTORY

Room	Type of Property	Replacement Cost	Receipt/Proof
Kitchen	Appliances:		
	Stove/oven	$ 600	Wards, 7/94
	Microwave	400	Penneys, 9/93
	Toaster	25	Gift
	Mixer/blender	125	Shaleys, 1/95
	Bread maker	250	K-Mart, 6/95
	Cabinets and contents:		
	Dishes	500	
	Pots and pans	500	
	Silverware	800	Oneida, 2/92
	Clock on wall	100	Gift
	Table and chairs	1,200	Dixons, 5/95
	Curtains	500	Wards, 8/94
Family Room	Bookcase, books	2,000	
	Couch and chair	1,000	Dixons, 2/95
	End tables/lamps	800	Dixons, 2/95
	Television	1,000	Mel's, 3/96
	Stereo	1,200	Mel's, 3/96
	Paintings	700	Dixons, 2/95
Bedroom	Antique bedroom set	5,000	Appraisal
	Clothing	2,000	
	Jewelry	500	
	Picture/mirrors	800	Dixons, 2/95
Garage	Lawn mower	900	Swath's, 3/94
	Garden tools	300	
	Camping equipment	800	Mel's, 3/96
	Bicycles	1,800	Jon's, 3/96
Utility Room	Washer/dryer	1,200	Sears, 3/95
	Cleaning supplies	100	

usable. A **coinsurance clause** requires the policyholder to carry insurance coverage equal to or exceeding 80 percent of the replacement cost of the building. If this condition is not met, then the insured receives less than the full amount of damages suffered. For example, suppose your house has an estimated value (replacement cost) of $100,000. Insurance of at least $80,000 is necessary. But suppose, to save on the premium, you insure for only $60,000. Subsequently there

Fig. 26-3

Items Not Insured

Items Not Covered by Most Homeowners Insurance Policies:

- Articles insured separately (floater) such as jewelry, collections

- Animals, birds, fish, and other pets

- Motorized land vehicles (licensed for use), except for lawn mowers and things used on the property exclusively

- Stereos, radios, CBs, cellular phones or CD players in vehicles

- Aircraft and parts of aircraft

- Property of renters, boarders, and other tenants (unless they are related to the owner and not paying rent)

- Business property in storage, such as samples

- Business property pertaining to a business that is conducted at the residence (separate insurance is required)

- Business property away from the residence

is a fire, and damages total $40,000. In this case, you would collect 60/80 (75 percent) of the loss ($30,000). The insurance company will base its payment on the portion of coverage carried.

Physical Damage Coverage

Physical damage may be caused by such hazards as fire, wind, water, and smoke. These hazards can cause destruction of your property or temporary loss of its use. The main component of homeowners insurance is protection against financial loss due to damage or destruction to a house or other structures. Your dwelling and attached structures are covered for fire and other damages. Detached structures on the property, such as a garage or shed, are also protected. Trees, plants, and shrubs are included in the coverage.

Loss or Theft Coverage

Loss or theft coverage protects household property and personal belongings that are either in your home or with you when you are away from home. Valuables are insured in the event of burglary, robbery, or other damage. (Loss or theft insurance is included with homeowners and renters policies.)

A **personal property floater** may be purchased to protect specific items of high value. With a homeowners policy, there are limits on coverage of personal property. For example, your policy may pay up to

Loss or theft coverage protects household property and personal belongings.

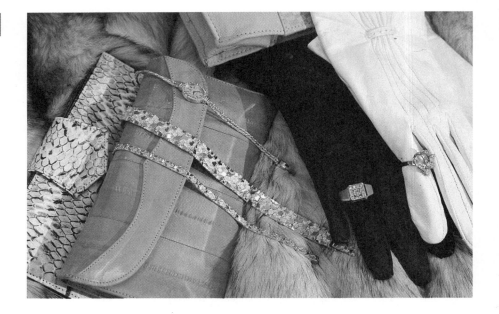

$1,000 for computers and related technology, $1,000 for jewelry, and $1,000 for collections. If, in fact, you have personal property worth more than these minimum amounts, you can protect them with a floater. A floater policy is basically a minipolicy. It covers high-cost personal property such as furs, fine jewelry, musical instruments, coin and stamp collections, art work, and the like. With a floater, property is protected without regard to its location at the time of loss. Rates are reasonable. For example, a camera worth $500 could be insured for about $20 a year. A floater requires a detailed description of the item and periodic appraisals to verify its current value.

Liability Coverage

Liability coverage protects you against expensive lawsuits arising from both property damage and bodily injury. For instance, if a guest in your home slips and falls, you may be held liable for medical expenses for a broken leg or other injuries. If you own a dog, you are responsible for acts of the dog. If the dog bites someone, you are covered for the medical expenses of treating the injury. If you damage your neighbor's home by burning leaves in your backyard, you are protected by personal liability coverage. If your child hits a baseball through a neighbor's window, you are covered for the physical damage caused.

All homeowners and landlords should carry liability insurance. Homeowners are responsible for acts occurring on their property, even acts involving *uninvited* persons. In most cases, a homeowner will not be held liable for damages when someone trespasses on her or his private property unless a trap is set with the intent to harm the trespasser.

personal perspective

U nderstanding an Insurance Policy

Many people who look at insurance policies find them difficult to read and understand. Consumers complain to state insurance commissioners that they do not know enough about insurance to know whether they are getting a good deal or a rip-off.

Most insurance policies contain a number of "standard" parts, including the declaration, the insuring agreement, the conditions, the exclusions, and endorsements.

1. **The Declaration.** This piece of paper is attached to the policy itself. It declares the property that is being insured, the dollar amounts of coverage and deductibles, and other basic information that applies specifically to one person's insurance policy. The declaration is different for every insurance policy.

2. **The Insuring Agreement.** This paragraph or section sets forth who is the insured and what coverages are specifically included in the policy. Often abbreviations are used that are explained in footnotes or small print.

3. **The Conditions.** This section explains the duties of the insured and of the insurance company. For example, it is the insured's responsibility to pay premiums on time and to meet conditions that were agreed upon in the setting of premiums. The insurance company will collect premiums, process claims, and pay the cost of damages as agreed.

4. **The Exclusions.** This section describes all circumstances that will not be covered. For example, intentional acts are not accidents and therefore may be excluded from coverage. Certain perils, property, and types of losses may also be specifically excluded, such as acts of war or civil disobedience.

5. **The Endorsements.** Any modification or addition to the insurance agreement is included as an endorsement. It should be noted that an endorsement can either add a coverage or delete a coverage. Endorsements can be added at a later date and serve to modify the original agreement.

The best protection, of course, is to read and understand all this information prior to signing and agreeing to pay the premiums.

critical thinking

1. Is an insurance policy a form of contract or agreement?

2. Why is it important to read through a policy, particularly the declaration and the insuring agreement?

3. What types of insurance policies have you seen, read, or examined carefully?

An **attractive nuisance** is a dangerous place, condition, or object that is particularly attractive to children, such as a swimming pool. If a child sneaks into a private pool without permission and is hurt, the homeowner will be held liable for damages and injuries. The owner is frequently responsible, even if steps are taken to prevent entry into the pool. (Liability coverage is included with homeowners and renters policies.)

utomobile insurance

All states have *financial responsibility laws.* These laws are intended to keep off the highways drivers who cannot pay for any property damage or injuries they cause. In most states, minimum automobile insurance is required for registration of a motor vehicle. If there is no insurance, a driver must put up tens of thousands of dollars in cash or personal property.

Automobile insurance provides protection to owners and operators of motor vehicles. It covers costs of damage to a motor vehicle, its owner, and any passengers. It also covers costs of repairs to other vehicles, medical expenses of occupants in other vehicles involved in an accident, and property damage (shrubs, trees, and fences). To these losses must be added those from theft. Each year at least one car in fifty is stolen. Many are found later, but most of them are damaged or stripped of parts.

Cost of Automobile Insurance

Automobile insurance is expensive. Premiums are based on a number of factors, such as model, style, and age of car; driver classification (age, sex, marital status, driving record); location (city, county) of driver and car; distances driven; purpose of driving (such as work); and the age and sex of other regular drivers of a car. Premium discounts are available for certain conditions, such as more than one vehicle insured with the same company, drivers education training, and good grades in high school (usually a B average or better).

A person's driving record includes the number and type of traffic tickets, called *infractions,* along with accident record. Arrests for serious traffic offenses, called *misdemeanors,* will result in increased insurance premiums. An infraction might be a parking ticket, failure to come to a complete stop at a stop sign, or an improper left hand turn. A misdemeanor would include speeding, driving without a license, or reckless driving. A serious traffic violation, such as drunk driving, hit and run, or leaving the scene of an accident, is a felony offense in many states. All these events not only increase your insurance premium, but remain a part of your driving record for at least three years. In many states, when drivers receive three or more tickets in a twelve-month period, they are required to take a drivers' safety course.

Except for vintage (antique) cars, the older the car, the less insurance that is required because the car is worth less. New and expensive cars cost more to insure because they are worth more (and would therefore be more expensive to repair or replace). Sports cars are more expensive to insure than family cars; young single drivers pay more for insurance than those over twenty-five and married; young male drivers pay more than their female counterparts. Certain geographic locations are considered more hazardous because of narrow roads, country roads, number of licensed drivers and cars in the area, and the local accident rates. The farther you drive on a regular basis (such as to work), the higher your insurance premiums. Who will be driving, primarily and occasionally, will also be a factor in determining cost. Adding a teenage driver to an existing policy will increase premiums. Another important consideration is the number of claims filed. When you file too many claims, your premiums increase.

Types of Automobile Insurance Coverage

There are five basic types of automobile insurance. These include liability, collision, comprehensive, personal injury protection (PIP), and uninsured/underinsured motorist. All types of insurance purchased in a single policy is known as *full coverage*. Figure 26-4 shows a comparison of coverages for automobile insurance.

Liability Coverage

Most states require all drivers to carry liability insurance. **Liability coverage** protects the insured against claims for personal injury or damage to another person or his or her property. However, the insured would receive nothing for his or her losses (either personal injury or damage to the vehicle). Payments under liability coverage are only for injuries and damages caused to others. It is important to note, however, that if an accident is not your fault, the liability coverage of the other driver will pay for damages to your car. If, however, the accident is your fault and all you have is liability coverage, your insurance will not pay for the damages to your car.

Liability insurance coverage is usually described using a series of numbers, such as 100/300/50. The numbers mean that the insurance company will pay up to $100,000 for injury to one person, $300,000

Fig. 26-4

Automobile Insurance

AUTOMOBILE INSURANCE

	Who Is Protected:	
	Policyholder	**Other Persons**
Liability coverage:		
Personal injuries	No	Yes
Property damage	No	Yes
Collision coverage:		
Damage to insured vehicle	Yes	No
No-fault provision	Yes	No
Comprehensive coverage:		
Damage to insured vehicle	Yes	No
Personal injury protection:		
Medical payments	Yes	Yes
Pedestrian coverage	Yes	No
Uninsured/underinsured motorist coverage:		
Bodily injury	Yes	Yes

total for all persons, and $50,000 for property damage in an accident. Premiums charged for liability insurance vary according to the amount of coverage.

Collision Coverage

To cover repair or replacement of your own car, you purchase **collision coverage.** This will pay for the damage to your car in the event you are at fault and the other driver's liability insurance does not pay. Most collision coverage has a deductible. For example, you may pay the first $100 or $500, as specified by your policy, for repairs, and the insurance company pays the rest. Because many minor traffic accidents involve damage that costs less than many deductibles, it is wise to have a larger deductible and pay lower premiums. In other words, paying the first $250 for each accident might be less expensive than having a $50 deductible and paying higher insurance premiums.

Comprehensive Coverage

Damage to your car from events other than collision or upset is covered by **comprehensive coverage.** Events other than collision include fire, theft, tornado, hail, water, falling objects, natural disasters, and acts of

Collision coverage covers repair or replacement of your car.

vandalism. For example, if your car is scratched while parked in a mall lot, or if it receives a broken window or dent from a flying rock or golf ball, your insurance pays for this type of damage. In the event someone breaks into your car and steals your camera, comprehensive coverage will pay replacement cost. Usually, there is a very small or no deductible for comprehensive coverage.

Personal Injury Protection (PIP)

Commonly known as medical coverage insurance, **personal injury protection** (PIP) pays for medical, hospital, and funeral costs of the insured and his or her family and passengers, regardless of fault. If the insured is injured as a pedestrian or bicyclist, this personal injury protection insurance will pay the medical costs. To reduce costs for insurance, buy a car with airbags, antilock brakes, and other safety devices that lower the risk of injury.

Uninsured/Underinsured Motorist Coverage

Uninsured/underinsured coverage protects you in the event you sustain a bodily injury because of the acts of an uninsured or underinsured motorist. An uninsured motorist does not carry required insurance. An underinsured motorist has policy limits that are too low to cover all of your injuries.

Your injuries are covered just as if the driver causing the accident had insurance. Typically, it pays for car rental, medical, and other costs that would have been paid by a fully insured motorist. Your insurance company will attempt to recover this amount from the uninsured or underinsured motorist. You should also know that uninsured motorist coverage protects you as a pedestrian if you are hit by an uninsured vehicle.

No-Fault Insurance

In many states **no-fault insurance** laws provide for the repair or replacement of your car by your insurance company, regardless of who is at fault at the scene of the accident. Payment for repairs is made by each insurance company to its own client. Repairs are made and paid for; then the insurance companies settle the costs later, based on which driver is at fault.

The basic idea behind no-fault insurance is solid: it could take years to settle a case and determine fault. Even then, a driver with no assets and no insurance will not be able to fix the car or pay for damages as a result of his or her negligence. It was also hoped that by reducing the number of lawsuits, more money could go to injured people and get to them faster.

A good no-fault law balances payment of benefits with lawsuit restrictions. There are a few good no-fault laws, such as the one found in Michigan, where accident victims get all of their expenses paid by their own insurance companies. The Michigan law restricts lawsuits, and victims can sue only if an accident results in death, permanent disfigurement, or serious impairment.

Assigned Risk Policies

If you have an accident that costs your insurance company large sums of money for property damage, injuries, or liability settlements, you may find that your insurance coverage is cancelled. The number of traffic citations and fines on your record may also cause your insurance company to cancel your policy. At that time, you may be forced to look for insurance elsewhere.

Every state has an *assigned risk pool* that consists of people who are unable to obtain automobile insurance. Some of these people are assigned to each insurance company in the state. As a member of an assigned risk pool, you will pay several times the normal rate for insurance premiums until you are able to establish a good driving record.

mbrella liability insurance

In the previous two sections, you will recall that liability insurance is needed by homeowners to protect them from claims of others who may be injured on their property, and that liability insurance is required in most states as minimum automobile coverage. For people who maintain required minimum liability coverage on their automobile and home, they can also purchase an *umbrella liability policy* to pick up where the other coverage left off. An **umbrella policy,** also called a personal catastrophe policy, supplements your basic personal liability coverage.

An umbrella policy would generally pay up to $1 million or $2 million for any accidental injuries caused to another person—while the insured is driving, for an accident that occurred on the insured's property, or in the course of the insured's employment. This type of policy protects you from extraordinary losses—extremely high claims because of unusual circumstances. For example, you may be involved in an automobile accident where a person receives a permanent injury. Medical costs may exceed $500,000 with additional costs for many years to come. As long as you carry minimum liability requirements on your automobile insurance, the umbrella policy would cover the rest.

Summary

Property insurance protects you from losses due to damage, theft, and liability. Renters policies protect personal possessions on the premises of someone else's property. A homeowners policy contains coverage for your place of residence and its associated financial risks, such as damage to personal property and injuries to others. A homeowner should document the value of his or her property through a household inventory. Personal property is protected by a floater when value exceeds standard amounts.

Overinsuring is unwise. Insurance companies will pay only the replacement cost of property. Insurance adjustors determine the value of damaged and destroyed property; insurance investigators look for evidence to sustain claims. Extended coverage (called an endorsement) is available for disasters or events not covered in a basic insurance policy.

Underinsuring property can be as unwise as overinsuring. A co-insurance clause requires that insurance coverage equal or exceed a percentage (usually 80 percent) of the replacement cost. If insurance is less, then only a percentage of the claim will be paid.

Driver classifications are assigned based on age, sex, marital status, driving record, and driving habits. The category you are in will determine the auto insurance rates you must pay. Accidents, tickets, and insurance claims will raise your premiums: If you have your insurance cancelled because of a poor driving record, you may be a part of an assigned risk pool where you will pay several times the regular rates for insurance.

Liability insurance on automobiles is required in most states. Cost of automobile insurance varies widely and is based on a number of factors. Collision, comprehensive, personal injury protection, and uninsured/ underinsured motorist coverage are also available for automobiles. When all these coverages are included, it is known as comprehensive coverage.

No-fault insurance was intended to reduce lawsuit costs and leave more money for accident victims. With no-fault laws, each insured receives benefit from his or her own insurance company. Long delays to determine fault are not needed.

An umbrella liability supplements basic personal liability coverage. Extended liability policies are sold in amounts of $1 million or more and are especially useful to individuals with substantial net worth.

ocabulary terms

Directions: Can you find the definition for each of the following terms used in Chapter 26?

attractive nuisance   *liability coverage*
coinsurance clause   *no-fault insurance*
collision coverage   *personal injury protection*
comprehensive coverage   *personal property floater*
endorsement   *renters policy*
homeowners policy   *umbrella policy*

1. Provides coverage for perils such as floods and earthquakes not generally covered by standard homeowners policies.

2. A policy clause requiring the insured to carry coverage equal to or exceeding 80 percent of the replacement value of the property.

3. Protection against claims for injury to a person or damage to property.

4. An automobile insurance program in which drivers involved in an accident collect medical expenses, lost wages, and related injury costs from their own insurance company.

5. Medical insurance coverage that pays for medical, hospital, and funeral costs of the insured and passengers involved in an accident, regardless of fault.

6. Supplementary personal liability coverage; also called a personal catastrophe policy.

7. Insurance that protects personal property and provides liability coverage for tenants.

8. Package that covers a wide range of risks for the owner of a home.

9. A special provision to increase amounts of coverage for specific property items such as jewelry or collectibles.

10. A dangerous place, condition, or object particularly attractive to children.

11. Automobile insurance that protects a person against accident-related damages to his or her own car.

12. Automobile insurance that protects a person against nonaccident related damages to her or his own car.

Facts and ideas in review

1. What are the three basic types of property insurance coverage?
2. Explain the differences between a renters policy and a homeowners policy.
3. Give several examples of an attractive nuisance.
4. Explain the principle of indemnity.
5. What are some items typically excluded from property insurance?
6. What do insurance adjustors and insurance investigators do?
7. Explain the concept of coinsurance.
8. What is the purpose of financial responsibility laws?
9. List several factors that affect the cost of automobile insurance.
10. How are infractions different from misdemeanors?
11. What is the purpose of automobile liability insurance?
12. Describe the difference between comprehensive physical damage coverage and collision coverage.
13. Why should a person carry uninsured motorist protection?
14. Explain the concept of no-fault insurance.
15. Why should a person purchase an umbrella policy?

Applications for decision making

1. Prepare a household inventory, listing only the contents of your room or one room in your home. Follow Figure 26-2 as an example. Next to each item, record its approximate value and indicate whether or not you have a receipt to prove its cost and a photo of each item.
2. Write a few paragraphs discussing the perils of overinsuring or underinsuring property. Be specific in the consequences that may result in either case. How can you be sure that you are insuring property for its appropriate replacement value? (Hint: Ask people who have property insurance how they determined value, such as the assessed valuation as provided on property tax rolls.)
3. Outline ways you can protect valuables from being stolen from your home or automobile. Complete research to determine the cost of protection devices or services.

4. Get a price quote for full coverage automobile insurance on the automobile of your choice. Determine ways to reduce premium costs through discounts or other methods. Write a paper reporting your results.

5. What type and how much liability coverage is required in your state for drivers of automobiles? How are financial responsibility laws enforced? For example, is vehicle insurance tied to vehicle registration? What are the fines or penalties if a driver is caught without insurance? You can get information on this subject from a driver's manual, or look in the library for relevant laws (statutes).

6. Interview an insurance agent about the need for umbrella liability insurance in your state. Ask questions about coverage availability, maximum policy limits, and premium costs. Also ask about exclusions—what situations would not be covered by the policy.

 ife situation problem solving

1. Your friend Allison is renting an apartment. She has nice furniture that she inherited from her grandparents. One day while you are having lunch, she mentions to you that last year the pipes burst in her apartment building and she was lucky that her valuable furnishings were not damaged. You ask if she has renters insurance, and she says no, the landlord has insurance. What do you advise her?

2. As a first-time house buyer, your friend Mark is considering what type of insurance to buy. Describe the types of insurance that Mark might consider. (Refer to Figure 26-1.)

3. Your neighbor owns a particularly valuable collection of antique plates. She estimates their value is more than $10,000. When talking about the plates, you learn that she has homeowners insurance but no personal property floater for the plates. Explain to her the reason for a floater.

4. Your friend Shelley owns a home that has a value of $80,000. Her insurance policy has an 80 percent coinsurance clause. She has the property insured for $40,000. Later that year, she experiences a fire that causes damages of $25,000. How much insurance will she be able to collect?

5. Your friend Ken is complaining about the high cost of automobile insurance. He really would like to own his own car but, at age 19, he feels he can't afford the insurance premiums. Discuss with him ways he can reduce the amount of insurance premiums.

6. Benito Mendoza carried the following insurance on his car at the annual costs shown:

Comprehensive physical damage	$ 80
Property damage liability ($25,000)	70
Bodily injury liability (100/200)	175
Collision ($250 deductible)	150
Total Premium	$485

As a result of an accident in which Benito was negligent, the driver of the other car was awarded $9,800 for injuries to himself and $2,100 in damages to his car. Benito's auto was damaged at a cost of $820. His medical bills were $135.

a. How much did the insurance company have to pay in claims as a result of the accident?

b. What is the maximum the policy would pay for injuries to the other driver?

c. Provided the premiums stayed the same, how many years' premiums would be required to equal the total paid by the insurance company as a result of this one accident?

objectives:

After reading and studying this chapter you will be able to:

27-1 Describe the need for health insurance, types of health insurance coverage, and health plans available to consumers.

27-2 Discuss the availability, need, and cost of disability insurance.

27-3 Explain the need for and types of life insurance plans that are available to American consumers.

In addition to homeowners and automobile insurance, individuals and families also need protection from losses due to sickness, diseases, injuries, or the death of a wage earner. These types of losses are serious because income is disrupted and the family must make lifestyle adjustments. In some cases, these types of losses result in bills that can be overwhelming and force a person into bankruptcy. In this chapter, you will learn about health insurance coverage and its importance to all people, about disability insurance and how it works, and about life insurance—who needs it and the best type to buy.

Health and Life Insurance

chapter 27

ealth insurance

In the last decade the cost of medical care, from office visits to hospital charges and laboratory tests, has escalated rapidly. Workers with no health insurance provided through employment have been unable to afford individual health insurance policies. Many millions of Americans have not received proper medical care because they had no insurance.

Employers who have provided health insurance coverage for employees have been faced with increases in insurance premiums, often 10 percent or more a year, and have searched for ways to control costs. This phenomenon has led to health care reform with a target of universal health care or insurance for all citizens. Many states have implemented health care reform in order to meet the needs of vast numbers of uninsured individuals and families.

The rapidly escalating cost of health care has become a national problem.

Insuring Against Losses

Health insurance is a plan for sharing the risk of financial loss due to accidents or illnesses that result in large medical bills. Health insurance reduces risk by spreading it among many individuals and groups. The insured pays a premium for the insurance, which guarantees coverage. Health insurance, like other forms of insurance, reduces the financial burdens of risk by dividing losses among many individuals. Health insurance is sold by insurance companies on a group or an individual basis.

The most common type of health insurance is **group health insurance.** Group plans share risk among a large number of people, usually employees. All those insured have the same coverage and pay a set premium for insurance. Pooling of resources in this manner allows for greater coverage and lower premiums. Some companies or groups pay the premiums as a fringe benefit to their members. More commonly, however, as in the case of employer and employee, the two share the premium costs. Over 70 percent of all health insurance is issued in the form of group health insurance plans. An individual's coverage cannot be canceled by the insurance company unless the person leaves the group or the group plan itself is terminated. Also, when employees covered under a health plan leave their employer, voluntarily or involuntarily, they are allowed to participate in the policy for a limited period of time (usually eighteen months) until they find another employer and insurance plan.

Individual health insurance policies can be purchased by individuals and families. The premiums are usually high. Most individual policies require a physical exam for coverage. Moreover, individuals may have to wait a certain length of time (usually ninety days) before coverage begins. (Members of group plans receive immediate coverage.)

Most states require that some type of individual policy be available for purchase by people who do not have group policies. States have high-risk insurance pools whereby people with preexisting conditions (such as diabetes) can buy insurance. Unfortunately, the premiums are often very high and placement on a waiting list can exclude a person from coverage when it is needed.

Supplemental health insurance is available in addition to group or individual plans. This type of policy would pay benefits after the individual or group plan is exhausted. Generally, it is designed to pay high deductibles and copayments (the first 20 percent that the insured must pay) as well as medical fees that are higher than a policy allows. For example, a group plan may pay up to $350 a day for a hospital room, but the charges may come to $400 per day. A supplemental policy would pay the difference of $50 per day.

If a couple or family has more than one group insurance plan, benefits are coordinated. **Coordination of benefits** limits reimbursement for expenses to 100 percent of allowable medical expenses. For example, if a couple has two policies—one through the husband's employer and one through the wife's employer—then one policy may pay 80 percent of the medical expenses and the other the remaining 20 percent. The couple would not be reimbursed for more than 100 percent of the expenses incurred.

Types of Health Insurance Coverage

There are several standard types of health insurance coverage: basic health insurance (medical, hospital, and surgical), major medical insurance, dental, and vision insurance. The main purpose of these kinds of coverage is to protect consumers from doctor and hospital bills that could ruin them financially. Figure 27-1 summarizes good health insurance coverages.

Fig. 27-1 **Health Insurance Coverages**	**What a Good Health Insurance Plan Provides:** • Basic coverage for hospital and doctor bills; a reasonable copayment of $5 to $15 per visit or 80 percent of reasonable charges • Cost of prescriptions, with a reasonable copayment of $5 to $15 per prescription • At least 120 days of hospital stay coverage, with insurance paying at least 80 percent with a stop-loss provision of $1,000 • A yearly deductible of $150 per person or $450 per family before medical and hospital benefits begin • No unreasonable exclusions; no preexisting conditions that would not be covered • At least a $1 million lifetime maximum for each family member (major medical) • Reasonable coverage for dental and vision care, with low deductible ($50 per person) and at least 80 percent coverage of all procedures, excluding orthodontics

Basic Health Insurance

Medical expense insurance helps pay for physician care that does not involve surgery. This type of coverage pays for office visits and routine services, such as X rays and laboratory tests. Hospital coverage pays for hospital bills for room, board, and drugs while in the hospital. Surgical coverage pays for part or all of a surgeon's fees for an operation. Usually the types of surgery are limited and must be necessary (not cosmetic or elective). The three types of insurance (medical, hospital, and surgical) are called *basic health insurance*.

Major Medical Expense Insurance

Major medical coverage provides protection against the large and catastrophic expenses of a serious injury or illness. Coverage is beyond basic health insurance and typically extends to a maximum of $100,000 to $1 million or more. For example, when a patient is admitted to the hospital for a bone marrow transplant, organ transplant, or some other major type of surgery, the cost can be $500,000 or more.

The major medical coverage often has a *coinsurance provision* requiring the insured to pay 20 percent of all bills. However, a *stop-loss provision* would generally provide that after the insured has paid $1,000 (or some specified amount) in deductibles and coinsurance payments, the rest would be fully paid by major medical.

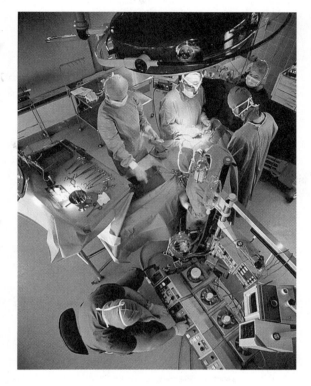

Major medical insurance provides protection against the large expenses of a serious injury or illness.

Dental and Vision Insurance

Many group plans also provide for dental coverage. Most dental plans have low deductibles and coinsurance requirements of 20 percent or more. They also pay maximum amounts, such as $1,500 per year per person, and cover only certain types of services, such as exams, X rays, and fillings. Some services, such as crowns or bridges, are often paid for at a much lower rate (such as 50 percent). In some cases, only certain types of services are covered. For example, the cost of an amalgam filling (metal) is far less than a porcelain filling. Most dental policies will pay only for amalgams except when the filling is in the front teeth. The insured must pay the difference as well as any costs exceeding the "prevailing fee range." For instance, if your dentist charges $130 for a porcelain filling, and your insurance allows only $75, then insurance will pay 80 percent of $75 and the insured pays a 20 percent copayment.

Vision insurance pays for medical exams and lenses. The insured can have an eye examination on a regular basis—once every few years—and purchase single-vision correction lenses. Typically not covered are sunglasses and contact lenses.

Private Health Plans

Employee health plans are grouped into two categories: unmanaged and managed. An *unmanaged (traditional fee for service) plan* allows employees to choose doctors and to be reimbursed for usually 80 percent of the expenses incurred after a deductible of $100 to $250 per patient. This is the most expensive of all plans because there is no strict control on costs or services.

The *managed plan* adds requirements such as preapproval for surgery or hospital admission, second or third opinions, and control over what types of services are provided and the maximum benefits allowed for those services. Preferred provider organizations and health maintenance organizations are examples of managed care plans.

A **preferred provider organization (PPO)** is a group of health care providers (doctors and hospitals, for example) who band together to provide health services for set fees. Patients must choose doctors from an approved list. There are limits on types of services that can be provided and fees that can be charged. There is usually a small copayment of $5 to $15 per office visit and for prescriptions.

A **health maintenance organization (HMO)** is a group plan offering prepaid medical care to its members. An HMO often has its own facilities and usually provides a full range of medical services. Employees must choose from the doctors on the staff of the HMO. The advantage to an HMO is that routine preventative care, such as routine physical exams, is generally covered. The idea of an HMO is to encourage people to come in for treatment before a minor ailment becomes a major problem. The HMO patient often pays no deductible or copayment; still, the costs of running an HMO are often lower than other health plans, resulting in savings to employers who enroll employees in an HMO.

Self-Insurance Plans

Some larger employers (with usually 100 employees or more) may elect to self-insure. Rather than contract with an insurance company, a company will collect insurance premiums from employees to pay medical benefits as needed. Based on mathematical probability, the plan works on the assumption that only a small number of employees and their families will need extensive health care in a given period of time; if medical costs exceed money in the plan, then the company pays the difference to cover the cost of medical care. Often self-insured companies contract with insurance companies to process claims made against the company's insurance plan.

Medicare and Medicaid

Medicare is health insurance provided to people currently age 65 and older. (For people born after 1960, the age for benefits will be 67.) Medicare is funded by employee payroll deductions (currently 1.45 percent of all money earned). Coverage is paid through the Social Security Administration. Like other plans, there are maximum benefits, exclusions, and other requirements. Retired persons pay a monthly premium for medicare insurance. *Medigap* insurance (a supplemental private insurance policy) often pays the amounts (deductibles and copayments) not covered by medicare.

Similarly, *medicaid* is a health insurance program available to people who are qualified under state welfare and public assistance programs. This program is designed to help families who are in poverty and are unable to afford health insurance or medical care. Like medicare, there are limitations and exclusions.

Income protection insurance

Disability insurance is a plan to provide regular income during a period when a person is injured or ill and unable to work. This type of insurance is frequently referred to as *income protection* because coverage compensates employees and their survivors from loss of income resulting from illness, accident, or death. Generally there are two types of disability insurance: short-term and long-term. *Short-term disability insurance* provides benefits for up to two years. For periods over two years, and up to retirement, *long-term disability insurance* is needed.

Of all types of insurance, disability insurance is the most overlooked. People think nothing can happen to them that will interrupt their earning power. Unfortunately, recovery from an accident or an illness can extend for several weeks or even months. Yet while you are disabled (unable to perform your job), your regular living expenses go on. Disability insurance benefits are payable when you are unable to work at your job; as soon as you are able to return to work, benefits cease.

Disability coverage requires a *waiting period*. In other words, benefits don't begin the day you are disabled. The waiting period may be from 30 to 180 days. (The longer the waiting period, the lower the premium.) During this time, an employee would likely be on sick leave and would be collecting regular pay.

Employees and their survivors are protected from loss of income through disability or income protection insurance.

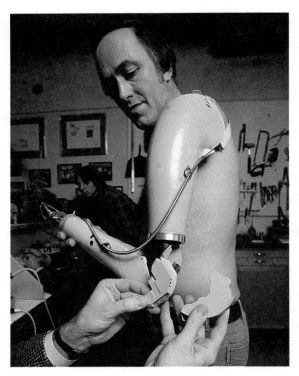

The maximum *duration of benefits* under most disability policies would be until age 65 or early retirement if you qualify. A few policies pay benefits for life if you become permanently disabled. In addition, the maximum amount you can collect is usually 50 to 75 percent of your regular pay. (The lesser the percentage, the lower the premium.)

Guaranteed renewability of coverage will protect you against cancellation if your health turns bad. Without this provision, an insurance company can refuse to renew your insurance. The premium for renewability is higher, but the coverage is well worth the extra cost.

Prior to disability insurance, people who missed work because of an injury or illness lost more from missed paychecks than from medical bills. Disability insurance was set up to protect against such loss of income. This kind of coverage is quite common today, and several hundred insurance companies offer it to individuals, employees, or both.

Before purchasing an individual disability insurance policy, remember that you may already have this insurance, such as from your employer and social security. In addition, you may also be eligible for income protection from the Veterans Administration (if you served in the military), civil service disability income (if you worked for the government), state welfare benefits, automobile insurance disability benefits, and many other potential sources depending on your situation.

Group Disability Insurance

Group disability insurance plans are generally the least expensive option. In many cases, the employer pays for part or all of the plan. Unfortunately, the insurance is good only as long as you work for the employer; when you leave, you lose all policy rights. In most cases, your employer pays part or all of the cost of this plan.

Social Security Disability Insurance

Most of the salaried workers in the United States participate in the social security program. You will recall from previous chapters that social security is more than retirement income. Social security is OASDI (old age, survivors, and *disability* insurance) as well as HI (health insurance—medicare). Because you have social security deducted from your paycheck, you are entitled to disability payments from social security in the event you cannot work. To qualify, you will have to prove the extent of your disability, fill out forms, and have medical exams as required by the Social Security Administration. Workers are considered disabled if they have a physical or mental condition that prevents them from doing any gainful work, and the condition is expected to last for at least twelve months or result in death. Your benefits are determined by your salary and by the number of years you have been covered under social security.

Workers' Compensation Insurance

This type of insurance covers your expenses if your injury or illness occurred at your place of employment or resulted from your employment. If you are partially or totally permanently disabled, workers' compensation will pay monthly benefits. Another benefit is a death benefit (a burial payment and an allowance for living expenses for survivors) for persons who are killed during the course of employment. Like social security benefits, these benefits are determined by your earnings and your work history.

ife insurance

Life insurance provides protection from the financial loss that might otherwise occur when someone dies. Most people buy life insurance to protect someone who depends on them from a financial loss caused by death. Consider the financial needs that will exist for a family after the death of a wage earner—and how much income will be needed to pay the ongoing expenses of daily living. The purpose of life insurance, then, is to protect others who are dependent on you as a source of income. Figure 27-2 is a list of purposes that are often identified for life insurance policies.

Like all types of insurance, life insurance is based on risk sharing and probability. To predict the likelihood of death occurring, insurance companies use *mortality tables*. Mortality tables are based on statistics

Fig. 27-2

**The Purposes of
Life Insurance**

Why You Should Purchase Life Insurance:

- to pay off a home mortgage and other debts at the time of death
- to provide lump-sum payment to children when they reach a specified age
- to provide an education or income for children
- to make charitable bequests after death
- to provide for retirement income
- to accumulate savings
- to make estate and inheritance tax payments
- to take care of children's needs as they are growing up
- to provide cash value that can be borrowed

gathered about length of life in this country. Based upon these tables and the age and sex of the insured, a premium is assigned that is based on the likelihood of death while the policy is in effect.

When purchasing life insurance, keep in mind that it is based on the assumption that the insured is of average health and physical condition. A person with a health problem, such as a heart condition, may be uninsurable. Life insurance premiums are low for young people because their risk of death is low.

To obtain life insurance, you must submit an application for insurance. The application usually has two parts—in the first part you state your name, age, sex, occupation, type of policy desired, how much coverage you want, and so on. In the second part, you give a detailed medical history and personal information. You may be required to have a medical examination, especially for large policies. The insurance company determines your insurability based on the application.

Group life insurance can often be purchased cheaply through an employer. However, when you terminate employment, you cannot take the coverage with you. Group insurance is term insurance, which is described on pages 658–659. A *group insurance plan* insures a large number of persons under the terms of a single policy without a medical examination. Employers often provide group life insurance as a fringe benefit.

Provisions of Life Insurance Policies

An important provision in every life insurance policy is the right to name your beneficiary. *Beneficiaries* are people who will inherit money at the death of the insured. Most married couples name each other as beneficiaries; children may also be named, or if the children are minors, an estate may be named to administer the money on behalf of the children. Life insurance policies are generally not taxable (for income tax purposes).

An **incontestability clause** is a provision preventing an insurance company from cancelling an insurance policy in force for a specified period of time (usually two years). After the specified period, the insurance company cannot dispute its validity during the lifetime of the insured for any reason, including fraud. A reason for this provision is that the beneficiaries should not be made to suffer because of acts of the insured.

A **suicide clause** provides that if the insured dies by suicide during the first two years a policy is in force, the death benefit will equal the amount of the premiums paid. After two years the suicide becomes a risk covered by the policy and the beneficiaries of a suicide receive the same benefit that is payable for death from any other cause.

A life insurance **rider** is any document attached to the policy that modifies the coverage by adding or excluding conditions or altering benefits. Riders are extra-cost features that insurance agents like to tack onto policies.

Guaranteed insurability riders give a policyholder the right to buy a new policy or additional coverage without showing evidence of good health. Many life insurance policies contain *accidental death* riders. In the case of accidental death, some riders allow *double indemnity*. This means that the beneficiary is paid twice the face amount of the

Most married couples name each other or their children as beneficiaries.

insurance. To collect this benefit, the insured must die within a certain time after the injury (and death must be directly related to the injury), and death must occur before the insured reaches age 60 or 65. A *waiver of premium* rider allows you to stop paying premiums and keep your coverage in force if you become disabled and cannot work. This rider usually does not kick in until you've been disabled at least six months.

Types of Life Insurance

There are two major types of life insurance policies: temporary insurance and permanent insurance. Temporary insurance exists only as long as the policy is in effect. Typically, there is no savings or cash value. With permanent insurance, however, a residual or cash value is present, and the insurance policy represents a form of savings plan.

Temporary Life Insurance

Term insurance is protection for a specified period of time, usually twenty years or up to age sixty-five. Term policies are sometimes called "pure" insurance because when you are through paying the premiums, the policy lapses. The insured receives protection for the specified period, but afterwards nothing remains. Term insurance pays death benefits only if the insured dies during the period covered. There are two types of term insurance: decreasing term and level term.

With *decreasing term insurance*, the amount of coverage decreases each year while the premium remains the same. A twenty-year decreasing term policy decreases in coverage each year until the value reaches zero at the end of twenty years. If the insured dies during the first year of the policy, it pays the full benefit (let's say $100,000). If the insured dies during the second year, death benefits decrease to $95,000. In other words, the coverage of the policy decreases gradually each year.

Level term insurance (also called renewable term) is renewable yearly, every five years, or every ten years. Some policies guarantee the insured the right to renew his or her coverage without passing a physical examination. When the policy is renewed, however, the premiums go up while the face value (the amount the policy will pay in the event of death) remains the same. A policy with a face value of $100,000 might have premiums of $150 the first five years, $175 for years six through ten, and $200 for years eleven through fifteen. The premiums increase because, as you get older, the risk of death to the insurance company is greater.

Another type of temporary life insurance is *credit life* or some version of it, such as mortgage life insurance. Credit life is used to repay a debt should the borrower die before doing so. You can obtain this type of coverage from the lender; however, in most cases it would be cheaper to buy term insurance.

point counterpoint

T erm Insurance versus Cash Value Insurance

Insurance agents and some personal financial planners make money (commissions) from the insurance products they sell you. Some will try to convince you to buy expensive life insurance containing special features, even if it is not the best financial choice for you. The sale of expensive life insurance means higher commissions for agents.

They will give you a computer print-out of how much money you will have saved, along with the insurance benefits in the event of death, compared to how much you would have without a cash value policy. But there are a couple of things they might not tell you, and when you have the full story, you might make a different decision.

First, consider the *time value of money*. When an agent tells you that setting aside a certain amount today will be worth so much in the future, he or she is giving you an example of the time value of money. In other words, as the money is paid into an insurance fund, it earns interest. Over a period of years, interest is compounded, so the cash value would grow at a more rapid rate. If you were to take the same amount of money and set it aside in a savings account, you would likely have just as much money—possibly even more—because you wouldn't be sharing the gain with the insurance company, and you wouldn't be paying commissions and fees.

Second, the agent is giving you a future value of money and comparing it to nothing. That is, the agent assumes that if you don't save through insurance, you would save absolutely nothing. Keep in mind that you have other options. You can buy cheaper term insurance and invest the savings. With some diligence on your part, you can earn a better rate of return than the insurance company provides.

Before you buy insurance, ask yourself these questions: Why do I need the insurance? If the answer is to pay for children's living expenses, then you must ask another question: Will I need the insurance after the kids are grown and gone? In other words, if your insurance needs decrease, then you have a temporary insurance need.

However, if you need long-term protection and a savings plan, then you may have a need for a cash value policy. In this case, it is best to buy insurance as soon as possible—you can get much lower premiums when you are young.

critical thinking

1. Have you ever purchased something—a good or service—because you felt pressured by a salesperson? Did you later regret the purchase?

2. What type of life insurance needs do you have currently? What type of needs do you think you will have in the next five years?

3. Can you explain the concepts of compound interest and the time value of money?

Term insurance policies can have additional features, such as optional conversion to a whole life policy or double indemnity. Additional features generally raise premiums, however, and beyond a certain age, term insurance may not be renewable. Therefore, term insurance is temporary protection. Benefits are paid only if the policyholder dies within the specified period of coverage. The main advantage of term insurance is its cost, which is very low compared to permanent coverage.

Permanent Life Insurance

Permanent insurance offers protection plus cash value. **Cash value** is the amount of money available to the policyholder to borrow during the life of the policy or at discontinuation of the policy. Permanent insurance policies build cash value and remain in effect for the insured's entire lifetime. There are four basic types of permanent life policies: straight life, limited-pay life, universal life, and variable life.

Straight life (also known as whole or ordinary life) is a policy under which premiums are paid throughout the life of the insured, and a stipulated sum is paid at death to a beneficiary. The amount of your premium depends primarily on the age at which you purchase the policy. One important feature of the straight life policy is the buildup of cash value.

Limited-pay life is a policy on which premiums are limited to a specific number of years (such as twenty years) or until age sixty-five. At the end of the payment period, the policy is considered "paid up." However, you remain insured for life and the company will pay the face value of the policy at the insured's death. Limited-pay policies build cash value. The policyholder can borrow against the cash value. This loan does not have to be repaid, but it will reduce the death benefits.

Universal life provides a savings plan in combination with life insurance for the policyholder. The policyholder gets two things—insurance, together with a guaranteed savings plan that gains cash value. The amount of insurance coverage can be changed more easily in a universal life policy than in a traditional policy. In other words, the face value of the policy can be reduced or raised without rewriting the policy. The interest rate earned on the cash value of the policy is geared to market rates. An increase in the cash value of a universal life policy reflects the rate of interest earned on short-term investments.

Variable life is similar to universal life. Universal life combines insurance with a savings plan; variable life combines insurance with investment options. Variable life policyholders pay fixed regular premiums. Part of the premium is invested by the insurance company in securities chosen by the policyholder. Because the policyholder can choose among investment opportunities, variable life is considered a "security" by the government. Policyholders designate what portion of the net premium (the amount left over after insurance expenses) is to be invested in stocks, bonds, or short-term money market instruments. Both the death benefit and the cash value rise (or fall) with the investment results. While a minimum death benefit is guaranteed, there is no guaranteed cash value.

Summary

The cost of medical care has risen dramatically in the last two decades. Today, it is difficult for families to afford health insurance except as it is provided by their employers. Group health insurance provides most of the health insurance coverage today.

Basic health insurance includes (1) doctor visits and routine service, (2) hospital, and (3) surgical expenses. Major medical insurance protects a person from large and catastrophic expenses of injury or illness. Dental insurance provides reimbursement for the expenses of dental services and supplies and encourages preventative dental care. Vision care is another aspect of many group health plans.

There are two major types of health insurance plans: unmanaged and managed. HMOs are the fastest growing type of managed care insurance plan. A preferred provider organization, or PPO, is one of a group of health care providers (doctors and hospitals, for example) who band together to provide health care services at a discount. In addition, medicare and medicaid are health insurance for retired people (65 and older) and for people who qualify for public assistance.

Disability insurance is the most often overlooked type of insurance. Disability insurance is designed to protect your income when you are unable to work due to an injury or illness. There are two types: short-term (up to two years) and long-term. In addition, social security and other disability benefits may be available.

Life insurance protects a family from loss when a wage earner dies. Life insurance policies can give protection for a limited period of time or for life. There are two main categories of life insurance: temporary (term insurance) and permanent (straight life, limited life, universal life, and variable life). Life insurance benefits are not taxable for income tax purposes.

27

Vocabulary terms

Directions: Can you find the definition for each of the following terms used in Chapter 27?

cash value
coordination of benefits
disability insurance
group health insurance
health insurance
health maintenance
  organization (HMO)

incontestability clause
life insurance
preferred provider
  organization (PPO)
rider
suicide clause

1. A method of integrating the benefits payable under more than one health insurance plan.
2. Provides payments to replace income when an insured is unable to work.
3. Any document attached to a policy that modifies its coverage.
4. A plan for sharing the risk of financial loss due to accident or illness.
5. Insurance protection from the financial loss that occurs when a wage earner dies.
6. A provision that prevents an insurance company from cancelling an insurance policy after a certain period of time, even for fraud.
7. Excludes death benefits for suicide within the first two years that a policy is in force.
8. The most common type of health insurance, which is a plan for sharing risk among a large group of people.
9. A group of health care providers who band together to provide health services for set fees.
10. A group health insurance plan offering prepaid medical care to its members.
11. An amount that increases over the years you own the life insurance policy and that you receive if you cancel the policy.

Facts and ideas in review

1. Why have health care costs risen so rapidly in the last decade?

2. What is the most common type of health insurance—individual or group policies? Why?

3. What is supplemental health insurance? Who should buy it?

4. What is covered by basic health insurance?

5. What is major medical insurance?

6. How is a managed plan different from an unmanaged (traditional) plan of health insurance?

7. What is the difference between an HMO and a PPO?

8. How is medicare different from medicaid?

9. What is the purpose of disability insurance?

10. What is meant by short-term and long-term disability insurance? Briefly describe each.

11. Name and describe at least four sources of disability (income protection) insurance.

12. Why would a person need to have life insurance?

13. Why do you suppose life insurance policies have suicide clauses?

14. What are the two types of term insurance? Explain each.

15. What are the three types of permanent insurance? Briefly describe each.

 pplications for decision making

1. Do a mini-research project gathering information about the costs of health care in the last decade. Magazines, newspapers, and books report the costs and trends. Write a paper describing what has been happening and who is to blame. (You will note that various sources blame each other.) Make your own determination based upon findings.

2. Interview a person who has recently had surgery or been in the hospital for several days or longer. Ask them about the type of services provided and the approximate cost per day of those services. Ask them how much of the cost was paid by insurance and how much (percentage or dollar amount) they will have to pay themselves. Write a report on your findings.

3. Obtain a brochure describing the benefits of a group health insurance plan. If you don't know someone who belongs to this type of plan, your local library will have information about nonprofit plans, such as Blue Cross or Blue Shield. Write a paper summarizing your findings—types of coverages, deductibles, copayments, exclusions, and so on.

4. Complete a research project on medicare or medicaid. Find out what types of medical/hospital/surgical and major medical coverages are provided and how much of these costs are paid by the patient. Based on your findings, do you feel that medigap insurance is a good value for a person on medicare?

5. Prepare an analysis of your disability needs, assuming that you are working full-time, are married, and have one child. Pick a career that you would like to have and use a realistic amount of income for a beginning worker (with 1 to 3 years of experience).

6. Examine the list of insurance needs shown in Figure 27-2. Can you add anything to this list? Can you delete anything? Prepare a list of insurance needs based on your personal situation as you imagine it in ten years.

 ife situation problem solving

1. Your friend is considering two career opportunities—one in which she will be an independent contractor and have no benefits provided, and one in which she would work as an employee of a company and have full health insurance as well as other benefits. Explain to her the importance of having health insurance benefits.

2. A young couple who lives near you is a dual-income family. Both have full medical coverage provided through their employers. They figure that this "double coverage" will pay off if they get injured or become ill because they can claim benefits twice. Explain to them the concept of coordination of benefits for group health insurance policies such as theirs.

3. A cousin of yours is working but cannot afford to buy an individual health insurance policy. His employer does not provide a group plan. Explain to him the importance of major medical coverage.

4. Your friend George is working full time at two jobs in order to make house payments and buy a new car. His wife Helen is working nights so she can care for the children during the day. George can purchase both short-term and long-term disability insurance for a small premium ($10 a month) through his employer's group insurance plan. Explain to them the importance of disability insurance.

27

5. As a young, unmarried person, you are contemplating college next year and the pursuit of a professional degree that will take six years or more to complete. A neighbor of yours sells life insurance and wants you to buy a universal life policy with a $100,000 face value. Explain to him what type of policy, if any, you would consider purchasing.

6. You and your spouse are in your mid-twenties. You are expecting your first child. Both of you are presently working. You hope to buy your first house in the next few years. Discuss your need for life insurance and the type of life insurance you would purchase now and five years from now.

financial checkup

6

Financial Checkup 5:
Managing Personal Risks

In this financial checkup, you will learn more about risk and insurance. You will also do some further exploring and assessing of insurance needs and plans for the future. You'll learn how to compute the true cost of insurance, how to file an insurance claim, what to do if you have an accident, what you can do to reduce health insurance costs, how to use mortality tables, and how to build a good lifetime insurance plan.

The True Cost of Insurance

When people buy insurance they usually feel that it is money spent for protection against the risks of financial uncertainty and unexpected losses. The alternative—being uninsured—represents large and undefined risks that can leave you feeling uncomfortable. Since the alternative of not being insured is usually unacceptable, most people are covered by some type of insurance most of their lives.

Let's look at automobile insurance first. A full-coverage policy would likely have these coverages:

Liability coverage, 100/300/50	$260
Collision coverage, $50 deductible	180
Comprehensive coverage, $50 deductible	120
Personal Injury Protection	80
Uninsured/Underinsured Motorist	60
Towing	15
Total annual cost	$715

If you make monthly payments, they would include an additional $2.50 per month (for the convenience of monthly billing), adding an extra $30 to your yearly insurance costs. To avoid this extra cost, pay semiannually or have automatic monthly deductions from your checking account.

If this motorist was willing to increase the amount of the deductibles, the savings could be considerable. Let's assume that a $250 collision deductible would reduce the cost of this coverage by $50 a year. Over a five-year period, total insurance costs would be:

Full coverage, $50 deductible:
$715 × 5 = $3,575

Full coverage, $250 deductible:
$665 × 5 = $3,325

Savings: $250

In five years, you would have saved enough in premiums to pay for the $250 in loss, should it occur. What's important is to check options for saving on insurance premiums, calculate the savings over time, and thus make an educated decision.

Another example of saving on the premium is shown in Figure FC5-1 where you would decide when it would be wise to drop collision coverage on your car.

Assuming the annual cost of collision insurance is $180:

1. If a car is new it is a good value—keep collision.

2. If a car is 5 years old then determine its value:
   If $3000 or over, it is a good value—keep collision.
   If less than $3,000, reduce coverage.

3. If a car is older than 5 years:
   If it is antique or has collector's value, keep collision.
   If it is worth $1,000 or less, drop collision coverage.

Once a car is below $3,000 in value, it is advisable to look closely at the need for collision coverage.

Fig. FC5-1

The Cost of Collision Insurance

Let's now compute the cost of a whole life insurance policy and compare the results to the purchase of term insurance. To do this, we must use the time value of money concept—the fact that money will grow over time because it is earning interest.

Suppose a young person, age 25, purchased a $100,000 face value whole life policy. The annual premium for this policy is $250. The policy will pay a guaranteed rate of 6 percent (on the policy's cash value) after the first year. At the end of the first year, there is no cash value. The entire premium is used to cover commissions and policy costs. After the first year, a portion of the premium covers the cost of insurance and the balance is deposited in a savings plan. The amount deposited accumulates as cash value.

In the example below, the death benefit remains at $100,000 over a five-year period. During this time, the cost of insurance rises slightly each year, leaving a smaller amount of the premium for savings.

unit

Assuming the 6 percent rate holds, the cash value of the policy after five years would be $626.28. (See the table that follows.)

Year	Premium	Insurance Cost	Savings Plan Deposit + Interest	Cash Value at Beg. Year
1	$ 250.00	$100.00	$ 0	$ 0
2	250.00	102.00	148 + 0	148
3	250.00	104.00	146 + $ 8.88	302.88*
4	250.00	106.00	144 + 18.17	465.05
5	250.00	108.00	142 + 19.23	626.28
Totals	$1,250.00	$520.00	$580 $46.28	$626.28

*(Assume the full premium is paid at the beginning of each year. To compute the interest earned at the end of Year 2, multiply $148 times 6 percent. Then add the deposits of $148 and $146 to interest earned of $8.88 to derive the Year 3 cash balance of $302.88.)

As an alternative, this person purchases a term insurance policy instead of whole life insurance. The term premiums are as follows: $100 (Year 1), $102 (Year 2), $103 (Year 3), $104 (Year 4), and $106 (Year 5). The difference between the whole life premium and the term premium is deposited at the beginning of each year in a 6 percent savings account. (Assume, of course, that $150 is invested in Year 1; $148, Year 2; $146, Year 3; $144, Year 4; $142, Year 5.) With whole life insurance, the cash value is $626.28. The accumulated value of the savings account at the end of five years would be $873.79. The difference is $247.51. (See the table that follows.) A higher savings balance can be achieved through buying term insurance and saving on your own.

Year	Beginning Balance	Deposit	Interest	Ending Balance
1	$ 0	$150	$ 9.00	$159.00
2	159.00	148	18.42	325.42
3	325.42	146	28.29	499.71
4	499.71	144	38.62	682.33
5	682.33	142	49.46	873.79**

**The total saved at the end of five years is $873.79.

Complete Worksheet 1 in the *Student Activity Guide* to compute the future value of savings between different life insurance policies. (This Worksheet is also shown at the end of this Financial Checkup.)

How to File a Claim

When you have sustained a loss, such as fire damage to your home, you now must file a claim. In order to receive compensation for the insured property, you must be organized and prepared before you file a claim. First, you should know your policy and its coverages, limitations, and exclusions.

You should keep receipts and other documentation of value. If you own any antiques, collectibles, or other items for which you have no receipt, you should have the items appraised so that you will have a certificate of authenticated value. Such an appraisal may cost you $50 or more, but it will save you considerable time when filing a claim.

If property is stolen, you should call the police and fill out a report. Without evidence of a break-in or other such documentation (like a police report), the insurance company has no way of knowing whether or not the incident took place. Remember, you must take ordinary precautions against break-in and theft. If, for example, you leave your car unlocked, the insurance company may not pay benefits for stolen property. You should have good notes about what was taken, any witnesses, time of day, what you observed, and so on.

If property is damaged, you will need to get repair estimates—usually more than one. Be sure to contact your insurance company right away, and have documentation and notes ready. The insurance adjustor will take your report and ask you questions. It's important to be clear and accurate when supplying information.

Figure FC5-2 is a sample claim form that you would fill out with an insurance company to report damage to property you have insured under a homeowner's policy. Fill out Worksheet 2 based on the hypothetical information provided. (This Worksheet is in the *Student Activity Guide* and also shown at the end of this Financial Checkup.)

What to Do If You Have an Automobile Accident

Sooner or later, it is likely to happen to you. Either as a driver or as a passenger, you may be involved in an automobile accident. Most accidents are the result of human error. The higher the speed, the higher the likelihood of a serious injury and damage to property.

If you are involved in an accident, there are several things you must do. Figure FC5-3 on page 671 lists standard procedures to follow. Your state may have additional things you should do, or not do, following an accident. You will find this information in your state's driver's manual or similar publication from the motor vehicles division or licensing department. You should be familiar with this information before an accident occurs.

Your state has accident reporting forms; get one and fill it out for a fictional situation. In most cases, you have only three days (72 hours) to fill out an accident report once you are in an accident.

How to Reduce Health Care Costs

Whether you have health insurance or not, it's important to minimize health care costs. The best way to avoid high medical costs is to stay

unit

Claim No._____

Name of Insured _____
Address _____
_____ Phone _____
Policy No._____ Agent _____

Describe what happened: _____
_____
_____
_____

Was a police report filed?_____ Case No. _____
(Attach copy)

Police officer taking report_____

Were there any witnesses?_____ List their names and addresses:
_____
_____

Description of property damaged_____
Value of property_____
Date purchased_____ Purchase price _____
Where purchased_____ Receipt?_____

Where is property now located (for inspection)?_____
_____
_____

_____   _____
Date   Signature of Insured

well. Corporations across America are realizing the importance of "wellness" programs in an attempt to keep their employees healthy. Here are some fundamental ways you can stay healthy:

1. Eat a balanced diet and keep your weight down.
2. Avoid smoking.
3. Don't drink to excess.
4. Get sufficient rest and relaxation.
5. Drive carefully; avoid and reduce risks where possible.

When you do visit doctors and use health care services, there are additional ways to minimize your costs and your insurance company's costs. Figure FC5-4 on page 672 lists some methods of reducing health care costs and maximizing the benefit from services that you can use.

Complete Worksheet 3 in the *Student Activity Guide* to answer questions about your responsibilities in helping to reduce health care costs. (This Worksheet is also shown at the end of this Financial Checkup.)

unit

If you are involved in a motor vehicle accident, standard requirements are as follows:

1. Stop your vehicle, turn off the ignition, and remain at the scene of the accident. If feasible, pull your car to the side of the road so you won't impede traffic.

2. Get the names and addresses of other drivers, passengers, and witnesses. Make notes of what happened, including time of day, weather conditions, roadway location, signal lights, and so on. Write down vehicle license numbers.

3. Fill out the necessary accident report forms within the time requirements in your state (usually 3 days). Give a copy of the report to your insurance company. Also obtain a copy of the police report, if any.

4. Provide assistance to persons who are injured; seek medical help if needed. Stay at the scene of the accident until all needed information is exchanged and all involved parties leave the scene.

5. Always have your insurance and vehicle registration information with you. Get insurance and vehicle registration information from the other driver; copy it from the documentation rather than taking it down orally.

6. Know the laws of your state. There may be additional requirements where you live.

Life Expectancy and Mortality Tables

In a current edition of an almanac, you will find both life expectancy tables and mortality tables. For example, a person born in 1994 was expected to live 72.0 years if a man or 78.8 years if a woman. For a person who was 45 in 1994, life expectancy was another 30.8 years for men or 36.0 years for women.

Another table shows life expectancies over time. For example, in 1920, the average life span was 54.1 years (53.6 for men and 54.6 for women). By 1970, the average life span had risen to 70.8 (67.1 for men and 74.7 for women).

Life expectancy and mortality tables are used by insurance actuaries in setting life insurance premiums. A mortality table matches age with a mortality rate and sets a premium accordingly. Figure FC5-5 is an excerpt of a mortality table from the American Council of Life Insurance.

unit

How to Cut Health Care Costs

When you are the patient, whether or not insurance is involved, you can maximize your health care dollars by:

1. Knowing your insurance coverage, limitations, and exclusions.

2. Taking insurance information with you when visiting a hospital or doctor's office and when picking up prescriptions.

3. Taking a list of questions with you to the doctor. Take notes so you will remember specific answers.

4. Giving your doctor information needed to make correct diagnoses. Write down symptoms, relevant past history, what you have done or taken so far, and related information.

5. Asking the doctor about short- and long-term side effects of prescriptions. Read prescription directions and information supplied by a pharmacist and/or the manufacturer.

6. Getting second (and third) opinions for any type of surgery or medication with serious risks or potential for side effects.

7. Predetermining fees and services that will be provided for treatments, surgeries, and lab work. Exclude tests or costs that you can cover in less expensive ways. For example, you can go to a local clinic and have a cholesterol test for $5 to $10. At a doctor's office, it can cost you five to ten times that amount.

8. Using generic medicines.

9. Being cautious and asking lots of questions. Remember: You are in charge of your health care and the doctor is assisting you, not the other way around! Take charge of your own life, nutrition, and lifestyle and know what it takes to stay healthy and strong.

Mortality Table (partial)

Age	Deaths per 1,000	Life Expectancy (Years)
25	1.11	59
30	2.33	48
40	3.21	37
45	4.58	33
50	5.86	28
55	8.44	21
60	12.88	18
65	17.22	15
70	26.10	13

unit 6

Building a Personal Insurance Plan

As you make choices about the type and amount of insurance you will purchase, keep the following guidelines in mind. They can save you money, time, and energy as you build your personal insurance plan:

1. To avoid billing fees, have premiums deducted automatically from your checking account, or pay them quarterly or semiannually.

2. Be sure to read through the policy carefully. If you discover a clause you do not understand, call your agent immediately for clarification.

3. Review policies regularly to see if the coverage meets your needs. As your family situation changes, you might wish to modify your life insurance coverage. As your car gets older, you should consider dropping collision insurance.

4. Consider carefully the outcome of switching insurance companies or changing policies. If you do, be sure you are approved for the new insurance—and that it is correct as represented—before dropping your old insurance.

5. Get to know your insurance agent. Use his or her expertise—ask lots of questions and be sure you understand all coverages, limitations, exclusions, and so on. Discuss your changing needs and get his or her recommendations, but make your own decisions.

6. Don't hold onto policies or companies for sentimental reasons. Be a wise comparison shopper. When you are certain you can do better with another company, and have taken proper precautions, move forward to secure a new policy.

7. Don't keep overlapping policies with the hope of making a quick profit off insurance claims. Group policies require coordination of benefits. Private policies that overlap coverage in a group policy can be very expensive.

8. Use deductibles wisely! By paying the first part of an expense yourself, you can save a bundle on insurance rates.

9. Keep your insurance up-to-date. Pay premiums promptly and take advantage of any discounts available. Ask regularly about what new discounts, such as for nonsmokers, are available to reduce premiums.

Complete Worksheet 4 in the *Student Activity Guide* to review what you have learned about preparing a personal insurance plan. (This Worksheet is also shown at the end of this Financial Checkup.)

WORKSHEET 1

Computing Future Value

Assume that you purchased a whole life policy for $100,000 and your premiums were $300 a year, with $150 covering insurance and $150 directed to your savings plan. The insurance cost increases by $3 every year. You are guaranteed 5 percent interest on your savings for the first five years, but will not earn interest until the end of the second year.

Required:

1. Prepare a table that lists how much total premium you will have paid in five years, total insurance cost for five years, and the balance in your savings portion at the end of five years for the whole life policy. (See page 668.)

2. How much would you have had in savings if you had bought a term policy for $150/year (for 5 years) and put the remainder in a savings account at your bank with interest compounding at the rate of 4 percent a year?

unit

WORKSHEET 2

Insurance Claim Form

Directions: Fill out the claim form below based on the following information. The insured is Mary B. Ownbey, who lives at 845 Oak Street, Wellington, Ohio 45887. Her phone number is (202) 555-0180. Her policy number is KN338-44-2281, and her agent is G. Smiley. Her home was broken into sometime between 8 p.m. and 2 a.m. (Friday evening) while she was away. The kitchen was vandalized (spray paint on the walls and eggs thrown on the floor); the carpeting in the dining room was stained as well. A police report was filed (Case 95-2288) by Officer K. Bridges. There were no witnesses. The walls in the kitchen must be scraped and painted; the carpeting must be cleaned or replaced if the stain cannot be removed. The value of the damage is estimated at $500. The house was painted last year ($100 for the kitchen walls); the carpet was new a year ago ($2,000 for the damaged carpeting). Both were purchased at Excel Interiors and she has a receipt. The property is located in the home at the above address. Use today's date.

Claim No. _____

Name of Insured_____

Address _____

_____ Phone_____

Policy No. _____ Agent_____

Describe what happened: _____

_____

_____

_____

Was a police report filed?_____ Case No. _____
(Attach copy)

Police officer taking report_____

Were there any witnesses?_____ List their names and addresses:

_____

_____

Description of property damaged _____

Value of property_____

Date purchased _____ Purchase price_____

Where purchased _____ Receipt?_____

Where is property now located (for inspection)? _____

_____

_____   _____
Date   Signature of Insured

unit

WORKSHEET 3
Reducing Health Care Costs

Directions: Answer the following questions about ways you can reduce health care costs.

1. Do you eat well-balanced meals and exercise regularly?

2. Do you get sufficient rest and relaxation?

3. Do you know your health insurance coverages, limitations, and exclusions?

4. Do you use generic prescriptions where possible? (Generic drugs are less expensive versions of brand-name drugs. Because there is no advertising or other expenses of mass marketing, the cost is lower.)

5. Do you shop around for the best prices in (a) dental work, (b) vision care and glasses, (c) prescriptions, (d) charges for office visits, and (e) supplies, vitamins, and other health care purchases?

6. List some things you and your family can do to reduce health care costs.

7. Explain why it is important to ask questions when you visit your doctor.

unit 6

WORKSHEET 4

Your Personal Insurance Plan

1. Explain the purpose of each of the following types of insurance.

   a. Homeowners insurance:

   b. Automobile insurance:

   c. Liability insurance:

   d. Health insurance:

   e. Disability insurance:

   f. Life insurance:

2. Based on your current situation, what types of insurance do you currently purchase?

   a. Homeowners insurance:

   b. Automobile insurance:

   c. Liability insurance:

   d. Health insurance:

   e. Disability insurance:

   f. Life insurance:

3. How do you anticipate your need for each of these insurance coverages will change in the next five years?

   a. Homeowners insurance:

   b. Automobile insurance:

   c. Liability insurance:

   d. Health insurance:

   e. Disability insurance:

   f. Life insurance:

4. List several guidelines for building a plan for purchasing all types of insurance.

unit 6

looking back . . .

In Unit 6, Risk Management, you learned about risk and ways to manage it. You learned about different types of risk and how to analyze and assess risks you face. While insurance is important, you should also consider reducing, avoiding, and self-insuring so that you can get the best value for money spent on insurance.

Automobile insurance is likely to be your first encounter with insurance. Liability coverage is required in most states; as you know, it only protects the other driver and his or her property. Remember to drive carefully and do whatever you can to take advantage of discounts available to you.

As a renter, you need a policy covering your personal property. A landlord cannot insure your personal possessions. When you buy your first home, you will find the main types of home insurance policies are the basic, broad, special, and condominium forms. These policies differ in the risks and property they cover.

Health insurance is protection that provides payment of benefits for covered sickness or illness. Group insurance is the least costly protection against economic losses due to illness, accident, or disability. Disability income insurance benefits provide regular cash income lost by employees as the result of an accident, illness, or pregnancy.

Most people buy life insurance to protect someone who depends on them from financial losses caused by their death. The amount of your premium depends primarily on the age at which you purchase the insurance. Temporary, or pure insurance, is the best buy. And the money you save by buying term insurance instead of permanent insurance can be invested or used to meet other needs.

unit seven

A PUBLICATION OF CONSUMERS UNION · NO ADVERTISING

Blazer, Explorer, Land Rover

KEEP AWAY FROM
DANGER—

AS WITH MOST ELECTRICAL APPLIANCES
DRYER ARE ELECTRICALLY LIVE EVEN W
TO REDUCE RISK OF DEATH BY EL
1. ALWAYS "UNPLUG IT" AFT
2. DO NOT PLACE OR STOR
   PULLED INTO TUB, TO
3. DO NOT USE WHILE
4. DO NOT USE NEAR
5. IF DRYER FALLS IN
   REACH INTO WAT

100% COTTON

MADE IN
U.S.A.

consumer rights and responsibilities

7

objectives: *After reading and studying the chapters and completing the exercises and activities, you will be able to:*

1 Describe the basic characteristics of the marketplace and the free enterprise system, identify fraudulent and deceptive practices, and wise consumer behavior.

2 List consumer legislation and sources of consumer protection; describe how to contact public officials to express opinions.

3 Discuss the court system of the United States and at the state level where consumers can get redress, along with other ways of finding remedies to consumer problems.

looking forward

Unit 7, Consumer Rights and Responsibilities, focuses on the role of consumers in determining what is produced and sold. For the average consumer, the modern marketplace presents many challenges. The number of products available is large. The products themselves are often complex, and the methods used to sell them are sometimes misleading. To cope, consumers need protection.

In Chapter 28, you will examine the market economy in which you live. It is an economy based on consumer sovereignty, or power. You will explore wise buying practices and uncover both your rights and your responsibilities in a fast-moving and competitive marketplace.

In Chapter 29, you will take a look at federal laws and agencies that have been formed in the past few decades to help protect you. You will learn about the Consumer Bill of Rights that was introduced by John F. Kennedy to protect consumers in the marketplace. In addition, you will discover many types of national, state, and local agencies that provide consumer assistance and information. In the event you ever want to express your opinion to an elected official, you will learn one way to do so.

In Chapter 30, you will learn about the legal system of the United States. The federal court system, along with state court systems, is a tiered network of courts for the handling of legal cases. You'll learn about how a trial happens—the personnel, the process, and the results. Sometimes a lawsuit isn't the best answer to a problem, so you will also discover other methods of reaching redress, from negotiating to small-claims courts and governmental assistance.

objectives:

After reading and studying this chapter you will be able to:

28-1 Understand the basic characteristics of the marketplace.

28-2 List and describe the three basic components of a free enterprise system.

28-3 Describe deceptive practices used to defraud consumers and explain how consumers can protect themselves.

28-4 Explain wise buying practices and consumer rights and responsibilities when making purchases and resolving problems.

terms to know:

market economy
producers
consumers
supply
demand
advertising
competition
price-fixing
purchasing power
transfer payments
bait and switch
referral sale
fake sale
lowballing
pyramid schemes
consumer redress

chapter

n the United States, we live and work in a free market economy—an economic system in which people's decisions act as votes. When consumers buy a particular product, they are casting their dollar votes for that product. After the "votes" are counted, producers know what people want. Because producers are always looking for goods and services that consumers will buy, the consumer plays a key role in determining what businesses produce. To cast your vote wisely in our economy, you need to be aware of fraudulent and deceptive practices and how you can protect yourself. You also need to know how to resolve problems when you encounter them. In brief, you will learn about the market economy and its components, and about how you can protect yourself from being taken advantage of.

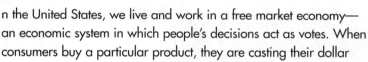

Role of the Consumer in the Marketplace

28

Characteristics of the marketplace

In the United States we have a **market economy.** A market economy is one in which producers and consumers are free to engage in business transactions. Both producers and consumers play an active role in the operation of the system. **Producers** are citizens and businesses that make products and services available for others to purchase. **Consumers** are citizens and businesses that purchase and use the goods and services produced for sale. Everyone is a consumer; that is, everyone must consume at least some goods and services produced by others in order to live. Many consumers are also producers; that is, they provide goods and services for others to consume.

Within a market economy, it is the consumer's role to maximize his or her satisfaction or *utility* for each dollar spent. Because you have limited resources (money), but unlimited and increasing needs and wants, as a consumer you should spend your money wisely.

The United States has a market economy involving producers and consumers.

On the other hand, it is the responsibility of producers to provide goods and services that will be purchased by consumers and meet their needs. In doing so, producers must make wise decisions so they can maximize their *profits*. In other words, producers will make certain decisions in order to find ways to sell more products for a profit.

Supply and Demand

Supply and demand are the key factors that determine what product or service is produced, in what quantity it is produced, and at what price it is sold. **Supply** is the quantity of goods and services that producers are willing and able to provide. **Demand** is the willingness and ability of consumers to purchase goods and services at certain prices.

Generally, if consumers demand a product (are willing and able to buy it at a certain price), producers will make it. The system works like this: Increased demand pushes up the price of the product. The high price brings large profits to the producers. High profits attract more producers and often cause current producers to make more of the product, increasing the supply. Attracted by profits, other producers start selling the same or similar products. But more supply means that consumers can pick and choose. In order to sell their product, producers must reduce their prices. Reducing prices in turn lowers profits.

Consumer Power

Consumers have the ultimate power in a market economy; consumers determine what is produced and at what price. Collectively, consumer buying decisions direct the production of goods and services. When consumers purchase a good or service, they are casting dollar votes for continued production of that good or service. If consumers refuse to buy a good or service, the price will drop. When the product or service still does not sell, it will no longer be produced. Producers will only supply those goods and services that people want and are able to buy. Thus, in our market economy, consumers actually exercise the power to determine what will be produced and at what price. There are, of course, exceptions to this rule, as in any economy; but generally the consumer plays a vital role in the marketplace through decisions to purchase or not to purchase goods and services.

Advertising is intended to influence consumer buying decisions.

Advertising

Producers also have power in a market economy because they can employ various techniques to affect consumer buying decisions. Advertising is perhaps the method most commonly used to induce consumers to want products. **Advertising** is the communication of product information through mass media to the consumer for the purpose of increasing the demand for a good or service. It can be informative and give important facts about quality goods and services. It can also be false and misleading and, unfortunately, damaging to the consumer's personal financial situation. In order to manage your personal finances successfully, you must learn to understand the role of advertising in our economic system and become a careful consumer.

 ssentials of a free enterprise system

Three basic conditions must exist for a free enterprise economy to function smoothly: competition, purchasing power, and informed consumers. If one of these conditions is missing or not functioning properly, the system begins to fail. The free enterprise system gains strength when each part of this triangle functions properly. Figure 28-1 illustrates the interplay of the three parts.

Fig. 28-1

Free Enterprise System

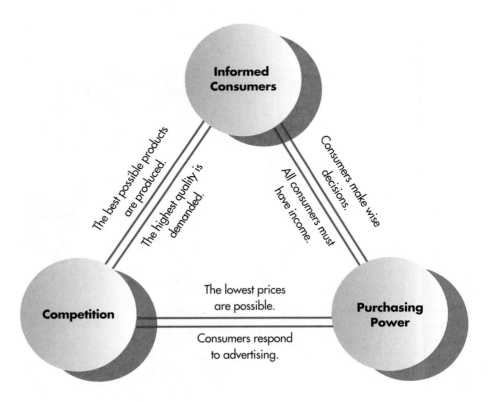

Competition

In order for prices to be based on supply and demand, competition is necessary. **Competition** occurs when there is more than one producer or supplier of a good or service. All producers must compete with each other to sell the same or similar products. When there is only one producer or supplier, a *monopoly* exists, and low-quality goods and services and high prices often result. When many producers compete to sell a product to the consumer, high-quality goods and services and low prices usually result.

It is not enough, however, for competition simply to exist. Competition must also be pure—without price-fixing or other controls. **Price-fixing** occurs when producers who are supposed to be competitors conspire to set the same prices on the same goods or services. There is no real competition because prices have been predetermined, or fixed. Price-fixing violates the principles of a free enterprise system, and it is illegal.

Purchasing Power

In our market economy, all consumers have purchasing power. **Purchasing power** is the amount of goods and services that can be obtained with a specific amount of money. In our country, virtually all persons have purchasing power. For instance, workers have income from their jobs. Children and minors have purchasing power through their parents.

Those persons who cannot or do not work may receive **transfer payments** from the government—money collected from employers and workers and distributed to those who do not work. Transfer payments may be "in kind" or "in cash." Food stamps and housing assistance are "in kind" benefits. Social security payments, veterans benefits, welfare and child assistance programs, and disability payments are examples of payments "in cash."

In this country, all persons have the ability to purchase goods and services. Purchasing power declines in a weak economy. That decline may be caused by *inflation*, in which prices increase faster than the value of goods and services. It may also result from a *recession*—a period in which production, employment, and income are declining.

Informed Consumers

A free enterprise system must have informed consumers who know their rights and responsibilities in the marketplace. When consumers make wise decisions, the system works to weed out inferior products and keep prices at acceptable levels. When consumers do not act in a responsible manner, prices increase.

raudulent and deceptive marketing practices

The marketplace is full of deceptive and misleading ways for suppliers to increase demand for a product—ways to induce consumers to buy goods and services of inferior quality or things they do not really need or want. Described in the following pages are a number of commonly reported fraudulent and deceptive marketing practices that all consumers should be aware of in order to protect themselves and their finances. In many cases, little can be done once the consumer has been duped into making a purchase. Dishonest sellers quickly disappear or deny wrongdoing. Therefore, consumers must educate themselves to recognize a potential fraud before they become victims. Prevention is still the best safeguard against financial misfortune.

Bait and Switch

The **bait and switch** technique is an insincere offer by a merchant who "baits" the buyer into the store by advertising an exciting bargain. When the customer arrives to purchase the advertised product, however, the merchant then switches the customer's interest to a more expensive product that will yield the merchant a higher profit. In some cases, the bait is a poor-quality product that is placed next to high-quality merchandise. The poor-quality bait is advertised to be of better quality than it is, giving the customer the idea that he or she is really getting a bargain. In other cases, when customers ask for the bait merchandise, they are told that it has been sold, but that comparable merchandise is available —for more money. Sometimes a crafty salesperson may try to convince the customer that he or she really does not want the bait item but rather a similar product of better quality—for more money. The bait and switch technique is a clever plan to get customers into a store to sell them more expensive merchandise than they had planned to buy.

A wise consumer knows products and prices. When a product is advertised at a special price, the consumer knows its quality and regular price. Product knowledge is gained by shopping around before making major purchases. In this way, consumers can protect themselves against the bait and switch technique.

Referral Sales

A **referral sale** means that the seller promises a money rebate, prize, or discount if the buyer can provide names of friends and acquaintances who are prospective customers. Such promises are illegal if actual

point counterpoint

B uy American

You may have read in newspapers and magazines about the trade deficit, about the disappearance of American manufacturing jobs, and about how we should "buy American first." In a global economy, products and services are available from around the world. And what you purchase will determine who will have jobs—and who won't. Let's look at both sides of the issue.

Side 1: Buy American—Your Job May Depend on It

When you buy goods and services, you support jobs. If you don't buy American cars, eventually there won't be any American cars. So who cares? You should! When people in America lose good-paying jobs, sometimes they can find other jobs and sometimes they can't. This will cost taxpayers added taxes to support the jobless. When good-paying manufacturing jobs are replaced with low-wage service jobs (the fastest-growing sector of the economy), there is less money to spend on the goods and services *you* produce. Therefore, as others lose their jobs and have less money to spend, you may be the next person to lose your job due to lack of demand.

Side 2: Buy the Best Value, Regardless of Who Makes It

The wide range of products available in a market economy makes it possible for almost everyone to satisfy their tastes. As a consumer, it is your job to maximize your utility, or satisfaction. If you buy a product that is not the best and the cheapest, you are not using your purchasing power wisely. Why should you buy a product that is inferior? Why should a company (such as an American car manufacturer) stay in business if it isn't producing the product you want to buy? In a market economy, consumers maximize satisfaction while producers maximize profits. Consumers have the right to buy only the best quality, lowest price products.

critical thinking

1. Do you buy American products first, or things made in your state first? Why or why not?

2. Do you agree that consumers have the right to purchase the best value, regardless of who makes the product? Why or why not?

3. Do you know of anyone whose job has been affected by changes in consumer buying decisions?

payment of the rebate, prize, or discount is not made. Delaying payment pending a sale, presentation, or other event is also illegal.

Referral sales techniques provide the seller with names, addresses, and telephone numbers of prospects. People on the referral list are expected to purchase the product because their friend gave the seller their names. Persons who volunteer the names and addresses of friends cannot expect appreciation from their friends. Sometimes friends are harassed by companies or organizations to purchase merchandise they do not want. Consumers should resist providing sellers with the names and addresses of their friends and acquaintances. The end of a friendship is a high price to pay for a discount or prize based on a successful referral.

Fake Sales

Probably the most common of all consumer frauds is the **fake sale.** A merchant advertises a big sale, but items are at regular price, or the price tags are disguised to show a price reduction when there actually is none. Often prices are increased just prior to the sale, and price tags are altered to show the so-called markdowns. The only way consumers can protect themselves from fake sales is to know products and prices and to plan purchases. Just because a flashy sign shouts "SUPER SAVINGS" does not mean that there are price reductions. Advertising campaigns, newspaper ads, and window signs may announce a big sale. Only a wise consumer is able to distinguish a real bargain from a fake sale.

Lowballing

Many repair businesses engage in the deceptive practice of lowballing. **Lowballing** is advertising a repair service at an unusually low price to lure customers, and then attempting to persuade consumers that additional services are needed. For example, when an appliance or implement is dismantled, other "necessary" repairs are discovered. The consumer is offered a special or regular rate for the additional repairs, and if the offer is refused, an extra fee is charged for reassembly.

Another form of lowballing is applying pressure, either bluntly or subtly, to convince an automobile owner that additional work is necessary for the safe maintenance of his or her car. For example, a repair shop may offer a special on brake relining. But when the brakes are inspected, several other "necessary" repairs are discovered. The customer may wind up with a front-end alignment, wheel balancing, or other repairs that are not really as urgent as the car owner is led to believe.

Consumers can protect themselves against this type of lowballing by stipulating that they want no repairs other than those agreed upon. Any repair other than the one specified must be authorized by the consumer after the repair shop has informed the consumer of the additional cost. Consumers should not pay for unauthorized work. Before having additional work done, the consumer should get a second opinion. The matter should be discussed with a spouse, a friend in the business, or someone who can offer an expert opinion. Consumers should indicate that no extra services or repairs beyond those advertised will be paid for without prior consent.

Another defense against lowballing is to deal with merchants you know or who are recommended to you by friends or relatives who have received good service. Check around with people who have had similar work done—ask neighbors, coworkers, and others. Check the reputations of businesses before you deal with them (call the Better Business Bureau in your area). In other words, ask questions and know what you need to have done before you take in your car or appliance for repairs.

Pyramid Schemes

Multilevel sales, called **pyramid schemes,** are selling schemes, illegal in many states, in which sellers are promised a lot of money quickly and with little effort for selling a product. A cash investment of some kind is usually required. The pyramid consists of managers or dealers at the top and a lot of middle and lower workers arranging parties, recruiting new salespersons, and selling products to friends and acquaintances. Having a lot of people selling products to their friends allows a manager to make big profits with little effort. However, the consumer finds it very difficult to make a profit or recover the initial cash investment because friends are unwilling to buy the product or service.

Pyramid schemes are often begun with a meeting in which a fast-talking and enthusiastic person convinces a group of people that they can make a fortune. They cannot lose; everyone can make it big! Unfortunately, the product is often not of high quality or even comparable quality to the same or similar products sold through regular retail outlets. In a relatively short time, there is neither profit nor sales because people will not buy the product more than once. Only persons at the top of the pyramid can expect to profit. The remainder, those persons at the bottom of the pyramid, are expected to continue mushrooming sales at an increasing pace. Increasing sales is not possible because the market becomes saturated, and sellers run out of friends who will buy the product.

The best defense against pyramid sales schemes is to remember that you cannot expect to make big profits without hard work. As the saying goes, "If it sounds too good to be true, it probably is." Before committing to such a plan, think it over for a week or two—and investigate the plan. Contact the Attorney General's Office, Consumer Affairs Division, to see if this practice is legal in your state. Talk to others who have purchased such merchandise; check with local consumer protection agencies; think it through. Ask yourself: Who will buy this product? Do I want to sell this to my friends and relatives? How much will I have to invest to get started? What happens if it doesn't work out? How much can I afford to lose?

Pigeon Drop

The term *pigeon drop* refers to any method used by experienced con artists to convince vulnerable people to invest in phony deposits, swampland real estate, or other swindles. People are said to be vulnerable when they are open to attack and easy to convince or persuade.

The pigeon is the unsuspecting consumer. People who have few defenses or little knowledge of such scams, but do have a source of money, are most often chosen. For example, older people on fixed incomes become the targets of fast-talking "financial experts." Older people may be asked to deposit their savings in an investment fund. These funds are then to be loaned out at high interest rates. Monthly payments are promised the pigeon for the use of his or her money. In some cases the pigeon is dropped (defrauded) immediately, and the trusted adviser disappears with the money. In other cases the swindler maintains an outwardly healthy business and pays dividends to the pigeon until it is no longer advantageous to do so. Then the swindler disappears with the investments. By maintaining a supposedly legitimate business for a period of time, the swindler can gain additional victims—friends eager to get in on the deal at the recommendation of the original pigeon. New victims are also dropped.

The best protection against this type of swindle is the local Better Business Bureau. The Bureau is equipped to investigate questionable schemes, so-called investment experts, and unsound business firms. Consumers should insist upon credentials, annual financial reports, and proof of past dealings. Trust in and trade only with ethical and established firms. Deposit your money in banks and savings and loan associations that are insured by the government.

Fraudulent Representation

Telephone or door-to-door sales made by persons who claim to represent well-known and reputable companies is a recent type of swindle. Consumers buy products or services and then learn that they have been sold rebuilt, stolen, or inferior merchandise with the reputable name on it. In some cases the product or service purchased is worthless or unusable. One such scam is the sale of discount coupons to be used in numerous restaurants and businesses. The coupons sound like a wise purchase because for a very reasonable price the buyer can save hundreds of dollars. But when the buyer presents the coupons for a discount or free merchandise, she or he discovers that the merchant has not authorized the coupon.

The buyer must be cautious in purchasing products or services from door-to-door salespersons.

Before buying a service or product from someone claiming to represent a major company, it is smart to check with the company. One phone call can save a lot of money. Don't feel compelled to buy a product when it is demonstrated. The local Better Business Bureau will have a record of salespeople who repeatedly engage in questionable practices.

Health and Medical Product Frauds

A common type of swindle involves deceptive advertising for expensive "miracle" pills, creams, and devices to enhance the consumer's health and beauty. Advertisements promise that these products can do everything, from growing hair on a bald head to helping a person lose ten pounds a week. The advertisements are designed to appeal to the typical consumer's desire to be healthy and attractive with little or no effort. Usually, deceptive health and medical advertisements carry endorsements and pictures of people who have found success using the product. Magazines, newspapers, and flashy tabloids often carry these advertisements. The manufacturers ask that you mail a sum of money to a post office address to receive one of the miracle devices or a quantity of pills or cream. Many times the money is accepted, but the product is not mailed to the consumer. If it is received, in most cases it is totally ineffective. Pills, creams, and similar products, when analyzed, may actually be sugar or an over-the-counter medication readily available for a much lower price in local stores.

Infomercials

An infomercial is a paid commercial advertisement of a product or service that includes testimonials, product demonstrations, and media presentation of the features of the item being offered for sale. These programs usually last fifteen to thirty minutes and target people with specific needs that are usually emotional—from weight loss to hair growth. While the product may be reputable, there is no guarantee, and claims about results may be greatly exaggerated. With infomercials, it is important to find out before you buy whether the business is reputable and the product works. Be cautious about giving credit card numbers over the telephone. Don't expect that because something "worked" for the paid actors describing the product on television that you will receive the same or better results.

he responsible consumer

Knowing the existence of various deceptive marketing tactics is the first step toward consumer responsibility. To keep our economic system running efficiently and to manage your personal finances successfully, you also need to learn how to protect yourself from becoming the victim of these fraudulent and deceptive practices. Prevention is the best protection; after you have been swindled, it is difficult to undo the financial damage you have suffered. In order to protect yourself, you must identify deceptive practices, use safeguards when buying, understand your rights and responsibilities, and seek redress when necessary.

Identify Deceptive Practices

When you hear certain types of claims, you should immediately be suspicious of possible deception. These warning signals include claims or offers made through advertising and by salespersons. Figure 28-2 lists common representations that catch your attention and are usually unreliable.

Watch Out When You Hear This:

1. Something can be obtained for free.
2. You will receive a free gift for an early reply.
3. You or your home has been specially selected.
4. High earnings can be made with no experience or little effort.
5. An advertising survey or questionnaire is being taken.
6. A no-obligation demonstration is offered.
7. You must decide immediately or lose the golden opportunity.
8. An incredibly low price is offered for a high-quality product.

Fig. 28-2

Warning Signals

Use Safeguards When Buying

The number of products available is large. The products themselves are often complex, and the methods used to sell them are sometimes misleading. To make wise buying decisions, follow these recommendations:

1. *Be aware of prices.* Know regular or "list" prices of common items. Terms often used in advertising, such as *manufacturer's list price* and

suggested retail price, and phrases such as "comparable value," "very important value," or "value $40, you pay only $35," attract your attention, but prices actually may not be reduced.

2. *Shop at several stores.* Comparative shopping is comparing quality, price, and guarantees for the same products at several different stores.

3. *Understand sale terminology. Sale* means that certain goods are offered at certain prices, but not necessarily at reduced prices. *Clearance* means that the merchant wants to clear out all the advertised merchandise, but not necessarily at a reduced price. *Liquidation* means that the merchant wants to sell immediately to turn the inventory into cash; again, prices may not be reduced.

4. *Avoid impulse buying.* Take a list with you when you go to the store or mall, and buy only what is on the list. Watch for displays of merchandise that attract your attention but are expensive and unnecessary.

5. *Plan your purchases.* Do not make major purchases during periods of emotional stress at the end of a crisis, during a time of loneliness or frustration, or at any time when your judgment is impaired.

6. *Compute unit prices.* Unit pricing is the determination of the cost per unit of items sold in quantity. The selling price is reduced to the lowest unit price. For example, to compare the price of a 15-ounce box with the price of a 24-ounce box, divide the price of each box by the number of ounces in each box. The result is the price per ounce of each box. The lowest unit price for products of comparable quality is the best buy. Figure 28-3 shows unit price computations.

Fig. 28-3	
Unit Pricing	Which is the better buy?
	A. 24 ounces for $2.59 or 15 ounces for $1.89?
	$2.59 ÷ 24 = 10.8 cents per ounce
	$1.89 ÷ 15 = 12.6 cents per ounce
	B. 3/89 cents or 6/$1.99?
	$ .89 ÷ 3 = 29.7 cents each
	$1.99 ÷ 6 = 33.2 cents each
	To determine unit pricing, divide the price by the number of ounces or units. This gives you a price per unit to compare to another price per unit.

7. *Read labels.* Know ingredients and what they mean. For example, a shirt that is 100 percent cotton will probably shrink, or if it is a dress shirt, it will probably have to be pressed each time it is worn. A product that says "Dry Clean Only" will be more expensive to maintain.

Read labels carefully on products you purchase, and check containers for damage.

8. *Check containers carefully.* Be sure packages have not been opened or damaged. Report any suspicious packaging defaults to the store manager.
9. *Read contracts.* Read and understand contracts and agreements before signing. Any warranties, guarantees, or other promises in writing should be retained for possible enforcement later.
10. *Compute total cost.* Check the total cost of an item, supplementary items (such as batteries), delivery charges, finance charges, and other add-on costs. In some cases, the base price may be lower but once added features are computed, the total cost exceeds other choices.
11. *Ask for references.* Ask for references from representatives of companies to be sure they really do represent the company. Call the company to check.
12. *Be loyal.* Patronize businesses that have good reputations and those at which you are a well-known customer. Tell others when

you have a good experience, and ask others for recommendations of doctors, accountants, repair services, and other businesses.

13. *Check up on businesses.* Check the validity of certifications, licenses, bonding, and endorsements. Use your local Better Business Bureau and state records divisions to be sure you are getting service from qualified and reputable professionals.

14. *Wait a day for major purchases.* Always wait at least twenty-four hours before making a major purchase. Be sure the purchase is not made on impulse and that you were not coerced into wanting the item. Many people change their minds after they have "cooled off" following a purchase.

Understand Your Rights and Responsibilities

Consumers who take precautions avoid many errors and later problems with their agreements and purchases. You are responsible for seeking information and advice to become knowledgeable of products and services before you buy. To protect yourself, practice doing the following assertive behaviors:

1. Be familiar with sources of information on goods and services, such as *Consumer Reports* and local agencies.
2. Read warranties and guarantees; ask questions so that you can fully understand performance claims. Get written guarantees and warranties whenever possible.
3. Read and understand care instructions before using a product.
4. Analyze advertisements about products before buying.
5. Insist upon enforcement of consumer protection laws—know how to get consumer redress.
6. Inform appropriate consumer protection agencies of fraudulent or unsafe performance of products and services. Do not hesitate to make your dissatisfaction known so that others may be helped and the product or service improved.
7. Suggest, support, and be aware of consumer legislation.
8. Report wants, likes, and dislikes as well as suggested improvements and complaints to dealers and manufacturers.

Seek Redress

When you have a complaint or need to solve a problem about a product or service, you have several consumer redress alternatives. **Consumer redress** is getting the action needed to resolve a problem with a product or service. Here are some suggestions for filing a complaint and resolving problems.

Complain first in writing to the person or company selling the product. Be specific about the problem. Produce evidence of the problem. Retain all warranties, sales slips, receipts, and related material. Send photocopies of necessary information to explain and support your position. Be firm; say that you are dissatisfied and explain why. Indicate the type of adjustment desired: refund, repair, replacement, or other action.

If the seller refuses to make an adjustment, then write to the manufacturer or distributor and state your complaint. Indicate that you previously wrote to the original seller of the product. Be specific. Enclose a copy of your letter of complaint to the company that sold you the product or service. Send photocopies of evidence, such as sales slips, warranties, receipts, or anything else that will help you support your position. Be firm and again state the type of adjustment you want. Specify a reasonable time limit in which to resolve the problem.

If the desired adjustment is still not made, file a complaint with the appropriate government agency for consumer protection. There may be more than one private or public agency to assist you in solving the problem.

Seek legal recourse when advisable. For claims of less than $1,000, small-claims court offers a much faster and less expensive process. Some states may have different dollar limits for small claims, but still have very effective small-claims court procedures. Because attorneys are not required for filing in a small-claims court, costs are lower. All that is required is payment of a small filing fee and appearance on the assigned court date. Small-claims courts are discussed in detail in Chapter 30.

In some cases, you may receive a judgment in your favor if a supplier has violated the federal Consumer Protection Act or a state law. You could be awarded attorneys' fees, court costs, minimum damages of $200, and punitive damages. An attorney could advise you of your chances of such a judgment. Class-action suits filed on behalf of a number of consumers who have the same complaint generally take many years to settle.

 ummary

In a market economy, consumers have power over what is made and sold. Every dollar spent is a vote cast for that product to be produced and sold. Demand for a product can be stimulated through effective advertising, but wise consumers weigh their choices and make good decisions.

One component of a market economy is competition. Markets must be reasonably competitive, allowing producers to compete with one another to offer the best value for the price. Consumers must be free to spend their money on whatever goods and services they wish. Everyone should also have access to adequate information so that alternatives can be known and wise choices made.

Consumers are exposed to many fraudulent and deceptive marketing practices. Bait and switch schemes get customers into a store; then customers are sold something they did not intend to purchase. Referral sales cost you friendships and get your friends on mailing lists. Fake sales lure customers who may not be aware of regular versus sale prices. Low-balling sells added services that are not needed. Pyramid schemes, illegal in many states, are built on promises of quick profits for small amounts of effort. Pigeon drops are highly organized schemes to take advantage of unsuspecting people; the representation appears to be genuine but in fact is fake. Health and medical product frauds involve millions of dollars of worthless products every year. Infomercials are emotional appeals that often do not meet expectations.

The responsible consumer identifies deceptive practices, uses safeguards when buying, and is proactive in taking steps to protect and assert rights in the marketplace. Consumer redress is getting satisfaction —a refund, repair, replacement, or other service—when you have been treated unfairly.

Vocabulary terms

Directions: Can you find the definition for each of the following terms used in Chapter 28?

advertising	*market economy*
bait and switch	*price-fixing*
competition	*producers*
consumer redress	*purchasing power*
consumers	*pyramid schemes*
demand	*referral sale*
fake sale	*supply*
lowballing	*transfer payments*

1. The action needed for a consumer to resolve a problem with a product or service.
2. Deceptive marketing practice whereby consumers are supposed to get others to sell to their friends.
3. A fraudulent practice whereby con artists convince people to invest in phony deals.
4. Advertising certain repairs at unusually low prices and then urging additional repairs and more costs upon the consumer.
5. An advertised "big sale" that really offers merchandise at regular prices.
6. A deceptive practice whereby the seller promises money, prizes, or discounts if the buyer provides names of friends.
7. A technique in which an item is offered for sale, but customers are urged to buy a similar item at a higher price.
8. Money given to citizens that was collected from other citizens.
9. Having money with which to buy goods and services.
10. Occurs when more than one producer or supplier of a good or service exists, and each tries to get the majority of consumers to buy its product.
11. A method of communicating information to the consumer to sell goods and services.
12. Willingness and ability of consumers to purchase goods and services at certain prices.
13. The quantity of goods and services that producers are willing and able to manufacture.
14. An economic system in which both producers and consumers play an active and vital role.
15. Citizens and businesses that purchase and use goods and services.

16. Citizens and businesses that make products and services available for others to purchase.

acts and ideas in review

1. Explain what is meant by this statement: Everyone is a consumer.
2. As the supply of a product increases, what happens to the price?
3. How do consumers have the power to determine what is produced and at what price?
4. What are the three parts of a free enterprise system?
5. How can the consumer be protected from bait and switch tactics?
6. What can you do to prevent lowballing?
7. Con artists prey on vulnerable people. What is meant by the term vulnerable?
8. List five warning signals that alert consumers to the possibility of deceptive marketing practices.
9. What are some safeguards to use when buying products and services?
10. List four ways that you, as a responsible consumer, can protect yourself in the marketplace.
11. What procedures should you follow to seek a solution to a problem with a product or service?
12. Why should you consider a small-claims court to resolve a consumer complaint?

pplications for decision making

1. Give an example of a recent product that has succeeded and a product that has failed because of consumers' influence.
2. Watch one hour of television in the early evening (between 7 and 8 p.m. is best) and record the number and types of commercials. What do the advertisements tell you about goods and services? Make a chart on a piece of paper listing each commercial and describing it as shown in the following example:

Time of Commercial	Product Advertised	Length of Commercial	Product Information Featured
7 p.m.	Toothpaste (NewBrite)	30 seconds	New flavor; old also available

3. How is the market price of a good or service affected by
  a. an increase in demand?
  b. a decrease in demand?
  c. an increase in supply?
  d. a decrease in supply?

4. Search through magazines, newspapers, and other sources for advertisements offering the following:
  a. something for nothing
  b. bonus for early reply
  c. offers of gifts and prizes
  d. other deceptive practices
  Collect the advertisements and bring them to class.

 ife situation problem solving

1. Compute the following unit prices (lowest units to compare values):
  a. 3/98 cents
  b. 4/$1.00
  c. 24 oz./$1.98
  d. 2 lbs./$2.19
  e. 3 lbs. 6 oz./$6.99
  f. 6/89 cents
  g. 3/$1.49

2. Copy the ingredients from the labels of the following products:
  a. pain pills
  b. breakfast cereal
  c. liquid cleaning product
  d. poisonous substance
  Are there any warnings on any of the above labels? What types of precautions are suggested?

3. Copy the words written on a warranty or guarantee for a household product that your family has purchased. What does the manufacturer agree to do? What exceptions are stated? What actions does the manufacturer state it will not agree to do?

4. Read through a copy of *Consumer Reports* in your library and answer the following questions:
  a. Who publishes the magazine?
  b. Who advertises in the magazine?
  c. In one issue, how many different types of products are tested and compared for quality?

d. Write a short (one paragraph) summary of an article that interested you from the issue of *Consumer Reports* that you read.

5. Assume that you bought a new hair dryer at a local department store last week. Write a letter of complaint because the hair dryer makes a strange rattling noise. Give factual information concerning the dryer and request a refund or other adjustment.

After reading and studying this chapter you will be able to:

29-1 Describe the provisions of the Consumer Bill of Rights.

29-2 Describe the provisions of significant federal consumer legislation.

29-3 Identify national sources of consumer information and assistance.

29-4 List and describe state and local agencies and private organizations that provide consumer assistance and information.

29-5 Explain how to contact public officials to express opinions.

terms to know:

redress
flammability
recall
generic
childproof
care labels
net weight
fraud
consumer advocate

For the average consumer, the modern marketplace presents many challenges. Consumers must be their own first line of defense. You must be aware of fraudulent and deceptive practices and seek redress when your rights as a consumer are violated. In many cases, however, you cannot protect yourself from products and ingredients that are unsafe, undependable, or even hazardous to your health. Consumer protection laws exist at all levels of government. You can contact federal, state, and local agencies to provide assistance and advice. In this chapter, you will learn about your rights as a consumer, the many types of consumer protection laws available to you, and government agencies responsible for enforcing those laws. In addition to government agencies, there are a number of private groups organized to work in the area of consumer protection.

Consumer Protection

chapter

29

The Consumer Bill of Rights was proposed in 1962 by President Kennedy.

ignificant federal consumer legislation

For many years the consumer's position in the marketplace was characterized by the phrase "buyer beware"; in other words, the consumer was given little assistance or protection against fraudulent practices. Since 1960, however, a number of major consumer-protection laws have been passed. One of the most important steps in the direction of consumer protection was the adoption of the Consumer Bill of Rights. The Consumer Bill of Rights was proposed by President Kennedy during his 1962 State of the Union Address, and later expanded by Presidents Nixon and Ford. It includes the following important provisions:

1. The right to safety—protection against products that are hazardous to life or health.
2. The right to be informed—protection against fraudulent, deceitful, or grossly misleading practices and assurance of receiving facts necessary to make informed choices.
3. The right to choose—access to a variety of quality products and services offered at competitive prices.

4. The right to be heard—assurance of representation of consumer interests in formulating government policy and of fair and prompt treatment in enforcement of the laws.
5. The right to **redress** (remedy)—assurance that buyers have ways to register their dissatisfaction and to have complaints heard. When a consumer gets redress, he or she is able to achieve satisfaction as the result of a complaint.
6. The right to consumer education—assurance that consumers have necessary assistance to plan and use their resources to their maximum potential.

Many laws have been passed to ensure that consumers get quality products and services for their hard-earned dollars. The most significant consumer laws enacted by Congress date from the 1930s through the 1970s. The laws explained on the following pages relate specifically to health and safety legislation and labeling and packaging.

Food, Drug, and Cosmetic Act of 1938

The Food, Drug, and Cosmetic Act of 1938 requires that foods be safe, pure, and wholesome; that drugs and medical devices be safe and effective; and that cosmetics be safe. The law also provides that these products be truthfully labeled. The weight or volume of the contents and name and address of the manufacturer must be on the label. The use of containers that are misleading because of size, thickness, or false bottoms is prohibited.

The FDA approves drugs before they can be sold. Requirements for saleability include years of research, testing, and proof of effectiveness and safety. While this process takes time and slows down the availability of drugs to consumers, it assures them that products meet standards of safety, purity, and usefulness.

Wool Products Labeling Act of 1939

Amended in 1965, the Wool Products Labeling Act of 1939 requires proper labeling of the amount and kind of wool contained in all products made of wool, except carpeting and upholstery. Percentages of new, reused, or reprocessed wool and other fibers, care of the product, and the identity of the manufacturer must be shown on the labels of products containing 5 percent or more wool. Similarly, the Fur Products Labeling Act (1951) prohibits mislabeling of fur products.

Flammable Fabrics Act of 1953

Amended in 1967, the Flammable Fabrics Act enabled the Consumer Product Safety Commission to set flammability standards for clothing, children's sleepwear, carpets, rugs, and mattresses. **Flammability** is the capacity for catching on fire. Interstate commerce of all wearing apparel made of easily ignited material is prohibited. The flammability standard for children's sleepwear requires that the garment will not catch fire when exposed to a match or small fire. The flame retardant finish must last for fifty washings and dryings. Proper care instructions to protect sleepwear from agents or treatments known to cause deterioration of the flame retardant finish must be on all labels.

Poultry Products Inspection Act of 1957

This act required the proper inspection of poultry. In 1967, the Wholesome Meat Act was also passed, which updated the Meat Inspection Act of 1906 and provided for stricter standards for slaughtering facilities of red-meat animals. Both of these acts protect consumers in the purchase of chicken and beef by standardizing inspection procedures.

Hazardous Substances Labeling Act of 1960

The Hazardous Substances Labeling Act, passed in 1960, requires that warning labels appear on all household products that are potentially dangerous to the consumer. In most cases, hazardous products are recalled. A **recall** is a procedure whereby the manufacturer stops production of a product and refunds the purchase price of items already sold. Sometimes a recalled product can be repaired so that it is no longer hazardous; it can then be returned to the consumer.

Kefauver-Harris Drug Amendment of 1962

As a result of the Kefauver-Harris Drug Amendment of 1962, drug manufacturers are required to file notices of all new drugs, which must be tested for safety and effectiveness before being sold to consumers. This amendment also provides for the manufacture and sale of generic drugs. **Generic** is a term used for a product having the same qualities or contents as a well-known brand-name product. A generic drug is usually less expensive than a brand-name drug because it carries no trademark registration. National brand names are usually more expensive than generic products because of the added costs of development, advertising, and marketing.

Cigarette Labeling and Advertising Act of 1965

The Cigarette Labeling and Advertising Act of 1965 added a requirement of warning labels of possible health hazards from smoking. Today these warning labels are even more specific. For example, original labels read: "Warning—cigarette smoking may be hazardous to your health." Current labels read: "Surgeon General's Warning: Quitting smoking now greatly reduces serious risks to your health."

Cigarette warning labels warn of the health hazards of smoking.

National Traffic and Motor Vehicle Safety Act of 1966

The National Traffic and Motor Vehicle Safety Act of 1966 established national safety standards for automobiles and for new and used tires. The National Highway Traffic Safety Administration of the Department of Transportation is charged with supporting and enforcing provisions of the act. Increasing public awareness of the need for safety devices, testing for safety, and inspecting vehicles for proper safety equipment are also responsibilities of the National Highway Traffic Safety Administration.

Child Protection and Toy Safety Act of 1966

As a further precaution against unfortunate accidents, the Child Protection and Toy Safety Act was passed in 1966. This act bans the sale of toys and children's articles containing hazardous substances and those that pose electrical, mechanical, or thermal dangers. These products can be inspected and removed from the marketplace.

Special labeling for children's products was required by this act, along with devices that are made childproof. **Childproof** devices are designed so that it is difficult for children to open them or use them in such a manner as to hurt themselves.

Fair Packaging and Labeling Act of 1966

This law requires that accurate names, quantities, and weights be given on product labels, and it applies to all types of consumer products, such as groceries, cosmetics, cleaners, and chemicals. It is the responsibility of the consumer to compare weights and sizes of products available, a much easier job when good, standard information is available for comparison purposes.

Permanent Care Labeling Rule of 1972

Effective since 1972, the care labeling rule specifies that clothing and fabrics must be labeled permanently with laundering and care instructions. Labels must give instructions sufficient to maintain a garment's original character. By carefully reading the labels on garments you purchase, you can estimate how much time or money will be required to maintain the garment. **Care labels** give instructions as to laundering or cleaning, wash and dry temperature, and other methods to preserve the product. They must stay attached and be easy to read for the life of the garment.

Toy Safety Act/Generic Drug Act (1984)

The Toy Safety Act of 1984 permits the Consumer Product Safety Commission to quickly recall toys and other articles intended for use by children that might present a substantial risk of injury. Similarly, the Generic Drug Act of 1984 speeds up the Food and Drug Administration approval process of generic versions of drugs whose patents have expired. These two laws attempt to protect the consumer more quickly than in the past by reducing roadblocks that would slow down safety recalls or keep drug prices high for consumers.

Sources of consumer protection

When you need assistance with a consumer problem, you may not be sure where to look. There are numerous sources available to you. Your first choice may not be the right one, but by asking, you will be referred to the appropriate agency of the federal, state, or local government, or to a specific consumer organization.

Federal Agencies

Numerous government agencies on the federal level provide information of interest to consumers. Some of these agencies handle consumer complaints, and others direct complaints to agencies or sources that address consumer issues. Some well-known federal agencies are described in the following paragraphs.

Department of Agriculture

Within the Department of Agriculture, there are a number of agencies that exist to meet various consumer needs. The Agricultural Marketing Service inspects food to ensure wholesomeness and truthful labeling, develops official grade standards, and provides grading services. For example, eggs must meet specific standards to be classified as extra large, jumbo, large, medium, or small. The Food and Nutrition

The Department of Agriculture inspects food to ensure its quality.

Service provides food assistance programs, such as the food stamp and school lunch programs, and information on diets, nutrition, and menu preparation. The Cooperative Extension Services provides consumer education materials (pamphlets and booklets) on such topics as budgeting, money management, food preparation and storage, gardening, credit counseling, and many more. Most of the materials are free.

Department of Commerce

The National Bureau of Standards is an agency within the Department of Commerce that sets measurement, product, and safety standards. All food packages must indicate whether the weight shown includes the packaging or is a **net weight**—the weight of the product without the container or package.

Department of Health and Human Services

Two of the many agencies within the Department of Health and Human Services are the Food and Drug Administration and the Office of Consumer Affairs. The Food and Drug Administration (FDA) is charged with enforcing laws and regulations preventing distribution of mislabeled foods, drugs, cosmetics, and medical devices. The FDA requires testing and approval of all new drugs; conducts testing of new and existing products for health and safety standards; provides standards and guidelines for poisonous substances; controls the standards for identification, quality, and volume of food containers; establishes guidelines for labels and proper identification of product contents, ingredients, nutrients, and directions for use; investigates complaints; conducts research; and issues reports, guidelines, and warnings about substances its researchers find to be dangerous or potentially hazardous to health.

The Office of Consumer Affairs represents consumer interests in federal agency proceedings, develops consumer information materials, and assists other agencies in responding to consumer complaints. Specific consumer complaints received by the Office of Consumer Affairs are referred to the appropriate government and private agencies for further assistance.

Consumer Product Safety Commission

The Consumer Product Safety Commission (CPSC) was created by an act of Congress that was signed into law in 1972. The purpose of the CPSC is to regulate all potentially hazardous consumer products.

Federal Communications Commission

The Federal Communications Commission (FCC) regulates radio and television broadcasting and interstate telephone and telegraph companies. In addition, the FCC establishes communications standards for and controls the quality of transmissions from radio stations, television networks, cable television networks, CB (citizens band) and ham radios, and any other transmissions through public airspace. What can or cannot be said or done over the air is regulated by the FCC. An advertisement may be discontinued or modified if the FCC determines that it is false or misleading.

Federal Trade Commission

The Federal Trade Commission (FTC) is concerned with protecting consumers from unfair methods of competition, false or deceptive advertising, deceptive product labeling, inaccurate or obsolete information on credit reports, and concealment of the true cost of credit. Anyone can file a complaint with the FTC by sending a letter accompanied by as much supporting evidence as possible.

United States Postal Service

The United States Postal Service operates the Postal Inspection Service to deal with the consumer problems pertaining to illegal use of the

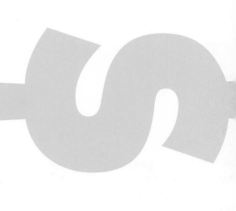

mail. The Postal Inspection Service enforces postal laws, protecting consumers from dangerous articles, contraband, fraud, and pornography. Through its Consumer Protection Program, the Postal Inspection Service resolves unsatisfactory mail-order transactions, even in cases where no fraud has occurred. **Fraud** is the intentional misrepresentation of information to consumers with the intent of deceiving them into buying something they would not otherwise purchase.

Federal Aviation Administration

The Federal Aviation Administration (FAA) is an agency of the U.S. Department of Transportation. It controls air traffic and certifies aircraft, airports, pilots, and other personnel. The FAA writes and enforces air safety regulations and air traffic procedures. Consumer protection and rights while flying on domestic aircraft are provided through the Civil Aeronautics Board (CAB), which keeps track of complaints, inspects aircraft, investigates accidents, and enforces safety regulations. Airline passengers have rights enforced by the CAB, such as the right to a nonsmoking seat. Any person requesting a nonsmoking seat must be accommodated. All airlines now have a no-smoking requirement on flights of less than two hours, a rule mandated through the CAB.

Federal Bureau of Investigation

The Federal Bureau of Investigation (FBI) is the chief law enforcement branch of the United States Department of Justice. The FBI investigates federal crimes such as bank robbery and kidnapping. It also collects evidence in lawsuits involving the federal government, as well as intelligence (information) about individuals or groups that are believed to pose a threat to national security. FBI investigators are called *special agents*. The FBI director is appointed by the President with approval of the Senate.

State and Local Assistance

Most states have a consumer protection agency, or the state attorney general may handle consumer affairs. In addition, many county and city governments have set up consumer protection agencies or offices. Their names and responsibilities vary, however. Consumer leagues and public interest research groups are also active at the state and local levels. These groups may publish newsletters, pamphlets, brochures, and handbooks on current consumer issues.

At the local level, consumers may also have access to legal aid societies, newspaper and broadcast action reporters, or consumer representatives on local utility or licensing boards. Independent consumer groups focusing on specific issues, such as food prices, may operate on the local level as well.

Private Organizations

The Better Business Bureau (BBB) serves as a clearinghouse of information about local businesses. Complaints against local businesses may be filed with the BBB. The merchant is given an opportunity to respond to the complaint; if he or she does not, the Better Business Bureau may advise the consumer to seek another form of redress. Information regarding the nature of complaints filed against local merchants is available upon request.

The BBB is not the only guardian of consumer interests in the business community. For example, the Major Appliance Consumer Action Panel (MACAP) is comprised of representatives of the home appliance industry and provides assistance in resolving or minimizing consumer problems in the purchase and use of home appliances. The automobile and furniture industries, all of which produce goods that represent significant investments for buyers, have voluntary consumer action panels.

Ralph Nader is one of the best-known consumer advocates.

Consumers may also seek the support of a **consumer advocate**— one who promotes or protects the causes or interests of consumers. Ralph Nader is the best-known consumer advocate. When Ralph Nader finds, through research and investigation, that an injustice or dangerous condition exists, he pursues it in behalf of all consumers. Ralph Nader may file lawsuits against companies or organizations to force them to meet safety standards, correct inequitable situations, or properly inform consumers of dangers in the use of their products.

Other consumer organizations help guide consumers in the marketplace. Two such organizations are Consumers' Research, Inc., and Consumers Union of the United States, Inc. Consumers' Research is an independent, nonprofit organization established for the purpose of providing the public with scientific, technical, and educational information.

personal perspective

When You Don't Want What You Bought

Sometimes you buy things and after you think it over, you change your mind. You may feel guilty and uncomfortable with the decision made under stress, persuasion, or other emotional condition.

In case "buyer's remorse" happens to you, you should know about laws that can help:

1. **Cooling-Off Period.** In many states, you will have the right to cancel a contract within three business days. The Federal Trade Commission's (FTC) three-day cooling-off rule lets you cancel, in person or by mail, until midnight of the third business day after the contract was signed. Even if you are not told of this right, you can exercise it. Contracts you can cancel are door-to-door sales contracts for more than $50; contracts made anywhere other than the seller's normal place of business (such as your home or at a trade show); a contract to join a health club or a membership campground; a contract to join a discount buying club (for records, tapes, compact discs, or books). After cancelling, your money must be refunded within ten days. The seller may keep up to 5 percent of the sales amount as a cancellation fee.

2. **Goods Ordered by Mail.** Goods not received in a timely manner can be refused by buyers. For example, if a mail-order company informs you that a product you ordered is "back ordered" and will arrive in six weeks, you have the right to refuse the product. Any amount prepaid must be refunded immediately.

3. **Goods Ordered from Telemarketers.** This type of sale falls under the three-day cooling-off rule. Most telemarketers will send a confirmation of the sale in the mail. You can refuse the item at this time if you act promptly.

4. **Computer-Generated Calls.** Some states prohibit computer-generated calls for selling goods and services. In other states, the purpose of all sales calls must be identified in the first thirty seconds.

5. **Unordered Merchandise.** When you receive something you didn't order, you do not have to pay for it. In fact, it is considered a gift.

critical thinking

1. Have you ever purchased goods and later regretted it? If so, did you try to return them to the seller? What happened?

2. Do you ask stores about their return policies when you buy gifts, clothes, and other purchases? Do you shop stores with good return policies?

3. Write a sample return policy for a department store.

Consumers' Research magazine presents articles on a wide range of topics of consumer interest. A not-for-profit organization, Consumers Union has the largest consumer testing facility in the world. Through its monthly magazine, *Consumer Reports*, Consumers Union gives test results and product ratings. To assure that all ratings are unbiased, all products tested are purchased by Consumers Union. No advertising is accepted, and no free products are accepted for testing from manufacturers. *Consumer Reports* also prints articles dealing with insurance, credit, and other items of consumer interest. An annual buying guide is also published by Consumers Union.

tate and federal information numbers

Many consumers are unaware of complaint-handling resources available through their own state governments. Each of the thirty-four states listed in Figure 29-1a and b maintains a toll-free 800 number for consumers to make inquiries or register complaints. Some offices handle complaints on almost any subject; others specify their area of interest. Hours of operation are listed for local time zones. Figure 29-2 on page 719 is a list prepared by the U.S. Government and available free of charge from the Consumer Information Center, Pueblo, Colorado.

Fig. 29-1a

State Consumer Toll-Free Numbers

ALABAMA (Montgomery)
Hours: 8:00–5:00
1 800 392-5658
In state only. Advice given over the phone. Complaints must be submitted in writing for action.

ARIZONA (Phoenix)
Hours: 8:00–5:00
1 800 352-8431
In state only. Handles complaints concerning possible fraud.

ARKANSAS (Little Rock)
Hours: 8:00–5:00
1 800 482-8982
In state only. Handles complaints concerning possible fraud or false advertising and will answer general inquiries.

CALIFORNIA (Sacramento)
Hours: 8:00–5:00
1 800 952-5210
In state only. Handles complaints concerning auto repair jobs.

1 800 952-5567
In state only. Information regarding solar energy uses/insulation.

Hours: 9:00–12:00; 1:00–4:00
1 800 952-5225
In state only. Takes general complaints.

COLORADO (Denver)
Hours: 8:00–5:00
1 800 332-2071
In state only. Handles complaints concerning possible price fixing or other antitrust matters.

CONNECTICUT (Hartford)
Hours: 8:30–4:30
1 800 842-2649
In state only. Handles all types of complaints and inquiries.

FLORIDA (Tallahassee)
Hours: 7:45–4:30 (recording after hours).
1 800 342-2176
In state only. Handles most types of complaints and inquiries.

GEORGIA (Atlanta)
Hours: 8:00–5:00
1 800 282-4900
In state only. Handles general complaints and inquiries.

ILLINOIS (Chicago)
Hours: 8:30–5:00
1 800 252-8972
In state only. Handles complaints and inquiries related to state tax, senior citizens relief tax and other matters.

1 800 252-8980
In state only. Handles complaints and inquiries on used car problems.

1 800 252-8903
In state only. Handles complaints and inquiries on public aid fraud.

INDIANA (Indianapolis)
Hours: 8:15–4:45
1 800 382-5516
In state only. Handles general consumer complaints and inquiries.

KANSAS (Topeka)
Hours: 8:00–5:00
1 800 432-2310
In state only. Handles general complaints and inquiries.

KENTUCKY (Frankfort)
Hours: 8:30–5:00
1 800 432-9257
In state only. Advice given over the phone. Will send complaint forms or refer.

LOUISIANA (Baton Rouge)
Hours: 8:30–5:00
1 800 272-9868
In state only. Handles general complaints and inquiries.

MASSACHUSETTS (Boston)
Hours: 9:00–5:00
1 800 632-8026
In state only. Handles energy related complaints and concerns

1 800 392-6066
In state only. Handles public utility complaints and inquiries.

MICHIGAN (Lansing)
Hours: 8:30–5:00
1 800 292-4204 (Bureau of Automotive Regulation)
In state only. Handles auto complaints.

1 800 292-5943 (Commissioner of Insurance)
In state only. Handles insurance related complaints.

1 800 292-9555 (Public Service Commission)
In state only. Handles utility related complaints.

MISSISSIPPI (Jackson)
Hours: 8:00–5:00
1 800 222-7622 (Governor's Hotline)
In state only. Consumer complaints are referred.

MISSOURI (Jefferson City)
Hours: 8:15–4:45
1 800 392-8222
In state only. Handles complaints involving fraud and misrepresentation in the sale of goods.

Fig. 29-1b	**State Consumer Toll-Free Numbers**

MONTANA (Helena)
Hours: 8:00–5:00 (answering service after hours)
1 800 332-2272
In state only. Refers complaints and inquiries to the proper state office.

NEVADA (Carson City)
Hours: 8:00–5:00
1 800 992-0900
In state only. Operator connects consumer with state agencies. Consumer must know which agency to request.

NEW HAMPSHIRE (Concord)
Hours: 8:00–4:00
1 800 852-3456 (Governor's Office of Citizens Services)
In state only. Handles complaints and inquiries concerning energy.

1 800 852-3311 (State Council on Aging)
In state only. Information about and for the elderly.

NEW JERSEY (Trenton)
Hours: 9:00–5:00 (recording after hours)
1 800 792-8600
In state only. Refers complaints and inquiries to the proper agency.

NEW YORK (Albany)
Hours: 7:30–4:30
1 800 342-3736
In state only. Handles consumer inquiries on all types of insurance coverage.

Hours: 9:00-5:00
1 800 522-8707
In state only. Refers consumer inquiries on utilities to the proper public service/utility.

Hours: 7:30–4:30
1 800 342-3823
In state only. Handles complaints concerning auto repairs performed within the last 90 days.

Hours: 9:00–4:00
1 800 342-3722 (recording after hours)
In state only. Answers inquiries about energy programs, conservation and regulations.

NORTH CAROLINA (Raleigh)
Hours: 8:00–5:00
1 800 662-7777
In state only. Receives inquiries about insurance coverage.

NORTH DAKOTA (Bismark)
Hours: 8:00–5:00
1 800 472-2600
In state only. Investigates allegations of consumer fraud.

Hours: 8:00–5:00
1 800 472-2927
In state only. Handles general consumer complaints

OHIO (Columbus)
Hours: 8:00–5:00 (recording after hours)
1 800 282-0515
In state only. Handles general complaints and inquiries.

OKLAHOMA (Oklahoma City)
Hours: 8:00–5:00
1 800 522-8555 (Capital Straight Line)
In state only. Handles general complaints and inquiries.

OREGON (Portland)
Hours: 8:00–5:00
1 800 452-7813
In state only. Will link caller to appropriate state agency.

SOUTH CAROLINA (Columbia)
Hours: 8:00–5:00
1 800 992-1594
In state only. Handles general complaints and inquiries.

SOUTH DAKOTA (Pierre)
Hours: 8:00–5:00
1 800 592-1865
In state only. Tie line. Must ask for specific division.

TENNESSEE (Nashville)
Hours: 8:00–4:30
1 800 342-8385
In state only. Handles general complaints and inquiries.

VERMONT (Montpelier)
Hours: 8:00–4:30
1 800 642-5149
In state only. Handles general complaints and inquiries.

VIRGINIA (Richmond)
Hours: 8:30–5:00
1 800 552-9963
In state only. Handles general complaints and inquiries.

WASHINGTON (Seattle)
Hours: 1:00–5:00
1 800 552-0700
In state only. Will mail out complaint forms or make referrals.

WISCONSIN (Madison)
Hours: 8:00–4:45
1 800 362-3020
In state only. Handles general complaints and inquiries.

Fig. 29-2   **Federal Toll-Free Information Numbers**

ALABAMA
Birmingham 205 322-8591
Mobile 205 438-1421

ALASKA
Anchorage 907 271-3650

ARIZONA
Phoenix 602 261-3313
Tucson 602 622-1511

ARKANSAS
Little Rock 501 378-6177

CALIFORNIA
Los Angeles 213 688-3800
Sacramento 916 440-3344
San Diego 714 293-6030
San Francisco 415 556-6600
San Jose 408 275-7422
Santa Ana 714 836-2386

COLORADO
Colorado Springs 303 471-9491
Denver 303 837-3602
Pueblo 303 544-9523

CONNECTICUT
Hartford 203 527-2617
New Haven 203 624-4720

FLORIDA
Ford Lauderdale 305 522-8531
Jacksonville 904 354-4756
Miami 305 350-4155
Orlando 305 422-1800
St. Petersburg 813 893-3495
Tampa 813 229-7911
West Palm Beach 305 833-7566
Northern Florida 1 800 282-8556
  (Sarasota, Manatee, Polk, Osceola,
  Orange, Seminole, and Volusia counties
  and north)
Southern Florida 1 800 432-6668
  (Charlotte, DeSota, Hardee, Highlands,
  Okeechobee, Indian River and Brevard
  counties and south)

GEORGIA
Atlanta 404 221-6891

HAWAII
Honolulu 808 546-8620

ILLINOIS
Chicago 312 353-4242

INDIANA
Gary/Hammond 219 883-4110
Indianapolis 317 269-7373

IOWA
Des Moines 515 284-4448
Other locations 1 800 532-1556

KANSAS
Topeka 913 295-2866
Other locations 1 800 432-2934

KENTUCKY
Louisville 502 582-6261

LOUISIANA
New Orleans 504 589-6696

MARYLAND
Baltimore 301 962-4980

MASSACHUSETTS
Boston 617 223-7121

MICHIGAN
Detroit 313 226-7016
Grand Rapids 616 451-2628

MINNESOTA
Minneapolis 612 349-5333

MISSOURI
Kansas City 816 374-2466
St. Louis 314 425-4106
Other locations within area code 314
  1 800 392-7711
Other locations within area codes 816
  & 417 1 800 892-5808

NEBRASKA
Omaha 402 221-3353
Other locations 1 800 642-8383

NEW JERSEY
Newark 201 645-3600
Paterson/Passaic 201 523-0717
Trenton 609 396-4400

NEW MEXICO
Albuquerque 505 766-3091
Santa Fe 505 983-7743

NEW YORK
Albany 518 463-4421
Buffalo 716 846-4010
New York 212 264-4464
Rochester 716 546-5075
Syracuse 315 476-8545

NORTH CAROLINA
Charlotte 704 376-3600

OHIO
Akron 216 375-5638
Cincinnati 513 684-2801
Cleveland 216 522-4040
Columbus 614 221-1014
Dayton 513 223-7377
Toledo 419 241-3223

OKLAHOMA
Oklahoma City 405 231-4868
Tulsa 918 584-4193

OREGON
Portland 503 221-2222

PENNSYLVANIA
Allentown/Bethlehem
  215 821-7785
Philadelphia 215 597-7042
Pittsburgh 412 644-3456
Scranton 717 346-7081

RHODE ISLAND
Providence 401 331-5565

TENNESSEE
Chattanooga 615 265-8231
Memphis 901 521-3285
Nashville 615 242-5056

TEXAS
Austin 512 472-5494
Dallas 214 767-8585
Fort Worth 817 334-3624
Houston 713 226-5711
San Antonio 512 224-4471

UTAH
Ogden 801 399-1347
Salt Lake City 801 524-5353

VIRGINIA
Newport News 804 244-0480
Norfolk 804 441-3101
Richmond 804 643-4928
Roanoke 703 982-8591

WASHINGTON
Seattle 206 442-0570
Tacoma 206 383-5230

WISCONSIN
Milwaukee 414 271-2273

For information and help with your questions about the federal government, use the toll-free information numbers given in Figure 29-2. These numbers will allow you to contact the nearest Federal Information Center (part of the U.S. General Services Administration). You can contact a center toll free if you live in any of the cities listed in Figure 29-2, or in a state with an 800 number shown.

ublic officials

National elected officials include the president and the vice president of the United States, serving four-year terms; United States senators, serving six-year terms; and the members of the United States House of Representatives, serving two-year terms. Governors of states usually are elected to four-year terms. Other state elected officials include the secretary of state, state treasurer, and state attorney general; superintendent of public instruction; labor commissioner; and state senators and representatives.

Each court (federal, state, and local) has at least one judge, and several clerks of the court assist in filing and information gathering. County elected officials include the county administrator, district attorney, sheriff, and tax assessor, plus a number of commissioners. Other elected local officials include the mayor, city council members, and city manager. These officials are available at county and city office buildings and meet regularly or are available to the public by appointment. The phone book lists various officials separately by state and by county, with each department listed alphabetically.

If you wish to communicate with a public official about a consumer issue, there are several ways to do so:

1. **In Person.** Appointments can be made during regular office hours as well as at meetings of government bodies, which are generally open to the public (except for executive sessions). There are opportunities to speak at almost all hearings.
2. **By Phone.** Brief calls at reasonable hours are generally effective. Your state may have a Wide Area Telecommunications Service (WATS) line, which enables citizens to call public officials toll free. You can leave a message, and your call will be returned. When calling Washington, D.C., remember time zone differences.
3. **By Wire.** Personal Opinion Messages may be sent to the president, vice president, U.S. senators and representatives, your governor, and the state legislators. The cost is $3.50 for 20 words, excluding

your name and address, unless there are additional signatures. You can call 1-800-648-4100 to send a message.

4. **By Letter.** An effective letter written to the appropriate representative states clearly the purpose of the letter; identifies a bill by proper name and number; refers to only one issue; and arrives while the issue is current. Give reasons for your position and avoid emotionalism. Ask for specific relief—what you want the public official to do.

In almost all cases, your contact with a public official will be answered. Telephone calls are generally returned within one or two working days. Letters are answered within a week or two.

ummary

Consumers today have many protections that have been created since the beginning of this century. There are numerous acts of federal legislation that protect us from unsafe and untested products and require proper labeling and disclosures so that consumers can make wise purchasing decisions.

Federal agencies also enforce consumer protection laws, from the Department of Agriculture to the U.S. Postal Service. These agencies set standards and enforce them for the general health and welfare of all citizens.

State and local agencies are also involved in consumer protection, along with private organizations that do research, publish comparisons, and warn consumers about deceptive practices and help consumers to get redress when they have been cheated. But ultimately it is the consumer's responsibility to know what help is needed and to find that help and exercise her or his rights in the marketplace.

29

 ocabulary terms

Directions: Can you find the definition for each of the following terms used in Chapter 29?

care labels	*generic*
childproof	*net weight*
consumer advocate	*recall*
flammability	*redress*
fraud	

1. A general term used for a product having the same qualities or contents as a well-known name-brand product.
2. The procedure whereby a manufacturer stops production and refunds the purchase price of items already sold.
3. The weight of a product without the container or package.
4. One who promotes or seeks to protect the causes or interests of consumers.
5. Labels on clothing that describe laundry and other special handling requirements.
6. The capacity of cloth or other product to catch on fire easily.
7. The procedure whereby a consumer achieves satisfaction regarding a consumer complaint.
8. The intentional misrepresentation of information in order to induce someone to buy something.
9. Referring to the safeguarding of a product so that it will not injure a small child.

 acts and ideas in review

1. What consumer protection action was proposed by President Kennedy in 1962?
2. List the six major items in the Consumer Bill of Rights.
3. What was the purpose of the Food, Drug, and Cosmetic Act of 1938?
4. How long must a flame-retardant finish last in children's sleep-wear as provided by the Flammable Fabrics Act of 1953?
5. Who tests all new drugs that are produced for sale in the marketplace?

6. What are the functions of the National Highway Safety Administration?

7. What was the major purpose of the Permanent Care Labeling Rule of 1972?

8. Which two major agencies are within the Department of Health and Human Services?

9. What types of communications, in addition to radio and television broadcasting, are controlled by the FCC?

10. What types of crimes are investigated by the FBI? Give examples.

11. If you have a complaint about airline service, whom should you contact?

12. What do the letters BBB stand for?

13. List and describe the four ways to communicate with an elected official.

 A pplications for decision making

1. Why are consumers encouraged to ask for generic products rather than brand-name products?

2. Does your state have a toll-free number to call for consumer inquiries or to register complaints? If so, what types of assistance are available? What is the federal toll-free information number nearest you?

3. Select any garment from your closet. Read the care label. What does the message indicate?

4. Cut the labels from three or four food products, such as soup, cereal, snacks, and processed foods. List the different types of information —such as quantity per serving, ingredients, and vitamin and mineral content—you find on the label. Are there ingredients you do not recognize? Is the nutritional value what you expected?

 L ife situation problem solving

1. List your state and local sources that can provide assistance with a consumer complaint.

2. Consult the Consumer Reports *Buying Guide* for the current year. Summarize three articles that are of interest to you.

3. Your local library contains much information about consumer problems and assistance. Visit the library and list in outline form what types of information are available for consumers who need information.

4. Attend a public hearing on a local issue—land use or zoning, for example—and write a report on who was present, what was discussed, and the conclusion reached. Hearings are held in city hall or county buildings and are open to the public for testimony and input.

5. Check your local newspaper for public notices of hearings by local government groups. List hearings that are scheduled. Which hearings are on issues affecting consumers? Exactly how would consumers be affected in each case? If possible, attend a hearing and prepare a report on it.

6. Check recent issues of the newspapers and news magazines for reports of proposed laws and regulations. Choose an issue that concerns you and investigate it. Prepare a letter to the appropriate official with your comments on the proposed law or regulation.

After reading and studying this chapter you will be able to:

30-1 Describe the organization of the legal system in the United States at federal, state, and local levels.

30-2 Explain the procedures involved from the time a complaint is filed until a judgment is entered by a court.

30-3 Define remedies available to consumers —from self-help through negotiating to filing a lawsuit and seeking governmental assistance.

terms to know:

court
jurisdiction
trial court
appellate court
civil court
criminal court
jury
docket
Statute of Limitations
plaintiff
defendant
counterclaim
depositions
judgment
equitable relief

The first step, as you have learned, in solving a consumer problem is to register a complaint. If your complaint is about defective merchandise or poor service, a personal visit may be the best way to handle the matter. A letter of complaint often works better when people in authority must be contacted. If these efforts fail, an attorney may be able to help you pursue legal action. Your last resort is a lawsuit, called a *civil action,* to get the type of remedy you want.

In this chapter, you will learn about the legal system in the United States and how to use it effectively. You will explore the process of filing a lawsuit and the steps from complaint through judgment. You will also learn about remedies and actions that are effective in settling disputes.

Legal Protection

chapter

30

Courts give redress to the injured and enforce punishment against wrongdoers.

ANGELES COUNTY COURTHO

COUNTY OF LOS ANGELES
COURT HOUSE

he legal system

The legal system in the United States is one based on common law. Common law refers to case decisions that are decided by courts and have the effect of law. At the base of our common law legal system are the courts. A **court** is a tribunal established by the government to hear and decide matters properly brought before it, to give redress to the injured or enforce punishment against wrongdoers, and to prevent wrongs.

There are many types of courts—federal, state, and local. Each court is empowered to decide certain types or classes of cases. This power is called **jurisdiction,** which is the legal right and authority of the court to hear and decide a case. A court may have original or appellate jurisdiction, or both. The court of original jurisdiction, or the first place a trial is heard, is called the **trial court.** A trial court has the authority to hear a dispute when it is first brought into court. A court having appellate jurisdiction is the appellate court. An **appellate court** has the authority to review the judgment of a lower court. **EN4-30**

Courts are also classified in terms of the nature of their jurisdiction. A **civil court** has the authority to hear disputes involving the violation of the private legal rights of individuals. Disputes between private citizens, private groups, companies, and corporations are heard in civil courts. In addition, all disputes against a branch of the government (local, state, or federal) as well as consumer complaints are heard in civil courts. A **criminal court** is for the trial of crimes regarded as violations of certain duties to society and disturbances of public peace and order. The government, representing all the people, prosecutes the alleged wrongdoer. Appeals can be made by the losing party in civil or criminal matters if it appears that an error or injustice has been committed.

Court Personnel

The assistance of many people is required for the efficient operation of our federal and state court systems. Included are persons in the direct employ of the courts, officers of the court, and sometimes a jury.

Judge

The judge is the presiding officer in the court and is either elected or appointed. Attorneys are usually selected by the parties in the dispute, but are sometimes selected by the judge, to present the issue in the case to the court.

Clerk

The duties of the clerk of the court are to enter cases on the court calendar; to keep an accurate record of the proceedings; to accept, label, and provide safekeeping for all items of evidence; to administer the oath to witnesses and jurors; and sometimes to approve bail bonds and compute the costs involved.

Reporter

The court reporter keeps a word-by-word record of the trial, usually through the use of a special recording machine. These trial records are available to each of the attorneys and are necessary for appeals.

Bailiff

Deputy sheriffs serve as sergeants at arms during court proceedings. Bailiffs maintain order in the courtroom at the instruction of the judge.

Jury

The **jury** is a body of citizens sworn by a court to hear the facts submitted during a trial and to render a verdict. A trial jury consists of not more than twelve persons. A juror must be of legal age, a resident of the county, and able to see and hear. Jurors are chosen from a list of local citizens—usually from tax or voter rolls.

The Federal Court System

The bases of federal jurisdiction are the United States Constitution and the laws enacted by Congress. The federal courts hear only matters that concern the nation as a whole—matters pertaining to constitutional rights, civil rights, interstate commerce, patents and copyrights, internal revenue, currency, and foreign relations. Other areas, such as crimes, contracts, and divorces, are left to the states in which the acts are committed. The federal courts may hear a dispute between citizens of two different states, but only if it involves $10,000 or more.

The United States Supreme Court

The Supreme Court is the top court of the federal court system and is located in Washington, D.C. The Supreme Court is the only federal court expressly established by the Constitution. Appeals from federal appellate courts and from state supreme courts that pertain to federal issues are heard by the Supreme Court. The Supreme Court chooses which cases it will hear. The Court sets its own **docket,** or schedule of cases, dates, and times for issues to be heard. Only cases of the greatest importance and national consequence are accepted. Thousands of actions are appealed every year, but the Supreme Court accepts only about 125 for consideration. There are nine Supreme Court justices, including a chief justice, who are appointed to their positions for life. No federal judge may be dismissed or impeached for any reason other than gross misconduct.

The Supreme Court is the only federal court expressly established by the Constitution.

Courts of Appeal

The United States, including the District of Columbia, is divided into twelve judicial circuits. Each of the circuits has a court of appeals. Each appellate court has from five to nine judges, who review final decisions of the district courts. The decisions of the courts of appeal are final in most cases.

District Trial Courts

The United States is divided into ninety federal districts, with a court assigned to each. Each district covers a state or a portion of a state. Consequently, some states may be home to more than one federal district court, while other states contain none. (These states are part of a federal district whose court is in a different state.) Each district court is a trial court, also divided into civil or criminal divisions. District courts are staffed by judges who hear cases individually, not as a panel.

Some issues are always considered federal issues, such as bankruptcy and crimes involving interstate commerce. For example, hijacking, kidnapping, bank robbery, and counterfeiting are all considered federal crimes and would be prosecuted in federal courts. Any criminal sentenced for a federal crime would be sent to a federal prison or penitentiary.

Special Federal Courts

Additional special courts have been established by Congress to hear only cases of a special nature. These special federal courts include the Court of Claims, Customs Court, Court of International Trade, Tax Court, Court of Military Appeals, and the territorial courts. If you wanted to sue the United States of America, you would file a claim in a U.S. district or special federal court.

State Court Systems

The greatest share of legal matters is handled in state court systems. This is not only because state systems outnumber the federal system by fifty to one, but also because there are limits placed on the federal system by the Constitution. The Tenth Amendment to the United States Constitution grants each state the sovereign power to enact and enforce state laws.

A state's laws are contained in its constitution and enacted by its own legislature. These laws are binding upon the citizens of a state and must not violate the U.S. Constitution. Each state has the power to run its own court system to decide issues that involve state laws. Each state establishes its own set of court procedures, determines court names, divides areas of responsibility among the various courts, and sets limits of authority among the state courts. Some issues are tried exclusively in state trial courts, such as divorce, probate, and adoption.

State Supreme Courts

In most states the highest court is the state supreme court, sometimes called the Court of Final Appeal. Ordinarily, the state supreme court has appellate jurisdiction. The decision of a state supreme court is final, except in cases involving the federal Constitution, laws, and treaties. In many states, there are appellate courts and one supreme court.

District and Circuit Courts

General trial courts, often called state district courts, circuit courts, or superior courts, decide matters beyond local courts. These courts hear civil cases involving large sums of money, criminal matters with major penalties, and cases that are appealed from local courts whose decisions are questionable. Judges at this level are usually appointed by the state governor, although some may be elected for terms of four to six years. Decisions from district courts may be reviewed by the highest state court.

County and City Courts

The lowest state court levels are found at the city or county level. These courts may also be called municipal or justice courts. Courts at this level have authority limited by geographic boundaries. Civil and criminal cases are heard at the local level. However, civil cases must be for small amounts only. In some states, the maximum amount in dispute in a civil case is $500. At the local level, disputes usually are heard and decided by judges, not by juries. In very small areas, a judge may be called a justice of the peace, who is an appointed, part-time official. Justices of the peace in other areas are elected officials. Special courts at the local level may be called police courts, traffic courts, small-claims courts, and justice-of-the-peace courts.

 court proceedings

The filing of a lawsuit involves many steps, costs, and outcomes. You will need an attorney who will advise you of your chances of winning your case, laws pertaining to your case, and what you need to do to prepare for trial. The services of a competent attorney will cost from $100 to $200 an hour, or more in some areas. Some attorneys will work on a contingency-fee basis, which means they receive fees only if you win the case. Your state bar association can supply names of attorneys who specialize in the area of your complaint. Your attorney will appear in court on your behalf and represent your interests. In all states there is a **Statute of Limitations,** which restricts the length of time in which court action may be taken on various complaints. For example, in many states personal injury lawsuits must be filed within two years from the date of the injury. A lawsuit filed after the two-year limit will be dismissed.

global connection

International Legal Disputes

Because we live in an *interdependent* world, individuals and businesses must be aware of the international implications of business dealings. They must know and understand the laws and customs of countries in which they do business for resolving international disputes.

When a dispute arises from an international transaction, one source of redress is the International Court of Justice (ICJ) located at the Hague, Netherlands. An individual or business has no standing before the ICJ; only nations may appear. Sometimes a nation will represent an individual or business with a claim against another country before the ICJ.

Once an issue is presented to the ICJ for resolution, the other nation is notified that a filing has occurred. That nation may choose to appear and argue the case. If it refuses to appear, that is the end of the matter.

This procedure was established by the United Nations Charter, which made the ICJ an agency of the United Nations. Each nation must agree to be bound by the court's decision. If a nation does not agree, then the ICJ has no jurisdiction to hear the case.

When ICJ is not an option, an individual can file a lawsuit in the foreign nation by filing a claim in the courts of that nation. Private persons can often get adequate relief in this manner. If, for example, a citizen of the U.S. files a lawsuit against a citizen of France and wins the lawsuit, the U.S. citizen could be awarded a *lien* against the property of the defendant in the United States or in France. (A lien is the right to hold goods or property until claims are paid.)

Recognizing foreign claims is usually a matter of *comity*. Comity is the principle that one country agrees to recognize the laws of another nation, and to respect the rights to claims made by citizens of the other nation against their own citizens. Comity is a matter of respect, good will, and courtesy between nations that are on good terms with each other.

critical thinking

1. Have you visited any foreign countries? How are laws different in foreign countries?

2. If you worked for a company that does international business, would you be willing to live in a foreign country as an employee? Why or why not?

Generally, a lawsuit involves the following steps: a complaint is filed; the defendant is served; trial date is set and a period of discovery follows; the case is tried; a judgment is entered; and costs are awarded.

Plaintiff Files Complaint

The person filing the complaint is known as the **plaintiff.** The plaintiff sees an attorney and discusses the facts of the case. The attorney considers the matter, conducts extensive research on similar cases, and advises the client of the prospect of winning the lawsuit. If the client (plaintiff) wishes to pursue the matter, the attorney draws up the necessary papers, which the plaintiff signs. Action is begun by filing the complaint with the clerk of the appropriate court. A filing fee of $125 to $250 is usually required. Generally, the complaint consists of a description of the acts complained of by the plaintiff and a request for relief.

Defendant Is Served

A certified copy of the complaint is served upon the defendant named in the lawsuit. The **defendant** is the person against whom the plaintiff is making a complaint. The local sheriff's department or a private company may be used to serve the defendant. Usually, several days are required to serve the defendant, who must be presented with the papers personally. A reasonable time in which to appear (file a response to the complaint) is then allowed the defendant. Ten days are allowed if the defendant is served in the same county; if in the same state, thirty days; outside the state, sixty days or more. The defendant must decide whether to default—not answer and automatically lose—or answer the complaint. If the defendant does not answer, the plaintiff will win the case by default judgment.

The defendant must first obtain the services of an attorney and discuss the case. Then the defendant's attorney prepares and files an answer to the complaint. A counterclaim asserting the plaintiff's guilt, and therefore liability in the matter, could be filed by the defendant. A **counterclaim** states that the defendant believes the plaintiff to be at fault and demands damages as a result of the plaintiff's actions. At this point, the defendant may also file a motion to dismiss (called a *demurrer*), which states that even if the plaintiff's complaint is true, the plaintiff is still not entitled to any relief. The defendant may also allege that there is insufficient evidence, improper jurisdiction, or other legal reasons why the matter should not be set for trial.

Trial Date Is Set

After the defendant's attorney has filed an answer to the complaint with the appropriate court, a date is set for the trial. The trial date is set several months before the matter can be heard. During the time before trial, much work must be done by the plaintiff and defendant and by their attorneys. Usually for six months to a year or longer, attorneys gather information, talk to witnesses, prepare legal arguments, take depositions, hire investigators, examine reports, and negotiate with the opposing party. (**Depositions** are sworn statements of witnesses taken before court appearances in order to preserve the memory of the issues.) Many cases are settled before going to trial because both parties realize the risk involved in a trial. If a settlement can be reached, a formal agreement is signed and the case is dropped.

Trial Takes Place

All defendants are entitled to request a jury trial in state courts where there is a possibility of a jail or prison sentence. In small issues, such as traffic tickets, a jury may be denied when incarceration is not a possible outcome. For a jury trial, several days may be necessary to question and choose a panel of jurors. Attorneys are careful to eliminate anyone who appears prejudiced, knows any person who will be present at the trial, or for any reason might not be able to reach an unbiased decision. Once the jury is seated, the trial begins.

Defendants are entitled to a jury trial when there is a possibility of a prison sentence.

The plaintiff's case begins first. Any evidence and witnesses to support the case are included in the presentation. The defendant then presents evidence and witnesses in defense against the plaintiff's allegations. Then the attorneys for both sides make closing arguments and the jury deliberates. A decision is reached and announced to the court by the foreman (chosen leader) of the jury.

In deciding civil cases, one side must simply prove their position by a *preponderance* of the evidence; in other words, convince the jury that their side is more believable. In deciding criminal cases, the prosecutor must prove his or her case *beyond a reasonable doubt*. All the defense has to do is prove that there is a reasonable doubt; the defense does not have to prove absolute innocence.

Judgment Is Entered and Costs Are Awarded

Based on the decision of the jury or the judge, a judgment is entered requiring the losing party to pay the decided amount. A **judgment** is an obligation or debt created by the decree (decision) of a court. The losing party has a limited time in which to appeal. A case heard in a state district court may be appealed to a circuit court. After the circuit court, the case may go to the state appeals court, and then to the state supreme court. Any matters involving national interests may be appealed to the United States Supreme Court, which may or may not choose to hear the case.

In addition to monetary damages, the plaintiff may seek what is known as equitable relief. **Equitable relief** is a legal action that allows a previous order to be rescinded, requires a situation to be restored to its previous state, or provides for the performance of a specific act. For example, you could ask the judge to allow you to withdraw from a legal contract. A judge may, in some situations, deny monetary damages to a plaintiff if the defendant will restore certain items to their rightful owner—the plaintiff. Equitable relief is often granted when a monetary judgment would not adequately serve to compensate an innocent or damaged party for injuries caused by the actions of the defendant. An action or restraint from action (equitable relief) may be more appropriate than monetary damages.

When one party wins a lawsuit, costs awarded to the winning party include the cost of filing papers with the court, the cost of having the sheriff or other officers of the court take official action, fees paid to witnesses, jury fees, and the cost of printing the record of the trial. Sometimes a reasonable attorney's fee is also awarded.

inding a remedy

If you are a victim of a consumer problem, you may want to review the courses of action available to you. Alternatives for redress are self-help, small-claims court, a private or class-action lawsuit, or assistance from a government or private agency to stop the objectionable practices and help you recover your money.

Self-Help

After you have carefully analyzed the problem and believe you are entitled to some type of relief, you can proceed to seek redress. Negotiating and withholding payment are two self-help techniques you may find effective.

Negotiating

A negotiated settlement is one voluntarily entered into by both sides. The buyer must be willing to give up some things in return for the seller's changing his or her position. In most cases, when consumers complain and want some type of settlement, the seller is willing to discuss the issues to reach some type of agreement so that the goodwill of the customer can be maintained. Negotiating is a process that requires tact and precision. You must know the problem, what you want done about it, and what you are willing to do to make a settlement. Negative emotions and statements will not facilitate an agreement.

A customer who has purchased a product that is faulty or otherwise unsatisfactory should seek an agreeable remedy with the merchant before pursuing legal remedies. Once the merchant is alienated from (unfriendly toward) the customer because of the customer's actions, the possibility of a negotiated settlement is reduced. Negotiated settlements are often much less expensive and easier to achieve than seeking legal relief. It is essential that the consumer follow up immediately after the damage has occurred. A long wait before seeking a remedy can sometimes result in no relief for damages. In addition, the mental and emotional energy required to pursue legal remedies can be very stressful and prolonged.

When two parties in a dispute cannot reach an agreement, *arbitration* may be used. The arbitrator is usually chosen by both parties, and both parties agree to accept the decision of the arbitrator. In some cases a panel is chosen—one arbitrator representing each party, and the two arbitrators choosing a third panel member. Arbitration services are expensive, but much less so than court action.

There are many alternatives to settling disputes in the courts. The Yellow Pages of your telephone book has listings for mediation and arbitration services. In addition, Figure 30-1 lists sources of information and assistance that you can contact by writing or calling.

The Yellow Pages has listings for mediation and arbitration services to resolve disputes.

Withholding Payment

As a consumer, you have rights when there is a purchase dispute. You must put your complaint in writing and explain clearly the reason why you are withholding payment on the disputed amount. The seller is compelled to respond to your complaint and has time limits in which to resolve the matter. You should pay all other amounts due as agreed. Do not withhold payment on amounts not in question, as this will weaken your position. Your credit cannot be damaged if you follow the proper procedures for questioning credit charges.

When merchandise is purchased with credit, you have more lever-age than if you pay cash, because the merchant is motivated to get payment for the merchandise that is already in your possession. Again, diplomacy is required.

Fig. 30-1	**Sources of Assistance**

Arbitration

The American Arbitration Association (headquarters)
140 W. 51st Street
New York, NY 10020
Call: 212-484-4000
Has offices in 25 cities (see your local telephone book).

Bar Referral

The American Bar Association can give the name and address of the nearest dispute resolution center. Write:
American Bar Association's Special Committee on Alternative Dispute Resolution
1800 M Street NW
Washington, D.C. 20036
Call: 202-331-2258
You will receive a list of 200 centers for $10.

Business Disputes

For free publications for businesses on saving money on legal disputes through use of a panel of dispute resolves, write:
Center for Public Resources
680 Fifth Avenue
New York, NY 10019
Call: 202-541-9830

Divorce Mediation

Divorce Mediation Research Project
1720 Emerson Street
Denver, CO 80218
Send $10 to receive a partial list of mediators who specialize in divorce.

Endispute
Suite 803
11 Dupont Circle NW
Washington, D.C. 20036
Call: 202-232-5368
Offices also in Chicago, Los Angeles, and San Francisco.

West Coast affiliate:
Judicial Arbitration & Mediation Service
P.O. Box 10333
Santa Ana, CA 92711
Call: 714-972-1616

Lawyer Tips

For tips on dealing with lawyers, write:
HALT
Americans for Legal Reform
Suite 309
201 Massachusetts Avenue NE
Washington, D.C. 20002
Call: 202-546-4558

Small-Claims Court

If the amount is relatively small, you might consider small-claims court. The matter will be heard quickly, but the decision is final. Fees are small. You must represent yourself—no attorneys are allowed—and there is no jury. The matter is decided by a judge. A request for a jury would remove the matter to a district or circuit court. Most states have a maximum amount of $500 to $5,000 in damages that can be recovered in a small-claims court.

Small-claims courts are usually easy to use. An instruction sheet that explains how to file a small claim is available at your county courthouse. You must know the name and address of the person with whom you have a problem. You must know the amount in contention and make a short statement of why you are entitled to the money.

Once your claim is filed, a copy of it is served upon the defendant. The defendant has ten days to appear. If the defendant contests (disagrees with) the claim, a hearing date is set. The hearing lasts about a half hour. The plaintiff presents his or her side of the case; the defendant does the same. You may bring in written statements or evidence as well as witnesses. You should summarize your position on one page and present it to the judge.

No record is made of the small-claims court hearing. It cannot be appealed—the judge's decision is final. The benefit of taking your dispute to small-claims court is financial: you pay no attorneys' fees. Court filing fees are small—$15 to $50 is common. The case is heard in a few weeks at most, giving you speedy relief. If the defendant does not appear, you win by default. The judge proclaims a judgment and the losing party is required to pay damages.

It is important in a small-claims court hearing that you be organized, calm, and specific about your complaint. If you are asking for $500 in damages, you must be prepared to show why you deserve that sum. The judge will ask questions of the plaintiff and defendant. Usually the judge will make an immediate decision or will take a fifteen-minute break and return with the decision.

Many people are experts at appearing in small-claims court. Collection agencies, for example, appear often in small-claims court and know exactly what will happen. If it is your first appearance, you may be nervous and unable to explain your position. Therefore, it is important to prepare yourself by outlining what you will say, gathering evidence you want to present, and summarizing your position. You may read your statement and give a copy to the judge.

In any small-claims action, the plaintiff must prove that the defendant's act was willful—in other words, that the defendant intended to defraud and knowingly and willingly proceeded to do so. The plaintiff must also prove that a loss was sustained as a result of the defendant's willful actions.

Private or Class-Action Lawsuits

You may wish to consider filing a private lawsuit. A private lawsuit is filed to resolve a dispute between an individual (or a business) and others. The lawsuit is called a civil case and is resolved by compromise or formal court trial. Most lawsuits are settled between parties before going to trial.

A civil lawsuit is filed to resolve a dispute between an individual (or business) and others.

If others are similarly affected, a class-action lawsuit may be appropriate. When more than one person is damaged because of the acts of another, a class-action lawsuit may be filed. In this case, a person sues another in behalf of himself or herself and all others. In a class-action lawsuit, all defendants are represented in one case; any judgment would be split among them.

In either event, lawsuits can be very costly and take several years to resolve. Be sure you are willing to take the risk and invest the time, money, and energy to resolve the matter in court.

Anyone can file a lawsuit. The advantages and disadvantages of doing so should be weighed carefully before you decide. Because of the courts' busy schedules, you may wait from one to three years after you have filed the complaint to appear in court. After a court renders a decision, the losing party may file an appeal. You cannot collect a judgment until the appeal is resolved. Therefore, it could be many years before you actually receive any monetary benefits from a lawsuit.

One can never be sure of winning a lawsuit. There may be unknown facts or conditions that will affect the outcome of the action. You may be unable to prove your case to the satisfaction of the judge or jury. One of your witnesses may refuse to testify or may change his or her opinions. For many possible reasons, things might not go as planned. Therefore, you should enter a lawsuit only if you can afford to lose the money you invest in it, and only if you believe there is much more involved than the money you stand to gain.

In some cases, you can convince a consumer protection group to file a lawsuit in your behalf. For example, the American Civil Liberties Union (ACLU) files lawsuits to protect the rights of groups of citizens. The ACLU collects money from donations to pay the costs involved in filing lawsuits. Many individuals cannot afford to pursue legal remedies without the help of such groups because of the expense involved.

Governmental Assistance

In addition to the sources of consumer assistance listed in Chapter 29, you may wish to seek help from a government agency to stop some objectionable practice and get your money back. In many cases, the cost to you is small, while the benefit to all consumers is great. Government agencies that have information and can assist you with a consumer complaint include the following sources as shown in Figure 30-2.

Automobiles	National Highway Traffic Safety Administration	
Collection, Credit	State Consumer Protection Division (at your state capitol)	
Drugs/Foods	Food and Drug Administration	
Household	Consumer Product Safety Commission	
Investment Fraud	Federal Trade Commission Securities and Exchange Commission	
Medical/Dental	State Board of Medical Examiners State Department of Commerce State Board of Dental Examiners State Health Division State Board of Pharmacy	
Medicare	Social Security Administration	
Misrepresentation/Fraud	State Consumer Protection Division Local District Attorney Local or State Better Business Bureau	
Transportation	Interstate Commerce Commission	
Warranties	Federal Trade Commission	

Fig. 30-2

Sources of Governmental Assistance

 ummary

When you cannot get redress through letters and personal contacts with retailers, creditors, manufacturers, or others, you can always turn to the legal system. The American legal system is based on *common law*. This is the law stated by judges in court opinions. There are federal courts, state courts, and local courts.

The federal court system consists of the United States Supreme Court, U.S. Courts of Appeal, and U.S. District (trial) Courts. State court systems consist of the state supreme court, district and circuit (trial) courts, and county and city courts.

Court proceedings begin with the filing of a complaint. The defendant is served and must appear. While the case is awaiting trial, a period called *discovery* begins. During this time, information is gathered, depositions are taken, and in most cases, the parties reach a settlement. If no settlement can be reached, the case goes to trial. The plaintiff presents his or her case first, followed by the defendant. The judge or jury renders a decision, and a judgment is entered for the winning party. Appeals can delay collection or enforcement of the judgment for months or even years.

To find the appropriate remedy, you may wish to negotiate or withhold payment in an attempt to reach an agreement. You may also use a small-claims court (no attorneys allowed) to get a quick answer. You can also consider a class-action lawsuit if there are many others like you who have been damaged, or you may ask for assistance from the ACLU or from the government.

Vocabulary terms

Directions: Can you find the definition for each of the following terms used in Chapter 30?

appellate court   *equitable relief*
civil court   *judgment*
criminal court   *jurisdiction*
counterclaim   *jury*
court   *plaintiff*
defendant   *Statute of Limitations*
depositions   *trial court*
docket

1. A legal action that allows a previous order to be rescinded, the restoration of a previous state, or the performance of a specific act.
2. A tribunal to hear and settle matters brought before it.
3. A tribunal for the trial of crimes regarded as violations of duties to society.
4. A tribunal having authority to hear disputes involving private individuals.
5. The legal right and authority to hear and decide a case.
6. A body of citizens sworn by a court to hear issues of fact and render a verdict.
7. A schedule of cases, dates, and times of issues to be heard by the court.
8. The original court that hears a dispute first brought into court.
9. The person who files a complaint and brings an issue before a court.
10. A tribunal having authority to review the judgment of a lower court.
11. A law that controls the length of time in which a court action must be taken or else the grievance must be forgotten.
12. The person against whom a complaint is made.
13. Written, sworn statements of witnesses, records of which are used in court at a later date.
14. An assertion by a defendant that the plaintiff is at fault.
15. An obligation or debt created by the decree (decision) of the court.

Facts and ideas in review

1. Describe what types of matters are heard before these courts:
   a. trial court
   b. appellate court
   c. civil court
   d. criminal court
2. List and briefly describe the officers of the court.
3. On what bases is the federal court system operating?
4. What is the highest court of the federal court system?
5. How many districts are there for federal district courts in the United States?
6. List several courts that are considered special federal courts.
7. What is the highest court in the state court system?
8. What are the lowest state courts? Give two examples.
9. List the six steps that occur when a court action is filed and carried through trial to a decision of a judge or jury.

Applications for decision making

1. Small-claims courts were set up to give the ordinary person "a say in court" for small matters otherwise not worth taking to court. Why are small-claims courts easy to use and, in some cases, more advantageous than a formal court proceeding?
2. A lawsuit is filed by the plaintiff. Explain what happens until a judgment is entered for the plaintiff.
3. A case that involves a dispute in a city is filed with the circuit court of a county in the same state. When the case is heard in a trial court, where can it be appealed?
4. As a store customer, you are dissatisfied with a product purchased. Explain the self-help remedies and actions to consider in resolving the dispute.
5. Investigate government agencies that have information and can assist you with consumer complaints. What type of complaint is each agency responsible for? Think of a past consumer complaint you or a member of your family may have had. Which agency would you choose for help with this consumer problem?

ife situation problem solving

1. Spend a half day at a local county courthouse. Make arrangements to observe a case being tried. Generally, you will not be allowed to leave the room until the court adjourns, nor will you be allowed to enter while court is in session. You may observe a civil or criminal case. Write a report on what you observe.

2. Visit your local law library located at the county courthouse, a public university, or at a law school if there is one in your area. List five types of references available. Look up the Statute of Limitations for filing lawsuits in your state and tell how long you have to file actions in the following situations:
   a. Wrongful death or injury
   b. Real property infringement
   c. Civil action where you are the injured party of a contract
   Also in your law library, you will find books that summarize cases tried and decided in your state. Find a case that interests you and summarize the issues involved, the court's decision, and your reactions.

3. Examine a lawsuit that has been filed. You can look at records of cases that have been filed in your county, although you will not be given copies free of charge. Read through each case and make notes about the plaintiff, the defendant, the issue at hand, what the plaintiff was asking, and how the matter was resolved.

4. Work in groups with fellow students to determine the appropriate legal remedy for each of the following situations.
   a. The plaintiff was driving his vehicle in a northerly direction when the defendant ran a stop sign going in an easterly direction and did severe damage to the plaintiff's vehicle, including personal injuries to the plaintiff.
   b. A person has paid money to a telemarketer for a product that was promised but never received. The caller said the product was high quality and that the company was a nonprofit organization to benefit disabled veterans.
   c. A local restaurant served food that caused people who ate there on a particular night to get sick. No one died, but several people were very sick for several days, causing medical bills amounting to several thousand dollars. When the cause of the illness was detected, the restaurant was required to make needed changes, and then it was allowed to reopen for business.

7

Case Problems:
Exploring Ethical Issues

In *ethics* we study what is morally good and bad, right and wrong. We seek to learn what makes actions right or wrong. As you will discover, deciding the difference can be a more complex process than it might seem at first.

In this section, you will analyze situations involving ethics in the marketplace and workplace. You will be asked to answer questions related to a specific case. Please record your answers in the space provided on the worksheets in the *Student Activity Guide*. In analyzing each case, you must (1) identify the problem, (2) apply relevant knowledge to the solution of the problem, and (3) draw a conclusion or reach a decision based on careful analysis of the problem. People base ethical decisions on their personal values and principles, which are developed through individual life experiences. Therefore, since everyone has different experiences, decisions about each case will probably vary. How many of your classmates do you suppose answered every question exactly the same?

CASE 1

Get Rich Quick

Charlie Adams is an energetic and ambitious high school student. He wants to make money to go on a great vacation during the summer. When he was reading the newspaper want ads last week, he discovered an ad called "Get Rich Quick." It read as follows:

> Want to make big money in a short time? All you have to do is call the toll-free number listed below. If you can talk on the telephone and you have only $500 to buy your own tele-kit, you can make as much as $5,000 in just two months! Why wait? Call today.

When Charlie called the toll-free number, he was given an address for sending his money. He was told that the plan is "foolproof." He is guaranteed to make all the money he needs for the vacation of his dreams. So Charlie mailed off the $500—all he had in his savings—and eagerly awaited the response. It's been over a month now, and Charlie has heard nothing.

1. What warning signals did Charlie Adams ignore?

2. What do you think will happen next? Will Charlie make $5,000?

3. What can Charlie do now? (Are there consumer protection agencies he can contact for assistance? What do you recommend?)

4. Can you find a similar ad in a newspaper, magazine, circular, or other source that seems too good to be true? Cut it out and attach it here. Write a sentence about what seems to be wrong with the ad.

unit

7

CASE 2

One Thing Leads to Another

Sally Adams works part-time. With her parents as cosigners, she was able to buy her first car. The car wasn't new, but it got her to work.

Sally knows that cars have to be maintained in order to run well. She took her car in last week for a tune-up and was told it would cost about $200, including parts. When she arrived to pick up the car, she was told that more work needed to be done and that she shouldn't drive the car too far before having it done.

So Sally returned and had more work done on her car. The bill came to $150. Sally saw on the repair order that the mechanic also noticed that her brakes needed relining. When she asked how much these items would cost, she was told another $75 to $100.

Now Sally is discouraged and thinks it's time to get rid of the car. All the repairs are just too much for her budget.

1. What type of scam appears to be going on here?

2. What should Sally have done differently?

3. What can Sally do now? What is your advice to her?

4. List some techniques to use when having work done on a car (or other property) to protect yourself from being overcharged.

CASE 3

Something for Nothing

Jared and Kayla work together for a fast-food restaurant. They are both good workers and have been employed for over a year. Each Christmas the company they work for has a big party for all employees. Gifts are given away to employees with outstanding service during the year.

Jared and Kayla's manager has worked for the company for over ten years. She discovered a way to falsify information in the computer to her advantage. She gets more than her fair share of gifts while others in the company do not get as much. Jared and Kayla accidentally discovered this scam. The manager encouraged Jared and Kayla to participate in the scheme.

"You too can get more gifts if you participate. If you try to turn me in, I'll have both of you fired," she said.

1. What is the ethical problem involved in this situation?

2. What are Jared and Kayla's options?

3. What would you do if you were in this situation? Why?

4. How might this case be an example of employee stealing in the workplace?

CASE 4

It's a Good Deal

When Jamal flew to see his relatives last year, he was able to earn enough air miles for a free ticket. The frequent flyer club rules are clear: The ticket is non-transferable.

Jamal bought a ticket for a flight across the country, but later discovered he couldn't go. A friend of his was planning a similar trip, so Jamal offered him the ticket for $100—much cheaper than the cost of a full fare.

When Jamal's friend tried to use the ticket on his return flight, the agent discovered that the ticket belonged to someone else. The airline refused to allow him on the plane without his paying the full price. When he told Jamal about the problem, Jamal said it wasn't his concern.

1. Discuss the pros and cons of Jamal's dilemma.

2. What's wrong with the owner of a ticket giving or selling it to someone else?

3. Would you participate in this type of a deal? Why or why not?

unit

CASE 5

Nobody Got Hurt

Loriann bought a new dress to wear for a special occasion. During the course of the evening, she spilled some juice on the dress and was unable to remove all of the stain. The stain was small and not really visible at first glance.

The next day, Loriann decided that she would probably never wear the dress again. Anyway, the dress didn't fit as well as she would have liked, so she decided to get her money back. That afternoon she returned the dress to the store. She claimed the dress was a gift that she didn't like. The store gave her credit for the dress, and Loriann bought something else.

When asked how she could do something like that, Loriann replied, "Why not? Nobody got hurt."

1. Was there anything wrong with what Loriann did? Did anybody get hurt? Who?

2. Why do some stores have lenient return policies? Why do some stores have "no return" policies?

3. What would you do if you worked in the store and knew what Loriann had done?

4. Discuss the ethical principles involved in this case.

looking back . . .

Unit 7, Consumer Rights and Responsibilities, focused on your rights and responsibilities as a consumer in the marketplace. Consumer groups made up of interested citizens have been formed at the national, state, and local levels. The interests of such groups include consumer education and information, political action, and even public protest. The interests and membership of these groups vary. However, they usually share a common belief—only through organized group action will consumers be heard and have their power felt.

Exercising your rights and responsibilities as an individual requires effort on your part. Reading labels, asking questions, checking references, and going slowly are only a few techniques that are effective in making good purchasing decisions. It's also important to be aware of the consumer laws and know which agency to contact when you need help. You should also keep up on proposed new legislation and be prepared to voice your opinion on matters that concern you.

The court system is there for your protection. Many people do not file lawsuits because of the expense and time involved. Nevertheless, you should be aware of your legal remedies, of court procedures, and of all your options for redress. Polishing your negotiation skills will help you solve problems before you get to the point of needing a lawyer.

1040EZ Tax Tables

These tax tables are provided for taxpayers to compute the amount of income tax liability they owe for the tax year. The 1040EZ tax tables are included with the instructions for preparing Form 1040EZ. After you file your first income tax return, these tables will be mailed to you each year from the IRS to assist you in preparing your tax return. The first year you must file a tax return, you can obtain the instructions and tax tables at a post office, state department of revenue office, or federal tax office in your area, or you can write or call the IRS to have them mailed to you. The tables are simple and easy to use once you compute your taxable income.

appendix a

Section 5—Tax Table

For persons with taxable income of less than $50,000

Example. Mr. Brown is single. His taxable income on line 6 of Form 1040EZ is $23,250. First, he finds the $23,250-23,300 income line. Next, he finds the "Single" column and reads down the column. The amount shown where the income line and filing status column meet ➡ is $3,644. This is the tax amount he must enter on line 8 of Form 1040EZ.

At least	But less than	Single	Married filing jointly
		Your tax is—	
23,200	23,250	3,630	3,484
23,250	23,300	(3,644)	3,491
23,300	23,350	3,658	3,499
23,350	23,400	3,672	3,506

If Form 1040EZ, line 6, is — / **And you are —**

At least	But less than	Single	Married filing jointly
		Your tax is—	
$0	$5	$0	$0
5	15	2	2
15	25	3	3
25	50	6	6
50	75	9	9
75	100	13	13
100	125	17	17
125	150	21	21
150	175	24	24
175	200	28	28
200	225	32	32
225	250	36	36
250	275	39	39
275	300	43	43
300	325	47	47
325	350	51	51
350	375	54	54
375	400	58	58
400	425	62	62
425	450	66	66
450	475	69	69
475	500	73	73
500	525	77	77
525	550	81	81
550	575	84	84
575	600	88	88
600	625	92	92
625	650	96	96
650	675	99	99
675	700	103	103
700	725	107	107
725	750	111	111
750	775	114	114
775	800	118	118
800	825	122	122
825	850	126	126
850	875	129	129
875	900	133	133
900	925	137	137
925	950	141	141
950	975	144	144
975	1,000	148	148

1,000

At least	But less than	Single	Married filing jointly
1,000	1,025	152	152
1,025	1,050	156	156
1,050	1,075	159	159
1,075	1,100	163	163
1,100	1,125	167	167
1,125	1,150	171	171
1,150	1,175	174	174
1,175	1,200	178	178
1,200	1,225	182	182
1,225	1,250	186	186
1,250	1,275	189	189
1,275	1,300	193	193
1,300	1,325	197	197
1,325	1,350	201	201
1,350	1,375	204	204
1,375	1,400	208	208
1,400	1,425	212	212
1,425	1,450	216	216
1,450	1,475	219	219
1,475	1,500	223	223

If Form 1040EZ, line 6, is — / **And you are —**

At least	But less than	Single	Married filing jointly
		Your tax is—	
1,500	1,525	227	227
1,525	1,550	231	231
1,550	1,575	234	234
1,575	1,600	238	238
1,600	1,625	242	242
1,625	1,650	246	246
1,650	1,675	249	249
1,675	1,700	253	253
1,700	1,725	257	257
1,725	1,750	261	261
1,750	1,775	264	264
1,775	1,800	268	268
1,800	1,825	272	272
1,825	1,850	276	276
1,850	1,875	279	279
1,875	1,900	283	283
1,900	1,925	287	287
1,925	1,950	291	291
1,950	1,975	294	294
1,975	2,000	298	298

2,000

At least	But less than	Single	Married filing jointly
2,000	2,025	302	302
2,025	2,050	306	306
2,050	2,075	309	309
2,075	2,100	313	313
2,100	2,125	317	317
2,125	2,150	321	321
2,150	2,175	324	324
2,175	2,200	328	328
2,200	2,225	332	332
2,225	2,250	336	336
2,250	2,275	339	339
2,275	2,300	343	343
2,300	2,325	347	347
2,325	2,350	351	351
2,350	2,375	354	354
2,375	2,400	358	358
2,400	2,425	362	362
2,425	2,450	366	366
2,450	2,475	369	369
2,475	2,500	373	373
2,500	2,525	377	377
2,525	2,550	381	381
2,550	2,575	384	384
2,575	2,600	388	388
2,600	2,625	392	392
2,625	2,650	396	396
2,650	2,675	399	399
2,675	2,700	403	403
2,700	2,725	407	407
2,725	2,750	411	411
2,750	2,775	414	414
2,775	2,800	418	418
2,800	2,825	422	422
2,825	2,850	426	426
2,850	2,875	429	429
2,875	2,900	433	433
2,900	2,925	437	437
2,925	2,950	441	441
2,950	2,975	444	444
2,975	3,000	448	448

If Form 1040EZ, line 6, is — / **And you are —**

3,000

At least	But less than	Single	Married filing jointly
		Your tax is—	
3,000	3,050	454	454
3,050	3,100	461	461
3,100	3,150	469	469
3,150	3,200	476	476
3,200	3,250	484	484
3,250	3,300	491	491
3,300	3,350	499	499
3,350	3,400	506	506
3,400	3,450	514	514
3,450	3,500	521	521
3,500	3,550	529	529
3,550	3,600	536	536
3,600	3,650	544	544
3,650	3,700	551	551
3,700	3,750	559	559
3,750	3,800	566	566
3,800	3,850	574	574
3,850	3,900	581	581
3,900	3,950	589	589
3,950	4,000	596	596

4,000

At least	But less than	Single	Married filing jointly
4,000	4,050	604	604
4,050	4,100	611	611
4,100	4,150	619	619
4,150	4,200	626	626
4,200	4,250	634	634
4,250	4,300	641	641
4,300	4,350	649	649
4,350	4,400	656	656
4,400	4,450	664	664
4,450	4,500	671	671
4,500	4,550	679	679
4,550	4,600	686	686
4,600	4,650	694	694
4,650	4,700	701	701
4,700	4,750	709	709
4,750	4,800	716	716
4,800	4,850	724	724
4,850	4,900	731	731
4,900	4,950	739	739
4,950	5,000	746	746

5,000

At least	But less than	Single	Married filing jointly
5,000	5,050	754	754
5,050	5,100	761	761
5,100	5,150	769	769
5,150	5,200	776	776
5,200	5,250	784	784
5,250	5,300	791	791
5,300	5,350	799	799
5,350	5,400	806	806
5,400	5,450	814	814
5,450	5,500	821	821
5,500	5,550	829	829
5,550	5,600	836	836
5,600	5,650	844	844
5,650	5,700	851	851
5,700	5,750	859	859
5,750	5,800	866	866
5,800	5,850	874	874
5,850	5,900	881	881
5,900	5,950	889	889
5,950	6,000	896	896

If Form 1040EZ, line 6, is — / **And you are —**

6,000

At least	But less than	Single	Married filing jointly
		Your tax is—	
6,000	6,050	904	904
6,050	6,100	911	911
6,100	6,150	919	919
6,150	6,200	926	926
6,200	6,250	934	934
6,250	6,300	941	941
6,300	6,350	949	949
6,350	6,400	956	956
6,400	6,450	964	964
6,450	6,500	971	971
6,500	6,550	979	979
6,550	6,600	986	986
6,600	6,650	994	994
6,650	6,700	1,001	1,001
6,700	6,750	1,009	1,009
6,750	6,800	1,016	1,016
6,800	6,850	1,024	1,024
6,850	6,900	1,031	1,031
6,900	6,950	1,039	1,039
6,950	7,000	1,046	1,046

7,000

At least	But less than	Single	Married filing jointly
7,000	7,050	1,054	1,054
7,050	7,100	1,061	1,061
7,100	7,150	1,069	1,069
7,150	7,200	1,076	1,076
7,200	7,250	1,084	1,084
7,250	7,300	1,091	1,091
7,300	7,350	1,099	1,099
7,350	7,400	1,106	1,106
7,400	7,450	1,114	1,114
7,450	7,500	1,121	1,121
7,500	7,550	1,129	1,129
7,550	7,600	1,136	1,136
7,600	7,650	1,144	1,144
7,650	7,700	1,151	1,151
7,700	7,750	1,159	1,159
7,750	7,800	1,166	1,166
7,800	7,850	1,174	1,174
7,850	7,900	1,181	1,181
7,900	7,950	1,189	1,189
7,950	8,000	1,196	1,196

8,000

At least	But less than	Single	Married filing jointly
8,000	8,050	1,204	1,204
8,050	8,100	1,211	1,211
8,100	8,150	1,219	1,219
8,150	8,200	1,226	1,226
8,200	8,250	1,234	1,234
8,250	8,300	1,241	1,241
8,300	8,350	1,249	1,249
8,350	8,400	1,256	1,256
8,400	8,450	1,264	1,264
8,450	8,500	1,271	1,271
8,500	8,550	1,279	1,279
8,550	8,600	1,286	1,286
8,600	8,650	1,294	1,294
8,650	8,700	1,301	1,301
8,700	8,750	1,309	1,309
8,750	8,800	1,316	1,316
8,800	8,850	1,324	1,324
8,850	8,900	1,331	1,331
8,900	8,950	1,339	1,339
8,950	9,000	1,346	1,346

Continued on next page

19-- 1040EZ Tax Table —*Continued*

If Form 1040EZ, line 6, is —		And you are —		If Form 1040EZ, line 6, is —		And you are —		If Form 1040EZ, line 6, is —		And you are —		If Form 1040EZ, line 6, is —		And you are —	
At least	But less than	Single	Married filing jointly	At least	But less than	Single	Married filing jointly	At least	But less than	Single	Married filing jointly	At least	But less than	Single	Married filing jointly
		Your tax is—				Your tax is—				Your tax is—				Your tax is—	
9,000				**12,000**				**15,000**				**18,000**			
9,000	9,050	1,354	1,354	12,000	12,050	1,804	1,804	15,000	15,050	2,254	2,254	18,000	18,050	2,704	2,704
9,050	9,100	1,361	1,361	12,050	12,100	1,811	1,811	15,050	15,100	2,261	2,261	18,050	18,100	2,711	2,711
9,100	9,150	1,369	1,369	12,100	12,150	1,819	1,819	15,100	15,150	2,269	2,269	18,100	18,150	2,719	2,719
9,150	9,200	1,376	1,376	12,150	12,200	1,826	1,826	15,150	15,200	2,276	2,276	18,150	18,200	2,726	2,726
9,200	9,250	1,384	1,384	12,200	12,250	1,834	1,834	15,200	15,250	2,284	2,284	18,200	18,250	2,734	2,734
9,250	9,300	1,391	1,391	12,250	12,300	1,841	1,841	15,250	15,300	2,291	2,291	18,250	18,300	2,741	2,741
9,300	9,350	1,399	1,399	12,300	12,350	1,849	1,849	15,300	15,350	2,299	2,299	18,300	18,350	2,749	2,749
9,350	9,400	1,406	1,406	12,350	12,400	1,856	1,856	15,350	15,400	2,306	2,306	18,350	18,400	2,756	2,756
9,400	9,450	1,414	1,414	12,400	12,450	1,864	1,864	15,400	15,450	2,314	2,314	18,400	18,450	2,764	2,764
9,450	9,500	1,421	1,421	12,450	12,500	1,871	1,871	15,450	15,500	2,321	2,321	18,450	18,500	2,771	2,771
9,500	9,550	1,429	1,429	12,500	12,550	1,879	1,879	15,500	15,550	2,329	2,329	18,500	18,550	2,779	2,779
9,550	9,600	1,436	1,436	12,550	12,600	1,886	1,886	15,550	15,600	2,336	2,336	18,550	18,600	2,786	2,786
9,600	9,650	1,444	1,444	12,600	12,650	1,894	1,894	15,600	15,650	2,344	2,344	18,600	18,650	2,794	2,794
9,650	9,700	1,451	1,451	12,650	12,700	1,901	1,901	15,650	15,700	2,351	2,351	18,650	18,700	2,801	2,801
9,700	9,750	1,459	1,459	12,700	12,750	1,909	1,909	15,700	15,750	2,359	2,359	18,700	18,750	2,809	2,809
9,750	9,800	1,466	1,466	12,750	12,800	1,916	1,916	15,750	15,800	2,366	2,366	18,750	18,800	2,816	2,816
9,800	9,850	1,474	1,474	12,800	12,850	1,924	1,924	15,800	15,850	2,374	2,374	18,800	18,850	2,824	2,824
9,850	9,900	1,481	1,481	12,850	12,900	1,931	1,931	15,850	15,900	2,381	2,381	18,850	18,900	2,831	2,831
9,900	9,950	1,489	1,489	12,900	12,950	1,939	1,939	15,900	15,950	2,389	2,389	18,900	18,950	2,839	2,839
9,950	10,000	1,496	1,496	12,950	13,000	1,946	1,946	15,950	16,000	2,396	2,396	18,950	19,000	2,846	2,846
10,000				**13,000**				**16,000**				**19,000**			
10,000	10,050	1,504	1,504	13,000	13,050	1,954	1,954	16,000	16,050	2,404	2,404	19,000	19,050	2,854	2,854
10,050	10,100	1,511	1,511	13,050	13,100	1,961	1,961	16,050	16,100	2,411	2,411	19,050	19,100	2,861	2,861
10,100	10,150	1,519	1,519	13,100	13,150	1,969	1,969	16,100	16,150	2,419	2,419	19,100	19,150	2,869	2,869
10,150	10,200	1,526	1,526	13,150	13,200	1,976	1,976	16,150	16,200	2,426	2,426	19,150	19,200	2,876	2,876
10,200	10,250	1,534	1,534	13,200	13,250	1,984	1,984	16,200	16,250	2,434	2,434	19,200	19,250	2,884	2,884
10,250	10,300	1,541	1,541	13,250	13,300	1,991	1,991	16,250	16,300	2,441	2,441	19,250	19,300	2,891	2,891
10,300	10,350	1,549	1,549	13,300	13,350	1,999	1,999	16,300	16,350	2,449	2,449	19,300	19,350	2,899	2,899
10,350	10,400	1,556	1,556	13,350	13,400	2,006	2,006	16,350	16,400	2,456	2,456	19,350	19,400	2,906	2,906
10,400	10,450	1,564	1,564	13,400	13,450	2,014	2,014	16,400	16,450	2,464	2,464	19,400	19,450	2,914	2,914
10,450	10,500	1,571	1,571	13,450	13,500	2,021	2,021	16,450	16,500	2,471	2,471	19,450	19,500	2,921	2,921
10,500	10,550	1,579	1,579	13,500	13,550	2,029	2,029	16,500	16,550	2,479	2,479	19,500	19,550	2,929	2,929
10,550	10,600	1,586	1,586	13,550	13,600	2,036	2,036	16,550	16,600	2,486	2,486	19,550	19,600	2,936	2,936
10,600	10,650	1,594	1,594	13,600	13,650	2,044	2,044	16,600	16,650	2,494	2,494	19,600	19,650	2,944	2,944
10,650	10,700	1,601	1,601	13,650	13,700	2,051	2,051	16,650	16,700	2,501	2,501	19,650	19,700	2,951	2,951
10,700	10,750	1,609	1,609	13,700	13,750	2,059	2,059	16,700	16,750	2,509	2,509	19,700	19,750	2,959	2,959
10,750	10,800	1,616	1,616	13,750	13,800	2,066	2,066	16,750	16,800	2,516	2,516	19,750	19,800	2,966	2,966
10,800	10,850	1,624	1,624	13,800	13,850	2,074	2,074	16,800	16,850	2,524	2,524	19,800	19,850	2,974	2,974
10,850	10,900	1,631	1,631	13,850	13,900	2,081	2,081	16,850	16,900	2,531	2,531	19,850	19,900	2,981	2,981
10,900	10,950	1,639	1,639	13,900	13,950	2,089	2,089	16,900	16,950	2,539	2,539	19,900	19,950	2,989	2,989
10,950	11,000	1,646	1,646	13,950	14,000	2,096	2,096	16,950	17,000	2,546	2,546	19,950	20,000	2,996	2,996
11,000				**14,000**				**17,000**				**20,000**			
11,000	11,050	1,654	1,654	14,000	14,050	2,104	2,104	17,000	17,050	2,554	2,554	20,000	20,050	3,004	3,004
11,050	11,100	1,661	1,661	14,050	14,100	2,111	2,111	17,050	17,100	2,561	2,561	20,050	20,100	3,011	3,011
11,100	11,150	1,669	1,669	14,100	14,150	2,119	2,119	17,100	17,150	2,569	2,569	20,100	20,150	3,019	3,019
11,150	11,200	1,676	1,676	14,150	14,200	2,126	2,126	17,150	17,200	2,576	2,576	20,150	20,200	3,026	3,026
11,200	11,250	1,684	1,684	14,200	14,250	2,134	2,134	17,200	17,250	2,584	2,584	20,200	20,250	3,034	3,034
11,250	11,300	1,691	1,691	14,250	14,300	2,141	2,141	17,250	17,300	2,591	2,591	20,250	20,300	3,041	3,041
11,300	11,350	1,699	1,699	14,300	14,350	2,149	2,149	17,300	17,350	2,599	2,599	20,300	20,350	3,049	3,049
11,350	11,400	1,706	1,706	14,350	14,400	2,156	2,156	17,350	17,400	2,606	2,606	20,350	20,400	3,056	3,056
11,400	11,450	1,714	1,714	14,400	14,450	2,164	2,164	17,400	17,450	2,614	2,614	20,400	20,450	3,064	3,064
11,450	11,500	1,721	1,721	14,450	14,500	2,171	2,171	17,450	17,500	2,621	2,621	20,450	20,500	3,071	3,071
11,500	11,550	1,729	1,729	14,500	14,550	2,179	2,179	17,500	17,550	2,629	2,629	20,500	20,550	3,079	3,079
11,550	11,600	1,736	1,736	14,550	14,600	2,186	2,186	17,550	17,600	2,636	2,636	20,550	20,600	3,086	3,086
11,600	11,650	1,744	1,744	14,600	14,650	2,194	2,194	17,600	17,650	2,644	2,644	20,600	20,650	3,094	3,094
11,650	11,700	1,751	1,751	14,650	14,700	2,201	2,201	17,650	17,700	2,651	2,651	20,650	20,700	3,101	3,101
11,700	11,750	1,759	1,759	14,700	14,750	2,209	2,209	17,700	17,750	2,659	2,659	20,700	20,750	3,109	3,109
11,750	11,800	1,766	1,766	14,750	14,800	2,216	2,216	17,750	17,800	2,666	2,666	20,750	20,800	3,116	3,116
11,800	11,850	1,774	1,774	14,800	14,850	2,224	2,224	17,800	17,850	2,674	2,674	20,800	20,850	3,124	3,124
11,850	11,900	1,781	1,781	14,850	14,900	2,231	2,231	17,850	17,900	2,681	2,681	20,850	20,900	3,131	3,131
11,900	11,950	1,789	1,789	14,900	14,950	2,239	2,239	17,900	17,950	2,689	2,689	20,900	20,950	3,139	3,139
11,950	12,000	1,796	1,796	14,950	15,000	2,246	2,246	17,950	18,000	2,696	2,696	20,950	21,000	3,146	3,146

Continued on next page

19-- 1040EZ Tax Table —Continued

Column headers for each section:

If Form 1040EZ, line 6, is —		And you are —	
At least	But less than	Single	Married filing jointly
		Your tax is—	

21,000

At least	But less than	Single	Married filing jointly
21,000	21,050	3,154	3,154
21,050	21,100	3,161	3,161
21,100	21,150	3,169	3,169
21,150	21,200	3,176	3,176
21,200	21,250	3,184	3,184
21,250	21,300	3,191	3,191
21,300	21,350	3,199	3,199
21,350	21,400	3,206	3,206
21,400	21,450	3,214	3,214
21,450	21,500	3,221	3,221
21,500	21,550	3,229	3,229
21,550	21,600	3,236	3,236
21,600	21,650	3,244	3,244
21,650	21,700	3,251	3,251
21,700	21,750	3,259	3,259
21,750	21,800	3,266	3,266
21,800	21,850	3,274	3,274
21,850	21,900	3,281	3,281
21,900	21,950	3,289	3,289
21,950	22,000	3,296	3,296

22,000

At least	But less than	Single	Married filing jointly
22,000	22,050	3,304	3,304
22,050	22,100	3,311	3,311
22,100	22,150	3,322	3,319
22,150	22,200	3,336	3,326
22,200	22,250	3,350	3,334
22,250	22,300	3,364	3,341
22,300	22,350	3,378	3,349
22,350	22,400	3,392	3,356
22,400	22,450	3,406	3,364
22,450	22,500	3,420	3,371
22,500	22,550	3,434	3,379
22,550	22,600	3,448	3,386
22,600	22,650	3,462	3,394
22,650	22,700	3,476	3,401
22,700	22,750	3,490	3,409
22,750	22,800	3,504	3,416
22,800	22,850	3,518	3,424
22,850	22,900	3,532	3,431
22,900	22,950	3,546	3,439
22,950	23,000	3,560	3,446

23,000

At least	But less than	Single	Married filing jointly
23,000	23,050	3,574	3,454
23,050	23,100	3,588	3,461
23,100	23,150	3,602	3,469
23,150	23,200	3,616	3,476
23,200	23,250	3,630	3,484
23,250	23,300	3,644	3,491
23,300	23,350	3,658	3,499
23,350	23,400	3,672	3,506
23,400	23,450	3,686	3,514
23,450	23,500	3,700	3,521
23,500	23,550	3,714	3,529
23,550	23,600	3,728	3,536
23,600	23,650	3,742	3,544
23,650	23,700	3,756	3,551
23,700	23,750	3,770	3,559
23,750	23,800	3,784	3,566
23,800	23,850	3,798	3,574
23,850	23,900	3,812	3,581
23,900	23,950	3,826	3,589
23,950	24,000	3,840	3,596

24,000

At least	But less than	Single	Married filing jointly
24,000	24,050	3,854	3,604
24,050	24,100	3,868	3,611
24,100	24,150	3,882	3,619
24,150	24,200	3,896	3,626
24,200	24,250	3,910	3,634
24,250	24,300	3,924	3,641
24,300	24,350	3,938	3,649
24,350	24,400	3,952	3,656
24,400	24,450	3,966	3,664
24,450	24,500	3,980	3,671
24,500	24,550	3,994	3,679
24,550	24,600	4,008	3,686
24,600	24,650	4,022	3,694
24,650	24,700	4,036	3,701
24,700	24,750	4,050	3,709
24,750	24,800	4,064	3,716
24,800	24,850	4,078	3,724
24,850	24,900	4,092	3,731
24,900	24,950	4,106	3,739
24,950	25,000	4,120	3,746

25,000

At least	But less than	Single	Married filing jointly
25,000	25,050	4,134	3,754
25,050	25,100	4,148	3,761
25,100	25,150	4,162	3,769
25,150	25,200	4,176	3,776
25,200	25,250	4,190	3,784
25,250	25,300	4,204	3,791
25,300	25,350	4,218	3,799
25,350	25,400	4,232	3,806
25,400	25,450	4,246	3,814
25,450	25,500	4,260	3,821
25,500	25,550	4,274	3,829
25,550	25,600	4,288	3,836
25,600	25,650	4,302	3,844
25,650	25,700	4,316	3,851
25,700	25,750	4,330	3,859
25,750	25,800	4,344	3,866
25,800	25,850	4,358	3,874
25,850	25,900	4,372	3,881
25,900	25,950	4,386	3,889
25,950	26,000	4,400	3,896

26,000

At least	But less than	Single	Married filing jointly
26,000	26,050	4,414	3,904
26,050	26,100	4,428	3,911
26,100	26,150	4,442	3,919
26,150	26,200	4,456	3,926
26,200	26,250	4,470	3,934
26,250	26,300	4,484	3,941
26,300	26,350	4,498	3,949
26,350	26,400	4,512	3,956
26,400	26,450	4,526	3,964
26,450	26,500	4,540	3,971
26,500	26,550	4,554	3,979
26,550	26,600	4,568	3,986
26,600	26,650	4,582	3,994
26,650	26,700	4,596	4,001
26,700	26,750	4,610	4,009
26,750	26,800	4,624	4,016
26,800	26,850	4,638	4,024
26,850	26,900	4,652	4,031
26,900	26,950	4,666	4,039
26,950	27,000	4,680	4,046

27,000

At least	But less than	Single	Married filing jointly
27,000	27,050	4,694	4,054
27,050	27,100	4,708	4,061
27,100	27,150	4,722	4,069
27,150	27,200	4,736	4,076
27,200	27,250	4,750	4,084
27,250	27,300	4,764	4,091
27,300	27,350	4,778	4,099
27,350	27,400	4,792	4,106
27,400	27,450	4,806	4,114
27,450	27,500	4,820	4,121
27,500	27,550	4,834	4,129
27,550	27,600	4,848	4,136
27,600	27,650	4,862	4,144
27,650	27,700	4,876	4,151
27,700	27,750	4,890	4,159
27,750	27,800	4,904	4,166
27,800	27,850	4,918	4,174
27,850	27,900	4,932	4,181
27,900	27,950	4,946	4,189
27,950	28,000	4,960	4,196

28,000

At least	But less than	Single	Married filing jointly
28,000	28,050	4,974	4,204
28,050	28,100	4,988	4,211
28,100	28,150	5,002	4,219
28,150	28,200	5,016	4,226
28,200	28,250	5,030	4,234
28,250	28,300	5,044	4,241
28,300	28,350	5,058	4,249
28,350	28,400	5,072	4,256
28,400	28,450	5,086	4,264
28,450	28,500	5,100	4,271
28,500	28,550	5,114	4,279
28,550	28,600	5,128	4,286
28,600	28,650	5,142	4,294
28,650	28,700	5,156	4,301
28,700	28,750	5,170	4,309
28,750	28,800	5,184	4,316
28,800	28,850	5,198	4,324
28,850	28,900	5,212	4,331
28,900	28,950	5,226	4,339
28,950	29,000	5,240	4,346

29,000

At least	But less than	Single	Married filing jointly
29,000	29,050	5,254	4,354
29,050	29,100	5,268	4,361
29,100	29,150	5,282	4,369
29,150	29,200	5,296	4,376
29,200	29,250	5,310	4,384
29,250	29,300	5,324	4,391
29,300	29,350	5,338	4,399
29,350	29,400	5,352	4,406
29,400	29,450	5,366	4,414
29,450	29,500	5,380	4,421
29,500	29,550	5,394	4,429
29,550	29,600	5,408	4,436
29,600	29,650	5,422	4,444
29,650	29,700	5,436	4,451
29,700	29,750	5,450	4,459
29,750	29,800	5,464	4,466
29,800	29,850	5,478	4,474
29,850	29,900	5,492	4,481
29,900	29,950	5,506	4,489
29,950	30,000	5,520	4,496

30,000

At least	But less than	Single	Married filing jointly
30,000	30,050	5,534	4,504
30,050	30,100	5,548	4,511
30,100	30,150	5,562	4,519
30,150	30,200	5,576	4,526
30,200	30,250	5,590	4,534
30,250	30,300	5,604	4,541
30,300	30,350	5,618	4,549
30,350	30,400	5,632	4,556
30,400	30,450	5,646	4,564
30,450	30,500	5,660	4,571
30,500	30,550	5,674	4,579
30,550	30,600	5,688	4,586
30,600	30,650	5,702	4,594
30,650	30,700	5,716	4,601
30,700	30,750	5,730	4,609
30,750	30,800	5,744	4,616
30,800	30,850	5,758	4,624
30,850	30,900	5,772	4,631
30,900	30,950	5,786	4,639
30,950	31,000	5,800	4,646

31,000

At least	But less than	Single	Married filing jointly
31,000	31,050	5,814	4,654
31,050	31,100	5,828	4,661
31,100	31,150	5,842	4,669
31,150	31,200	5,856	4,676
31,200	31,250	5,870	4,684
31,250	31,300	5,884	4,691
31,300	31,350	5,898	4,699
31,350	31,400	5,912	4,706
31,400	31,450	5,926	4,714
31,450	31,500	5,940	4,721
31,500	31,550	5,954	4,729
31,550	31,600	5,968	4,736
31,600	31,650	5,982	4,744
31,650	31,700	5,996	4,751
31,700	31,750	6,010	4,759
31,750	31,800	6,024	4,766
31,800	31,850	6,038	4,774
31,850	31,900	6,052	4,781
31,900	31,950	6,066	4,789
31,950	32,000	6,080	4,796

32,000

At least	But less than	Single	Married filing jointly
32,000	32,050	6,094	4,804
32,050	32,100	6,108	4,811
32,100	32,150	6,122	4,819
32,150	32,200	6,136	4,826
32,200	32,250	6,150	4,834
32,250	32,300	6,164	4,841
32,300	32,350	6,178	4,849
32,350	32,400	6,192	4,856
32,400	32,450	6,206	4,864
32,450	32,500	6,220	4,871
32,500	32,550	6,234	4,879
32,550	32,600	6,248	4,886
32,600	32,650	6,262	4,894
32,650	32,700	6,276	4,901
32,700	32,750	6,290	4,909
32,750	32,800	6,304	4,916
32,800	32,850	6,318	4,924
32,850	32,900	6,332	4,931
32,900	32,950	6,346	4,939
32,950	33,000	6,360	4,946

Continued on next page

19-- 1040EZ Tax Table —*Continued*

If Form 1040EZ, line 6, is —		And you are —		If Form 1040EZ, line 6, is —		And you are —		If Form 1040EZ, line 6, is —		And you are —		If Form 1040EZ, line 6, is —		And you are —	
At least	But less than	Single	Married filing jointly	At least	But less than	Single	Married filing jointly	At least	But less than	Single	Married filing jointly	At least	But less than	Single	Married filing jointly
		Your tax is—				Your tax is—				Your tax is—				Your tax is—	
33,000				**36,000**				**39,000**				**42,000**			
33,000	33,050	6,374	4,954	36,000	36,050	7,214	5,404	39,000	39,050	8,054	6,130	42,000	42,050	8,894	6,970
33,050	33,100	6,388	4,961	36,050	36,100	7,228	5,411	39,050	39,100	8,068	6,144	42,050	42,100	8,908	6,984
33,100	33,150	6,402	4,969	36,100	36,150	7,242	5,419	39,100	39,150	8,082	6,158	42,100	42,150	8,922	6,998
33,150	33,200	6,416	4,976	36,150	36,200	7,256	5,426	39,150	39,200	8,096	6,172	42,150	42,200	8,936	7,012
33,200	33,250	6,430	4,984	36,200	36,250	7,270	5,434	39,200	39,250	8,110	6,186	42,200	42,250	8,950	7,026
33,250	33,300	6,444	4,991	36,250	36,300	7,284	5,441	39,250	39,300	8,124	6,200	42,250	42,300	8,964	7,040
33,300	33,350	6,458	4,999	36,300	36,350	7,298	5,449	39,300	39,350	8,138	6,214	42,300	42,350	8,978	7,054
33,350	33,400	6,472	5,006	36,350	36,400	7,312	5,456	39,350	39,400	8,152	6,228	42,350	42,400	8,992	7,068
33,400	33,450	6,486	5,014	36,400	36,450	7,326	5,464	39,400	39,450	8,166	6,242	42,400	42,450	9,006	7,082
33,450	33,500	6,500	5,021	36,450	36,500	7,340	5,471	39,450	39,500	8,180	6,256	42,450	42,500	9,020	7,096
33,500	33,550	6,514	5,029	36,500	36,550	7,354	5,479	39,500	39,550	8,194	6,270	42,500	42,550	9,034	7,110
33,550	33,600	6,528	5,036	36,550	36,600	7,368	5,486	39,550	39,600	8,208	6,284	42,550	42,600	9,048	7,124
33,600	33,650	6,542	5,044	36,600	36,650	7,382	5,494	39,600	39,650	8,222	6,298	42,600	42,650	9,062	7,138
33,650	33,700	6,556	5,051	36,650	36,700	7,396	5,501	39,650	39,700	8,236	6,312	42,650	42,700	9,076	7,152
33,700	33,750	6,570	5,059	36,700	36,750	7,410	5,509	39,700	39,750	8,250	6,326	42,700	42,750	9,090	7,166
33,750	33,800	6,584	5,066	36,750	36,800	7,424	5,516	39,750	39,800	8,264	6,340	42,750	42,800	9,104	7,180
33,800	33,850	6,598	5,074	36,800	36,850	7,438	5,524	39,800	39,850	8,278	6,354	42,800	42,850	9,118	7,194
33,850	33,900	6,612	5,081	36,850	36,900	7,452	5,531	39,850	39,900	8,292	6,368	42,850	42,900	9,132	7,208
33,900	33,950	6,626	5,089	36,900	36,950	7,466	5,542	39,900	39,950	8,306	6,382	42,900	42,950	9,146	7,222
33,950	34,000	6,640	5,096	36,950	37,000	7,480	5,556	39,950	40,000	8,320	6,396	42,950	43,000	9,160	7,236
34,000				**37,000**				**40,000**				**43,000**			
34,000	34,050	6,654	5,104	37,000	37,050	7,494	5,570	40,000	40,050	8,334	6,410	43,000	43,050	9,174	7,250
34,050	34,100	6,668	5,111	37,050	37,100	7,508	5,584	40,050	40,100	8,348	6,424	43,050	43,100	9,188	7,264
34,100	34,150	6,682	5,119	37,100	37,150	7,522	5,598	40,100	40,150	8,362	6,438	43,100	43,150	9,202	7,278
34,150	34,200	6,696	5,126	37,150	37,200	7,536	5,612	40,150	40,200	8,376	6,452	43,150	43,200	9,216	7,292
34,200	34,250	6,710	5,134	37,200	37,250	7,550	5,626	40,200	40,250	8,390	6,466	43,200	43,250	9,230	7,306
34,250	34,300	6,724	5,141	37,250	37,300	7,564	5,640	40,250	40,300	8,404	6,480	43,250	43,300	9,244	7,320
34,300	34,350	6,738	5,149	37,300	37,350	7,578	5,654	40,300	40,350	8,418	6,494	43,300	43,350	9,258	7,334
34,350	34,400	6,752	5,156	37,350	37,400	7,592	5,668	40,350	40,400	8,432	6,508	43,350	43,400	9,272	7,348
34,400	34,450	6,766	5,164	37,400	37,450	7,606	5,682	40,400	40,450	8,446	6,522	43,400	43,450	9,286	7,362
34,450	34,500	6,780	5,171	37,450	37,500	7,620	5,696	40,450	40,500	8,460	6,536	43,450	43,500	9,300	7,376
34,500	34,550	6,794	5,179	37,500	37,550	7,634	5,710	40,500	40,550	8,474	6,550	43,500	43,550	9,314	7,390
34,550	34,600	6,808	5,186	37,550	37,600	7,648	5,724	40,550	40,600	8,488	6,564	43,550	43,600	9,328	7,404
34,600	34,650	6,822	5,194	37,600	37,650	7,662	5,738	40,600	40,650	8,502	6,578	43,600	43,650	9,342	7,418
34,650	34,700	6,836	5,201	37,650	37,700	7,676	5,752	40,650	40,700	8,516	6,592	43,650	43,700	9,356	7,432
34,700	34,750	6,850	5,209	37,700	37,750	7,690	5,766	40,700	40,750	8,530	6,606	43,700	43,750	9,370	7,446
34,750	34,800	6,864	5,216	37,750	37,800	7,704	5,780	40,750	40,800	8,544	6,620	43,750	43,800	9,384	7,460
34,800	34,850	6,878	5,224	37,800	37,850	7,718	5,794	40,800	40,850	8,558	6,634	43,800	43,850	9,398	7,474
34,850	34,900	6,892	5,231	37,850	37,900	7,732	5,808	40,850	40,900	8,572	6,648	43,850	43,900	9,412	7,488
34,900	34,950	6,906	5,239	37,900	37,950	7,746	5,822	40,900	40,950	8,586	6,662	43,900	43,950	9,426	7,502
34,950	35,000	6,920	5,246	37,950	38,000	7,760	5,836	40,950	41,000	8,600	6,676	43,950	44,000	9,440	7,516
35,000				**38,000**				**41,000**				**44,000**			
35,000	35,050	6,934	5,254	38,000	38,050	7,774	5,850	41,000	41,050	8,614	6,690	44,000	44,050	9,454	7,530
35,050	35,100	6,948	5,261	38,050	38,100	7,788	5,864	41,050	41,100	8,628	6,704	44,050	44,100	9,468	7,544
35,100	35,150	6,962	5,269	38,100	38,150	7,802	5,878	41,100	41,150	8,642	6,718	44,100	44,150	9,482	7,558
35,150	35,200	6,976	5,276	38,150	38,200	7,816	5,892	41,150	41,200	8,656	6,732	44,150	44,200	9,496	7,572
35,200	35,250	6,990	5,284	38,200	38,250	7,830	5,906	41,200	41,250	8,670	6,746	44,200	44,250	9,510	7,586
35,250	35,300	7,004	5,291	38,250	38,300	7,844	5,920	41,250	41,300	8,684	6,760	44,250	44,300	9,524	7,600
35,300	35,350	7,018	5,299	38,300	38,350	7,858	5,934	41,300	41,350	8,698	6,774	44,300	44,350	9,538	7,614
35,350	35,400	7,032	5,306	38,350	38,400	7,872	5,948	41,350	41,400	8,712	6,788	44,350	44,400	9,552	7,628
35,400	35,450	7,046	5,314	38,400	38,450	7,886	5,962	41,400	41,450	8,726	6,802	44,400	44,450	9,566	7,642
35,450	35,500	7,060	5,321	38,450	38,500	7,900	5,976	41,450	41,500	8,740	6,816	44,450	44,500	9,580	7,656
35,500	35,550	7,074	5,329	38,500	38,550	7,914	5,990	41,500	41,550	8,754	6,830	44,500	44,550	9,594	7,670
35,550	35,600	7,088	5,336	38,550	38,600	7,928	6,004	41,550	41,600	8,768	6,844	44,550	44,600	9,608	7,684
35,600	35,650	7,102	5,344	38,600	38,650	7,942	6,018	41,600	41,650	8,782	6,858	44,600	44,650	9,622	7,698
35,650	35,700	7,116	5,351	38,650	38,700	7,956	6,032	41,650	41,700	8,796	6,872	44,650	44,700	9,636	7,712
35,700	35,750	7,130	5,359	38,700	38,750	7,970	6,046	41,700	41,750	8,810	6,886	44,700	44,750	9,650	7,726
35,750	35,800	7,144	5,366	38,750	38,800	7,984	6,060	41,750	41,800	8,824	6,900	44,750	44,800	9,664	7,740
35,800	35,850	7,158	5,374	38,800	38,850	7,998	6,074	41,800	41,850	8,838	6,914	44,800	44,850	9,678	7,754
35,850	35,900	7,172	5,381	38,850	38,900	8,012	6,088	41,850	41,900	8,852	6,928	44,850	44,900	9,692	7,768
35,900	35,950	7,186	5,389	38,900	38,950	8,026	6,102	41,900	41,950	8,866	6,942	44,900	44,950	9,706	7,782
35,950	36,000	7,200	5,396	38,950	39,000	8,040	6,116	41,950	42,000	8,880	6,956	44,950	45,000	9,720	7,796

Continued on next page

19-- **1040EZ Tax Table** —*Continued*

If Form 1040EZ, line 6, is —		And you are —		If Form 1040EZ, line 6, is —		And you are —	
At least	But less than	Single	Married filing jointly	At least	But less than	Single	Married filing jointly
		Your tax is—				Your tax is—	

45,000

At least	But less than	Single	Married filing jointly
45,000	45,050	9,734	7,810
45,050	45,100	9,748	7,824
45,100	45,150	9,762	7,838
45,150	45,200	9,776	7,852
45,200	45,250	9,790	7,866
45,250	45,300	9,804	7,880
45,300	45,350	9,818	7,894
45,350	45,400	9,832	7,908
45,400	45,450	9,846	7,922
45,450	45,500	9,860	7,936
45,500	45,550	9,874	7,950
45,550	45,600	9,888	7,964
45,600	45,650	9,902	7,978
45,650	45,700	9,916	7,992
45,700	45,750	9,930	8,006
45,750	45,800	9,944	8,020
45,800	45,850	9,958	8,034
45,850	45,900	9,972	8,048
45,900	45,950	9,986	8,062
45,950	46,000	10,000	8,076

46,000

At least	But less than	Single	Married filing jointly
46,000	46,050	10,014	8,090
46,050	46,100	10,028	8,104
46,100	46,150	10,042	8,118
46,150	46,200	10,056	8,132
46,200	46,250	10,070	8,146
46,250	46,300	10,084	8,160
46,300	46,350	10,098	8,174
46,350	46,400	10,112	8,188
46,400	46,450	10,126	8,202
46,450	46,500	10,140	8,216
46,500	46,550	10,154	8,230
46,550	46,600	10,168	8,244
46,600	46,650	10,182	8,258
46,650	46,700	10,196	8,272
46,700	46,750	10,210	8,286
46,750	46,800	10,224	8,300
46,800	46,850	10,238	8,314
46,850	46,900	10,252	8,328
46,900	46,950	10,266	8,342
46,950	47,000	10,280	8,356

47,000

At least	But less than	Single	Married filing jointly
47,000	47,050	10,294	8,370
47,050	47,100	10,308	8,384
47,100	47,150	10,322	8,398
47,150	47,200	10,336	8,412
47,200	47,250	10,350	8,426
47,250	47,300	10,364	8,440
47,300	47,350	10,378	8,454
47,350	47,400	10,392	8,468
47,400	47,450	10,406	8,482
47,450	47,500	10,420	8,496
47,500	47,550	10,434	8,510
47,550	47,600	10,448	8,524
47,600	47,650	10,462	8,538
47,650	47,700	10,476	8,552
47,700	47,750	10,490	8,566
47,750	47,800	10,504	8,580
47,800	47,850	10,518	8,594
47,850	47,900	10,532	8,608
47,900	47,950	10,546	8,622
47,950	48,000	10,560	8,636

48,000

At least	But less than	Single	Married filing jointly
48,000	48,050	10,574	8,650
48,050	48,100	10,588	8,664
48,100	48,150	10,602	8,678
48,150	48,200	10,616	8,692
48,200	48,250	10,630	8,706
48,250	48,300	10,644	8,720
48,300	48,350	10,658	8,734
48,350	48,400	10,672	8,748
48,400	48,450	10,686	8,762
48,450	48,500	10,700	8,776
48,500	48,550	10,714	8,790
48,550	48,600	10,728	8,804
48,600	48,650	10,742	8,818
48,650	48,700	10,756	8,832
48,700	48,750	10,770	8,846
48,750	48,800	10,784	8,860
48,800	48,850	10,798	8,874
48,850	48,900	10,812	8,888
48,900	48,950	10,826	8,902
48,950	49,000	10,840	8,916

49,000

At least	But less than	Single	Married filing jointly
49,000	49,050	10,854	8,930
49,050	49,100	10,868	8,944
49,100	49,150	10,882	8,958
49,150	49,200	10,896	8,972
49,200	49,250	10,910	8,986
49,250	49,300	10,924	9,000
49,300	49,350	10,938	9,014
49,350	49,400	10,952	9,028
49,400	49,450	10,966	9,042
49,450	49,500	10,980	9,056
49,500	49,550	10,994	9,070
49,550	49,600	11,008	9,084
49,600	49,650	11,022	9,098
49,650	49,700	11,036	9,112
49,700	49,750	11,050	9,126
49,750	49,800	11,064	9,140
49,800	49,850	11,078	9,154
49,850	49,900	11,092	9,168
49,900	49,950	11,106	9,182
49,950	50,000	11,120	9,196

$50,000 or over— use Form 1040

1040A Tax Tables

These tax tables are provided for taxpayers to compute the amount of income tax liability they owe for the tax year. The 1040A tax tables are included with the instructions for preparing Form 1040A. After you file your first income tax return, these tables will be mailed to you each year from the IRS to assist you in preparing your tax return. The first year you must file a tax return, you can obtain the instructions and tax tables at a post office, state department of revenue office, or federal tax office in your area, or you can write or call the IRS to have them mailed to you. The tables are simple and easy to use once you compute your taxable income.

appendix b

Section 5—Tax Table

For persons with taxable incomes of less than $50,000

Example. Mr. and Mrs. Green are filing a joint return. Their taxable income on line 22 of Form 1040A is $23,250. First, they find the $23,250-23,300 income line. Next, they find the column for married filing jointly and read down the column. The amount shown where the income line and filing status column meet is $3,491. This is the tax amount they must enter on line 23 of Form 1040A.

At least	But less than	Single	Married filing jointly *	Married filing sepa-rately	Head of a house-hold
			Your tax is—		
23,200	23,250	3,630	3,484	4,105	3,484
23,250	23,300	3,644	(3,491)	4,119	3,491
23,300	23,350	3,658	3,499	4,133	3,499
23,350	23,400	3,672	3,506	4,147	3,506

If Form 1040A, line 22, is — At least	But less than	And you are — Single	Married filing jointly *	Married filing sepa-rately	Head of a house-hold	If Form 1040A, line 22, is — At least	But less than	And you are — Single	Married filing jointly *	Married filing sepa-rately	Head of a house-hold	If Form 1040A, line 22, is — At least	But less than	And you are — Single	Married filing jointly *	Married filing sepa-rately	Head of a house-hold
			Your tax is—						**Your tax is—**						**Your tax is—**		
$0	$5	$0	$0	$0	$0	1,300	1,325	197	197	197	197	2,700	2,725	407	407	407	407
5	15	2	2	2	2	1,325	1,350	201	201	201	201	2,725	2,750	411	411	411	411
15	25	3	3	3	3	1,350	1,375	204	204	204	204	2,750	2,775	414	414	414	414
25	50	6	6	6	6	1,375	1,400	208	208	208	208	2,775	2,800	418	418	418	418
50	75	9	9	9	9	1,400	1,425	212	212	212	212	2,800	2,825	422	422	422	422
75	100	13	13	13	13	1,425	1,450	216	216	216	216	2,825	2,850	426	426	426	426
100	125	17	17	17	17	1,450	1,475	219	219	219	219	2,850	2,875	429	429	429	429
125	150	21	21	21	21	1,475	1,500	223	223	223	223	2,875	2,900	433	433	433	433
150	175	24	24	24	24	1,500	1,525	227	227	227	227	2,900	2,925	437	437	437	437
175	200	28	28	28	28	1,525	1,550	231	231	231	231	2,925	2,950	441	441	441	441
200	225	32	32	32	32	1,550	1,575	234	234	234	234	2,950	2,975	444	444	444	444
225	250	36	36	36	36	1,575	1,600	238	238	238	238	2,975	3,000	448	448	448	448
250	275	39	39	39	39	1,600	1,625	242	242	242	242						
275	300	43	43	43	43	1,625	1,650	246	246	246	246		**3,000**				
300	325	47	47	47	47	1,650	1,675	249	249	249	249	3,000	3,050	454	454	454	454
325	350	51	51	51	51	1,675	1,700	253	253	253	253	3,050	3,100	461	461	461	461
350	375	54	54	54	54	1,700	1,725	257	257	257	257	3,100	3,150	469	469	469	469
375	400	58	58	58	58	1,725	1,750	261	261	261	261	3,150	3,200	476	476	476	476
400	425	62	62	62	62	1,750	1,775	264	264	264	264	3,200	3,250	484	484	484	484
425	450	66	66	66	66	1,775	1,800	268	268	268	268	3,250	3,300	491	491	491	491
450	475	69	69	69	69	1,800	1,825	272	272	272	272	3,300	3,350	499	499	499	499
475	500	73	73	73	73	1,825	1,850	276	276	276	276	3,350	3,400	506	506	506	506
500	525	77	77	77	77	1,850	1,875	279	279	279	279	3,400	3,450	514	514	514	514
525	550	81	81	81	81	1,875	1,900	283	283	283	283	3,450	3,500	521	521	521	521
550	575	84	84	84	84	1,900	1,925	287	287	287	287	3,500	3,550	529	529	529	529
575	600	88	88	88	88	1,925	1,950	291	291	291	291	3,550	3,600	536	536	536	536
600	625	92	92	92	92	1,950	1,975	294	294	294	294	3,600	3,650	544	544	544	544
625	650	96	96	96	96	1,975	2,000	298	298	298	298	3,650	3,700	551	551	551	551
650	675	99	99	99	99							3,700	3,750	559	559	559	559
675	700	103	103	103	103		**2,000**					3,750	3,800	566	566	566	566
700	725	107	107	107	107	2,000	2,025	302	302	302	302	3,800	3,850	574	574	574	574
725	750	111	111	111	111	2,025	2,050	306	306	306	306	3,850	3,900	581	581	581	581
750	775	114	114	114	114	2,050	2,075	309	309	309	309	3,900	3,950	589	589	589	589
775	800	118	118	118	118	2,075	2,100	313	313	313	313	3,950	4,000	596	596	596	596
800	825	122	122	122	122	2,100	2,125	317	317	317	317						
825	850	126	126	126	126	2,125	2,150	321	321	321	321		**4,000**				
850	875	129	129	129	129	2,150	2,175	324	324	324	324	4,000	4,050	604	604	604	604
875	900	133	133	133	133	2,175	2,200	328	328	328	328	4,050	4,100	611	611	611	611
900	925	137	137	137	137	2,200	2,225	332	332	332	332	4,100	4,150	619	619	619	619
925	950	141	141	141	141	2,225	2,250	336	336	336	336	4,150	4,200	626	626	626	626
950	975	144	144	144	144	2,250	2,275	339	339	339	339	4,200	4,250	634	634	634	634
975	1,000	148	148	148	148	2,275	2,300	343	343	343	343	4,250	4,300	641	641	641	641
	1,000					2,300	2,325	347	347	347	347	4,300	4,350	649	649	649	649
						2,325	2,350	351	351	351	351	4,350	4,400	656	656	656	656
1,000	1,025	152	152	152	152	2,350	2,375	354	354	354	354	4,400	4,450	664	664	664	664
1,025	1,050	156	156	156	156	2,375	2,400	358	358	358	358	4,450	4,500	671	671	671	671
1,050	1,075	159	159	159	159	2,400	2,425	362	362	362	362	4,500	4,550	679	679	679	679
1,075	1,100	163	163	163	163	2,425	2,450	366	366	366	366	4,550	4,600	686	686	686	686
1,100	1,125	167	167	167	167	2,450	2,475	369	369	369	369	4,600	4,650	694	694	694	694
1,125	1,150	171	171	171	171	2,475	2,500	373	373	373	373	4,650	4,700	701	701	701	701
1,150	1,175	174	174	174	174	2,500	2,525	377	377	377	377	4,700	4,750	709	709	709	709
1,175	1,200	178	178	178	178	2,525	2,550	381	381	381	381	4,750	4,800	716	716	716	716
1,200	1,225	182	182	182	182	2,550	2,575	384	384	384	384	4,800	4,850	724	724	724	724
1,225	1,250	186	186	186	186	2,575	2,600	388	388	388	388	4,850	4,900	731	731	731	731
1,250	1,275	189	189	189	189	2,600	2,625	392	392	392	392	4,900	4,950	739	739	739	739
1,275	1,300	193	193	193	193	2,625	2,650	396	396	396	396	4,950	5,000	746	746	746	746
						2,650	2,675	399	399	399	399						
						2,675	2,700	403	403	403	403			Continued on next page			

* This column must also be used by a qualifying widow(er).

19-- Tax Table—*Continued*

If Form 1040A, line 22, is —		And you are —				If Form 1040A, line 22, is —		And you are —				If Form 1040A, line 22, is —		And you are —			
At least	But less than	Single	Married filing jointly *	Married filing separately	Head of a household	At least	But less than	Single	Married filing jointly *	Married filing separately	Head of a household	At least	But less than	Single	Married filing jointly *	Married filing separately	Head of a household
		Your tax is—						Your tax is—						Your tax is—			
5,000						**8,000**						**11,000**					
5,000	5,050	754	754	754	754	8,000	8,050	1,204	1,204	1,204	1,204	11,000	11,050	1,654	1,654	1,654	1,654
5,050	5,100	761	761	761	761	8,050	8,100	1,211	1,211	1,211	1,211	11,050	11,100	1,661	1,661	1,661	1,661
5,100	5,150	769	769	769	769	8,100	8,150	1,219	1,219	1,219	1,219	11,100	11,150	1,669	1,669	1,669	1,669
5,150	5,200	776	776	776	776	8,150	8,200	1,226	1,226	1,226	1,226	11,150	11,200	1,676	1,676	1,676	1,676
5,200	5,250	784	784	784	784	8,200	8,250	1,234	1,234	1,234	1,234	11,200	11,250	1,684	1,684	1,684	1,684
5,250	5,300	791	791	791	791	8,250	8,300	1,241	1,241	1,241	1,241	11,250	11,300	1,691	1,691	1,691	1,691
5,300	5,350	799	799	799	799	8,300	8,350	1,249	1,249	1,249	1,249	11,300	11,350	1,699	1,699	1,699	1,699
5,350	5,400	806	806	806	806	8,350	8,400	1,256	1,256	1,256	1,256	11,350	11,400	1,706	1,706	1,706	1,706
5,400	5,450	814	814	814	814	8,400	8,450	1,264	1,264	1,264	1,264	11,400	11,450	1,714	1,714	1,714	1,714
5,450	5,500	821	821	821	821	8,450	8,500	1,271	1,271	1,271	1,271	11,450	11,500	1,721	1,721	1,721	1,721
5,500	5,550	829	829	829	829	8,500	8,550	1,279	1,279	1,279	1,279	11,500	11,550	1,729	1,729	1,729	1,729
5,550	5,600	836	836	836	836	8,550	8,600	1,286	1,286	1,286	1,286	11,550	11,600	1,736	1,736	1,736	1,736
5,600	5,650	844	844	844	844	8,600	8,650	1,294	1,294	1,294	1,294	11,600	11,650	1,744	1,744	1,744	1,744
5,650	5,700	851	851	851	851	8,650	8,700	1,301	1,301	1,301	1,301	11,650	11,700	1,751	1,751	1,751	1,751
5,700	5,750	859	859	859	859	8,700	8,750	1,309	1,309	1,309	1,309	11,700	11,750	1,759	1,759	1,759	1,759
5,750	5,800	866	866	866	866	8,750	8,800	1,316	1,316	1,316	1,316	11,750	11,800	1,766	1,766	1,766	1,766
5,800	5,850	874	874	874	874	8,800	8,850	1,324	1,324	1,324	1,324	11,800	11,850	1,774	1,774	1,774	1,774
5,850	5,900	881	881	881	881	8,850	8,900	1,331	1,331	1,331	1,331	11,850	11,900	1,781	1,781	1,781	1,781
5,900	5,950	889	889	889	889	8,900	8,950	1,339	1,339	1,339	1,339	11,900	11,950	1,789	1,789	1,789	1,789
5,950	6,000	896	896	896	896	8,950	9,000	1,346	1,346	1,346	1,346	11,950	12,000	1,796	1,796	1,796	1,796
6,000						**9,000**						**12,000**					
6,000	6,050	904	904	904	904	9,000	9,050	1,354	1,354	1,354	1,354	12,000	12,050	1,804	1,804	1,804	1,804
6,050	6,100	911	911	911	911	9,050	9,100	1,361	1,361	1,361	1,361	12,050	12,100	1,811	1,811	1,811	1,811
6,100	6,150	919	919	919	919	9,100	9,150	1,369	1,369	1,369	1,369	12,100	12,150	1,819	1,819	1,819	1,819
6,150	6,200	926	926	926	926	9,150	9,200	1,376	1,376	1,376	1,376	12,150	12,200	1,826	1,826	1,826	1,826
6,200	6,250	934	934	934	934	9,200	9,250	1,384	1,384	1,384	1,384	12,200	12,250	1,834	1,834	1,834	1,834
6,250	6,300	941	941	941	941	9,250	9,300	1,391	1,391	1,391	1,391	12,250	12,300	1,841	1,841	1,841	1,841
6,300	6,350	949	949	949	949	9,300	9,350	1,399	1,399	1,399	1,399	12,300	12,350	1,849	1,849	1,849	1,849
6,350	6,400	956	956	956	956	9,350	9,400	1,406	1,406	1,406	1,406	12,350	12,400	1,856	1,856	1,856	1,856
6,400	6,450	964	964	964	964	9,400	9,450	1,414	1,414	1,414	1,414	12,400	12,450	1,864	1,864	1,864	1,864
6,450	6,500	971	971	971	971	9,450	9,500	1,421	1,421	1,421	1,421	12,450	12,500	1,871	1,871	1,871	1,871
6,500	6,550	979	979	979	979	9,500	9,550	1,429	1,429	1,429	1,429	12,500	12,550	1,879	1,879	1,879	1,879
6,550	6,600	986	986	986	986	9,550	9,600	1,436	1,436	1,436	1,436	12,550	12,600	1,886	1,886	1,886	1,886
6,600	6,650	994	994	994	994	9,600	9,650	1,444	1,444	1,444	1,444	12,600	12,650	1,894	1,894	1,894	1,894
6,650	6,700	1,001	1,001	1,001	1,001	9,650	9,700	1,451	1,451	1,451	1,451	12,650	12,700	1,901	1,901	1,901	1,901
6,700	6,750	1,009	1,009	1,009	1,009	9,700	9,750	1,459	1,459	1,459	1,459	12,700	12,750	1,909	1,909	1,909	1,909
6,750	6,800	1,016	1,016	1,016	1,016	9,750	9,800	1,466	1,466	1,466	1,466	12,750	12,800	1,916	1,916	1,916	1,916
6,800	6,850	1,024	1,024	1,024	1,024	9,800	9,850	1,474	1,474	1,474	1,474	12,800	12,850	1,924	1,924	1,924	1,924
6,850	6,900	1,031	1,031	1,031	1,031	9,850	9,900	1,481	1,481	1,481	1,481	12,850	12,900	1,931	1,931	1,931	1,931
6,900	6,950	1,039	1,039	1,039	1,039	9,900	9,950	1,489	1,489	1,489	1,489	12,900	12,950	1,939	1,939	1,939	1,939
6,950	7,000	1,046	1,046	1,046	1,046	9,950	10,000	1,496	1,496	1,496	1,496	12,950	13,000	1,946	1,946	1,946	1,946
7,000						**10,000**						**13,000**					
7,000	7,050	1,054	1,054	1,054	1,054	10,000	10,050	1,504	1,504	1,504	1,504	13,000	13,050	1,954	1,954	1,954	1,954
7,050	7,100	1,061	1,061	1,061	1,061	10,050	10,100	1,511	1,511	1,511	1,511	13,050	13,100	1,961	1,961	1,961	1,961
7,100	7,150	1,069	1,069	1,069	1,069	10,100	10,150	1,519	1,519	1,519	1,519	13,100	13,150	1,969	1,969	1,969	1,969
7,150	7,200	1,076	1,076	1,076	1,076	10,150	10,200	1,526	1,526	1,526	1,526	13,150	13,200	1,976	1,976	1,976	1,976
7,200	7,250	1,084	1,084	1,084	1,084	10,200	10,250	1,534	1,534	1,534	1,534	13,200	13,250	1,984	1,984	1,984	1,984
7,250	7,300	1,091	1,091	1,091	1,091	10,250	10,300	1,541	1,541	1,541	1,541	13,250	13,300	1,991	1,991	1,991	1,991
7,300	7,350	1,099	1,099	1,099	1,099	10,300	10,350	1,549	1,549	1,549	1,549	13,300	13,350	1,999	1,999	1,999	1,999
7,350	7,400	1,106	1,106	1,106	1,106	10,350	10,400	1,556	1,556	1,556	1,556	13,350	13,400	2,006	2,006	2,006	2,006
7,400	7,450	1,114	1,114	1,114	1,114	10,400	10,450	1,564	1,564	1,564	1,564	13,400	13,450	2,014	2,014	2,014	2,014
7,450	7,500	1,121	1,121	1,121	1,121	10,450	10,500	1,571	1,571	1,571	1,571	13,450	13,500	2,021	2,021	2,021	2,021
7,500	7,550	1,129	1,129	1,129	1,129	10,500	10,550	1,579	1,579	1,579	1,579	13,500	13,550	2,029	2,029	2,029	2,029
7,550	7,600	1,136	1,136	1,136	1,136	10,550	10,600	1,586	1,586	1,586	1,586	13,550	13,600	2,036	2,036	2,036	2,036
7,600	7,650	1,144	1,144	1,144	1,144	10,600	10,650	1,594	1,594	1,594	1,594	13,600	13,650	2,044	2,044	2,044	2,044
7,650	7,700	1,151	1,151	1,151	1,151	10,650	10,700	1,601	1,601	1,601	1,601	13,650	13,700	2,051	2,051	2,051	2,051
7,700	7,750	1,159	1,159	1,159	1,159	10,700	10,750	1,609	1,609	1,609	1,609	13,700	13,750	2,059	2,059	2,059	2,059
7,750	7,800	1,166	1,166	1,166	1,166	10,750	10,800	1,616	1,616	1,616	1,616	13,750	13,800	2,066	2,066	2,066	2,066
7,800	7,850	1,174	1,174	1,174	1,174	10,800	10,850	1,624	1,624	1,624	1,624	13,800	13,850	2,074	2,074	2,074	2,074
7,850	7,900	1,181	1,181	1,181	1,181	10,850	10,900	1,631	1,631	1,631	1,631	13,850	13,900	2,081	2,081	2,081	2,081
7,900	7,950	1,189	1,189	1,189	1,189	10,900	10,950	1,639	1,639	1,639	1,639	13,900	13,950	2,089	2,089	2,089	2,089
7,950	8,000	1,196	1,196	1,196	1,196	10,950	11,000	1,646	1,646	1,646	1,646	13,950	14,000	2,096	2,096	2,096	2,096

* This column must also be used by a qualifying widow(er).

Continued on next page

19-- Tax Table—*Continued*

If Form 1040A, line 22, is —		Single	Married filing jointly *	Married filing separately	Head of a household
At least	But less than				Your tax is—
14,000					
14,000	14,050	2,104	2,104	2,104	2,104
14,050	14,100	2,111	2,111	2,111	2,111
14,100	14,150	2,119	2,119	2,119	2,119
14,150	14,200	2,126	2,126	2,126	2,126
14,200	14,250	2,134	2,134	2,134	2,134
14,250	14,300	2,141	2,141	2,141	2,141
14,300	14,350	2,149	2,149	2,149	2,149
14,350	14,400	2,156	2,156	2,156	2,156
14,400	14,450	2,164	2,164	2,164	2,164
14,450	14,500	2,171	2,171	2,171	2,171
14,500	14,550	2,179	2,179	2,179	2,179
14,550	14,600	2,186	2,186	2,186	2,186
14,600	14,650	2,194	2,194	2,194	2,194
14,650	14,700	2,201	2,201	2,201	2,201
14,700	14,750	2,209	2,209	2,209	2,209
14,750	14,800	2,216	2,216	2,216	2,216
14,800	14,850	2,224	2,224	2,224	2,224
14,850	14,900	2,231	2,231	2,231	2,231
14,900	14,950	2,239	2,239	2,239	2,239
14,950	15,000	2,246	2,246	2,246	2,246
15,000					
15,000	15,050	2,254	2,254	2,254	2,254
15,050	15,100	2,261	2,261	2,261	2,261
15,100	15,150	2,269	2,269	2,269	2,269
15,150	15,200	2,276	2,276	2,276	2,276
15,200	15,250	2,284	2,284	2,284	2,284
15,250	15,300	2,291	2,291	2,291	2,291
15,300	15,350	2,299	2,299	2,299	2,299
15,350	15,400	2,306	2,306	2,306	2,306
15,400	15,450	2,314	2,314	2,314	2,314
15,450	15,500	2,321	2,321	2,321	2,321
15,500	15,550	2,329	2,329	2,329	2,329
15,550	15,600	2,336	2,336	2,336	2,336
15,600	15,650	2,344	2,344	2,344	2,344
15,650	15,700	2,351	2,351	2,351	2,351
15,700	15,750	2,359	2,359	2,359	2,359
15,750	15,800	2,366	2,366	2,366	2,366
15,800	15,850	2,374	2,374	2,374	2,374
15,850	15,900	2,381	2,381	2,381	2,381
15,900	15,950	2,389	2,389	2,389	2,389
15,950	16,000	2,396	2,396	2,396	2,396
16,000					
16,000	16,050	2,404	2,404	2,404	2,404
16,050	16,100	2,411	2,411	2,411	2,411
16,100	16,150	2,419	2,419	2,419	2,419
16,150	16,200	2,426	2,426	2,426	2,426
16,200	16,250	2,434	2,434	2,434	2,434
16,250	16,300	2,441	2,441	2,441	2,441
16,300	16,350	2,449	2,449	2,449	2,449
16,350	16,400	2,456	2,456	2,456	2,456
16,400	16,450	2,464	2,464	2,464	2,464
16,450	16,500	2,471	2,471	2,471	2,471
16,500	16,550	2,479	2,479	2,479	2,479
16,550	16,600	2,486	2,486	2,486	2,486
16,600	16,650	2,494	2,494	2,494	2,494
16,650	16,700	2,501	2,501	2,501	2,501
16,700	16,750	2,509	2,509	2,509	2,509
16,750	16,800	2,516	2,516	2,516	2,516
16,800	16,850	2,524	2,524	2,524	2,524
16,850	16,900	2,531	2,531	2,531	2,531
16,900	16,950	2,539	2,539	2,539	2,539
16,950	17,000	2,546	2,546	2,546	2,546

If Form 1040A, line 22, is —		Single	Married filing jointly *	Married filing separately	Head of a household
At least	But less than				Your tax is—
17,000					
17,000	17,050	2,554	2,554	2,554	2,554
17,050	17,100	2,561	2,561	2,561	2,561
17,100	17,150	2,569	2,569	2,569	2,569
17,150	17,200	2,576	2,576	2,576	2,576
17,200	17,250	2,584	2,584	2,584	2,584
17,250	17,300	2,591	2,591	2,591	2,591
17,300	17,350	2,599	2,599	2,599	2,599
17,350	17,400	2,606	2,606	2,606	2,606
17,400	17,450	2,614	2,614	2,614	2,614
17,450	17,500	2,621	2,621	2,621	2,621
17,500	17,550	2,629	2,629	2,629	2,629
17,550	17,600	2,636	2,636	2,636	2,636
17,600	17,650	2,644	2,644	2,644	2,644
17,650	17,700	2,651	2,651	2,651	2,651
17,700	17,750	2,659	2,659	2,659	2,659
17,750	17,800	2,666	2,666	2,666	2,666
17,800	17,850	2,674	2,674	2,674	2,674
17,850	17,900	2,681	2,681	2,681	2,681
17,900	17,950	2,689	2,689	2,689	2,689
17,950	18,000	2,696	2,696	2,696	2,696
18,000					
18,000	18,050	2,704	2,704	2,704	2,704
18,050	18,100	2,711	2,711	2,711	2,711
18,100	18,150	2,719	2,719	2,719	2,719
18,150	18,200	2,726	2,726	2,726	2,726
18,200	18,250	2,734	2,734	2,734	2,734
18,250	18,300	2,741	2,741	2,741	2,741
18,300	18,350	2,749	2,749	2,749	2,749
18,350	18,400	2,756	2,756	2,756	2,756
18,400	18,450	2,764	2,764	2,764	2,764
18,450	18,500	2,771	2,771	2,775	2,771
18,500	18,550	2,779	2,779	2,789	2,779
18,550	18,600	2,786	2,786	2,803	2,786
18,600	18,650	2,794	2,794	2,817	2,794
18,650	18,700	2,801	2,801	2,831	2,801
18,700	18,750	2,809	2,809	2,845	2,809
18,750	18,800	2,816	2,816	2,859	2,816
18,800	18,850	2,824	2,824	2,873	2,824
18,850	18,900	2,831	2,831	2,887	2,831
18,900	18,950	2,839	2,839	2,901	2,839
18,950	19,000	2,846	2,846	2,915	2,846
19,000					
19,000	19,050	2,854	2,854	2,929	2,854
19,050	19,100	2,861	2,861	2,943	2,861
19,100	19,150	2,869	2,869	2,957	2,869
19,150	19,200	2,876	2,876	2,971	2,876
19,200	19,250	2,884	2,884	2,985	2,884
19,250	19,300	2,891	2,891	2,999	2,891
19,300	19,350	2,899	2,899	3,013	2,899
19,350	19,400	2,906	2,906	3,027	2,906
19,400	19,450	2,914	2,914	3,041	2,914
19,450	19,500	2,921	2,921	3,055	2,921
19,500	19,550	2,929	2,929	3,069	2,929
19,550	19,600	2,936	2,936	3,083	2,936
19,600	19,650	2,944	2,944	3,097	2,944
19,650	19,700	2,951	2,951	3,111	2,951
19,700	19,750	2,959	2,959	3,125	2,959
19,750	19,800	2,966	2,966	3,139	2,966
19,800	19,850	2,974	2,974	3,153	2,974
19,850	19,900	2,981	2,981	3,167	2,981
19,900	19,950	2,989	2,989	3,181	2,989
19,950	20,000	2,996	2,996	3,195	2,996

If Form 1040A, line 22, is —		Single	Married filing jointly *	Married filing separately	Head of a household
At least	But less than				Your tax is—
20,000					
20,000	20,050	3,004	3,004	3,209	3,004
20,050	20,100	3,011	3,011	3,223	3,011
20,100	20,150	3,019	3,019	3,237	3,019
20,150	20,200	3,026	3,026	3,251	3,026
20,200	20,250	3,034	3,034	3,265	3,034
20,250	20,300	3,041	3,041	3,279	3,041
20,300	20,350	3,049	3,049	3,293	3,049
20,350	20,400	3,056	3,056	3,307	3,056
20,400	20,450	3,064	3,064	3,321	3,064
20,450	20,500	3,071	3,071	3,335	3,071
20,500	20,550	3,079	3,079	3,349	3,079
20,550	20,600	3,086	3,086	3,363	3,086
20,600	20,650	3,094	3,094	3,377	3,094
20,650	20,700	3,101	3,101	3,391	3,101
20,700	20,750	3,109	3,109	3,405	3,109
20,750	20,800	3,116	3,116	3,419	3,116
20,800	20,850	3,124	3,124	3,433	3,124
20,850	20,900	3,131	3,131	3,447	3,131
20,900	20,950	3,139	3,139	3,461	3,139
20,950	21,000	3,146	3,146	3,475	3,146
21,000					
21,000	21,050	3,154	3,154	3,489	3,154
21,050	21,100	3,161	3,161	3,503	3,161
21,100	21,150	3,169	3,169	3,517	3,169
21,150	21,200	3,176	3,176	3,531	3,176
21,200	21,250	3,184	3,184	3,545	3,184
21,250	21,300	3,191	3,191	3,559	3,191
21,300	21,350	3,199	3,199	3,573	3,199
21,350	21,400	3,206	3,206	3,587	3,206
21,400	21,450	3,214	3,214	3,601	3,214
21,450	21,500	3,221	3,221	3,615	3,221
21,500	21,550	3,229	3,229	3,629	3,229
21,550	21,600	3,236	3,236	3,643	3,236
21,600	21,650	3,244	3,244	3,657	3,244
21,650	21,700	3,251	3,251	3,671	3,251
21,700	21,750	3,259	3,259	3,685	3,259
21,750	21,800	3,266	3,266	3,699	3,266
21,800	21,850	3,274	3,274	3,713	3,274
21,850	21,900	3,281	3,281	3,727	3,281
21,900	21,950	3,289	3,289	3,741	3,289
21,950	22,000	3,296	3,296	3,755	3,296
22,000					
22,000	22,050	3,304	3,304	3,769	3,304
22,050	22,100	3,311	3,311	3,783	3,311
22,100	22,150	3,322	3,319	3,797	3,319
22,150	22,200	3,336	3,326	3,811	3,326
22,200	22,250	3,350	3,334	3,825	3,334
22,250	22,300	3,364	3,341	3,839	3,341
22,300	22,350	3,378	3,349	3,853	3,349
22,350	22,400	3,392	3,356	3,867	3,356
22,400	22,450	3,406	3,364	3,881	3,364
22,450	22,500	3,420	3,371	3,895	3,371
22,500	22,550	3,434	3,379	3,909	3,379
22,550	22,600	3,448	3,386	3,923	3,386
22,600	22,650	3,462	3,394	3,937	3,394
22,650	22,700	3,476	3,401	3,951	3,401
22,700	22,750	3,490	3,409	3,965	3,409
22,750	22,800	3,504	3,416	3,979	3,416
22,800	22,850	3,518	3,424	3,993	3,424
22,850	22,900	3,532	3,431	4,007	3,431
22,900	22,950	3,546	3,439	4,021	3,439
22,950	23,000	3,560	3,446	4,035	3,446

* This column must also be used by a qualifying widow(er).

Continued on next page

19-- Tax Table—*Continued*

If Form 1040A, line 22, is —		And you are —			
At least	But less than	Single	Married filing jointly *	Married filing separately	Head of a household
		Your tax is—			

23,000

At least	But less than	Single	Married filing jointly *	Married filing separately	Head of a household
23,000	23,050	3,574	3,454	4,049	3,454
23,050	23,100	3,588	3,461	4,063	3,461
23,100	23,150	3,602	3,469	4,077	3,469
23,150	23,200	3,616	3,476	4,091	3,476
23,200	23,250	3,630	3,484	4,105	3,484
23,250	23,300	3,644	3,491	4,119	3,491
23,300	23,350	3,658	3,499	4,133	3,499
23,350	23,400	3,672	3,506	4,147	3,506
23,400	23,450	3,686	3,514	4,161	3,514
23,450	23,500	3,700	3,521	4,175	3,521
23,500	23,550	3,714	3,529	4,189	3,529
23,550	23,600	3,728	3,536	4,203	3,536
23,600	23,650	3,742	3,544	4,217	3,544
23,650	23,700	3,756	3,551	4,231	3,551
23,700	23,750	3,770	3,559	4,245	3,559
23,750	23,800	3,784	3,566	4,259	3,566
23,800	23,850	3,798	3,574	4,273	3,574
23,850	23,900	3,812	3,581	4,287	3,581
23,900	23,950	3,826	3,589	4,301	3,589
23,950	24,000	3,840	3,596	4,315	3,596

24,000

At least	But less than	Single	Married filing jointly *	Married filing separately	Head of a household
24,000	24,050	3,854	3,604	4,329	3,604
24,050	24,100	3,868	3,611	4,343	3,611
24,100	24,150	3,882	3,619	4,357	3,619
24,150	24,200	3,896	3,626	4,371	3,626
24,200	24,250	3,910	3,634	4,385	3,634
24,250	24,300	3,924	3,641	4,399	3,641
24,300	24,350	3,938	3,649	4,413	3,649
24,350	24,400	3,952	3,656	4,427	3,656
24,400	24,450	3,966	3,664	4,441	3,664
24,450	24,500	3,980	3,671	4,455	3,671
24,500	24,550	3,994	3,679	4,469	3,679
24,550	24,600	4,008	3,686	4,483	3,686
24,600	24,650	4,022	3,694	4,497	3,694
24,650	24,700	4,036	3,701	4,511	3,701
24,700	24,750	4,050	3,709	4,525	3,709
24,750	24,800	4,064	3,716	4,539	3,716
24,800	24,850	4,078	3,724	4,553	3,724
24,850	24,900	4,092	3,731	4,567	3,731
24,900	24,950	4,106	3,739	4,581	3,739
24,950	25,000	4,120	3,746	4,595	3,746

25,000

At least	But less than	Single	Married filing jointly *	Married filing separately	Head of a household
25,000	25,050	4,134	3,754	4,609	3,754
25,050	25,100	4,148	3,761	4,623	3,761
25,100	25,150	4,162	3,769	4,637	3,769
25,150	25,200	4,176	3,776	4,651	3,776
25,200	25,250	4,190	3,784	4,665	3,784
25,250	25,300	4,204	3,791	4,679	3,791
25,300	25,350	4,218	3,799	4,693	3,799
25,350	25,400	4,232	3,806	4,707	3,806
25,400	25,450	4,246	3,814	4,721	3,814
25,450	25,500	4,260	3,821	4,735	3,821
25,500	25,550	4,274	3,829	4,749	3,829
25,550	25,600	4,288	3,836	4,763	3,836
25,600	25,650	4,302	3,844	4,777	3,844
25,650	25,700	4,316	3,851	4,791	3,851
25,700	25,750	4,330	3,859	4,805	3,859
25,750	25,800	4,344	3,866	4,819	3,866
25,800	25,850	4,358	3,874	4,833	3,874
25,850	25,900	4,372	3,881	4,847	3,881
25,900	25,950	4,386	3,889	4,861	3,889
25,950	26,000	4,400	3,896	4,875	3,896

26,000

At least	But less than	Single	Married filing jointly *	Married filing separately	Head of a household
26,000	26,050	4,414	3,904	4,889	3,904
26,050	26,100	4,428	3,911	4,903	3,911
26,100	26,150	4,442	3,919	4,917	3,919
26,150	26,200	4,456	3,926	4,931	3,926
26,200	26,250	4,470	3,934	4,945	3,934
26,250	26,300	4,484	3,941	4,959	3,941
26,300	26,350	4,498	3,949	4,973	3,949
26,350	26,400	4,512	3,956	4,987	3,956
26,400	26,450	4,526	3,964	5,001	3,964
26,450	26,500	4,540	3,971	5,015	3,971
26,500	26,550	4,554	3,979	5,029	3,979
26,550	26,600	4,568	3,986	5,043	3,986
26,600	26,650	4,582	3,994	5,057	3,994
26,650	26,700	4,596	4,001	5,071	4,001
26,700	26,750	4,610	4,009	5,085	4,009
26,750	26,800	4,624	4,016	5,099	4,016
26,800	26,850	4,638	4,024	5,113	4,024
26,850	26,900	4,652	4,031	5,127	4,031
26,900	26,950	4,666	4,039	5,141	4,039
26,950	27,000	4,680	4,046	5,155	4,046

27,000

At least	But less than	Single	Married filing jointly *	Married filing separately	Head of a household
27,000	27,050	4,694	4,054	5,169	4,054
27,050	27,100	4,708	4,061	5,183	4,061
27,100	27,150	4,722	4,069	5,197	4,069
27,150	27,200	4,736	4,076	5,211	4,076
27,200	27,250	4,750	4,084	5,225	4,084
27,250	27,300	4,764	4,091	5,239	4,091
27,300	27,350	4,778	4,099	5,253	4,099
27,350	27,400	4,792	4,106	5,267	4,106
27,400	27,450	4,806	4,114	5,281	4,114
27,450	27,500	4,820	4,121	5,295	4,121
27,500	27,550	4,834	4,129	5,309	4,129
27,550	27,600	4,848	4,136	5,323	4,136
27,600	27,650	4,862	4,144	5,337	4,144
27,650	27,700	4,876	4,151	5,351	4,151
27,700	27,750	4,890	4,159	5,365	4,159
27,750	27,800	4,904	4,166	5,379	4,166
27,800	27,850	4,918	4,174	5,393	4,174
27,850	27,900	4,932	4,181	5,407	4,181
27,900	27,950	4,946	4,189	5,421	4,189
27,950	28,000	4,960	4,196	5,435	4,196

28,000

At least	But less than	Single	Married filing jointly *	Married filing separately	Head of a household
28,000	28,050	4,974	4,204	5,449	4,204
28,050	28,100	4,988	4,211	5,463	4,211
28,100	28,150	5,002	4,219	5,477	4,219
28,150	28,200	5,016	4,226	5,491	4,226
28,200	28,250	5,030	4,234	5,505	4,234
28,250	28,300	5,044	4,241	5,519	4,241
28,300	28,350	5,058	4,249	5,533	4,249
28,350	28,400	5,072	4,256	5,547	4,256
28,400	28,450	5,086	4,264	5,561	4,264
28,450	28,500	5,100	4,271	5,575	4,271
28,500	28,550	5,114	4,279	5,589	4,279
28,550	28,600	5,128	4,286	5,603	4,286
28,600	28,650	5,142	4,294	5,617	4,294
28,650	28,700	5,156	4,301	5,631	4,301
28,700	28,750	5,170	4,309	5,645	4,309
28,750	28,800	5,184	4,316	5,659	4,316
28,800	28,850	5,198	4,324	5,673	4,324
28,850	28,900	5,212	4,331	5,687	4,331
28,900	28,950	5,226	4,339	5,701	4,339
28,950	29,000	5,240	4,346	5,715	4,346

29,000

At least	But less than	Single	Married filing jointly *	Married filing separately	Head of a household
29,000	29,050	5,254	4,354	5,729	4,354
29,050	29,100	5,268	4,361	5,743	4,361
29,100	29,150	5,282	4,369	5,757	4,369
29,150	29,200	5,296	4,376	5,771	4,376
29,200	29,250	5,310	4,384	5,785	4,384
29,250	29,300	5,324	4,391	5,799	4,391
29,300	29,350	5,338	4,399	5,813	4,399
29,350	29,400	5,352	4,406	5,827	4,406
29,400	29,450	5,366	4,414	5,841	4,414
29,450	29,500	5,380	4,421	5,855	4,421
29,500	29,550	5,394	4,429	5,869	4,429
29,550	29,600	5,408	4,436	5,883	4,436
29,600	29,650	5,422	4,444	5,897	4,447
29,650	29,700	5,436	4,451	5,911	4,461
29,700	29,750	5,450	4,459	5,925	4,475
29,750	29,800	5,464	4,466	5,939	4,489
29,800	29,850	5,478	4,474	5,953	4,503
29,850	29,900	5,492	4,481	5,967	4,517
29,900	29,950	5,506	4,489	5,981	4,531
29,950	30,000	5,520	4,496	5,995	4,545

30,000

At least	But less than	Single	Married filing jointly *	Married filing separately	Head of a household
30,000	30,050	5,534	4,504	6,009	4,559
30,050	30,100	5,548	4,511	6,023	4,573
30,100	30,150	5,562	4,519	6,037	4,587
30,150	30,200	5,576	4,526	6,051	4,601
30,200	30,250	5,590	4,534	6,065	4,615
30,250	30,300	5,604	4,541	6,079	4,629
30,300	30,350	5,618	4,549	6,093	4,643
30,350	30,400	5,632	4,556	6,107	4,657
30,400	30,450	5,646	4,564	6,121	4,671
30,450	30,500	5,660	4,571	6,135	4,685
30,500	30,550	5,674	4,579	6,149	4,699
30,550	30,600	5,688	4,586	6,163	4,713
30,600	30,650	5,702	4,594	6,177	4,727
30,650	30,700	5,716	4,601	6,191	4,741
30,700	30,750	5,730	4,609	6,205	4,755
30,750	30,800	5,744	4,616	6,219	4,769
30,800	30,850	5,758	4,624	6,233	4,783
30,850	30,900	5,772	4,631	6,247	4,797
30,900	30,950	5,786	4,639	6,261	4,811
30,950	31,000	5,800	4,646	6,275	4,825

31,000

At least	But less than	Single	Married filing jointly *	Married filing separately	Head of a household
31,000	31,050	5,814	4,654	6,289	4,839
31,050	31,100	5,828	4,661	6,303	4,853
31,100	31,150	5,842	4,669	6,317	4,867
31,150	31,200	5,856	4,676	6,331	4,881
31,200	31,250	5,870	4,684	6,345	4,895
31,250	31,300	5,884	4,691	6,359	4,909
31,300	31,350	5,898	4,699	6,373	4,923
31,350	31,400	5,912	4,706	6,387	4,937
31,400	31,450	5,926	4,714	6,401	4,951
31,450	31,500	5,940	4,721	6,415	4,965
31,500	31,550	5,954	4,729	6,429	4,979
31,550	31,600	5,968	4,736	6,443	4,993
31,600	31,650	5,982	4,744	6,457	5,007
31,650	31,700	5,996	4,751	6,471	5,021
31,700	31,750	6,010	4,759	6,485	5,035
31,750	31,800	6,024	4,766	6,499	5,049
31,800	31,850	6,038	4,774	6,513	5,063
31,850	31,900	6,052	4,781	6,527	5,077
31,900	31,950	6,066	4,789	6,541	5,091
31,950	32,000	6,080	4,796	6,555	5,105

* This column must also be used by a qualifying widow(er).

Continued on next page

19-- Tax Table—*Continued*

If Form 1040A, line 22, is —		And you are —			
At least	But less than	Single	Married filing jointly *	Married filing separately	Head of a household
		Your tax is—			

32,000

At least	But less than	Single	Married filing jointly	Married filing separately	Head of a household
32,000	32,050	6,094	4,804	6,569	5,119
32,050	32,100	6,108	4,811	6,583	5,133
32,100	32,150	6,122	4,819	6,597	5,147
32,150	32,200	6,136	4,826	6,611	5,161
32,200	32,250	6,150	4,834	6,625	5,175
32,250	32,300	6,164	4,841	6,639	5,189
32,300	32,350	6,178	4,849	6,653	5,203
32,350	32,400	6,192	4,856	6,667	5,217
32,400	32,450	6,206	4,864	6,681	5,231
32,450	32,500	6,220	4,871	6,695	5,245
32,500	32,550	6,234	4,879	6,709	5,259
32,550	32,600	6,248	4,886	6,723	5,273
32,600	32,650	6,262	4,894	6,737	5,287
32,650	32,700	6,276	4,901	6,751	5,301
32,700	32,750	6,290	4,909	6,765	5,315
32,750	32,800	6,304	4,916	6,779	5,329
32,800	32,850	6,318	4,924	6,793	5,343
32,850	32,900	6,332	4,931	6,807	5,357
32,900	32,950	6,346	4,939	6,821	5,371
32,950	33,000	6,360	4,946	6,835	5,385

33,000

At least	But less than	Single	Married filing jointly	Married filing separately	Head of a household
33,000	33,050	6,374	4,954	6,849	5,399
33,050	33,100	6,388	4,961	6,863	5,413
33,100	33,150	6,402	4,969	6,877	5,427
33,150	33,200	6,416	4,976	6,891	5,441
33,200	33,250	6,430	4,984	6,905	5,455
33,250	33,300	6,444	4,991	6,919	5,469
33,300	33,350	6,458	4,999	6,933	5,483
33,350	33,400	6,472	5,006	6,947	5,497
33,400	33,450	6,486	5,014	6,961	5,511
33,450	33,500	6,500	5,021	6,975	5,525
33,500	33,550	6,514	5,029	6,989	5,539
33,550	33,600	6,528	5,036	7,003	5,553
33,600	33,650	6,542	5,044	7,017	5,567
33,650	33,700	6,556	5,051	7,031	5,581
33,700	33,750	6,570	5,059	7,045	5,595
33,750	33,800	6,584	5,066	7,059	5,609
33,800	33,850	6,598	5,074	7,073	5,623
33,850	33,900	6,612	5,081	7,087	5,637
33,900	33,950	6,626	5,089	7,101	5,651
33,950	34,000	6,640	5,096	7,115	5,665

34,000

At least	But less than	Single	Married filing jointly	Married filing separately	Head of a household
34,000	34,050	6,654	5,104	7,129	5,679
34,050	34,100	6,668	5,111	7,143	5,693
34,100	34,150	6,682	5,119	7,157	5,707
34,150	34,200	6,696	5,126	7,171	5,721
34,200	34,250	6,710	5,134	7,185	5,735
34,250	34,300	6,724	5,141	7,199	5,749
34,300	34,350	6,738	5,149	7,213	5,763
34,350	34,400	6,752	5,156	7,227	5,777
34,400	34,450	6,766	5,164	7,241	5,791
34,450	34,500	6,780	5,171	7,255	5,805
34,500	34,550	6,794	5,179	7,269	5,819
34,550	34,600	6,808	5,186	7,283	5,833
34,600	34,650	6,822	5,194	7,297	5,847
34,650	34,700	6,836	5,201	7,311	5,861
34,700	34,750	6,850	5,209	7,325	5,875
34,750	34,800	6,864	5,216	7,339	5,889
34,800	34,850	6,878	5,224	7,353	5,903
34,850	34,900	6,892	5,231	7,367	5,917
34,900	34,950	6,906	5,239	7,381	5,931
34,950	35,000	6,920	5,246	7,395	5,945

35,000

At least	But less than	Single	Married filing jointly	Married filing separately	Head of a household
35,000	35,050	6,934	5,254	7,409	5,959
35,050	35,100	6,948	5,261	7,423	5,973
35,100	35,150	6,962	5,269	7,437	5,987
35,150	35,200	6,976	5,276	7,451	6,001
35,200	35,250	6,990	5,284	7,465	6,015
35,250	35,300	7,004	5,291	7,479	6,029
35,300	35,350	7,018	5,299	7,493	6,043
35,350	35,400	7,032	5,306	7,507	6,057
35,400	35,450	7,046	5,314	7,521	6,071
35,450	35,500	7,060	5,321	7,535	6,085
35,500	35,550	7,074	5,329	7,549	6,099
35,550	35,600	7,088	5,336	7,563	6,113
35,600	35,650	7,102	5,344	7,577	6,127
35,650	35,700	7,116	5,351	7,591	6,141
35,700	35,750	7,130	5,359	7,605	6,155
35,750	35,800	7,144	5,366	7,619	6,169
35,800	35,850	7,158	5,374	7,633	6,183
35,850	35,900	7,172	5,381	7,647	6,197
35,900	35,950	7,186	5,389	7,661	6,211
35,950	36,000	7,200	5,396	7,675	6,225

36,000

At least	But less than	Single	Married filing jointly	Married filing separately	Head of a household
36,000	36,050	7,214	5,404	7,689	6,239
36,050	36,100	7,228	5,411	7,703	6,253
36,100	36,150	7,242	5,419	7,717	6,267
36,150	36,200	7,256	5,426	7,731	6,281
36,200	36,250	7,270	5,434	7,745	6,295
36,250	36,300	7,284	5,441	7,759	6,309
36,300	36,350	7,298	5,449	7,773	6,323
36,350	36,400	7,312	5,456	7,787	6,337
36,400	36,450	7,326	5,464	7,801	6,351
36,450	36,500	7,340	5,471	7,815	6,365
36,500	36,550	7,354	5,479	7,829	6,379
36,550	36,600	7,368	5,486	7,843	6,393
36,600	36,650	7,382	5,494	7,857	6,407
36,650	36,700	7,396	5,501	7,871	6,421
36,700	36,750	7,410	5,509	7,885	6,435
36,750	36,800	7,424	5,516	7,899	6,449
36,800	36,850	7,438	5,524	7,913	6,463
36,850	36,900	7,452	5,531	7,927	6,477
36,900	36,950	7,466	5,542	7,941	6,491
36,950	37,000	7,480	5,556	7,955	6,505

37,000

At least	But less than	Single	Married filing jointly	Married filing separately	Head of a household
37,000	37,050	7,494	5,570	7,969	6,519
37,050	37,100	7,508	5,584	7,983	6,533
37,100	37,150	7,522	5,598	7,997	6,547
37,150	37,200	7,536	5,612	8,011	6,561
37,200	37,250	7,550	5,626	8,025	6,575
37,250	37,300	7,564	5,640	8,039	6,589
37,300	37,350	7,578	5,654	8,053	6,603
37,350	37,400	7,592	5,668	8,067	6,617
37,400	37,450	7,606	5,682	8,081	6,631
37,450	37,500	7,620	5,696	8,095	6,645
37,500	37,550	7,634	5,710	8,109	6,659
37,550	37,600	7,648	5,724	8,123	6,673
37,600	37,650	7,662	5,738	8,137	6,687
37,650	37,700	7,676	5,752	8,151	6,701
37,700	37,750	7,690	5,766	8,165	6,715
37,750	37,800	7,704	5,780	8,179	6,729
37,800	37,850	7,718	5,794	8,193	6,743
37,850	37,900	7,732	5,808	8,207	6,757
37,900	37,950	7,746	5,822	8,221	6,771
37,950	38,000	7,760	5,836	8,235	6,785

38,000

At least	But less than	Single	Married filing jointly	Married filing separately	Head of a household
38,000	38,050	7,774	5,850	8,249	6,799
38,050	38,100	7,788	5,864	8,263	6,813
38,100	38,150	7,802	5,878	8,277	6,827
38,150	38,200	7,816	5,892	8,291	6,841
38,200	38,250	7,830	5,906	8,305	6,855
38,250	38,300	7,844	5,920	8,319	6,869
38,300	38,350	7,858	5,934	8,333	6,883
38,350	38,400	7,872	5,948	8,347	6,897
38,400	38,450	7,886	5,962	8,361	6,911
38,450	38,500	7,900	5,976	8,375	6,925
38,500	38,550	7,914	5,990	8,389	6,939
38,550	38,600	7,928	6,004	8,403	6,953
38,600	38,650	7,942	6,018	8,417	6,967
38,650	38,700	7,956	6,032	8,431	6,981
38,700	38,750	7,970	6,046	8,445	6,995
38,750	38,800	7,984	6,060	8,459	7,009
38,800	38,850	7,998	6,074	8,473	7,023
38,850	38,900	8,012	6,088	8,487	7,037
38,900	38,950	8,026	6,102	8,501	7,051
38,950	39,000	8,040	6,116	8,515	7,065

39,000

At least	But less than	Single	Married filing jointly	Married filing separately	Head of a household
39,000	39,050	8,054	6,130	8,529	7,079
39,050	39,100	8,068	6,144	8,543	7,093
39,100	39,150	8,082	6,158	8,557	7,107
39,150	39,200	8,096	6,172	8,571	7,121
39,200	39,250	8,110	6,186	8,585	7,135
39,250	39,300	8,124	6,200	8,599	7,149
39,300	39,350	8,138	6,214	8,613	7,163
39,350	39,400	8,152	6,228	8,627	7,177
39,400	39,450	8,166	6,242	8,641	7,191
39,450	39,500	8,180	6,256	8,655	7,205
39,500	39,550	8,194	6,270	8,669	7,219
39,550	39,600	8,208	6,284	8,683	7,233
39,600	39,650	8,222	6,298	8,697	7,247
39,650	39,700	8,236	6,312	8,711	7,261
39,700	39,750	8,250	6,326	8,725	7,275
39,750	39,800	8,264	6,340	8,739	7,289
39,800	39,850	8,278	6,354	8,753	7,303
39,850	39,900	8,292	6,368	8,767	7,317
39,900	39,950	8,306	6,382	8,781	7,331
39,950	40,000	8,320	6,396	8,795	7,345

40,000

At least	But less than	Single	Married filing jointly	Married filing separately	Head of a household
40,000	40,050	8,334	6,410	8,809	7,359
40,050	40,100	8,348	6,424	8,823	7,373
40,100	40,150	8,362	6,438	8,837	7,387
40,150	40,200	8,376	6,452	8,851	7,401
40,200	40,250	8,390	6,466	8,865	7,415
40,250	40,300	8,404	6,480	8,879	7,429
40,300	40,350	8,418	6,494	8,893	7,443
40,350	40,400	8,432	6,508	8,907	7,457
40,400	40,450	8,446	6,522	8,921	7,471
40,450	40,500	8,460	6,536	8,935	7,485
40,500	40,550	8,474	6,550	8,949	7,499
40,550	40,600	8,488	6,564	8,963	7,513
40,600	40,650	8,502	6,578	8,977	7,527
40,650	40,700	8,516	6,592	8,991	7,541
40,700	40,750	8,530	6,606	9,005	7,555
40,750	40,800	8,544	6,620	9,019	7,569
40,800	40,850	8,558	6,634	9,033	7,583
40,850	40,900	8,572	6,648	9,047	7,597
40,900	40,950	8,586	6,662	9,061	7,611
40,950	41,000	8,600	6,676	9,075	7,625

* This column must also be used by a qualifying widow(er).

Continued on next page

19-- Tax Table—*Continued*

41,000 / 42,000 / 43,000

If Form 1040A, line 22, is —		And you are —			
At least	But less than	Single	Married filing jointly *	Married filing separately	Head of a household
		Your tax is—			
41,000					
41,000	41,050	8,614	6,690	9,089	7,639
41,050	41,100	8,628	6,704	9,103	7,653
41,100	41,150	8,642	6,718	9,117	7,667
41,150	41,200	8,656	6,732	9,131	7,681
41,200	41,250	8,670	6,746	9,145	7,695
41,250	41,300	8,684	6,760	9,159	7,709
41,300	41,350	8,698	6,774	9,173	7,723
41,350	41,400	8,712	6,788	9,187	7,737
41,400	41,450	8,726	6,802	9,201	7,751
41,450	41,500	8,740	6,816	9,215	7,765
41,500	41,550	8,754	6,830	9,229	7,779
41,550	41,600	8,768	6,844	9,243	7,793
41,600	41,650	8,782	6,858	9,257	7,807
41,650	41,700	8,796	6,872	9,271	7,821
41,700	41,750	8,810	6,886	9,285	7,835
41,750	41,800	8,824	6,900	9,299	7,849
41,800	41,850	8,838	6,914	9,313	7,863
41,850	41,900	8,852	6,928	9,327	7,877
41,900	41,950	8,866	6,942	9,341	7,891
41,950	42,000	8,880	6,956	9,355	7,905
42,000					
42,000	42,050	8,894	6,970	9,369	7,919
42,050	42,100	8,908	6,984	9,383	7,933
42,100	42,150	8,922	6,998	9,397	7,947
42,150	42,200	8,936	7,012	9,411	7,961
42,200	42,250	8,950	7,026	9,425	7,975
42,250	42,300	8,964	7,040	9,439	7,989
42,300	42,350	8,978	7,054	9,453	8,003
42,350	42,400	8,992	7,068	9,467	8,017
42,400	42,450	9,006	7,082	9,481	8,031
42,450	42,500	9,020	7,096	9,495	8,045
42,500	42,550	9,034	7,110	9,509	8,059
42,550	42,600	9,048	7,124	9,523	8,073
42,600	42,650	9,062	7,138	9,537	8,087
42,650	42,700	9,076	7,152	9,551	8,101
42,700	42,750	9,090	7,166	9,565	8,115
42,750	42,800	9,104	7,180	9,579	8,129
42,800	42,850	9,118	7,194	9,593	8,143
42,850	42,900	9,132	7,208	9,607	8,157
42,900	42,950	9,146	7,222	9,621	8,171
42,950	43,000	9,160	7,236	9,635	8,185
43,000					
43,000	43,050	9,174	7,250	9,649	8,199
43,050	43,100	9,188	7,264	9,663	8,213
43,100	43,150	9,202	7,278	9,677	8,227
43,150	43,200	9,216	7,292	9,691	8,241
43,200	43,250	9,230	7,306	9,705	8,255
43,250	43,300	9,244	7,320	9,719	8,269
43,300	43,350	9,258	7,334	9,733	8,283
43,350	43,400	9,272	7,348	9,747	8,297
43,400	43,450	9,286	7,362	9,761	8,311
43,450	43,500	9,300	7,376	9,775	8,325
43,500	43,550	9,314	7,390	9,789	8,339
43,550	43,600	9,328	7,404	9,803	8,353
43,600	43,650	9,342	7,418	9,817	8,367
43,650	43,700	9,356	7,432	9,831	8,381
43,700	43,750	9,370	7,446	9,845	8,395
43,750	43,800	9,384	7,460	9,859	8,409
43,800	43,850	9,398	7,474	9,873	8,423
43,850	43,900	9,412	7,488	9,887	8,437
43,900	43,950	9,426	7,502	9,901	8,451
43,950	44,000	9,440	7,516	9,915	8,465

44,000 / 45,000 / 46,000

If Form 1040A, line 22, is —		And you are —			
At least	But less than	Single	Married filing jointly *	Married filing separately	Head of a household
		Your tax is—			
44,000					
44,000	44,050	9,454	7,530	9,929	8,479
44,050	44,100	9,468	7,544	9,943	8,493
44,100	44,150	9,482	7,558	9,957	8,507
44,150	44,200	9,496	7,572	9,971	8,521
44,200	44,250	9,510	7,586	9,985	8,535
44,250	44,300	9,524	7,600	9,999	8,549
44,300	44,350	9,538	7,614	10,013	8,563
44,350	44,400	9,552	7,628	10,027	8,577
44,400	44,450	9,566	7,642	10,041	8,591
44,450	44,500	9,580	7,656	10,055	8,605
44,500	44,550	9,594	7,670	10,069	8,619
44,550	44,600	9,608	7,684	10,083	8,633
44,600	44,650	9,622	7,698	10,098	8,647
44,650	44,700	9,636	7,712	10,114	8,661
44,700	44,750	9,650	7,726	10,129	8,675
44,750	44,800	9,664	7,740	10,145	8,689
44,800	44,850	9,678	7,754	10,160	8,703
44,850	44,900	9,692	7,768	10,176	8,717
44,900	44,950	9,706	7,782	10,191	8,731
44,950	45,000	9,720	7,796	10,207	8,745
45,000					
45,000	45,050	9,734	7,810	10,222	8,759
45,050	45,100	9,748	7,824	10,238	8,773
45,100	45,150	9,762	7,838	10,253	8,787
45,150	45,200	9,776	7,852	10,269	8,801
45,200	45,250	9,790	7,866	10,284	8,815
45,250	45,300	9,804	7,880	10,300	8,829
45,300	45,350	9,818	7,894	10,315	8,843
45,350	45,400	9,832	7,908	10,331	8,857
45,400	45,450	9,846	7,922	10,346	8,871
45,450	45,500	9,860	7,936	10,362	8,885
45,500	45,550	9,874	7,950	10,377	8,899
45,550	45,600	9,888	7,964	10,393	8,913
45,600	45,650	9,902	7,978	10,408	8,927
45,650	45,700	9,916	7,992	10,424	8,941
45,700	45,750	9,930	8,006	10,439	8,955
45,750	45,800	9,944	8,020	10,455	8,969
45,800	45,850	9,958	8,034	10,470	8,983
45,850	45,900	9,972	8,048	10,486	8,997
45,900	45,950	9,986	8,062	10,501	9,011
45,950	46,000	10,000	8,076	10,517	9,025
46,000					
46,000	46,050	10,014	8,090	10,532	9,039
46,050	46,100	10,028	8,104	10,548	9,053
46,100	46,150	10,042	8,118	10,563	9,067
46,150	46,200	10,056	8,132	10,579	9,081
46,200	46,250	10,070	8,146	10,594	9,095
46,250	46,300	10,084	8,160	10,610	9,109
46,300	46,350	10,098	8,174	10,625	9,123
46,350	46,400	10,112	8,188	10,641	9,137
46,400	46,450	10,126	8,202	10,656	9,151
46,450	46,500	10,140	8,216	10,672	9,165
46,500	46,550	10,154	8,230	10,687	9,179
46,550	46,600	10,168	8,244	10,703	9,193
46,600	46,650	10,182	8,258	10,718	9,207
46,650	46,700	10,196	8,272	10,734	9,221
46,700	46,750	10,210	8,286	10,749	9,235
46,750	46,800	10,224	8,300	10,765	9,249
46,800	46,850	10,238	8,314	10,780	9,263
46,850	46,900	10,252	8,328	10,796	9,277
46,900	46,950	10,266	8,342	10,811	9,291
46,950	47,000	10,280	8,356	10,827	9,305

47,000 / 48,000 / 49,000

If Form 1040A, line 22, is —		And you are —			
At least	But less than	Single	Married filing jointly *	Married filing separately	Head of a household
		Your tax is—			
47,000					
47,000	47,050	10,294	8,370	10,842	9,319
47,050	47,100	10,308	8,384	10,858	9,333
47,100	47,150	10,322	8,398	10,873	9,347
47,150	47,200	10,336	8,412	10,889	9,361
47,200	47,250	10,350	8,426	10,904	9,375
47,250	47,300	10,364	8,440	10,920	9,389
47,300	47,350	10,378	8,454	10,935	9,403
47,350	47,400	10,392	8,468	10,951	9,417
47,400	47,450	10,406	8,482	10,966	9,431
47,450	47,500	10,420	8,496	10,982	9,445
47,500	47,550	10,434	8,510	10,997	9,459
47,550	47,600	10,448	8,525	11,013	9,473
47,600	47,650	10,462	8,538	11,028	9,487
47,650	47,700	10,476	8,552	11,044	9,501
47,700	47,750	10,490	8,566	11,059	9,515
47,750	47,800	10,504	8,580	11,075	9,529
47,800	47,850	10,518	8,594	11,090	9,543
47,850	47,900	10,532	8,608	11,106	9,557
47,900	47,950	10,546	8,622	11,121	9,571
47,950	48,000	10,560	8,636	11,137	9,585
48,000					
48,000	48,050	10,574	8,650	11,152	9,599
48,050	48,100	10,588	8,664	11,168	9,613
48,100	48,150	10,602	8,678	11,183	9,627
48,150	48,200	10,616	8,692	11,199	9,641
48,200	48,250	10,630	8,706	11,214	9,655
48,250	48,300	10,644	8,720	11,230	9,669
48,300	48,350	10,658	8,734	11,245	9,683
48,350	48,400	10,672	8,748	11,261	9,697
48,400	48,450	10,686	8,762	11,276	9,711
48,450	48,500	10,700	8,776	11,292	9,725
48,500	48,550	10,714	8,790	11,307	9,739
48,550	48,600	10,728	8,804	11,323	9,753
48,600	48,650	10,742	8,818	11,338	9,767
48,650	48,700	10,756	8,832	11,354	9,781
48,700	48,750	10,770	8,846	11,369	9,795
48,750	48,800	10,784	8,860	11,385	9,809
48,800	48,850	10,798	8,874	11,400	9,823
48,850	48,900	10,812	8,888	11,416	9,837
48,900	48,950	10,826	8,902	11,431	9,851
48,950	49,000	10,840	8,916	11,447	9,865
49,000					
49,000	49,050	10,854	8,930	11,462	9,879
49,050	49,100	10,868	8,944	11,478	9,893
49,100	49,150	10,882	8,958	11,493	9,907
49,150	49,200	10,896	8,972	11,509	9,921
49,200	49,250	10,910	8,986	11,524	9,935
49,250	49,300	10,924	9,000	11,540	9,949
49,300	49,350	10,938	9,014	11,555	9,963
49,350	49,400	10,952	9,028	11,571	9,977
49,400	49,450	10,966	9,042	11,586	9,991
49,450	49,500	10,980	9,056	11,602	10,005
49,500	49,550	10,994	9,070	11,617	10,019
49,550	49,600	11,008	9,084	11,633	10,033
49,600	49,650	11,022	9,098	11,648	10,047
49,650	49,700	11,036	9,112	11,664	10,061
49,700	49,750	11,050	9,126	11,679	10,075
49,750	49,800	11,064	9,140	11,695	10,089
49,800	49,850	11,078	9,154	11,710	10,103
49,850	49,900	11,092	9,168	11,726	10,117
49,900	49,950	11,106	9,182	11,741	10,131
49,950	50,000	11,120	9,196	11,757	10,145

* This column must also be used by a qualifying widow(er).

(**50,000 or over** — use Form 1040)

The Internet

What Is the Internet?

The microcomputer made its debut in the American home in the late 1970s. Technology advances since that time have been rapid and extraordinary. In the early 1980s, the Internet was born. It was designed for specialized uses and users; it permitted selected groups (such as educational researchers and the military) access to information that made their work much faster and easier. Today, millions of computer users worldwide are connected to the Internet; it's still a rapidly growing network that provides all types of people with access to all types of information from their very own computer station at home or at work. If you can find a computer terminal that is connected to the Internet, you too can "surf the net" and obtain a wide range of information from an astounding list of sources.

As we learn more about the Internet, let's first examine some of the vocabulary and background about networks and how they operate.

Nets and Networks

When individual computers are linked together to share information, a **network** (or "net") is created. Individual computers, called stand-alones, are limited in the information they can store and information that can be shared with others. By linking, or networking, computers together, each computer station can access a larger amount of information. A network can be small—just a few computers—or it can be very large—thousands of computers linked together.

The Internet is a "network of networks." In other words, it is not a single network, but rather a giant network of more than 50,000 smaller networks. The **server** (or "host") stores and controls large volumes of information that can be downloaded or copied to individual networked computer stations. The purpose of the Internet is to bring to you the resources of the world and enable you to access all types of information from your computer station.

Any person or company that wishes to join a super network such as the Internet must have special software called "client software." When you link from your computer (as the client) to the server (Internet), you are entering "cyberspace," an electronic realm filled with choices for you to explore, play, purchase, exchange information, or just "hang out."

You Must Have an Address

Before you (the client) can be recognized by the Internet (your host) in a process called logging in, you must have an Internet address. Your address is a name that is converted to numbers by DNS (Domain Name System) computers. Your address often includes your name, your work site, or some other specific identifier, such as:

joanr@clack.bused.edu

Every name on the net is different so that you can receive mail called electronic mail (e-mail). Electronic mail means you can leave messages for people and receive messages from people on your computer once you have accessed the Internet.

The e-mail address has several important qualities:
- The @ sign means "AT."
- A period (.) means "DOT."
- There are no spaces in the name.
- All letters should be lowercase.
- Each group of letters should specify or identify the user or client, as distinguished from all other potential users.

Several common Internet e-mail address categories include a "domain extension" that identifies the type of user, such as the following:
.mil military
.edu educational
.com commercial
.org organizational
.gov governmental
.net network provider

What Is on the Net

The Internet is on every continent; it reaches schools in more than 140 countries around the world. Also on the Internet are government agencies, libraries, colleges, military bases, and millions of clients accessing all types of information, called **resources** in cyberspace. Resources include people, places, hosts, and data you can find when surfing the net.

When you connect your computer to the Internet resources, you come **online**. When you use online services like Internet, you can shop, pay your bills, take classes, book a trip, search databases for specific types of information, send mail, receive mail, download information, and browse through thousands of libraries and electronic stores throughout the world.

Let's look at some of the basic resources that are on the Net. The most common and widely used is the e-mail application, which lets you receive and send memos, notes, letters, and even software packages using your Internet address. Another resource is called "FTP" (File Transfer Protocol), which allows you to transfer files from distant computers to your computer. Telnet is a resource that allows you to log in to a distant computer host in another state or country and use that computer as if you were there! The World Wide Web and Gopher allow you to seek and talk to friends and sources around the world. As you can see, the applications are incredible and far-reaching.

Online Access to the Internet

Being "online" means that you are able to search a host computer and download to your own computer a wide variety of information—news, mail, articles, graphics, references, and even video games. You can also chat with a friend electronically, pay your bills, and subscribe to all types of services that are added to the Net each month. Some futurists believe that online access is the wave of the future. Today people feel the need to communicate and be aware of what's going on—they read newspapers and magazines, watch television, attend meetings, and so on. The people of the future will view being online as equivalent to these modern-day tools. At the very least, online services will drastically change the way goods and services are bought and sold, shown and delivered, to the consumer.

Students will find that the Internet has vast opportunities. You can browse through libraries, ask opinions of experts, and call information to your screen and print it, using what are called **hypertext** links. Hypertext allows you to select a word with your mouse and then jump to another document that contains more information on the same topic. When you see a hypertext word that you like or want to know more about, simply click on that "keyword" and jump to the document that has the information you want.

Today's Internet connections are also colorful. Your screen captures the very essence of the image you want to see, depending on the type of screen you are using. Full sound and video are also available, as the computer's capacity has increased substantially—both in quantity that can be used and stored, and in speed at which the computer can perform its assigned tasks.

Today's Online Services

Today there are many companies offering online services. Large communications corporations from Microsoft to AT&T realize that consumer business is changing. People want new conveniences and will welcome cyberspace shopping. In truth, all of cyberspace is open to those who want to set up shop—as subscribers and producers—eager to meet their markets in a new and exciting format.

America On-line is a rapidly growing service; CompuServe (a subsidiary of H&R Block) is a vast and profitable enterprise. Prodigy, a joint venture between IBM and Sears, is also carving a niche. Another important online service is Microsoft Network. The Microsoft Network is designed to fully harness the power and ease of Windows 95. These and other services will come and go. But it should be noted that the major customers of these services are business users rather than individuals. It is thought that most people are still oblivious to the emergence and potential of this new consumer service industry—something that may change in the near future when consumers discover incredible personal finance uses and applications from Quicken (to balance your checkbook and keep records) to ordering a pizza.

There may be several reasons why the consumer isn't quite ready for today's online services. Let's examine some reasons for consumer reluctance to enter cyberspace:

1. *The cost.* Online services cost ranges from $10 to $30 a month for a set period of time, such as five hours a month. Extra time is billed on a per-hour basis.
2. *Inconvenience.* While time may be saved ultimately (when the system is fully available for all types of goods and services), today it ties up the family phone and consumes a large amount of time in procedures such as downloading.
3. *Technical problems.* Technical problems are always a part of new technology that has not been fully tested. People get discouraged when the product or service doesn't perform exactly as expected—with minimal learning and maximum ease and convenience. Churning (people leaving online services) is expensive as sellers must find replacements in addition to other new customers.
4. *Difficulty.* The Internet is often difficult to use. Just when you think you've gotten through to the right source, your connection to the

Net might crash. Cryptic messages such as "REFUSED CONNEC-TION" may pop up for a number of reasons, such as too many requests for the same information.

5. *Lack of security*. Probably the greatest problem to overcome with the Net is its lack of privacy. When consumers and businesses complete transactions, credit card numbers and other private data are sent via the Net, making it vulnerable to theft. Software is being developed that will make the transactions safer, but hackers are swiftly circling behind it, thereby making any safety measures short-term in effectiveness.

Competition Is Fierce

Like all new and potentially lucrative fields of profit, online services and nets are in a highly competitive and volatile field. So far the companies that have grown the fastest are **access providers** or those who allow access to the Net. For a monthly fee, the consumer can connect his or her computer to the Internet by making a telephone call. Also, many companies offer programs to users of the net to help them find their way around.

What will the future hold for Internet? According to most experts, the competition will continue to be fierce. Those companies that can best serve consumers' needs will, at least for a short time, make enormous profits.

Photo Credits

Photo by Alan Brown/Photonics: pages 205, 250, 410, 476, 581, 693

Photograph by Al Greening, San Francisco, CA: page 152

Location Courtesy of AlphaGraphics: page 386

Photograph by Andrew Sims, Camden, ME: page 433

BETTMANN: page 706

Copyright © Cathlyn Melloan/Tony Stone Images, Inc.: page 141

Copyright © Charles Gupton/Tony Stone Images, Inc.: pages 106, 455

Copyright © Charles O'Rear/Westlight: page 654

Copyright © Chronis Jons/Tony Stone Images, Inc.: page 648

Copyright © C. Sims/SuperStock, Inc.: page 395

Copyright © Dale Durfee/Tony Stone Images, Inc.: page 240

Copyright © Daniel Bosler/Tony Stone Images, Inc.: pages 534, 564

Copyright © Dennis O'Clair/Tony Stone Images, Inc.: page 28

Copyright © D. and J. Heaton/Westlight: page 731

Copyright © D. Muscroft/SuperStock, Inc.: page 104

Copyright © Doris De Witt/Tony Stone Images, Inc.: page 639

Copyright © E. Faure/SuperStock, Inc.: page 304

Copyright © Elan Sun Star/Tony Stone Images, Inc.: page 583

Photo by Erik Von Fischer/Photonics: pages 266, 277, 300, 305, 321, 415

Federal Reserve Bank of Cleveland: page 307

Copyright © Frederick Myers/Tony Stone Images, Inc.: page 17

Copyright © G. Hunter/SuperStock, Inc.: page 332

GM Card: page 383

Photo by Guennadi Maslov/Photonics: pages 709, 715, 736

Copyright © Jean Claude Grelier/Tony Stone Images, Inc.: page 651

Jeff Greenberg, Photographer: pages 59, 78, 184, 193, 245, 265, 271, 281, 325, 380, 397, 407, 419, 438, 439, 454, 502, 515, 537, 541, 546, 558, 563, 612, 621, 629, 685, 739

Copyright © Jim Pickerell/Tony Stone Images, Inc.: pages 340, 506

Copyright © Keith Wood/Tony Stone Images, Inc.: page 587

Copyright © L. Chiger/SuperStock, Inc.: page 136

Copyright © Mark E. Gibson: pages 348, 449, 530, 577, 615, 634, 684

Copyright © Michael Rosenfeld/Tony Stone Images, Inc.: page 221

Copyright © Myrleen Cate/Tony Stone Images, Inc.: page 480

Location courtesy of Northland Volkswagen: page 555

NYSE: page 292

Copyright © Peter Lamberti/Tony Stone Images, Inc.: page 330

Copyright © Phil Jason/Tony Stone Images, Inc.: page 247

Copyright © Randy Faris/Westlight: page 689

Copyright © R. Dahlquist/SuperStock, Inc.: page 326

Copyright © R. Heinzen/SuperStock, Inc.: page 93

Copyright © R. Llewellyn/SuperStock, Inc.: page 618

Copyright © Robert E. Daemmrich/Tony Stone Images, Inc.: pages 29, 53, 166, 733

Copyright © Roger Tully/Tony Stone Images, Inc.: page 287

Copyright © Ron Lowery/Tony Stone Images, Inc.: page 4

Copyright © R. W. Jones/Westlight: page 139

Courtesy of Sayett Technology, Inc.: page 73

Copyright © The Stock Market/Al Francekevich: page 342

Copyright © SuperStock, Inc.: pages 210, 349, 426, 520, 691

Copyright © Thomas Del Brase/Tony Stone Images, Inc.: page 408

Courtesy of Toyota Motor Manufacturing, U.S.A., Inc.: page 85

UPI/BETTMANN: page 714

Copyright © V. Hobbs/SuperStock, Inc.: page 219

Copyright © Walter Hodges/Westlight: pages 101, 355, 501

Copyright © W. Cody/Westlight: page 261

World Bank Photo: page 24

A

20/10 rule. Never borrow more each year than 20 percent of your yearly take-home pay, and never agree to monthly payments that are more than 10 percent of your monthly take-home pay. (p. 446)

401(k) plan. An employer-based plan whereby employees set aside money for retirement that is sometimes matched by employers. (p. 347)

403(b) plan. A retirement account for employees of schools, tax-exempt organizations, and government units. (p. 347)

Abrasives. Cleaning agents in car polishing compounds that contain strong chemicals or are coarse and can cause surface damage. (p. 564)

Abstract. A summary of all known previous transactions involving a piece of real property. (p. 519)

Acceptance. In a real estate transaction, when an offer is accepted by the seller exactly as it is stated. (p. 536)

Account executive (stockbroker). A professional who works for a brokerage firm, buying and selling securities for clients. (p. 244)

Actuarial table. A table of premium rates based on ages and life expectancies. (p. 613)

Actuary. One who calculates insurance and annuity premiums, reserves, and dividends; a specialist on insurance statistics. (p. 613)

Adjustable rate mortgage (ARM). A mortgage in which the interest rate starts low but changes as the loan progresses. (p. 599)

Adjusted balance method. A method of computing finance charges in which creditors add finance charges after subtracting payments made during the billing period. (p. 435)

Adjusted gross income. Income minus allowable exclusions (such as IRAs and alimony). (p. 160)

Administrative agencies. Governmental groups established by Congress and authorized by the executive branch of government that have the power to enforce administrative laws. Example: Social Security Administration. (p. 105)

Advanced degrees. Degrees earned through specialized, intensive post-baccalaureate programs. (p. 14)

Advertising. The communication of product information to the consumer for the purpose of increasing demand for the product or service. (p. 686)

Agency bond. A government-guaranteed bond sold by a secondary mortgage market company. (p. 306)

glossary

Agency. A company that represents more than one type of insurance and more than one insurance company. (p. 621)

Agent. A trained professional salesperson who acts for the insurance company in negotiating, servicing, or writing an insurance policy. (p. 613)

Agricultural Marketing Service. A division of the Department of Agriculture which inspects food to ensure wholesomeness and truthful labeling. (p. 711)

Alimony. Money paid to a former spouse for support, usually as a lump sum or regular payment for a set period of time. (p. 589)

Allowances. Persons who are dependent on your income for support (you get one withholding allowance for each). (p. 92)

Annual percentage rate (APR). The rate of interest charged on installment contracts. (pp. 390, 432)

Annual percentage yield. The true or effective rate of interest when compounding is taken into effect. (p. 243)

Annual report. Information about a company that allows a potential investor to make an investment decision. (p. 267)

Annuity. A contract or agreement whereby money is set aside for a specified period of time, at the end of which you begin receiving payments at regular intervals. (pp. 270, 345)

Appellate Court. A court having appellate jurisdiction (able to hear a court that has been appealed from a trial court where it was first heard and decided). (p. 726)

Appreciation. The increase in property value while a person owns the property. (p. 544)

Aptitude. A natural physical or mental ability that permits you to do certain tasks well. (p. 24)

Arbitration. A process of hearing a dispute by an impartial person or persons who make a decision which is binding on the parties who agree to the process of arbitration. (p. 735)

Architect's fee. The cost for drawing up plans to build a house. (p. 601)

Assets. Items of value that a person owns. (p. 185)

Assigned risk pool. People who are unable to get automobile insurance. (p. 640)

Attractive nuisance. A dangerous place, condition, or object that is particularly attractive to children. (p. 636)

Auction market. A stock market where buyers and sellers are brought together; the stockbroker earns a commission based on sales. (p. 285)

Audit. The examination of your tax records by the Internal Revenue Service. (p. 155)

Automatic deductions. Authorized deductions from your checking account, such as for insurance premiums, safe deposit box fees, or other payments. (p. 251)

Average daily balance method. A method of computing finance charges in which creditors add your balances for each day in a billing period, and then divide by the number of days in the period. (p. 436)

Back-end load. A mutual fund where you pay a commission when you sell your shares. (p. 321)

Bait and switch. A technique to get buyers to purchase more expensive merchandise by luring them with cheaper products. (p. 688)

Balance due. The total amount that remains due on a loan, including both principal and interest. (p. 384)

Balanced fund. A mutual fund that invests in a mixture of stocks and bonds to minimize risk. (p. 319)

Bankruptcy. Legally insolvent; not capable of paying bills. (p. 448)

Basic health insurance. Includes medical, hospital, and surgical insurance coverages. (p. 650)

Basic needs. Food, clothing, water, and shelter. (p. 479)

Bear market. A market characterized by falling prices of 15 percent or more, with a bleak outlook. (p. 284)

Bearer bond (coupon bond). A bond not registered by an issuing company. (p. 301)

Beneficiary. 1. A person who benefits from a trust or inheritance. (p. 352) 2. A person named on an insurance policy to receive the benefits (proceeds) of the policy. (pp. 613, 656)

Benefits. 1. Sums of money to be paid for specific types of losses under the terms of an insurance policy. (p. 613) 2. Sick pay, vacation time, and other company-provided supplements to income. (p. 8)

Better Business Bureau (BBB). A state and local group that serves as a clearinghouse of information about local businesses. (p. 693)

Billing (closing) date. The last date of the month that any purchases or payments made are recorded in a charge account. (p. 384)

Blank endorsement. The signature of the payee written on the back of the check exactly as it appears on the front of the check. (p. 215)

Blue chip stocks. Stocks in the biggest, most established, and consistently profitable companies in the United States. (p. 280)

Body (of a letter). The content part of a letter, containing attention, interest and desire, and action. (p. 48)

Bond fund. A mutual fund that invests in government, corporate, or tax-exempt bonds with different maturities. (p. 319)

Bonds. Debt obligations of corporations or government. (p. 268)

Borrower. The person who borrows money or uses another form of credit. (p. 384)

Broker. A person who buys and sells stock on an exchange, in behalf of a buyer (investor). (p. 284)

Budget. An organized plan whereby you match your expected income to your expected outflow. (p. 181)

Bull market. A rising stock market (volume and prices) which is characterized by optimism. (p. 284)

Call option. The right to buy stock or futures contracts at a fixed price until the expiration date. (p. 332)

Callable bond. Bonds that can be recalled, or paid off, before their maturity date. (p. 301)

Canceled checks. Checks the bank has processed. (p. 205)

Capacity. The ability to repay a loan from present income. (p. 406)

Capital. Property possessed that is worth more than debts owed. (pp. 384, 406)

Capital gains. Profits from sale of assets, such as stocks, bonds, or real estate, that are not taxed until the asset is sold. (p. 309)

Car title. A document that lists the legal and registered owners of a vehicle. (p. 560)

Care labels. Labels found on clothing and other products that tell the new owner how to properly take care of them so that they will last. (p. 710)

Cash flow (positive). The excess of income over underlying mortgage and other expenses of owning real estate. (p. 539)

Cash value. The amount of money available to a policyholder to borrow during the life of the policy or payable upon discontinuation of a life insurance policy. (pp. 613, 660)

Cashier's check. A check written by a bank on its own funds. (p. 218)

Certificate of deposit. A time certificate representing a sum of money deposited for a set length of time, such as six months. (p. 246)

Certified check. A personal check that the bank guarantees to be good. (p. 218)

Chapter 11 bankruptcy. A proceeding for businesses to reorganize their debt structure. (p. 450)

Chapter 13 bankruptcy. The wage earner's plan of bankruptcy, wherein debtors keep all of their property and repay a portion of their debts over a period of time under a court-enforced plan. (p. 451)

Chapter 7 bankruptcy. A straight bankruptcy proceeding that wipes out most, but not all, debts. (p. 451)

Character. A trait of creditworthiness indicating a responsible attitude toward paying debts. (p. 406)

Checkbook register. A record of deposits to and withdrawals from a checking account. (p. 211)

Checking account. A banking service wherein money is deposited into an account, and checks are written to withdraw money as needed. (p. 205)

Cherry picker. A customer who buys only loss leaders and super sale items. (p. 491)

Child support. Money paid to a former spouse for support of dependent children. (p. 159)

Childproof. The process of making a product safe for children to use. (p. 709)

Civil Aeronautics Board (CAB). A federal agency which keeps tracks of complaints, inspects aircraft, investigates accidents, and enforces safety regulations. (p. 713)

Civil court. A court with authority to hear cases involving private legal rights of citizens. (p. 726)

Claim. A demand for payment for a loss under the terms of an insurance policy. (p. 613)

Closed-end credit. A contract for the loan of a specified amount in which the contract issued tells the amount of purchase, the total finance charge, and the amount of each payment. (p. 391)

Closing costs. The fees and charges paid when a real estate transaction is completed; also referred to as settlement costs. (p. 538)

Codicil. A document that explains, adds, or deletes provisions in your existing will. (p. 352)

Coinsurance clause. A feature of homeowners policies requiring the property owner to insure equal to or exceeding 80 percent of the replacement cost of the property. The homeowner must pay for part of the losses if the property is not insured for the specified percentage of the replacement value. (p. 632)

Collateral. Personal property pledged to a lender to secure a loan. (pp. 384, 406)

Collectibles. Collections of rare and valuable items, such as coins. (p. 330)

Collective bargaining. The process of negotiating the terms of employment for union members. (p. 142)

Collective values. What is important to society as a whole. (p. 481)

College placement center. Source of career counseling available at colleges or technical training institutes. (p. 15)

Collision coverage. Automobile insurance that will cover costs of repairing or replacing your own car, even if you are at fault. (p. 638)

Comity. The principle that one country agrees to recognize the acts (and court decisions) of another country. (p. 731)

Commercial property. Land and buildings that produce lease or rental income. (p. 322)

Common stock. A class of stock whereby the person who owns the stock shares directly in the success or failure of the business. (p. 277)

Company advertising. Advertising intended to promote the image of a store, company, or retail chain. (p. 490)

Competition. A situation where there is more than one producer or supplier of a good or service. (p. 687)

Complimentary close. The appropriate phrase that courteously ends a business letter. (p. 48)

Compound interest. Interest paid on the original principal plus the accumulated interest. (p. 242)

Comprehensive coverage. Insurance that pays for damage to your car from events other than collision or upset. (p. 638)

Compressed workweek. A work schedule which shrinks the days worked but contains the same total hours; for example, four days, 10 hours each, totaling a 40-hour week. (p. 138)

Conditions. Existing debts, employment stability, and other circumstances that affect a person's ability to meet financial obligations. (p. 406)

Condominium. Individually owned unit in an apartment-style complex. (p. 324)

Consideration. Something of value that each party to a contract must receive. (p. 191)

Construction loan. A loan provided by a contractor that finances construction and is paid off when the building of a house is completed. (p. 601)

Consumer advocate. One who promotes and protects the causes or interests of consumers. (p. 714)

Consumer finance company. A general-purpose company that extends mostly consumer loans to customers buying consumer durables. (p. 394)

Consumer redress. Getting action to resolve a problem with a product or service. (p. 698)

Consumer Reports. A magazine published by Consumers Union that tests and rates products for effectiveness, quality, and safety. (p. 716)

Consumers. Citizens and businesses that purchase and use goods and services produced for sale. (p. 684)

Contacts. Relatives, friends, people you have worked for, and others who may be able to provide inside information on job openings. (p. 32)

Contract. A legally enforceable agreement between two or more parties to do or not to do something. (p. 187)

Convertible bond. A bond that can be exchanged for common stock at maturity. (p. 302)

Coordination of benefits. A method of integrating the benefits payable under more than one health insurance plan so that the benefits received from all sources are limited to 100 percent of allowable medical expenses. (p. 649)

Cosigner. A person with an acceptable credit rating who promises in writing to repay a promissory note if the maker fails to do so. (p. 195)

Counterclaim. A claim for damages by the defendant against the plaintiff; an assertion that the plaintiff is at fault. (p. 732)

Counteroffer. In a real estate transaction, a revised offer from the seller that is then accepted or rejected. (p. 536)

Coupon bond. See Bearer bond.

Court. A tribunal established to hear and decide matters brought before it; to give redress to the injured; to enforce punishment against wrongdoers; to prevent wrongs. (p. 726)

Court personnel. Those who work in the courts to assure fair trials, including the judge, clerk, reporter, bailiff, and jury. (p. 727)

Coverage. Protection provided by the terms of an insurance policy. (p. 613)

Creative listening. A type of listening in which all ideas are considered, and the working parts of each are saved. (p. 71)

Credit. The privilege of borrowing something now, with the agreement to pay for it later, or borrowing money with the promise to pay it back later. (p. 380)

Credit bureau. A company that operates for profit in the business of accumulating, storing, and distributing credit information. (p. 404)

Credit card advance. Money borrowed against a credit card limit. (p. 394)

Credit file. A summary of a person's credit history. (p. 404)

Credit history. The complete record of your credit performance. (p. 404)

Credit life. A policy that pays off a debt obligation (such as a mortgage or installment loan) if you should die. (p. 658)

Credit report. A written report issued by a credit bureau that contains relevant information about a person's creditworthiness. (p. 405)

Creditor. Any person to whom one owes money or goods. (p. 384)

Cremation. A process of reducing a body to ashes in a high-temperature oven. (p. 368)

Criminal court. A court for the trial of crimes regarded as violations of duties to society. (p. 727)

Critical listening. A type of listening in which you differentiate fact from fiction. (p. 71)

Cumulative preferred stock. A stock issue whose unpaid dividends accumulate and must be paid before any cash dividends are paid to common stockholders. (p. 279)

Custom. A long-established practice that may be considered an unwritten law. (p. 484)

Cyclical stocks. Stocks that follow the business cycle of advances and declines in the economy. (p. 280)

Database management. The storage and use of information so that all or part of it can be recalled, combined, and manipulated. (p. 199)

Database. 1. Central storage area used by a computer. 2. A computer program that allows the storage and use of information so that parts or all can be recalled, combined, and used. (p. 199)

Debentures. Corporate bonds that are backed not by corporate assets but by the general credit of the company. (p. 301)

Debt collector. A person or company hired by a creditor to collect the balance due on an account. (p. 417)

Debt load. The amount of outstanding debt at a particular point in time. (p. 465)

Debtor. One who owes money to another. (p. 448)

Decreasing term insurance. The policy has a constant premium, but the benefits decrease during the term of the policy. (p. 658)

Decree. A final statement of a dissolution of marriage. (p. 590)

Deductible. A specified amount subtracted from covered losses; the insurance company pays only the amount in excess of the deductible. (p. 613)

Deductions. 1. Amounts subtracted from gross pay. (p. 126) 2. Expenses the law allows the taxpayer to subtract from gross income. (p. 160)

Deed. A document that transfers title to real property. (p. 537)

Defendant. The person against whom a plaintiff has filed a complaint. (p. 732)

Defensive stocks. A stock that protects investors against the risks of varying economic conditions (business cycles). (p. 280)

Deferred billing. A service to charge customers whereby purchases are not billed to the customer until a later date. (p. 385)

Defined-benefit plan. A plan that specifies retirement benefits, based on wages earned and years of service. (p. 346)

Defined-contribution plan. A plan that specifies a minimum contribution but no promise of a particular benefit at retirement. (p. 346)

Demand. The willingness and ability of consumers to purchase goods and services at certain prices. (p. 685)

Demand deposit. An account that lets you demand portions of your deposited funds at will. (p. 205)

Demurrer. A legal document which asks the court to dismiss a complaint if based on insufficient evidence, improper jurisdiction, or other legal reasons. (p. 732)

Deposit. A pledge, or down payment. A refundable payment made to secure an apartment. (p. 504)

Deposition. A written, sworn statement of a witness which can take the place of court testimony and serves to preserve evidence. (p. 733)

Depreciation. 1. Loss in value of a vehicle during its lifetime. (p. 559) 2. In real estate, the using up of property value. (pp. 328, 544)

Direct investments. Investments in which the investor holds legal title to a property. (p. 322)

Disability insurance. A plan to provide regular cash income (75 percent to 80 percent of regular pay) to persons who are unable to work due to injury or illness. (p. 653)

Discharged debt. A debt that is no longer owed after declaration of bankruptcy. (p. 450)

Discount. A reduction made to the face value of a bond to entice buyers. (p. 303)

Discount bonds. Bonds purchased at less than face value. (p. 269)

Discount broker. An account executive who charges a smaller fee or commission than full-service brokerage, but gives no advice in buying and selling decisions. (pp. 267, 306)

Discovery. The period of time before a case can be tried during which evidence is gathered and preserved. (p. 742)

Discretionary income. Money that is left over when the bills have been paid. (p. 242)

Discrimination. The act of making a difference in treatment or favor on a basis other than individual merit. (p. 419)

Disinherit. To exclude a person who would ordinarily be entitled to an inheritance. (p. 353)

Disposable income. The money you have to spend or save as you wish after taxes, social security, and other required and optional deductions have been withheld from your gross pay. (p. 181, 480)

Dissatisfier. Conditions and policies that create dissatisfaction and produce low employee morale and low productivity. (p. 82)

Dissolution of marriage. A divorce proceeding based on no-fault laws. (p. 588)

Diversification. Holding a variety of securities so an occasional loss in one can be offset by gains in others. (p. 261)

Dividends. A distribution of money or stock that a corporation pays to stockholders. (p. 278)

Docket. A schedule of cases, dates, and times for cases to be tried in court. (p. 728)

Dollar-cost averaging. The process of making regular payments or investing the same amount periodically. Sometimes shares cost more, but average cost is smoothed out over time. (p. 289)

Dormitories. Buildings that contain many small rooms with beds, dressers, closets, and study areas. (p. 500)

Double indemnity. Paying double the face value of a life insurance policy, usually because of accidental death. (p. 657)

Down payment. An amount given as security for a loan to ensure that other remaining payments will be made. (p. 433)

Downward communication. A form of communication used by employers to keep employees informed and to give them job-related information and feedback about their performance. (p. 74)

Drafts. Checks used to withdraw money from an account. See also Share draft account. (p. 205)

Driver classification. Categories of drivers by age, sex, marital status, driving record, and driving habits. (p. 636)

Due date. The date on or before which a credit payment is due. (p. 384)

Duplex. A building with two separate living quarters. (p. 324)

Early withdrawal penalties. Fees charged to depositors who take money from their account before a minimum time period has expired. (p. 249)

Earnest money. In real estate, a portion of the purchase price that the buyer deposits as evidence of good faith to show that the purchase offer is serious. (p. 535)

Earnings per share. A corporation's after-tax earnings divided by the number of shares of common stock outstanding. (p. 283)

Easement. The right or privilege one party has to use the land of another person for some special purpose. (p. 533)

Economy. A system or structure of economic life in a country. (p. 485)

Efficiency apartments. Small, inexpensive living spaces; also known as studio apartments. (p. 501)

Eminent domain. The right of the government to take away privately held real property. (p. 532)

Empathy. Ability to see another's point of view. (p. 75)

Employee expenses. Costs paid by employees and not reimbursed by employers. (p. 10)

Employee services. Special perks or features offered to employees to enhance employment and motivate workers. (p. 133)

Employment application. A preprinted form which must be filled out when applying for employment. (p. 54)

Encumbrance. A claim, right, lien, or other liability against property. (p. 532)

Endorsement. A written document that modifies a policy in some way, perhaps adding or deleting coverage. (p. 631)

Entrepreneur. One who organizes, manages, and assumes the risks of a business or enterprise. (p. 11)

Equitable relief. A legal decision permitting some action or denying some action, rather than giving monetary damages as the result of a lawsuit. (p. 734)

Equity. Ownership interest in property; the value of a home less the amount still owed on the mortgage. (pp. 327, 518)

Estate. All that a person owns, less debts owed. (p. 349)

Estate planning. The process of planning for a person's last wishes, together with minimizing taxes and other costs. (p. 349)

Estate tax. A tax levied by the federal government against the value of an estate. (p. 356)

Eviction. The removal of a tenant from property that was rented. (p. 516)

Exclusions. Circumstances or losses that are not covered under the terms of an insurance policy. (p. 613)

Exempt status. A claim on Form W-4 that allows you to have no federal tax withheld from your paycheck. (p. 92)

Exempted property. An item of value or a possession that a bankrupt person is allowed to retain a certain equity in because it is considered necessary for survival. (p. 451)

Exemption. An allowance a taxpayer claims for each person dependent on the taxpayer's income. (p. 156)

Experience. Knowledge, skills, and practice gained for direct participation in a job. (p. 31)

Extended coverage. An added coverage, such as earthquake insurance, to an existing policy. (p. 631)

Face amount. The death benefit of a life insurance policy. (p. 613)

Face value. The amount a bondholder will be repaid when the bond matures or is due. (p. 300)

Fake sale. An advertised sale that represents regular-priced merchandise. (p. 690)

Family financial planning. A set of common financial goals for a family unit. (p. 582)

Family of funds. A mutual fund account that allows you to choose more than one type of mutual fund and switch back and forth. (p. 318)

Federal Aviation Administration (FAA). A federal agency of the U.S. Department of Transportation that controls air traffic, airports, pilots, and other personnel. (p. 713)

Federal Bureau of Investigation (FBI). A federal agency of the U.S. Department of Justice that investigates federal crimes such as bank robbery and kidnapping. (p. 713)

Federal Communications Commission (FCC). A federal agency that regulates radio and television broadcasting and interstate telephone and communication devices. (p. 712)

Federal court system. Consists of federal trial courts, appellate courts, and the U.S. Supreme Court. (p. 728)

Federal Trade Commission (FTC). A federal agency that protects consumers from unfair methods of competition, false or deceptive advertising, deceptive product labeling, and other consumer issues. (p. 712)

Fee simple. An ownership interest in property. (p. 532)

Fee-for-service. Unmanaged health care plan allowing choice of doctors and 80 percent coverage after deductibles. (p. 652)

Finance charge (handling charge). The total dollar amount you pay to use credit. (p. 384)

Finance company. Small loan companies that charge high rates of interest to use their money. (p. 394)

Financial advisers. Trained professional planners who give overall investment advice. (p. 267)

Financial maturity. The point in life when one can concentrate on one's own financial plan. (p. 340)

Financial pages. The financial section of a newspaper that includes financial data, such as stock prices, bond prices, and other investment information. (p. 264)

Financial plan. A formal budget document that specifies one's current financial situation, along with goals and methods of achieving them. (pp. 181, 582)

Financial responsibility laws. State legislation that requires drivers to prove their ability to cover the cost of damage or injury caused by an automobile accident. (p. 636)

Financial services. Companies that gather raw financial data about public corporations. (p. 266)

Fixed expenses. Expenses that remain constant. (p. 184)

Fixed-rate mortgage. A mortgage in which the interest rate remains constant over the life of the loan. (p. 599)

Fixture. An item of personal property that is permanently attached to real property. (p. 529)

Flammability. The capacity of a product to catch on fire. (p. 708)

Flextime. A variation of starting times for employees. (p. 137)

Floating a check. The practice of writing a check on insufficient funds and hoping to make a deposit to cover the check before it is cashed. (p. 206)

Floorbrokers. Stockbrokers who are members of a stock exchange and may do business at the exchange (buy and sell stocks). (p. 284)

Follow-up. A final contact, usually a thank-you letter, made after a job interview and before the interviewer makes a decision. (p. 61)

Food and Drug Administration (FDA). A federal agency charged with enforcing laws and regulations of foods, drugs, cosmetics, and medical devices. (p. 711)

Form W-2, Wage and Tax Statement. A form that lists income earned during the year and all amounts withheld by the employer in your behalf. (p. 95)

Form W-4, Employee's Withholding Allowance Certificate. A form completed for income tax withholding purposes. (p. 92)

Formal Wedding. A wedding ceremony where guests and participants wear formal clothing, which includes long gowns and tuxedos. (p. 580)

Fraud. Intentional misrepresentation of material facts that are relied upon by a person who is then damaged from making a decision or entering a contract. (p. 713)

Fringe benefits. Specific extras, which are in addition to gross pay, such as vacation time, sick leave, personal leave, health insurance packages, and so on. (p. 142)

Front-end load. A mutual fund where you pay a commission on your purchase and sometimes on dividend reinvestments as well. (p. 321)

Full disclosure. To reveal to a purchaser in complete detail every possible charge or cost involved in the granting of credit. (p. 415)

Furnished. An apartment that includes the basic furnishings: bed, sofa, chairs, table, lamps, etc. (p. 505)

Futures contract. An agreement made today for commodities bought and sold in the future. (p. 331)

Futures market. A transaction that allows people to know in advance what they will be paid in the future. (p. 332)

Gems. Natural precious stones such as diamonds, rubies, sapphires, and emeralds. (p. 329)

General obligation bond. A bond that is backed by the full faith and credit of a governmental unit. (p. 305)

Generic. A product marketed without a brand name or store name. (p. 708)

Gift tax. A tax levied on the person giving a gift to another person in excess of $10,000 in a year. (p. 357)

Global fund. A mutual fund that purchases international stocks and bonds as well as U.S. securities. (p. 320)

Goal. A desired end toward which efforts are directed. (p. 30)

Grace period. The period following the due date of an unpaid premium during which the policy is still in effect (usually thirty days). (p. 614)

Gross income. All taxable income received, including wages, tips, salaries, interest, dividends, unemployment compensation, alimony, and so forth. (p. 158)

Gross pay. The total salary before any deductions are made. (p. 124)

Group health insurance. A method of sharing health-related risks among a large group of people, usually employees of a company or non-profit organization. (p. 649)

Growth funds. Mutual funds that invest in the common stock of established companies as well as in new companies and industries. (p. 319)

Growth stocks. Stocks issued by a corporation that will provide future returns rather than income in the short term (income stocks). (p. 280)

Guaranteed renewability. A guarantee that coverage cannot be canceled if a person's health turns bad. (p. 654)

Hazard. A condition that increases the likelihood of some loss. (p. 614)

Health insurance. A plan for sharing the risk of financial loss resulting from an accident or illness. (p. 648)

Health Maintenance Organization (HMO). A health insurance plan that directly employs or contracts with selected physicians, surgeons, and dentists to provide an individual with health care services in exchange for a fixed, prepaid monthly premium. (p. 652)

Hearing. The physiological sensory process of receiving auditory sensations. (p. 69)

Heirs. Persons who are entitled to inherit from a decedent. (p. 352)

High-yield funds. Mutual funds that invest primarily in lower-rated bonds. (p. 319)

Highballing. An excessively high offer for a trade-in vehicle. (p. 556)

Holographic will. A legal, handwritten will. (p. 350)

Homeowners policy. A type of insurance available to the owner of a home; policies cover more than fire, such as theft, damage to contents, and injuries to guests (both invited and uninvited). (p. 629)

Horizontal communications. Less formal communication among employees of equal rank. (p. 74)

Human relations. Getting along with others. (p. 75)

Identity. Who and what you are. (p. 23)

Incentive pay. A way to encourage employees to do more and better quality work. (p. 133)

Income fund. A mutual fund that specializes in income-producing securities which consistently pay good dividends. (p. 319)

Income stocks. Stocks that have a consistent history of paying high dividends. (p. 280)

Incontestability clause. A provision that prevents an insurance company from canceling insurance after a specified period of time. (p. 657)

Indemnification. Putting an insurance policyholder back in the same financial condition as before a loss occurred. (p. 613)

Indirect investments. Investments in which the investor appoints a trustee who holds legal title on behalf of the investor or group of investors. Example: REIT. (p. 325)

Individual retirement account (IRA). A plan that allows workers to set aside up to $2,000 per year in tax-deferred savings. (p. 343)

Industry advertising. Advertising intended to promote a general product group, without regard to where these products are purchased. (p. 490)

Inflation. The increased cost of living. (pp. 260, 328)

Informal wedding. A wedding ceremony that can be held outside, in a church, or elsewhere with no special dress requirements for the wedding party or guests. (p. 580)

Infractions. Traffic violations, or tickets. (p. 636)

Inheritance tax. A tax levied by a state against the person who inherits money from a decedent. (p. 356)

Initiative. A quality that allows you to do things on your own, without being told to. (p. 100)

Innovations. New ideas, methods, or devices that bring about change. (p. 482)

Insolvent. Unable to pay debts or meet legal obligations of contracts. (p. 448)

Installment loan. A loan to be repaid in fixed payments that include principal and interest. (p. 391)

Installment purchase agreement. A written agreement to make regular payments on a specific purchase. (p. 391)

Insurable interest. Financial interest that a person has in the life of another or in property. (p. 617)

Insurable risk. A financial loss that can be determined. (p. 616)

Insurance. A cooperative system of sharing the risk of financial loss. (pp. 612, 614)

Insurance adjusters (claims adjusters). People who determine the value of property that was damaged or destroyed. (p. 631)

Insurance company. A business that, for a fee, issues policies to protect individuals and companies against some kind of loss. (p. 612)

Insurance investigators. Professionals who look for evidence of destroyed or damaged property and investigate the filing of fraudulent claims. (p. 631)

Insured. The person, partnership, or company protected against loss (not always the owner of the policy). (p. 614)

Inter vivos. A living trust. (p. 352)

Interdependent. The concept that people, groups, and even nations depend on each other and cannot act without considering how their actions will affect others. (p. 731)

Interest. Money paid for the use of money; earnings on a savings account. (p. 242)

Intestate. A condition where a person dies without a valid will. (p. 350)

Investment. Outlay of money in the hope of realizing a profit. (p. 257)

Investment company. A firm that, for a management fee, invests pooled funds of small investors in different types of securities. (p. 318)

Investment grade. High-quality bonds. (p. 308)

Investment portfolio. A group or collection of investments, including cash, CDs, stocks, and so on. (p. 320)

Investment strategy. A plan that examines potential returns and rates investments according to desirability. (p. 366)

Investor services. Companies that provide financial information about companies to investors. (p. 266)

Involuntary bankruptcy. A financial situation that occurs when creditors file a petition with the court, asking the court to declare a debtor unable to pay bills. (p. 450)

Itemized deductions. A listing of allowable deductions on Schedule A of Form 1040, such as medical expenses, mortgage interest and tax payments, and charitable contributions. (p. 160)

Itinerary. A detailed schedule of events, times, and places for a vacation or trip. (p. 584)

Job analysis. A procedure that lists the positive and negative attributes of a given career choice. (p. 8)

Job interview. A procedure in which you are asked questions about yourself, your experience, and your education, to which you respond verbally. (p. 58)

Job rotation. A technique used to train employees to be efficient in more than one specialized area. (p. 138)

Job sharing. A process in which two people share what was originally a full-time job, including salaries and benefits. (p. 138)

Joint endorsement. The signatures, on the back of a check, of both persons named as payees on the front of the check. (p. 214)

Joint ownership. Two or more persons holding joint title to property. (p. 355)

Joint tenants with rights of survivorship. Legal arrangement whereby if one partner dies, the other automatically inherits his or her interest in a property. (p. 355)

Judgment. A legal obligation or debt created by decree (decision) of a court. (p. 734)

Junk bonds. Corporate bonds with a low or no investment rating. (p. 308)

Jurisdiction. The legal right and authority of a court to hear and decide a case. (p. 726)

Jury. A body of citizens sworn by the court to hear the facts submitted during a trial and to render a verdict. (p. 727)

Keogh. A retirement account available to self-employed persons. (p. 344)

Labor union. A group of people who work in the same or similar occupations, organized for the benefit of all employees in these occupations. (p. 140)

Landlord. The owner of real estate who rents or leases the property to another person. (p. 327)

Layaway. A credit plan whereby merchandise is laid away in your name, and you make regular payments and claim the merchandise when it has been paid for in full. (p. 392)

Lease. The legal document that defines the conditions of a rental agreement. (p. 512)

Leasing. A contractual agreement to make monthly payments for the use of a car for a set period of time, with no ownership interest. (p. 558)

Lemon laws. Laws, enacted by thirty-three states, that provide redress to purchasers of defective cars. (p. 567)

Letter address. The part of a letter that shows the name and address of the person or company to whom you are writing. (p. 48)

Letter of application. A letter written to a potential employer asking for a job interview. (p. 43)

Letter of reference. A statement, in letter form, written by someone who can be relied upon to give a sincere report on your character, abilities, and experience. (p. 54)

Level term insurance. The benefits payable remain constant, but the premiums increase gradually each time the policy is renewed for another term. (p. 658)

Leverage. Borrowing money to make purchases; only a small part of the purchase price is your own cash. (pp. 286, 327)

Liabilities. Amounts of money that are owed to others. (p. 185)

Liability coverage. Protects the insured from claims for bodily injury or damage to another person's property. (p. 637)

Liability risks. The possibilities of loss due to accidents or negligence. (p. 616)

Lien. A claim against property by a creditor or other person who has a judgment against a person. (p. 533)

Life estate. Passing title to property but retaining the right to live on the premises. (p. 357)

Life insurance. Insurance protection from the financial loss that occurs when a wage earner dies. (p. 655)

Lifestyle. The way people choose to live their lives, based on the values they have chosen or rejected. (p. 24)

Limited partnership. A group of investors who pool their money to buy high-priced real estate; often called a real estate syndicate. (p. 326)

Limited-pay life. A whole life policy on which the premiums are paid for a specified number of years. (p. 660)

Line of credit. A pre-established amount that can be borrowed on demand. (p. 385)

Liquidity. The quality of being easily converted to cash. (p. 246)

Listening. An active process or skill that requires mental concentration and effort. (p. 69)

Loan sharks. Unlicensed lenders who charge very high and usually illegal interest rates. (p. 396)

Lobbying. Supporting legislation and political action that is beneficial to a certain profession. (p. 144)

Locked in. The state of feeling trapped in a job because you cannot afford to take the cut in pay that may accompany starting over. (p. 31)

Long-term disability insurance. Provides regular cash income for more than two years, but usually not past age 65, for employees unable to work as the result of an accident, illness, or pregnancy. (p. 653)

Loss. An unexpected reduction or disappearance of an economic value; the basis of a valid claim for repayment under the terms of an insurance policy. (p. 614)

Loss leader. An item of merchandise marked down to an unusually low price, sometimes below cost, to attract customers into the store. (p. 491)

Lot and block. Property legal description based on a plat map of a city assessor's office. (p. 530)

Lowballing. 1. Advertising one service, then adding others (repairs) that are not necessary or not expected. (p. 690) 2. An excessively low offer for a trade-in vehicle. (p. 556)

Major Appliance Consumer Action Panel (MACAP). A private organization in the home appliance industry that provides assistance in settling consumer problems with home appliances. (p. 714)

Major medical expense insurance. Provides coverage for the large and catastrophic expenses resulting from a serious injury or illness. (p. 650)

Managed care plan. A group health insurance plan that provides comprehensive health care to members. Examples include preferred provider organizations and health maintenance organizations. (p. 652)

Market economy. An economic system whereby both producers and consumers play an active role in determining what is produced and sold and at what price. (p. 684)

Market value. The highest price a property will bring in a competitive and open market. (pp. 281, 519)

Marketable. A term describing work of a quality such that an employer can use or sell it. (p. 99)

Maturity. The time when a corporation repays borrowed money. (p. 300)

Maturity date. The date on which you must renew a certificate, cash it in, or purchase a new certificate; the date on which a bond's principal amount must be repaid in full. (pp. 246, 302)

Medicaid. Government sponsored health insurance provided to qualified persons on public assistance and welfare programs. (p. 653)

Medicare. Federal health insurance for those aged 65 or over; program also covers those who have received social security benefits for disability for two consecutive years or more, even if under age 65. (p. 653)

Medigap. A supplemental private health insurance policy that pays deductibles and copays not covered by Medicare. (p. 653)

Metes and bounds. A type of legal description that identifies a parcel of property by specifying its shape and its boundaries. (p. 530)

Micromarketing. A strategy to target specific customers to meet their specific needs. (p. 493)

Minimum wage. The legally established lower limit on wages employers must pay. (p. 107)

Minors. Persons under the age of legal majority. (p. 95)

Money market fund. A combination savings-investment plan in which the deposit holder (brokerage firm) invests your money in a variety of financial instruments. (p. 246)

Monopoly. A situation where there is only one producer of a product or service. (p. 687)

Month-to-month rental agreement. An agreement, oral or written, to rent property at a specified price on a month-to-month basis. (p. 512)

Mortality tables. Life expectancy tables for males and females in various age categories. (p. 655)

Mortgage. A long-term loan on a specific piece of property, such as a home or other real estate. (pp. 325, 519)

Mortgage bond (secured bond). A corporate bond secured by various assets of an issuing firm. (p. 302)

Motion. A formal proposal that an action be taken. (p. 117)

Motivators. Incentives that inspire workers to produce more and better quality goods and services. (p. 82)

Multiple listing service. A real estate service agency composed of real estate offices that list and sell property. (p. 535)

Municipal bonds. Bonds issued by state and local government units, called "munis." Earnings are tax-free. (p. 304)

Mutual assent. Agreement to all terms of the contract by all parties to the contract. (p. 190)

Mutual fund. A company which pools the money of many investors to buy a large selection of securities that meet the fund's stated investment goals. (p. 270)

National Bureau of Standards. An agency within the Department of Commerce that sets measurement, product, and safety standards. (p. 711)

Negative cash flow. Rental income is less than the costs of repairs, maintenance, and the underlying mortgage. (p. 327)

Negotiable instrument. A document that contains promises to pay monies and is legally collectible. (p. 194)

Net pay. The amount left after all deductions have been taken out of your gross pay. (p. 127)

Net weight. The weight of a product without the container or package. (p. 711)

Networks (networking). Communication lines established for people to talk to each other and share information. (p. 17)

No-fault insurance. Drivers involved in an accident collect medical expenses, lost wages, and related injury costs from their own insurance company, regardless of who is at fault. (p. 640)

No-load funds. Mutual funds that do not charge commissions. However, there are annual maintenance charges and service fees. (p. 321)

Odd-number pricing. The practice of putting odd numbers on price tags, such as 99 cents rather than $1.00. (p. 490)

Offer. An agreement that lets the seller (owner) of real property know you want to buy his or her home. (p. 535)

Office of Consumer Affairs. A federal agency that represents consumer interests in federal agency proceedings, develops consumer information materials, and assists in responses to consumer complaints. (p. 712)

Open-ended credit. Credit wherein the lender places a limit on how much a qualifying customer can borrow during a given period. (p. 387)

Option. The right, for a fee, to buy or sell stock at a predetermined price. (p. 332)

Over-the-counter (OTC) market. A network of stockbrokers who buy and sell securities of corporations that are not listed on a securities exchange. (p. 285)

Overbooked. A situation that occurs when an airline has sold tickets for more seats than are available. (p. 588)

Overdraft or NSF (not-sufficient-funds check) check. A check written without sufficient money in an account to cover it. (p. 206)

Overtime. Hours worked over the regular hours in a workweek; usually more than 40 hours in a five-day period. (p. 124)

Oxidize. Lose color and shine in the paint of a vehicle. (p. 564)

Packs. High-priced, high-profit dealer services that add little or no value to a car being purchased. (p. 557)

Par value. Stated value. The basic price for which stock was originally issued. (p. 281)

Participating preferred stock. A class of preferred stock that shares profits with common stock (beyond the guaranteed rate). (p. 278)

Participation certificate. An investment in a pool of mortgages that have been purchased by one of several government agencies. (p. 327)

Pawnshop. A legal business in which loans are made against the value of specific personal possessions. (p. 396)

Penny stock. A stock that sells for less than $5 a share. (p. 280)

Peril. An event whose occurrence can cause a loss. (p. 614)

Personal factors. Factors in a person's life that influence spending and preferences, such as resources, position in life, customs, background, religion, values, and goals. (p. 484)

Personal injury protection. Automobile insurance coverage that pays for medical, hospital, and funeral costs of the insured and his or her family and passengers, regardless of fault. (p. 639)

Personal investing. The use of savings to earn a financial return. (p. 258)

Personal property floater. An addendum to an insurance policy that protects specific items of property. (p. 633)

Personal property. Items that are not permanently attached to real property but are removed when property is sold (cars, lawn mowers, furniture). (p. 529)

Personal resources. Time, money, energy, skills and abilities, and available credit. (p. 484)

Personal risks. Possible losses involving income or standard of living. These could include premature death, illness, disability, old age, and unemployment. (p. 615)

Personality. Personal qualities and traits that make each person unique. (p. 25)

Pigeon drop. A method used to convince vulnerable people to invest in phony schemes. (p. 692)

Plaintiff. The person who files a complaint and begins a legal process called litigation or trial. (p. 732)

Point system. A method used in rating consumers' creditworthiness wherein a credit applicant is given points for employment, amount of income, length of residence, type of residence, and other factors. (p. 411)

Police power. The right of the government to enact laws and enforce them for the public health, safety, morals and general welfare. (p. 532)

Policy. A written insurance contract. (p. 612)

Policyholder. The person who owns, or holds, an insurance policy. (pp. 612, 614)

Polishing compound. A substance that is used to clean an automobile's surface scratches, scuffs, and stains. (p. 564)

Positive cash flow. When rental income exceeds underlying payments, repairs, and maintenance of real property. (p. 327)

Postal Inspection Service. An agency of the U.S. Postal Service that deals with consumer problems pertaining to illegal use of the U.S. mail. (p. 713)

Power of attorney. A legal document giving another person the power to do something in your absence. (p. 352)

Preapproval. Finding out how much money you will be qualified to borrow before making a purchase. (p. 554)

Precious metals. Expensive and rare metals such as gold, silver, and platinum. (p. 328)

Preferred Provider Organization (PPO). A managed care health plan that combines the best elements of the traditional (fee-for-service) and HMO systems. (p. 652)

Preferred stock. The type of corporate stock in which dividends are fixed, regardless of the earnings of a company. (p. 278)

Premium. 1. The sum of money the policyholder agrees to pay to an insurance company periodically (monthly, quarterly, annually, or semiannually) for an insurance policy. (pp. 612, 614) 2. When bonds sell for higher than their par value, the amount above par is called a premium. (p. 303)

Preponderance. Where one party to a lawsuit better convinces the jury than the other side of the lawsuit. (p. 734)

Previous balance method. A method of computing finance charges in which creditors give you no credit for payments made during the billing period. (p. 435)

Price-fixing. A situation that occurs when competitors agree on prices rather than operate on a competitive basis. (p. 687)

Prime rate. The rate of interest lenders offer their best commercial (business) customers. (p. 429)

Principal. 1. The amount of money deposited by the saver; the total amount that is financed or borrowed and on which interest is computed. (p. 430) 2. The amount of money set aside by a saver that will earn interest. (p. 242)

Probability. The mathematics of chance; the chance of a loss occurring. (p. 613)

Probate. A court proceeding in which a will is validated and processed to be sure the wishes of the testator are met. (p. 355)

Producers. Citizens or businesses that make products and services available for sale. (p. 684)

Product advertising. Advertising intended to convince consumers to buy a specific good or service. (p. 489)

Productivity. A measure of the output of a production unit during a specific period of time. (pp. 4, 82)

Professional organizations. Groups that collect dues from members of a profession and provide support services. (p. 144)

Progressive taxes. Taxes that increase in proportion to income. (p. 151)

Promotion. The opportunity to advance, accept more responsibility, and work your way up in a company. (p. 9)

Proof of loss. The written verification of the amount of a loss that must be provided by the insured to the insurance company before a claim can be settled. (p. 614)

Property risks. The possibilities of loss or harm to personal or real property. (p. 615)

Property settlement agreement. A document specifying the division of property and assets agreed to by both parties to a divorce and entered into court for the judge's approval. (p. 589)

Proportional share. A percentage of a bankrupt's assets paid to a creditor, based on the total debt owed the creditor. (p. 450)

Proportional taxes. Taxes for which the tax rate remains constant, regardless of the amount of income. (p. 151)

Prorate. To divide proportionately over a period of time (interest or handling charge, for example). (p. 384)

Proration. A division of expenses between people who benefit. For example, a new owner who buys a property and lives in it half a month will owe half a month's mortgage interest. (p. 538)

Prospectus. Detailed financial information about a mutual fund company or a company issuing stock. (p. 320)

Proxy. Voting rights as a stockholder that are assigned to another person. (p. 278)

Public corporation. A corporation whose stock is traded openly in stock markets and may be purchased by an individual. (p. 277)

Purchasing power. The ability to buy goods and services. (p. 687)

Pure risk. Any personal, property, or liability risk that will cause a loss if certain events (perils) occur. The financial loss can be determined and is therefore insurable. (p. 616)

Put option. The right to sell stock or futures contracts at a fixed price until the expiration date. (p. 332)

Pyramid schemes. Selling schemes with promise of big money for those who find others to sell products. (p. 691)

Rate. The interest charge, expressed as a percentage of the principal. (p. 430)

Reaffirmation. When debtors agree to pay some or all of their debts after bankruptcy is completed. (p. 452)

Real estate investment trusts (REITs). Similar to a mutual fund, your money is pooled with other people's money; these funds are invested in real estate or are used to make construction or mortgage loans. (p. 326)

Real property. Land and anything that is permanently attached to it, such as buildings, fences, and sidewalks. (p. 529)

Rebate. A program to refund a portion of purchase amounts, or give away prices in accordance with amount purchased. (p. 439)

Recall. A procedure whereby the manufacturer stops production and refunds items previously sold or fixes them so they are no longer hazardous. (p. 708)

Recession. The economy slows down and manufacturers slow production (there are layoffs); an economic downturn of two or more quarters. (p. 280)

Reconciliation. The monthly process of matching the bank's records with the checking account balance. Outstanding checks and deposits are considered along with other charges and additions to the checking account. (p. 212)

Recorded plat. A map of subdivisions on file in the county recorder's office. (p. 530)

Redress. The act of consumers in getting satisfaction for a claim or other action relating to a purchase. (p. 707)

References. People over 18, not related to you, who have known you for at least one year and can report on your character and achievements. (p. 53)

Referral sale. A sale based on one person giving names of friends and acquaintances to get a rebate or other prize. (p. 688)

Registered bond. A bond that is recorded in the owner's name by the issuing corporation. (p. 300)

Registration fee. The cost of having a car licensed in a state so it can be driven. (p. 560)

Regressive taxes. Taxes that decrease in proportion to increases in income. (p. 151)

Renters policy. A type of insurance for people who rent that includes personal property protection, additional living expenses, and personal liability coverage. (p. 629)

Reservation. An advance commitment that assures a traveler will receive a service. (p. 585)

Residual value. Current balance left on a lease (monthly payments will apply only a small portion to principal). (p. 558)

Restrictive endorsement. An endorsement that restricts or limits the use of a check. (p. 216)

Resume. A summary of personal information, education, experience, additional qualifications, and references of a person seeking a job. (p. 48)

Retail stores. Stores that purchase goods from wholesalers and sell directly to customers. (p. 393)

Retraining. Learning new and different skills in order to remain employable. (p. 14)

Return address. The part of a letter that shows the writer's street address, city, state, ZIP Code, and date of the letter. (p. 44)

Revenue. Money collected by the government from citizens and companies in the form of taxes. (p. 151)

Revenue bond. A municipal bond that is repaid from the revenue (income) generated by a special project. (p. 304)

Reverse mortgage. An arrangement that allows a homeowner to receive monthly payments for a set period of time from a financial institution. When the house is sold, or the homeowner dies, the loan must be repaid. (p. 341)

Rider. A document attached to a life insurance policy that modifies coverage by adding or deleting a benefit. (p. 657)

Risk. 1. Potential for loss in an investment. (p. 260) 2. The possibility of a loss that faces a person or property covered by insurance. (pp. 612, 614)

Risk assumption. Self-insuring; paying for losses personally. (p. 618)

Risk avoidance. Avoiding situations involving risk. (p. 618)

Risk management. A plan to reduce financial loss. (p. 617)

Risk reduction. Taking measures to lessen the frequency or severity of losses that may occur. (p. 618)

Salary. The amount of monthly or yearly pay. (p. 8)

Sales agreement. The legal document that contains the specific details of a purchase. (p. 556)

Sales finance company. A manufacturer-related company that makes loans through authorized representatives. (p. 394)

Salutation. The letter greeting, using a person's name sometimes followed by a colon. (p. 48)

Secured loan (or secured debt). A loan that is guaranteed by a pledge of property or other assets to assure the creditor of repayment. (pp. 384, 429)

Securities exchange. A marketplace where brokers who are representing investors meet to buy and sell securities. (p. 284)

Securities. A broad range of investment instruments, including stocks, bonds, and mutual funds. (p. 244)

Self-actualization. A level at which workers meet their needs for accomplishment and satisfaction. (p. 83)

Self-assessment inventory. A listing of your strong and weak points and plan of action. (p. 15)

Self-esteem. Feelings of self-worth about ourselves and our accomplishments. (p. 83)

Semiformal wedding. A wedding ceremony held in the afternoon or early evening, with less formal wear required of guests. (p. 580)

Semiprecious stones. Garnets, spinels, opals, etc., that are purchased as investments. (p. 330)

Seniority. The policy that the last ones hired should be the first ones laid off. (p. 142)

Service charge (carrying charge). The amount charged borrowers by merchants or banks for servicing or carrying an account or loan. (p. 384)

Service credit. Credit for a service rendered (telephone, doctor). (p. 392)

Share account. A savings account at a credit union; the shares are ownership interest in the credit union. (p. 245)

Share draft account. A "checking" account offered to members of a credit union. Instead of checks, "drafts" are written against the member's account. (p. 218)

Short-term disability insurance. Provides income protection up to two years if a person is unable to engage in gainful employment. (p. 653)

Simple interest. Interest computed on the principal only. The formula for computing simple interest is $I = P \times R \times T$ (p. 429)

Simple will. A short form (one or two pages) that lists spouse and/or children as beneficiaries and documents a simple division of property. (p. 350)

Simplified employee pension plan (SEP). An individual retirement account funded by an employer. (p. 271)

Social Security Act. The first national social insurance program, enacted in 1938 to provide retirement for the elderly, survivors benefits for a deceased worker, disability income for the injured worker, and health insurance for the retired worker (OASDHI—old age, survivors, disability, and health insurance). (p. 105)

Social security number. Account number issued to each citizen for purposes of identification on tax returns; used for record of earnings which have been taxed by OASDHI. (p. 92)

Special agents. Investigators for the FBI. (p. 713)

Special endorsement (endorsement in full). An endorsement that instructs the bank to pay the amount of a check to a third party. (p. 215)

Specialists. Brokers to the floor-brokers (assisting with buying and selling securities). (p. 284)

Speculative risk. An event that may result in a loss or gain and is therefore uninsurable. (p. 616)

Spreadsheet. Computer software that sets information into columns and rows. (p. 199)

Standard deduction. A base amount allowed according to filing status in lieu of itemizing deductions on an income tax return. (p. 160)

Standard policy. The contract form that has been adopted by many insurance companies, approved by state insurance divisions, or prescribed by law (modifications are made to suit the needs of the individual). (p. 614)

Statute of limitations. A legal restriction that limits the length of time in which a court action may be taken. (p. 730)

Sticker price. The manufacturer's suggested retail price of a car appearing on the car window. (p. 554)

Stock. Ownership in a corporation; stock can be common or preferred. (p. 268)

Stock exchange. The location where stocks are bought and sold. (p. 284)

Stop payment order. A request that the bank not cash or process a specific check. (p. 222)

Stop-loss provision. A requirement that after the insured has paid a specified amount, such as $1,000, the policy pays 100 percent of the remaining cost. (p. 651)

Straight life. A whole life policy under which premiums are paid throughout the life of the insured, and the face value is paid at death. (p. 660)

Strike. A process whereby the members of a union refuse to work until an agreement is reached. (p. 143)

Subscriber. A creditor who pays an annual fee to a credit bureau for use of its credit reports. (p. 405)

Suicide clause. Provides that death benefits will not be paid for a suicide occurring within the first two years of a policy. (p. 657)

Supplemental health insurance. An individual policy, in addition to other group or individual plans, that pays deductibles, copays, and whatever else other plans will not pay. (p. 649)

Supply. The quantity of goods and services that producers are willing and able to manufacture. (p. 684)

Survivorship. Putting title to property in joint ownership. (p. 355)

Sympathetic listening. Technique of listening empathetically without offering advice. (p. 70)

Target audience. A specific consumer group to which advertisements are directed. (p. 489)

Tax avoidance. Strategies to reduce taxes, such as selling securities for a loss to offset gains on the sale of securities. (p. 309)

Tax evasion. Willful failure to pay taxes. (pp. 155, 309)

Tax shelter. A legal method of avoiding paying taxes on present earnings. Real estate is a good tax shelter because the owner can deduct expenses against rental income. (p. 544)

Tax shifting. Moving forward income and deductions to the next year when they will do you more good. (p. 309)

Tax-deferred investment. Income from an investment that is taxed at a later date. (p. 309)

Tax-exempt investment. There will be no tax on the earnings of this type of investment, either now or in the future. Example: municipal bonds. (p. 309)

Taxable income. Adjusted gross income minus deductions, exemptions, etc. (p. 160)

Technology. Advances resulting from improvements in technical processes. (p. 4)

Tenant. One who rents or leases property from a landlord. (p. 500)

Term insurance. Life insurance that offers protection for only a specified period of time and then lapses. (p. 658)

Testamentary trust. A trust that comes into being on the death of the trustor. (p. 352)

Testator. A person who makes a will. (p. 350)

Thank-you letter. A follow-up tool used to remind the employer of your interest in the job, written after the job interview. (p. 61)

Time. The period the borrower will take to repay a loan. (p. 430)

Time sharing. Real estate property rights represented by rights to use the property for usually one or two weeks a year. (p. 543)

Trading stamps. Stamps given to customers for purchases and redeemed for merchandise at a later date. (p. 492)

Transfer payments. Money or in kind distributions to persons who are unable to provide for themselves. (p. 687)

Travel agency. An authorized agent for all airlines to issue tickets and make travel reservations on behalf of a traveler. (p. 586)

Treasury direct. The purchase of Treasury bills, notes, or bonds directly through the Federal Reserve System. (p. 307)

Trial court. The first court to hear a case or trial (a court of original jurisdiction). (p. 726)

Trust. A legal document giving a person or institution custody of someone's assets for distribution to a third party. (p. 352)

Trust will. A long and complicated will, prepared by an attorney, that lists provisions for holding property, assets, and money for minor children and others. (p. 350)

Trustee. A person named to manage money or property for another. (pp. 325, 350)

Trustor. A person who creates a trust. (p. 352)

Umbrella policy. A policy that pays for damage caused by acts of negligence on the part of a property owner after coverage under other policies has been exhausted. (p. 641)

Under undue influence. Pressured or otherwise influenced to do or not to do something. (p. 353)

Unearned premium. The portion of a paid premium that has not been earned by the insurance company and is returned to the policyholder when a policy is canceled. (p. 614)

Unemployment insurance. Insurance that provides benefits to workers who lose their jobs through no fault of their own. (p. 106)

Unfurnished. A rental unit that does not include furniture or furnishings. (p. 505)

Uninvited persons. Trespassers on one's property for whose actions the owner is not liable. (p. 634)

Universal life insurance. A permanent insurance plan designed to let a policyholder pay premiums at any time in virtually any amount. The amount of the insurance benefit can also be more easily changed than in a traditional policy. The policy combines insurance and savings elements. (p. 660)

Unlisted number. A telephone number that is not listed in a telephone directory. (p. 522)

Unmanaged (traditional) plan. Insurance coverage that allows employees to choose any doctor and be reimbursed for medical, surgical, and hospital expenses. (p. 652)

Unsecured debt (or loan). Debt for which there is no collateral; only the borrower's signature serves as security for a loan. (p. 450)

Unused credit. The amount of credit above what you owe that you could charge, to a maximum amount. (p. 437)

Upgrading. Advancing to a higher level of skill. (p. 12)

Upholstery. Covering on seats, such as cloth, vinyl, or leather. (p. 565)

Upward communication. The transmission of information from employees to their supervisors and employers. (p. 74)

Usury laws. Laws setting maximum interest rates that lenders may charge. (p. 396)

Utility. Electric or water service to an apartment or living unit. (p. 505)

Values. The things in life that are important to you. (p. 23)

Variable expenses. Expenses that change according to needs and short-term goals. (p. 184)

Variable life insurance. A permanent insurance plan designed to let a policyholder choose among several investment options. (p. 660)

Vehicle emission test. A standard test required by large cities and urban areas to control pollution emitted from vehicles. (p. 556)

Vested. Status of having worked long enough to have the right to at least a portion of the benefits you have accrued under an employer pension plan (within certain limits) even if you leave the employer before you retire. (pp. 136, 346)

Voluntary bankruptcy. A financial situation that occurs when a debtor files a petition with a federal court asking to be declared unable to meet his or her debts. (p. 450)

Voluntary compliance. The expectation that all employed citizens will prepare and file income tax returns. (p. 155)

Wage and Hour Act. Also known as the Fair Labor Standards Act of 1938. A law providing minimum wage and hours standards, such as overtime, and other worker protection clauses. (p. 107)

Waiver of premium. A rider that allows you to stop paying insurance premiums and keep your coverage in force if you become disabled and are unable to work. (p. 658)

Warranty. A guarantee (usually written) from the manufacturer or distributor of a product that specifies the conditions under which the product can be returned, replaced, or repaired. (p. 196)

Wedding party. The active participants in a wedding ceremony— bride, groom, best man, maid of honor, and so on. (p. 578)

Whole life insurance. See Straight life insurance.

Will. A document that gives directions as to how the decedent wishes his or her property to pass upon death. (p. 349)

Work characteristics. Daily activities at work, such as indoor or outdoor work or working with people or alone. (p. 10)

Work history. A record of all jobs held and the length of time spent with each employer. (p. 35)

Workers' Compensation. Benefits paid to workers and their families in the event of injury, illness, loss of income, or death that occurs as a result of a job or working conditions. (p. 108)

Yield. The rate of return earned by an investor who holds a security, such as a bond or stock, for a stated period of time. (p. 243)

Zero-coupon bond. A bond that is sold at a price far below its face value, makes no annual or semi-annual interest payments, and is redeemed for its face value at maturity. (p. 310)

D